United States Congress

Arguments before the Committee on patents of the Senate and

House of representatives

United States Congress

Arguments before the Committee on patents of the Senate and House of representatives

ISBN/EAN: 9783337175610

Printed in Europe, USA, Canada, Australia, Japan

Cover: Foto ©Suzi / pixelio.de

More available books at **www.hansebooks.com**

ARGUMENTS

BEFORE THE

COMMITTEE ON PATENTS

OF THE

SENATE AND HOUSE OF REPRESENTATIVES,

IN SUPPORT OF, AND SUGGESTING AMENDMENTS TO, THE BILLS (S. No. 300 AND H. R. 1612) TO AMEND THE STATUTES IN RELATION TO PATENTS, AND FOR OTHER PURPOSES.

APRIL 3, 1878.—Ordered to be printed.

WASHINGTON:
GOVERNMENT PRINTING OFFICE.
1878.

CONTENTS OF ARGUMENTS BEFORE SENATE COMMITTEE.

VI

CONTENTS.

Page.

CONTENTS OF ARGUMENTS BEFORE HOUSE COMMITTEE.

. [See index, page xv, *infra*.]

APPENDIX.

[See index at end of volume.]

S. 300.

NOVEMBER 14, 1877.—Mr. WADLEIGH asked and, by unanimous consent, obtained leave to bring in the following bill; which was read twice and referred to the Committee on Patents.

MARCH 5, 1878.—Reported by Mr. WADLEIGH with amendments, viz:
Omit the parts in [brackets] and insert the parts printed in *italics*.

A BILL to amend the statutes in relation to patents, and for other purposes.

Be it enacted by the Senate and House of Representatives of the United States of America in Congress assembled, That from and after the passage of this act no profits or damages in any suit at law or in equity *hereafter commenced* for the infringement of a patent shall be recovered which shall have accrued more than four years next preceding the commencement of such suit: *Provided*, That where a party, in order to preserve his right of recovery, finds it necessary to institute a number of suits involving the same issues, and he is proceeding with good faith and with reasonable diligence to bring one of them to final judgment, any court in which any of them are pending may, in its discretion, grant a stay of proceedings from time to time in any such other cases pending before it : *Provided also*, That *the limitation herein provided for shall not apply to* rights of action existing at the passage of this act [may be enforced by] *on which* suits *shall be* brought within [four] *two* years thereafter, if not previously barred by laws already existing ; but nothing in this section contained shall revive any right of action already barred, nor prolong the right to sue on any cause of action already existing.

SEC. 2. In all cases where the patentee has elected to license other persons generally to use his invention, in like manner to that in which it was used by the defendant, or where it appears to the court or jury that, from the nature of the invention, it is for the interest of the patentee that other persons generally should use the same in like manner and pay him a license fee therefor, the measure of the plaintiff's damages shall be the same, both at law and in equity, and no account of profits or savings *from use* shall be allowed, *except in case of a use by therewith partially or completely making a product for sale*. If a license-fee has already been established by a reasonable number of transactions of a character applicable to the case at bar, that shall be adopted as the measure of said damages ; but if not, then the court or jury shall determine the [same] *damages* from all the evidence in the case. In taking an account of profits in any case, the defendant shall not be charged with any saving he may have made, [unless it has] *if he shall show that it has not* enabled him to realize an actual profit in that part of his business connected with the use of the invention. And the court shall determine what proportion of such profit is due to the use of said invention, and what proportion to the other elements from which such profit was derived, capital and personal services excepted ; and the proportion of actual profit so found to be derived from the use of the invention shall be the measure of the profits to be recovered. But, if in any case, it shall appear to the court that the damages or profits, ascertained as above, shall be inadequate to give the plaintiff a just compensation for the injury done by the infringement, or shall be in excess of such injury, the court shall have power to increase or diminish the amount to such an extent as may be just and reasonable. *And whenever the court shall be of the opinion that the suit of the plaintiff, or the defense of the defendant, was vexatious, or the infringement was willful, the court may award against the defeated party such sum, by way of counsel fees and expenses, as it shall deem just and reasonable: Provided,* That the provisions of this section shall not apply in any case in which a decree for an account or assessment of damages has, at the date of the passage of this act, already been pronounced. Nothing contained in this section shall affect the right of the plaintiff to an injunction, *nor to recover in a suit in equity, in addition to the profits to be accounted for, the damages the complainant has sustained by the infringements complained of.*

SEC. 3. In all patent causes, after a decree has been made upon the merits of the case, in favor of the complainant, establishing the validity of a patent, finding an infringement thereof by the defendant, and ordering an account or an assessment of damages, the court in which the cause is pending may, if it shall see fit, authorize the defendant to appeal forthwith from such decree; and thereupon, if such an appeal shall be taken and perfected within such time as the court shall prescribe, it shall be competent for the *said* court to stay proceedings in whole or in part during the pendency of such appeal, and to require from the defendant a bond, with sureties, to answer the final decree in the cause, or to dispense with such bond, as it shall see fit.

SEC. 4. The several courts vested with jurisdiction of cases arising under the patent laws may, at any time during the pendency of any patent cause, grant or suspend the issuing or operation of an injunction upon such terms as the court may impose, and *subject to such rules and regulations as the Supreme Court may establish,* shall have like power after an appeal of said cause, and while the same is pending in the Supreme Court.

SEC. 5. Section forty-nine hundred and sixteen of the Revised Statutes is hereby amended so as to read as follows: Whenever any patent is inoperative or invalid, by reason of a defective or insufficient specification, or by reason of the patentee claiming as his own invention or discovery more or less than he had a right to claim as new, if the error has arisen by inadvertence, accident, or mistake, and without any fraudulent or deceptive intention, the Commissioner shall, on the surrender of such patent and the payment of the duty required by law, cause a new patent for the same invention [shown in the model or drawings, or described in the original specification or its amendments, and to which he would have been entitled,] and in accordance with the corrected specification, to be issued to the patentee, or in the case of his death, or of an assignment of the whole or any undivided part of the original patent, then to his executors, administrators, or assigns, for the unexpired part of the term of the or ginal patent. Such surrender shall take effect upon the issue of the amended patent. The Commissioner may, in his discretion, cause several patents to be issued for distinct and separate parts of the things so shown or described, upon demand of the applicant, and upon payment of the required fee for a reissue for each of such reissued letters patent. The specifications and claim in every such case shall be subject to revision, [and] restriction, *and rejection,* in the same manner as original applications are. Every patent so reissued, together with the corrected specification, shall have the same effect and operation in law, on the trial of all actions for causes thereafter arising, as if the same had been originally filed in such corrected form, except as otherwise provided in this act; *but no new matter shall be introduced into the specification not shown, contained, or substantially indicated in the specification or drawings of the original application or its amendments.* In any suit at law or in equity upon a patent hereafter reissued, the defendant, having given notice or pleaded the same in the manner set forth in the forty-nine hundred and twentieth section of the Revised Statutes, may prove in defense to the whole patent, or any of the claims thereof, that the new patent, or any claim thereof, is not for the same invention shown [in the model or drawings, or described in the original specification or] *contained or substantially indicated in the specification or drawings of the original application and* its amendments, and to which he would have been entitled.

SEC. 6. No machine or other article made prior to the surrender of a patent, and the issue thereupon of a new patent, which, or the use of which, did not infringe such surrendered patent, shall be held to be an infringement of any of the claims of the new patent not existing when such machine or other article was made. All rights of action accruing to a patentee, his executors, administrators, or assigns, for profits and damages on account of any infringement of a patent, prior to its surrender for a reissue, shall remain unaffected by such surrender, and no suit shall be barred or abated by such surrender, and all suits at law or in equity may be maintained for the recovery of such damages or profits in the same manner as if said surrendered patent had expired by its own limitation: *Provided,* That nothing contained in this section shall apply to letters patent reissued prior to the date of the passage of this act.

SEC. 7. Whenever a patent has been issued to one person for an invention actually made by him jointly with another or others, or a patent has been issued to several persons for an invention made by only one or more of them, and such error has arisen through inadvertence, accident, or mistake, the Commissioner, upon the application and oath of the true inventor or inventors, and, with the written consent of all the owners of said patent, entered of record, may correct the mistake as a clerical error. No new patent shall be issued in such case, but the correction shall be entered upon the old patent, or the record thereof, or both, and said patent shall thereafter, for all purposes, be regarded as having been properly issued, in its corrected form, at the date of its original issue. Upon such correction, a fee of twenty dollars shall be paid, under such regulations as the Commissioner of Patents may from time to time prescribe.

SEC. 8. Any person who may wish to perpetuate testimony to be used in any patent suit then pending, or which may thereafter be brought, may do so, subject to the following rules and conditions: He may file a bill or petition in the circuit court of any district in which the parties having a right to sue for infringement of said patent, or against whom he shall desire to use testimony to be taken hereunder, or any of them, reside or may be found, setting forth the date, number, and subject of the patent, and the name of the patentee, the names and residences of the several parties interested in said patent, so far as known to him, the names of witnesses proposed to be examined, *the facts proposed to be proved by each,* and his desire to perpetuate testimony, as aforesaid.

On the said parties being brought into court in the usual way, the court, *if it deems it just and reasonable so to do,* may enter an order or orders in the case, directing *before whom and* when and where, either within or without the district, the evidence shall be taken. Both par·

ties may attend at the same time and place or times and places so designated by the court, or at such times and places as they may agree,
and [then and there introduce such legal testimony of said witnesses
as they may se* fit, which] *the petitioners may then and there introduce
such legal testimony of such witnesses as they may see fit relating to the facts
set forth in the petition ; and thereupon, in relation to or in rebuttal or
avoidance of the matters put in evidence by the petitioners, the respondents
may introduce the legal testimony of such of said witnesses as they, or any
of them, may see fit to call, and as the court, upon application in the same
proceeding may permit.* The examination shall be by interrogatories, and
all objections *of mere form to such interrogatories shall be raised at the
time or deemed to have been waived.* The evidence, when so taken, shall
be *certified by the persons taking the same, and by him, or them, respectively, returned to the court, and* filed among the records of the court;
and the same, or duly certified copies thereof, shall thereafter be received, *so far as admissible,* in all suits on said patent to which the said
petitioners, or the said defendants, or any of them, or those claiming
by, through, or under them, shall be parties ; but the witnesses, if living, may be recalled in said suits, and re-examined or cross-examined,
as the case may be, by any party. And the complainant or petitioner
in any such proceeding shall, within twenty days after the filing in court
of any such petition, file in the Patent Office a certificate of the clerk
of the court, setting forth when and where such petition was filed,
together with the date and number of the patent, and the name of
the patentee, which certificate shall be entered of record by the Commissioner of Patents in the assignment records of the Patent Office.
Any number of persons, whether jointly interested or not, may join in
said petition ; and, if necessary, several petitions may be filed, at the
election of the petitioners, in different districts where any other parties
interested in said patent reside or may be found. Each party to said
petition shall pay the costs of taking his own testimony, but all the
costs of court shall be paid by the petitioners ; but the court may, in its
discretion, assess upon the complainant or petitioner any part or all
of the legal costs, and also a reasonable allowance for travel and attendance : *Provided,* That no deposition taken under this section shall be
used, except as against persons who are parties to such proceeding *and
actually served with personal notice,* or those claiming under them by interest acquired subsequent to filing said certificate in the Patent Office :
And provided, That no such deposition shall be used in any action at
law when the witness is alive, competent to testify, and within the
United States during any time when his testimony could be regularly
taken in the cause, *except that if the party producing it in such case shows
any sufficient cause then existing for using the same, it may be admitted ;
but whenever testimony taken hereunder by the petitioners shall be used, testimony taken in the same proceeding by the respondents, in relation to or in
rebuttal or avoidance of the matters referred to by said evidence of the petitioners, may be used by the party against whom said evidence of the petitioners is used.*

SEC. 9. Upon the petition of any person interested adversely to any
original, reissued, or extended patent, and upon proof that the owners
thereof, or persons entitled to bring suits thereon against the petitioner
where the owners are not so entitled, have knowledge of infringement
thereof, and unreasonably delay or neglect to bring suit in which the
validity of said patent may be tried, to the injury of the petitioner, any
court of the United States having jurisdiction of patent causes, upon
notice as hereinafter provided and due hearing, may authorize such peti-

tioner to bring a bill in equity to declare void said patent, or any claim thereof, for any of the causes which by law may render the, same invalid, whether relating to the original patent or any reissue or extension. And a decree rendered in said suit, declaring void said patent, or any claim thereof, shall be conclusive in favor of all persons against all the parties defendant in said suit who may have been duly served or appeared therein. It shall be the duty of the clerk of the court where such suit was pending, within twenty days from the rendition of a final decree adjudging said patent or any claim thereof to be void, to make and send to the Commissioner of Patents a certificate setting forth the names of the parties, the date and number of the patent, and the name of the patentee, and the number of the claims so adjudged to be void; which certificate shall be recorded by the Commissioner of Patents with the records of assignments, and notice of such decree shall be given in connection with such publications and notices as the Commissioner may make of the expiration of patents.

Such petition and bill shall name as defendants all persons who appear by the records of the Patent Office to be owners of said patent, or to have an interest therein, except that licensees holding by licenses not exclusive in their character as to territory or purpose need not be made parties.

Said petition and bill shall be brought in the district where a plurality in interest of the owners of the legal title to the patent reside or are found; but if equal interests are held by owners in different districts, each of which is greater than the interests of owners in any other district, then said petition and bill may be brought in either of said districts. Upon the filing of the petition, an order of notice shall issue to those defendants who are found within the said district, and also to those not to be found therein, directing them, on a day therein to be designated, to appear and show cause, if any they have, why the prayer of said petition should not be granted, and to appear, plead, answer, or demur to such bill as the court shall permit to be filed thereupon. And if the court shall allow such petition and such bill to be filed, no additional service shall be necessary upon those defendants who were served under the petition. Such order shall be served in the same manner that subpœnas in equity are now served, or in such other manner as the court may order. If any defendant does not appear, show cause, plead, answer, or demur within such time as the court, by special order or general rules, may prescribe, it shall be lawful for the court, upon proof of said notice and of the performance of the directions contained therein, to entertain jurisdiction, and to proceed upon said petition and bill in the same manner as if such defendant had been served with process within the district, and had made default.

From a final decree in such suit, an appeal may be taken to the Supreme Court in the same manner provided by law for appeals in other patent causes in equity.

SEC. 10. Whenever any person shall be injured by a claim by the owners of any patent, or the parties entitled to sue thereon, or their agents, that he is infringing the same, made publicly or by notice to customers or consumers, and no suit shall, *within a reasonable time*, be brought and prosecuted to enforce such claim, he may file a petition in equity, in any court of the United States having jurisdiction of patent causes, to compel the person making such claim, or on whose behalf it is made, to bring or cause to be brought a suit on said patent, to test its validity and the question of its infringement by those acts which are so claimed to constitute an infringement. The petitioner shall file affidavits in support of the allegations of his petition, and the court, upon sufficient cause shown, shall order the defendant to appear at a day named, to show cause why the prayer of the petition should not be granted. On the return day of said order of notice, the defendant shall file his answer, with dffidavits in defense; and the petitioner may file affidavits in reply within such time as the court may fix. If, upon a hearing on the petition, answer, and affidavits, the court shall deem it just and reasonable, it shall pass an order requiring the respondent to bring a suit as aforesaid, within a time named, and in default thereof to be enjoined from thereafter making or prosecuting in any manner, against the petitioner, or those claiming under him as purchasers of any specific article, machine, or composition of matter, the claim which is found and adjudged by the court to be the basis of the petition; and upon such default, the court may issue an injunction accordingly.

SEC. 11. On each and every patent for an invention issued after the passage of this act, there shall be paid to the Commissioner a duty, as follows, namely: Fifty dollars to be paid on or before the first day of January occurring next after the expiration of four years from the date of the *original* patent, and one hundred dollars on or before the first day of January occurring next after the expiration of nine years from the date of the *original* patent; and in default of any such payment, the patent shall expire on the first day of April next thereafter. But the Commissioner, for good cause shown, may allow the payment to be made at any time before such first day of April, in which case the patent shall not become void. The Commissioner shall annually, in the month of April, publish a list of the patents which have expired for non-payment of duties. Patents issued under this law shall contain a notification of the annual duties to be paid, and the time of such payments. *It shall be the duty of the Commissioner to keep a record of said payments; and a receipt therefor, or a certificate that the payment has been made, sealed and executed in the manner provided by law for certified copies, shall be conclusive evidence of the payment; and, upon request, it shall be the duty of the Commissioner to cause such a certificate to be indorsed upon or annexed to the letters patent.*

SEC. 12. Section forty-eight hundred and ninety-eight of the Revised Statutes shall be, and hereby is, amended to read as follows: Every patent, or any interest therein, shall be assignable in law by an instrument in writing; and the patentee or his assigns or legal representatives may, in like manner, grant and convey an exclusive right under his patent to the whole or any specified part of the United States, or an exclusive license thereunder, for any specified purpose or territory. An assignment, grant, conveyance, or exclusive license, as aforesaid, shall be void as against any subsequent purchaser, mortgagee, or licensee for a valuable consideration, without notice, unless it is recorded in the Patent Office within [one] *two* months from the execution thereof, or before the execution of such subsequent grant, conveyance, or license. And all licenses and all powers of attorney and agreements made under or relating to any letters patent, may, if desired, be recorded in the Patent Office, and any duly certified copy of the record of the same may be used in evidence in all cases where the copy of the record of any assignment so certified may now by law be used.

SEC. 13. When there are two or more joint owners or owners in common of any patent, a license from any one of said owners shall be good and valid in law, and shall vest in the licensee a right to use the said invention, but not exclusively, according to the terms of said license, unless the conveyance or other instrument creating such joint ownership, or ownership in common, recorded at the Patent Office before the éxecution of said license, shall provide that no license shall be valid unless executed by all of such owners, or a specified portion thereof in number or interest, or unless an agreement to that effect shall be made by said owners and filed for record before the execution of said license.

SEC. 14. Whoever, *with intent to defraud,* conveys any interest in any patent or grants any license thereunder, knowing that the interest or right so purporting to be granted or conveyed has been previously granted in whole or in part to another, without, before the payment, either by note or otherwise, of the consideration, or any part thereof, informing the grantee or grantees of the existence and nature of such incumbrance or prior right, so far as he has actual knowledge thereof, shall, for every such offense, be punished by imprisonment not exceeding one year, or by fine not exceeding one thousand dollars.

SEC. 15. Section four hundred and seventy-nine of the Revised Statutes shall be, and hereby is, amended so as to read as follows: The Commissioner of Patents, Assistant Commissioner, and the chief clerk, before entering upon their duties, shall severally give bond, with sureties, to the Treasurer of the United States, the first two in the sum of ten thousand dollars each, and the last in the sum of five thousand dollars, conditioned for the faithful discharge of their respective duties, and that they shall render to the proper officers of the Treasury a true account of all money received by virtue of their offices.

SEC. 16. Section four hundred and ninety-three of the Revised Statutes shall be, and hereby is, amended so as to read as follows: The price to be paid for uncertified printed copies of specifications and drawings of patents shall be determined by the Commissioner of Patents, within the limits of actual cost as the minimum, and fifty cents as the maximum price, *and for uncertified manuscript copies the reasonable cost of making the same;* and the price to be charged for certified copies shall be the same as for uncertified copies, with the addition of twenty-five cents for the certificate and seal.

SEC. 17. Section eight hundred and ninety-two of the Revised Statutes shall be, and hereby is, amended so as to read as follows: Copies of any records, books, papers, drawings, or models, belonging to the Patent Office, and of letters patent authenticated by the seal and certified by the Commissioner, Assistant Commissioner, or Acting Commissioner of Patents, shall be evidence in all cases wherein the originals could be evidence; and any person making application therefor, and paying the fee required by law, shall have certified copies thereof.

SEC. 18. Section forty-eight hundred and eighty-five of the Revised Statutes shall be, and hereby is, amended so as to read as follows: The final fee due upon the allowance of a patent shall be paid within six months after the sending of the notice of such allowance to the applicant or his agent, and if the fee be not paid within such time the patent shall not be issued. Every patent shall issue, bear date, and take effect as of a day certain, to be fixed by the Commissioner of Patents, not later than the second calendar week after the payment of the final fee; and until the day of issue the application shall be within the jurisdiction of the Commissioner: *Provided,* That no application on which the final fee has been paid, after notice of allowance, shall be withheld from issue because of interference with any application filed subsequent to the payment of the final fee, as aforesaid.

SEC. 19. Section forty-eight hundred and eighty-seven of the Revised Statutes shall be, and hereby is, amended so as to read as follows: No person shall be debarred from receiving a patent for his invention or discovery, nor shall any patent issued subsequent to March second, eighteen hundred and sixty-one, be declared invalid, by reason of its having been first patented in a foreign country upon the invention of the same person, unless the same has been introduced into public use in the United States for more than two years prior to the application ; but all applications hereafter to be made for patents for inventions which shall have been patented in a foreign country upon the invention of the same person shall be made within two years after the date of such foreign patent.

[SEC. 20. Section forty-eight hundred and ninety-four of the Revised Statutes shall be, and hereby is, amended so as to read as follows : All applications for patents shall be completed and prepared for examination within two years after the filing of the application, and in default thereof, or upon failure of the applicant to prosecute the same within two years after any action therein, of which notice shall have been sent to the applicant or his agent, they shall be regarded as abandoned by the parties thereto.]

SEC. [21.] 20. Section forty-eight hundred and ninety-five of the Revised Statutes shall be, and hereby is, amended so as to read as follows: Patents may be granted and issued to the assignee of the inventor or discoverer, and they may be reissued to the owner or owners of the entire interest in the patent; but the assignment must first be entered of record in the Patent Office. And in all cases of an application by an assignee for the issue of a patent, the specification shall be signed and sworn to by the inventor or discoverer ; and in all cases of an application for a reissue of any patent, the application may be made and the corrected specification sworn to and signed by the owner or owners, *or in case of death or disability, his or her legal representative*, of the entire interest in the patent.

SEC. 21. *Any person who has an interest in an invention or discovery, whether as inventor, discoverer, or assignee, for which a patent was ordered to issue upon the payment of the final fee, but who fails to make payment thereof within six months from the time at which it was passed and allowed, and notice thereof was sent to the applicant or his agent, shall have a right to make an application for a patent for such invention or discovery the same as in the case of an original application. But such second application, in order to be a continuation of the original application, must be made within two years after the allowance thereof. But no person shall be held responsible in damages for the manufacture or use of any article or thing for which a patent was ordered to issue under such renewed application prior to the issue of the patent. And upon the hearing of renewed applications preferred under this section, abandonment shall be considered as a question of fact.*

[SEC. 22. Section forty-eight hundred and ninety-seven of the Revised Statutes shall be, and hereby is, repealed ; but in the case of any patent which, prior to the passage of this act, has been ordered to issue, and has been forfeited for non-payment of the final fee, the renewed application provided for by said section may be made within six months from the passage of this act.]

SEC. [23] 22. Section forty-nine hundred of the Revised Statutes shall be, and hereby is, amended so as to read as follows : It shall be the duty of all patentees, and their assigns and legal representatives, and of all persons making or vending any patented article for or under them, to give sufficient notice to the public that the same is patented, either by fixing thereon the word "patented," together with the year the patent was granted, and number of the patent, or when, from the character of the article, this cannot be done, by fixing to it, or to the package wherein one or more of them is inclosed, a label containing the like notice; and in any suit for infringement, by the party failing so to mark, no profits or damages shall be recovered by the plaintiff, except on proof that the defendant was duly notified of the infringement, and continued, after such notice, to make, use, or vend the article so patented : *Provided,* That profits or damages shall not be forfeited for failure to mark the number of the patent on a patented article or its label, unless such failure shall occur at a period later than six months after the passage of this act: *And provided further,* *That this section shall only be applicable to patents hereafter granted.*

SEC. [24] 23. Section forty-nine hundred and four of the Revised Statutes shall be, and hereby is, amended so as to read as follows : Whenever an application is made for a patent, or for the reissue of a patent, which, in the opinion of the Commissioner, would interfere with any pending application, or with any unexpired patent, he shall give notice to the parties in interest, [as the case may be,] and shall direct the examiner of interferences to proceed to determine the question of priority of invention ; and the Commissioner may issue a patent to the party who is adjudged the prior inventor, unless the adverse party appeals from the decision of the examiner of interferences, or of the board of examiners-in-chief, [or of the Commissioner or Assistant Commissioner, as the case may be,] within such time, not less than twenty days, as the Commissioner shall prescribe: *Provided,* That after the final decision between the parties to an interference, the application of the successful party shall not be put into interference with any application filed subsequent to the closing of the testimony taken on behalf of the successful party in the interference so decided; but the patent shall issue to the successful contestant and then, if desired by the subsequent applicant or applicants, an interference may be had with said patent: *And provided further,* That in the case of reissues no interference shall be declared with any patent of later date than that sought to be reissued, except when the original application for such subsequent patent is shown by the office records to have been of prior date to the [application of the] patent sought to be reissued, nor with any application for a patent filed subsequent to the date of the patent sought to be reissued; but, if desired by such subsequent applicant or patentee, on an application for reissue, an interference may be had with the reissued patent after the same shall have been issued.

SEC. [25] 24. All laws and parts of laws inconsistent with the foregoing provisions are hereby repealed.

ARGUMENTS

BEFORE THE

COMMITTEE ON PATENTS,

UNITED STATES SENATE,

IN SUPPORT OF AND SUGGESTING AMENDMENTS TO THE BILL
(S. No. 300) TO AMEND THE STATUTES IN RELATION
TO PATENTS, AND FOR OTHER PURPOSES.

ARGUMENTS

COMMITTEE ON PATENTS,

UNITED STATES SENATE.

THURSDAY, *November* 15, 1877.

The Committee on Patents having invited parties interested in the bill to amend the statutes in relation to patents, and for other purposes, to appear, the following gentlemen were present:

Chauncey Smith and J. J. Storrow, of Boston, appeared in support of the bill; Albert H. Walker, of Chicago, on behalf of certain inventors and patentees; J. H. Raymond, of Chicago, for certain railroad interests; Henry D. Hyde, of Boston, for the Shoe and Leather Association of Boston; C. S. Whitman and W. C. Dodge, of Washington, for the Patent Office Bar Association; George H. Christy, of Pittsburgh, for car-brake manufacturers; T. L. Livermore, of Boston, for the bill, and suggesting amendments to it; Charles F. Stansbury, president of the Patent Office Bar Association; Hon. M. D. Leggett, formerly Commissioner of Patents; Edward H. Knight, formerly official editor of Patent Office; John E. Hatch, of Cincinnati; Charles Colahan, of Cleveland, Ohio, inventor and manufacturer; Wm. Wheeler Hubbell, of Philadelphia, inventor and patentee; and J. M. Blanchard, of Washington.

Messrs. SMITH and STORROW submitted the following:

MEMORANDUM OF THE PRINCIPAL CHANGES INTRODUCED BY A BILL TO AMEND THE STATUTES IN RELATION TO PATENTS AND FOR OTHER PURPOSES.

SECTION 1. There is now no statute of limitations applicable to patent causes. This proposes that no recovery shall be had for an infringement more than four years old, leaving the right to sue for what has been done within four years where the infringement has continued. It allows the court, where many suits are brought on one patent, to have one brought to trial, and meanwhile stay proceedings in the others.

SEC. 2. There are now two ways of recovering in cases of infringements. In an action at law, the plaintiff recovers " actual damages." (R. S., § 4919.) Upon a bill in equity, the court considers that the defendant has by the wrongful use of the plaintiff's invention realized gains and profits, and treats him as trustee thereof for the benefit of the plaintiff and orders him to account for them. (*Burdell* v. *Denig*, 92 U. S., 720.) A court of equity may also give damages where the in-fringer has so conducted his business that the profits do not give ade-quate compensation. (§ 4921.) If the patentee has elected to enjoy his invention by granting the right to use it to those who will pay him a license-fee, and others have bought that right to a sufficient extent to establish a market-value for it, then the " actual damages " which he suffers from the infringement are, generally speaking, measured by the license-fee which he would otherwise have received for the use. (*Burdell* v. *Denig*, 92 U. S., 720; *Packet Co.* v. *Sickles*, 19 Wall., 618; *Birdsall* v. *Coolidge*, 93 U. S., 70.) Where no such license-fee has been established, then the amount of his recovery depends upon all the evidence in the case. This section does not change the rule of damages, but contem-plates the application of the same rule to cases where, from the nature of the invention, the patentee cannot use it himself, but must enjoy his right by allowing others to use it for a license-fee. A railroad-switch would be an example of such a case. (*Seymour* v. *McCormick*, 16 How., 480.) It further provides that in cases where, by the election of the patentee, signified by his course of dealing or by the nature of the in-vention, the patentee's gain comes through use by others, these rules of damages shall apply, and no " account of profits shall be allowed." One reason for this is the fact that such a rule, generally speaking, will give a just compensation for the wrong done ; another reason is that an account of profits in such cases is very expensive to take, and does not give a satisfactory result, because it cannot be told with the certainty required in accounting how much of the profit of a large business en-terprise is due to each particular device which may be employed in the course of it.

In estimating profits, the court started upon the idea of holding the defendant a trustee for the plaintiff of what he had received by the use of the invention. Where the infringement consists of the manufacture and sale of a patented article, the rule is applied easily. *Mowry* v. *Whit-ney*, 14 Wall., 620, was the case of the employment of an improved pro-cess in one step of the manufacture of an article which was not pat-ented, and which could be produced, though at greater expense, by another unpatented process. The court decided that the plaintiff should not have all the profits actually realized in the manufacture, but only such portion as represented the saving in cost made by the use of the plaintiff's process over the use of the old process.

In *Mevs* v. *Conover*, 11 Official Gazette, 1111, the court, following the language of *Mowry* v. *Whitney*, rather than the spirit of the decision, held that the *saving* must be the rule of profits, though, in fact, the busi-ness resulted in a loss instead of a profit, upon the ground that the de-fendant would have lost more if he had not used the plaintiff's inven-tion. Certainly, this was a departure from the ground of treating the defendant as trustee of money actually in his hands. The second clause of this section is intended to relieve the court from decisions which they have felt to work injustice (*Packet Co.* v. *Sickles*, 19 Wall., 618), and to put the rule on its true basis. To avoid the evil of an inflexible rule, the third clause allows the court to increase or diminish the amount of the recovery ; not for the purpose of giving vindictive damages, but to give a "just compensation."

Sec. 3. In patent suits in equity, the court first determines the valid-ity of the patent and the question of infringement; it then orders an account. An appeal cannot be taken unless the account has been com-pleted. The accounting is very expensive, and consumes much time, and if the decision as to validity or infringement is revised, or even modified, on appeal, it becomes useless. This section authorizes the court, in such cases, to permit the appeal to be taken at once.

SEC. 4. This preserves in the circuit court, pending an appeal, the same power over the parties, with relation to the injunction, which it had before the appeal.

SEC. 5. As the law now stands, the Commissioner may grant a reissued patent for "whatever was described, suggested, or substantially indicated in the original specifications, drawings, or Patent-Office model," as constituting "the same invention as that embraced and secured in the original patent." (*Seymour* v. *Osborn*, 11 Wall., 544, 545.) The courts first held that the action of the Commissioner in issuing a patent could not be revised. Then they held that they would compare the two specifications, in order to ascertain whether the reissue was for the same invention as the original, and have evidently been struggling with the rule originally and improvidently laid down. The new section allows the Commissioner to reissue the patent upon the papers and model on which the original was issued, and no others, and allows the correctness of his *ex-parte* action in this respect to be re-examined in litigated cases, substantially as the validity of an original patent can be re-examined.

SEC. 6. The law requires that patents should state what the inventor claims as new; all that is not so claimed the public may lawfully use. If the patentee amends his claim by a reissue, and these new claims cover a machine which was not covered by the claims in existence when it was made, the patentee may prevent the use of the same machine which the defendant lawfully built and invested his money in.

In order to amend his patent, the law obliges the patentee to surrender it and take out a new one. The courts have held that the destruction of the patent by surrender destroys his existing right of action for past infringement.

The amendment takes away from the reissue its retroactive character in both respects.

SEC. 7. If a patent is issued to two on the invention of one, or to one on the invention of two, this mistake may be corrected as a clerical error by the consent of all the inventors and owners.

SEC. 8. A provision for taking testimony *in perpetuam* in patent cases introduced, because the general law applicable to all cases is not adequate in patent causes.

SEC. 9. Allows suits to be brought to repeal and annul patents which are void.

Existing laws afford no adequate remedy.

(See Opin. of Attorney-General of November 19, 1874, Patent Office Gzette, vol. 6, p. 723; *Attorney-General* v. *Rumford Works*, 9 ib., 1062.)

SEC. 10. Supplies a remedy for cases where a person injures the business of another, by advertising that it infringes a patent, and yet refuses to bring a suit in which the validity of the patent or the question of infringement can be tried.

SEC. 11. Many patents are for inventions which, on trial, prove worthless, but which stand in the way of subsequent valuable improvements. This section imposes on all patents a fee of $50 at the end of four years and $100 at the end of nine years, and non-payment of either kills the patent. If the patent is of any value, the fee is not a hardship; if it is not of sufficient value, it will thus be got out of the way. This feature is found in all foreign systems, and weeds out three-fourths of the patents, after actual trial has shown their value or worthlessness. I is believed to be of great advantage to the public and to inventors of really useful improvements.

SEC. 12. This requires exclusive licenses to be recorded in the same manner as technical grants, because, practically, the two are equivalent. It shortens the time allowed for recording assignments from three months to one month. Improvements in the mail-service since 1836 justify this. It allows all agreements about patents to be recorded, and makes certified copies from the record to be legal evidence.

SEC. 13. The law now is that each joint owner of a patent may grant licenses without the consent of the other. The object of this amendment is to give full effect to an agreement between them as to which shall exercise this power, if the agreement be in writing, signed by all the parties, and recorded.

SEC. 14. This punishes, by not exceeding one year's imprisonment or $1,000 fine, whosoever sells as unencumbered a patent which he actually knows he has no power to sell and convey. This is new.

The following sections amend those which regulate proceedings in the Patent Office:

SEC. 15. This requires the Assistant Commissioner of Patents to give the same bond as the Commissioner.

SEC. 16. This establishes the price for Patent-Office copies in no case to be less than actual cost.

SEC. 17. The old statute allowed certified copies of papers to be used as evidence wherever the originals would be competent. The amendment extends the provisions to models, and also allows the Assistant Commissioner to sign the certificate.

SECS. 18, 22. Sections 4885 and 4897 allow six months' grace for payment of the final fee, and then two years more in addition by means of a renewed application. This amendment consolidates the two sections and abolishes the two years' allowance.

SEC. 19. The law about granting patents in this country to those who have patented their inventions abroad has been changed several times, particularly by the act of March 2, 1861, in a manner which has caused considerable confusion. This section establishes what is believed to be a just and reasonable rule. It retains the provision that a foreign patentee cannot come here to get a patent for an invention that has been in use here for two years, and adds a new requirement, that if he makes it known by patenting it abroad he must apply here within two years, or it can be used by the public.

SEC. 20. This amends section 4894, by making two years' neglect to prosecute an application conclusively equivalent to an abandonment thereof.

SEC. 21. At one time, the surrender of a patent and the application for a reissue were required to be sworn to by the assignee and at another time by the inventor. This amendment leaves it to be sworn to by the assignee. The oath is of no importance, because the action of the Commissioner is to be based on the sworn statements filed by the inventor on his original application. To require his oath to the new application, is to enable him to extort money from the person who has already bought and paid him for the invention.

SEC. 24. The law has always required the patentee to mark on the article the date of the patent. About 300 patents a week are now issued, all bearing the same date. This amendment requires him to add the number of his patent, in order that it may be identified.

SEC. 25. This amends section 4904, about interference applications in the office, so as to include reissue applications and make the law about them substantially conform to what the decisions have established about them, except that, in determining whether an interference contest shall be ordered, reference is to be had solely to the dates of the original applications.

SEC. 26. Repeals all inconsistent laws. Careful provisions have been added to each section which relates to substantial rights as distinguished from the form of remedy so that the changes introduced by this bill shall not be retroactive.

Respectfully submitted, by

CHAUNCEY SMITH.
J. J. STORROW.

WASHINGTON, *November* 15, 1877.

ARGUMENT OF CHAUNCEY SMITH, Esq.

Mr. CHAIRMAN AND GENTLEMEN OF THE COMMITTEE : I had the honor last year, just before the close of the session, to appear before this committee in opposition to a bill which had been brought from the House to the Senate and referred to this committee. In appearing before the committee at that time, I stated, if I remember correctly, that while I deemed the provisions of that bill unwise and not calculated to promote the interests of the country, or even well adapted to promote the objects which the person had in view who brought the bill before Congress, I still desired to have it understood that I did not appear to oppose all amendments to the patent law or to contend that in its present condition it was all that could be desired; and it will be remembered that I then submitted several propositions, in addition to those which had been embraced in the bill before the committee, which I deemed important. I suggested such considerations as seemed to me legitimately to bear upon the question, and which, in my judgment, would justify some important modifications of the patent law.

The result of that hearing, if I understood it, was that, to some extent at least, the committee seemed to consider as worthy of attention the propositions which I submitted. I believe in part, if not in full, they favorably reported them to the Senate.

No final action, however, was taken, and with the understanding that the committee had obtained leave to sit during the recess I early planned with some of those with whom I was associated to lay before the profession and those interested in patents, as far as we conveniently could, the action which had been taken in Congress and some propositions for further amendments to the bill. I think Senator Wadleigh was aware of my intention to do this, and thought it might be well to secure in this way, as far as we could, the opinions of the members of the bar, especially of those who had had experience in the practice and administration of the patent law.

Some time in the summer, therefore, there was a pamphlet prepared in Boston and sent out under my name—although a very large part of it was not peculiarly my work—inviting those to whom it was sent to consider its provisions, and, if they saw fit, to communicate with myself, or others who were known to be interested in this matter, and state their views upon the proposed amendments of the patent law.

There was no suggestion as to what our own views were, no arguments intended to secure a favorable expression of opinion, but merely the expression of a desire to know what the wishes, judgment, and ex-

2 P

perience of the members of the bar familiar with the workings of the
patent law might be upon the various amendments.

There was a brief preface stating the subject-matter of the pamphlet.
After stating the object of the contents of the pamphlet, it reads as follows:

"The third paper herewith printed, containing several provisions in
addition to those embraced in either of the preceding papers, is submitted
for the purpose of obtaining opinions in relation to the subject from
those interested in patents or in the administration or improvement of
the patent law, and especially the opinions of lawyers whose practice
has given them an opportunity to observe the practical working of the
law as it now is.

"The chairman of the committee of the Senate has expressed a desire
to have these opinions obtained, so far as can be done, and at the request of many gentlemen I have taken this method of obtaining them.
I shall be glad to receive any communications on the subject. Attention is especially invited—

"1. To the proposed limitation of the time within which damages or
profits may be recovered, contained in the first section.

"2. To the provision contained in the second section (two forms of
which are given) in relation to the measure of damages and the rule for
estimating profits in certain cases.

"3. To the provisions of the fourth section in relation to rights of
action under claims in reissued patents which were not in the original
patent, and to the loss of existing rights of action by a reissue.

"4. To the provisions of the eighth section requiring the payment, at
certain intervals, of fees in order to preserve such patents as are found
to be worth preserving."

Soon after issuing that pamphlet I received communications from
some gentleman upon the subject, and finally an invitation was extended
to me to visit gentlemen in Chicago for the purpose of conferring on the
subject of amending the patent law.

I went there in the latter part of September. I met Mr. Raymond,
and the counsel for the Western Railroad Association, Mr. Payson, and
several other gentlemen from different parts of the country, many of
them counsel for the railroad companies who had been supposed to have
an especial interest in the passage of the act brought here last year, but
among them many counsel familiar with the practice of the patent law.

We sat down together and discussed the subject for seven days, as
earnestly and as candidly, I think, as any gentlemen ever could discuss
a question of the importance of this. We met, differing widely in our
views; we parted, having come to a very substantial agreement in our
views. We had done this, not by concessions on our side of what we
deemed to be valuable, for the purpose of securing a like concession from
other parties, in order that we might present a bill which might be regarded as a compromise bill, but we came to the conclusions which we
did from an honest conviction that in our discussions we ought to weigh
the objections most carefully which had been presented on one side or
the other; and I believe that the result of our discussions there was an
agreement based upon a conviction, shared by all alike, that we had been
compelled to concede nothing to each other as the price of other concessions, but that we had discussed the subject in the utmost fairness and
arrived at valuable results. As soon as we had done that we prepared a
revision of the proposed amendments, embracing more than had been
contained in the first pamphlet, and this revision, in turn, was printed,

and sent to all gentlemen who had received the original pamphlet, and to a large number besides.

I think several hundred copies were distributed in this way, without any other suggestion than to say that what the pamphlet contained was the result of our deliberations, and that if anything could be elicited by way of objection or approval, or by way of addition thereto, we should be glad to receive it.

The result which we hoped to reach by this method of addressing the public was in some degree realized. We received written and verbal communications from many, and expressions of satisfaction to a considerable extent with the work which had been done. Some criticism has been made. Some have doubted the wisdom of all its provisions which we have thought proper to present here. Generally, however, I may say that the result of our labor has been received by the profession much more favorably than we had any reason to expect from gentlemen who were not in possession of the views which we entertained personally and of the reasons upon which we had presented the proposed amendments.

I come, therefore, with some degree of confidence before this committee to say that I feel justified in the conclusion that the work which we have presented to the public, and which we now come before the committee and Congress for the purpose of securing favorable action upon, has received a very general approval from those who have the largest interest in the working of the patent law, either for it or adversely to it, and from those who have had the largest experience and the best means of judging as to the value of its provisions. Such, Mr. Chairman, is the history of this bill.

Before considering its provisions in detail, I should be glad if the committee would indulge me in a few observations upon the general expediency of the proposed amendments, especially with reference to their bearing upon the general working of the patent law.

The Constitution of the United States provides that "Congress shall have power to promote the progress of the useful arts by giving to inventors, for a limited period, the exclusive right to their respective inventions"; and, in pursuance of this power, in 1790 a patent law was passed, and the country has been in the possession of a patent law ever since. That law was repealed three years subsequent to its passage and a new one substituted, which remained in force with some amendments until 1836. The law then underwent a complete revision. The whole theory of our system was changed in several important particulars. Previously to that, patents had been granted to any one who applied for them, no supervision being exercised over the issue of a patent except as to its form. No power existed on the part of the Secretary of State, as I understand it, or the Attorney-General or officers who had it on charge, to reject an invention if the applicant saw fit to take his patent.

In 1836, as I said, the law underwent a complete revision. The most important new feature of it was the institution of the Patent Office under the charge of an officer whose duty it was, before issuing a patent, to examine the alleged invention and to form a judgment as to its value and as to the fact whether or not it was an original invention with the party laying claim to it. This feature of our system has remained in force ever since. It has been adopted by other countries, and is now about being adopted in England. It has been adopted, as I understand, in Germany, though I have not personally examined the matter. It has secured the assent of other countries, as I am informed.

This law has remained in force without much substantial change until the present time. It is true, the law underwent revision in 1870, but its features were not essentially changed, and some changes were effected upon the revision of the statutes in 1874; but they were not material. Substantially, then, we are subject now to the law which has been in operation since 1836.

Has this law vindicated the wisdom of the original provision of the Constitution and the provisions of the law itself in promoting the progress of the useful arts? I cannot entertain a doubt that those who have witnessed its operations must come to the conclusion that, whatever its faults may have been, its advantages to the public have been immense and were never greater than at the present day. It has, as I believe, stimulated invention to a high degree. It has produced the most extraordinary and wonderful inventions in our own country which the world has ever seen. It has interwoven new inventions with every branch of our national industries.

During the first ten years of the existence of the patent law, only about two hundred and fifty patents were granted; at the present time something like 15,000 are granted in a year. They embrace every branch of human industry. They cover the whole field of our manufactures, and not of our manufactures alone, but of agriculture. It would not be possible to-day to raise a bushel of wheat in this country without taking advantage of modern inventions. If the plow itself was not a patented plow, it yet would be a plow which embraced in the iron or steel used in its construction patented productions or the result of patented machinery. If, for the sake of the experiment, we discarded the plow for the more primitive spade, we should still find ourselves in the use of patented inventions. Turn whichever way we will, our daily life is beset, so to speak, with modern inventions.

I remember when my mother was a spinner, and spun and wove the cloth with which she clad her children. She walked backwards and forwards at her wheel, drawing out a thread of some two or three yards in length, and doing for a day's work an amount of travel which, I think, amounted to between three and four miles. Some little time since I was in a manufactory watching the operations of a boy tending a machine which drew out 600 threads at a time, each of them longer than the threads which my mother drew, twisting them and winding them up on the spindle in less time than she could do it; and on inquiry I found that that was a machine of limited capacity; that other machines existed which drew out 1,500 threads at once. Upon inquiry I became satisfied that it would not be extravagant to say that the value of human labor to-day in spinning was a thousand-fold what it was in my early days.

Weaving has shared in the general progress, not, perhaps, quite to that extent, but still to such an extent that, as a domestic art, it has ceased to exist. Have we ever reflected upon the wonders involved in the production, at the present day, of a yard of cotton cloth? The cotton must be raised. How much machinery is involved, except as it may be involved in the preparation of the soil, in planting the cotton. I do not know, but it is no sooner gathered than it is brought within the reach of some invention. Among the earliest of those of which the patent-law of this country keeps a record is Whitney's cotton-gin. At the very next stage of its progress it comes under the action of patented machines for baling it. These bales, in their turn, are fastened by patent fasteners now in use, and which are deemed of such importance that large manufactory interests are involved in them. It is brought to our mills in the East for manufacture by railroads, the fruit of inventions of later years, and by steamships which did not exist at the commencement of this century. It finds its way to our mills to be taken from the cars into the mills by patent derricks, or elevators. It is cleansed by patented machinery; it is spun by a whole long list of patented inventions to reach its final form; it is woven into cloth which numbers, it is a modest calculation to say, one hundred threads to the inch. I think the number is more than double that; but even at that number we would find that the length of thread in a yard of cloth was more than seven thousand yards, and yet, when this length of thread has been twisted and woven, it is sold, it may be, for not over four cents a yard. At the several stages of its progress, it has passed under the influence of recent patented inventions.

I stood, not long since, in a print shop where this cloth comes to receive its final finish by receiving upon its surface figures devised by artists of the highest character, giving to it a beauty which Solomon in all his glory could not command in his day, and I wondered at the amount of invention which was concentrated at the point where the roll which imprinted the figure, the cloth, and the chemical dye which imparted it were brought together. Along one line I traced this series of inventions which I have been describing, having reference to the production of cotton and weaving it into cloth. I went into an adjoining room and found artists engraving the rolls. I knew that these rolls were produced by improved processes, the result of chemical investigation and of mechanical invention such as the world was entirely ignorant of a few years previous. I found the artists engraving designs which were themselves the result of high artistic progress in their departments. I watched the applications of the dyes, and I knew there was a long line of invention which had placed them within the reach of man, and a whole series of processes by which these designs of skilled artists could be imprinted on the cloth, which went out of the mills to be sold at seven or eight cents a yard.

I could cite numerous examples of the same kind. Invention has given us the telegraph, a thing unknown a few years since. It has given us all the varied products of rubber, unheard of till within the life of all aged men now living. It has given us the reaper and the mowing-machine and the thrasher. Why, the very words that were used in agriculture in my boyhood now no longer have their original meaning. Reaping is not what it used to be. A reaper formerly was a man using a sickle; it is now a machine. A thrasher is not a man using a flail; it is a machine driven by a steam-engine, devouring the grain on the Western fields faster than two teams can bring it from the field within their reach.

I took occasion to say while I was in consultation with the gentlemen in Chicago that the papers the past season had been filled with the importance to this country of securing the European markets for the grain which was raised on the Western prairies. It was deemed a matter of national importance. The struggle was to be, whether this country or the fields of Russia were to supply the demand for the manufacturing centers of Europe. There are three classes of men, I said to those gentlemen, who are especially interested in the progress of this national industry. They are the farmers who raise the grain, the millers who grind it, and the railroads which transport it; and upon the progress of invention which shall enable them to lay down a bushel of wheat or a barrel of flour at our Eastern wharves at a few cents more or less, may depend our hold upon those vast markets. If there are any classes of men to-day who are hostile to patents, it is just these three classes of men whom I have named as being most especially interested in this great branch of national industry. Let me turn wherever I will, I find similar illustrations.

Let me allude to one, because it is of historic interest. Adam Smith, in his "Wealth of Nations," refers to the manufacture of pins, as practiced in his day, to illustrate the great advantages of the division of labor, and tells us that there were eighteen operations to be performed in the manufacture of pins. Generally they were each performed by a single individual, but sometimes, where the number of workmen was not sufficiently large, one individual at different times performed different operations. He had seen, he said, an establishment where ten men were engaged in manufacturing pins. They were able, by the great skill which they had acquired, to make twelve pounds of pins in a day, and as each pound, he said, contains on an average four thousand pins, the product of a day's labor was forty-eight thousand pins, where, without this advantage derived from the division of labor, ten men would not, perhaps, have been able to produce over twenty pins each a day. All that is changed now. In a room not much larger than this, a short time since, I saw forty machines at work, not much larger than sewing-machines. They were in the charge of four men, who kept them in repair, supplied them with material, and took away their product. That was all they had to do, and when the material was once fed to the machines the machine went on doing its duty with more precision than it would if it had been a living person. Each machine was turning out pins at the rate of 160 a minute, and thus the establishment was producing pins at the rate of about four millions a day. Nothing remained to be done with the pins after they left the machine except to treat them chemically for the purpose of coloring them and to stick them on papers. Strange as it may seem, it cost more to put them on papers than to make them. Invention, I believe, has changed that, so that now pins are stuck on the papers without the aid of human fingers. And, most wonderful of all, these pins, cut from wire, pointed, headed, colored, and put on papers, with all the expense attending their sale, were sold for between 3 and 4 cents per pound more than the wire cost out of which they were made. Pins themselves are of comparatively modern invention. I believe Queen Elizabeth did not have them. Who would dispense with them now? They enter into our daily habits, so that it would be regarded a deprivation to be without them; and yet a little addition to their cost would place them beyond the reach of many persons. Now they are so cheap that nobody can afford to be economical of them.

Within a few years there has been a form of pin invented for the benefit of the infant portion of the community, a toilet pin which protects the point. It is a wire pointed at one end and cunningly twisted, so that one end serves as a shield for the point of the pin. It was pointed out to an English lady at our Patent Office as one of the most interesting inventions that we had to present. Why was it not invented long before? It waited three hundred years before getting itself invented after pins were introduced. No one would imagine it involved invention, and yet, though the need always existed, it was not until some happy thought brought it to the mind of some lucky inventor that it was brought to the world; and no person now would think of dispensing with it.

Shall I pass over the various modifications—the various inventions of comparatively a trifling character—and come to one which I think will be deemed the wonder of the world, which even now is exciting the wonder, not merely of those who do not understand it, but even more, the wonder of those who believe they understand it.

You have all heard of the telephone, recently introduced, by which, Mr. Chairman, I believe that if you had the communication established you could talk with your friends in San Francisco as readily and as easily as I now talk with you. If I was called upon to produce evidence that this invention was due directly to the influence of the patent laws, I have a witness here whom I could put upon the stand to testify to you that, knowing its history, he knew well that Mr. Bell at least would never have invented that device, that wonderful contrivance, unless it had been for the hope that through the patent law he would reap a rich reward for his devotion to this invention.

Some years ago I appeared before a committee of the House upon a matter connected with the telegraph. The president of the Western Union Telegraph Company was there opposing the measure which I had either the honor or misfortune to advocate. I was endeavoring to impress upon the committee the conviction that our telegraph communications might be greatly improved; that there were inventions lying in the land, unused by the Western Union Company, which would enable them to perform that service for the country for less than half what it was done for then. I was asked what these inventions were. I enumerated several. My friend Mr. Hubbard, here present, will remember that I mentioned among others the duplex telegraph, a device by which messages are sent at the same time over the same wire in opposite directions, or, if need be, two sets of messages in the same direction. You should have seen the look of incredulity which passed over the faces of the members when I stated that this could be done; you should have seen the smile of contempt on the face of Mr. Orton as he referred to inventors. I said, "Mr. Orton, you ought, I think, to know, but apparently you do not know, that this invention has been in daily use between Boston and New York for six months; it is only because a man, who has made an improvement in the invention in the hope of the reward which will come from it, is himself the president of a weak telegraph company, and he is able to maintain the field as a competitor with you only by means of this invention."

Mr. Orton left the room, as I have been assured, with the determination that he would not rest until he had possessed himself of that invention; and he did obtain it, and now, to-day, spread all over the land, are machines in operation which not only send double messages, but which send quadruple messages over the wires; and this great controversy in New York a few weeks since between the two rivals was based upon the desire of each to possess the advantages of that invention.

Shall any one say to me that inventions would be made if there were no patent laws? Why are the inventors so ready to come forward and take the advantages of the patent law unless they make their inventions in view of the protection they afford? Any gentleman who has practiced long with inventors knows that no contracts are more common than those which have reference to future inventions where parties stipulate, on the one hand the inventor and the other hand the man possessed with means, that the inventor shall set himself to work to evolve an invention which is to be the joint property of the two. Would such contracts ever be made if the patent law was not in force? If this day there should be a change in the Constitution which should give to Congress the power, not to promote the useful arts, but to retard and hinder them, and Congress was called upon to carry out that provision of the Constitution, what would be its first step except to repeal the patent law?

What else would it be necessary to do? Would not every one instinct-ively feel that except for the stimulus of patent law there would be no need to invoke any legislation to retard and destroy inventions?

You need not impose a penalty on a man for making an invention. Take away from him the hope of reward, and the trouble and labor and expense of making inventions will be quite sufficient to prevent anybody from making them. I affirm, therefore, that if it is a desirable thing to promote the progress of the useful arts, it is a necessary and indis-pensable thing to provide a patent law which shall. afford protection to inventors; and not to them alone—hardly to them primarily—but to those who are called upon when inventions are made to invest the ne-cessary capital to bring them out and demonstrate their value.

This is one of the most important functions of the patent law; for, except for this, inventions might lie around you as thick as hoar-frost in an autumn morning, and people would not invest the money required and take the risks which they have to incur if they knew the fruits would be seized by their neighbors the next day, and they should have to go into competition loaded with the weight of the expenditure which had been necessary in order to bring the inventions before the public. Not alone for the inventor does the patent law exist; not alone for the manufacturer or the capitalist, but primarily for the country; but for the country only through and by the influence and the protection which the patent law has upon and gives to the men of genius and the men of capital. Look at the history of Canada. She started into the race with us and other countries under the belief that she could take inven-tions of other countries, and especially of her inventive neighbor at the south, without paying for them. She made provisions for protecting her own inventors, but no foreigner could take the benefit of the patent law in Canada, if I understand it right. The inventions would not go there. The inventions which were made here and proved to be profit-able could not be transported to Canada, because nobody would take the risk and be subject to the free competition of a man who spent no money upon them; consequently their system was changed, and our inventors have the Canadian field, and now are this day going there with their inventions simply because the introduction of them is attended with the hope of reward.

How many of our industries have grown up to a magnitude which makes them important far beyond what I have said. We are seizing the watch manufacture of the world. Switzerland went home from here last year in dismay at the prospect that this industry of hers would be swept from her hands. Her commissioners went home to recommend the establishment of a patent law.

I know of no more striking illustration of what can be reached in the progress of time by the continued efforts of inventors than this very matter of the watch and clock manufacture. Go down through the streets of this city—or any other city, I suppose, in this country—and you will find in their shop-windows, at any time, bushels—I use the term not extravagantly—bushels of a little cheap clock, which will keep good time, which is tasteful in its appearance, and serves all the purposes of the domestic clock; and you can buy it for $1.25.

One other illustration, Mr. Chairman, and I will leave this subject. We all know that engineering has received an accession to its powers within a few years which seems to enable it to defy all obstacles which nature may interpose in its path. Its additional power has been gained through two important inventions; one is the steam-drill, the other is nitro-glycerine. One of them struggled into existence. It received its full development in the work attending the Hoosac Tunnel. A steam-drill, it is true, had been introduced in the Mont Cenis Tunnel. It was an exceedingly expensive instrument to use, and has been entirely supplanted by what is now known as the "Burleigh drill." When I was called upon some years since to investigate the invention involved in that drill, I found that there were almost a hundred, certainly scores, of men who had attempted to occupy that field, but the attempt had not been successfully attained until the time I indicate—during the progress of the work on the Hoosac Tunnel. When it was accomplished, the invention was so simple that you could hardly lay your hand upon the feature which distinguished Burleigh's drill from all the fruitless efforts which had been made before. But now it enables us to pierce mountains which human power would never have dreamed of. It opens to us at far less cost the boundless resources of the Western mountains. Not by that alone, however, for alongside of it is the invention of nitroglycerine, which, when it was discovered a few years ago, was looked upon as so dangerous to human life that it would be impossible to train it to the service of man. It seemed to be created by nature for no other purpose than to fill the world with alarm. It has now become as harmless as a little child at play until it is called upon to perform its work; and it does it then with a power which human imagination had no conception of until this agent was introduced.

I had placed upon the sheet of paper before me a variety of other illustrations, and I think those that I have named are by no means the most marked. They are, however, I believe, those in which you can trace most directly and emphatically the influence of the patent law. I am perfectly well assured that Mr. Burleigh would never have invented the Burleigh drill unless he had hoped for a reward through the working of the patent law; for he had not got the invention onto paper, even, before he started for Washington to secure his patent.

I will now ask the attention of the committee to the special provisions of the bill.

I am reminded that I omitted to state, in giving the history of this bill, that some of its provisions were planned and presented by the members of the Patent Bar Association, relating particularly and especially to the practice of the Patent Office; and others who were associated with us and myself limited our labor principally to provisions relating to the administration of the law after patents are issued. As I proceed I will call attention to some of those provisions.

It may seem strange, Mr. Chairman, yet the fact is so, that there is no statute of limitation which bars the right of action on suits for the infringement of a patent. This omission probably has arisen from the fact that the law of the United States does not provide statutes of limitation except under the general provision which places actions in the Federal courts under the law of the State courts in that particular. There has been some conflict of decisions in the courts as to whether the statutes of the several States in relation to limitations of actions generally would apply to the actions for the infringement of a patent; most of the decisions, I think, however, have been adverse to the application of these laws. I think it must be taken, therefore, that there is no statute of limitations applicable to it.

The bill which was presented here last year provided that no recovery should be had in actions for an infringement of a patent for more than one year prior to the giving of a notice of infringement. I suggested in the hearing before the committee at the last session that that, in the first place, was inadequate to cut off the right of action, because it°could be preserved by giving notice; and if notice had been given, no length of time was interposed as a bar to the action. I suggested, too, that, in my judgment, an evil would arise from that of very serious magnitude, and that was, that parties having a right of action, or thinking they might have a right of action, would feel it necessary to give notice universally. That, of itself, is a matter which is attended with considerable injury sometimes, because a claim that a right of action exists for infringement is necessarily an uncertain one, and people often find themselves embarrassed in their business who are innocent infringers, if infringers at all, by the influence which such notices have upon the willingness of people to trade with them.

I suggested then that the true remedy was a statute of limitations, and the first section of this bill, that I have the honor to call the attention of the committee to, is a statute of limitations. It provides that no damages shall be recovered for a period of more than four years prior to the bringing of the suit. There has been a general expression of opinion so far as I know, or have been able to learn, that there should be some statute of limitations provided. There has been a considerable difference of opinion as to what the true limit should be. Some have thought that it should be six years from the expiration of the patent, which would carry it over a period of twenty-three years. Others have thought that the right of action should expire with the patent. Some gentlemen have suggested that it should either be shorter than four years or as long as six. Some find the principle by which they thought it should be governed in the analogy of actions upon contract, which usually run for six years. Others think it should be treated more in the nature of a tort; and in this case the statute is generally shorter.

Legally, an infringement of a patent is a tort, and it would naturally, if mere names were to be observed, fall under the shorter limitation. We have thought that there are good reasons why there should not be a very short period of limitation, because the length of time which is requisite to bring a suit on a patent to a hearing for the purpose of testing the validity of the patent is necessarily long, occupying two or three years before the circuit court, sometimes longer; and if it goes to the Supreme Court, generally from three to five years. It seemed wise then, it seemed judicious, to give such a length of time as would enable the patentee to bring his suit to test the validity of his invention without the necessity of bringing a multitude of suits in order to preserve his right of action; and thinking that generally it might be assumed that that question might be determined in four years, we have suggested that as the proper time.

In order, however, to give a party the right without unnecessary expense to preserve his rights of action by bringing a suit, we have introduced a proviso giving the courts power, whenever the bringing of a suit becomes necessary, to suspend the progress of all others while one suit is going forward in good faith to test the questions at issue, thus giving a party the power to protect his rights without subjecting either plaintiffs or defendants to the expense which attends the prosecution of a suit to final judgment.

The last proviso is one which relates to causes of action now in existence, upon which I suppose I need not spend time.

Senator MORGAN. It has occurred to me that there should be an exception incorporated in the first section; and that is, to limit the operations of the bar in the statute to those persons using such patent for their personal account, and not for the sale of the invention or the manufacture of patented machines or parts of machines for sale. Probably a person ought not to be held liable to account for damages who had been using the patent in good faith upon his own account and in his own business; but if he had been engaged in speculation he ought not to be entitled to the benefit of that statute. I think there ought to be an exception as to that class of persons who have willfully and for profit invaded the rights of the patentee.

Mr. SMITH. I can only say, in respect to that, that I think, if the issue of good faith were presented, it would be a difficult issue to try, and one which would be claimed to exist in all cases; and that no person ever infringes a patent or does any other thing in the ordinary course of business except for profit.

Senator MORGAN. My question is not one of good faith, but for personal use and personal advantage, without sale or attempt to derive profit by sale of the manufactured patented machines or parts of a machine.

Mr. SMITH. I suppose your objection relates to the use of the machines, like the mowing-machine or the reaper, and alludes to such a case as the purchase by a farmer without any knowledge.

Senator MORGAN. Where a man in California or Oregon has invented a machine, patents and introduces it there, has capital to carry it on there, and another party in Georgia or some other distant point, Maine, for instance, becomes furnished with the information which enables him to manufacture such machines, and he does so, and disposes of them along the Atlantic coast, that man ought to be punished, of course, for his invasion of the rights of the patentee; whereas, if such a person were to use a patent unwittingly, I may say, while he violates the patent rights of the inventor, he uses it for his own purposes.

Senator WADLEIGH. Your idea is that this first section should apply to cases where a man makes a personal use of the thing, but not to a case where he manufactures for profit—that there should be a longer limitation, if anything?

Senator MORGAN. It ought to be an exception.

Mr. SMITH. That there should be no right of action against the party for personal use?

Senator MORGAN. No; limit it to four years against that person, but increase the length of the bar against the person who uses it for profit.

Mr. SMITH. I think that is a suggestion which is deserving of consideration; though it does not strike me as practical to apply it in such a way as will not subject the users of machines, if there is a short bar, to the necessity of being sued in order to preserve the rights of action; and it has been one part of our effort to place the rule so that litigation may be rendered unnecessary to as large an extent as possible. I am, however, very glad of the suggestion.

Senator WADLEIGH. Your view is that if the owner of the patent allows it to go into use by parties who have purchased of those who have manufactured for profit, thereby the plaintiff is foreclosed from bringing a suit against them?

Mr. SMITH. I do not understand that that is the suggestion. The suggestion is that if parties who purchase machines or use inventions themselves are liable to be sued, and must be sued, say within one year, the necessity for bringing suits against them will be greatly increased, because parties will not allow their rights to expire or become barred when they know of them; whereas, under the longer statute of limitations, the question at issue may be decided in one suit, and will serve as a guide in the settlement and disposal of other causes afterward.

Senator WADLEIGH. Senator Morgan is not disposed to shorten the time at all.

Senator MORGAN. I am satisfied with the four years. I have never seen a statute that was not liable to some exceptions. In the course of judicial investigations exceptions are grafted upon them.

Mr. SMITH. There are some cases where there would be some necessity for a longer provision. There are classes of cases where some injustice would be done if limited to four years. I had not thought of that method of meeting with the objection; and if it should be deemed advisable, I certainly do not at present see any reason for objecting to it. If the committee will pardon me, I will now yield to other gentlemen, resuming my remarks hereafter.

ARGUMENT OF A. H. WALKER, Esq.

GENTLEMEN OF THE COMMITTEE: I was much pleased with the eloquent eulogy Mr. Smith pronounced upon the patent law as it now stands. He *delivered* the encomium; *I* will apply it. I will do so by urging the committee to change the law with great caution, lest, according to the old fable, it kill the goose that laid the golden eggs.

My remarks will be confined wholly to the second section of the proposed act. In order to its proper understanding, I will review the law as it now exists. There are at present two methods, in either of which a patentee may proceed to enforce a money recovery for the infringement of his patent. He may proceed at law and recover " *damages,*" *i. e.,* what *he has lost* by reason of the infringement, or he may proceed in *equity* and recover the infringer's "*profits,*" *i. e.,* what the infringer has *gained* by his wrongful acts.

These remedies are based on wholly different theories; the first being an action of trespass on the case, and the other a bill in equity based on the idea that the infringer is a constructive trustee *de son tort* for the benefit of the patentee as to whatever gain the former has derived from the infringement. They are also adapted, each, to a different class of patents. The value of a patent on a *bed*, for example, consists wholly in *making* and *selling* it. These things can be done by one man about as well as by another, and therefore, in *such* cases, the recovery of "*damages*" is an adequate remedy.

The *hot-air blast* is an example of a patent the value of which, on the other hand, consists wholly in its *use*. Formerly blast-furnaces were fed only with cold air. Afterward it was discovered that by simply introducing hot air into the furnace a superior quality of iron could be produced. That invention was patented. There was no particular machinery by which hot air could be produced, but the hot-air process was patented. Now, in that kind of invention the monopoly consisted wholly in the *use*, and could not at all consist in the *making* and *selling*, because nothing could be *made* which could be patented, but it was simply the *use* that constituted the value of the patent.

I fancy the time will come when the locomotives will be run by water instead of coal. Water is the most combustible thing in the world; hydrogen being very inflammable, and oxygen being the great sustainer of combustion. The problem is merely to separate the two gases. When our coal-fields are exhausted, I fancy our engines will be propelled by the combustion of water; and I presume when that invention is perfected, it will be analogous to the hot-air blast. It will consist in some simple application of a previously well-known means, and not in the invention of machinery.

If my conjecture proves to be correct, the value of that invention will consist only in its *use;* not in *making* and *selling* of machinery.

Now, suppose I should happen to be the inventor of that wonderful thing, and all the world, seeing that water is cheaper than coal, use it, and the railroad running from Baltimore to Philadelphia says, "We will not get a license, but we will go on and use it, and see whether Walker will make us pay." That thing is constantly done by railroads in using inventions. Suppose I sue the railroad company running from Baltimore to Philadelphia at law for damages, they put in a plea that they have not injured me at all by the use of the invention. Why? Because if they had not used water to run their locomotives they would have used coal, and if they had not used water or coal, I could not have run the locomotives over the road.

They have not deprived me of anything I would otherwise have had, and therefore, when I sue at law, I recover nothing. But it is not for the benefit of the *user* of the patent that the Government of the United States has conferred the exclusive privilege of it; and here that privilege is taken away from me and conferred upon the railroad company. The benefit inures to the railroad, and I am not to be rewarded in any manner for that invention, merely because I could not use the invention if they had not used it. In such a case my only remedy consists in the fact that a *trust* exists in behalf of the inventor, and the Supreme Court has held the doctrine that the user of the patent is a *trustee* for the benefit of the owner of the patent, and whatever money the former derives from the use of that invention, be it more or less, he holds as such trustee, and is bound to pay that money over to the owner of the patent.

That is the doctrine of equity. In 1870 a statute was enacted by Congress in which this distinction between the recovery of damages and the recovery of profits was recognized. Congress enacted that, in addition to the *profits* heretofore recoverable in equity, the court, sitting on the chancery side, shall have power to give the recovery of the *damages* that the patentee has suffered.

That looks like a great injustice, in that it would give the patentee a double recovery; but the Supreme Court of the United States in the case of *Birdsall* v. *Coolidge,* 3 Otto, 68, has construed that enactment to mean that the patentee might have in equity whichever one is largest, whether the profits or damages, and if it turns out on the hearing that the profits which he would derive in equity are smaller in amount than the damages on the other side, the profits shall be increased by having added to them such proportion of the damages as is necessary to swell the aggregate amount of the damages he would have recovered at law. Therefore, the construction which the Supreme Court has put on the act of 1870 removes every element of injustice, and that act provides nothing new except that the party may get damages in *equity,* and he is not forced to go on the other side of the court and file a declaration, but he gets the same kind of relief in equity that he formerly could get only by beginning a second suit.

Senator MORGAN. Is it the result in practice that these cases under that act go to courts of equity instead of law courts?

Mr. WALKER. Very largely. As the act is construed, it only produces a difference of tribunal, although upon a reading of the statute it seems to be grossly unjust. However, this bill does not propose any change in that law. What this bill proposes to do in the second section is to *abolish the recovery of profits altogether*, and limit the recovery to the damages which the patentee has suffered. I am sure it will be seen that I am right in that when I call attention to the last clause of the second section before the proviso. There are several complicated methods, not easy to be understood by anybody not an adept in such matters, by which the profits and damages are to be assessed in accordance with the provisions of this section, and then it says:

"But if, in any case, it shall appear to the court that the damages or profits, ascertained as above, shall be inadequate to give the plaintiff a just compensation for the *injury* done by the infringement, or shall be in excess of such *injury*, the court shall have power to increase or diminish the amount to such an extent as may be just and reasonable."

That means this: When, in accordance with the plan laid down in the first two paragraphs of that section, profits do happen to be assessed *as* profits, on the idea of trusteeship, now enforced by the Supreme Court of the United States and the circuit courts of the United States, if it turns out that those *profits* amount to more than the *damages* that would be recoverable at law, they have to be reduced to the damages recoverable in law. Therefore the effect of the section is that the recovery of profits under the doctrine of trusteeship is abolished, and the only recovery is the exact amount of damages.

Now, suppose I should go on and invent my method of running steam-engines by water, and should sue the Baltimore and Ohio Road for infringing it. Under this bill I could not get anything more than a nominal recovery, because the bill abolishes the recovery of profits under the theory of trusteeship, and, whether I should proceed in equity or in law, all I could get would be *damages*. I cannot prove that I have been *injured* other than in a nominal way by reason of such infringement, and they will say, "We have not hurt you at all; we have not deprived you of anything because we have used this invention on our locomotives. The locomotives belong to us and you have no control over them, and you could not have used the invention on our road."

The only remedy on any theory of "damages" is a license-fee in such cases. I could, indeed, refuse to allow these people to use my invention unless they gave me a license-fee, but, unfortunately for that measure of damages, license-fees can only be established by agreement between the infringers who use the patent and the patentee. The railroad companies have nothing to do except to refuse to establish the license-fee, and they cut me off entirely from that only possible method of recovery under this bill.

It seems to me to be very unjust, and contrary to the spirit of patent laws, to reward infringers, and deprive inventors of that reward which the Constitution of the United States supposes they are to have.

This bill is a bill for the reward of torts, not of genius; for the encouragement of wrong-doing, not the encouragement of invention; inasmuch as it takes away the lion's share of the benefit derivable from the vast proportion of the inventions made in this country, and confers that lion's share upon the wrong-doer. It gives the patentee only a very small proportion of the benefit that is derived from the use of his improvement during the life of the patent. It does that thing in all cases where the invention is of such a character that it can be used by the infringer more profitably than by the inventor.

There is a large proportion of the patents granted by the United States which come under that category. The infringer may make twice as much money out of the use of an improvement as the inventor can, and in all such cases, under the doctrine of trusteeship, the recovery of profits is twice as much as the recovery of damages; and as this bill proposes to abolish the recovery of profits and confines the recovery solely to damages, in all such cases it confers upon the infringer the largest proportion of benefit arising from the patent.

Senator MORGAN. I suppose the gentlemen who prepared this bill had your argument in view when they inserted this clause: "The court shall have power to increase or diminish the amount to such an extent as may be just and reasonable."

Mr. WALKER. I do not know exactly what they meant by that language, but I understand they meant "just and reasonable" in view of the *damages* to which the patentee was entitled, and not "just and reasonable" in view of the trusteeship relating to *profits*.

Senator MORGAN. Does it not give to the chancellor power, in assessing the damages or profits, to regulate the assessment by his opinion of what is "just and reasonable," either in the nature of profits or in the nature of damages? Is not that jurisdiction actually conferred by this clause in the bill?

Mr. WALKER. I have thought a good deal about that, and I believe no chancellor would take the responsibility of giving me profits on the theory of trusteeship. The bill is not expressed clearly. My idea is that chancellors are reluctant to exercise any discretion, and they do not do it unless it is clearly conferred; and therefore the practical construction would be given to the act, by every court to the attention of which it might be called, that they are to increase or diminish the assessment with reference to *damages*, and not at all with reference to this principle of *trusteeship* for *profits*.

Senator WADLEIGH. But the bill provides:

"But if, in any case, it shall appear to the court that the damages or profits, ascertained as above, shall be inadequate to give the plaintiff a just compensation for the injury done by the infringement, or shall be in excess of such injury, the court shall have power to increase or diminish the amount to such an extent as may be just and reasonable."

Mr. WALKER. "Just and reasonable" with reference, as I apprehend, to the idea of *damages*. If it turn out on trial that the damages shall amount to $1,000 and the profits to $10,000, and I have proved up my profits at $10,000, the defendant will say, "Your honor will please exercise the discretion conferred by this act and reduce the $10,000 down to $1,000, inasmuch as the $1,000 represents the *damage* which the patentee has suffered," and he will insist that that is the true construction of the law. I hope the committee, whatever it does, will express itself clearly, because there is nothing more vexatious and troublesome than the construction of an act the meaning of which cannot be known for many years. It is my deliberate opinion that the courts would hold that the discretion conferred is to reduce the assessment down to *damages*, and that the just and reasonable thing contemplated by the bill is the just and reasonable *damages*, and that it has no reference at all to *profits*.

Senator MORGAN. As the words "damages" and "profits" are only divided by the disjunctive conjunction " or," which is copulative in this connection, the meaning in that case is plain. " But if, in any case, it shall appear to the court that the damages or profits, ascertained as above," &c. And in either case, whether damages or profits, "the court shall have power to increase or diminish the amount to such an extent as may be just and reasonable.

Mr. WALKER. Just and reasonable, to make it conform to the idea of the *injury*.

Senator WADLEIGH. Just and reasonable under all the apparent circumstances.

Senator MORGAN. Just and reasonable as to the damages or profits. I do not see any obscurity.

Mr. WALKER. My idea of the law is this: Whenever you figure it on the theory of profits or damages and it turns out that the latter amount is more than enough to *compensate* the patentee for the *injury* he has suffered, the court has the discretion to reduce it down to the amount of injury he has suffered.

Senator CHAFFEE. The clause says, "damages or profits."

Mr. WALKER. Certainly, "damages *or* profits," but the fore part of the section provides for assessing damages and assessing profits. Now, the bill goes on to provide that, when the whole thing is figured up, the equity account shall be reduced to reasonable *compensation*, and compensation means *damages* and *not* profits, on the theory of trusteeship. However, the committee undoubtedly will be able to draught the bill so as to express it clearly. Very likely I am wrong about it, but it is clear to my mind that no bill ought to be enacted which abolishes the recovery of profits, because when the recovery of profits is abolished, in every case applying to inventions of such a character that they can be more profitably used by the infringer than by the inventor, the result of the abolition of the recovery of profits is that the infringer will have three-quarters or nine-tenths of all the advantages of the invention, in exact contravention of the theory of the patent law, which proposes to confer the advantages upon the *inventor* and his assignees.

Senator WADLEIGH. Take the railroad-brake.

Mr. WALKER. That is an illustration.

Senator WADLEIGH. In that case it was estimated that the invention, which was a very simple one indeed, under the law in reference to taking the amount of profits as the basis of compensation, was worth sixty millions of dollars.

Mr. WALKER. That was a grossly exaggerated estimate.

Senator WADLEIGH. Suppose it was true?

Mr. WALKER. I will argue that. Suppose it was true. Suppose the damages that would be recoverable on the theory of a license, or any other theory of damages, would amount to $100,000 instead of $60,000,000 (and, in point of fact, for many years the railroad companies did reap $60,000,000 from the invention), this bill says the patentee shall recover the $100,000, and that the infringers shall keep all the balance.

Senator WADLEIGH. The bill says that the patentee shall recover such amount as the court shall deem just and reasonable, taking into view not only the injury, but the profits derived from the invention.

Mr. WALKER. I wish the bill said that. I cannot find it.

Senator CHAFFEE. In the fore part it says: "The measure of the plaintiff's damages shall be the same, both at law and in equity, and no account of profits or savings shall be allowed."

Senator MORGAN. That is in regard to the license-fee.

Mr. WALKER. The license-fee is applied by the bill to all cases, like the use of water as a fuel and the use of the brake. This bill provides that where the invention is of such a nature that the inventor desires to license other parties to use it, owing to the fact that he is not in a situation to use it all himself, under such circumstances, both in law and in equity, no profits shall be allowed at all. Senator Chaffee made the correct remark in that regard, that in all such circumstances no recovery of the profits could be allowed at all according to the bill.

With regard to the invention of the future, the burning of water instead of coal, no profits could under any circumstances be allowed to the patentee at all, but he would be remitted to his license-fee, if he could persuade enough railroad companies to establish a license-fee; and if not, the jury would have to assess, according to this bill, compensation for the *injury* that the patentee had received; and in making that assessment they would be precluded by the very language of the bill from taking into consideration at all the benefit the infringers had derived from the use of the patented improvement.

The CHAIRMAN. Your position, as I understand it, is that the law should now stand as it is, as construed by the Supreme Court?

Mr. WALKER. Yes, sir.

The CHAIRMAN. And that it needs no alteration?

Mr. WALKER. And that it needs no alteration.

Senator MORGAN. Is it altered by this bill?

Mr. WALKER. O, most materially.

Senator MORGAN. In what particular?

Senator WADLEIGH. It is altered in this respect. As the law now is, it gives the inventor either profits or damages, whichever may be largest.

Senator MORGAN. I understand that it gives the inventor the election.

Senator WADLEIGH. But in this case, whichever may be the largest, he cannot have that as the measure of his compensation unless the court determine that under the circumstances it is just and reasonable.

Senator MORGAN. The court always has that substantially under its charge by its power to grant a new trial. They cannot impose enormous damages on the conscience of the court merely by the fact that the jury found it so, and the court may make a new decree. The power of granting a new trial being brought to the attention of the court, the proper relief may be obtained without difficulty.

Mr. WALKER. But these profits are never recoverable by jury, and therefore the power of granting a new trial would not exist at all.

Senator WADLEIGH. In reference to the first clause of the second section, so far as that relates to license, I suppose you understand it to apply only to cases where the license granted has been granted where the transaction is one where the inventor understands he is getting about what is right for the use of his invention. Then you could not take a case and bring it in to show the transaction as the establishment of a license-fee where the license had been granted mainly or partially for the purpose of giving the inventor the use.

Mr. WALKER. I think if there were enough cases of the latter kind they would establish a license-fee under the rule of the courts.

Senator WADLEIGH. You do not understand the granting of license for the purpose of getting the invention into use, but it would furnish evidence as to what license-fee should be in this case.

Mr. WALKER. I think they might, because this section says if the license-fee has been established, that shall be the measure of compensation.

Senator WADLEIGH. But if the license-fee has already been established by a reasonable number of transactions of a character applicable to the case at bar, that would be sufficient. Now, would not that clause "of a character applicable to the case at bar," prevent a transaction where a license was granted simply or mainly to get the invention into use?

Mr. WALKER. Yes; it would prevent that. That hardship would not result, but it is true, gentlemen of the committee, that inventors in the early years of their monopoly are often ignorant of the real value of their inventions. It is frequently far more valuable than they suppose, and very often they grant licenses for a very small fraction indeed of the real value of the invention. This bill provides that if they have granted a moderate number of licenses, according to the law as it now stands in reference to the establishment of a license-fee, that thereafter that shall be the sole measure of recovery, and if it turns out that the infringers make ten times as much as they supposed they would make or as the inventor supposed they would make, he shall be confined to what in the early days of the patent he, with their concurrence, agreed as the amount he was willing to receive, and that they shall pocket the balance.

Mr. SMITH. What do you understand the law to be now?

Mr. WALKER. I understand that under some circumstances the license-fee can be changed from time to time, but that the power to change the license-fee from time to time does not enable the patentee to fix a license-fee adequate to the value of the invention in cases where the invention can be used far more profitably by the infringer than it can be used by him. The courts have understood for twenty-five or thirty years, and understood very well, that *damages* cannot be made to conform in amount to the *profits* recoverable on the theory of trusteeship. In the case of *Livingston* v. *Woodward* the question was illustrated. That was the first case in which any recovery of money for the infringement of a patent was had in equity, and there the elective principles were hinted at. In 2 Otto, 716, and 3 Otto, 68, Justice Miller and Justice Clifford have fully explained the philosophy of elective recoveries.

I think no lawyer will dispute this proposition, that if it is deemed desirable that the infringer should pay to the inventor whatever benefit he has derived, it cannot be brought about with any degree of uniformity except by the doctrine of trusteeship, owing to the fact that, unlike other kinds of personal property, the patent is frequently of more value to one man than to another. A horse may be worth a hundred dollars to me, and it may be worth a hundred dollars to my brother Smith. My patent may be worth a hundred dollars to me, and a thousand dollars to him. Shall he take away and pocket the $900, in exact contravention of the philosophy of the patent law which conferred upon *me* the exclusive benefit of my invention for a limited time? That gross injustice can only be prevented by allowing the courts of equity to proceed as they have done and to say to Brother Smith, "You have made a thousand dollars by the use of Mr. Walker's property, and if he chooses to treat you as a trustee and ask you to pay over that thousand dollars, without interest, you cannot complain." There is a *particular* injustice in reference to this matter when rights of action have already accrued. It is well settled that rights of action that are vested are as much property as tangible property is. If anybody disputes that proposition, Cooley on Constitutional Limitations will disabuse his mind. Several of my clients have a number of valuable improvements in locomotives and various improvements in railroads. Those improvements have been infringed fifteen or twenty years by the railroad companies. The rights of action for infringers' profits have accrued. We file bills, and ask them to pay over the amount of profit derived. Our rights of action have vested; they are as much property as any other kind of property, the only difference being it is in the tortuous possession of another party. It is held in trust by the parties who derived the profit by means of their own wrong-doing, and I have now only to sue in equity to force them to pay it over to my clients. This bill puts a stop to that, and says that the remedy of a bill in equity shall be no longer at our disposal for the recovery of that property.

The fifth amendment of the Constitution provides that " no person shall be deprived of property without due process of law." I say my clients' property cannot be divested, whether it be a chose in action or a thing in possession, by an act of Congress; and if it cannot be divested by act of Congress, then, inasmuch as this bill refers to our actions which have already accrued as well as those hereafter to accrue, it is obnoxious to the fifth amendment to the Constitution of the United States, which provides that they shall not be deprived of property without due process of law.

Senator MORGAN. I suppose you would want to amend the last proviso by inserting that " the provisions of this act shall not apply in any case to any right of action under existing laws."

Mr. WALKER. That is it exactly, and that is all the amendment I have to suggest, " that the provisions of this section shall not apply in any case in which the right of action has already accrued."

Senator MORGAN. What do you consider the meaning of the words in the twenty-third line of the second section, " capital and personal services excepted ?"

Mr. WALKER. I understand that was intended by Brother Smith to meet what he deems to be an unjust decision of the Supreme Court in the case of *Mevs* v. *Conover*, in 4 Otto. That was a patent for sawing wood. It turned out that the man who infringed the patent and sawed wood lost money, but the Supreme Court held that he would have lost 50 cents per cord *more* if he had not infringed the patent, and therefore he had to pay over the difference. I understand that the whole clause was intended to meet the doctrine laid down by the Supreme Court in that case.

Mr. SMITH. That particular clause was intended to place the rule exactly where the law now is, that the infringer of a patent is not to be allowed for the use of his capital and personal services.

Mr. WALKER. Mr. Smith would be far more competent to explain what he meant by this language than I, but evidently it has no connection with the argument I am making, viz, that where rights of actions for profits on the theory of trusteeship have accrued, this bill, as far as it acts on those rights of action, is in contravention of the fifth amendment of the Constitution of the United States. It is an act of confiscation. It says, " Because you have not your money in your pocket, but it is in the hands of parties who ought to pay it over to you, and you can only get it by certain proceedings in equity, we will confiscate it by depriving you of the only remedy you have to obtain it."

It is frequently said that Congress could do anything so long as it did not interfere with rights by *name*, and that only when they take away property by *name* do they violate the fifth amendment; but the Supreme Court has twice, and perhaps oftener, stated that whenever the law-making power passes a law which in any manner abridges the *remedy* existing prior to the passage of that law for the recovery of property or rights, it is as much in contravention of the fifth amendment of the Constitution as though it took away the right by *name*. I will furnish the committee with the reference to the cases in which that is decided.

This, then, is my argument in reference to rights of actions heretofore accrued. If anybody has infringed my patent, all the benefit he has derived from the use of that patent is *my* property in *his* possession, and I have only to file a bill in equity to make him pay over to me that exact sum, and that without any regard whatever to the amount of injury I have received.

That is the explicit declaration of the Supreme Court, and it has been the law for a great many years. I say, under the circumstances, my clients have a right at this moment (a good many suits are already begun) to recover these profits that belong to them according to law. But now this bill comes in and says, " You shall not have your remedy for recovering those profits at all; you can sue them at law and get *damages*, which is an entirely different thing, but you will have no remedy in equity to recover those *profits*." I say, inasmuch as it takes away the *remedy*, it takes away the *right* as much as though it took away the right by name, and I can furnish the members of the committee . with ample authorities to substantiate that doctrine. Therefore I say the bill ought to be amended, if it is desirable to pass a constitutional law, and one that will undergo the scrutiny of the courts, in precisely the form that Senator Morgan suggests.

Senator WADLEIGH. Your idea is that a man's right to his invention is precisely the same as his right to his horse, or any other property belonging to him ?

Mr. WALKER. I would so hold if I had time to argue the question.

Senator WADLEIGH. Is there not this distinction : While a man has a right to put his horse into his own barn, and not use it himself, he has no right to lock up his invention and let nobody use it. It is his duty to let his invention go out to the world.

Mr. WALKER. He has no such duty with reference to the period of his monopoly at all. The only duty he has is to spread the description of the invention on the records of the Patent Office, so that *after* the monopoly has expired, whether it be in fourteen, or seventeen, or twenty-one years, it will be free to the world. He has no duty to publish that invention, or introduce it during the life of the monopoly; and if he chooses to let it lie as useless, there is no law or reason why he shall not be permitted to do so.

Senator WADLEIGH. Suppose, for instance, a foreign inventor comes here from a foreign country, and he procures a patent for an invention which materially affects the cost of important manufactures. He procures that patent in this country for the benefit of his manufactories abroad, and, for reasons which he sees fit to act upon, he does not allow any one in this country to use his invention at all, but lets it be used for the benefit of foreign countries entirely.

Mr. WALKER. I understand such a hardship as that ought to be guarded against by refusing such a man a patent.

Senator WADLEIGH. The Patent Office cannot divine what his intention is and know what he is going to do with it.

Mr. WALKER. That is purely a theoretical case. No inventor or patentee ever does that thing. The theory of the law is that during the life of the monopoly, which is limited, the patentee may do whatever he chooses with his property, and after that period it is free to the world. There is no decision of the courts, and no language that can be quoted from any statute, which confers upon the inventor anything like a *qualified* property in his patent during the life of the monopoly. As I understand the theory of the law, it is his *absolute* property during the life of the monopoly and is *not* qualified. Indeed, that is the language of the Constitution itself, viz, that the right is *exclusive*. If he is bound to sell that property at reasonable prices, it would not be *exclusive ;* and whether Congress *could* include the less in the greater and make a *modified* monopoly, and base it upon the *exclusive* direction of the Constitution, certainly Congress has not done so. The Constitution provides that the patentee shall have the *exclusive* right to his invention for a limited time, and, in conformity, Congress has enacted a series of laws conferring the *exclusive* right upon the patentee. No law can be pointed out which makes it *not* exclusive. This bill may be said by some persons to be doing a wise thing in making it a modified and qualified right. Perhaps it may be said that it would be a wise thing if the Constitution were changed; but, at the present, the Constitution says Congress may protect patentees by conferring an *exclusive* privilege upon them; and, in conformity with the Constitution, exclusive privileges *have* been conferred. I say when, under those exclusive privileges, rights of action have accrued, and are therefore perfectly vested property as much as *anything* is property, the members of this committee will see, if they read page 362 of Cooley on Constitutional Limitations, that they have no right to interfere with it. But this bill comes in and deprives us of those rights of action, and, therefore, deprives us of our property, and is therefore in contravention of the fifth amendment of the Constitution.

Senator MORGAN. What part of the fifth amendment?

Mr. WALKER. That no person " shall be deprived of * * property * * without due process of law."

Senator MORGAN. That relates to the methods of procedure; but is there any prohibition on the power of Congress to take from any man the benefits of what you call a vested right under law?

Mr. WALKER. In the case of *Barron* v. *The City of Baltimore*, 7 Peters, that precise point came within the decision of the Supreme Court, and Chief-Justice Marshall held that that amendment was enacted as a restraint on the law-making power of Congress.

Senator MORGAN. With reference to rights under contract?

Mr. WALKER. With reference to any matters referred to in the fifth amendment.

Senator MORGAN. As to taking a man's property without due process of law?

Mr. WALKER. Without due process of law.

Senator MORGAN. I understand that. Suppose we should know of a case in which there was a very great amount of damages recoverable by a patentee whose patent was believed to be wholly and equitably unjust and a great burden to the country. Do you deny the right (notwithstanding you brought an action) to take away the benefits of existing laws so far as they give the power to recover such damages?

Mr. WALKER. I certainly do.

Senator MORGAN. I have a series of cases in my mind which would have a tremendous influence upon certain sections of this country. A man took out a patent for a process of killing cotton-worms with a mixture of Paris green, flour, &c. As soon as the discovery was known, of course everybody resorted to it. Every cotton-grower in my State who had the money to use it went to work and got Paris green and flour and mixed them up, and they killed the cotton-worms, and in many instances saved vast amounts of cotton. Suits are pending now in regard to that. Upon certain assumptions or premises which are furnished in the different cases, those men would have the right to recover the profits and damages out of the cotton-planters for the use of this discovery. Under the circumstances, if we have the power to prevent it, I think it is our duty to prevent the recovery of the great damages or great profits which may have accrued to the planters in these cases and to confine the parties to the recovery of a proper license-fee.

Senator WADLEIGH. The second section of this bill provides for that.

Senator MORGAN. I know the second section of the bill would provide for that, but I was referring to our constitutional power to enact such a section as to pending cases.

Mr. WALKER. This monopoly that was granted for this discovery was only a limited one in point of duration, and after the expiration of the monopoly, if it is a great blessing to the cotton-fields of the South, it will be used by them. Is it, after all, such a gross injustice that this great benefit, although enormous for a short time, should be conferred upon the man who discovered it, in order that invention may be encouraged and the public have the free use and benefit of the discovery for centuries afterward ?

Senator WADLEIGH. Somebody else would have discovered it.

Mr. WALKER. Mr. Smith said that for three centuries this simple thing of the toilet-pin was not thought of. It is easy to see that the simplest invention may be unknown for a long time.

Senator WADLEIGH. I believe it was in evidence that this brake was invented by several workmen in railroad-shops, who did not apply for a patent, and it went into use on those roads.

Mr. WALKER. In point of fact that brake was invented by but one or two persons, independently of the true and first inventors and after they invented it.

Mr. SMITH. In the case put relating to Paris green, would you claim that the owner of the patent for the Paris green had a vested right to the whole of the cotton-crop, without allowing anything for the use of the capital ?

Mr. WALKER. Of course not. I do not understand that the law as it now stands would have given it.

Mr. SMITH. Could you take the profit into account in any other way ?

Mr. WALKER. He would have a vested right in all the profits that came from the use of the Paris green.

Senator MORGAN. In some cases the remedy was applied when three-fifths of the cotton-crop was destroyed, and a great deal was rescued, and sometimes it was almost entirely rescued by the use of this preparation. That would be profits in the way which has been mentioned, because it was that much saved to the planter. There are various actions pending in some parts of the country for the recovery of these very profits. Is it to be admitted here that Congress has not the power, in the readjustment of the patent law, to deprive those persons of the profits which they claim were realized by the planter in the use of this invention and in the saving of his crops ?

Mr. WALKER. I take the ground that there are only three or four links to that question, and that the conclusion is inevitable that Congress has no power whatever to deprive the inventor of those profits.

Senator MORGAN. I should be very much obliged to you for a brief on that point ; for my strongest disposition is, if it could be prevented, not to allow this man to obtain profits on these vast cotton-crops, saved by the application of so simple a thing as that.

Mr. WALKER. I will repeat (as perhaps my brief will not be brought to the attention of all members of the committee) my proposition, that where rights to recover profits in equity have *vested*, Congress has no power whatever to *divest* them, and that depends on these circumstances: First, that those rights are as much property as anything tangible is property ; and you will find the law on that point in Cooley on Constitutional Limitations. Secondly, that. *being* property, the fifth amendment provides that property shall not be taken away without due proeess of law; and, thirdly, due process of law has frequently and constantly been held to mean judgments, proceedings, and decrees of courts, and never acts of Congress or of any other legislative body. Fourth, the Supreme Court decided, in *Barron* v. *The City of Baltimore*, that that amendment was designed expressly to prevent Congress from doing that thing; and, further, that the conclusion is positive and certain that where rights of action for profit have *accrued*, Congress has no power whatever to take away that right, or in any manner limit or abridge the remedies by which those profits may be recovered.

I take it, the gentlemen of the committee were not sent by their constituents to Washington for the purpose of passing laws which will be held to be unconstitutional by the Supreme Court. It is the duty of Congress to pass wise laws, but those laws should be always constitutional. No object would be gained by passing the bill as it now is, except to promote litigation and raise a large crop of questions that would be finally settled only by the Supreme Court, and on the principles I have enunciated they would confirm our rights. If the bill presented to this committee is clearly unconstitutional, the committee will see such unconstitutional features and they will sift them out and adopt those that *are* constitutional.

Members of the committee may think if they were making a constitution they would make it differently, but still I fancy they will conform to the Constitution as it *is* and pass no laws not in conformity with it.

Therefore, I say in behalf of my clients that I take no interest in the question except that I do not want to see my clients put to the expense of having such a provision held to be unconstitutional by the Supreme Court. Litigation is tedious; litigation is expensive; litigation is long, and life is short. If that bill were passed to-morrow, I could file a bill in equity contravening it in some circuit court in the West or in the East, and in the course of five years I would get a decision of the Supreme Court that in as far as the second section applied to the rights already accrued it would be null and void, and in contravention of the fifth amendment of the Constitution. The parties infringing patents would have the trouble of fighting the question, which would be finally settled adversely to them. No good would come of it, and nothing would be accomplished except delay and increased litigation and perplexity by raising the question. We would merely be forced to put it through all the stages of litigation in order that the provision might be held to be unconstitutional by the Supreme Court.

The committee adjourned until to-morrow at 10 o'clock a. m.

FRIDAY, *November* 16, 1877.

The committee met at 10 o'clock a. m., pursuant to adjournment.

ARGUMENT OF CHAUNCEY SMITH RESUMED.

Mr. SMITH. I approach now, Mr. Chairman, the consideration of confessedly the most difficult branch of the patent law; that is, the subject of the damages in suits at law and the rule in regard to the recovery of profits in suits in equity. The patent law, the statute I mean, prescribes no rule of damages, and no rule in regard to the recovery of profits. There is, indeed, a provision that, under certain circumstances, the courts may increase to the extent of threefold the amount of actual

damages found by a jury; and there is a provision that a court of equity
in taking an account of profits may also proceed to ascertain the damages in addition to the profits. Neither of these provisions, however,
prescribes a rule under which or by which the profit shall be ascertained
in the one case or the damages in the other.

The difficulty of prescribing any rule is inherent in the nature of the
subject. Inventions are of such various characters that the modes in
which they are to be used must be widely varied. The rights which an
inventor has to determine for himself in what mode he shall use his invention, will materially affect the damages which he might suffer from
an infringement. He may have an invention which it is impossible for
him to use personally, or even to manufacture. It is one upon which he
must rely for reaping any reward upon inducing other people to adopt
it. Another invention may be of such a character that he may engage
in the manufacture of the article covered by the invention, and reap
his profit from the sale of the article, endeavoring to hold the monopoly
in his own hands, and to supply the community with all of the article
which they desire to use. Such might have been the case with Howe's
sewing-machine. He may on the other hand elect, in view of the large
amount of capital which is requisite to carry on the manufacture and
supply the community, to license other parties upon a royalty for the
manufacture, they paying him for the right under the invention. Such
in fact was the mode in which Howe reaped mainly his profits upon
the sewing-machine. In one case he might reap by the aid of his capital and his skill in business a very large profit on each machine. In
the other case he might reap only a small profit on each machine, but
it would be the profit due directly to the invention, and not increased
by his personal skill and ability in the management of a business or
by the capital which he invested in its employment. Another case
which may arise—and you will readily see it presents a difficult
case for estimating damages—is where an inventor may have some
invention upon, for instance, a sewing-machine, or a reaping-machine,
or a steam-engine, or a printing-press, which gives the machine an
additional value to the public. He may be a manufacturer, and through
the aid of that invention he may seek by giving it to the public, by
selling his machine at no enhanced price, to reap his reward through
the sale of a larger number of machines which the public are open to
manufacture. Mr. Corliss made some valuable improvements upon
the steam-engine. New England and the whole country is deeply indebted to him for the improvements which he not only made, but which
he stimulated other people to make, by the competition he forced them
to encounter. His mode of dealing with the patent was, not to allow
other persons to manufacture under a royalty; not to allow them to
put his invention on machines which they might build. He did not
even sell his machines, in many cases, for a price enhanced by virtue
of his invention. Sometimes he sold them for a fixed price in money.
An ordinary and a very beneficial way to the community was to go to
a person using a steam-engine and ascertain how much it costs him for
fuel. Taking the records of his books for a series of years, and ascertaining that for the power he used it cost him so much money per
year, he would offer to take out his steam-engine, put in a new one
with his improvement, taking for his pay a certain fraction of the price
which in one, two, or three years the man should save by the introduction of it. So that the party got a better engine for nothing. Not only
that, he got a premium for putting it in, because he received a larger
share of the saving than Mr. Corliss himself did. Mr. Corliss made his

profit iu the sale of the whole engine. Suppose an iufringer came in and iuterfered with the possibility of his making those arrangements, you can see that the damages which he would suffer, I do not mean legal damages as estimated by the courts, but the loss, the injury, might be very serious.

A question akin to this arose in the case of *Seymour* v. *McCormick*, where the manufacturer had the control of a patent which increased the value of the reaping-machine, which he sold, however, at the same price, perhaps, with other manufacturers. He made, perhaps, really little or no profit upon the particular feature which was the subject of the patent; but he made, as usual, a considerable profit on the machine at large; and he claimed in a suit for the infringement of that patent that he was entitled to recover what he had lost, not merely by the sale of so much of the machine as was covered by the patent, but the profit which he would have made if he had held the whole machine under his patent, upon the theory that if the defendant had not used his iuvention, he himself, the plaintiff, would have had the opportunity to sell the machine, and not the defendant.

It appeared in fact in that case that the plaintiff had been in the habit, however, of granting licenses to other manufacturers to use his invention at a specified price. The court held in that case that the damages could not be estimated by reference to the loss of the profits on the whole machine; that that was too remote, and that in some way they must arrive at that proportion of damage which was due to the use of that particular feature of the machine, and there having been an established royalty, the Supreme Court held that that must be taken as the damages in that class of cases.

Beyond this, I believe there is no fixed rule in law. Even that is a flexible rule; for upon an examination of the cases it will be found that the courts will consider in each particular case whether the royalty which has been established is one which is "applicable under all the circumstances to the case at bar."

I pass from the consideration of the damages at law, because I do not understand that the section which we have under consideration makes any change in the rule of recovery at law, and I do not understand that, in the administration of the patent-law in suits at law, any cause of complaint has arisen which calls for a statute. I suppose that no defendant ever yet had a verdict found against him with which he was satisfied; but there has been no just cause of public complaint under the rule as applied to suits at law.

I think I have before stated that the difficulty of administering this branch of the law had been so great that the courts and the legal profession had abandoned the law side of the court and sought the benefit of the equity side primarily, because it was easier to investigate the questions arising under the patents before a judge than before a jury, and especially because a court of equity could grant relief by injunction, which a court of law cannot grant. But when the law side of the court was abandoned for the equity side, it was soon found that there were cases were the plaintiffs were not content to rest with the remedy of an injunction, but sought to go further, as justly they might in many cases, and obtain a recovery in money, and the court of equity lent its assistance to plaintiffs in such cases by sending the cause to a master to ascertain the profits which had been made by the defendant, upon the theory, repeatedly stated by the courts, that the defendant was to be held as a trustee for the money in his hands.

In the case of *Dean* v. *Mason*, in 20 Howard, I think, the plaintiff

undertook to charge the defendant not simply with the profits he had
actually made by infringing the Woodworth patent on the planing-machine, but to charge him with such profits as he ought to have made
in the exercise of reasonable skill in the use of the invention. The
same principle was implied in an earlier case. They sought to charge
him as a trustee for the use of the invention, as a trustee under a contract is often charged for the profitable employment or for reasonable
skill in the employment of property which he holds of his *cestui que trust.*
The court repudiated that doctrine. They held that he was to be charged,
not as a trustee for the use of the invention, not as holding the invention in his hands as a trustee under a contract, but only for the money
which had actually come into his hands as the fruit of the invention;
and against that rule it seems to me there could be little cause of complaint, although cases might arise where the recovery would be large.
A case did arise afterward in Providence, where, under the application
of that rule, the defendants were charged with some two or three hundred thousand dollars profits, made in the use of an invention.

I have never, however, heard that there was any cause of complaint
against the rule there laid down, which embraces this peculiarity and
has reference to a clause in the section where they held that the defendant
in that case could not be allowed to set off against the profit which he
had made interest on the capital which he had invested, neither could
he be allowed to set off a claim for personal services and for the skill
which he had brought to the management of the business, following in
that case the analogy of the rules of equity in regard to trustees, that
they are not to be allowed to make a profit out of the funds of their
cestui que trusts by charging for their services or for capital which may
be employed alongside of that of the *cestui que trust* in the unlawful use
of it.

Some time after this the case which was referred to yesterday of
Mowry v. *Whitney* arose, and I beg the attention of the committee
especially to this case because I think it gave rise to all the complaints
which have arisen in regard to recovery in suits in equity since that
time. It gave rise to a necessity, if there is a necessity, for the very
amendment which we have brought before you in the second section of
this bill. The defendant there had manufactured car-wheels and annealed them by a process which was covered by the plaintiff's patent.
He had made a profit of about $95,000, if I remember correctly; over
$90,000 certainly.

The plaintiff undertook to charge him for the whole amount of that
profit, on the ground that the car-wheel, substantially, when it was subjected to the process of annealing, was not of so much value as it had
cost up to that time, and that if sold for any purpose to which it could
be applied at that time, it would have sold for less than it had cost;
that profits began to arise from that point, and were therefore due to
his invention because the annealing was all, substantially, that remained
to be done. Under that rule he claimed $95,000, which he said had been
made by the use of his invention.

It appeared, however, that the defendant, and the plaintiff himself, I
believe, sold car-wheels made by this process at no higher price than
those which were annealed by other processes which were open to the
world to use; and the court held, apparently, and I think with good
reason, for the purpose of preventing an injustice or a hardship under
the rule as it was previously laid down, that that portion of the profits
which had been made should be determined by ascertaining how much
advantage the defendant had gained in reaping those profits from the

especial mode of annealing wheels as compared with any of the other modes of annealing wheels. The invention did not rest broadly on the annealing of wheels. It rested only on the special process of annealing wheels. The plaintiff could not therefore put into his pocket as the fruit of his invention that which was due to annealing generally, but could only take that part of the profits arising from the annealing of wheels which was due to his particular process of annealing.

Unfortunately, as I think, in laying down this rule, however, the court stated it in terms which were capable of the greatest hardship, if not of injustice. They said that the defendant was to be chargeable with the advantages which he had reaped from the use of the invention, which in that case was well enough; but it would often appear, and I think has subsequently appeared in different cases, that in attempting to reach those advantages by comparing the cost of the process under the patent with the cost of other known processes, they laid down a rule which would sweep into the plaintiff's profits moneys which the defendant never dreamed of possessing, and could by no possibility have possessed. I will repeat again an illustration which I have repeated so many times that I am almost ashamed of it, and yet it so strongly illustrates the fallacy of the rule, whether we can state that fallacy in the words or not, that I cannot forbear its introduction here. It was given to me by Mr. Hillard of Boston, when I was engaged in taking an account of profits before him, and where the defendant in that particular case, which arose before the case of *Mowry* v. *Whitney*, claimed that just such a rule as was laid down in *Mowry* v. *Whitney* should be applied; because in that particular case he held that he should be charged with a less amount than under the rule which we sought to charge him with.

There was, said Mr. Hillard, a time when the art of printing was new, and it might have been covered by a patent. If the first man who printed the Bible had been an infringer of the patent, and had been brought up to an account under the rule which has been subsequently laid down in the case of *Mowry* v. *Whitney*, he as master, if he had been sitting in that case, would have found himself confronted with this state of facts : That the only mode of making books before that was by the pen ; that the Bible, a large book, eagerly sought by a large class of people, was so expensive that there were few people in Europe who could command a copy, and that in point of fact the person who might have been the defendant in that case had sold the whole edition at a price so cheap that the ecclesiastics of that day charged him with being in conference with the devil. Now, the whole edition which he sold probably brought him a less sum of money than it would have cost to have made a single copy of the Bible by hand ; and if he had been charged for each copy of the Bible which he sold, made by the art of printing, the cost of each one of them written out by hand, there was not a kingdom in Europe which could have responded in damages.

I need not say that we all see that the application of such a rule would be unjust, because you would be charging under the guise of profits, under the rule which allowed you only to charge that which the defendant had received, with a sum of money infinitely larger than he had ever dreamed of receiving.

The application of the doctrine of *Mowry* v. *Whitney* to cases arising in the West illustrate that rule. There are two patents now or recently in force under which several defendants at the West, railway companies, have been charged, or are liable to be charged, with infringement. One of them is known as the swedge-block patent. Somebody had invented a kind of an anvil, I will call it, upon which the ends of injured rails could be restored to their original form and integrity much more conveniently than by any other device (as it was claimed) then known—much more conveniently than with a common anvil.

. The defendants in those cases had infringed by using machines varying somewhat from that described in the patent, but which the owners of the patent still claimed came within the scope of the patent; and when driven to take an account, the rule of *Mowry* v. *Whitney* was applied. The master ascertained what it would have cost to mend those rails by any known process of mending them open to the parties to use, and he found a large amount—a million and a half of dollars, I think—against some of the companies. The case came to the Supreme Court, and was decided last year. There was an attempt made to show that the railroad companies never had made any such amount of profit as that; there was an attempt made to show that that mode of mending rails even was not a profitable mode, and could not be made a profitable mode; that the companies had better have abandoned their rails and had them re-rolled, and laid down new rails. But the court refused to listen to that suggestion.

Still another case is known as the *Tanner brake case*, where it is claimed—I do not know with how much justice—that if the plaintiff is allowed to recover under the rule laid down in *Mowry* v. *Whitney*, the sum would amount from the several roads to fifty or sixty million dollars. And yet the service is one which the plaintiff sought in vain to induce the railroad companies to adopt to any great extent at five dollars a mile. What he may eventually get out of it I do not know. He has not yet received the fifty or sixty million dollars. In fact, I believe he has not been able to receive enough yet to pay his counsel.

My own judgment was that, though the rule of *Mowry* v. *Whitney* was wrong in principle, the Supreme Court would at least limit it to those cases where profits had actually been made, and would consider it as a rule only for ascertaining the proportion of actual profits which the defendants had made; and I was unwilling to believe, until forced to believe it by the decision in the case of *Mevs* v. *Conover*, decided last winter, and reported in the Official Gazette, where they held that the defendant should be charged with that difference, under the rule of *Mowry* v. *Whitney*, between what it cost him to split wood by the machine and what it would have cost him to split it by hand, although he had lost money in selling his wood. They charged him for money constructively in his hands, although in the case of *Dean* v. *Mason* they had refused to charge him with what he ought to have made by a reasonable use of the invention.

How these two decisions can be reconciled I am unable to understand. But it leads me here to observe, that if any such rule is in existence, any rule which entitles the plaintiff to the whole amount of the advantage derived from his invention, it is, I think, unsound for another reason; and that is, that in the introduction of inventions to the public use the case rarely, if ever, occurs where an inventor is able to place in his own pocket any considerable amount of the value which the community derives from his invention, and any rule which undertakes to place in the plaintiff's pocket a very much larger sum of money than he could possibly have made if he had been allowed to practice his invention in his own way, must, I think, involve in som eway some lurking fallacy.

Take this case of *Mevs* v. *Conover*: I do not know the special circumstances which surround it, but I can easily imagine that the defendant was compelled to sell his wood at a lower price than it cost, and not wholly because he managed his business unskillfully, but because the price of wood in the market, split perhaps by the aid of this very invention, and by licenses lawfully using, had been reduced so much in consequence of the invention, that he had to follow the market and sell it at the same price.

Now, who got the benefit of it, if that was the state of the fact and it is a state of facts that might easily arise? Not the man who split the wood and sold it at the price which had been determined by the introduction of the invention to the public. The defendant in that case did not put into his pocket the advantage of the invention. The public got it; and there are few cases where a plaintiff, as I said before, can reap the whole value of an invention.

I know of one case, in which I think the facts are substantially these : A machine has been for many years in successful operation in Massachusetts for the manufacture of a particular class of shoes. I believe it cost ten years of the labor of some of our most skillful inventors— more than one—and more than one hundred thousand dollars in money to bring that machine up to a useful point. It is safe to say that no man would have ventured upon that expenditure unless he had hoped at the end to reap not only a reward for daily services, but a rich reward under the operation of the patent law. It has proved to be a very profitable invention. I believe that under it something like 25,000,000 pairs of shoes have been made in a year of a class which previously sold at $4 a pair, but which could be manufactured so much cheaper by this process that they have sold at $3 a pair; the public getting the benefit of an article which they desired to use, and which they could use more largely than before, of $1 on each pair of shoes.

The owners of that patent have charged as a royalty and received less than two cents a pair on all the shoes made. That is a striking, and no more than a fair, illustration of the ordinary operation of the patent law, which goes to show that the inventor is in no case enabled to reap anything like the amount of benefit which the community derive out of an invention.

Take, again, the Howe sewing-machine, a monopoly which was—and I think not without justice—toward the latter portion of its term complained of. Machines of the best class, suited to general use, were for many years sold for about $60. It was complained of as a hardship that the American people were compelled to buy them at that price when they could be built for $15 or $20; and yet if you had undertaken to estimate as to each particular machine how much its owner made by the use of that machine even at $60, estimating it by the rule in *Mowry* v. *Whitney*, and to ascertain the difference between the cost of doing upon the machine all that the machine was capable of doing and the cost of doing the same amount of sewing by hand, it would be found that the machine paid for itself perhaps a hundred fold even at that price.

I think Mr. Howe, when he applied for the extension of his patent, was compelled to admit that he had received in net profits nearly $500,000 for his invention; and yet he was also enabled to show that, at that date even, the advantage to the country could not be estimated at less than many millions of dollars. It was upon the proof of this state of facts that he was entitled to receive his extension.

It has seemed to me, Mr. Chairman, in view of the case of *Mevs* v. *Conover* especially, that the Supreme Court had tied itself down to a rule, which the circuit courts feel bound to follow, which cannot be administered without great hardship and great injustice; and I have, therefore, felt no hesitation in asking this committee to consider a rule which

should release the courts from a bond under which they have bound
themselves, so that they might reach some rule which would not work
such cases of extreme hardship.

I have felt the danger of undertaking to prescribe in terms any rule
to meet a case of such difficulty as this. I have felt that unless the
exigency were pressing it would be better to—

hear those ills we have,
Than fly to others that we know not of.

And while I think I can see my way clear to the application, without
injustice, of the rule which we have endeavored to state, in all cases
which I can bring to my mind, I am yet by no means confident that
cases may not arise now unanticipated upon which the rule may operate
with as much hardship as any rule that has ever been suggested. Yet
I think there is good reason why this committee and those who are interested in improving the patent laws should make the attempt.

The first clause of this second section does not, I think, change the
rule of recovery in cases at law. It only provides that in a certain class
of cases the courts of equity shall administer the rule of the courts of
law, and shall not take an account of profits in form; but that they
shall, in such way as they have the power of doing, ascertain what the
damages would be under the rule in law in like cases.

So far, I think, there is no danger to be apprehended from the suggestion made yesterday, that we might be interfering with vested rights.
I understand we are leaving the rule at law just as it now is, and that
we are only saying to a court of equity that it shall adopt the same rule,
and shall not seek to administer justice through the machinery of an
account. There are suggestions in several of the cases which have been
brought before the courts that the taking of an account of profits was
merely a mode of reaching the damages, and to be limited eventually
by the amount which the party was entitled to recover as damages. If
my suggestion is correct, the objection to this part of the section will
not be found to have force.

Whether we have been successful in happily choosing the language
under which the courts will be called upon to act, I cannot with certainty say. The only part of the first branch of the section as to which
I have entertained any doubt—and I shall not attempt to discuss it—
is that part commencing in the fourth line, which reads as follows:

Or where it appears to the court or jury that, from the nature of the invention, it is
for the interest of the patentee that other persons generally should use the same in like
manner and pay him a license-fee therefor, the measure of the plaintiff's damages shall
be the same, both at law and in equity.

We have endeavored to guard this language cautiously, so that it
shall not bring within its scope cases which would operate with hardship upon plaintiffs. There are gentlemen present who will present objections to this feature of the bill, and I do not care now to discuss it. I
will leave it to those gentlemen to state their objections; and when they
are clearly brought out, if we see that the bill can be improved by a
change, no persons will be more happy to adopt the suggestion than we
shall. If necessary, another gentleman, following me, will attempt to
show that this language is as well chosen as any which could be adopted.

The second branch of the section commences on page 2 of the Senate
bill, line 14, and is an attempt to relieve the courts from the operation
of the rule in *Mowry* v. *Whitney* by stating that in taking an account
they shall only charge the defendant with profits on account of a saving
when such saving has enabled him to make an actual profit; that one

of the facts which must be ascertained is the actual profits which the defendant has made by the sale of the invention or in the branch of business in which the invention has been used; that having ascertained that fact, the court shall then, by appropriate modes of investigation, ascertain what proportion of the actual profits made is justly chargeable to the use of the invention, and that the defendant shall be charged with that amount, and no more.

We have, in addition to this provision, which does seek to control the mode of taking an account in equity, a provision which is intended to place the whole subject of damages within the discretion of the court, so that they shall feel that in no case they shall be compelled, under a particular rule, to give a judgment for an amount which is greater than the injury done to the plaintiff, or which is really less than the injury which has been inflicted upon him.

We have introduced also a proviso that the provisions of this bill shall not apply to cases which have actually been sent to an account. I think the suggestion which was made by Mr. Walker yesterday, that the damages which a party is entitled to recover for an infringement are to be treated as vested property, is entitled to much weight. I confess that I have great difficulty in coming to the conclusion that his right to recover those damages is not a right of property which the court must respect. But I have been able to persuade myself that the rule which we have laid down will not come within that objection. I have already suggested one of the answers to one branch of it. The answer in respect to the second branch which we have introduced, the one relating to profits, or my answer to it, is that we are endeavoring, not to change the rule of profits, but to compel the courts to administer the true rule, because, as I have intimated already, I have never believed that that rule was a sound one. It may perhaps be regarded as a provision for declaring what is already the law. To my mind, at all events, it is not a change which affects any rights that the plaintiff can now say are vested in him.

Mr. WALKER. You are now speaking, I suppose, only of the second paragraph of the section?

Mr. SMITH. That is all, sir. I have one further suggestion which may be entitled to some consideration, and that is that the subject of damages generally is unquestionably within the discretion of Congress. It may lay down a rule of recovery, I think, without doubt, if it seems wise to do so. If it should appear that this rule, if adopted, would interfere with rights already vested in some plaintiff, the court I think would not hold that provision unconstitutional, but would simply hold that the case did not come within the scope of the provision, although it was not specially excepted by the terms of the act; and for myself I should not feel quite at liberty to exclude a defendant from the possibility of reaching the benefit of this rule under the suggestion that under some possibility the court might hold that he was not entitled to the benefit of it.

I perhaps ought to make this suggestion, that I believe the defendants in most of the cases which have arisen, or which are likely to arise, would find in the circumstances of the case qualifications which would prevent the rule of *Mowry* v. *Whitney* from operating with too great hardship. No more striking illustration of that arises than in the very swedge-block cases. Three or more defendants were sued for using machines which were each unlike the others, but each of them the plaintiff charged was an infringement. The court finally held that one or two of those machines were not infringements of the patent; that they were things which were open to the world to use, and the defendants in those cases escaped liability on the ground that there was no infringement. If the defendants in the other cases, instead of attempting to defeat the patent, had allowed its validity and had claimed before the master that there were two other machines which were open to them to use, and that they were only to be charged with the difference between the cost of mending the rails by their own machine and by these other two machines, they would have escaped scot-free.

So in many cases it will be found that the special circumstances are such that the defendant will escape from the operation of the rule. Take, Mr. Senator Morgan, the suggestion which you made yesterday in regard to the use of Paris green for killing the army-worm. I am unable to believe that any man can hold a valid patent for the use of Paris green in that way. If he can have any patent at all, it must be for the use of some combination of Paris green with some other substance, either inert, for the purpose of more readily applying it, or having some specific action of its own.

Senator MORGAN. That was the nature of the patent I spoke of—a patent for a combination.

Mr. SMITH. If there was any other known mode of applying Paris green for killing insects, especially in combination with anything else, those plaintiffs must come under that qualification of the rule and recover only for what they can show their particular combination is better than any other known combination. But the case that you suggest is a striking illustration of what might arise where the plaintiff, claiming that he was entitled to all the advantages which arise from the use of an invention, might put a whole cotton-crop into his pocket against the defendant, although he would undoubtedly himself be perfectly content to sell his new powder for a price which might not give him $5 an acre.

Mr. RAYMOND. Excuse the interruption. Do you draw distinction between a combination which is patented and any other compound which the public are entitled to use?

Mr. SMITH. Any other compound which the defendants are entitled to use, at least where Paris green forms the poisonous element.

Mr. RAYMOND. It does not cover all other combinations of that character, but simply that compound.

Mr. SMITH. The Supreme Court has not yet decided whether a party is to be held chargeable for the whole use of an invention when he might legitimately buy another patented article and use it in its place, although the rule as stated, perhaps, would exclude that.

I pass on, Mr. Chairman, and I will now pass hastily over the remaining sections to section third.

Senator MORGAN. Before you do that, I should like to suggest a difficulty, not with a view of having it answered now, but one that occurs to my mind in reference to the second section. In the concluding clause of that section you give the court power to increase or diminish the damages in any case at law or in equity, as I understand, according to its discretion, making that the final decision and the judgment of the court. It is a discretionary decision, as I understand. It is, of course, a judicial decision, but somewhat discretionary. We have power lodged in the court; and where is the necessity of having any rules for regulating the processes or methods by which the court shall arrive at the amount of the damages to be ascertained in a given case?

Mr. SMITH. Perhaps that might be so. The last clause might be all that is required, and I am not sure that I should not have preferred to leave the section in that way if I could have felt sure that the courts would feel as much at liberty to apply a rule of that kind as they would if it was incorporated into the law itself.

I desire, Mr. Senator, in this connection, to read a passage from a reported case, which will show why we thought it necessary to introduce some provision of this kind and indicate the spirit of the amendment which we propose to make. It is the case of the *Packet Company* v. *Sickles*, a case at law, where the court used this language:

The rule in suits in equity of ascertaining, by a reference to a master, the profits which the defendant has made by the use of the plaintiff's invention, stands on a different principle. It is that of converting the infringer into a trustee for the patentee as regards the profits thus made, and the adjustment of these profits is subject to all the equitable considerations which are necessary to do complete justice between the parties, many of which would be inappropriate in a trial by jury. With these corrective powers in the hands of the chancellor, the rule of assuming profits as the groundwork for estimating the compensation due from the infringer to the patentee has produced results calculated to suggest distrust of its universal application even in courts of equity. (19 *Wallace*, pp. 617, 618.)

It has seemed to us—I speak now for those with whom I have been in conference—that notwithstanding the powers which the court had, they still felt their hands tied to some extent by the rules which they themselves had laid down, and that it would be of service to them, perhaps, to prescribe by statute a rule which should clearly place in their hands in all cases the power of administering justice under the particular case; and yet I am not quite certain that except for these considerations I should not have preferred to introduce simply the last clause of the section and leave the matter there.

Mr. HUBBELL. Allow me to make a suggestion. To enable the gentleman to turn his mind to that point—I see that it struck the Senator as it has struck me—I suggest that instead of this special legislation to the court, which is always objectionable—

In the estimation of damages or profits under a patent the owner shall have a right only to recover a just compensation for his invention, and his time, ingenuity, and expense bestowed upon the same, with a right to a penalty not exceeding three times the amount in all, in the discretion of the court, and due allowance shall be made for the capital, labor, and circumstances under which the invention has been used in the estimation of damages and compensation—

it would be better to leave all the details to the court and not legislate specially for the court. That is a judicial question. I wish to turn your attention to that. I shall urge this instead of that whole section.

Mr. SMITH. Thank you. The rule which was presented last year for estimating damages provided that a reasonable license-fee should be ascertained having reference to time, ingenuity, and expense expended upon the invention. I then suggested, and I think the suggestion is a pertinent one, that such a rule would operate with extreme hardship upon defendants in many cases, because there are many inventors who spend more time upon an invention than it proves to be worth, and to transfer to a defendant the cost of an invention, instead of allowing it to rest upon the plaintiff, would be an act of hardship.

I will pursue this thought a little further. When in consultation with Mr. Paison, the counsel for the railroad association, we were discussing the propriety of attempting to place in the hands of the court power to ascertain what a reasonable compensation was. I asked what elements he would take into account, whether it should be simply what it cost to the inventor, and, if so, what proportion of this cost should be charged upon the defendant before the court; whether he was to take the whole of it, or whether it was in some way to be apportioned between that de-

fendant and all other defendants known or unknown to the court, in
which case it would be, of course, utterly impossible to apply the rule,
and the defendant might be charged with very much more than he
ought to be charged with, on the assumption that there might not be
half as many infringers as might actually arise.

I suggested, further, that one element would be to take into account
the value of the invention to the public—to those who used it, but that
there would be danger under that rule that the defendant would be
charged with ten times as large a proportion of the actual benefit to the
public as the plaintiff, as an inventor, ever now receives under the operation of the ordinary laws of trade; so that it seemed to me not only
unwise, but might, in many cases, be unjust to attempt to charge a
defendant his proportion of the value of an invention to the whole public at large; because he would, in that case, be charged with an amount
which no inventor now expects to reap if he is left in the undisturbed
enjoyment of his invention.

Section 3 was suggested by Mr. Gifford, of New York. It provides
for a hardship pressing mostly upon a defendant, but oftentimes felt
by a plaintiff, arising in this way: Upon the final hearing of a suit in
equity, if it is held that the defendant does not infringe the patent,
although it may be valid, the plaintiff may appeal at once to test the
question of infringement before the Supreme Court, because no account
intervenes. If, however, the defendant is charged as an infringer under
the decision of the court, an account is to be taken, because no appeal
can be taken until a final decree is reached, and the decree upon the
original hearing is merely an interlocutory decree. The parties therefore, must go through, in the case of a finding in favor of the plaintiff,
with a long and very extensive accounting in many cases before there is
any possibility of reaching the Supreme Court to determine the only
question which may be of any importance, and that is the question of
infringement, or the validity of the patent. We have, therefore, provided in this section that the court, in its discretion, may allow the defendant to appeal at once, and not await the finding of the court below
upon the question of damages.

We hesitated much before introducing it, not that from any reason
related to the administration of the patent law it would not be a very
beneficent provision, but from an apprehension that it might send more
business to the already overcrowded Supreme Court; but upon a discussion with the gentlemen in Chicago, who had in various States seen
the operation of a rule similar to that in their State jurisprudence, we
came to the conclusion that it would be more likely to diminish the work
of the Supreme Court than to increase it.

Senator MORGAN. Is it intended to apply that to equity cases alone?

Mr. STORROW. One gentleman has suggested that after "causes," in
the first line, the words "in equity" should be inserted.

Senator MORGAN. Is not that the rule now in all equity causes, that
when there is a final decree settling the equities between the parties an
appeal lies to the Supreme Court, and then you do not have to await
the stating of an account?

Mr. SMITH. No, sir; that decree is held to be only an interlocutory
decree in patent causes, and the Supreme Court would not allow an
appeal. That rule is well settled, and it seems to me that both for plaintiffs and defendants it is well to place in the hands of the circuit court the
power of sending a case up for a decision on the important questions
without waiting to incur the expense of taking an account, which may
after all prove entirely fruitless.

Section 4 provides for placing in the hands of the circuit courts power to alter or amend the injunction after an appeal has been taken to the Supreme Court, for in many cases great hardship arises from imposing on a defendant an injunction which he must obey during all the lapse of time while the case is pending in the Supreme Court, and where he may suffer a hardship against which he can have no relief.

It is not necessary that I should discuss these sections, because I think their scope is sufficiently indicated by them. I pass over the fifth section, not because it does not deserve some comment, but because it was introduced by the Patent Bar Association, who will address the committee upon that subject, only remarking that I think it states the rule of law as it now stands with a single exception, that it places in the hands of the court an enlarged authority to inquire, in the case of reissued patents, as to the character of the reissue. As I have already taken more time than I ought to take, I must pass hastily over this, trusting that other gentlemen will bring the attention of the committee to them.

Section 6 contains two provisions, one clearly for the benefit of defendants in patent causes, and calculated to relieve them from a serious hardship. As the law now stands, a patentee may take his patent and neglect to claim some feature of the invention which he had a perfect right to claim. So long as his patent stands in that way, the world is entitled to use it, because he is held to disclaim all which is not specially claimed. Under that state of things a party may resort to the patent, and having ascertained that a certain thing is not claimed, may incorporate it into a machine. On a reissue of the patent, although no damages can be recovered for infringement prior to that time, he may be enjoined from the use of the machine after that time, although he lawfully built it, and it became his property. This section is intended to relieve him from that liability to injury by providing that he may continue to use the machine as though he had constructed it under a special license. It also provides a remedy in another class of cases which operated with hardship on the plaintiff, because by the surrender of his patent he lost his right to prosecute for infringements which had occurred previously to the act of surrender. We see no reason why he should not be allowed to recover, if he has a valid claim under his original patent, in the same way that he would be entitled to if his patent expired by its own limitation instead of by act of surrender.

I intended to trace hastily the other provisions of the bill; but, having consumed so much time, I will close my remarks with a single observation. I received last night, from a gentleman in Boston, Mr. Maynadier, a patent lawyer, a communication addressed to me upon the subject of these amendments. As it is in print, I will hand to each of the members of the committee a copy of it.

The CHAIRMAN. The committee propose to take all the time that is necessary for the full discussion of this bill, and do not propose to limit you. We can have other meetings if necessary.

Mr. SMITH. I am greatly obliged to you, Mr. Chairman, for the suggestion, and yet I think there is nothing which makes it of much importance for me to continue my address. I wish to say that I also received from Mr. Latrobe, of Baltimore, a letter, not in print, but which I think is deserving consideration, which I will also place in your hands.

The CHAIRMAN. Do you wish this incorporated in your argument by the reporter?

Mr. SMITH. No, sir; I only hand it to you as the opinion of a gentleman whose opinions are entitled to consideration. I should be g'ad if the committee saw fit to print it.

The CHAIRMAN. We can have it printed.

(The letters of Mr. Latrobe and of Mr. Maynadier refer to a previous draught of the bill; the changes since made meet some of their suggestions.)

Mr. SMITH. Mr. Chairman, I am greatly obliged for the kindness of the committee in listening to me with such attention. I cannot close without expressing the hope that the work which we have been enabled to bring before you will receive the approval of the committee, and, after it, of Congress, and that through it the country—not inventors only, but the whole country—will find that the true objects of the Constitution are secured by promoting, more effectually than heretofore, "the progress of the useful arts."

<hr />

APPENDIX TO MR. SMITH'S ARGUMENT.

Letter of Mr. Latrobe.

BALTIMORE, *October* 31, 1877.

MY DEAR MR. SMITH: I have taken my first leisure to go over the amendments to the patent laws proposed by the committee of which you are chairman; and that I take an interest in the subject is best proved by my troubling you with this letter.

SECTION 1. I am not quite sure about four years as the statutory limit for recovery in a suit on a patent. I know more than one case where more than six years have elapsed between the commencement of a suit and the final decree of the Supreme Court. Ought not an inventor to be permitted to test his patent's worth before you oblige him to sue? I would make the limitation six years at least. True, your section authorizing an appeal before an account helps matters, but I think I would prefer the six years to the four of your section 1.

SEC. 2. Are you quite right in leaving it to either court or jury to fix what ought to be the price of a license? True, you leave it to the party to fix a license-fee "by a reasonable number of transactions." But, if not, then "the court or jury shall determine the same from all the evidence." Is not my invention as much my property as my house, and am I not the sole judge of the value of the latter? I am not sure that the law, as decisions have made it, is not all that is wanted just now. I have a case where I would like just such a section as your number 2. But—

SEC. 3. Very good indeed.
SEC. 4. All right.
SEC. 5. Supplies a defect.
SEC. 6. The last clause of this section is very proper. I wish it were law *now*, to meet a want I have. Are you satisfied that the first part of the section is quite as clearly expressed as it might be? I found myself *studying* before I quite made it out. I think that I would have used some such form of words as this, "A license by one of two or more patentees shall have the same effect as a license executed by all, unless their power in this respect is controlled by some instrument recorded in the Patent Office."
SEC. 7. It may be hypercritical, but is there any necessity for the words at the top of page 7 beginning at "before" and ending "thereof"?
SEC. 8. All right.
SEC. 9. I doubt this. It may be old-fashioned, but I hesitate before

I am willing to interfere with a patentee's right to deal with his property at his discretion. Suppose a patentee *permits* his patent to be infringed—suppose, as is often the case, he is not able to bear expenses of litigation—what right have *I* to call upon court or jury to determine whether a delay to sue is reasonable or not? Other objections suggest themselves. Is not the present remedy sufficient in case of a patent assailable on any legal ground?

SEC. 10. This is assimilating our patent law to the English and French systems. I am not sure whether this is desirable or not. You know as well as I do the struggles which some of the most meritorious patentees have had in introducing their inventions to the notice of the public. I have now a suit on a valuable patent, the owners of which were, you may say, paupers at the expiration of four years from the date of their patent, which now has but five years to run. I am not sure about section 10.

SEC. 11. All right.

SEC. 12. All the alterations proposed here are good, especially that to 4916.

Most truly,

JNO. H. B. LATROBE.

CHAUNCEY SMITH, Esq.

LETTER OF MR. MAYNADIER.

BOSTON, *November* 12, 1877.

DEAR SIR: I have examined the pamphlets received from you, the last, entitled "Revision of the Proposed Amendments to the Patent Law," with such care that I can make the following statement of my opinion in regard to the matter:

SECTION 1. Some limitation is, in my opinion, needful, and four years is reasonable.

SEC. 2. It is too late now, perhaps, to object to taking the established license-fee as the *measure* of damages; but I have no doubt that it is always unjust to put an unsuccessful defendant on the same footing with those persons who are honest enough to admit a just claim before they are compelled to do it.

It seems to me that full justice will be done if the equity doctrine as to profits be done away with, and the matter be left under the rules of law, now pretty well settled, as to damages.

Under the present decisions it is safe to say the license-fee will be held the measure of damages in all cases where such ruling is not flagrant.

I am so fully persuaded that much wrong arises to both parties from the present system of holding the infringer liable not only as a tort-feasor, but also as trustee, that I beg attention to this matter.

I suggest that section 2 be changed as follows: Strike out lines 16 to 27 (p. 3), both inclusive, and also the words "or profits" in line 29, and insert after line 15, "The infringer shall not be charged as trustee, but in all suits in equity the complainant shall have the usual discovery and account, so far as relates to the extent of infringement, to aid in showing the actual damages."

It seems to me also that both rules for estimating profits (the one now established and the one suggested) are open to grave objections.

For example: Suppose the infringer has used the patented machine so improvidently that he has lost money, *i. e.*, that he has sold the product of the patented machine below cost (it may be, and often is, in competition with the owner of the patent); in that case the proposed rule would be less just than the present rule (*Mowrey* v. *Whitney*), under which the master finds the actual saving by using the patented machine over any other means or method open to the infringer, whether the infringer sold the product at a profit or at a loss. It seems to me that the profits the infringer may have *actually made* can have no relation whatever to the amount he may have saved by using the patented machine instead of some other machine which he had a right to use. If the product cost five dollars when the patented machine is used, and would have cost six made in any other way, it is obvious (*if* the rule established be just) that the infringer has saved one dollar; and this whether the product be sold at a profit or at a loss.

The rule now established has no relation to the profits actually made; but determines the profits for which the infringer is charged by ascertaining the saving. Why change it, not at all in the case of an infringer who so keeps up the price of the product that he actually realizes as much as or more than the amount saved by the use of the patented machine, but radically in the case of an infringer who so undersells that he actually realizes no profits at all?

Why not abolish it altogether? for it necessitates an issue which is absurd, viz: What would have happened if the defendant had done something else than he did? it being, in at least ninety-nine cases in a hundred, absurd to suppose that the defendant would have done this "something else."

The third and fourth sections (pp. 4 and 5) are of great importance, and should have been enacted in the first patent act. This is also true, in a measure, of section 7. Should not the words "in equity" be inserted after "jurisdiction" in line 2, section 4?

Section 5 (p. 5) seems to me eminently just, and to make a much-needed change. Lines 1 to 8 of section 6 (pp. 5, 6) seem unnecessary. The rest of this section may be of value as declaratory.

Sections 8 and 9 seem to me very desirable additions to the present law. Lines 41–43 of section 9 (p. 10) seem to need revision, as they do not cover the case of two or more equal owners not in the same district; nor the case of three or more owners, no two of whom owning "*the greater part* of the patent" (*i. e.*, more than one-half) reside in the same district.

I have not fully considered the tenth section (p. 11), but I have long been of opinion that some method should be devised for ridding the community of several classes of patents before the expiration of the full term. One of these classes embraces patents not valid, but which, it is hoped by their owners, cannot be *proved* invalid after the lapse of a few years. Another, and a very large class, embraces patents for inventions of a very low grade. Another class embraces what may be termed speculative patents, *i. e.*, those obtained by skillful but oversanguine inventors, not for present use, but with the hope that some day they may be important; these are mostly mere notions imperfectly thought out, and never embodied except in a crude model.

The provisions of the tenth section would probably work a remedy, but it would certainly work great hardship in some few cases, viz, that of the really great inventors, too far ahead of their times to be appreciated, and too poor to pay the taxes; but most of these men are defrauded as the law now stands.

Section 11 (p. 12) will be of great value in the few cases where it is applicable.

Very respectfully,

J. E. MAYNADIER.

CHAUNCEY SMITH, Esq.

SUGGESTIONS OF COMMISSIONER SPEAR.

Mr. SMITH. I understand that the Commissioner of Patents approves the bill. I should like to have the committee hear him.

Mr. SPEAR. I would prefer to put my suggestions in writing on some other day than to-day. On the whole, the bill meets with my hearty approval. There are some features relating more particularly to matters concerning the Patent Office and the conduct of business in the office, which I should like to make some comment upon, and I will do so to-morrow or some later day in writing.

The CHAIRMAN. You prefer a submission in writing?

Mr. SPEAR. Yes, sir.

ARGUMENT OF T. L. LIVERMORE.

Mr. CHAIRMAN AND GENTLEMEN: I disarrange the order because I fear that I must leave earlier than I anticipated. I deem it a great fortune of mine that I was called on by the learned counsel, who opened this subject to the committee, to participate in the deliberations of himself and his associates on this amendment, an honor which perhaps my experience does not fully warrant. At the same time, having been called upon to do so, and conceiving that no counselor careful of his own standing could feel at liberty to advocate class or special legislation, knowing that my associates in this matter have not such a feeling, and having full permission from them to express my individual views dissenting in some degree from the provisions of the bill, I take the liberty of now suggesting two or three amendments, which, I think, ought to be made to the bill as presented.

I am glad to do so before the gentlemen who represent the Bar Association of the District of Columbia speak, because in what I have to say on one section I shall criticise something that they have offered in the bill. I shall be glad to have them have an opportunity to reply to it.

The first remarks that I desire to present are with regard to the second section. The first paragraph of that section I will read:

" In all cases where the patentee has elected to license other persons generally to use his invention, in like manner to that in which it was used by the defendant, or where it appears to the court or jury that, from the nature of the invention, it is for the interest of the patentee that other persons generally should use the same in like manner and pay him a license-fee therefor, the measure of the plaintiff's damages shall be the same, both at law and in equity, and no account of profits or savings shall be allowed. If a license-fee has already been established by a reasonable number of transactions of a character applicable to the case at bar, that shall be adopted as the measure of said damages; but if not, then the court or jury shall determine the same from all the evidence in the case."

The first three lines in the bill as presented by the gentlemen here, substantially the first three lines of the Senate bill, propose to enact, as Mr. Smith has said, what has already been decided to be the law by the courts, and I agree that that provision is just; that "in all cases where the patentee has elected to license other persons generally to use his invention," that license-fee should be the measure of damages; provided that, in addition to that, interest is added from the time when the infringement began, because if the patentee licensed them early he would obtain his license-fee and have the use of that money during the whole period since the time when the machines began to be used.

But suppose an infringer for four years or ten years has availed himself of the invention without paying a license-fee, then it evidently would not be right that he should get off at the end of ten years by simply paying the license-fee, when the patentee, if the man had paid the license-fee in the beginning, would have had the benefit of the capital in the mean time. I am inclined to think that the courts would now, as the law stands, add interest; and I think that the provision in the last part of the clause giving the court power to increase the damages would probably result in that adding of interest. So that those first three or four lines I agree to.

Then we come to this provision in the second section:

" Or where it appears to the court or jury that, from the nature of the invention, it is for the interest of the patentee that other persons generally should use the same in like manner and pay him a license-fee therefor, the measure of the plaintiff's damages shall be the same, both at law and in equity, and no account of profits or savings shall be allowed."

I understand that that is framed with the purpose of meeting a class of cases where, for instance, a man has invented a switch for a railroad and evidently cannot use it himself because he cannot run a railroad for his own profit individually ; or in a case like that suggested by Senator Morgan, where an improvement like a combination of Paris green with something else for the purpose of having it safely handled and used is the subject of the patent, and that improvement is one which evidently must be used by the public generally in order to bring profit to the patentee. Of the nature of the invention itself, it is one which must be licensed to other people to be used in order to give the patentee any profit. I agree that in such cases, where it is an improvement like that, like the Paris-green combination, it might result in enormous injustice to have an account of the profits which the defendants made taken under the rules which perhaps the courts are bound by now; and that in those cases where, from the nature of things, it must be held to be the intention of the patentee that his improvement shall be used by the public because it is an improvement out of which he cannot make profit unless it is used by the public, a reasonable license-fee should be the measure of damages.

So far I agree to it. But suppose that there is an improvement like that of Mr. Corliss, which was suggested here, which, from the nature of things, he can use more profitably himself; and suppose that he conceives that it is for his interest to use it more profitably ; suppose that he has not at the time that case comes to trial been able to begin the introduction of this improvement, as he contemplates, and a case comes to a court, and he sets up in his declaration that he intends to practice the invention himself, and not license others to apply his invention to machines ; suppose that some jury takes a different view or some judge takes a different view, and because it cannot be demonstrated by evidence of practical experience that it would be for his profit to have others use it or introduce it or sell it, instead of himself, they limit him to some imaginary proper license-fee.

In those cases the rule would be unjust, and to my mind that would come very near to infringing upon that provision of the Constitution which provides that Congress may legislate to secure to inventors the exclusive use of their inventions, because the exclusive use in that case which they can secure to him is the use which he can make of it. In the other cases the exclusive use is that use which is the only one that can be profitable, to wit, the use by the public under license from him.

To my mind, this part of this section operates with a level rule. It touches Mr. Corliss's case as well as the case of the farmers in Alabama; and I think there should be a discrimination, and to that end I would suggest that all that part of the Senate bill beginning at the word "or," line 3, and ending with the word "allowed," line 10, second page, should be stricken out; or that this amendment should be made, that the word "for," in line 5 of the Senate bill, and line 5 of the bill presented, should be stricken out; the word "interest" in the same line stricken out, and the word "intention" inserted in place of the word "interest;" and after the word "damages," in the eighth line of the Senate bill, and the eighth line of the proposed bill, the words "for using, but not for selling," inserted; so that the paragraph would either be entirely stricken out, and leave the law as it is to-day in cases where no license-fee has been established, or else that it should read in this fashion:

"Or where it appears to the court or jury that from the nature of the invention it is the intention of the patentee that other persons generally should use the same in like manner and pay him a license-fee therefor, the measure of the plaintiff's damages for using, but not for selling, shall be the same both at law and in equity."

That, to my mind, would effect that discrimination which is the only one that would be just, to wit, in those cases where the thing might be used by the public to make a profit for the patentee, like the use of Paris green, or the railroad-switch, the court should be at liberty to infer that it was his intention to have the public use it, for there could be no other inference; and in those cases where it was possible that he himself only could apply the improvements to his machines, and sell them, as his own powder, or the machines for the production of given articles, in those cases the law should be left as it is to-day.

In stating the case upon my proposition, I think I have stated all the argument upon it that is necessary, and I will pass from that section.

Section 5, which is one that Mr. Smith has said was framed by the Patent Bar Association, is another one which I think is open to criticism, and very serious criticism; and before I read that, in order that the committee may have before their minds clearly the situation to which that section is intended to apply, let me state briefly what the law as to reissues is to-day, as interpreted by the courts, and as we suppose it would be interpreted by them.

If a man in describing his invention has omitted to make a complete description of it, or has omitted to state fully and completely all that he might claim as novel in his invention, he may surrender his patent and apply to the Commissioner of Patents for a new patent, called a reissue, and that new patent may be issued with a new description of his machine, and with new claims and new features that he did not claim before; and, to make that new description under the law and the practice of the courts as it stands to-day, the Commissioner of Patents is authorized to, and must, as I conceive, allow the patentee to go to the model which is on file in the Patent Office and make a new drawing from that model, putting in new features which did not appear in the drawing of the original patent, no matter if it is half the machine, and upon that new drawing make a new specification and a new description, and upon that new description make new claims.

Now it is not quite settled, as I understand, by the courts, whether in making an amended specification the applicant may resort to the original specification which he filed in the Patent Office when he applied for his original patent, for an amended description or not. It often happens that the Commissioner, in passing upon his application, requires certain parts of his description to be stricken out, for one cause or another, so that the specification or description of the inventor, as annexed to the original patent, may omit many features which were described in the original description filed. It is not clearly settled, I think, by the courts to-day that an applicant for a reissue may resort to that original description to enlarge the description of the reissued patent which he proposes to take. This section is one designed to authorize and require the Commissioner to permit the applicant to resort to that original specification, and confirming the law, in addition, as it now stands. Section 5 of this bill provides:

"Section forty-nine hundred and sixteen of the Revised Statutes is hereby amended so as to read as follows: Whenever any patent is inoperative or invalid, by reason of a defective or insufficient specification, or by reason of the patentee claiming as his own invention or discovery more or less than he had a right to claim as new, if the error has arisen by inadvertence, accident, or mistake, and without any fraudulent or deceptive intention, the Commissioner shall, on the surrender of such patent and the payment of the duty required by law, cause a new patent for the same invention"—

And now comes the clause to which I object—

"shown in the model or drawings, or described in the original specification or its amendments"—

To wit, the specification originally filed in the office and not that annexed to the original patent necessarily—

"and to which he would have been entitled, and in accordance with the corrected specification, to be issued to the patentee, or in the case of his death or of an assignment of the whole or any undivided part of the original patent"—

And it goes on to provide then substantially what the law provides now. The last paragraph of this section provides that—

"In any suit at law or in equity upon a patent hereafter reissued, the defendant, having given notice or pleaded the same in the manner set forth in the forty-nine hundred and twentieth section of the Revised Statutes, may prove in defense to the whole patent, or any of the claims thereof, that the new patent, or any claim thereof, is not for the same invention shown in the model or drawings, or described in the original specification or its amendments, and to which he would have been entitled."

I understand that that part of the section is framed to meet this state of affairs: The law, as it now stands, requires the Commissioner to amend the new specification by the model on file; and it is a serious question whether it is not the law as laid down by the courts that that decision of the Commissioner is conclusive, so that a defendant in a suit is not at liberty to allege and prove, by way of defense, that the model did not contain the new features embodied in the new patent; and this last half of the section, if the law is to remain as it now is, is a beneficial provision, and one which I can heartily approve; but with the amendments, which I think ought to be made, this last part that I have just read is entirely unnecessary, as it seems to me.

Now I will come to the operation of the law as it is to-day, and as it would be in a greater degree if this amendment allowing the specification of the new patent to be amended by the original specification were incorporated in the law. To-day the law is that the patentee may have secured unto him for seventeen years the exclusive right to any invention which he will fully describe and set out upon the records of the Patent Office and indicate as his invention, if he will so fully describe it that after the term of his monopoly has expired the public may come in and from his description make the invention. The law also prescribes that he shall indicate just what part of the thing described he claims as his new invention, so that the public may be informed, that they may not infringe his patent.

Now a man comes in, having invented twenty things, we will say; by blundering, by design, or from any other cause, he describes two of them and leaves out eighteen. Eighteen that are embodied in his model he leaves out of his specification, or eighteen that are in his specification the examiner strikes out, or he strikes them out voluntarily, so that he describes only two and claims only two, and that patent goes forth to the people of the United States.

A man then inspecting the records of the Patent Office, inspecting the patent, which is all the law requires him to inspect, finds that these eighteen things which he sees embodied in some machine are open to the public—are not claimed. He sets up a factory; he goes to making machines, embodying these eighteen things. Some day a new patent comes out describing the eighteen things and claiming them, and his business is ruined. That is unjust. It results from the fact that the patentee may resort to that model, which is here in the Patent Office, to incorporate a new description and new claims into his new patent.

One of the provisions of this bill is that a reissue shall not be retroactive, so as to prevent machines which have already been built from being used; but it does not provide that a business which is erected shall not be tipped over. A whole factory, equipped for the manufacture of machines, can be stopped notwithstanding this provision; and, further than that, there is this opportunity, this incentive, this wide door open for fraud.

Why, look at these little models in the Patent Office. Many of them represent a walking-beam, for instance, by a piece of metal no bigger than a pen-holder; a thing which may be broken, twisted, bent, altered in various ways by the fingers. Other pieces are represented by little pieces of wood glued to other pieces of wood. They may come apart. Material alterations may be made by accident or by design in those models. No man can tell whether the models originally were filed as they appear to-day. Perhaps—and upon these alterations I speak advisedly from instances which I know have happened—upon those models, altered in that fashion, new descriptions of new inventions, which never existed in the mind of the patentee, are incorporated into the new patent and the public are made to suffer.

And if these amended specifications can be made from the original specifications, a dash of a pen through a word, the interlineation of a word, the use of a little acid, numbers of devices which unscrupulous men may resort to, can alter those specifications so as to alter the whole character of the original invention. Now, to my mind, the opportunity should be removed, the temptation should no longer be afforded, and the public should be protected by not only preventing these proposed alterations, but by striking out of the law the provision that allows the new specification to be amended by the model; and, to that end, I would strike out of section 5 of the Senate bill lines 11 and 12 and the first two words of line 13 : " shown in the model or drawings, or described in the original specification or its amendments, and to which he would have been entitled."

The same in lines 12, 13, and 14 of the proposed bill of the gentlemen.

I would add to that section, in line 18 of the Senate bill, and line 19 of the proposed bill, after the word " upon," the words: " But the specification shall be amended only by itself, or the drawings, or the patent."

I wish to state, in addition, that this provision of the second section, which I have objected to, was not contained in the Senate bill reported last session.

It has been urged with reference to the permission which already is accorded, and which it is proposed to accord, to amend a reissue by the model and by the old specification, that great hardship results to the inventor often by reason of his employing an incompetent solicitor, who does not prepare the specification upon the patent as finally issued in accordance with his real invention, as shown in his model, and that, therefore, this privilege should be accorded to the patentee.

My reply to that is this: The specification of a patent, which is published as a part of the patent, forms a part of the contract between the patentee and the public—by the public, on the one hand, that he shall have a monopoly of what he discloses for a certain term, and by the patentee, on the other hand, that he will disclose then and there all that he claims, so that the public may not be misled by false lights; and if he suffers hardship on account of the ignorance or incapacity of the attorney whom he employs, he suffers but the same hardship which every contracting party suffers who has a contract unskillfully drawn by reason of employing incompetent attorneys. In the case of an ordinary contract, no lawyer would urge that the other contracting party should suffer because of the ignorance of the first one's attorney.

I also wish to add that I am heartily with this proposed bill, as advocated by Mr. Smith, in all particulars, excepting the two that I have mentioned. I have given it a good deal of study, and it seems to me that this bill goes a very long way to cure the evils which have resulted from the administration of the patent law, and to prevent the injustice which has been done to the public, and to secure more complete justice to the patentee than it has hitherto been possible to secure under the law as it stands. More than that, I think this bill is nearly a complete bill. I think it deals with nearly all the remedies which in practice we have found ought to be provided upon the one hand for the patentee, and the protection which we have found ought to be provided on the other hand for the public.

ARGUMENT OF C. S. WHITMAN.

Mr. Whitman. Mr. Chairman and gentlemen: I was rather unexpectedly called upon to represent the view of the Bar Association in regard to certain proposed amendments of the patent laws. I propose to occupy as little of your very valuable time as possible; I will therefore call your attention immediately to the fifteenth section of the bill, page 15 of the Senate print, bill No. 300. As section 15 now stands, it provides that " section 479 of the Revised Statutes shall be, and hereby is, amended, so as to read as follows: The Commissioner of Patents, Assistant Commissioner, and the chief clerk," &c.

The new words contained in the section are the words "Assistant Commissioner" following the word " patents"; also after the words " United States" in the sixth line the insertion is made of the words " the first two." The effect of the introduction of the words " Assistant Commissioner" is to require the Assistant Commissioner of Patents to give a bond as well as the Commissioner of Patents. Both the Commissioner and the chief clerk are now required to give bond in a certain amount prescribed by the act. Very frequently the Assistant Commissioner of Patents performs the duties that are incumbent upon the Commissioner of Patents, day after day and perhaps week after week. If the Commissioner of Patents gives bond there seems to be no good reason why the Assistant Commissioner should not do so. The Commissioner of Patents gives bond in the sum of $10,000, and the chief clerk in the sum of $5,000. Under this amendment the Commissioner and the Assistant Commissioner would both give bonds in the amount ot $10,000.

Senator CHAFFEE. What is the object of their giving bond ?

Mr. WHITMAN. As the section states, " for the faithful discharge of their respective duties, and that they shall render to the proper officers of the Treasury a true account of all money received by virtue of their offices."

If a bond is required of the Commissioner for the faithful performance of his duties, why should not a bond be required of the Assistant Commissioner, who performs the duties of the Commissioner sometimes for two weeks or a month during the absence of the former ?

Senator CHAFFEE. I do not see why it is required of the Commissioner to give bond. It is a mere matter of form.

Mr. WHITMAN. The mere effect of the amendment would be to make the law uniform.

Mr. STANSBURY. He is a receiving and a disbursing officer.

Mr. RAYMOND. The Commissioner of Patents receives sixty thousand dollars a year in small sums.

Senator MORGAN. It is stated that he receives large amounts in very small sums.

Mr. WHITMAN. He is a receiving and disbursing officer. As I understand it, he receives all moneys paid into the office for fees; that is to say, fifteen dollars when the application is filed and twenty dollars when the patent is issued. This money is placed in his custody. I am not conversant enough with the red-tape of the office to state just how much authority he has over the money.

Senator CHAFFEE. I supposed it went into the control of the Secretary of the Interior.

Mr. LIVERMORE. It all goes to the Commissioner of Patents and he turns it into the Treasury.

Mr. WHITMAN. It is always paid to the Commissioner of Patents or his order.

Mr. STANSBURY. It is deposited in bank every day to the credit of the Commissioner of Patents, and then turned over to the Treasury afterward at certain specified times.

Mr. WHITMAN. The next section of the law to which I will call your attention is section 16, immediately following. It reads as follows as amended:

" Section 493 of the Revised Statutes shall be, and hereby is, amended so as to read as follows: 'The price to be paid for uncertified printed copies of specifications and drawings of patents shall be determined by the Commissioner of Patents, within the limits of actual cost as the minimum, and fifty cents as the maximum price."

The only change in the law here effected is in the use of the words "actual cost." The law read before, instead of " actual cost," " ten cents." The amendment merely enables the Commissioner of Patents to go into the wholesale as well as the retail business. Heretofore he has been in the habit of charging the same price at wholesale as at retail in selling these copies of patents. You make an application to the Patent Office for a copy of the specification and drawing, or for ten copies. They charge you ten cents apiece, or a dollar for ten copies. You make application for five hundred or five thousand copies, if they could furnish you so many, and they charge you the same price. These copies of specifications and drawings are of great interest to the manufacturers of the country, and to the inventors, for very frequently they wish to investigate the state of the art to which an invention relates, and they write on to the office for tens, and hundreds, and perhaps thousands, of copies. These drawings have been photolithographed, and a whole class can be ordered at once. For instance, a stove manufacturer may order every patent relating to stoves. If he writes to the office for one copy, it may be worth ten cents to the office to select that one copy and put it in the mail and send it to him. It requires the same character of work for one copy that it would require to send ten thousand copies. This provision of the bill merely enables the Commissioner of Patents to charge the inventors and manufacturers of the country a less amount than ten cents. This amendment was inserted at the suggestion of the Commissioner of Patents. Instead of furnishing them as now at ten cents a copy, he might furnish them at three cents a copy. The benefit of course would be altogether to the public.

There is also a further change in that section. All after the word "price" in line 7 is new matter, as follows: "And the price to be charged for certified copies shall be the same as for uncertified copies, with the addition of twenty-five cents for the certificate and seal."

They are in the habit of charging now ten cents per hundred words for printed copies. They charge the same price for printed copies that they used to do in old times, before the specifications were printed, for written copies, and the payment of this amount is frequently very onerous to parties engaged in litigation. It is necessary for litigants sometimes to provide themselves with large numbers of certified copies of office-records, and the statute as it now stands compels a litigant in patent cases to pay a tax to the government for conducting litigation, which seems to be rather an improper mode of taxation. This amendment merely provides that the office-copies, certified, shall be furnished at their actual cost.

Senator MORGAN. What is the meaning of "fifty cents as the maximum price?" I do not understand that.

Mr. WHITMAN. It is supposed that perhaps a copy of the specification and drawing might cost fifty cents under certain circumstances.

Senator MORGAN. It might cost more, might it not.

Mr. WHITMAN. I can hardly conceive that it would cost more than that.

Mr. STORROW. Fifty cents is the maximum of the present law now.

Mr. WHITMAN. Section 17 of the bill, on page 16, reads as follows:

"Section eight hundred and ninety-two of the Revised Statutes shall be, and hereby is, amended so as to read as follows: Copies of any records, books, papers, drawings, or models belonging to the Patent Office, and of letters patent authenticated by the seal and certified by the Commissioner, Assistant Commissioner, or Acting Commissioner of Patents, shall be evidence in all cases wherein the originals could be evidence; and any person making application therefor, and paying the fee required by law, shall have certified copies thereof."

The only change in this section from the old law is the insertion of the words "or models" in line 4, after "drawing." The Commissioner of Patents has been in the habit for years of furnishing these certified models to the courts in litigated cases. The question seems to have arisen, however, whether they could be actually used as evidence; whether or not it requires any statutory provision in order that they may be used as evidence. You, gentlemen of the committee, can judge better than I. Anyhow, it renders the law certain in that respect, and puts models on the same footing as other records of the office which may be certified to.

Then there is another change in this section. In line 6, after the word "Commissioner," the words "Assistant Commissioner" are inserted. This is done in order to enable the Assistant Commissioner of Patents to certify models or records when the Commissioner of Patents is absent or engaged. The Commissioner of Patents may be engaged in listening to an important hearing, or in transacting some other positively necessary business of the Patent Office, and in the course of his duties he may be interrupted by the requirement that he should certify to some paper which perhaps might be instantaneously required. This provision merely allows the Assistant Commissioner to perform that duty. The Assistant Commissioner sits in an adjoining room, and it is much more convenient in many instances to apply to him to perform this duty than it would be to apply directly to the Commissioner.

I call your attention to section 19, on page 17. That section reads as follows:

"Section forty-eight hundred and eighty-seven of the Revised Statutes shall be, and hereby is, amended so as to read as follows: No person shall be debarred from receiving a patent for his invention or discovery, nor shall any patent issued subsequent to March second, eighteen hundred and sixty-one, be declared invalid, by reason of its having been first patented in a foreign country upon the invention of the same person, unless the same has been introduced into public use in the United States for more than two years prior to the application; but all applications hereafter to be made for patents for inventions which shall have been patented in a foreign country upon the invention of the same person shall be made within two years after the date of such foreign patent."

The law, as it stands, has led to a great deal of confusion and difficulty on account of a limitation therein limiting American patents to the term of the foreign patent. For instance, if I should take out a patent in Great Britain, where a patent merely runs for fourteen years, in the month of May, and afterward, in the month of June, if I should come over to the United States and take out a patent here, the United States would limit me to a fourteen years' patent, whereas I would be entitled to a seventeen years' patent if the patent had been taken out here first. There does not seem to be any sense or logic in such a provision of law at all. It can be very easily illustrated. Suppose I, an American, give all the world a right to use my invention. I say to the English, French, and Germans, and to the people all over the world, "You may have a right to use my invention for nothing," and then take out a patent in the United States for seventeen years. The United States freely grants that patent without limiting the term thereof; but if I go over to England and deprive the English people of using that invention for fourteen years, the United States says to me, "Your American patent shall only be issued for fourteen years"; that is, if you allow the English people to use your invention they will give you a patent for seventeen years, but if you deprive them of using your invention for fourteen years, they limit the American patent to fourteen years.

This provision also leads to difficulties in other directions. Foreign

64

MR. C. S. WHITMAN.

patents are not what American patents are. A foreign inventor may take out a series of fifteen or twenty foreign patents before he has perfected his invention to such an extent as to take out what we call a patent. They often file an application for a patent where we would file a *caveat;* for when a man merely makes an inchoate or incomplete invention, he may file an application at the British patent-office and receive a British patent. He comes over here afterward and files an application in the United States, and the question presents itself to the Commissioner of Patnts how he is to limit the American patent. He may embody everyth ng contained in these fifteen patents in his American patent, and the looseness with which they grant patents abroad renders it almost impossible, in some instances, to limit the American patent to the foreign patents. They grant patents in England without any examination whatever, and leave it to the courts afterward to determine the validity of the patent.

There seems to be very strong reasons in favor of this amendment. It is customary with the Commissioner of Patents, immediately after the issuance of a patent, to forward to the British patent-office a complete copy of that patent, and of all patents issued. For instance, here are three hundred patents issued in a week. As soon as a steamer can take those patents to England they are published in Chancery Lane, in the British patent-office, and are open to the inspection of the English people, and in fact to all Europe. It is as good a publication to defeat a patent as could possibly be made. Now, the American inventor a short time afterward may go to England to take out a patent. They grant him a patent, of course, because they give patents to anybody without any examination, but when he goes into the courts with that patent afterward he is informed that his invention was published in England perhaps a week or a month before he took out the patent, and that his English patent is good for nothing. Consequently, American inventors are actually prevented by this section of the law to a certain extent from taking out foreign patents. If the inventor takes the other horn of the dilemma and, instead of taking out the patent in this country first, takes out a patent in England and comes back to the United States to take out his American patent, Uncle Sam informs him that he can only give him a patent for less than fourteen years on account of his having taken out the patent abroad first. So what is he to do? He must run all those risks. There is one practice, however, that skillful attorneys follow, and that unskillful attorneys sometimes fail to follow: that is, after the invention has been allowed by the American Patent Office, or when the inventor has received what is called the notification of the allowance which is sent out by the Commissioner of Patents before the patent is granted, he may make application abroad and tie up his application here in the American Patent Office until his foreign patents are granted. But that is a matter of a great deal of difficulty and trouble. In some foreign governments it is very difficult to obtain a patent; for instance, it is very difficult to obtain a patent in Prussia. The application of the inventor may be held up for years in that country, and for a lesser time in France or England. In the mean time he is obliged to hold up his application in the Patent Office here. For these reasons the proviso has been stricken out. The question has sometimes arisen in my mind why it was ever introduced into the patent law, or how it ever came there. It may be worth while to give a *resumé* of the legislation on that subject: As long ago as 1839 a law was passed which I am confident was the first law limiting the term of an American patent.

That law limited the term of an American patent to fourteen years from the date of the English patent. It was not as the law stands now; it did not limit the patent to the term of the foreign patent having the shortest term. A patent abroad, for instance, may have a term of five years, and it would cut down the American patent to a term of five years. The old law of 1839 contained a provision that an American patent should extend for fourteen years from the date of the foreign patent. That, I believe, continued to be the law until 1861. In 1861 a law was passed providing that *all* patents thereafter issued should extend for the term of seventeen years from the date of issue. The construction of that section seems to be that all patents issued between 1861 and 1870 would extend for the term of seventeen years. Along came the legislators again in 1870 and changed the law. In 1870 the patent laws were completely codified, and all sections before in force were repealed. It was a complete codification of the patent laws, and in that codification it was provided that where an American or foreign inventor takes out a patent in the United States his term shall be limited to the term of the foreign patent. That law creates needless difficulties at the Patent Office, and in fact throws a cloud upon every patent which the Patent Office issues. How is any one of the patent lawyers about here, in investigating a patent case and looking up the title of a patent, to know the term of that patent? They do not limit it at the Patent Office; it may really be for a term of five or six years, if a foreign patent has been taken out, and they give a patent for seventeen years. You take that patent and read it: John Smith is granted the right of his invention in the United States for seventeen years. In the mean time there may have been half a dozen patents in different parts of Europe limiting the term of the patent of John Smith, so that in fact the proviso throws a cloud upon every patent issued from the Patent Office. I hardly think that I need say anything more to show the necessity of changing that section of the law.

I now have the honor to call your attention to section 21 of the Senate bill, which provides that—

"Section 4895 of the Revised Statutes shall be, and hereby is, amended so as to read as follows: Patents may be granted and issued to the assignee of the inventor or discoverer, and they may be reissued to the owner or owners of the entire interest in the patent; but the assignment must first be entered of record in the Patent Office. And in all cases of an application by an assignee for the issue of a patent, the specification shall be signed and sworn to by the inventor or discoverer;' and in all cases of an application for a reissue of any patent, the application may be made and the corrected specification sworn to and signed by the owner or owners of the entire interest in the patent."

This change in the statute merely restores the law as it formerly existed. It restores the law to the condition in which it was from the year 1836 to the year 1870. From the year 1836 to the year 1870 (and if I am not correct in the date I hope some brother here will correct me) any assignee might take out a reissue; for instance, a patent is taken out by John Smith. Four years afterward John Smith assigns his invention to Thomas Jones. Thomas Jones finds that the invention is defective and insufficient, and that, although he may have paid thousands of dollars for the patent, it is inoperative and invalid and of no use to him. He finds it necessary to obtain a reissue of the patent. The patent law, as it existed from 1836 to 1870, allowed Thomas Jones, in taking out a reissue, to make the application, but our legislators, for some reason best known to themselves, in 1870 (when several modifications of the patent law seem to have crept in that nobody seems to understand) made this change, providing that after the passage of the law of 1870 an application must be made and the oath taken by the original inventor himself. Suppose John Smith to be the orginal inventor, and that he assigns his invention to some manufacturing company or large interest that may, perhaps, pay for it a hundred thousand dollars, for that amount has been paid for patents. They afterwards find that his invention is worthless, and go to him and say, " Well, Mr. Smith, we want you to make a new oath and assist us in taking out a reissue." Mr. Smith quietly steps aside and says, " Well, gentlemen, give me a hundred thousand dollars, and I will do it. I do not think you will take out that reissue unless I make the oath, and if you will give me a hundred thousand dollars I will take the oath for you and make the application." That is no imaginary, but a very common, case. The inventor parted with his invention, has parted with all pecuniary interest in it, but human nature naturally prompts him to make more money if he can, with, perhaps, a little bit of the rascal at the botton of his disposition, and he requires $100,000, or any other amount of money, before he will sign those papers. This provision of the bill merely restores the law to where it stood from 1836 to 1870, and allows the assignee to make the application and to make the oath. Perhaps in the mind of a patent lawyer the question might arise as to whether the assignee of a patent could make the oath; but a good law and similar provision seems to have been in force since 1836, at least in regard to executors. Since 1836 an executor has been allowed to make oath in the case of the death of an inventor.

Senator MORGAN. What oath would he have to take?

Mr. WHITMAN. He would merely have to make an oath that the patent was inoperative and invalid, and did not cover the invention as it originally existed.

Mr. LIVERMORE. And that the party's application for the reissue covers the invention of the patentee.

Senator MORGAN. That is, after all, a question to be settled by the Commissioner.

Mr. WHITMAN. He swears he believed him to have been the first inventor.

Senator MORGAN. His swearing to it does not prove it.

Mr. WHITMAN. That seems to have been the law from 1836 to 1870; and it was a law which passed under the scrutiny of some of the ablest counsel in the country, and some of the ablest judges who ever lived, in this or any other country; among them, such men as Chief Justice Taney and Joseph Story. They seem to have found no difficulty in the matter, and I do not know why there should be any.

Senator MORGAN. Still there must have been some prominent reason for a change in the law. I do not know what it was.

Mr. KNIGHT. If the gentleman will permit me, the codification was made under the act by which the three commissioners were appointed— Judge James, Judge Cushing, and Judge Johnson. They commenced on the work, Judge Johnson taking patents and admiralty. They divided it in that way, among themselves. I recollect that Judge Johnson showed me his codification of the law up to the point he brought it. Their commission was signed by President Lincoln, and it expired, and the work was not done. Others were appointed. Of the original three codifiers, Judge James was retained. The late Commissioner, S. S. Fisher, was largely instrumental in giving the law the shape which it eventually assumed under the Revised Statutes, so far as relates to patents. It is believed that these discrepancies crept in accidently. It was not the intention of the codifiers to make any change of the law, but that it should be a true and genuine codification of the law as it stood. The commission had no right to change it, and probably did not intend to change the law; but when it was passed upon in a mass by Congress, it of course took shape as the law of the land.

Mr. WHITMAN. I think that brother Knight has presented the correct view of the case, that when Congress passed the law of 1870 they supposed they were merely codifying the law, and crystallizing the various acts into one statute, but some of these amendments did creep in, in a way that nobody seems to understand.

But, gentlemen, I do not propose to make any speech here to-day. I merely read over these sections of the bill in order to call your attention to the changes and modifications which are made by it in the existing law. However, there have been some remarks made by brother Livermore in regard to one section of the statute which I will notice. I had not supposed that it was a part of my duty in coming here to-day to undertake to explain or define the fifth section. I do not exactly understand it myself. The ideas as expressed by Mr. Livermore, it strikes me, are very correct. The trouble which he suggests, however, seems to me to be obviated by another section of the act. Now, the trouble in regard to reissues seems to be this: An original application for a patent consists of a specification, a drawing, and a model. That is what the inventor first puts in the office. The inventor, as a matter of fact, frequently sees nothing but the model. It may be that he is not a man who would be skilled enough in the art of mechanical drawing to understand it if he should see it, for the reading a mechanical drawing is an art in itself; or he may not perhaps understand the use of language sufficiently well to thoroughly comprehend a specification; but he does understand the model. There is no doubt about that. That is placed before him. Brother Livermore seems to look upon a model as being altogether the very worst evidence of an invention which can possibly be adduced. So far from the model being worse evidence than the specification and drawing, it strikes me that you could have none better. It is something which the inventor sees, and which perhaps he makes himself. The drawing may be changed from the model, and the specification may use all manner of language about the drawing, but there is the model as originally made by the inventor, and what better evidence can there possibly be of the invention?

Now, it was a practice of the Patent Office (and I hope I will be corrected if I am wrong) from 1836 to 1870 to allow a party to reissue his patent and cover anything that was shown in the model. I think the practice was at that time to look upon the model as being the best evidence. A man would frequently put his case in the hands of an unskillful attorney; his specification might not be properly drawn and his drawing not properly prepared. He would come back years afterward and go to his old original model as the best evidence of his invention. A drawing would be made to correspond with the model, and a specification would be drawn describing the drawing. He would not get anything more of course than what was in the original invention; whereas if he relied on the drawing and cast the model aside he might get something not shown in the original invention, for the drawing might have been filed at the Patent Office, prepared perhaps not under the eye of the inventor, and it might not agree with the model. If you throw the model aside and reissue on the drawing, it is possible that errors might creep into the patent.

That is the way the law existed from 1836 to 1870. Until that time the party was required by law to furnish a model. The law of 1870 did away with that requirement, and the inventor was not required by law to furnish a model; but the Commissioner of Patents makes a rule of the Patent Office requiring him to furnish a model. He may, however, in any case where he sees fit, dispense with the model, and in a good many cases, at least as far back as 1871 and 1872, the Commissioner did dispense with it.

There seems to be no difficulty in the mind of Mr. Livermore in regard to the reissue so far as the drawing and specification are concerned. Mr. Livermore holds, as I understand him, that the party may go back to the drawing and take everything that there is there and reissue his patent in such a way as to cover it. If I do not represent his views correctly I am willing to be corrected. His view is that the inventor may go to the specification and find anything that is described in the specification and reissue his patent in such a way as to cover it; but Mr. Livermore would deprive the inventor of going back to the model and reissuing the patent in accordance with it. He would deprive him of availing himself of the best evidence that could possibly exist of the original invention, and forbid him to reissue the patent in such manner as to cover what was shown in the model.

As I said before, errors might be found in the drawing or in the language of the specification which the inventor did not intend to make, but if the inventor made his model, as is frequently the case, or if it was made under his eye, as is most generally done, what better evidence of the invention could there possibly be?

But, after all, perhaps Mr. Livermore's views are right; at least I do not stand here to combat them. The trouble about the case is simply this: The genius of the patent law requires, as I understand it, that when a patent is issued the world shall know what that patent covers. The model does not constitute a part of the patent. It may be filed away in secret places in the Patent Office, or it may be in the public model-room of the office. That is a matter of option with the Commissioner. He may keep it there in the cases, if he chooses, or he may put it away. As a matter of practice he does, I believe, keep the models in the model-cases. Now, the public know nothing at all about this model, but they have a right to know, and do know, everything that issues under the seal of the Patent Office and is published broadcast over the land. They know all there is in the specification, forming a part of the patent, or they can know it very easily. Now, we give the inventor the right to reissue and cover anything that is described in his original specification and described in his original drawing, not because that specification and drawing are the best evidence of the invention, but because it is what the inventor has published to the world. The difficulty which Mr. Livermore speaks of is not imaginary. I know of just such a case. The trouble would seem to be this: The party files with his application his model, his drawing, and his specification, at the Patent Office. He takes out his patent, and it may be said, first, that his model does not agree with his drawing or specification when filed at the office. The Commissioner may dispense with the model or not, as he sees fit. He therefore may take out a patent for what is not really shown in the model. The model may differ from the drawing, under the present law. He goes on for six or eight years. He finds that certain devices which are shown in his model that has been deposited in the Patent Office are largely used all over the country. Perhaps he finds that all the harvesters of the western country use a certain device shown in his model which is filed away in the Patent Office. Perhaps he finds that some large manufacturing interest has been established upon what has been deposited in the model-room of the Patent Office, but what did not constitute a part of the patent according to the specification and drawing. He goes back to the Patent Office, or goes to his attorney, or solicitor, and takes out a reissue covering what was shown in that model—covering not what was shown in his original specification or in his original drawing and what the world is supposed to know all about, but covering something that was placed in the custody of the Commissioner of Patents and something that the Commissioner of Patents might do with as he chose. He then takes out his reissued patent and flirts it in the face of the manufacturers of the country, or the farmers on the western prairies and says, "Here, gentlemen, you are all using my harvester and you must pay me for it." That seems to have been the difficulty in the patent law that Mr. Livermore speaks of as needing correction, and he also mentioned the fact that perhaps gentlemen connected with the Bar Association might oppose it. I assure him most earnestly that I have no wish to oppose his views as I understand them.

I believe I have nothing more to say upon the question, gentlemen. Mr. Dodge, a member of the association, and Mr. Christy, a patent lawyer of prominence in Pittsburgh, desire to make some remarks to the committee, I understand.

ARGUMENT OF W. C. DODGE.

Mr. CHAIRMAN AND GENTLEMEN OF THE COMMITTEE: Before proceeding to discuss the proposed bill, I desire to make a few remarks on the policy and effect of a patent law. Among a certain class, of late, there has been considerable opposition to our patent system, and that feeling has found expression in both the Senate and House. I have observed, however, that this opposition generally assumes the form of self-interest, and is a demand for class legislation of the worst kind. On the part of the Grangers it was first a demand that articles which they wanted to use should not be patented, and subsequently, that patents should be granted only for such a time as would suffice to demonstrate the utility of the invention, and that then they should be free to the public, the inventor to be rewarded by a grant of money from the public treasury. On the part of the railroads it is a demand that they shall be allowed to appropriate any invention they please, and then to have the law so changed as practically to prevent their being compelled to pay for them.

Then there is another class, very small, thank God, who denounce all inventions as a curse; and it is but a few weeks since a paper here at the capital asserted that the invention of the steam-engine and the sewing-machine were two of the greatest evils that ever befell mankind.

Another writer recently gave it as his opinion that while "no doubt a good deal of good grows out of the industry and ingenuity set to work (by patents), it is at least an even chance that the evil is greater," and that the "inventors stimulated by patents are *men of second or third rate ability as inventors*, whose skill consists rather in formulating an ingenious application which may give them a patent that will enable them to levy tribute on same form of industry," and then clinches his argument, as he supposes, by the statement that such men as Franklin, Watt, Fulton, and Stephenson did not take patents on their inventions because they were "not actuated by a love of gain, but worked solely for the public weal."

A little examination will show how utterly unfounded are these and all similar statements.

Franklin made his invention, which was an improvement on the German open stove, in 1745, and he subsequently invented the lightning-rod; but as he died in 1790, and as our first patent law was not passed until after he died, it is not easy to see how he could have patented them if he would.

Watt not only patented his steam-engine, but he also patented all his subsequent improvements. Not only this, but his patent was *extended by act of Parliament for twenty-five years.*

As to Stephenson, he patented every invention he made, the list of which can be seen in the record of English patents from 1815 to 1841.

So, too, with Fulton. The State of New York granted his partner, Livingston, and himself the exclusive right to navigate the waters of that State by steam, which act was extended from time to time, until finally it was declared illegal by the Supreme Court, in the case of *Gibbons* vs. *Ogden*, because it was a violation of the right conferred by the Constitution upon Congress; but that was after his death. In 1809 Fulton took out his first patent, and in 1811 he took out another. In addition to all this, in 1846 Congress passed an act giving to his heirs the sum of $76,300, a fact so little known that when a bill was pending before the Senate a few years since to remunerate the heirs of Jethro Wood for his invention of a modern plow, a Senator said, "If the government desires to do anything of the kind, why does it not do something for the heirs of Fulton, who never received a cent?"

If any one doubts that our patent-system has been a great benefit to the nation, he need only to look at our condition at the commencement of the Revolution, when the laws of the mother country prohibited the establishment within the colonies of any iron-rolling mill, lumber-slitting mill, and the manufacture of hats or woolen goods of any kind, unless shipped in British vessels and sold to British merchants or in the British colonies, and then look at the condition of the country to-day.

It is no longer a question that patents do stimulate inventions, and that inventors are of immense benefit to the nation; and hence it is that nearly all civilized nations have patent laws, and that all the greatest and best inventions originate in those countries which offer protection to the inventor. As an illustration of a country without a patent system, take Switzerland. For lo! these many years, generation after generation, the Swiss have been almost a nation of watch-makers. One would naturally suppose, therefore, that all the valuable improvements in time-keepers would have originated with them. But not so; on the contrary, nearly every valuable improvement in time-keepers has originated in England, France, and the United States. Why? Simply because they have patent laws, and Switzerland has none. What object is it for a man to spend his time and money inventing an improvement, if the moment it is done his neighbor can appropriate it? What farmer would sow or plant if the moment his crop was grown his neighbors could step in and "reap where they had not sown?" Or, which of these public-spirited railroad companies, now asking you to change the patent laws for their special benefit, would invest their capital in building their roads if when built, the dividends were to go into other pockets than their own?

As an illustration of what an inducement will accomplish, take the chronometer. That little article, of such inestimable value to the commerce of the world, was the result of a prize offered by the British Government of $100,000 for any means by which the longitude of a vessel could be determined within ten miles. Harrison worked at it for forty years, and in 1767 he won the prize of $100,000. It is recorded that he made one so perfect that it varied but one second and a quarter in ten years.

To-day we make more and better watches and clocks than any other nation, and why? Simply because our intelligent mechanics, stimulated by our patent system, have not only invented valuable improvements in them, but have also invented machinery whereby they can be made far better and cheaper than they possibly can be by hand. The result is not only that the price of these articles has been greatly reduced, but they are so much better that the Swiss have not only copied them, but have also copied the trade-marks used on them. So great has been the revolution wrought in this business that the Swiss commissioner to our Centennial, himself a large manufacturer of watches, on his return home, told his people that *they must either adopt our system or give up the business.*

And what is true of this is equally true of nearly every other branch of manufactures. Our improvements in machinery for the manufacture of boots and shoes have so cheapened and expedited their production that to-day we are selling them in Europe, especially in Holland and Germany, notwithstanding their cheaper labor; and only a few days since I read the statement that no less than twenty-eight factories, stocked with American machinery, had been established there since our Centennial.

To-day American-made tin-ware is being sold in Birmingham, notwithstanding the tin comes from Cornwall, and pays freight here and back, besides the duties on it. Why? Because we make it by machines produced by our inventors, enabling us to make it cheaper, if not better, and because the superior skill of our artisans enables them to produce the articles in styles and forms which render them much neater and more convenient for use.

To-day British dealers and manufacturers everywhere are excited over the fact that American hardware is fast displacing theirs, not only in Europe, but in Central and South America, where heretofore they have held undisputed sway.

Almost from the first we have supplied Europe and the Central and South American countries with sewing-machines, nearly two-thirds of the entire product of our country being exported; and to-day you will find American knitting-machines in many a German household; while for years past American locomotives have coursed over the plains of Russia, and to-day the American sleeping-car is crowding its way on to all the principal railroads of Europe.

Sir Robert Peel once said it was "the destiny of the United States to feed Great Britain, and the destiny of Great Britain to clothe the United States." Even if that was true then, it is not so now, for not only do we clothe ourselves, but we are beginning to send our clothes to England, and that, too, while feeding her to a greater extent than ever before.

How English opinion has been changed in this respect is shown in the following extract from a recent report of Harris Gastrell, secretary of the British legation, made to his government upon the state of our textile industries. After giving at great length the statistics, showing our production, the number of hands employed, wages paid, and the capital invested, he closes with this statement:

I cannot close this report without recording the fact that, in every important branch of industry referred to in the course of the previous pages, *the American manufacturers seemed to be ever gaining on their competitors of the Old World* by availing themselves to the utmost of every advantage of *improved process* or *labor-saving machinery* which American or other inventors may offer.

There can be little doubt but the *celerity with which all such advantages are thought out and then introduced into general use,* is owing to the constant pressure of high rates of wages, *and the comparative certain protection of capital invested in inventions.*

Neither can I close without observing how favorably the great industries of the United States would probably compare with the best organized of the competing industries of Europe. The past history and present development of the textile industries is an earnest of a prolific future. Whether or not a reduced cost of living shall ever be attained, I cannot doubt that, under sound conditions of production, *American industry will not only supply its home market, but will also become a formidable competitor in foreign markets in many articles.*

How soon that competition abroad may take place in this or that industry is not for me to conjecture. But I think that the data in this report are sufficiently full and correct to enable others to predict that time in respect to the cotton and woolen industries.

I have italicised a portion of the above to call special attention to what I consider the more important of the statements made. The "celerity with which inventions are made and introduced" and the "comparative certain protection of capital invested in inventions" is the key to the whole subject, and *for all that we are indebted to our patent laws.* Need I say more as to the beneficence of our patent system, or the importance of preserving it in its integrity?

The result of all' this is to keep at home a large amount of gold formerly sent abroad to pay for foreign manufactures, while giving employment to large numbers of our people, who in turn add to the demand for the products of our farmers, and give employment to our railroads.

Who believes, who can believe for a moment, that this state of affairs ever could have existed but for our splendid patent system?—a system, I hesitate not to say, which is the best the world has ever seen, and as evidence of that fact I may state that other countries are adopting it, some already having done so, and others about to do so.

It is not at all a new idea to find now and then some thoughtless persons who rail at the patent system, as being the source of "odious monopolies," and who believe that its repeal would be a benefit to the public, but it is a most singular fact that now, just when, through our Centennial, our inventions are being introduced all over the world, there should arise this hue and cry against the patent laws. And what is more singular still, is the fact that the Granger element, which was organized to fight the railroads, should now be co-operating with the latter in the effort to limit the rights and remedies of inventors.

It may not be amiss to see what has been the result of similar efforts elsewhere. In 1862, and again in 1871, there was adopted by the British Parliament a resolution, as follows:

Ordered, That a select committee be appointed to inquire into the law and practice and the effect of grants of letters patent for inventions.

That resolution was introduced by a member whose firm had been made to pay quite an amount in damages for the use of a patented invention which they had appropriated without leave or license of the owner; and it is a striking coincidence that this movement to change our laws was inaugurated by the railroad combination, who, as they tell you, have in like manner been mulcted in heavy damages for a similar appropriation of patented inventions, and which the owners would gladly have sold or licensed them to use for far less than the sum awarded by the courts. As proof of this it is stated that the owner of the swage-block patent, for the use of which these companies complain they have been made to pay an exorbitant price—over $100,000—offered

to let that same company have the use of his patent for its whole term
for $1,000, which they agreed to pay, but when the papers were to be
executed, the company insisted on the party taking pay in the bonds of
the company, worth only ninety cents on the dollar, and because the
owner of the patent refused to be thus swindled out of one-tenth of the
price agreed upon, they refused to complete the arrangement, and told
him they would use it in spite of him, and he might help himself if he
could. I submit that it does not become parties who have acted thus
to now come here crying like a whipped school-boy, and ask Congress
to change the law simply to relieve them from the consequences of their
own willful violation of the law.

But to return to the result of the parliamentary investigation. The
committee consisted of twenty-one members, headed by the attorney-
general, and it was authorized to send for persons and papers. The
investigation was continued through two sessions, the committee calling before it a large number of the most prominent manufacturers,
inventors, and others, from not only their own country, but also from
other countries of Europe, and one or two from the United States.
Their report contains the testimony in full, and makes two quarto volumes of nearly 500 pages. The result of that investigation was, that
instead of recommending the abolition of patents, the committee recognized and reasserted the right of inventors in their inventions, and
that a just patent law was of great benefit to the nation, and finally
recommend, in effect, *the adoption of the American system.*

I cannot leave this subject without calling the attention of this committee especially to the following propositions laid down by that committee in their final report, viz:

1. That the privilege conferred by the grant of letters patent promotes the progress
of manufactures by causing many important inventions to be introduced and developed more rapidly than would otherwise be the case.

2. That the same privilege leads to the introduction and publication of numerous
improvements, each of a minor character, but the sum of which contributes greatly to
the progress of industry.

4. That it does not appear that the granting of pecuniary rewards (as proposed by
the Grangers) could be substituted, with advantage to the public interest, for the temporary privilege conferred by letters patent.

6. That protection should only be granted for what is shown by an investigation to
be new; that is, by adopting the American system of examination as a novelty.

10. That the duties payable on patents should be so adjusted as to encourage inventors to the utmost to make known their inventions, &c.

12. That inasmuch as the property created by the patent law, and the questions
arising under it, are peculiar, *there should be special courts* for their determination.

For a more detailed statement, I beg to refer this committee to the
report itself, a copy of which I had the pleasure of presenting to its
then chairman a year ago. It contains many other valuable facts and
suggestions, but which want of time will not now permit me to mention.
I may add, however, that it closed with a recommendation of an international patent system, and a request that Her Majesty's Government
take steps looking to that end, and that a resolution to the same effect
was adopted by the representatives of the different countries at the
patent congress held at the World's Fair at Vienna. Since that time
Canada has adopted our system, and Germany has done substantially
the same during the past season; and even Brazil and other countries
are about moving in the matter, being stimulated thereto by the wonderful evidences presented at the Centennial of the benefits of our system.

Before leaving this branch of the subject I desire to add a few words
in reference to the ideas of those who oppose patents, and to whom I
have already referred.

As to that class who insist that all inventions are a curse, it is hardly worth while to spend time to argue. They belong to the *communistic* class, the same class who destroyed Cartwright's loom, Arkwright's spinning-jenny, and who, under the direction of the trade-union of Lyons, destroyed the Jacquard loom, an invention so wonderful that when its author was presented to the great war minister Carnot, himself a splendid engineer and mechanician, he exclaimed, "Are you the man who can do what the Almighty cannot, tie a knot in a stretched string?" They belong to the same unreasoning class who during the past season created the riots and worked such wide-spread destruction throughout our own land. With such to attempt to reason is to cast pearls before swine, and therefore I pass them by.

In reply to the writer who says that those who are stimulated to make patentable inventions by a hope of gain are second or third rate inventors, I instance the whole list of inventors who have taken patents, at home and abroad. Take such men as Dr. Nott, Evans, Blanchard, Whitney, Goodyear, Colt, Howe, Singer, Wilson, Morse, McCormick, Perkins, Fairbanks, Bigelow, and Ericsson, Siemens, Bessemer, Fowler, Whitworth, Jacquard, Nasmyth, Arkwright, Fulton, Watt, Stephenson, Earl of Stanhope, Hargreaves, Crompton, Bell, and Jethro Wood, of whom a Senator on the floor once said, "I am fully satisfied that no citizen of the United States has conferred greater economical benefit on his country than he; none of her benefactors have been more inadequately rewarded." If, as asserted, men like these are but second or third class inventors, then where, in Heaven's name, do you find the first-class inventors?

People generally have but a faint idea of the amount of labor and money that is expended in producing and perfecting inventions. They seem to think that they come as a matter of course, or that they are the result of a mere lucky thought, requiring neither study nor expense for their completion. Nothing can be further from the truth. As an illustration, take a few of the cases testified to in the parliamentary report before mentioned. It is there shown that Mr. Holden spent sixteen years and $250,000, and his partner, Mr. Lester, as much more, on their wool-combing machine, and that altogether there was expended on the invention before final success not less than *ten millions of dollars!*

Mr. Howard testified that he and his partner, Mr. Fowler, M. P., expended on their invention of the steam-plow $300,000, and that it was not done as "a work of philanthropy, but from the hope of gain." And he added, "I think that it is good public policy on the part of the state to stimulate the faculty of invention in those who possess it, inasmuch as by invention the public is greatly benefited, and I think the patent law has the effect of stimulating inventors." And when asked if he, as a manufacturer, had not been placed at a disadvantage in those countries which had no patent laws, he replied, "No; and I attribute it mainly to one great fact, namely, that *the two great manufacturing nations of the world, England and America, maintain a patent law.*" He further stated that, as a result of their patent system, he found that their manufacturers were always ahead of those countries which did not protect inventors; that in his own branch of business he had found by his travels in Prussia they were at least seven years behind the English, and that in Holland, *where there was no patent law, there was no progress.*

Siemens testified that he left his own country and went to England simply because he could secure protection for his inventions there, but could not in Germany.

Bessemer, the inventor of Bessemer steel, testified as follows: "My experience during the whole of this time (the years that he was experimenting) has shown me clearly that if I had no patent law to fall back upon, I, as an engineer, could never have first spent two and a half years of my time and $20,000 over mere experiments, which, if they had failed, would have been an entire loss to me. Altogether I made an outlay of $100,000 (gold); but of course I had a large stake to play for. I knew that steel was selling at $250 to $300 per ton, and I knew that if it could be made by my plan it could with profit be sold at $100 per ton. But had it not been for the law, securing my right in my invention by a patent, I could never have hoped, as a simple manufacturer, to recoup myself; and I should never have dared to embark in the iron trade, that I knew nothing of, and compete with every manufacturer, who could use my invention without the cost and risk that I myself had had, because he would have known everything at once, while I had to dig it out at great cost. Instead of having an advantage over the trade, I should have had the manifest disadvantage of having spent more capital to produce a given result than any man who followed me; but with the protection of a patent law, I felt no hesitation, and so strong was my belief in the ultimate success of my invention, in spite of the unfavorable opinion of the trade, that I persisted."

The result of that invention was that the production of steel in Great Britain was raised from 51,000 tons in 1851 to 300,000 tons in 1871. At the same time the price was reduced to $125 per ton, thus making a saving to the public of $22,227,500 in that twenty years, to say nothing of the benefits to all the world for all time to come. I think it is safe to say that fully ten millions of capital is invested in the Bessemer-steel business in this country to-day, and it may double that amount. As a consequence, steel rails are furnished at about the former price of iron rails, and their importation has almost ceased, thus retaining at home the vast sums formerly sent abroad for their purchase, besides giving much better and safer roads.

Mr. Mundella testified that he " was quite clear that inventions never would be proceeded with without patent laws." Mr. Wright, a large manufacturer, testified as follows: "I think I may, without exaggeration, say that *a very great part of our prosperity is owing to the inventions protected by patents.*" Of the same tenor was the testimony of Messrs. Hasseltine, Johnson, Carpmael, Sir William Grove, Lord Romilly, Webster, Ashton, Newton, Nasmyth, and others, all of whom testified to the benefit of the patent law, and that thereby their manufacturers were enabled to keep twenty years ahead of competing nations who did not thus protect inventors. Mr. Woodcroft testified that his experience showed that without a patent law inventions would not be produced, and as proof he instanced the colonies of New South Wales, Victoria, Ceylon, Cape of Good Hope, New Zealand, and Trinidad, all of which had recently adopted a patent law, simply " because they *could not get inventions without patent laws.*"

J. Stuart Mill advocated the patent system; and Jeremy Bentham, in his Manual of Political Economy, says that, " protection of inventions is as necessary as protection against thieves;" and he adds: " He who has no hope that he shall reap, will not take the trouble to sow; for that which one man has invented all the world can imitate," thus showing the greater necessity for the protection of this species of property.

As a prominent law-writer has well said, property in patents is the most difficult of all kinds of property to defend. It cannot be defended like lands or ordinary personal property by possession or force, because of its intangibility; and a thousand different persons may infringe it in a thousand different places at the same instant. Said Commissioner

Mason in his report for 1855: "The present insecurity of the property of inventors, even after patents are obtained, is a source of great discouragement and often of peculiar hardship."

Commissioner Holt, in his report for 1857, after speaking of the lawlessness of infringers, says: "The eyes of Argus would not suffice to discover, nor the arms of Briareus suffice to resist, the assaults of so omnipresent a foe as it is the lot of the patentee to encounter. The insolence and unscrupulousness of capital, subsidizing and leading on its mercenary minions in the work of pirating some valuable invention held by powerless hands, can scarcely be conceived of by those not familiar with the records of such cases as I have referred to." And he advocated a limitation of time, after which the validity of the patent should not be called in question.

Said Commissioner Bishop, in his report for 1859: "There is no species of property in this country subject to the same hazards and uncertainty as property in patents."

Said Commissioner Fisher: "No class of our citizens has done more for the glory and substantial prosperity of the nation than the mechanics and inventors of the United States, and they have never been favored children."

Said Judge Holt, in his report for 1858: "A class of men who have given to their native land and to the world the cotton-gin, the steam-engine, the electric telegraph, the reaper, the planing and the sewing machines—inventions whose beneficent influences tell with measureless power upon every pulsation of our domestic, social, and commercial life—may well be pardoned for believing their wants should not be treated with entire indifference by that body which represents alike the intellect and heart, as it does the material interests of the great country of which they are citizens—the Congress of the United States."

With such evidence as this before it, I trust this committee will hesitate long before it recommends any change of the law which shall either abbreviate the rights of inventors or render their invasion by infringers more easy.

As to the idea that patents are the "odious monopolies" that some represent them, it is simply absurd, and shows that those who apply to them this term do not know what they are talking about. How can that be a monopoly which is open to every citizen, and even to every foreigner? All alike can have the benefits of the patent law by complying with its conditions. It is far less of a monopoly than is the patent which the government gives freely to every citizen who will settle upon and improve a quarter-section of the public lands. In the latter case the occupant gives nothing to the public, and gets a title in fee-simple, which he and his heirs can have the benefit of forever; while the inventor, who does give something to the public, gets a title for seventeen years only, *a mere lease for that which he created !*

The odious monopolies, or those properly so called, such as were given in the time of Queen Elizabeth, conferring on some favorite the exclusive right to sell steel, salt, starch, paper, &c., by which the cost to the people was increased in some instances a thousand per cent., *took from the public rights which it possessed, and gave nothing in return ;* while, on the other hand, *an inventor gives to the public something it never before had, and takes nothing from it.*

"Invention," says Mr. Ray, "is the only power on earth that can be said to create. It enters as an essential element into the process of the increase of national wealth, because that process is a creation, and not an acquisition. Hence the most frequent cause of the increase of national wealth is the increase of the skill, dexterity, and judgment, and of the mechanical contrivances, with which national labor is applied."

"How," says Commissioner Holloway in his report of 1863, "can the exclusive privilege to sell salt in Elizabeth's time, which added not one bushel to the production, but which enriched the monopolist and robbed the community, as was the fact, by raising the price from sixteen pence to fifteen shillings, and the exclusive right of Whitney to the cotton-gin, which has added hundreds of millions to the products and exports of the country, be both branded with equal justice with the odious name of monopoly?"

The fact is, the patent law was established to prevent just such odious monopolies, by providing that no one shall be protected in the right to his own invention even, except on condition that he shall fully explain it to the public so it can use it, and then, after a brief period, give it freely to the public forever. With even more truth might it be said that it is an odious monopoly for the farmer to gather the crop he has raised, or the mechanic to occupy the house he has made.

Since the commencement of this hearing the cable brings us the following in reference to patents in Switzerland:

Public sentiment in Switzerland is beginning to look with favor upon patent laws; and the loss of a good deal of their watch-making trade, mainly because inventors could not be protected, has caused considerable feeling on the subject. Federal Councilor Droz has prepared a bill for a patent law, which has been published in the Swiss journals, and thus is presented to the people. Patents of importation will be granted to inventors living abroad only on the principle of reciprocity. The maximum duration of a patent is to be fifteen years.

And thus it will be seen that Switzerland too has awakened to the importance and necessity of protecting inventors in order to keep abreast of her competitors in the onward march of the age.

Having thus traveled rapidly over a very wide field, I now ask the attention of the committee to the few provisions of this bill which it is made my duty to explain.

I propose to occupy your time but very briefly, and only upon some sections which Mr. Whitman has not referred to, which I had more of a hand in preparing than he, and which, therefore, he wished me to present to you. I will just call your attention to section 5. I will say upon this subject, on which he was just speaking, and which was referred to by my friend Mr. Livermore, that when we had that subject before the association originally we struck out the words "or model" entirely, for reasons very similar to those given by Mr. Livermore; but there is now another or additional reason for striking out these words, and that is the late fire in the Patent Office, which has destroyed about one-half of all the models there, about 87,000, I think. So that with reference to those patents it is impossible of course that they shall be reissued by the models. The question is, as a matter of policy, whether we shall let the law stand in its present shape, and have one rule for those patents where the models were destroyed, and another rule for those patents where the models are not destroyed. My own view is, that it would be better to strike out entirely all reference to models. Yet the inventors and the majority of our association say this (and there is a great deal of force in what they say), that the model was the object which the inventor best knew, and the thing upon which he was most entitled to his patent; and if he did not get a particular thing in his drawing or specification originally, it is no reason why he should be cut off from it on reissue. The same might be said of other features as well as those in the model, perhaps not in the drawing and not claimed in the patent; and if he reissues by the drawing, he would cut him off just as much, and there would be no difference in that respect. After all, it seems to me it is more a question as to what it is politic to make the law than anything else. However, there is this consideration, that one-half of the models were burned, and, therefore, if you insert the words "or models" you will have one rule applied to one-half the patents and another rule to the other half. But, as a matter of justice and right, I can see no reason at all why the inventor should not be allowed to cover whatever was his original invention, and whatever might have been patented originally. I can see very grave reasons why he should not be allowed to do it under the law as it was, because when he takes out the reissue he would hold the infringer liable for machines and articles which were made before he ever notified the world that he claimed them as his invention. That certainly was very unjust, and that we propose to prohibit by another section.

Senator MORGAN. Will you refer us to the section of the old statute which is proposed to be here amended?

Mr. DODGE. The section relating to reissues, section 4916.

I will state for the information of the committee that, as this law stands now, we can reissue and claim anything shown in the model or in the drawing. The way Mr. Livermore proposes to change it, or as it would be changed if you leave out the word "model," is that you may reissue and amend the patent by anything shown in the drawing or specification. In other words, this change in the law would substitute the specification for the model. Formerly, prior to 1861, it was the practice of the office to allow reissues for anything shown in the drawing, model, or specification, and in addition to that to allow parties to furnish proof. *aliunde* of features which were not shown in either of the three. That was the practice of the Patent Office until the decision of the Supreme Court in the Carhart Melodeon case, in which they decided that the reissue in which had been put a feature not shown in the model, drawing, or specification, but which the man originally had as a part of his invention, was void; and since that time the office has not permitted anything of that kind. In the act of 1870 the law was changed so that the inventor could only claim by a reissue what was shown in the drawing or model. If you strike out the word "model," it will simply leave a drawing or specification.

Mr. LIVERMORE. The published drawing or specification.

Mr. DODGE. That was not the intention. The intention was to allow him to go as far as the papers which he originally filed showed that he was entitled to, on reissue.

Mr. LIVERMORE. That is what I object to, among other things.

Mr. DODGE. Then there would not be much of an object in the reissue.

Mr. LIVERMORE. That is the foundation of the claim.

Mr. DODGE. The very object of the reissue very frequently is to get a more complete and full description of the invention as the foundation for a claim. If he cannot change the specification, I cannot see what he gains by the reissue.

Mr. LIVERMORE. I would allow him to amend by describing anything shown in the drawing, because that is published to the world, but I would not allow him to go back to the specification filed in the Patent Office, and which is never published.

Mr. DODGE. I get your idea perfectly. Now, I want to call attention to section 11, which, although it did not originate with us, is one that probably will create as much excitement among the inventors of the country as any section in the bill, and that is the one providing for the payment of two duties upon a patent in order to keep it alive; a provision which we advocated (that is, myself and some of the older residents here) when the act of 1870 was passed, and which we are decidedly in favor of; that is, I am personally in favor of it, and I think quite a number of the solicitors are, for the reasons which have been stated, to get out of the way these old dead patents. It happens in the course of our experience that we find a man takes out a patent for what he supposes will be a good invention. He has never made a machine or tested it. Probably 9 out of 10 of the things patented never have been embodied in full-sized working-machines prior to being patented. A man gets an idea of an invention, goes to work and makes a model, and goes to the Patent Office to secure his patent. After he gets that done he solicits capitalists to manufacture the article. A manufacturer very frequently goes to work and spends $10,000, it may be, in the first machine, and experiments with it, and he finds that it proves a failure. If so, of course, that is the end of that patent. The inventor abandons all thought of it, and goes off and turns his attention to something else. By and by there comes along another man who, taking up the same idea, goes to work and makes a machine which proves to be perfectly successful and gets a patent on it. He organizes a company, getting $100,000 or $300,000 or $500,000 of capital invested in the manufacture of that machine. It is put before the public, and it operates successfully.

Then comes along what I call one of these patent sharks or patent speculators. He goes down to the office and rakes that class over with a fine-tooth comb to see if he cannot find an old patent which can be reissued to cover this successful machine. He comes across the old defunct patent and goes and buys it. The owner, of course, is glad to get what he spent on it, and he may take a hundred dollars for it. Very frequently the man is dead, and he will go to the widow or heirs, and they will take anything he offers them for it. He reissues that patent. Being an *ex parte* proceeding, of course nobody knows anything about it. He reissues it just as Judge Grier stated of that hat-body case, that it was put through the *enlarging* process, not for the purpose of protecting what that patentee invented, but for the purpose of covering other inventions. He has the specifications and claims prepared with special reference to covering this successful machine, and when he gets his patent he goes to the manufacturer and says, "You are infringing my patent." The manufacturer examines the matter, and it seems to be a clear case. Or he refers to his attorney or counsel, and they examine it, and they tell him that they think he is infringing the patent; and then he has either got to pay that man what he chooses for the privilege of going on with his business, or else he has to shut up shop.

If the man who gets out this reissue cannot make the manufacturer come to terms, he will go around to his different customers all over the country and threaten them with suits of infringement, and thus destroy or break up his business.

The proposed law cuts off that sort of thing. This provision will do more to prevent fraudulent reissues than any other provision in the whole bill, because that original inventor, of course, will not keep his patent alive after this failure of it. That will be the end of it. If he does not pay this fee at the end of four years it is out of the way. Hence, I think, this provision will do more to prevent fraudulent reissues, which have done more to give rise to the predjudice against patents than any other provision in the law. But you will find a great deal of objection to it from the inventors on account of the amount of the fee. The object is not revenue. That is not what is wanted, because they have a million and a hundred odd thousand dollars lying in the Treas-

ury now, paid by the inventors of the country, over and above the expenses of the Patent Office, and it would be unjust to tax them further
    Therefore, it seems to me that the fee might be very materially
reduced. It does not matter what the amount is, whether it be five or
ten dollars, but only some amount which the man must pay or have his
patent die. I should say that five and ten dollars would be amply sufficient for all purposes, instead of fifty and a hundred dollars. It strikes
me, if there is to be any difference in the terms, as they have four years
for the first term and five for the second, that the first term is the one
that ought to be the longer. When a man has made an invention he
has only got the work laid out. Then the difficulty is to introduce it to
the public, and there are a hundred reasons why he cannot do it. In
the first place, there may be a patent that has a few years to run, and he
cannot use his invention until that patent has expired.
    One of the most successful inventions our manufacturers are using
to-day, and on which they have netted probably not less than a million
dollars of profit, is an invention of my own, which I sold to a manufacturing company, and for four years I could not stir with it. I endeavored to sell it for anything I could get for it, simply because there
was a patent which had four years to run, and which we believed would
be extended for seven more. The manufacturers said to me, "We cannot use it; what is the use of buying it?" I could not do a thing with
it myself because it required large capital. That is the way with almost
all these inventions. The inventor hardly ever works the thing himself,
and the difficulty is to get capital interested in it and to have it introduced, because all these manufacturers have their capital invested in
the manufacture of some article with all the machinery, tools, and appliances adapted to that article, and they say: "What is the use of
throwing away all that we have invested to introduce something else?
So long as nobody else does that, what is the use of it? We can sell
these articles just as well without your patent as with it."
    Hence I would make the first term the longer term, so as to give a
man a good chance to get his patent introduced and to realize from it,
if he can. If then he fails, and does not care to pay the duty, let the
thing go.
    In England they pay fifty pounds at the end of three years, and a
hundred pounds at the end of seven years, and a failure to pay either
of course forfeits the patent. In other countries it is an annual tax; an
annuity in most of them. We find at the end of the first period of three
years in England a large proportion of the patents die out. They do
not choose to pay the fifty pounds to keep the patent alive, and at the
end of seven years probably not ten in a hundred are preserved.
    Mr. STANSBURY. Ninety per cent. die out.
    Mr. DODGE. At any rate, the larger portion of them die out. They
do not prove to be valuable, and hence the inventors do nothing with
them.
    I will say, in reference to section 16, of which my colleague spoke,
that there is one point where I am afraid you did not get a clear idea.
The law prescribing the price to be paid for copies was fixed before we
commenced printing the patents. It was fixed in the act of 1861, making the price ten cents per hundred words. We commenced printing
patents November 27, 1866. They did not change the law in that
respect from that time on. The act of 1870 did not change the fee at
all; so that we pay now the same price for certified copies of printed
specifications as was paid for written specifications. I will give a case
to illustrate that. For instance, I buy a printed copy of a patent for
25 cents. I want to have it certified for use in a suit. It happens

to be a voluminous one. After they have put on the certificate which is a blank form, and the seal, the price amounts to over $30; and the Commissioner says, " Under the law, I cannot help it; I must charge you ten cents per folio." That provision of the law is a mere oversight, and the suggestion of amendment comes from the Commissioner. He, however, I believe, has a little amendment which he wants made to that section ; but that he will point out himself, and I will not take your time.

The next is section 18.

Senator MORGAN. Before going any further, can you state what are the present charges under section 11 ?

Mr. DODGE. There never have been any under our law. It is an entirely new idea introduced into the system.

Senator MORGAN. The entire section is new, then ?

Mr. DODGE. Yes, sir ; it is entirely new. That did not originate with us; but I wanted to call attention to these facts, because we are all interested in making the bill perfect.

As the law stands to-day, you will find a man who fails to prosecute his application in the office for two years after any action had on it, forfeits his application; but he may come in and file a new one at any time. The party who has had his patent allowed, and has let six months go by without paying the final fee, forfeits his application, and if he neglects for two years to renew his application, he is cut off entirely from ever having a patent for it. So that the man who has an invention which the office says is patentable is placed on a worse footing than the man to whom the office says, " You have no invention."

There are two sections in the original law on this subject, one referring to neglect to act on a case rejected, and one to a case where forfeiture is incurred by neglect to pay the final fee. We finally came to the conclusion to cut off at the end of six months the party who failed to pay the fee. One object is to make the parties more attentive and not to let these cases lie along, so that the public may know what patents are liable to come out. But the opinion of the Commissioner is, and I think it is the opinion of the majority of our association, that this provision should be changed so as to put the two classes upon precisely the same footing and allow them to renew it at the end of two years by paying a new fee and filing a new application. That the Commissioner will speak himself to you about.

There are in section 18 some very important provisions. I may say that the practice in the office has grown up by accretion, not really by any statutory provisions, and they are changed with every new Commissioner. As Commissioner Leggett said, it is, and probably will continue to be, a political office. We have averaged ten Commissioners since Mr. Lincoln's election, some of whom were lawyers, others were not, not even members of the bar, and the result of it is that we have all sorts of decisions and all sorts of practice. It is like a clock-pendulum, here she comes and there she goes, all the time swinging from one extreme to the other, until we do not know, as was said, when we go to bed at night where we will be when we get up in the morning, so far as the decisions and the practice of the Patent Office are concerned.

When Commissioner Leggett was in, he established the rule that when a party paid his final fee, which, under the statute of 1861, was not to be done until the patent was issued, he then having complied with all the requirements of the statute, his patent should issue ; that it should not be stopped by the interference of somebody who came in after that time.

There are about two weeks between the time of the payment of the final fee and the time the patent is delivered. That time is occupied in preparing the drawing and specification, and everything, in the office. That time elapses after the party has paid his final fee, before the patent is made up, signed, and sealed. Commissioner Leggett established the rule that it ceases to be an application and becomes a patent after the final fee is paid. At present the patent is dated two weeks before delivery, and it commences to run, and is actually in operation under the law, two weeks before the document is in existence, and before the party can get possession of it.

Now the office has swung away to the other extreme, and they have stopped patents even after they were signed and all made up and ready for delivery, after they had commenced to run. We want, if possible, by statute to fix definitely the time when the case ceases to be an application and becomes a patent—a time definite, within which the patent shall issue after the party has complied with all the requirements of law. Hence we say here, which is new matter, in line 7 :

"Every patent shall issue, bear date, and take effect as of a day certain, to be fixed by the Commissioner of Patents, not later than the second calendar week after the payment of the final fee."

What we mean by a day certain to be fixed is this: They have in the office what they call an issue day for each week. All patents are dated on a certain day. That, of course, must be in the discretion of the Commissioner, according to the facilities and necessities of the office. Now Tuesdays are issue days and Fridays are make-up days. He will probably designate Tuesday as the day when the patents will take effect, and they are to be delivered on that day ; not delivered two weeks hence and liable to be stopped in the mean time. But we go further. Suppose that although the man has complied with all the requirements and the patent is made up, the Commissioner ought not to issue patents which he knows the courts will hold to be void. Hence we leave it entirely under his jurisdiction by the next succeeding words: "And until the day of issue the application shall be within the jurisdiction of the Commissioner."

That is done for two reasons: First, they may find a reference which they had not found before and which is a perfect answer to it; and if they do, they will give that as an answer, and the man will then abandon the case. The Commissioner should not issue a patent which could be of use to no one. There may be a case of fraud brought to the attention of the Commissioner of which he is bound to take notice, and in that case he ought not to be compelled to issue a patent. But we go on with this proviso restoring the rule as practiced by Mr. Leggett:

"Provided, That no application on which the final fee has been paid, after notice of allowance, shall be withheld from issue because of interference with any application filed subsequent to the payment of the final fee, as aforesaid."

It leaves it in his jurisdiction for all other purposes. That party may have his interference after the patent has issued, if he wants. The idea is to make these parties hurry up; not to let them lay back four, five, and six months, or a year or two years, and then come in and stop a more energetic party who has been industrious in trying to get his patent.

I want also to add one word in reference to what my friend said about section 19, and that is as to having our patents terminate by the expiration of foreign patents. There is one fact not generally understood, and that is, that we cannot have a valid patent abroad after the patent has been taken out here. I have within the last month received word from England that the English patent office has held that the introduction of one of our printed specifications there is a bar to the inventor himself from taking a patent there subsequently, because the invention is thus published within the kingdom.

In the second place, we cannot have a valid patent at all in France if the thing is made public in any way or anywhere previous to the filing of the application there. Therefore, generally, when a party comes to us and says, "I have an invention which I want patented here, and also in England, France, and Belgium" (those being the three principal countries in which inventors take out foreign patents, because those are the great manufacturing countries of Europe), our practice is to file an application here and let it lie until we send over there and file an application, and as soon as we know that the application is filed there we have the patent issued here. Then the American patent will take date before the foreign patent and will not lose that three years; but here is the trouble: Under these foreign systems they have no examination, but the grant of patents is a matter of course, and the patent will issue in so many days or weeks from the time the papers are filed, whether the inventor wants it to issue or not. Consequently the inventor has no control over the patent after it is filed in the office.

Here it is not so. We are liable to all sorts of delays, and are kept waiting for one or two years by references and appeals or by an interference, but in the mean time the foreign patents have gone out in advance, when we did not mean to have them go out in advance, and thus against the party's desire and intention he is deprived of three years of his American patent. That is one reason why we propose to change that section.

Section 20 is substantially the same as the law is now, making all rejected applications which lie for more than two years without any action forfeit. I think there are only one or two changes in the section, and they are not of any consequence.

The last section, section 24, is one of the most important, relating to reissues.

Senator MORGAN. Is not two years a very long time to allow the application to be completed?

Mr. DODGE. Two years was adopted simply because that had been adopted under the act of 1861, and applied in various conditions all the way through. Under the law now the party is required to complete his application within two years. That was done for this reason: Before the act of 1861, parties would file their specification and drawing in the office and not pay their fee. It served as a perpetual caveat without paying anything for it, and the office became cumbered with applications of that kind. Hence they said, "You shall complete your application in two years or we will cut you off"; and so when the act was before Congress in 1870, and discussed at great length, they concluded to apply it all the way through.

Senator WADLEIGH. Has there been any difficulty or inconvenience under the act of 1870 on account of the two years' rule?

Mr. DODGE. No, sir.

Senator WADLEIGH. It has worked well?

Mr. DODGE. It has worked well, and we found no difficulty, except in the revision of the statutes; they changed the language of the statute in such a way as to put the man whose patent was allowed in a worse condition than the man whose patent was rejected. In one case it made him abandon his application, and in the other it made him forfeit his invention. We want to put them both on the same footing.

Section 24, amending section 4904 of the Revised Statutes, relates to reissues, and that is a very important section; because, as I said before, the great difficulties and the prejudices that exist to-day among our granger friends and those opposed to patents generally, have arisen under abuses of the provisions of the statute relating to reissues, which abuses grow rather out of the maladministration of the law or the failure to properly administer it in the Patent Office. But there are certain things that can be cured by statute. We have followed as near as possible the original phraseology of the statute which has been in existence since 1836, with the exception of the proviso which comes in in line 15:

"*Provided*, That after the final decision between the parties to an interference, the application of the successful party shall not be put into interference with any application filed subsequent to the closing of the testimony taken on behalf of the successful party in the interference so decided; but the patent shall issue to the successful contestant, and then, if desired by the subsequent applicant or applicants, an interference may be had with said patent."

That relates to original applications. Then there is another proviso, which is new, commencing in line 23. The first proviso relates to ordinary interference upon new applications. This proviso relates to an interference where a man comes back to reissue his patent:

"*And provided further*, That in the case of reissues no interference shall be declared with any patent of later date than that sought to be reissued, except when the original application for such subsequent patent is shown by the office-records to have been of prior date to the application of the patent sought to be reissued, nor with any application for a patent filed subsequent to the date of the patent sought to be reissued; but, if desired by such subsequent applicant or patentee, on an application for reissue, an interference may be had with the reissued patent after the same shall have been issued."

What we have sought to do there is to correct two most outrageous practices that have grown up in the office. It originated in this way: A party comes in and makes an application for a patent. After his case is allowed (and perhaps he may have been there a year or a year and a half) another party comes along and makes application for the same invention. They are put into interference, and it will take from six to twelve months to get through that interference, and it is very expensive.

After it is all done and the case has been decided by the examiner of interferences, the unsuccessful party appeals to the board of examiners. They set a time for the hearing, and after they have decided, there is a limit of appeal given of thirty days, and just before that time the unsuccessful party will appeal again to the Commissioner, and in that way he may keep this party tied up a long time after the original interference is decided. Then, just as the patent is about to issue, this unsuccessful party, perhaps, if a manufacturer, gets one of his workmen to come in and make another application for the same thing, which will again put the inventor in an interference, and then he has got to fight all over the ground again and his patent is tied up just as before.

After waiting until the last day, and when he has gone through all the stages, in comes a third applicant, and he will be put into interference. In that way cases have been tied up there until the unsuccessful party, who knew he could not get a patent and did not expect to get a patent but wanted to keep the inventor out of his patent until he could supply the market, has done that; and when the market has been wholly supplied for the next ten years the patent will issue; so that, if the party gets a patent ultimately, it is of little or no use to him.

The Commissioner says that is a most gross outrage, but that under the present law he has no power to prevent it. He cannot compel parties to give security for costs nor prevent this outrage against applicants.

Senator WADLEIGH. He would have an action on the case at common law against him, I suppose.

Mr. DODGE. I am stating now just an actual fact. Take these street-cars here; this sliding car-door. Stephenson, the manufacturer, of New York, is the one who manufactured it. He supplied it to nearly all the street-railroads in the United States, keeping the inventor out of his patent three years, filing unsuccessful applications, one after another. By these means a wealthy man can ruin a poor inventor, who cannot afford to employ a man to travel around the country to take testimony at an expense of twenty-five dollars a day, while the wealthy man has plenty of means at command and can do it. Now we want to stop that abuse.

The reason for making a distinction between applications for original patents and for reissues is this : that where a man has his patent and he is tied up in the office by an interference on application for a reissue, it takes so much out of the life of the patent, nor can he bring suit or hold them responsible as infringers or collect damages from those infringing in the mean time.

A case in point will illustrate that. There was a patent taken out a few years ago on a certain stove-board. Is consisted simply of a sheet of zinc spun over the edge of a wooden frame or body in such a way as to hold the wooden parts in and allow them to expand and shrink freely without wrinkling the metal at all, there being no screws or nails in the wood. It was held entirely by the zinc being spun over the edge of it. That patent was taken out by Mr. Westlake, of Chicago. We secured the patent for him. He first had a party to manufacture under it for two years. They went into the manufacture very largely, fitting up a shop for it; one of those brass-manufacturing companies in Chicago. They put out, prior to the Chicago fire, about sixty thousand of those, which they retailed at two dollars or two dollars and a half apiece. After the fire, in about six months, they got started again.

They brought suit against a party who commenced to make the same thing in Chicago, and Judge Drummond held, or intimated rather, that, while they had a good invention, the patent did not cover it. They then dropped that suit and came to the office for a reissue of the patent; and after it was allowed, and just as it was ready to issue, in came another applicant from the same place claiming the same thing. Our case was stopped and tied up with an interference for eighteen months, and the attorney on the other side boasted that they were then filling one order for ten thousand of the articles, for which we never could get any damages, of course.

All of this came up in testimony, and it turned out ultimately that this party did not expect to get a patent, that that was not his object, but that the object was to flood the market and put the money in his pocket ; and he admitted afterward on the stand, in that very case, that he had knowledge of the existence of our patent for more than two years before he filed his application, which, under the statute itself, was a bar to the grant of a patent to him. That is the reason for that provision there.

I believe, gentlemen, I have said all I desire to say.

ARGUMENT OF G. H. CHRISTY.

Mr. CHRISTY. Mr. Chairman and gentlemen of the committee, I desire to call attention to a few verbal alterations which I think should be made in the bill, and also comment on one or two points connected with the general policy of the law. And, first, I will refer to section 1 of the Senate bill, which relates to the matter of limitation. I think the limitation is wise. The only question is as to the time. My own impression is that four years is a little too short. I think that it should be five or six years. That, however, is purely a matter of discretion or judgment. Some limitation is wise. In the act of July 8, 1870, it was made six years from the expiration of the patent, and that provision continued in force until the Revised Statutes went into operation, and for some reason or other that provision was left out. This provision makes it four years prior to the date of bringing the suit. As this is rather an experiment in the way of legislation, I think it should be made as broad as possible, and five or six years should be allowed.

Passing to the second section, my friend, brother Livermore, referred to some alterations which he desired to have made in the first four or five lines. I have an amendment to suggest in the same lines and for substantially the same purpose, and I will call the attention of the committee to the language in order to get at my meaning:

"In all cases where the patentee has elected to license other persons generally to use his invention in like manner to that in which it was used by the defendant."

There is *one* case in which a license-fee is to be the measure of damages. Now, then, it provides another case:

"Or where it appears to the court or jury that, from the nature of the invention, it is for the interest of the patentee that other persons generally," &c.

Thus there are two provisos. One is, when the patentee has fixed a license-fee himself; the second is, when it shall appear for the interest of the patentee, based on the nature of the invention. I will take, for illustration, the Pullman car. Suppose Pullman to be the first inventor of that; it is obvious that it was optional with him to resort to one of two ways to use the invention: either to sell licenses to the roads to build their own cars, involving his improvements, in which case he would have fixed a license-fee, or to do, secondly, as he has done—build the cars himself, and run them on the roads. The bill here, in reference to such a matter, makes the *nature of the invention* the sole test, whereas it should be the nature of the invention and the manner in which the patentee has chosen to work the invention.

Following down, in line 13 in the same page, the word "same" occurs. I should like to ask the committee to strike that out and insert the word "damages." The word "same" may refer to one of three things—the *license* which is specified in line 9: "If a license-fee has already been established by a reasonable number of transactions of a character applicable to the case at bar, that shall be adopted as the measure of said damages; but if not, then the court or jury shall determine the same."

The word "same" may relate to "*license*," which is the subject of the preceding sentence; it may refer to "measure," in the line preceding; or it may refer to "damages." Now, when, in shaping the law, ambiguity can possibly be avoided, I submit it had better be done. I suppose the intention was to mean damages.

Mr. RAYMOND. It means license.

Mr. CHRISTY. I had two Boston lawyers last night to help me in getting at the meaning of that section, and *they* said that this word meant "damages"; here is a Chicago lawyer who says it means "license." If you go into court on that language, how are you going to construe it? If it means "license"—and that is what I understood it to mean when I first read it—I am opposed to the whole section. If it means "damages," I have no particular objection to it; but there is an ambiguity which arises right on the face of the paper.

Senator WADLEIGH. It has to be read with a view to what you intended to effect. The court and jury are to determine what? The case is brought to recover damages; they are to determine, then, the damages that the case is brought to recover.

Mr. CHRISTY. That is the construction I want to have given to it.

Senator WADLEIGH. I do not think the courts will find any difficulty about it.

Mr. CHRISTY. Very well, if the committee are satisfied.

On page 3, in lines 30, 31, 32, and 33, there is this proviso: "*Provided*, That the provisions of this section shall not apply in any case in which a decree for an account or assessment of damages has, at the date of the passage of this act, already been pronounced."

I heartily approve of the correction suggested, I think, by Senator Morgan, and advocated by brother Walker, of the Chicago bar, to make it read: "*Provided*, That the provisions of this section shall not apply in any case in which a right of action has already accrued."

I never examined the question, but I think brother Walker's position there is the correct one, that legislation cannot affect the right of parties to damages which have already accrued. I think that alteration there would be a wise one.

Senator WADLEIGH. Let me ask you, on that point, is not the legislature to prescribe the mode in which the damages shall be arrived at?

Mr. CHRISTY. I will say to the committee that I have not specially examined that subject, and am not prepared to give a legal opinion upon that point. I only say my impression is that Mr. Walker's position is correct. I would not undertake to go into a discussion without first making a careful examination of the subject.

Mr. WALKER. I have given a great deal of study to that question, and it is not a question of the mode of arriving at the damages at all. There are now two separate recoveries, one of profits on the theory of trusteeship, the other of damages by the parties in an action on the case, they having no philosophical or legislative connection with each other whatever; and when you have abolished profits you have not chan.ed the mode of arriving at damages, because profits are not damages any more than a horse is a mule. They are not connected in such a way as that, and when you have abolished the recovery of profits you have simply abolished the recovery of something that the law now gives us.

Senator WADLEIGH. My idea would be this: that when any procedure, either at law or in equity, is brought by a patentee to recover for an infringement of his right, what he gets is the damages for that infringement, not in the common-law sense of the word, but really damages arrived at in the one case by process of law, and in the other case by proceedings in equity.

Mr. WALKER. Are you using "damages" in the sense of "compensation" now?

Senator WADLEIGH. Not at all.

Mr. SMITH. The Supreme Court once used language almost to that effect.

Senator WADLEIGH. I speak generally, of course, without any reference to a particular case.

Mr. WALKER. In two cases in the Supreme Court, one in which the opinion was delivered by Justice Clifford in 1876, and the other in which the opinion was delivered by Justice Miller in 1875, they expressly stated the philosophy of the two recoveries, and clearly indicated that the two recoveries have no connection whatever, and that the recovery of profits in equity is not a recovery of damages in any sense.

Senator WADLEIGH. I understand perfectly well it is not in one sense.

Senator MORGAN. Is not the real distinction this: whether damages that arise under the common law for any injury done to the person or for compensation, whether compensatory or punitive, are damages that belong rightfully to the party as property?

Mr. WALKER. Exactly.

Senator MORGAN. Damages given by statute, as I understand, are always under the control of the legislature, and by a repeal or modification of the statute you can always strike out damages without doing harm to the party at all.

Mr. WALKER. But this recovery arises wholly on common-law principles and never belongs to the legislature at all.

Senator WADLEIGH. They take the ground that inasmuch as the defendant has used or held the property of the plaintiff, therefore he must account to the plaintiff for whatever profits he may have received from the property.

Mr. WALKER. Under the doctrine that he is a trustee.

Senator WADLEIGH. Yes; under the common-law or equity doctrine.

Mr. WALKER. Of trusteeship.

Senator WADLEIGH. He is trustee of the plaintiff.

Mr. WALKER. And without any regard to the damages.

Senator WADLEIGH. I understand that perfectly well, but that is simply one way of giving the plaintiff compensation against a wrong-doer.

Mr. WALKER. If you will take pains to read the latest decision of the Supreme Court, they say that is not compensation.

Senator WADLEIGH. Well, what is it?

Mr. WALKER. It is not compensation for the injury he has received at all. It proceeds on the theory that the infringer has taken the property of another man and made money out of it, and that the money according to natural principles belongs to the man that owns the property, and they subject it to a trust and make him a constructive trustee, and he has to pay it over without any regard to any question of compensation, and without any regard to any question of damages.

Senator WADLEIGH. I understand that perfectly well.

Mr. CHRISTY. I wish to refer to one or two points which have arisen in the discussion already, but I do not propose to review very much of what has been said. As I understand this cotton-worm case (although I have not examined the patent), as stated by Senator Morgan, somebody has a patent on a mixture of Paris green and flour. I apprehend, so far as this second section has any bearing on a case of that kind, it simply amounts to this, that that man has a patent on the mixture, and when he makes and sells the mixture his right under his patent has expired, and that property then, when sold, goes into the common mass of property, and he has no claim in reference to any utility which may arise out of the application of it from the products of the soil, any more than a physician selling a patent medicine has a right to the profit which may result from the benefit of the medicine to the human system, or any more than in the case of a patent (if such a thing should be in the future) for regulating the weather by arranging the orderly succession of storm and sunshine, any more than the patentee of a method of securing that result could claim that he is entitled to all the benefits flowing from the operation of nature's laws the action of which is so prearranged. In this case of the cotton worm I say that the infringer of the patent is liable to the extent of making that mixture; that up to that point he is liable. He is liable purely for the profits on the mixture, the profits which the patentee would have reaped if he himself had made the mixture and sold it; but as to giving him the profits on the entire crop, it is certainly going further than any courts yet have gone with the doctrine of consequential damages, to say that if by virtue of a good season, a favorable sun, or a favorable climate, the cotton crop has turned out well after you have killed the worms, therefore the man who patented the mixture which killed the worms should himself have all the benefit flowing from such favorable season. There is, I apprehend, no danger of the courts going to that extent.

Now, in reference to the point upon which my brother Smith has spoken at considerable length, as to holding an infringer as a trustee, even though the money which the courts charge him with has never actually come into his possession, it looks like a hard doctrine in the way the Supreme Court laid it down, at first sight, but the question arises in this class of cases: An infringer will adopt a patented device; he will put it on a machine (and I am speaking from experience, for I have had to deal with such cases); he will sell that machine at so low a price that no profits can by any possibility come into his possession. Now, then, because he has not only infringed, but also, by his own voluntary act, has put himself in a position where he cannot pay money because it is not actually in his possession, therefore he must go scot-free; I say *that* is an extremely absurd law, and I take it that that is substantially the doctrine condemned in the case he referred to.

Mr. SMITH. I did not suppose the party ought not to be liable in damages. My objection was to the absurdity of an application on the theory of profits when a man had no profits.

Mr. CHRISTY. When a man conducts a tortious business (for an infringement is a tort) in such a manner that he not only sinks his own property, but sinks the property which he ought to have acquired as the result of the tort, I say it is no injustice to hold him accountable for the money which he ought to have made had he conducted his business properly, and that he should be held accountable to the patentee for that money.

Passing now to section 5, that is this reissue section. With the permission of the committee I desire to consider that section along with section 21, which my brother Whitman commented on, in reference to applications for reissue being sworn to by the assignee. I will state generally, because it is the foundation of the conclusions I want to reach, it was found as a matter of history that along about 1864 and down to 1869, when the law was such that any party desiring to do so could go and buy up an old patent, educe from it in some manner or other, by some mental operation of his own, some invention which would cover somebody else's manufacture, that such an assignee could resort to this privilege of reissue, making oath that he verily believed that John Smith was the inventor of what he himself imagined the invention to have been. He goes into the Patent Office and gets a patent accordingly. The Patent Office at that time had drifted very far in that direction, allowing assignees to come in and make claims, fraudulent on their face, unjust to the public, which did not constitute a part of the invention as originally patented. I can give an illustration of that. In a suit brought by the *The Pullman Company* v. *The Woodruff Company,* which I had the honor in part to defend, the suit was based on a reissued patent to T. T. Woodruff. The reissue was taken out by an assignee. In that suit I got an affidavit from T. T. Woodruff, the inventor and original patentee, that, in his own opinion, he was not the inventor of claims 1, 2, and 3, I think, of the reissued patent. There is just the evil which arose at that time. That patent was reissued in 1869, I believe. Now, then, the law of 1870 was passed which corrected that defect, or that evil, rather, by closing up the doors in part, or the facility with which reissued patents could be obtained, and, among other things, it required that the corrected specification, the specification on which the reissue was to be based, must be sworn to by the inventor if he was alive. We have lived since that time under that law. I am not aware in my own practice of any serious difficulties arising under it, but this section now is drawn for the purpose of reopening that door and letting in again the very evils which the act of July 8, 1870, was designed to correct. I am most strenuously opposed to doing that. My brother Whitman, I think, says he does not know how that provision of the law got in there. The fact is, that law was drawn under the supervision, I think, of the late Hon. S. S. Fisher, known to you all ; the late Hon. Mr. Jenckes, of Rhode Island, then chairman of the House committee ; Mr. Bakewell, of Pittsburgh, and I do not know how many others. It was revised by them time and again and carefully prepared, and prepared, among other things, for the express purpose of stopping this fraudulent reissue business which was almost, in one sense, sapping the foundation of our patent system ; and to-day the outrageous character of some of the reissues is one of the most serious causes of complaint against our patent system in this country. In my opinion the true policy of the law now is, instead of reopening those doors and making these fraudulent reissue cases possible again, to shut them a little tighter, and, perhaps, as brother Livermore suggested, strike off the model part of it.

Now, then, giving as I think the true history of the way in which these amendments came into the law of 1870, that they were made to correct a then existing evil, I think that it is not the best thing to be done at the present stage of litigation to strike out the alterations then made and restore the law as it was and let those evils come in again.

I am not satisfied with lines 10, 11, and 12 of this section 5 which relates to this reissue question ; but at the same time I do not know how to make it any better, unless you abolish the whole model system, which I am inclined to think would be a good plan, and require the drawings to be made to a scale, or require reduced working-drawings, and then there could be no mistake in what you mean. One of the difficulties is this, and the necessity of models arises from this fact, that drawings are frequently made by unskillful draughtsmen; hence they are often crude in their character, and it is difficult sometimes to make out in complicated devices just exactly what the drawing was intended to show. Members of the committee will understand that when a paper is drawn by a lawyer you can know what it means; but if it is drawn by a man unfamiliar with legal terms you sometimes find it difficult to understand what it means. In the same way a drawing made by a professional draughtsman can generally be understood by those skilled in the art, while with a drawing made by a man unskilled in making drawings it is sometimes difficult to tell what the drawing means. When we have that class of drawings to deal with it is exceedingly important to refer to the model in order to correct some defect in the drawing on account of the unskillfulness of the man who made it. I think the best way to remedy the evil is to abolish the model system altogether, and require drawings to be made to a scale accurate in all their parts, or reduced working-drawings, which amounts to the same thing; and then there will be no difficulty in telling what the invention means, because it can only mean one thing, and it is more accurate in that respect than the English language itself.

Section 5 provides that "the Commissioner shall, on the surrender of such patent, and the payment of the duty required by law, cause a new patent for the same invention," &c. The law as it is drawn now, as I understand it, provides for determining whether the invention in the reissue is the same as that in the original, by a comparison of the two documents, and that the reissue must be based on the original patent. This section, however, provides that you can base the reissue on the model or the drawings, or the original specification or its amendments. It is opening the door very wide to say you may correct by reference to the original model *or* original drawing *or* original amendments; and I say in that respect as this section is drawn it is open to greater objection than the law of 1839, which was amended by the act of July 8, 1870. While I am opposed to this section, I am free to say I do not know how to make it any better, unless it is by striking out the model system altogether.

Passing on, if the committee please, to section 8: In the patent law there is one remedy by which the patentee may sue the infringer, either at law or in equity. This bill provides for three other and distinct remedies. First, the infringer may file a bill against the patentee for the repeal of the patent, and it is a wise provision; I have no objection to it. Secondly, he may, if he so desires, take a rule on the patentee in case he is threatening, &c., to compel the patentee to bring a suit and test the infringement. Now, there is a third remedy (just as if two remedies for an infringer were not enough), that the infringer may file a bill for the purpose of perpetuating testimony. I submit that it is unreasonable to provide three remedies as against one form of wrong, and particularly I object to the remedy of perpetuating testimony. I have, I think, a perfectly good objection to it, and that is, it is a legal proceeding unnecessary, because there are two other remedies to be used instead of it, and it is highly objectionable, from the fact that it is not followed by any adjudication. Testimony is to be taken and filed in court; a copy, I suppose, is to be sent to the Patent Office, and there it stands on the record. The parties are subjected to a long job of taking testimony, or a short one, as the case may be, and to the expense of it, and so far as determining their rights is concerned they are not one inch farther forward then when they started. As to going through litigation without an adjudication and without deciding something, it strikes me that it is contrary to the policy of our laws. Hence, section 8, I think, had a great deal better be stricken out.

Senator WADLEIGH. Would not the same objection that you make apply to taking testimony *in perpetuam* in any case at common law or in equity?

Mr. CHRISTY. It would, provided you had these other remedies. I understand that in common-law cases, &c., the party accused, who stands in the position of a defendant, is unable to compel the plaintiff to bring suit. Now, this act provides that the defendant may compel

the plaintiff to bring suit on his patent, or he may file a bill to repeal
the patent.

Mr. SMITH. Only in certain cases.

Mr. CHRISTY. I say under certain circumstances. My point is this:
that those two provisions give the infringer enough remedy for any
wrong that he may be supposed to suffer under it, and it is wholly unnecessary and contrary to the policy of the law, after giving him remedy
enough, to superadd another which is not going to do anybody any
good.

Mr. LIVERMORE. Would you deprive the patentee of the right of perpetuating testimony?

Mr. CHRISTY. I think he can do that now.

Mr. SMITH. He may want to preserve the evidence of his own invention, or he may want to preserve the evidence of something he may suppose will be of use to him.

Mr. CHRISTY. I think he can do that now under an ordinary bill to
perpetuate testimony, and as to making an additional provision to give
the infringer another remedy when one is enough and the bill gives him
two others, I think it wholly unnecessary. I think, under the Revised
Statutes as they stand now, the ordinary remedy by bill to perpetuate
testimony will give the patentee all the remedy he wants. However,
that is only a matter of judgment, and I will pass along.

I have been requested by brother Hatch, of Cincinnati, to suggest an
amendment on page 8 of the Senate bill, in line 47. The committee will
notice the proviso:

" *Provided,* That no depositions taken under this section shall be used
except as against persons who were parties to such proceeding, or those
claiming under them," &c.

It is to insert after the word " proceeding" the words " and were
served personally with notice." They might be made parties by virtue
of an advertisement under a rule of court, or something of that kind.
Testimony should not be used against any parties except such as were
served with personal notice. If the section is adopted at all, that
amendment, it strikes me, should be inserted.

At this point I will reply to some suggestions made by brother Whitman in reference to the relationship of American and foreign patents.
I want to give a little bit of history here, and I think it will throw some
light on the matter. Along in 1869 and in 1870, perhaps, when Mr. Fisher
was Commissioner of Patents, the patents under which the Bessemer
process of making steel has been conducted in this country, some of
them at least, expired. The Musbet patent, and perhaps some of the
first Bessemer patents, and one or two others, expired. The Bessemer-
steel business was largely conducted in this country, and with great
profit to the English patentees. They came here, under our law as it
stood then, and made applications for extensions for the additional term
of seven years. Mr. Commissioner Fisher, in examining the case, found,
as a matter of fact, that the English patents for the same inventions
had expired, and decided that it was contrary to the policy of our law
to grant to a foreigner an extension for an invention in this country when
the nation from which he came enjoyed the right to do the thing which
it was sought to be protected here. In other words, the English could
make Bessemer steel with impunity and without a tax; and he held that
it was wrong to tax the Bessemer-steel interest in this country with a
tribute to the English patentees, under the circumstances. That illustrates exactly the difficulty met with in this class of cases. The law, I
suppose, as originally drawn, was only intended to apply to a foreign

patentee; but, through an inaccuracy in drawing it, it was made to apply also to American inventors. I should like the committee to consider the propriety of adding an amendment to section 19, so as to limit it to foreign inventors, those not citizens of the United States. I understand our law discriminates now as against all patentees holding patents in foreign countries, be they foreigners or Americans. I propose now to amend the bill in such a way as that it shall discriminate as against all foreign patentees taking patents in this country only.

Mr. DODGE. Provided the foreign patents are taken first.

Mr. CHRISTY. Yes. Of course I cannot state all the conditions. I propose to add this, and I have noted it in my copy: "But if such person" (that is, the patentee under such circumstances) "is not a citizen of the United States, his patent shall be so limited as to expire at the same time with the foreign patent; or if there be more than one, at the same time with the one having the shortest term; but in no case for more than seventeen years."

I think the committee will find the decision of Mr. Commissioner Fisher in the Mushet case based on good grounds. These cases are published in the Decisions of the Commissioner, and I think the Mushet case is the one most fully discussed. I think the committee will agree with Mr. Commissioner Fisher that it is contrary to the policy of our law to grant protection in this country for inventions after the patents for the same inventions have expired over there. Take this Bessemer steel interest. After the foreign patents had expired, if they were still in force here our American manufacturers would be working at a disadvantage; they would have to pay royalty to the English patentee when the English manufacturing public could manufacture Bessemer steel royalty free, because the English patent had expired.

Mr. WHITMAN. Suppose the foreigner took out a patent here and did not take out a patent there?

Mr. CHRISTY. I should say, as is commonly said, that that is not a supposable case. My knowledge of foreigners leads me to believe—and I have considerable knowledge of them—that they consider that their country is a little better than any other country on earth—and perhaps we do not differ with them in that respect—and that no case was ever known where a foreign patentee took out a patent in this country before he took it out in his own.

With thanks to the committee for their attention, I have nothing further to offer.

ARGUMENT OF H. D. HYDE.

Mr. HYDE. Mr. Chairman and gentlemen of the committee, I have but a few words to say. I am here representing the Shoe and Leather Association of Boston.

As you have already seen, most of the gentlemen who have appeared before you and advocated this bill, or amendments to it, have spoken from the stand-point of the inventor. While the bill is drawn with reference to the rights of all parties, the interests of the inventors have naturally drawn together here the lawyers who have appeared and presented their views. I have been requested to appear here in behalf of a very large body in the State of Massachusetts who are users and not the owners of inventions, and to ask that you may give to them, in the consideration of this question, the relief which they feel they are entitled to have.

One of the difficulties which the users of inventions find is where, having occasion to use machinery, purchasing it of reliable parties, they find, after it has gone into use, that demands are made for patents, covering some portion of the machine, and they are thus often subjected to litigation. It is often impossible for them to know what their rights are except through very expensive litigation, in which they have little or no interest, and which they certainly never would have incurred or been led into had they known the result that would have followed.

There are two sections of this bill which are sought to furnish a remedy to that class of people. I suppose the bill that passed the House, and to which the attention of this committee was originally called, arose from a class of people situated similarly to those whom I represent here. The two sections of the bill to which I shall speak, and only those, are the first and the eleventh; that is, to the statute of limitations and the provision that patents shall expire unless renewal fees are paid from time to time.

The first section is the statute of limitations. That I find incorporated in the bill, and I have every reason to believe that the committee will report some statute of limitations. I desire to particularly emphasize that matter before the committee, and, if you should differ upon other portions of the bill, or if at any stage of it it should be found that the Senate or the other branch should differ, I would impress upon you that this is a section which should be preserved, and that, if possible, the passage of it should be secured.

I do not come here as representing a section of people who cry out against the patent laws. We believe in them. The industry that I represent is the largest to-day that we have in Boston. That industry never could have existed without the patent law. We live and prosper under its beneficence. On the other hand, we ask to be protected from certain evils which we do not believe impair the efficiency of the law, but which subject it to certain opposition, and which cause complaints to be raised against it which we believe are just.

All concede, I believe, now, that some statute of limitations as in other forms of action should be passed. There has been placed in this bill a period of four years. What is the wisest period of any statute of limitations it is somewhat difficult to say. It is not upon any abstract principle that you can determine any question of limitation. It is that period which upon the whole shall best preserve the rights of all parties. Of course if the period be too short you only invite litigation, lest men should multiply suits for the mere purpose of preserving their rights. If it is too long, the benefit of a statute of limitations is lost. Now, what is the wisest limit, what is the best statute of limitations under these circumstances for this law, is for the committee to determine. Four years have been inserted here. The gentlemen whom I represent have discussed this matter a good deal, and they have felt that a shorter period should be established, and both favor and urge the period of one year. They say that a short period amply protects the owners of patents, and that while they innocently infringe and have no knowlege of the existence of patents those who own the patents are always on the alert to discover infringers, and may always avail themselves of their rights.

I call the attention of the committee to it that, out of all the discussions on this section, they may fix that statute of limitations which shall be wisest.

Now, passing on to the eleventh section, that also is a section very important. It is incorporated in the patent laws of other countries, but I believe in this country it has never heretofore been a portion of the patent law. I entirely dissent from what has been said by Mr. Dodge, that the fee should be a nominal fee; the benefit of it is to weed out inventions which are of no value, which only live to vex people engaged in legitimate business. One of the serious difficulties to-day is that of a patent which has lain dormant five, ten, or fifteen years, and has even expired, being used for the purpose of provoking litigation, or for the purpose of collecting damages, or for the purpose of injuring in some way a party that may have unwittingly used it. If an invention has value, if it really comprises anything of worth, the parties are perfectly willing to pay the renewal fee. If it has no value, and if in four years it has not been put into any use, or found to have no value, it ought to expire; or at least, if the man desires to keep it alive, he ought to be willing to pay a sum as large as is mentioned in this bill. In England the fee for a first renewal is £50—five times what it is here; and for a second renewal it is £100—five times again what it is here. Here it is put at $50 and $100. If the invention is valuable, any man will be willing to pay that sum. If it is worthless, then, if he wants to keep alive a worthless patent merely to vex the community, he ought to be required to pay as much as that sum.

I have looked over other portions of the bill presented here, and I sincerely hope that the committee will recommend the bill as it has been presented substantially; but these two sections, as representing the users of inventions, not the owners of inventions, I desire especially to emphasize before this committee, because I believe when those two remedies are furnished the great outcry against the patent law will have been silenced, and those situated as the persons I represent, as users who enjoy the benefit and beneficence of law, will still be allowed to continue to enjoy those privileges, and will not be subjected to the hardships to which they sometimes have been in the past.

The committee adjourned until to-morrow at 11 o'clock a. m.

SATURDAY, *November* 17, 1877.

The committee met at 11 o'clock a. m., pursuant to adjournment.

ADDITIONAL ARGUMENT OF W. C. DODGE.

Mr. DODGE. With the permission of Mr. Smith, I wish to occupy the attention of the committee about ten minutes, explanatory of a feature stated yesterday about which I said nothing, because I did not think there would be any opposition to it, which is, to allow the assignee to make oath in the case of a reissue. Our friend Mr. Christy, the committee will recollect, stated that that provision was put into the law of 1870, as he understood, to prevent some fraud or to meet cases of that kind. In the first place, I happen to have had a good deal to do with that act in 1870, and I have here in my hand the original draught of that bill, as draughted by the late Commissioner Fisher.

The CHAIRMAN. What is the section of the proposed act to which you refer?

Mr. DODGE. It is the last clause of section 21 of the bill, which provides:

And in all cases of an application by an assignee for the issue of a patent, the specification shall be signed and sworn to by the inventor or discoverer; and in all cases of an application for a reissue of any patent, the application may be made and the corrected specification sworn to and signed by the owner or owners of the entire interest in the patent.

That was always the law until the act of 1870. It was then changed by some means which no person has discovered. It was not in the original draught, prepared by the late Commissioner Fisher, which I have here. [Exhibiting.] There is the section and there the amendments which he proposed. That provision is not among them, as you will see. It was not put in there by the House committee or by the Senate committee, and as to its being ultimately passed by the conference committee, I inquired of every member of the conference committee and not one of them could tell how it originated or why it was put in. Commissioner Fisher denounced it from the beginning. He said it would simply be the means of enabling the party selling a patent to blackmail the assignee; and that we find to be the actual fact. During the past year and a half we were applied to by the president of one of our large manufacturing concerns to reissue a patent which he had bought. We prepared a reissue application, and, under this act, he was obliged to go to the original inventor and ask him to make the oath. He refused to do so unless he was paid $5,000, and we were obliged to pay him $5,000 cash in hand before he would sign the paper. There was no process by which he could compel him to do it in the courts. I am happy to say that Commissioner Leggett is here to-day, and he will confirm all that I have said upon this subject, for every Commissioner, from the time the law was passed to the present, including the present Commissioner, has considered that that provision was a great hardship in the law, and that it ought to be remedied. It was found to work such a hardship that at the next session of Congress there was passed an explanatory provision, as you will see by the Revised Statutes, defining that it does not apply to any patent which was assigned prior to the passage of the act. Therefore we have two rules now, a rule applying to patents assigned prior to the passage of the act of July, 1870, where the assignee who makes the application may make the oath, and in the other case, relating to those patents which have been assigned since that time, the owner of the interest must go to the original inventor to make the oath and sign the specification.

Yesterday the question was asked what that oath was. I have brought here some copies of the rules for the benefit of the Senate committee. The oath is simply this:

STATE OF   , County of   , ss :

A. B. and C. D., the above-named petitioners, being duly sworn (or affirmed), depose and say that they verily believe that, by reason of an insufficient specification, the aforesaid letters patent granted to E. F. are inoperative; that the said error has arisen from inadvertence, accident, or mistake, and without any fraudulent or deceptive intention, to the best of their knowledge and belief; that the entire title to said letters patent is vested in them, and that they verily believe the said E. F. to be the first and original inventor of the invention set forth and claimed in the foregoing amended specification; and that the said E. F. is now deceased.

A. B.
C. D.

You see they are required to swear that he is dead. It works a hardship in another way also. It often happens, and we have a case in point (which Mr. Bond could testify to if he were here), in which a manufacturing concern in Chicago own a patent which they bought of the inventor. They found they could not protect their manufacture under the patent as it stood, and that it was necessary to reissue the patent. In looking for the inventor, all they have been able to ascertain is that he has gone to Europe. They cannot make oath that he is dead, for in fact they know he is not, in all reasonable probability, and at the same time they are tied up, and cannot move one step, simply because they cannot find the inventor. It has been a constant source of annoyance and of hardship from the time the act went into operation, and I was surprised to hear my friend Christy say yesterday that it was not objected to and did not work hardship. So far as I know, the objection has been universal, in the office and out of the office, and its change has been urged or recommended by every Commissioner from Mr. Fisher down to the present occupant.

ARGUMENT OF M. D. LEGGETT.

[Ex-Commissioner of Patents.]

Mr. LEGGETT. Mr. Chairman and gentlemen, it was my desire to be present at all the meetings of the committee this week, but duties in courts that I could not control have prevented my attendance, and consequently I do not feel that I ought to occupy your time. I do not desire to go over points that have been discussed, and I do not know what has been discussed and what has not. I do not believe that it would be in my power to enlighten the committee on the various matters so ably presented by the several gentlemen who have already spoken. If any member of the committee or any gentleman present desires to ask my opinion on any particular point, of course I am very willing to give the results of my own observation and experience.

On the point that has been presented this morning, I will simply say that I fully indorse all that Mr. Dodge has said. I see no good whatever in that provision of the law, and it is often made a very onerous tax upon the owners of patents; it is made a source of black-mailing to an enormous extent. Since I have gone out of the Patent Office some three years ago or a little over, I have been engaged exclusively in the practice of patent law before the courts. We have found it necessary very often to reissue our patents before we can commence suits on them. This is sometimes done for the purpose of disclaiming certain parts of an invention. We find that the original patent was too broad; that the claims called for an invention of greater scope than the inventor had a right to cover, the consequence being that, if we should bring suit and go into court on our patent, as originally granted, our patent would be defeated; and therefore it is necessary in such cases to limit the patent and bring it down to just what the inventor had a right to have patented, with the exception of sustaining his patent. Before we can reissue a patent, for the purpose of getting it in such perfected condition, the original inventor must be found, although he may have no earthly interest in the patent at all. The inventor has sold his patent, received a full consideration for it, and therefore has no further interest in it. Yet, as the law now stands, the inventor must be found and his signature obtained to the application for a reissue. In several cases that have come up in my practice the assignees of a patent have been obliged to pay a bonus, and a considerable bonus, to the inventor. In one instance I was informed that the bonus was as a high as $5,000, and

in no iustauce was it less than $50 for this simple matter of the inventor
giving his signature to a reissue application. The law gives him the
power of bleeding the owner of a patent just to that extent. The patent may be utterly worthless unless he will sign his name to the application for a reissue. He has no interest in the patent, directly or indirectly. He rarely examines the papers. He is not obliged to give the
matter any attention, and his siguature is all that he is asked to give;
yet he cau bleed the assignee to the full extent of the value of the patent, if he so desires. I see, as I said, no earthly good that can grow
out of the preseut law, but there is constant evil; aud the evil is such
that now I often advise my clients, when they take an assignment of a
patent, to draught a reissue in blank and make the party sigu it, and
that stands sometimes for years before it is filed.

Senator CHAFFEE. Why could not the patentee give a power of attorney to the assignee ?

Mr. LEGGETT. There is no provision in the law that will allow him
to sign an application for a reissue by power of attorney.

Senator WADLEIGH. A power of attorney would be revocable at any
time, of course.

Mr. LEGGETT. If the patentee should give a power of attorney, he
could revoke it. The inventor is obliged to subscribe the oath and
swear to the facts set forth in the application, and that cannot be done by
power of attorney. There is no provision in the law by which an attorney can sigu for the applicant. All such signatures have always
been refused by the office. We have had cases also where the inventor
has gone, nobody knows where he is, and it has been utterly impossible
to find him with all the means that have been used. Yet we have every
reason to suppose that he is living, and the matter becomes a hardship
to the assignee, and a very great hardship, as without the signature of
the inventor the reissue could not be secured.

Your honors have given attention enough to this matter to understand that invalid patents are often granted. The examiners and the
Commissioner examine the applications for patents as thoroughly as
they can with the lights before them, but all they have is the record of
the Patent Office, the machinery there, and what is represented there
iu regard to the invention. If evidence sufficieut to overthrow the
prima facie case of the applicant is not found within the records of this
office and is not within the personal knowledge of any of the officers,
the Commissioner must grant the patent. Under the law, he caunot do
otherwise. The law compels the granting of the patent, provided the
application complies with the conditions prescribed. Now, when we
come to enforce our patent, we may discover that a portion of the thing
patented has been constructed by others prior to the date of the patent.
That part which has been coustructed at such earlier date is not original
invention of the patentee. We have a clean invention outside of this
machiue. It therefore becomes necessary to reissue a limited patent, so
as to exclude all claims covering the machine which had been manufactured and used at such prior date; otherwise, should we go iuto court,
our patent must be defeated.

Senator MORGAN. Do you mean that where the patent covers a claim
that is not lawful, all the other claims which it covers are vitiated by
that fact ?

Mr. LEGGETT. No, sir; not necessarily that; but there may be a
single claim in the patent so broad as to cover clearly a machine that
had been constructed and used prior to the date of the invention of the
patentee, and our patent may be defeated on that very ground. In

that case we give up our broad patent and obtain a narrower one, because we are not entitled to a broad one. Everything is not found at the Patent Office. There has been an effort on the part of the government to get everything there they can, but a great many valuable improvements have never been patented, and, consequently, there is no trace of them in the office. Our mechanics and manufacturers have knowledge. of such matters, and patentees must restrict their patents so as to avoid any conflict with such prior machines.

Senator CHAFFEE. I should like to ask you a question at this point in regard to the best manner of issuing a patent, whether upon a model, or whether it would not be better to have perfect and complete drawings made, so as to explain every point that the inventor claims a patent for; that is, to use drawings instead of models. Which would be the better way, to use the models or to use the drawings?

Mr. LEGGETT. I will say that my experience in the four years I was in the Patent Office (and I have had some experience before the courts prior to that time and since) is, that while originally I thought that models were mere traps, curiosities, interesting to the public to look at, the more I have given my attention to the matter, the more firmly I am of the opinion that they are absolutely necessary for the protection both of the community and of patentees. The Patent Office could get along better without them than the courts. The examiners in the Patent Office are experts in reading drawings. The matter of reading a drawing is an art, just as much as the reading of German or French. If you take a man not accustomed to the reading of drawings, they are blank pages to him. He cannot make the lines of a drawing stand out and portray the invention, because he has not been educated to it. We find actually in experience that there is not to exceed one in five, at most, and probably not so large a proportion, of our best judges on the bench who get any just conception of a machine by the drawing.

Senator CHAFFEE. In a case before a court, an expert could take the drawing and make a model for the court.

Mr. LEGGETT. That is where the greatest trouble comes in precisely. If you would go before the courts and try three or four patent suits and have experts and mechanics construct machines to represent the drawings, you would find that they would come in with different and distinct machines to represent the same drawings. They will come in with two or three distinct machines, and each expert will swear that the model he presents correctly represents the drawing, and the judge is in a greater quandary than he would have been if he had never seen the machine at all.

Senator CHAFFEE. Would not that be the case with the model itself in court? Would not forty experts come in and give the testimony differently in regard to the same model?

Mr. LEGGETT. I have found no practical difficulty on that point. With the help of the drawings and the machine itself I have not yet found a case where experts would mislead the judge. We have no judge on the bench that I know of who would be troubled in that way. I will state the case of one of the clearest legal minds that we have on the bench. He is sharp and penetrating, and transacts a vast amount of business quickly, readily, and accurately. He is one of our very best lawyers. His decisions are a charm to lawyers everywhere, because they are succinct and sharp. I had the privilege of trying a patent case before him. My opponent was one of the best mechanical lawyers in the country, one of our leading patent lawyers. He argued the case for two days, and argued it so clearly that, although I went into court thinking

I had a perfect case, that could not be wrenched from me, when he got through he had made his view of the matter, it seemed to me, so very clear to the court that I felt a little down about it. He did not use a model, although there was one setting on his desk. The drawings were so plain and clear, that they seemed to show everything. He had a large drawing before him; there was a small drawing before the court, and another small drawing before himself, while I had one in my hands, these drawings representing the machine in question. The court listened. At the end of the second day, just before the closing hour, he rested, and the court adjourned for me to commence the next morning. I was stopping at the same hotel where the judge stopped. As I stepped in to supper he invited me to his table. He said he wanted to see me at his room after supper. I went to his room, and then he said to me, " I have a confession to make that I am ashamed of. I have listened two days to this case with all the ability that I have. Last night I sat up almost all night on it, for I was ashamed that I did not get the thing in my head. I must confess that I do not know anything about it, not a bit more than I did before one word was said. You will argue for two days, and I will not know anything more about it then." That was his confession ; and the reason of his confession was, because the model had not been used. I told him that the opposing counsel had made it so vivid and clear that I had been frightened in the presentation of it and felt hurt. Said I, "There is no earthly difficulty." Said he, " I will tell you what the difficulty is : I cannot understand the drawing ; they are just straight lines on paper. I cannot see any machine on it at all." I told him if he would send for the model I would go and look up the attorney on the other side. He consented to it. I did so. I sent to the court-room and got the model and papers. I looked the attorney up and he came in. We spent about half an hour in explaining it to the judge, and he said it was just as clear to him as a thing could be. I presented my side of the case and submitted my argument in a couple of hours the next day, and then went home the next morning and was never troubled with any further argument. Some judges do not find any difficulty. Judge Chipman will take and read a drawing with great vividness ; it stands up and is a machine to him. It was so with Judge Woodruff. He would pick up a drawing and read it as he would read a printed page ; it was all luminous to him; but those are exceptions ; and the only way to avoid confusion and difficulty is to have the model itself from the Patent Office, or a certified copy of it that shall be an exact copy. The inventors and the mechanics will attempt to introduce some slight modification, the party on the other side will make a departure the other way, and the drawing may sustain one side or it may sustain the other side. Experts will swear one way and experts will swear the other way, and the judge is confounded, worse confused, and knows no more when he has done with the case than when he commenced.

Senator CHAFFEE. Then a good mechanic can make a model from a good drawing and make it as perfect as the drawing itself ?

Mr. LEGGETT. He can do it if it is a working-drawing ; but working-drawings it would be very expensive to the government to reproduce.

Senator CHAFFEE. I was thinking whether it would not be better to have these patents issued from such drawings, because the drawings could be preserved more securely than the models.

Mr. LEGGETT. The government is in the habit of reproducing the drawings, and it seems to be necessary for the public that they should be reproduced. The great mass of patents require but a single sheet of drawings; but if you require working-drawings six or eight sheets would be necessary. Sometimes a single drawing will answer, if you have a model that represents it. Therefore, it would cost the government for every patent that is issued six or eight or ten times what it costs now to the government to issue those patents, and it would amount to from $75,000 to $100,000 a year probably. That would be a pretty expensive luxury, even if it was a luxury, while in fact it would be a great hardship to inventors. It is often that the principle in an invention is clearly shown in a model, and it is clearly shown in the drawing. Were they to get a working-drawing, it must be absolutely reduced to practice first, and to reduce it to practice would require an amount of expenditure that three-fourths of the inventors could not afford, and the consequence would be that the poor inventor would be always shut off. He cannot reduce the invention to practice, and must have help to do it, and the capitalist will not give him help until he has obtained his patent. Capitalists will not invest in experimenting until the patent has been granted. They are willing to experiment when they can be secure in case the experiment is successful. Reducing the machine to absolute practice before applying for the patent would become a necessity, provided you required working-drawings.

Senator CHAFFEE. I should like to ask what your idea is about this limitation. What would be a proper time, in your judgment?

Mr. LEGGETT. So far as the time is concerned, I approve of the bill which has been offered here. I think it is about as nearly correct as we can get it. I am not entirely satisfied with this presentation so far as the mode of getting at damages is concerned. The second section I think, perhaps, will need a little careful consideration. I presume it has been discussed already to an extent. I think that there should be a pretty broad discretion left to the courts, and that the discretion should be broader than it is now. Upon the finding of the master the court should have power, I think, to decrease or diminish as the justice of the special case would seem to demand. They may now increase, but when they come in with exorbitant amounts, they have no authority to diminish, and I think they should have authority both ways in reference to that matter. The measure of damages is very hard to fix. It is hard to say that it shall be just this or just that. A man may go to work and he may manufacture without a license. I may have a patent, and I may license parties here and in different parts of the country. Another man refuses to take a license from me, and goes to work and makes the machine without paying the royalty, and defies my patent. He thinks I am too poor to sue, for my license-fee is small; but finally my other licensees refuse to pay royalty; for they say if this man can manufacture without paying a license, we will not pay either. Therefore, I find myself driven to the absolute necessity of commencing suit against this infringer in order to collect my licenses from the other licensees; for they will not pay a license if he who defies my patent goes into the market and puts the article into trade without paying the tax. He can compete with the licensees and undersell them in the market. If all I can be permitted to recover from him is simply the ordinary license-fee which I am getting from willing licensees, I have wasted all the money in enforcing a single right that years have given me in the licenses of the others. It may be a small matter, but the court ought to have discretion in a case of that kind to compensate me for the expense I have been put to in order to enforce a right that the infringer determined not to respect until the court should enforce it. We have it in all other interests, and

the courts can compensate us to some extent further than just to measure the damage. This section seems to measure the damage by the
license-fee. I do not think you should make that the determination of
the whole thing, with no power to increase or decrease the measure of
damages.

Mr. SMITH. The last section remedies that.

Mr. LEGGETT. That applies to cases where there is no license-fee, I
understand.

Mr. SMITH. No, sir; to all cases provided for by statute.

Mr. LEGGETT. I have not given the subject much attention; but if
that is already in the bill, no other modification will be needed.

In reference to reissues, I want to just emphatically indorse the provision here, especially that portion of it in regard to manufacturers.
To make it clear, I will cite an illustration. Suppose that I am a manufacturer, and I want to manufacture a certain article, say a steam-
pump. I know a certain man who has a patent on a steam-pump. I
look over his patent to see what I have a right to make. I do this
honestly. The patent is published for that purpose. I do not want to
infringe the rights of the patentee, and therefore I carefully consider
his claims and find out what he has secured to him. It is presumed
that everything shown and described in his patent that is not covered
by the claim is either the property of a prior patentee or else it belongs
to the public. The Supreme Court has held that to be the presumption, that where a patentee fails to claim only a portion of a machine,
he thereby acknowledges that the remaining portion is not his invention.

Senator CHAFFEE. Is it the habit of the Commissioner to make a reissue for the purpose of enlarging on inventions?

Mr. LEGGETT. Not to enlarge on inventions, but to enlarge the
claims; that is, a man has come in originally and has obtained a narrow
patent on a specific construction. It was the blunder of his attorney,
because he could have obtained a wider patent. An attorney may present a claim for an invention and restrict it to all its peculiarities and
be sure of getting a patent, when, if he would lay a broad claim to it,
that would cover the principle of the construction, he would not get a
patent so easily. Very often they take out a narrow patent, and afterward, by a reissue, get a broader claim, to which they were entitled at
first.

Senator CHAFFEE. The Commissioner requires proof of that.

Mr. LEGGETT. No, sir; no proof is required, because the proof must
exist in the original documents. Unless the Commissioner finds that
the invention was clearly shown in the original application, no proof
will help him to grant the patent. He must find it in the original application, or he cannot grant it at all.

Senator MORGAN. I am very little acquainted with the patent law,
and particularly with the practice of the patent law; but it has occurred
to me since the argument has been going on that this matter of the
reissue of a patent is more analogous to proceedings to amend a judgment or a record *nunc pro tunc* than anything else, and that it ought
to go on the same principles. A court is asked to correct a mistake
made in a cause where the cause has gone into a final judgment. The
court refers back to the record, to everything that appears of record, and
from that, and that alone, it finds its authority to make such a correction as would do the sort of justice that ought to have been done by its
judgment in the first instance. Now, the Commissioner of Patents, in
looking back to see whether a patent ought to be reissued, it seems to

me, ought to be permitted to go to the model, to the claim, and to every part of the claim, to every paper in the case, in order to determine from all of these, and from nothing less than all of these, exactly what was the nature of the patent that ought to have been issued in the first instance ; and, it seems to me, any interference in striking out or removing from the consideration of the court any part of this record which the party has made in the model, or the claim, or any other proceeding, would be an invasion of his rights.

Senator CHAFFEE. That is exactly my idea about it.

Mr. LEGGETT. That is the practice.

Senator MORGAN. If there is anything in this bill to change that application of these principles of law, I should like to have it pointed out and discussed.

Mr. LEGGETT. I do not understand that there is anything in the bill of that character. I understand that the intention has been to make the reissue harmonize precisely with that idea.

Mr. COLAHAN. If, in his original application, he had disclaimed entirely the main feature he wishes to obtain a reissue upon, should that record have any effect?

Senator MORGAN. That would be a waiver, an abandonment of the claim.

Mr. LEGGETT. On that point I have held that it was an abandonment of the claim. I took occasion once, when Commissioner of Patents, to make a thorough examination of that point, and I held that, by the common-law principle or practice of estoppels, when a man had, in his original application, disclaimed that a certain thing was his invention, he should never be permitted to come back again into the office and claim that it was his invention, because actions had been based upon it subsequently, and the well-known law of estoppels comes in and applies.

Senator MORGAN. You have never become dissatisfied with that decision?

Mr. LEGGETT. I have never become dissatisfied with it; but the supreme court of the District of Columbia overruled me, an appeal being taken to it, 'and the consequence is that from that day to this the practice of the office has been otherwise.

Mr. HUBBELL. Might he not have made a mistake in the disclaimer?

Mr. LEGGETT. He may have made a mistake in the disclaimer, but he should abide by it in a case so solemn as that.

Mr. SMITH. I think in one decision—I do not know where it is—it was held that where a party had made a mistake in a disclaimer as to the facts on which he disclaimed, he might recall it. That was not exactly the case here.

Mr. LEGGETT. That is not precisely the case here. The courts have held that a mistake in the disclaimer, like all other mistakes, might be corrected in the record; but the case I had in mind was a very bald one. There was an interference declared between two parties, and the question was which was the first inventor. One party had bought up both patents, but he thought one of them better than the other. He went to one of these parties and solemnly·asserted that he was not the first inventor; that the other man was; and he disclaimed the original authorship of the invention. He did this to go into court with the other patent, and when he went into court and was defeated on the patent he came back to the Patent Office to revive this patent which he had already disclaimed. I refused to grant it, and the court overruled my decision.

Senator CHAFFEE. This matter of reissue rests wholly with the Commissioner?

Mr. LEGGETT. Yes, sir; he is limited only by the statute.

Senator CHAFFEE. He can grant a reissue or not, in his discretion?

Mr. LEGGETT. Yes, sir; but an appeal, of course, lies from him to the supreme court of the District.

Senator CHAFFEE. Suppose he refuses to grant a reissue?

Mr. LEGGETT. They can go to the supreme court of the District. The law provides that an appeal may be taken to that court from any decision made by the Commissioner except in a matter of interference. From a decision on an application for a patent or for a reissue, an appeal lies to the supreme court of the District of Columbia sitting in banc.

The point that I am speaking of particularly will be retained as a feature in that section. Suppose that I am a manufacturer, as I was going to say; I look into a patent to see what is there. I find that a certain machine that I want to make is not claimed. The inventor has talked about it; he describes it; but he goes and claims something else. Now the courts have held that, for the time being, the patentee is not protected in anything not claimed, as the failure to claim a thing operates as an actual disclaimer of it. The law provides that he may go back, if he has made a mistake, and claim it. That is right enough; but I have gone to work in the mean time, as a manufacturer, and built the machine; I have put it into my factory; I have invested my money in the use of it; and it was legal when I built it—perfectly so. The law sustained me fully in the building of it and in the investment of my money. Every step was legal, honest, upright, and straightforward; but yet, when he gets a reissue of the patent under the law, he may come in and enjoin me from any further use of the machine, and thereafter it must stand idle.

Senator MORGAN. That is in violation of the fixed and settled rule of law, that where a party has to go to a court of any sort, shape, size, or description, and ask the relief of that court to correct his own errors, or to correct errors that have crept into the record by any oversight, the rights which have vested in the interim must remain rights, and are beyond the power of the court to break down or control.

Mr. LEGGETT. That is law everywhere else except in the law of patents, which has provided otherwise; consequently the statute needs correcting, I think, in that respect; that is, where a machine has been made under such circumstances the party should have the right to use the machine if he has constructed it when it was perfectly legal on his part to construct it. Patentees cannot collect damages for what was done before the reissue, but after the reissue has been obtained they may prevent any further use being made of the machine by an injunction. That I think is wrong. I think it is wrong in principle; it is a hardship to the manufacturing interest; it is a hardship to everybody, and there is no honesty in it.

I am not particularly pleased with another feature in the same bill, which provides that if any mistake was made in the original patent, the patentees may go back and reissue, and may claim what was shown in the drawing or model as described in the specification. The law heretofore has been that it must be shown either in the drawing or in the model, but a description of the matter to be claimed was not sufficient to allow a claim to be allowed in a reissue. It seems to me there is justice in the provision of the law as it now stands. In these reissues more deviltry, if I may be permitted to use the phrase, creeps into the practice of the patent law than everything else put together. Reissues ought to be guarded carefully, and yet the right to reissue should be maintained, I think, carefully; but at the same time it should be restricted so as to shut every bar that can be shut against knavery in the practice in this respect.

A drawing is a definite, certain thing. That is not ambiguous. A model is a definite, certain thing. That has the same meaning always and no other meaning. Language is ambiguous. It may mean one thing to-day and it may mean another thing to-morrow. There may be an indefinite phrase used by which the man meant nothing particular at the time, but afterward he finds that somebody has come in and made something that that language might cover. He goes back and reissues his old patent because he has got a new idea and that language can be construed to cover that idea. If his model shows it, the idea was in his head at the time the model was constructed. If the drawing shows it, the idea was in his head when the drawings were prepared. But he may, or his attorney for him may, carelessly use language when the thought of a different construction never entered in his head at all.

For that reason it seems to me the principle should be shown either in the model or in the drawing before he should be allowed to take out any reissue. Upon that point, however, I am not so strenuous. I suppose it would change the law in this respect, that if the principle is found in either one of the three, either the specification, the drawing, or the model, it could be embraced in a reissue.

Mr. SMITH. I should like to have Mr. Leggett express to the committee his judgment upon that section which provides that there shall be the payment of a fee to prevent a patent from dying, and I should like to have his opinion as to what the effect of that provision would be.

Mr. LEGGETT. That provision I am very strenuously in favor of also. In one of my annual reports to Congress during the time that I was Commissioner, I urged very strongly that there should be a tax levied. Among the greater evils that grow out of the patent practice is, that they nose about among old rusty patents that never have been of any account at all, and certain parties make it their business to buy up old patents because they cover something that has gone into general use, after the patent has been sleeping eight, ten, twelve, or fourteen years perhaps, lying perfectly dormant. The thing has been discovered by almost everybody and it has gone into use, but it is not used by the inventor, because he obtained his patent and let it go. It is a fault of inventors often when that they take no interest in a thing except in inventing it. When they have invented a thing they drop it in chasing a new thought, and thus they go from one thing to another and never think of their former inventions. Somebody finds such an invention that has been patented and neglected and buys it at a song, and then he will go through the country and bleed the people. I have in mind one case where a man looked up an old patent which covered a gate. Almost every farmer in Indiana and Illinois who had a gate was infringing that patent. This man went around and made them pay from $5 to $20 each, or they must go to court. He bought this old patent and probably did not pay more than $5 for it, and he made $10,000 or more out of it.

If a patent is good for anything, it can afford to pay a tax at the end of five years. If you require a tax at the end of five years, a large number of patents in existence would die on that day. In my opinion, but a small proportion of the patents issued are patents that would live through such a tax. You can understand how the proposed law would clear up the fog banks and leave a very open sea; and people would know where they stood if we had some method to get rid of the patents which are regarded by the owners of them as worthless; and taxation would accomplish that object.

Mr. HUBBELL. Can this government do that, when the grant of a patent is not a prerogative right of the government? It is a right parted with by the States, and vested specifically in the United States for a certain purpose. Can the government defeat that purpose by levying a tax?

Mr. LEGGETT. The Constitution provides, I believe, that patents shall be granted for a limited time to inventors. The government may grant patents for one year, or two years, or five years, or fourteen years, or twenty years, or fifty years. It is within the province of Congress to do that; and if they grant a patent for fourteen years, and provide that on certain conditions it may expire in five years, I see no infringement of the constitutional power.

Senator MORGAN. Is there any question of taxation in it? Is the taxing power invoked at all? Is it not a question of restriction upon the license you give?

Mr. LEGGETT. That is all. The taxing power is not invoked at all. It is a restriction in the conditions imposed upon the license. I do not know why Congress may not fix it just as they would fix the original fee. They might charge $35 when a man takes out a patent, and $50 more at the end of five years.

Senator MORGAN. It is not a tax?

Mr. LEGGETT. It is not a tax.

I am much obliged to the committee for the attention they have given to my remarks.

ARGUMENT OF J. H. RAYMOND.

Mr. RAYMOND. Mr. Chairman and Senators of the committee, I shall be gratified by any interruption whatever from any member of the committee, and by any such interruption from gentlemen present, as shall correct any misstatement of law or of fact which I may through inadvertence or ignorance make in the course of my remarks. I shall devote myself in the general and special considerations mainly to the provisions of the first two sections. I desire to emphasize the extreme care, as well as the marked ability, with which this bill was drawn. It is not an exaggeration to say that the very highest talent in this department of law has been employed in considering it for two years, putting upon it recently consultations of about sixteen or eighteen days of continuous, constant hard work. Every word in the bill means something, and so far as was practicable it has been desired that every circumstance which ought to be should be provided for and met by the law proposed.

I desire at the outset to correct the idea, which has probably grown out of the fact that I have been active during the past two years in advocating radical amendments to the patent law, that I or the interests which I represent are inimical to the patent system. I cannot afford time, in the little it is proper for me to occupy, to say the much that I desire upon the important questions before the committee to exhibit the details of my motives and purposes in order to correct this mistaken idea. I desire the committee to take my most solemn and earnest assurance that there is nothing in my personal ambition and convictions, in my professional and business connections, or in the purposes of my principals, which would knowingly militate against the efficient and honest administration of a wise and equitable patent system.

I make this explanation thus earnestly, though thus briefly, specially because I deem it my duty on this occasion to make some criticisms upon the present patent laws and their administration.

My friend and senior, Mr. Smith, at the commencement of this discussion, asked the question, and answered it in a manner that did honor to his great experience and marked ability, "Has history vindicated the wisdom of the patent provisions of the Constitution and of the statutes?" I answer as to the Constitution, without reservation, "Yes." As to the statutes as in force for the last seventeen years, I answer, without hesitation or reservation, "No;" and it is my hope to show the committee that the present statutes, as now construed, with the rules of practice and recovery adhered to by the courts, are to the public in many respects great evils. That the law is in many respects a failure, is sufficiently evidenced by the petitions that come up from the people for its amendment, and by the wide-spread, extreme, and dangerous dissatisfaction among the people, which threatens at no distant day, in the absence of radical amendments, to repeal and destroy the whole system.

I shall cite some of the features which are complained of, some of which this bill proposes to remedy. I state as a proposition of my own conviction that 90 per cent. of all the infringements of patents are innocent infringements. That will be disputed by some; but no one intelligent in these matters will dispute that a very large majority of the infringements are innocent, unknowing infringements.

First, then, as to these provisions which have become burdensome to the people. The only limitation which the Federal law has known upon actions or recoveries in patent suits was that enacted in 1870, it being a statute of limitation of six years. The patents to which that applied are largely those granted prior to March, 1861—fourteen-year patents, that were extended as a mere matter of form in a large number of instances. Therefore those patents run twenty-one years. Patents which are now alive by virtue of those extensions, adding that statute of limitations, have a life-time of twenty-seven years within which their owners could bring suits.

Postulating, then, that these infringements, in a large majority of cases, are innocent infringements—not only innocent in their start, but continuously so for from twenty to twenty-seven years—for that whole use the people of this country are now called upon to answer in profits and savings on the equity side of our courts.

The nature of the title which is now given to a patentee is that of a close monopoly. If the owner of the patent is a manufacturer and desires to keep the control of his patented invention in his manufactory by the use and operation of the law of injunctions, the result only can be extravagant prices for the product of that machine, if it is a machine patent. There is no law which requires that the patent should go into use. A man may take his patent and lock it up in his closet and keep it there seventeen years. There is no power to get it out. The result is such instances as that of necessary use on the Southern plantations of the Paris-green compound already referred to, and the case of the millers of the Northwest in this middlings-purifier controversy, where, in order to use that patented process, one mill in Indianapolis is put under $250,000 bond by a justice of the Supreme Court of the United States in lieu of an operation of the injunction, the court thinking that he would be a little tender with that infringer in that respect; in both of which cases the users have been innocent infringers, yet are now liable as tort-feasors in immense damages.

It is generally conceded that these matters of reissues are great evils. Reissues are gotten out largely to cover inventions of other people which were made subsequent to the date of the original patent, which the original patentee knew nothing about in the world; or, in the second place, to cover some part of the model or drawings which is put in origi- nally as a mere matter of mechanical skill to make the machine complete, an element to which the inventor did not attach at all the merit of in- vention, but which afterward he finds going into use in other machines and other combinations. He reissues his patent to obtain a patent on what was put in originally as a matter of mechanical skill, a matter of accident, in order to complete the model and to show the operation of other things which he did invent and claim as his invention.

Devices innocently in use at the time of the reissue, not infringing the original patent, are made infringements of the reissued patent. This the bill partially provides for. Senator Morgan suggests that where a pat- ent is reissued any vested right in the public should be maintained, which certainly is sound, if it was possible to do it; but it cannot be done. While by the provisions of this bill, if at the date of the reissue I am using a single machine or a single process in my business which did not infringe the original patent, I am entitled to use that specific machine until it is worn out, and I may repair it but may not replace it, still if the reissued patent covers that machine or process, it certainly interferes with my business, and the vested rights I had under the orig- inal patent I am not entitled to except for a limited period, and that limitation hanging over me of course to a large extent destroys my business.

Instances have been named to the committee where reissues were gotten out on no other basis (and it is not a fictitious case) than that of a fraudulent alteration of a model in the Patent Office.

After a good deal of study, and I think honest, unprejudiced study, in this regard, I have come to this conclusion (although I admit there are two sides to it, and I am not altogether satisfied about it), that the only practical way of *properly* protecting the people against the reissue of patents is to abolish them altogether, and I would do so, if it were left to my discretion, to-day. Every gentleman in this room will admit that the reissue of patents has resulted in more evil than any other thing known to the Congressional acts. There is no possible doubt about that. There is no doubt, either, but that almost any restriction which the committee and Congress may put upon the reissue of patents would be a wise restriction. The legislative power of the government cannot err in that direction, in my judgment, and it would not err if Congress went to the extent of abolishing reissued patents entirely.

Taking up some of the features of the patent law which have come to be burdensome among the people, I will state that I have in my office claims which are made against the railroad companies which I repre- sent that I know to be perfectly fraudulent, for one reason or another. The patents have years to run, and the testimony upon which I am de- pendent to show that these claims are not valid depends upon witnesses fifty, fifty-five, sixty, and sixty-five years old. There is no way of per- petuating that testimony now, and the assignees (and the strictures which are put upon those who hold patents, and not upon the patentees and inventors, but upon the assignees), in a number of instances, are waiting for our inventors to die, in which case we would be remediless.

We desire to perpetuate testimony, and for additional reasons we desire to have the other provision as to invalidating patents.

In the next place, there is a large community of men who are traveling about the country notifying A, B, and C that "your business is conducted upon a plan that infringes my patent, and you must desist." They advertise the fact in the country, so that if I know that these men have a choice of action against either the user or the manufacturer, I am prevented from buying of the manufacturer, because ordinarily the claimant would choose to sue me, the user, rather than the manufacturer. Such notices are served all over the country, and they interfere with our commercial relations to a great extent.

Again, the claimant, not daring to publicly advertise that he has a claim upon this manufacture or business, will send out agents all over the country among the farmers, the millers, or the carpenters, or other artisans, and they will say, "Here is the patent which you are infringing." Described in the specifications, or possibly in the claims, is the device which the farmer or the artisan uses. There is the broad seal of the United States upon it, and the agent says, "I must receive compensation for the infringement." The farmer says, "I have been using that article for twenty-five years." The agent says, "I cannot help it; this man invented this patented article and got it up before your inventor, and we can prove it." The farmer says, "I cannot suffer a lawsuit," although he may know it to be a fraudulent claim. The agent says, "Give me $50 and I will give you a license." The amount of money is paid. This kind of blackmailing under the law amounts to millions of dollars annually.

There are some of these provisions that we cannot remedy *in toto*, but the people are feeling these burdensome features of the patent law; and the object of my citation of some of these burdensome features is to show that radical amendments are necessary, and that the patent law is not a sacred thing to be touched with delicate fingers. In the interest of the conservative element of the country I appeal to the committee that radical amendments should be made now, or else the unintelligent abuse of the patent law by the public will be carried to a greater extent, and the outcry will get so great in a short time that it cannot be controlled even by the legislative power of the government.

Senator CHAFFEE. Suppose the limitation were made for a year, would not that cut off these abuses?

Mr. RAYMOND. I will presently try to show why it should not be made one year, but I think four years too long. It should be three years.

In the next place, inventions are stolen from Canada as they come over to Detroit, Buffalo, and elsewhere. I know an instance, which is an example of many other cases. An invention is made in Canada, but not patented or described in any printed publication there, but is seen by some one who makes it the subject of an application for an American patent as his own invention. There is no way of destroying a patent in this country for an invention so stolen. Of course the same circumstances apply to England, France, and Germany.

Again, he who doubts that the policy of the government and the policy of the patent law is to give notice of these monopolies to the public, certainly has not read the statutes with intelligence. The government goes as far as it is practicable to go, in my opinion, in this direction in publishing the printed copies of patents, and in requiring the stamping of patented articles. And yet the people are supposed to know (they are bound to know the law) the full force and effect of the 15,000 patents granted annually, whereas in fact they do not know anything about it.

That, in my opinion, is about fifteen times as many patents as ought to issue. Corporations and large business interests can afford and are obliged to pay patent attorneys about $10,000 per annum to advise them as to the force and effect of the patents bearing upon their particular interests. If an individual desires the same service in an isolated case, the necessary report on the state of the art and an opinion thereon by a competent attorney costs him from $500 to $1,000. I do not know why it is, but the hardest thing I have to explain to railroad-men in my business is how one patent can be perfectly valid and yet infringe another patent. Probably the failure is with me in not making my explanation clear enough. All inventions run in lines. There is a certain progress and a steady improvement in all the arts, and, as I shall show in the course of my remarks, not by virtue of the patent law exclusively. These lines of invention are what is called "the art." Mr. A. starts on one of these lines of invention to remedy an existing evil. He studies over the matter and gets one element. It makes no difference whether it is a machine or a process that is to be patented. His patent is inapplicable; it is not used at all; but he started in the right direction, and the claim of his patent covers one element of the final solution of the difficulty.

Mr. B. builds upon that, perhaps independently of A. so far as personal knowledge is concerned, and adds a second element. He has to use the first element, and consequently he gets a combination claim in his patent. He does not solve the difficulty. Mr. C. adds still a third element to the other two, traveling in the same line, not necessarily knowing what the others have done. He builds upon their work, but traveling in the same line his machine or process necessarily involves the two elements invented by these other men, and Mr. C. gets a combination claim for his three elements. Now, you cannot use Mr. C.'s patent without paying Mr. C. for it, but neither can you use Mr. C.'s patent without paying also Mr. A. and Mr. B. C.'s patent is perfectly valid. He has a good claim for those three elements, but his patent is subject to the other two patents, the first of which covers one element and the second covering two elements.

Senator CHAFFEE. How can he get a patent if the same thing has been patented previously?

Mr. RAYMOND. They give him a combination claim, subject to the other two patents. No man can use this article without being subject to C.'s patent; neither can they use it without being subject to the other two patents. The question of infringement or of mechanical equivalents is the nicest question that exists in the patent law. It is a question which no layman can safely pass upon himself, even in the simplest case. He must have legal assistance. Yet those questions arise in every one of those 15,000 patents granted annually. The association of which I have the honor to be an executive officer has got to-day $50,000,000 in litigation in patent cases, and there is not one dollar of that litigation that is based upon the use of a device that we have not once bought and paid for, and paid the patentee.

Mr. WALKER. Mr. Raymond——

Mr. RAYMOND. I will not suffer an interruption.

Mr. WALKER. You stated that you would suffer an interruption when you made a misstatement of facts.

Mr. RAYMOND. I will withdraw that statement, then. The Tanner brake, which Mr. Walker represents, is a brake that in a few instances was used on cars, but I am within bounds in saying that the thing never went into use. It is used to day on some cars, but, comparatively, it is fair to say it never went into use. We are using the Stevens, the Hodge, the Eames, the Westinghouse, the Loughridge, and the Smith brakes, and have paid for them all; yet Mr. Walker, as the attorney for his father-in-law, Mr. Sales, sues the Northwestern Railway Company for the first element, the idea of connecting the two trucks of the car, and gets a judgment for $46,000, and the case is now pending in the Supreme Court. If extended to all railroads in the country on the basis of their liability under that patent, which is estimated, not on a basis of their mileage or gross runnings, but on the basis of their actual use of double-acting brakes, this decree would amount to over $62,000,000. I did not intend to enlarge upon that idea, but these relations of infringement are so difficult and embarrassing, and they are so constantly and uniformly arising, that the public have some rights and embarrassments in these matters which the patentee is bound to respect, and the patentee has no such sacred rights in these matters as that we are precluded from handling them very roughly in suggesting a statute to meet such difficulties.

I should like to notice, because I think the time has come when it should be noticed, and noticed very severely, the issue of patents out of the Patent Office for the most insignificant things in the world; and not only for the most insignificant things in the world, but the most insignificant things in the world are sometimes patented two or three times in the Patent Office. Within the last six months I applied for a patent in the Patent Office for a peculiar device, and reference was given to a patent for the same device in an attachment of thills to a wagon, constructed in exactly the same manner, without any qualification, producing exactly the same results—this being one in a railroad-switch. I said to my friend, "You ought not to have any patent, but I think I can get you one; I will try." I prepared a brief and sent it to the examiner. The examiner then sent me another reference of the use of the same thing, producing the same results, in exactly the same manner, in a sulky for a race course.

Senator CHAFFEE. Still they issued another patent?

Mr. RAYMOND. They issued another patent in another class. The examiner in one class probably did not happen to see this prior patent for a sulky for a race-course in another class. I cannot explain how it happens, but I am stating a fact that happened within the last three months. The second time being referred to this identical thing producing identically the same results in another connection, I wrote another brief and sent it to the examiner. I will not give the argument that I used before him. There was no sense or reason in it in the world.

Senator CHAFFEE. Then you were not very scrupulous?

Mr. RAYMOND. No, I am bound not to be, in securing and protecting all the rights the law may give my client. But I will pay my respects to that idea in a moment.

Senator CHAFFEE. Is that the case with all the rest of the patent lawyers?

Mr. RAYMOND. Yes, sir; with every one of them, without a single exception, in my opinion. But I sent my brief on and got a patent on the railroad-switch. Now as to the suggestion of Senator Chaffee: I came, two years ago, to the conclusion that there was no logical sequence following through the patent law from the commencement, nor yet was there a great deal of conscience in it. Of course there is conscience in the practice of patent law. A man came into my office the other day who had no claim in the world in law. He had in fact and morally a claim. He had been swindled out of a monopoly of a very valuable invention which we wanted to use. I gave him a hundred dollars, simply because he did not have money enough to get out of town. In another case, a man comes in with a case against us which he ought to maintain, but which some technicality of the Patent Office gives us a right to use. I know of no other basis, and there is no other basis, than that the law said thus and so. My conscience in patent matters is the patent statute enacted by Congress, and I cannot substitute anything else. If a man has a legal claim against us (as in one instance that comes to my mind, where there was not the first shadow of a moral right), if the law gives it to him, I say, " You have a claim;" and in the case to which I refer I paid $34,000 where, morally, the man had no claim at all. Another man comes in to whom I ought to pay $40,000 on conscientious grounds, but I say, " The law does not give it to you, and I cannot give it to you."

If the committee please, I have noted eight or nine other respects in which the patent law is very burdensome to the people; but I will pass them over. I think it sufficiently appears that the influence of the public sentiment upon members of Congress and the honorable members of this committee must convince you that there is a very, very radical wrong being perpetrated under the patent law, and it is radical amendments that are desired.

It is hardly germane to the particular questions before the committee that I should discuss the measure and the merit of the patent law in attaining the civilization which we now enjoy; yet, as these questions have been discussed, and as they materially affect important provisions of the bill under discussion and the stand-point from which they should be judged, I will submit brief considerations in this connection.

Although we are told eloquently of the offices performed by the patent laws in attaining our present civilization, yet their exact measure in this respect is never given us except in the glowing terms of glittering generalities. That they perform important offices in this respect, none should deny; that they perform principal and primary offices, none should believe. In considering the causes of our happiness, peace, and prosperity, and as well the assurances of the permanence thereof, my habit of mind is to place as the corner-stone the Christianity that gives us an eternal and immutable foundation by which to measure and on which to base our civil and social laws; to then add as the foundation the general principles of our government, involving the sovereignty of the individual, a government for the people and by the people, rotation in office, opposition to centralization of power, and the perfect enjoyment of the inalienable rights; then to build on as the frame-work the institutions of our civil liberty, involving the right of trial by a jury of peers, the right of public assemblage and free discussion, and the public education of the masses; then to place as the pillars the expressed constitutional guarantees of this religion, these principles, and these institutions; and I finish my building with the statutory provisions directed to the executive and judicial servants of the government, among which I find regulations which govern the right of property which our Constitution gives in one kind of the products of the genius and intellects of the people. We have gone far, and indeed have wellnigh exhausted the list of causes of our rapid progress and present civilization, before we come to the patent system. Yet it should have its place. There is an Infinite Power behind our progress. There are those who, viewing only some threatening political cloud or temporary commercial embarrassment, feel and insist that the world is moving

backward; who, harping upon the good days gone by, would bid Liberty
to turn her back upon the future—

> To clank her chains and
> Swear 't was music.

But a candid review of the wonderful progress, and patriotism, and
peace that have characterized the last twelve years of American history
must satisfy all that there is an indefatigable energy and an indomitable
progress in the people, which is due primarily to their physical and
mental characteristics as developed by the political principles and institutions of the government, and secondarily to the statutory provisions
which encourage development in character, in knowledge, and, indeed,
in invention.

This leads me to my second question in this connection: Is the proper
measure of the reward to be given to the inventor the full amount of
the benefit conferred by him upon the public, as has been the basis of
the remarks that have preceded me, or is it to be established by some
other, and by what other, rule? The laws and the decisions that have
obtained up to the present time have gone upon the basis that the inventor should have, as a measure of his recovery, the benefit that he
had conferred upon the public; and it is the logical consequence of that
spirit, that opinion, that our laws and decisions have made the measure
of recovery as burdensome as it now is.

I wish to direct the attention of the committee, also, to this fact, that
the measure of damages which you shall enact in this bill will establish
the commercial values of all patented articles. If I have a patent upon
an article and want to sell it, whether I am a manufacturer or simply
selling licenses, the price that I will take depends primarily and almost
exclusively upon what I can recover from those who are obliged to use
the invention. In establishing this measure of damages you are establishing an extensive list of commercial values.

One of the gentlemen who has participated in the arguments before
the committee cited the reward that was paid to Mr. Howe, and of the
difficulties that he encountered. A more striking illustration of that is
the difficulties, the trials, the annoyances, the anxieties—almost the
starvation—of Goodyear. I appreciate all those things, and agree that
such men should be rewarded handsomely. They cannot be compensated, but they should be rewarded. But there are instances of the
other kind. Why should Mr. Singer, a man knowing nothing in the
world about sewing-machines, except to see his wife operate one, engaged
entirely in other pursuits, sitting by his fireside reading a paper, when
in five minutes, as quick as thought, by a mere accident, comes to him
the idea that he subsequently patented. Why should he, under such
circumstances and within a few years, be paid thirteen millions of dollars as his reward?

If you will excuse the assumption, consider that I occupy the position
of the government for a moment. In our common law of this country,
as in the institutions of the government, there is not the first suggestion
of a patent system. More, a patent system is directly contrary to the
spirit of our common law (not that of England), and it is directly contrary to the institutions of our government. But for a purpose, for a
particular purpose, i. e., the good of the public, the government says to
the inventor, "Invent; go ahead; we will give you a right of property for
a limited period in the product of your brain. We will give you a reward as an incentive simply that the benefits of your work may be
reaped by the public." It is a mistaken idea that pervades almost every

provision of the patent law, that the inventor should be compensated
for his invention in the measure of its value to the public. Take, for
instance, my watch, an American movement, which cost eighty-five dollars, which, during six months loses only fifty-eight seconds—a watch
of a sort that within my recollection would have cost six hundred dollars. Is the difference to be paid to the patentee? Are watches still
to be six hundred dollars, and the patentee to get the difference? Take
a locomotive on a railroad : the utilization of steam for transportation
has been patented in all its parts; even the cone of the smoke-stack has
been patented. If you are to pay upon any basis whatever that shall
come anywhere near the benefit of the patents to the public, it would
cost any one of us a thousand dollars to go home, and the people would
have to pay it.

What, then, is the proper stand-point from which to look at this second section relating to the measure of the reward which a patentee
should get? I admit it is a matter of the utmost difficulty to fix; but
the stand-point from which we must start in considering the subject is,
that it is not the benefit conferred by the patentee upon the public, but
what the public, in view of the encouragement it gives to the patentee,
can afford to pay, taking into consideration all the commercial laws of
supply and demand, of easy times, of good wages, &c., and it is not
from the other stand-point of the benefit that has been conferred upon
the public. I said in an argument last year before this committee that
there were decrees in the Supreme Court representing values of patents
of forty millions of dollars, fifty millions of dollars, and, in one case,
of sixty-two millions of dollars. Is there any patent in the country
worth sixty-two millions of dollars? Was a patent ever issued that was
worth sixty millions of dollars, or forty millions of dollars, or thirty millions of dollars? There is no possible doubt that patents have conferred
that amount of benefit upon the world in a great many instances, but
can the world afford to pay it under the circumstances of its grant, and
the conditions and reasons for its grant?

I pass, then, these general considerations of the measure of recovery,
to note the nature of the title which a patentee holds, and to complain,
if I had the time and the ability, bitterly and forcibly against that title.
As I have said, the inventor can lock up his invention in his closet, and
keep it there for seventeen years, and deprive the public of it. In the
case of almost every important invention, the same invention is gotten up
contemporaneously by other persons. In almost every important case
litigation has resulted, for the reason that other men—in one instance
sixteen other men—at so near the same time made the same invention
that they had to go into the courts to determine which was the first
inventor.

In view of that fact, and in view, as I have shown, of the benefits of
the patent law (and the wonderful progress of invention is not yet found
out); in view of the indomitable energy and characteristic of our people, is it right that we should give anybody a close monopoly on any invention? I certainly say no, although the provisions of this bill do not
go to that extreme. Upon that point, and upon the question of reissues,
I occupy extreme ground, for which, perhaps, I am entitled to the reputation that I am inimical to the patent law; but I occupy those positions
after very long and earnest consideration. Take, for instance, the patents of the Pullman Palace Car Company, which have been referred
to here; they are in litigation, which, I hope, will continue, and determine the merits and demerits of that controversy. It is an infliction
upon the public, that I will not attempt to measure, that Mr. Pullman
or his company should have, by virtue of anything, although he holds it

by a slender thread, if he holds it at all, a monopoly upon usiug sleep-ing-cars in this country, and that we are forced to make such contracts with him as please him, or else respond to him in damages for the in-fringement of his patent. I do not characterize it as a *crédit mobilier* in the disgraceful sense of the word, but it is a *crédit mobilier* in every good sense of the word. It is a fifth wheel. It is a ring within a ring. I have been trying to demonstrate the fact that it is the right duty of the railroad companies to do their own business, and it does not belong to the Pullman Palace-Car Company, or any fast freight-line, or any other extraneous company. Why should Mr. Pullman, by reason of having a patent on the triangular space in the roof for the upper berth, which is his most important patent, the validity of which is least questioned, prevent the railroad companies from using any kind of sleeping-cars that the public will accept? Take the Westinghouse brake: why should we be obliged to buy any power-brake of Westinghouse or Lockridge or Eames or Smith, and, in order to be able to protect the lives and property of the people, pay them $150 for what it costs them $10 or $12 to make in the first instance, and then be obliged to buy every part that wears out, whether the piston or the rubber tube, from the manufactory of the patentee, and pay him a like profit? To be sure, we are doing our best to get the money out of the people that we have to pay; but I say it is an outrage, and that so far from receiving such profits upon the manufacturing, they ought to receive a reasonable patent royalty, and be subject to the competition in manufacturing that characterizes all other branches of trade.

These remarks are pertinent to this bill, because I will frankly admit that there is couched in the second section a provision that in some in-stances goes to that extent. The delicacy and ethics of being a *tort-feasor* in patent matters is something that does not secure many. The public will infringe a man's patent and become *tortfeasor*, if they can get out of it by reasonable damages, especially if they are forced to in-fringe the patent by the inexorable laws of trade. This first clause is put on to meet that case in certain instances. That is the thing we in-sist upon. These other gentlemen with whom I have been in consulta-tion have tried to narrow it down so as only to meet certain cases, viz, " where it is for the interest of the patentee that persons generally should use his device "—which cuts out Westinghouse and Pullman and others who have established the manufacture, because this is not for their interest. But where a man has a patent on a railroad article which he wants to sell, it is only of value to him in that the railroads use it and not he. In all such cases if a license-fee is established, that shall be the measure of damages, and if one is not established the court and jury shall ascertain the measure of damages.

I will stop to note the ambiguity of the word " same " in the fifteenth line. There is no ambiguity. You cannot read it and construe it gram-matically without making it refer to the license-fee. Brother Christy said if it did refer to the license-fee, he was opposed to the bill. I would oppose that section in every possible way if it did not refer to the license-fee, as he thinks it does not.

Senator CHAFFEE. Then there must be some ambiguity about it.

Mr. CHRISTY. My opinion is it refers to damages, and I understood some members of the committee also to say that it did.

Senator WADLEIGH. That is my view.

Mr. RAYMOND. The bill provides—

If a license-fee has already been established by a reasonable number of transactions of a character applicable to the case at bar, that shall be adopted as the measure of said damages; but if not, then the court or jury shall determine the same.

You eliminate the parenthetical clause and that is what it means. Now, what is the meaning?

Mr. CHRISTY. Leave it to the committee.

Senator WADLEIGH. I think it had better not be left in doubt, at any rate.

Mr. RAYMOND. I do insist, as the most important part of my argument, as the thing which the people of this country and of the eighty-one railroad companies that I represent do insist upon, that by some means we shall be admitted to the use of these devices without having to account for them by this wicked and absurd rule of profits and savings.

Senator MORGAN. My idea of the grammatical construction of the clause is unquestionably that the word " same" refers to damages, but it would be impossible to give it that construction for the reason that the jury cannot ascertain or determine the measure of damages. It is a question of law for the court.

Senator WADLEIGH. But my brother Raymond has insisted that it referred grammatically to license-fee.

Mr. RAYMOND. That semicolon there is a very awkward thing to get over. I did not see that before; but I will submit to the committee an amendment which will make it mean license-fee; for I will state that that part of this section is put in there at our earnest solicitation, and I would make it stronger if it was proper. That to us is the gist of this bill. We must have some relief in this matter. It is a necessity that the public should have relief not only through us (we are simply public servants), but in their own private affairs.

I want to cite another instance covering the Westinghouse brake and the Miller platform, which are of the most valuable inventions now in use by railroad companies, being absolutely essential, we think, to the preservation of life and property. There are about thirty railroad companies in this country that use neither. They are new roads, just built; built on bonds, and they cannot afford it, they say. Why? The Westinghouse brake costs them, say, $150, and the Miller platform, say, $100 a car. The president of the road says, " I cannot afford to make such a contract as that with Mr. Westinghouse and pay this enormous sum to put a brake on all the cars of this road, and I will make an insurance company myself. When I kill a man it costs $5,000; if I cut off his leg it costs ten or twelve thousand dollars. The interest upon that is so much. I can better afford to insure myself against these catastrophes than to buy this invention." It is an actual fact that upon that ground about thirty railroads in this country to-day do not use these inventions. It is the public that are suffering in that respect. The reasoning is good. To be sure it is said you could indict any one of them for manslaughter if you could prove it, but the president of the road has been driven into that position by the close-monopoly character of the title which you give to the patentee and which you should not maintain, in my opinion, in any instance, for it is unquestionably, on the ground of every construction which I have named since the commencement of my argument, contrary to the public policy that the patentee should have a close monopoly upon his patent in any instance.

To give some color for maintaining that he should have such a monopoly, the case of the pin-machine is frequently used. We will suppose that there are fifty manufacturers throughout the country manufacturing pins by hand, and that I have a machine about as big as this table by which I can supply the full demand myself and control the market. The machinery makes the pins and polishes them and puts them into papers, and runs them off into a basket, and you have simply to have one man here, they being supplied automatically, to push the paper as they are rolled up.

The interest of the patentee, the selfish interest, is that he should have a close monopoly upon that machine, and that he should make all the pins that are made in this country; that he should establish the price which we must pay for pins, sustaining his right by the operation of an injunction, and keeping others from using the machine. I respectfully submit if there is any ground upon which he should maintain that title and that close monopoly; it is diametrically opposed to all principles of public policy.

The bill which we introduced in the commencement of the Forty-fourth Congress provided that anybody could use any patented inventions by depositing bonds in the circuit court where he resided, in such sum as the court might dictate, to respond to the owner of the patent. That provision is not in this bill, but these remarks are applicable to this bill, because the second section of the first paragraph of the bill is intended to go to that extent in cases where it is for the interest of the patentee that the invention should go into use. I should like to make it broader. At the same time I submit, although the radical conclusion of my argument goes further than the bill, that I think it is judicious and wise to be at this time conservative in this very radical amendment of the patent laws, and that this is as far as we should go at present. In any amendment which may be proposed to the bill, I do insist and desire that that second clause of the first paragraph should be left in such a way as that, by the use of these patents, the users should be liable only to a license-fee, and not to the profits and savings.

I will notice one or two of the points that have been made during the argument, and only one or two. First, as to Mr. Walker's point as to vested rights. I intended to prepare a brief for the committee on the question of damages, but all is found in Mr. Smith's pamphlet, page 20, and the cases are there referred to which are in point.

I also had it in mind to quote from Cooley's Constitutional Limitations, and from other authorities, which I have not time to do, to show that profits in equity and damages at law in patent suits constitute a single recovery. There is not the difference between them that there is between a horse and a mule, as Mr. Walker has suggested. They are one and the same thing.

The provisions of this proposed statute go not to the right; they do not take it away; but to the manner, mode, and the extent of recovery. There can be no possible question in my mind but that Congress, and even the legislatures of the States under the prohibitions of the Constitution which do not apply to Congress, can alter any such measure, or mode, or extent at will. Especially is that true when the right sought to be enforced is not a common-law right, but is based upon statutory provisions. Patents only exist by virtue of the wise provisions in the Constitution, and, as I think, the unwise present provisions of the statute. I had the honor to submit these considerations to the Judiciary Committee of the House last year, and they passed upon these questions separately, and unanimously sustained these views, and especially because of this additional consideration. The Constitution says that Congress may grant an exclusive monopoly for a limited time. That is not a prohibition upon Congress from making anything less than an exclusive monopoly, but it is an express grant that they may give to the patentee anything less than an exclusive monopoly, on the familiar principle that the greater includes the less. There is no doubt in my mind, and I am unusually strong in my opinion on that point, but that this provision is perfectly constitutional and perfectly wise. At least the most that Mr. Walker contended for is that it is a case not perfectly well settled in the courts, and because of that it should go there to be settled.

Mr. WALKER. You misstate me.

Mr. RAYMOND. I shall not submit to an interruption.

Mr. WALKER. I cannot be misrepresented. I made no such statement of fact. It is not worth while for you to misrepresent me.

Mr. RAYMOND. What misstatement did I make?

Mr. WALKER. You stated that I admitted that it was a doubtful question. I admitted no such thing. I submitted a brief to the committee, and I claimed that, beyond all question, such retroactive effect would be unconstitutional, and the only interest I took in the controversy was that my client should not be put to the expense of going to the Supreme Court to particularly affirm my positive view.

Mr. RAYMOND. I must have been unfortunate in my language if I said that Mr. Walker so stated. I intended to say that the least he could maintain was that it was a doubtful question, not perfectly well settled in the courts. I submit that that question cannot be settled except by the courts. Of course it is a purely judicial question. If the present measure of damages or the present statute of limitations or any other provision of the patent law is unjust, iniquitous, is it proper that Congress, the legislative branch of the government, should decide a judicial question and preclude us from going to the courts to decide this question?

Senator MORGAN. Still there is a great difference between Congress giving retroactive effect to a statute and providing for future difficulties. If it is a question of policy, it is one that ought to be very gingerly dealt with. If they are not under a constitutional obligation to take away from these people rights already accrued, it seems to me a strong and hazardous movement to undertake to do it.

Mr. RAYMOND. I would not take away their right. But I cite the committee to the arguments in Cooley's Constitutional Limitations, and of Chancellor Kent upon retroactive statutes of limitation, starting in the first place with the theory that the statutes of limitation have been looked upon as a disgraceful defense to interpose and have been gingerly granted, whereas they should not be; maintaining the dignity of that defense and of the policy in certain circumstances of making statutes of limitation retroactive. If there is a radical wrong existing under these statutes and it is possible to make the remedy retroactive as to this measure of damages (but not as to the right of recovery) and as to the statute of limitations, it seems to me right as a question of policy to do it rather than perpetuate a wrong of the past, if it is an original wrong. I do not pretend to say that it is settled that these provisions would have a retroactive effect at all. I simply say that they should retroact in view of the necessities of the case if it is possible to make them, and that in my opinion the true policy would be to say nothing in this bill about it at all, but let that question come up and be settled in the courts after the enactment of the bill. I certainly cannot see why, where there is so wide a question of difference and so wide a discretion on these two provisions, we should be precluded from trying that question in the courts.

I will not spend any further time with the suggestions that have been made, except that I want to indorse most emphatically everything that my brother Livermore said about the reissues, and everything that Mr. Hyde said iu his address.

Senator MORGAN. On this subject of the statute of limitations in the first clause of the bill, I think I shall find myself compelled by my convictions to suggest an amendment to it. My idea, suggested perhaps very indefinitely the other day, has been matured since your argument has been proceeding by the use of a word which I think you have very aptly used in the course of your discussion of this section—the word "innocent." I shall propose, I think, that the section shall read as follows:

That from and after the passage of this act no profits or damages in any suit at law or in equity for the innocent infringement of a patent shall be recovered which shall have accrued in one year—

I do not commit myself to one year—

next preceding the commencement of such suit, and all other cases more than six years next preceding the commencement of the suit.

Discriminating between an innocent infringement and one not innocent. As I propose to offer such an amendment, I should like to suggest it for the benefit of the gentlemen of the bar who are present, in order to get their opinion, if they please to give it, in any form that they choose, as to whether the word "innocent" in that connection would be a sufficiently definite word to reach the object I wish to accomplish. Is the word "innocent," as understood in the practice of the patent law in reference to infringements of a patent, a sufficiently definite legal term to be incorporated into a statute of this kind? To say "for the innocent infringement of a patent" would avoid great circumlocution, if we could get one word to embody the idea.

Mr. RAYMOND. I had planned to submit a number of points to the committee on this section, and the first was that the statutes of limitation that have been in force, and that have survived any length of time, have been statutes of repose, and should be; and it is directed to the suggestion which the Senator has just made, as well as to the suggestion which was made the other day, that the statute of limitations should not apply to those who willfully, and more or less maliciously, infringe patents. All these arguments which I have hinted at are characteristic of, and reasons for, statutes of limitations as they have immemorially existed. The history of the statutes of limitation would insist that it should be a positive unlimited statute of repose. As to the first point, of a willful infringement, let me refer you to the cases that have arisen under the bankrupt law, wherein, without any modification of the statute itself, or conditions in the statutue, the courts have held that a willful failure did not come under the statute of limitations at all, and that the statute did not bar against such things; and I am clearly of opinion that where you can establish a willful infringement of a patent, this first section would not apply at all.

Senator MORGAN. There is nothing in the first section to indicate it, because it includes all infringements.

Mr. RAYMOND. The point I am making is that all statutes of limitation are of that character, and courts created the exception, for this reason, that it is impossible to put into the statute provisions and exceptions which will be certain, and clear, and satisfactory. Take, for instance, the bill proposed last winter, which provided that no damages should be recovered except for a year prior to the notice of infringement.

Senator MORGAN. I notice that when the courts create exceptions to any statute of limitations, they always accompany them with jeremiads against the legislature for not having more sense to include that which ought to have been included in the act. I do not say the word "innocent" is a proper word to be used. It looks like a contradiction of terms to say the innocent infringement of a man's patent.

Senator WADLEIGH. Is there any exception to the statute of limitations except what is based on fraudulent concealment that would be cause of action by the defendant?

Mr. RAYMOND. There is no exception in the statute. Even fraudulent concealment is not a matter of statutory provision.

Senator WADLEIGH. I do not think the courts hold so in all the States, but that fraudulent concealment is a cause of action and prevents the statute from running. It is so held in my State.

Mr. STORROW. Not any concealment, but intentional concealment.

Senator WADLEIGH. Fraudulent concealment.

Senator MORGAN. I should like to have the bill passed in such shape as to be understood by the Supreme Court as to what Congress means, and, more than that, I think there is justice in discriminating in the statute in reference to the man who has innocently infringed another's patent and one who has willfully infringed it. I threw out the suggestion in order to get an opinion on that point.

Mr. RAYMOND. The suggestion, which I did not intend to close with until just now, was in reply to the suggestion that was made the other day and assented to by Brother Smith, to take the last clauses of this second section, giving to the courts the widest discretion, and leave it at that. That would be to us a tremendous relief. Judge Drummond, in the swage-block case, reduced the decree from $1,700,000 to $416,000, and said he felt himself bound by the rules of the court and by the statute, and be admitted that that was a ridiculous decree, and said he would have reduced it more if he could.

The point that I am making is, that it is not safe to leave the measure of damages to be established by the courts. This has been demonstrated in the most emphatic way you can demonstrate it by the history of their action in the past. This whole country for the last ten years has been patent-mad, courts and all. They have treated-patentees as they would treat idiots and insane people, and as they used to treat married women. They have built up a series of rules, wherein they prostitute the doctrine of trusts entirely as the measure of damages for recovery, and it will take them ten years to get over it by their own operation. It is a crying necessity that the legislative part of the government should lay down some rules to amend and modify the rules they abide by, and to repeal those rules of practice and recovery which should not obtain at all.

It has been suggested that the inventor should never lose, and the infringer should never gain. The inventor never does lose. What he gets is not a measure of compensation, but is clear gain, is a reward. The infringer should always gain, or there is no reason in law or in logic for the existence of a patent law. I will submit some additional considerations to the committee, and thank the committee for listening to my remarks, which have been heterogeneous.

Senator WADLEIGH. I want to ask you whether or not the parties you represent would prefer this bill to be as it is now, or whether they would prefer to have the period of limitation amended, as suggested by Senator Morgan?

Mr. RAYMOND. If you will pardon me I will say that, as to the duration of the limitation, it does seem that a man should not be precluded and shut off from recovery while he is litigating his patent; that is to say, the only rule that I know of, except a mere general judgment and discretion, and guess at what ought to be the time, is that the statute of limitations should be measured by the time it takes the patentee to establish the validity of his patent, not the time it takes him to go through with that litigation, or, as will be the case after this bill passes, under the second section, to get through with the jury trial, because they will go back to the law for damages, where they belong. Except in very extraordinary cases, which should not be taken into consideration, the longest that equity suits take to establish the validity of a patent, that is, to go to an interlocutory decree, which is just as satisfactory as the final decree on that subject, is about three years; and I can see no reason in the world for making the statute longer than three. But, to cover these exceptional cases, to be conservative in all this radical amendment, and to get a law the enactment of which will be sustained by the people in all its branches, to which no serious or strong objections can be made, I heartily support the provision of the law as it stands, of four years, but certainly there is no good consideration for extending that time in any case.

Senator MORGAN. It is not the doctrine of notice which arises from *lis pendens*. It does not seem that there ought to be any exception to the statute after the party has brought suit.

Senator WADLEIGH. Suppose the party was entitled to a limitation of one year under the law; would not the word " innocent" in that case apply only to a party who did not know that he was infringing a valid patent, and in that case would not the question of innocence or no innocence be one which the court would send to a jury?

Senator MORGAN. The jury would have to pass upon it in every case.

Mr. RAYMOND. Yes, sir.

Senator WADLEIGH. In that case would not your clients be very liable to find juries who would say they were not innocent, and therefore you would have six years instead of four?

Mr. RAYMOND. Six years is not retained.

Senator MORGAN. Six years would be retained in the amendment.

Mr. RAYMOND. That applies to a reversal of the doctrine that now obtains, that we must know the law—must know all the patents that are issued. The word " innocent" would have no legal signification in that section. It cannot be used without some further statutory provision taking away and annulling the presumption of law that he ought to know all about these fifteen thousand annual patents. Then, again, the question of proving what is innocent and what is not is almost impossible.

Senator MORGAN. I inferred from the manner you spoke that it was understood among patent lawyers that there was a clear legal line of distinction between " innocent" and " willful."

Mr. RAYMOND. It is perfectly well understood among patent lawyers when talking together, but it has no legal signification whatever.

I do want to say one word about the suggestion made by Brother Christy that there are three provisions here : one for the annulling of patents, one for the perpetuation of testimony, and one to compel the patentee to bring suit, any one of which, in his opinion, would be sufficient. Take the case of a railroad company sued for a device used on their road twenty years ago. If lucky, we find one or two men who remember what the device was. They make a drawing or a model of it and submit it to the attorneys. They say that is not an infringement; but I do not want that man to commence suit and involve me in litigation and decide the question of the validity of the patent, for I have no interest in that question.

I do not want to commence a suit against him to annul his patent, because I have no interest in that in the world. What I want is simply to perpetuate the testimony of these two men to show that the machine I used twenty years ago was not an infringement of the patent.

Then it was said that the section of the Revised Statutes as to perpetuating testimony is sufficient. It is not for this, if for no other reason, that under that section two persons not jointly interested could not join in such a petition without a statutory provision for it, and the merchants, the dentists, the railroad companies, the farmers, any class of employment in any section would want to join in any petition to perpetuate testimony showing the invalidity of a patent in any suit to annul a patent or to compel a patentee to bring suit. The latter provision was put in for the remedy of an evil which exists in New England much more than in the West, of advertising that a man's business is an infringement of another's patent, for which the proper remedy is to compel that man to bring a suit; for, in that case, you will see it would be ridiculous to give the man against whom the claim is made and upon whom the notice is served the affirmative in a suit wherein the validity of another's patent was in question. The one charging infringement wants to manage his own case, of course, and he wants to be plaintiff in the case where the validity of the patent is concerned. Therefore, the only way to bring that to a point is to enact that third provision, which will compel him to bring his own suit and manage it. There is an undoubted necessity for each one of these provisions, and they are not additional provisions, one lapping upon the other, giving the infringer of the patent or the defendant in a suit additional advantages over a poor patentee.

Mr. HUBBELL. Would he not have a right to an action on the case at common law for damages?

Mr. RAYMOND. Certainly. Then, as to those limitations in the first section of the bill, nothing in the bill prevents the right of an injunction; and if it is the theory of the law that I may have a close monopoly of my pin-machine I have this remedy, and I do not care what the statute of limitations is; I can stop further operations by an injunction. If a man has willfully infringed on my patent, and I know it, I can stop him by an injunction, if I have such a claim as we ought to recognize in the statute.

Senator MORGAN. The patentee might choose to let the infringer go on in the business and prefer not to stop him.

Mr. SMITH. The courts have held that that is an implied license.

Senator MORGAN. If he does not bring suit within a reasonable time?

Mr. SMITH. Yes, sir; if he allows a man to go on and build up his business and allows all his money to be invested. Judge Shipman ruled that it was an implied license.

Mr. RAYMOND. The limitation and the demarkation of what makes a stale claim in patent law, of what would be an equitable limitation, has not been defined by the courts at all, as I am advised by older and better counsel. We are going to make that defense in some important suits in the West for the first time.

Senator MORGAN. It looks to me that there ought to be a statute of limitations of some sort.

The committee adjourned until Monday, November 19, at 1.30 o'clock p. m.

MONDAY, *November* 19, 1877.

The committee met at 1.30 p. m., pursuant to adjournment.

ADDITIONAL ARGUMENT OF J. H. RAYMOND.

Mr. RAYMOND. Mr. Chairman and Senators, in my remarks on Saturday I broke from the line of argument I intended to occupy and did not return to it, and therefore omitted some considerations which are to me of importance. I shall be very brief this morning, simply touching upon points upon which I would otherwise like to dwell.

First, as to what my brother Dodge said, that the amount of the penalty or annual tax upon patents should be $5 and $10 instead of being $50 and $100, as fixed by this bill, I desire to say we are following a well-established precedent abroad by not making it a mere nominal sum. In the second place, the grant of a patent by the government to anybody is at the very least either a taxation upon or a deprivation to the public which should not be continued in any instance unless the invention, which is the subject of that taxation or deprivation, is of sufficient value so that the inventor could well afford to pay a considerable fee. In the third place, we want the feeling to be among patentees that this provision is not one under which they may carelessly put a finger into their vest-pocket and hand over a little small change, but that it is something of importance and dignity, worth enacting by the Congress of the United States, predicated upon a certain value in the patent and its benefit to the public, and that they must put a hand into their pocket-book to get it. In the fourth place, the result of this provision would be the annulling of a large number of patents that are good for nothing except as the bases for infringement suits.

Following the illustration in the argument which I made on Saturday, that there is a large class of patents extant that do not cover practical machines, but contain principles upon which other more practical inventors have builded, and which are infringed by the other patented devices, and are good for nothing except to be bought and speculated upon by those who are justly called patent sharks—those practically useless patents come into value only at a very late stage in their history, after the line of inventions has proceeded to a practical result. Those patents are a curse to the public, and by this fee, if you make it large enough, we would get rid of them before the progress of invention has come to that stage where a practical inventor gets up something which the public desire to use, and patents it, so that the public, buying of him, may buy and pay for what they get with one transaction. That is one of the greatest evils in the present law. Amendments are proposed in the House of Representatives to-day which provide that the government shall not issue a patent unless upon the face of the patent shall be stamped the names and numbers and dates of those patents which are infringed by it, so that the public may have notice. That, of course, is an impracticable provision. There are other provisions of the same character proposed, tending to cure the evil, one of which is that not the user but the vendor, the manufacturer, the middle-man, should be responsible for these damages, which is alike impracticable.

There are certain evils about the patent system for which no one has been wise enough to suggest practical remedies. One evil is that of which I am speaking, and a very great remedy in that direction is to put upon these useless patents (useless except for the purpose of infringement suits) a taxation that shall rid the public of them before the line of invention to which they belong shall proceed to that point where some other man, building upon the first patent, shall create a demand in the public for the thing which he has invented and patented.

I desire also to call attention and to emphasize the argument made by my brother Livermore, that the assignee of an invention should not make oath to the facts of the invention at the time of reissue. Whether the oath he makes is upon information or belief, or upon his positive knowledge, is not a material point. It is in the bill which is presented by myself and my friends to the committee, but at the time that provision was put into the bill, I strongly protested against it, and reserved the right to oppose it before the committee, as I have not time to do this morning. It seems to me an absolute absurdity, ridiculous upon its face, that the assignee of the patent should make oath either on information or belief, on any ground, as to what the inventor did invent in the first place.

Then I revert to the argument I tried to make on Saturday, namely, that these reissues of patents are a greater cause of evil than any other element of the patent law, and that it is impossible for the committee or for Congress to err in the direction of putting restrictions upon reissues.

It was suggested also by my brother Livermore, I think, that a provision should be added to this section as to the measure of damages, adding interest to the judgment until recovery. A judgment, as is well known, carries with it costs and interest; it is a complete, well-rounded thing. A decree in equity, which is the result of most patent suits, is a specific direction, and carries interest with it only when it is included in the decree in express terms. I see no reason for abolishing that distinction between a judgment and a decree. Then, again, it is the policy of the Supreme Court of the United States, as laid down in their rules, and as contained in all the mandates which they issue to the courts below, that interest shall be received upon judgments or decrees according as the statutes and laws of the States from which the cases come shall allow interest or not. That seems to me a well-devised rule, and I see no reason for altering it. In other words, I see no reason for incorporating any provision in this bill as to interest, for the reason that the law and the present rules of the Supreme Court sufficiently and wisely provide for it.

I desire to submit one or two additional considerations upon the first and second sections of the bill. I desire to call attention to, and emphasize, the argument of Mr. Hyde, that if the statute of limitations is too long, it results in absolute loss and irreparable injury to the defendant, whereas if it is too short, it only results in a multiplicity of suits.

I revert again to the part of my argument on Saturday citing the provisions of the bill before Congress last year as to notices. There is no cheaper, no easier, no more effective way by which a patentee can give notice to the public and to infringers of his rights than by commencing suit. I do not think that the committee can err in that direction as to the statute of limitations resulting in a multiplicity of suits, especially in view of the proviso that is in the bill to the effect that if the patentee be in good faith contesting one suit in which is involved the validity of his patent, the rule of law that the plaintiff is always in court may be avoided by the court granting a stay of proceedings in any pending case.

I think I may assume safely that the argument has demonstrated that the statute of limitation which may be adopted by the committee should be an absolute statute, *strictissimi juris*, and that it should be a statute of repose. The history of statutes of limitation which have sur-

vived show that it is policy always to include in statutes of limitation
no conditional provisos that are not absolutely necessary in the special
cases. Are any such conditions in the case before the committee? I
think I may well assume that no provision or condition has been suggested to which insurmountable objections have not in turn been presented; for instance, the words "innocent infringement" would leave
the statute open to wide discussion and debate in the construction of
it, the words proposed not having any legal signification at all; in
which discussion and debate and determination by the court we would
be liable to lose the effect of the statute which is desired by the committee, by Congress, by the public, and by all the gentlemen present.
Then, again, in making a distinction in the statute between the vendor
and the vendee, the middle-man and user, you are simply transferring, if
that provision be adopted, the burden of the present law from the consumer to the middle-man—from one class to another; and it does not
affect at all the real ethics of the case. Now, the patentee has a right
of action against either the manufacturer, the seller, or the user. Because the user in one case is a railroad corporation, or in another case
a large miller, or in another a large manufacturer, he prefers to sue
him. In another case the users are the farmers or the mechanics scattered abroad through the country, whom he may easily black-mail, if the
case is a fraudulent one, or from whom he may easily get damages in a
large amount, if the case is not a fraudulent one, by sending agents
through the country to collect damages from them. You are not remedying the evil any by transferring the burden of it from the consumer
either to the middle-man, the vendor, or the manufacturer.

With that, I leave the subject of a statute of limitations, confident
that the committee will come to the conclusion that no other change is
necessary than such amendments as may be suggested by the discretion
of the committee in shortening or lengthening the time of the running
of the statute. The length of the statute should be determined largely
by the measure of damages which the plaintiff would recover.

I desire to suggest, in that connection, that while now all suits are contested in equity courts, if this second section should be adopted in its
present shape substantially, suits will be brought hereafter on the law
side of the courts, which present a more speedy and satisfactory remedy
than the equity courts now provide; and the necessity for a long statute to avoid pressing an interested patentee would not be the same in
that instance as it is now, whereas the patentee is subjected to long
equity litigation in every case by reason of its offering him so great a
reward.

I come, then, with these brief considerations, to the second section,
and suggest that any provision that may be adopted that would result
in reducing patent royalties and recoveries to reasonable and certain
amounts would benefit inventors by increasing the number of settlements in a degree that I hesitate to estimate. Almost all patent claims
now are fought by those who are able to fight them. I speak of the
public. I do not speak of large manufacturers or railroad companies,
because they employ counsel by the year to advise them in these matters
and they are governed by their advisers as to what the law is; but as
to the public generally, everybody who can afford to do it on general
principles fights a patent. Why? Because the recovery is so ridiculously high at the end, and therefore the demands made by the patentees
are so ridiculously high in the first instance. If the recoveries are reduced to a reasonable and certain amount, like a license-fee, the demands
made in the first instance by patentees would not be anything like so

great, and the number of settlements would be increased in a ratio that I hesitate to estimate.

It was suggested the other day, as I think the argument was put by my brother Walker, that the abolition of profits in equity cases, either entirely or wholly, would be in fact a premium upon torts. That is an *argumentum ad hominem* which perhaps requires some attention. It is equivalent to my saying to the committee that if, in the opinion of the legislative branch of the government, the penalty of death for murder is ridiculously and wickedly excessive, and entirely contrary to the public policy (as undoubtedly is this measure of recovery of profits in equity proceedings in patent causes), if the legislative branch of the government should come honestly to that conclusion as to the death penalty for murder, and therefore should substitute imprisonment for life, would that be a premium upon murder? I do not feel at liberty to make any further argument in favor of the entire abolition of profits in patent cases, or of close monopolies in patents, than is necessary to sustain the second clause of the first paragraph of second section, which I hope will practically have this effect in the particular cases in which those I represent may become interested.

If, then, in these cases the measure of recovery were reduced to the damages—and that is the intention of the first paragraph, although I believe you will come to see that as it reads it does not mean that, and for that purpose I shall submit to the committee some amendments to the second section which will make it plainer in that regard—if in certain cases the recovery in patent litigation is limited to the damages which in turn shall be solely determined by the license-fee, think for a moment what then the patentee would get, and compare his recompense or reward (I care not which you call it for the present purpose) with the recompense that is paid in the theory of reward and of compensation to any and every other product of the intellect, or that is paid for professional service that is created and rewarded by statutory provisions, as for instance the judges of our Supreme Court, the judges of our circuit and district courts, the members of the legislative branches of government, both National and State, and the executive officers of the government. Taking any other instance that you may find where the value of the property in the service is created by statutory provisions and the reward also is created by statutory provisions, I ask the question, would not the damages which the patentee would recover, if limited to his damages, and in turn as the measure of damages if limited to the license-fee, be the best compensated man in the world who holds that kind of property?

In the statement with which I conclude I desire the critical examination and careful criticisms of the members of the committee and the gentlemen present, for I desire to submit some propositions concerning the Paris-green compound case that has been referred to during the argument. I shall be very glad to be corrected if I am mistaken in the statements that I make, for they are strong statements. The patentee of the Paris-green compound for killing a worm that was destroying a large part of the cotton-crop was the first to invent such a compound that would accomplish this and without damaging the cotton. We will suppose that at the time of his invention compounds were known and used which produced like effect, but also damaged the crop to a considerable extent. Go further and suppose that another subsequently invented and patented a compound which did not involve the ingredients or principles of combination of the Paris-green compound, and therefore did not infringe the first patent, and that the planters, for the purposes of defense upon the question of damages in a suit under the first patent, had acquired rights under the second patent. Making that a strong case, then it must be admitted that under the mildest form of the present rules of recovery in equity the owners of the Paris green patent would recover from the planter the full market-value of that proportion of the crop saved by the use of the Paris-green compound which he would not have saved by the use of other compounds subsequently patented.

I go further and give the rather immaturely considered opinion (but I am sure this morning that I am correct therein) that the planter having bought rights under the second patent for the purposes of evading what would be considered the rights of the first patentee, and not for the purposes of use, because from the necessities of the case he is obliged to use the Paris-green compound, the courts would not admit him to the above comparison, but would hold him for the full market-value of the proportion of the crop saved by the Paris-green compound, which would have been lost by the use of any compound at that time public property and free to the use of any one.

Even in the case I stated, where there was a subsequent patent, that would accomplish the purpose, although not so well and perhaps not so economically. The comparison was not between the Paris-green compound and the other patent, although the planter might have bought rights under the other patent, but the comparison is between the results of the use of the Paris-green compound and the results of the use of any other compound which at that time was free to all the public to use and was public property.

Mr. WALKER. Do you mean to say that is law now ?

Mr. RAYMOND. I do, and I say that is the law in the case in which you are interested.

Mr. WALKER. I submit to the gentlem(of the committee that that is a very important statement of law.

Mr. RAYMOND. I ask gentlemen present to criticise that statement of law after I get through. I cite the case of *Emigh* v. *The Chicago, Burlington and Quincy Railroad*, and the swage-block cases, which were decided last May in the Supreme Court. I may say that some of those swage-block cases will go back into the Supreme Court on another question, and it is intended, if possible, to raise the question there. I do not think this is good law, but it has been held so in the cases cited. It has been held repeatedly by Judge Drummond in the Tanner-brake case, which my friend Walker represents, that the comparison was not between the Tanner-brake patent and the other patents which the road had bought the right to use, but it was between the Tanner-brake patent which was issued in 1852 and any other device (the old single brake) which the public were entitled to use at the time of the infringement of that patent. The courts have held this doctrine in cases in which I am interested, and so far as I am aware have not reversed it. This rule is not changed by the provisions of the bill, if only the fact is added that in the cultivation of that part of his crop affected by the worm the planter has made a profit of one dollar, for this abominable rule of profits is repealed only in cases (and I now refer to line 16 of the second section) " where the invention has enabled the defendant to realize an actual profit in that part of his business connected with the use of his invention." If he has not realized an actual profit of one dollar, or more, in that part of his business connected with the use of his invention, then the rule of profits does not apply under the provisions of the statute as proposed ; but if he has made a profit of one dollar or more, the rule of profits, as it now obtains in courts of equity, will apply, unless, perchance, he escapes, as I hope to escape in a large number of cases, through the provision in line 5 of this section, that " where it is for the interest of the patentee that other persons generally should use the same in like manner, the damages, measured by the license-fee, shall apply." I do not think the case would come under this latter provision. If, as in the case of a pin-machine cited the other day, or in the case of a sewing-machine, or sleeping-car, or any other case where there is a close monopoly—that is not a legal term, but the gentlemen present understand perfectly well what I mean—where it is for the interest of the patentee, and he desires to be the only manufacturer, and, in addition to such royalty as his caprice may establish, to reap a manufacturer's or middle-man's profit thereon; if it is for his interest that he should be the sole manufacturer or the sole vendor, then, again, you see, under the provisions of the second section, that it is not for his interest that other persons generally should use the device, as in the case of the Paris-green compound to which I referred. We hope to escape from this rule of profits, because, in the case of railroad devices, it is " for the interest of the patentee," &c., except in the Westinghouse brake, the Pullman palace-car, and a limited number of cases—perhaps there are some half dozen others that I might mention—where they have invested a million of dollars or more in the manufacture, and it is to their interest to maintain what I call a close monopoly in the patent. In the army of inventions that are presented to railroad companies, the man has simply the broad seal of the United States in his hands, and wants us to manufacture and introduce the article. In such a case the license-fee would apply, and, so far, we are getting relief by this bill.

I will submit my amendment, to cure the ambiguity suggested by brother Christy, as to what the word " same " means. I have adopted the language of the pamphlet which was prepared in my office in Chicago by the consultation there, and which was scattered among the members of the profession. It was subsequently altered within the last two weeks, by my consent, to be sure. I have also included another sentence, which is entirely new to our consideration, which came to my mind this morning. I would amend section 2 by striking out, in line 8 (I refer to the bill as printed by the Senate), the words " shall be the same," and by inserting after the word " equity," in said line, the words " shall be the price of said license-fee." I would also amend section 2 by striking out the words " the same," in line 13, and by inserting, in lieu thereof, the words " what would be a reasonable license-fee." That is the intent of what is in the pamphlet prepared at the consultation in Chicago. Then I want to suggest, and it is a new thought to me, to add, at the end of the sentence in line 14, after the word " case," the words " and that shall be the full measure of the plaintiff's recovery." That is what we mean, and we ought to say it. I believe in the old Irishman's maxim, " If you mean it, say it; and if you don't mean it, say so." Then the section would read, commencing with the third line—

or where it appears to the court or jury that, from the nature of the invention, it is for the interest of the patentee that other persons generally should use the same in like manner and pay him a license-fee therefor, the measure of the plaintiff's damages, both at law and in equity, shall be the price of said license-fee, and no account of profits or savings shall be allowed. If a license-fee has already been established by a reasonable number of transactions of a character applicable to the case at bar, that shall be adopted as the measure of said damages; but if not, then the court or jury shall determine what would be a reasonable license-fee from all the evidence in the case, and that shall be the full measure of the plaintiff's recovery.

I have no doubt in my own mind, unless I am very much mistaken, but that was the intent in the original section among those who prepared the bill. If it was not, I should be very glad to be corrected.

ADDITIONAL ARGUMENT OF CHAUNCEY SMITH.

Mr. SMITH. Are you aware that throughout all the discussion here last spring, and in Chicago, I contended that the introduction of the words "reasonable license-fee" was not the sound rule, and that it was an unsound rule, onerous even for the railroad companies that were interested? and instead of saying that that was the understanding, you will see that it was contrary to my views. I have always contended that that is an illegal phrase, and I do not believe, if it is ever adopted, that it would apply to railroad cases.

Mr. RAYMOND. We must certainly understand that the word "same" in the 13th line refers to license-fee, and not to damages.

Mr. SMITH. We discussed the propriety of using the words "license-fee," and finally dropped the phrase throughout the bill.

Mr. RAYMOND. I would be very content to strike out the word "same" and make it "license-fee."

Mr. SMITH. It might lead to this, that in determining what a reasonable license-fee was, you would resort to the advantages which the defendant had derived from the use of the patent, and that it would be reasonable for him to pay the full benefit of what he got. That is one view that might be contended for. The court, in assessing damages, look to the injury of the plaintiff, not to the benefit derived by the defendant mainly, and I have no idea that that rule can be introduced without working greater hardships to the defendant, except in cases of account, than the present rule. I should myself regard it so, and certainly the idea of introducing the words "reasonable license-fee" as an element to be taken into account in determining the damages, was one that we discussed in Chicago, and it was finally dropped.

Mr. RAYMOND. I was absent at my home, you will remember, when the discussion took place on that point.

Mr. SMITH. I remember. I cannot believe it would be your interest to introduce such a phrase as that, because it would carry you at once to the advantages that the defendant had derived as an element to determine what was reasonable for him to pay.

Mr. WALKER. Your idea of the bill, as it now stands, is that that is excluded?

Mr. SMITH. Perhaps not excluded as one means of determining damages, because the courts sometimes look to that. Still it is not a controlling element.

Mr. WALKER. That is only resorted to when the other means fail.

Mr. SMITH. That, I think, is so. The courts have sometimes allowed juries to look at the advantages which the defendant has derived, not as determining the measure, but as one element that might be resorted to in determining the damages. Any rule which introduces the element of a reasonable license-fee would, I think, carry the case just where parties stand in making a trade, and that directly involves the question of advantage to the defendant. Parties meet to trade. The thing they talk about is what value it would be to one party to buy, and how much he can afford to pay for what he is going to get.

Mr. HATCH. Looking at this matter, not from the point of the infringer or the railroad company, but from the point of the inventor, would it not be proper to have the word "reasonable" in the law, so that if there is to be a license-fee assessed it should be a license-fee that would be reasonable? Do you suppose that there is to be an unreasonable license-fee assessed? Consider the inventor, as well as the infringing railroad that comes in and proposes to take what it desires and use it and then settle for it afterward.

Mr. SMITH. The word "reasonable" introduces no idea that the law does not write there without the word. I do not think it is a proper rule to undertake to substitute in courts of law or equity for the phrase "damages," which has a pretty well settled signification. Take the price of an article. Whether you call that the price or the reasonable price, its value to the defendant is not the proper element in these cases of claims for damages. I only meant to say that I thought my brother Raymond had fallen into a mistake in saying that it was the intention at the consultation that the words reasonable license-fee should be used. We discussed that subject very fully, and came to the conclusion that the phrase should be dropped. You will recollect that I suggested here last year that the phrase "license-fee" was misleading, and that no one could tell where it would lead. Our object was, as I understood it, to take away the right to an account in a large class of cases, and limit the parties, both at law and in equity, to the establishment of damages by the appropriate means, recognizing that in a very large class of cases that rule has been already settled to mean an established license-fee. It takes away all danger of excessive recoveries under the guise of profits and substitutes therefor, as I think, the more conservative rule of law in damages where the object of the court or where the inquiry of the court is to view the damages which the party has suffered, and only incidentally what the defendant has realized.

Mr. HUBBELL. You say that where a man has an exclusive right granted to him under the Constitution, where the inventor has not licensed the party, and perhaps does not wish to license him, they are to have the privilege of taking his invention and using it, and then they are to be rated as though he had licensed them, and they are to be assessed on the ground of a license-fee, and not as compensation, or as damages? You use the term "license fee." License-fee would express volition on the part of the patentee, when there is no volition on his part that you should use the invention at all. Probably he has his own ideas and reasons for not allowing others to use his invention at all, and why should they pay him only a license-fee? What right have you to take his invention, in which he has the exclusive right, and rate it on the ground of a license-fee when he is giving no license? What right has the law to do it? What right has Congress to do it, when the Constitution does not give you a limited or restricted right in any way, but says that it shall be an exclusive or an absolute right? Here you would give it this conditional, contingent, and defeasible character by putting the inventor upon the ground of a licensor, when he is not a licensor.

Mr. SMITH. That is the ground where I understand the law now puts him in that case where he has not established a license-fee, because the law undertakes to fix damages by evidence in the case; and in equity it goes beyond that, and says he may recover profits that are clearly to be recovered. We propose to exclude the courts from inquiring into profits, and confine them to damages.

Mr. HUBBELL. Why put a bridle on the judicial power? Why not let them take all the facts and circumstances of the case, as in other causes, and fix that compensation which the Constitution recognizes as a compensation for the use of the invention?

Mr. SMITH. I think we come as near that as possible. Damages at law do not in all cases certainly, and probably in very few cases, reach the whole measure of the plaintiff's injury. There is a great deal of injury in many cases. The plaintiff may suffer a great deal of damage which is too remote to be reached. The law does not undertake to reach all the damage which the plaintiff may have suffered; therefore we wanted to confine the scope of the law as far as possible, and only step outside in the last clause when the rules for damages were plainly so injurious or so excessive in one direction or another as to do injustice. Our object was to make as little change in the law as possible, as we understood it, except in the matter of accounting in a class of cases, and yet place in the hands of the court a corrective power over the results of the rules of law when they plainly did injustice to the parties.

Mr. HUBBELL. The judicial power has that right anyhow.

Mr. SMITH. Not quite. The Supreme Court said in the case I quoted here that the chancellor in equity had a wide scope, but that the rules led to results which made them hesitate about their application, and, as I think, plainly indicated that they had not quite the freedom which sometimes might be desirable. We were seeking to place in their hands greater liberty than they seem now to think they possess.

Senator MORGAN. Mr. Smith, I should like to call your attention, for the purpose of getting the views of the bar and any gentlemen who may see proper to present their views, to this inquiry, which seems to me to affect the question of the statute of limitations and also the question of the admeasurement of damages: A person who uses a patented invention is treated in the adjudications under the patent law as a trustee *in invitum.*

Mr. SMITH. In equity?

Senator MORGAN. Yes, in equity. Now, is it not a principle of the law of trusts that a trustee *in invitum,* who holds under color of title, or who holds in absolute innocence, is not charged with profits unless he has actually realized profits; and ought not that principle of law to be applied to the patent system?

Mr. SMITH. I should hesitate to say that that is a general principle in all cases, but I am quite sure it was the principle which the courts started with in patent causes, and which ought to be the rule in patent causes. That, I believe, answers your inquiry.

Senator MORGAN. That answers my inquiry. It seems to me the adoption of such a principle as that in patent law, both in reference to the statute of limitations and in reference to the admeasurement of damages, would meet a great deal of difficulty that has been suggested here.

Mr. SMITH. I am free to say that the case of *Dean* v. *Mason* shows that no party should be held responsible in equity for profits unless he had made profits, because they there held, if he had not made as much as he ought, he was not chargeable for his lack of diligence.

Senator MORGAN. That would depend upon the motives, the *animus,* with which he took that property. If I take another man's property willfully, knowing it is not mine, out of which he could have made profits, and deprive him of the opportunity of doing so, I ought to be chargeable with everything that that man could have made by a proper use of the property ; but if, under color of title or entire innocency of his right, I take his property, and they charge me as trustee against my will, though I have not voluntarily put myself into that position, I ought not to pay profits unless I actually realize profits.

Mr. SMITH. That, I understand, is the law now; but it does not go so far as the case which you put, as you seem to think it might be carried, or at least it did not until this recent decision in *Mevs* v. *Conover,* 11 Official Gazette, p. 1111. Our object in this provision, if we have happily expressed it, is to bring the court back and limit them to a case where profits have actually been made, the trust attaching (if I can make the distinction plain) not to the invention in the hands of the party, but to his fruits of the use of it. I think the law really was, until the courts pushed it to an extreme, that they never contemplated in the outset just what you expressed in regard to the equitable cases.

FURTHER REMARKS OF J. H. RAYMOND.

Mr. RAYMOND. I desire to thank the committee for the patience and consideration which they have shown me, and I think it proper certainly that the committee should receive the thanks of the public for the great consideration that they have given this important question.

ADDITIONAL REMARKS BY A. H. WALKER.

Mr. WALKER. I wish to say a single word, with the permission of Mr. Storrow, in reference to a point that occurred in the course of remarks here and in regard to another point suggested by Senator Morgan. I refer him to the case of *Livingston* v. *Woodworth*, in 15 Howard, which was a case that came before the Supreme Court, in which this equitable recovery of profits was sought. The circumstances of that case were these: The infringer used unlawfully the Woodworth planing-machine. It was an equity case. On the trial, it turned out that, with proper management, he might have made a dollar a thousand on all the boards he planed. That was one fact. Another fact was developed that he made, in point of fact, only fifty cents a thousand. Mr. George T. Curtis was of counsel for the complainant in that case, and he urged, on the principles of trusteeship, that the defendant was bound as a trustee not only for what he did make, but that he was bound as such trustee to use due diligence to make all he could. He obtained a decree from the court below for the full dollar a thousand. When the case reached the Supreme Court of the United States, the Supreme Court of the United States used almost precisely the same language that Senator Morgan used this morning. The Supreme Court of the United States said this infringer was an innocent infringer, and, being an innocent infringer, he should be required only to pay over in equity the exact sum he received; and if, under any circumstances, it was deemed desirable or proper or just for the complainant to get the full amount he might have received, he should proceed at law, by an action on the case, on the theory that he had been injured to that amount, inasmuch as it was then supposed that every time the infringer planed a thousand feet of boards he deprived the owner of the patent of the opportunity to plane them, and therefore the infringer injured him to the extent of the profit that the owner of the patent might make.

Senator MORGAN. I suppose that would depend upon whether he was there ready with the machine to do the planing.

Mr. WALKER. Exactly. That doctrine never has been held, so far as I know, in any case in this country except in 1857 in the case of *Pitts* v. *Hall*, and a few years afterward in the case of *Seymour* v. *McCormick*, the Supreme Court held that it is of very limited application in actions at law.

Several remarks were made by brother Raymond to which I wish to refer. The idea that the patent law as it now stands makes a man who uses a machine upon which there are two or more patents pay more than once for the benefit he has derived, that is, pay all or a portion of what he has derived, to one patentee, and then afterward be forced to pay all or a portion to another patentee. To enforce that, he has said this morning that the courts held that when the owner of a patent proceeds in equity to recover profits, and when the case is referred to a master to take an account of those profits, the master is directed to take an account of what he would have derived by the use of this machine over and above what he derived by the use of any machine then open to the public and free to the world. Brother Raymond endeavored to exclude the idea that this measure of compensation was not confined to machines open to the public, but machines that were patented and which the infringer had no right to use, could also be set up as a standard of comparison. Now, in point of fact, the Supreme Court never has made an infringer pay two patentees for the same thing. He referred to the case of *Emigh* v. *The Railroad Company*. That is a case in point and illustrates this matter to a dot. The brakes about which we have heard so much, and which are used on almost all cars in the United States, are subject to three patents, the Tanner, Hodge, and Stevens, in their successive order. The Tanner brake was the first successful double brake ever used. Hodge invented an improvement on Tanner, and in addition to the benefit that was conferred upon the public by the invention and patent of Tanner, he conferred another benefit upon the public. Stevens took another step and perfected the art by inventing his particular combination of levers. Stevens's assignees brought suit in equity against the Burlington Road many years ago for profits, and all the profits claimed was the amount of the benefit he had conferred upon the Burlington Road over and above what they would have received by using the next best machine. He did not pretend to recover the entire profit derived from the use of that invention. It was precisely the case of a horse, saddle, and a pair of stirrups. When the Tanner brake was invented it conferred upon the public the horse. When Hodge invented the improvement, it put the saddle on the horse; and Stevens by his improvement added a pair of stirrups to the horse and saddle. A horse is very good even without a saddle or a pair of stirrups, but it is better to ride on a horse with a saddle and stirrups. Now, a saddled horse is better than an unsaddled one, and a saddled horse with stirrups is still better than a saddled horse without stirrups. All that Stevens ever asked in equity is the benefit that has been derived from the use of the stirrups; all that Hodge ever asked on his patent is the benefit derived from the use of the saddle with stirrups. Tanner said, "You have paid for the stirrups and the saddle honestly, and now pay me for the horse which never was claimed by Hodge or Stevens." There does not seem to be any confusion or any injustice in that. All the companies are called upon to pay is the whole, and to pay it to the right men. The value of the horse is divided up into three parts; but in some instances they have paid Stevens and have not paid the other two; in some instances they have paid Hodge, and have not paid the other two. In some instances they have paid Tanner, and have not paid the other two, and in some instances they have not paid anybody at all.

Senator MORGAN. There is not any question on that point when you go into equity, because the master might separate between the three patentees. The question would arise in an action at law for damages.

Mr. SMITH. That has been done by the Supreme Court.

Mr. WALKER. My remark was intended to meet brother Raymond's remark, which I presumed, although it did not intend to create that impression, might make the impression that an infringer is bound to pay more than once for the same thing.

I wish to say just another word about the doctrine of trusteeship and the theory upon which I understand it. Suppose that Senator Booth has got $50,000 in government bonds, and he thinks that he may die. He wants some good man as an executor of his estate, and he makes his will, appointing Jay Gould, of New York, his executor. That of course is a very absurd supposition, but it answers my purpose. He imposes no duty upon his executor except to cut the coupons off the bonds, and pay them over from time to time to the heirs of Senator Booth. Jay Gould says, " I have more points on stocks than any man alive, and I will do better for Senator Booth's heirs than he thought I could possibly do. I will take that money and invest it in some sort of stocks that I know exactly how to manipulate, and instead of making 6 or 7 per cent. a year I will make 50 per cent. per annum, and then I will pay over 25 per cent. of this profit to the heirs, and keep the other 25 per cent. for my trouble." He goes on and the thing turns out as he expected. He makes 50 per cent. per annum. The heirs learn of it and file a bill against him to require him to pay over the $50,000 and the last cent of profit he has derived, on the theory that he is a trustee not only for the exact amount of money which Senator Booth confided to his care, but also for the profit he derived from the use of the money. Mr. Gould puts in an answer and says, " Those heirs could not speculate on Wall street any more than they could fly; they do not know a single point about these things. There is not a man in the world who could have made that money except myself. Is it possible, because I used my remarkable talent and splendid experience in making 50 per cent. upon the investment, that I am bound to pay it over to a lot of people who could not have done it to save their lives ? No ; if I give them one-half that is abundantly liberal." In such circumstances equity says, " That is no defense; you must pay over to the *cestui que trustent* the last cent of money you have derived from its use." The railroad companies have infringed our patents. Take the swage-block patent; that is a remarkable case. I happen to know that the Lake Shore and Southern Michigan Railroad agreed to take out a license for the sum of $1,000, and when they came to pay a thousand dollars they desired to pay it in bonds of their own, depreciated to 90 per cent., so that the owner only would have received $900 instead of a thousand dollars. The inventor would not give the license for that sum, and the railroad never took out a license. He sued them in equity and got a decree against them, for the exact profit which they received, of over $130,000.

Mr. RAYMOND. The doctrine of profits carried it up to $291,000.

Mr. WALKER. That was the doctrine as the master understood it, but not the doctrine of profits as Judge Davis and Judge Drummond understood it. They understood that the master had made errors in applying the law, and cut down the decree more than one half. I say under these circumstances, when that company had the chance to buy that improvement for a thousand dollars some fifteen years ago, and then when they attempted to defeat the patent for a great many years, and finally when the patent was held to be valid and it was held that they were infringers in the Supreme Court this last year, is it an injustice and a wrong that they should be required to pay over to that patentee the exact amount of money they pocketed by the use of the property ?

Senator MORGAN. The difference in the cases is that one is an express trust under seal, and the other is a case of implied trust.

Mr. WALKER. You will see that implied trusts are subjected to the same considerations as express trusts. The distinction exists, but it is not a controlling consideration.

Senator MORGAN. I think in the case of an implied trust a man gets credit for the application of his skill, and in the other case he does not.

Mr. WALKER. If you are right about that, I am wrong. It is my impression that there is no such distinction between constructive and express trusts. I did not quote the illustration as an authority that should bind, but to illustrate the principle. As I understood, there is no such distinction as the Senator indicates between constructive and express trusts. There are many distinctions, but I do not understand that that distinction is laid down. But it is an illustration of our position, that when infringers have derived money from the use of our improvements the highest considerations of equity require that they should pay that money over to the men who own the improvements, and not be permitted to keep nine-tenths of it in their pockets. Particularly in cases where the rights of action have already accrued it is wholly improper and unconstitutional to deprive us of a right to sue for and recover that which the law says we are now entitled to have.

Mr. RAYMOND. I want to say in regard to Mr. Walker's first illustration (of course there is no opportunity for me to cite authorities to sustain my proposition) that the practical trouble is this: We have been presented—not the railroad companies, but all here—with the horse, saddle, and stirrups complete, and we have paid for it and closed our bargain, but find out afterward that the man we were dealing with was only the owner of the stirrups.

ARGUMENT OF J. J. STORROW.

Mr. STORROW. I shall endeavor, Mr. Chairman and gentlemen of the committee, if I have to use any illustrations in the course of the argument, not to refer to anything in which I have, or any one here has, any special personal interest in controversy to-day, because if I undertake to look out for the good of mankind and insist in the first place upon going to my office and looking out of my own window, I am afraid there is a great deal that I should miss and a great deal that I should see in a very peculiar and one-sided manner. I do not expect under this law, and none of us expect, that we shall entirely do away with all cases of hardship. We cannot do that under any system of government which depends upon law and due process of law, that is, rules laid down in advance for the guidance of judges, instead of the mere unrestrained conscience of the judge himself; and yet we would not give up that system, although the practice of an Eastern cadi allows greater mental freedom and in some individual cases perhaps greater justice. There will still be cases, in spite of any changes we make in the law, where practitioners at the Patent Office will impose upon the office and induce it to grant patents which ought not to be granted, where attorneys will get out patents that are worthless, which they know are anticipated, and betray their client for the sake of winning a fee from him, although they know that when such a patent is obtained it will be mere waste paper in his hands, or only useful to defraud the public. There will be cases undoubtedly where defendants will willfully infringe patents. Nay, there will be cases

where rich defendants will band themselves together and say to the
patentee unless he will sell his invention to them at a price agreeable to
them, that they will drag him for ten years through the courts at an expense which is a flea-bite to them but ruinous to him.

I do not look to amendments in the law simply or chiefly to get rid of
those cases of hardship. I do not think that the way to stop abuses of
rights is to destroy the rights themselves. I think we have to look a
little to an educated public and private sentiment which will cause
counsel and clients to understand that though they look to the law to
ascertain what their rights are, they must look to their consciences to
ascertain when and how, to what extent, and in what manner it is
decent and seemly for them to exercise those rights, whether of attack
on the one side or of defense on the other side.

These remarks lead me directly to a consideration which Mr. Senator
Morgan suggested the other day—and it is of a good deal of importance—
the distinction between innocent and willful infringers. It is of importance not only under the statute of limitations, but still more, I think,
upon a good many other questions—questions of damages, or questions
of the amount of recovery against infringers. The difficulty we have
in applying that, or putting that distinction into the statute, is this:
Who is an innocent infringer? We must take the phrase, not in the
moral sense, I think, but in a legal sense: some distinction that can be
seen by the law as distinguished from morals. If a man studies my
patent carefully, with good, competent advice, and concludes that the
machine he is about to build, and, thereupon, does build, does not infringe
my patent, I do not think he has done any moral wrong; yet, certainly,
he is not legally innocent. His fault has been that he misread the statement of my claim, which the court, finally pronouncing the decree
against him, says was so clear and precise and definite that he ought to
have known it and understood it. On the other hand, there is the case
that occasionally, though, I think, not very often, happens, where a man
has invented an improvement himself, and built a machine in accordance
with it, totally ignorant that any one else had previously invented and
patented that improvement. That case may justly be said to be thoroughly innocent morally and I think legally.

Senator MORGAN. I am satisfied the word "innocent" would not be
sufficiently definite.

Mr. STORROW. I go a little further. I cannot make the idea itself
sufficiently definite.

Senator MORGAN. Perhaps the words "knowingly and willfully"
should be used.

Mr. STORROW. The word "innocent" does have in equity a pretty
definite meaning. We know what an "innocent purchaser" is, and the
kind of defense that is set up under that name. There is an element in
those case in equity which cannot be put into patent cases. That
element is this: the innocent purchaser is one who has been led into his
position by some act or omission on the part of the plaintiff. If the
plaintiff has refrained from recording his deed; if he has got an equitable
interest and has failed to bring in the legal title, or put a mark upon the
legal title; if he has made a promissory note payable to bearer; there is
an act or an omission on the part of the plaintiff calculated to lead the
defendant to change his position. We cannot incorporate that into the
patent law, because in these cases there is never any act or acquiescence
by the plaintiff authorizing, or impliedly authorizing, the infringement,
except in a few cases that have been referred to, where a man by long
acquiescence or by sitting by and seeing the work go on seems to ap-

prove it; but for these cases equity already affords a sufficient remedy. The difficulty is, we think, that the idea which, by the word innocence, or some other, we should like to express, turns upon the state of heart, the state of mind, the state of knowledge of the infringer himself. Now, if you require the court and jury in every case, in order to find out whether the statute of limitations applies, to determine the condition of heart and mind and knowledge of the infringer, you make that statute, which ought to be a statute of repose, introduce into the trial of every case where it is invoked an issue of the most difficult and complicated character; you make the question of the application of the statute depend upon the verdict of the jury or the judgment of the court upon the most difficult question, I think, which ever comes before tribunals, a question which relates to the intention and purpose and secret knowledge of the defendant himself. It is for that reason that, although we should like to see the distinction put into the statute of limitations, and we should like to see it put into the section about damages, we have not been able to find ourselves in a position where we could suggest any way in which that end could be reached without, on the whole, doing more harm than good.

Senator MORGAN. My suggestion had reference to the time of the bar : First, that there ought to be a distinction made between those who are knowing and willful infringers and those who are not, in regard to the time of the bar. I think that there ought to be an absolute statute of limitations in regard to these patent suits.

Mr. STORROW. Now let me take a case which is perhaps the most frequent in patent suits, and see if we can apply that distinction in a practical way. Suppose one of the clients of my brother Hyde, who spoke here the other day, and represented the shoe-manufacturers of Massachusetts, to go into market and undertake to buy the latest piece of shoe machinery, with all the latests improvements in it. He buys it at a fair price in the market, meaning to get all the inventions known to the community in that machinery. He does not take the trouble to find out who owns the inventions, but he buys from a party without knowing, except by inquiry from him, and without going to the proper sources of information to find out who does own the invention. He cannot be said to be an innocent purchaser. The man would have the latest invention, and yet he does not mean to take the trouble of finding out who owns it. If a man buys a horse or buys a piece of land in that way, he gets no title. That is only one of a great many cases that arise; and I think you see the difficulty of laying down any rule, which shall be in the nature of a rule, to determine between one and the other.

Senator MORGAN. The case you have stated is where he buys a patented invention.

Mr. STORROW. I have put the case where a man buys a machine, desiring to get the shoe-machine or the reaper with the latest improvements, not knowing or inquiring whether it is patented or not, or inquiring merely of the man from whom he buys it, and, being told that it is covered by his patent, is satisfied, and does not inquire further.

Senator MORGAN. There never was any relief for that in respect to a question of title. A man has to take the risk of every title he buys. There is no doubt about that. If he buys it from the wrong man he is just that far mistaken. There is certainly, however, a very great class of cases to which that idea will not apply. A gentleman mentioned here, and it seems to be a fact, that when the art has progressed to a certain extent, half a dozen men in half a dozen days or half a dozen mouths may become possessed of the idea which is suggested perhaps by the very state of the art. It leads to a further improvement and a most important and valuable one. One of these men takes out a patent for it. Another, living, it may be, a thousand or three thousand miles away, builds a machine and uses it without knowing that the other party has taken out a patent. They are both equally inventors; they are both exercising equally a faculty beneficial to the country; but I think the man who is innocent in that case ought not to be mulcted in damages from the fact that he exercises his ingenuity or skill or ability in the invention or maturity of the machine. There must be cases of that sort that ought to be protected against, it seems to me.

Mr. STORROW. There are cases of that kind, but I do not think they get in the courts and cause trouble very often. I think the amount of damages covered by those cases is very small. Those are the only cases it seems to me to which you can properly apply the idea suggested by the word "innocent." There is one distinction between the different classes of infringers and the different classes of plaintiffs which I think it might possibly be right to make. There is no doubt that many defenses and many claims are, if not exactly malicious in the common-law sense of the word, at any rate oppressive and vexatious. If we could find any way by which the court should be authorized to make a handsome allowance for expenses and counsel-fees against the party, either a vexatious plaintiff or a vexatious defendant, who had made a frivolous and vexatious claim or a frivolous and vexatious defense, it seems to me that would be a step in the right direction. We have considered that matter somewhat. I am not quite prepared to say how it ought to be remedied or whether a remedy ought to be provided. In our circuit we have not had much trouble from that class of suits. In other places I believe they have had.

Senator MORGAN. It seemed to me in regard to the second section that it would be well to modify the language so as to give the power to the court, instead of increasing or diminishing damages at its pleasure, to tax the parties with costs and reasonable attorney-fees and make that in the nature of compensation or in the nature of punishment for the frivolous proceedings or defense.

Mr. STORROW. For my part I should be glad to see that made a part of the section. I think there is one suggestion with reference to that class of suits which I may make. It seems to me, from what I have seen and heard, that that class of suits and defenses more often arises where counsel defend or prosecute the action on shares. I understand that in some parts of the country that is done very much. In our part of the country it is not considered reputable or decent to do it, and it is never or very rarely done indeed.

Senator MORGAN. It ought to be punished criminally in the patent laws, I think.   ·

Mr. HATCH. It is a very common practice in the West.

Mr. SMITH. Some counsel of eminence, I know, have been subjected to considerable scandal on account of this practice.

Mr. STORROW. The scandal is not confined to the patent law, I am sorry to say. I wish it could be put down, and entirely stopped in the whole country.

There is another distinction between this statute of limitations and the ordinary State statutes, which is somewhat onerous upon plaintiffs. If I have a piece of land, or a thousand bales of cotton, or a contract for the payment of money, I know where it is, and I can watch it; I know when my rights are invaded; but if I have a patent right, it is situated, so to speak, in every village in the United States. I cannot watch it everywhere. An infringement may go on for years before I can know of it. We tried to insert some provision to meet cases of infringement which the plaintiff did not know of, but we found we could not introduce any provision which did not seem to lead to greater hardship or injury than the good that would result from it.

Mr. SMITH. When the defendant willfully and falsely concealed the infringement the statute should not apply.

Mr. STORROW. I have no doubt in that case the statute does not run against it. The Supreme Court have so decided. The bankrupt law provides that certain actions must be brought in two years. Under the old bankrupt law, which contained the same phrase, it was decided by Judge Curtis that willful concealment took the case out of the statute, and the Supreme Court, a couple of years ago, affirmed the same doctrine, though there was no word of exception in the statute.

There is another distinction between this and an ordinary State statute of limitations which is of importance. In most of the States, so far as I know, the State statute of limitations does not run if the defendant is out of the State. Under the patent law the plaintiff has got to go everywhere in the United States where a defendant lives, or where any infringer lives, to look him up and to sue him where he finds him, and the statute of limitations runs, although the infringer may live on the other side of the Rocky Mountains. That is onerous, but we have not seen any way to avoid it. We thought the way was to take all these cases together, without viewing any one of them alone, and fix a term of years which we thought on the whole would do the least hardship.

Senator MORGAN. Do you propose, by any section ingrafted on this statute, that the exception shall be determined by judicial decision hereafter?

Mr. STORROW. An exception as to willful concealment may be left to the rules of law administered by the courts, and that, I think, had better be left alone. Any exception which should distinguish between willful and innocent infringement, if you could find a way to do it satisfactorily, would have to be put in by enactment, because I do not think the court would undertake to make that distinction.

Senator MORGAN. I should be afraid to venture on it unless it was the general opinion of the profession that it ought to be done.

Mr. STORROW. We have studied the question, and we have not been able to arrive at any way.

Mr. HUBBELL. How do you know that the court would decide that concealment in patent cases would stop the running of the statute?

Mr. STORROW. Because they have decided it under other laws.

Mr. HUBBELL. That is no rule in patent cases.

Senator MORGAN. It is established upon the principle, I suppose, that no right can be predicated upon a fraudulent act.

Mr. STORROW. That is true. They rested upon the ground that that principle has always been the law in England under the statute of limitations, and they think it a very good rule, and will adhere to it.

Something has been said about the peculiar remedies for patent cases. I am not aware of any remedies given for the infringement of patent-rights different from those given for the infringement of other rights. The old statute (and the present one has impliedly continued it) provides that a patentee may have a jury and bring an action of trespass on the case, and have actual damages for the infringement of his rights. That is no more than a man would have in any case of trespass, or for any disturbance of an easement, or an incorporeal hereditament. Another statute gave equity jurisdiction to cases arising under the patent law, but it did not prescribe what recovery the patentee should have in such suits. It left that to the same principles which for a hundred or two hundred years had regulated equity jurisprudence.

Senator MORGAN. Allow me to inquire whether there is any good reason why the action for damages at law should not be abolished so as to let the parties go into equity for whatever remedies they have in regard to infringements, damages, profits, and everything of the sort?

Mr. STORROW. I do not know that there is any great advantage in an action at law, but I do not see any advantage in abolishing it.

Senator MORGAN. The action at law is abandoned by the profession and by litigants, and why not abolish it?

Mr. STORROW. I know but one action at law within the last ten years actually tried in our circuit. We all go into equity, not because the remedy is so much better, but because the court is more intelligent than twelve jurors.

Senator MORGAN. At all events, you go there.

Mr. STORROW. We go there. I understand in other parts of the country they try actions at law.

Mr. WALKER. We can get the same remedy in equity as at law under the act of 1870.

Senator MORGAN. I think were a patentee to go into court with a patent which was very valuable to the community at large, he would have a better chance for damages before a jury.

Mr. STORROW. He would, but he can get damages in a court of equity.

Senator MORGAN. Then why not go there in the first instance?

Mr. STORROW. We do.

Senator MORGAN. Then why not abolish the action at law entirely, so as to let every party go into equity, and thereby avoid all the difficulty that arises between damages and profits?

Mr. SMITH. I tried an important case at law, I think, in 1865, and I believe that is the last one.

Mr. STORROW. The sugar case?

Mr. SMITH. Yes, sir.

Mr. STORROW. That was taken from the jury before verdict, and turned into a bill in equity, to be heard on the short-hand report of the evidence, with some additions?

Mr. SMITH. Yes; we took it into equity.

Mr. RAYMOND. There are suits at law now pending. Mr. Walker has one that I know.

Mr. SMITH. There are suits pending, but there is no actual trial.

Mr. HUBBELL. How can you establish the possession which equity requires when you have no license-fees and no verdict of the jury? You must show possession in a suit in equity either by a license granted or by its use, or by the verdict of a jury; and if you have neither, how are you going to support a bill in equity?

Mr. SMITH. The patent furnishes sufficient evidence of possession.

Mr. HUBBELL. It must be acquiesced in by licenses. If you can show the verdict of a jury, there is possession; but suppose there is neither, then where is the possession? The *prima-facie* title of the patent the courts have never received as sufficient evidence in equity unless it was supported by a license.

Mr. WALKER. The court might send the issue out to a jury to be tried.

Mr. SMITH. They can send the case out to a jury, as Judge Nelson did, in order to find some issues of fact and to determine whether the judge should issue an injunction or not, and when the jury got back he coolly set the verdict aside and issued the injunction. The courts of equity entirely disregard, I think, the verdict of a jury as being of not much value in establishing the rights in a patent case.

Senator MORGAN. Ought there to be any real impediment in the law to a chancellor determining the extent of the infringement of a patent as well as a jury?

Mr. SMITH. They do determine it every day.

Mr. STORROW. There is not the least difference.

Mr. HUBBELL. They must show the possession by a license.

Mr. STORROW. No, sir; there is no such law at all. The remedies which a patentee has are these: He may bring his action at law, and in that action may recover actual damages. He may bring a bill in equity. In that bill in equity, after the court has sustained the validity of his patent and found that there has been some infringement, the statute provides that the case may be sent to a master to assess damages or to take an account of profits, and he may recover whichever of those two is the larger. That is the settled law on that point. Then at the end of this suit in equity he can have an injunction to prevent further infringement. Now, what the gentleman refers to is this: that if you present to the court at the outset a patent which has neither been adjudicated by a court nor sustained by long use, they will not grant you an injunction until they have fully heard the case on the merits. If, on the other hand, the validity of your patent has been sustained in a well-contested suit or by a very large acquiescence and a great many people paying you royalties under it, the court will consider that that makes a *prima-facie* case, and they grant an injunction *pendente lite*.

Mr. HUBBELL. They will decide it is an infringement, and then send it to a master?

Mr. STORROW. The statute authorizes and the practice is universal to send the case to a master to assess damages.

Mr. HUBBELL. After the court has decided that the patent was infringed.

Mr. STORROW. No account is to be taken unless the plaintiff has a claim. Undoubtedly the patent is not conclusive proof of the claim, but it is put in as making a *prima-facie* case, and is good until rebutted.

Mr. RAYMOND. Is it not your opinion that the predominance of suits in equity over suits in the law courts is on account of the additional recoveries rather than the facilities?

Mr. STORROW. No, sir; I think it is on account of the facility afforded more than anything else.

Mr. SMITH. I am sure that the amount to be recovered does not lead parties to choose equity rather than law. It is impossible to try a suit before a jury and get a decision that is of any real value.

Mr. STORROW. The sugar case that Mr. Smith referred to was tried eighteen days before a jury, and with witnesses brought up, experts, examined on the stand. No twelve jurors will be found in the world who could understand a complicated process of machinery under those circumstances. The only way to try these cases is to take evidence and print it, so that it can be studied by the counsel in preparing their argument, and by an intelligent court in deciding it. It is not the advantage of a larger recovery in the court of equity so much as the mental superiority of the court over a jury.

Mr. HUBBELL. Senator Morgan's idea cannot be carried out unless they say the patent shall be *prima-facie* evidence.

M. STORROW. They have said so.

Mr. HUBBELL. I know the courts have said so, as distinguished from the old requirement of making the patentee prove it useful, but still it is very different. If Congress shall say that the presentation of the title of a patent shall be *prima-facie* evidence of its validity in all respects, then a case could go into equity at once.

Mr. STORROW. I come to the second section. The two rights of recovery which now exist are the right to recover damages and the right to recover profits, and both may be exercised in a suit in equity, or one in equity and one at law. I should be sorry to see the right to recover profits given up. I think that nothing tends so much to check willful infringement as to cause the infringer to understand perfectly that he cannot make a dollar by his violation of the plaintiff's right. At the same time, under the guise of an account of profits, the courts have given an account of what was not properly profits, and we have endeavored by the second clause of this section to bring the rule down exactly to what Mr. Senator Morgan has suggested ought to be the rule, that they were not to be treated as trustees of profits unless they had the profits in their pockets, and that they were to be held accountable only for such portion of the profits arising from the use of a whole machine as were justly due and attributable to the particular element of the machine which belonged to the plaintiff, the same allowance being made for all other elements. That, I understand, ought to be the law now, but it is not, and we have put it in express terms in the second clause of this section which relates to profits. The first clause of this section, in the first part of it, provides that in certain cases there shall be no account of profits.

Although, as I said, I think the account of the profits is very useful in many cases, there are cases where it cannot conveniently be employed, and they are generally stated as cases where the use of the plaintiff's invention does not show itself in profits realized, but rather by greater ease and convenience in carrying on the business, or as some incidental or collateral advantage. An illustration once put by the Supreme Court is the case of a patent switch, so contrived that if the switch is misplaced the train will not be thrown from the track; it costs more to build and to repair than the old; it requires as many switchmen; but some day it may save life. The patentee ought to be paid, but how can the gain in dollars to the railroad that uses it? There is another difficulty in ascertaining profits by an account in the case where the use of the plaintiff's invention is not the main purpose, the substance of the defendant's business, but is only some subsidiary and merely incidental matter. It is absolutely impossible by any rule of accounting that can be devised to trace through a complicated business and find out just how much of the ultimate results are due to a particular device employed. We have endeavored to meet that difficulty by saying, in the class of cases referred to in the first provision of the section, that no account of profits shall be taken, but the plaintiff shall have his damages merely. As to the first part of that provision, referring to cases where the patentee has shown by his acts and manner of dealing with the patent that it is of that class, no doubt exists in the mind of the gentlemen who have considered it that the clause properly expresses a just rule. As to the second class, where there have not been dealings enough to determine whether the patentee has elected to treat his patent as of that class, then we have undertaken to say that the court or jury should ascertain from the nature of the invention itself whether it is one in which, although the patentee has not yet set up such a course of dealing, he must necessarily set it up.

The objections which have been made to that I do not think lie so much to the principle of it as in the suggestion that the clause is so drawn that the courts may abuse it, and hold the patentee as coming under that class, when, truly and justly, it is not for his interest and not his desire to use his patent in that manner, but rather to manufacture the article himself and sell it. It has seemed to us, with one alteration which has been offered, that, of all the suggestions made, none of them met the alleged difficulty or expressed the principle more clearly than the words we have used; and it has not seemed to us there would be any serious difficulty in the construction of the claim as it now stands. Mr. Christy and Mr. Hatch made the suggestion that after the word "damages," in the eighth line, "and pay him a license-fee therefor, the measure of the plaintiff's damages," we should insert the words "for infringement by using, but not by selling;" so that it would not apply to a case where a defendant has made a patented article and sold it where there would be no difficulty in ascertaining the profits, but to the case where he has used it.

Senator MORGAN. You seem to think that the difficulty lies in the ascertainment by the jury, or the court, whether the patent ought to be classed with those for which a license-fee ought to be charged ?

Mr. STORROW. Yes, sir.

Senator MORGAN. Could it be obviated by requiring that the Commissioner of Patents, when the patent is issued, should define that ?

Mr. STORROW. No, sir; that would be the worst possible tribunal, because, when a patent is issued, you cannot tell what is the use to be made of it; and such a decision would always be *ex parte.*

Mr. RAYMOND. Do you understand that the words "the same" refer to damages?

Mr. STORROW. I will come to that. I was going to discuss that somewhat at length; but it has been discussed so much by Mr. Smith in the last hour that I do not think I need add anything. It seems to me unquestionable that it refers to damages; but it does not seem to me to be very material which it refers to. The object of going to the court or jury is to find how many dollars the defendant is to pay the plaintiff. Now, to say to the court or jury you are to determine how many dollars the defendant is to pay from all the evidence in the case, or to say to them you are to determine the measure of the amount from all the evidence, and then by multiplication ascertain that number of dollars, seems to be much the same thing. It is like saying to a man, you shall have four pecks of potatoes or you shall have a bushel-basket full. What the court and jury have got to begin on is all the evidence in the case; what they have got to result in is a verdict or decree; and the more things you interpose between the two, the more ways they have got to go up-hill and come down again, the greater chances there are for the court or jury to lose their way and go wrong.

We have added to this section, in the last clause but one, a provision that the court may increase or diminish the amount of recovery which has been arrived at by the rules. One suggestion which was made was, suppose we put that in alone and leave out everything else? The answer to that is that the court in arriving at the amount of the plaintiff's recovery does not take abstract principles, but is governed by rules of law; and the difficulty which we reach is that, although in estimating damages probably the rules of law are right, yet, in estimating profits to which that clause of the section applies, the courts have found themselves fettered by rules which they themselves have declared lead to hard and onerous results. We thought that, in order to give the courts full power to break away from those rules, in the first place we must say, as we have in the distinction between savings and profits, that that rule was wrong, and then say that, after the verdict had, or the decree rendered in accordance with the established rules of law, "if you clearly think it is unjust or improper, you may have additional power to change it." We thought under that provision they would exercise the power. This is not entirely a new experiment. The old act of 1793, I think, provided that the plaintiff should recover three times the usual license-fee. Then the statute was changed to provide that he should recover three times his actual damages. Then in 1836 that was repealed, and it was provided that, after a verdict of the jury had found the actual damages, the court might multiply it by three. The construction which the courts have put upon that generally is that the actual amount of damages found by the jury was presumed to be a perfect, exact, and entire compensation, and that they would not increase it except in cases of malice or vindictiveness. I am not aware of any cases, though possibly there may have been some, where it has been increased for any other cause. We have thought fit to re-enact that and give them power both to increase and diminish; because if you merely gave them power to increase, that might seem not for the purpose of justice, but of vindictiveness and malice. Giving them the power to increase or decrease would seem to be for the purpose of justice.

Mr. RAYMOND. Is there not this distinction about the meaning of the words "the same" in the first paragraph, that in the first part of it, namely, where the person has established a license-fee, by his own commercial transactions that shall be the measure of his recovery, whereas you define the words "the same" in the second paragraph, where no license-fee is established, to mean his damages? Without any reason, therefore, you allow such other rules as the courts do sometimes adopt in addition to the rules of the license-fee in estimating the damages to come in. My idea was, whether the license-fee was established or not in the cases described in that first paragraph, that the license-fee should be the measure of the damages independent of any other consideration, while it is a fact that sometimes in cases at law they have ascertained the profits of the defendant as one element from which to establish the damages of the plaintiff, when the license-fee was not established. My point is that the word "same" should be consistent with the other part of the section, and limit him to the license-fee, which is not a license-fee established in the light of profits, but a license-fee established on the basis of commercial transactions, just such a license-fee as he would have established himself if he had gone at it to do so; that in one case you allow other elements, profits, or savings, and what not, for the estimation of his damages, whereas in the first case, as is contemplated in the second clause, you allow the same elements only to enter into the license-fee.

Mr. SMITH. If you call it a license-fee, under the rule it is to be used just as damages would.

Mr. RAYMOND. But still that is a technical license-fee, and you cannot, I understand, go into an account of the profits.

Mr. HUBBELL. My understanding is that it fixes the amount of damages on the basis of the license-fee.

Mr. RAYMOND. That is exactly the thing I am after, damages as assessed on the basis of the license-fee, where it is the basis exclusively.

Mr. STORROW. When we were discussing this matter in Chicago we had present a gentleman who at first I thought was extremely hostile to patents, Judge Osburn, the leading counsel, I think, for the Michigan

Central Railroad. He had been for many years a judge of the supreme court of Indiana or Illinois. He was present while we were discussing this matter of damages, and had a great deal to say about it, and he finally told us that his experience judicially and at the bar was that the more rules the legislature laid down as to the measure of damages the more trouble they got the courts into, and you had better leave it to the courts on all the evidence rather than to fix a definite rule. I think everybody knows with regard to patents, with regard to compensation for infringement, license-fees, and everything else, the patentee's receipts are be based in a general sense on the value of the invention to the people who want to use them. That is the theory on which the law goes. The patentee has an exclusive right, not because Congress supposes he will exclude everybody from the benefits of it, for such a thing never happened, but because, having the exclusive right, he will immediately proceed to grant licenses and to sell his patent to everybody or to those persons who may wish to use it for a compensation. It is perfectly true, as was said here the other day, that almost everything in this room was the result of a patented process. I think it would be the better way to say that almost everything in this room has been cheapened by a patented machine or a patented process, for it is perfectly true, in the first place, that the exclusive benefit or use of a patent is only given for a limited period to the inventor, and, in the second place, it is known to be true by every one who has had any experience in the matter that the inventor gets but a very small percentage of the public benefit which is derived from the use of his invention. The only way in which the inventor can introduce his invention is to say that he will take but a small portion and let the public get the rest of the benefit. I think it is perfectly well understood among the gentlemen here, as well as by the people, that it is very seldom the inventor gets five per cent. of the benefit derived from the use of his invention. There are cases where one or two per cent. is all they get, and they are contented because they can thus cheapen and so popularize the article. Its original cost may be reduced from a dollar to ten cents, and they know that to let the public get the benefit is the true way to make money, because their time is limited and their object is to introduce the invention while the monopoly lasts rather than afterward.

The theory of that statute is like the universal theory of law that the damage to the plaintiff, the amount of the plaintiff's recovery, is to be based primarily on the market-value of that which the defendant took. Where that market-value has been fixed by the sale of licenses there is no difficulty. But where there has been no sale of licenses, no actual dealing to fix the market-value, you cannot do otherwise than to have some regard to the value of the invention. You cannot make a rule that will fix any other basis in the absence of actual dealing than something or other referring to the value of the invention to users of it.

The next clause in that section which is of importance is the proviso declaring to what cases this section shall apply. That clause was put in by us after deliberation. In the first place, it follows the precedent of all previous statutes relating to patents. The rule of damages and the rule of recovery has been changed from time to time; but in every case the section has been so drawn as to apply to existing causes of action; not only that, but the statute of 1836, which changed the old law, and gave the plaintiff the actual damages, with power in the court to increase it, instead of in all cases three times the actual damage expressly provided that that provision should apply to existing suits; the last section of it so declares. I am not aware that the question ever arose in the courts under that act. I understand there is a case pending now in the Supreme Court, where a question similar to it will arise under the act of 1870, and be argued in the course of the winter; but that precedent being in all the statutes, we thought we might safely follow it without exposing this statute to be overturned as unconstitutional, leaving it to the court in this case, as in all other cases, to determine whether the statute shall be construed to be retroactive, and, if so, how far it shall be retroactive. Our view is that the statute should retroact on existing causes of action, for this reason : The vested right of the patentee does not seem to us to be the right to any particular measure of damages. The right of the patentee is to the exclusive use of his invention. Everything else relates to the remedy for the infringement or invasion of that right. I have no doubt that the legislature, generally speaking certainly, can change the remedy for the invasion of existing rights, so long as they do not by changing it substantially impair the right itself or prevent the party from a free exercise of the full enjoyment of it, and I do not think that there is any sound distinction between a change before the infringement and a change afterward. Can you say that this statute, which declares that the rule of damages shall be what it now is, that the rule of profits shall be one which is clearly just, and which adds to that the provision that the results to which those rules lead may be changed in any particular case where it is necessary to give a just compensation— can you say that a statute which provides all those remedies for the past and which leaves the courts power to issue an injunction against a future infringement, is a statute which so far deprives a man of remedy as to substantially impair the right which the man has in the exclusive use of his invention ? It seems to us it cannot. There is a case which states the whole doctrine, though it is not a patent case. It is *Bronson* v. *Kinzie* (1 Howard, 317). In that case the Supreme Court say :

It is difficult, perhaps, to draw a line that would be applicable in all cases between legitimate alterations of the remedy and provisions which, under the form of remedy, impair the right. But it is manifest that the obligation of the contract and the rights of a party under it may, in effect, be destroyed by denying a remedy altogether, or may be seriously impaired by burdening the proceedings with new conditions and restrictions, so as to make the remedy hardly worth pursuing. And no one, we presume, would say that there is any substantial difference between a retrospective law declaring any particular contract or class of contracts to be abrogated and void and one which took away all remedy to enforce them, or incumbered it with conditions that rendered it useless or impracticable to pursue it.

The committee will bear in mind that we are not discussing the question whether the man shall recover a sum of money which the defendant had previously *contracted* to pay, for any change—the slightest change—in a *contract* may properly be said to impair its obligation, for it is making a new contract. We are discussing the remedy which the law has changed from time to time since the government first created it and gave to the patentee the power to vindicate himself, to protect himself against an invasion of his right. There is one authority which seems to me to have a very strong bearing on this point. In a contract to pay money and interest, the amount of interest to be recovered is to be governed by the law of the country of the contract, because the promise to pay interest is a part of the promise given; but if the promise be to pay a sum of money and nothing said about interest, then the interest you recover is not in fulfillment of the contract to pay, but is damages for its violation. The Supreme Court of the United States have decided (*Foster* v. *Goddard*, 17 Wall.) that in such a case as that the rate of interest to be recovered by way of damages is to be governed by the law of the place of trial and of the time of trial. I am unable to see under that decision why the amount to be recovered for the invasion of a patent right may not be settled by the law of the forum, and consequently that the remedy may be changed by the law of the forum.

Senator MORGAN. I do not see any constitutional difficulty at all, since the patent is given by statute.

Mr. STORROW. I do not think that makes any difference, because the patent, once granted, becomes property, and the right of the patentee is vested. But I think that respect for the doctrine of vested rights is so essential to the well-being of society that in case of doubt the legislature may well hesitate to invade it or to do anything which seems like invasion. I think there is another reason. In making a general revision of the patent law we ought to be careful to see to it that nothing creeps in which can be thought to be suggested by a private desire to give a new defense to an existing suit, and so for our moral satisfaction we might change the clause so that the section shall not apply to existing suits.

I think there would be an objection to changing it so that it shall not apply to existing causes of action. Infringements are continuous; and in a suit to be brought next year, if I have got to try the question of damages and profits up to date under one rule, and in the same suit the question of damages and profits or the mode of bringing the suit or taking the account from this date forward under another rule, I shall produce some practical inconvenience which ought not to be incurred unless there is strong reason for it. Those are reasons which have actuated it.

Senator MORGAN. You would confine the saving clause to pending suits, not to existing causes of action ?

Mr. STORROW. That would be the proper change. My own opinion is, that the courts would so construe it that when a contest between parties has become the subject of existing litigation, it has passed out of the legislative control and into the control of the judicial power. I think they would construe it in that way. There is a case very much to the point in 7 Johnson, where Judge Kent and the other judges give their opinion. It was an action against a sheriff for an escape—a technical escape—of a debtor, outside of one set of limits and inside another, if I remember. At the time the action was brought, the statute was so framed that the sheriff was undoubtedly liable. Everybody admitted it to be unjust. During the action the legislature changed the statute, and put it back as it was before; and the Supreme Court held that although the language was strong enough to make the act retroactive they would construe it not to be retroactive, because they would not permit the defendant to have a defense which he had not when he was called into court. They rested that on a line of old English decisions, which were that when the plaintiff had brought a case and had a good cause of action, it would not be just to create a new defense, and send him out of court, and mulct him in costs. So far as the technical objection went, that would not apply here, because our change would not defeat the action, and would only modify the amount to be recovered in it.

Mr. WALKER. Do you understand that this statute does materially change the amount to be recovered in many cases ?

Mr. STORROW. I think that under it the amount to be recovered as profits would be brought back to what we conceive to be the true rule, and not the unjust and erroneous rule which is laid down in *Mevs* v. *Conover*. I think if that case were brought now under the new law, instead of getting fifty cents a cord, the patentee would have got no profits in equity. He would have got his damages, however. Whether those damages would have been greater or less than what he got as profits is a question depending on the circumstances of the case. He would, under section 2, have got damages, and as much more as the court thought necessary in the way of just compensation.

Mr. WALKER. Then in many cases it would materially change the amount of dollars and cents recovered.

Mr. STORROW. There are cases in which it will.

The only other topic that I believe I want to speak about is the question of reissues. The object of a reissue is to correct the patent, and make it what it ought to be. No one who has ever encountered the difficulties of drawing or construing a specification will doubt that that power ought to exist somewhere. It seems at first sight a very simple thing for a man who has made an invention to state it on paper, but that is not all the statute requires. The statute requires that the inventor shall state, in the first place, his invention as distinguished from the machine in which he has embodied it. Then he must state and describe the particular method in which he has hitherto applied it, or the best method known to him for applying and utilizing it. Then he may go on and, in some general language, state his invention in terms which shall distinguish it from every other invention. It is not altogether an easy matter to describe a complicated machine; but that is not the chief difficulty. After a man has described the machine he has actually constructed, the difficulty arises in stating what is the principle of the invention as distinguished from the accidental form in which at that moment the principle has become embodied; and then, afterward, in stating in proper language that which distinguishes his invention from all other inventions; because if he makes his statement too broad, and claims more than his invention, his claim is void for having been anticipated. If he makes it too narrow, everybody who wishes to practice his invention and get the benefit of it can do so and not infringe the claim of the patent, and, therefore, the infringement would not be illegal.

I do not know that I can better illustrate the difficulty of that than by stating to you the questions that arise in a patent cause. The principal question in a patent cause is, in the first place, as to the validity of the patent. That generally depends upon a comparison of the machine the patentee built with a pre-existing machine. The other important question is infringement. That is a comparison of the patentee's machine with the defendant's machine. The whole object of a patent suit with reference to those two questions is to ascertain, from an examination of those different devices, what it is that constitutes the true principle of each, because if you find the principle of one in the other, then the courts hold they are the same. Now, to the trial of a patent cause we bring the services of skilled counsel and experts, the great labor and study and learning of the court, and then we find great difficulty in coming to a result; and when we have got a result through the learning of the circuit court, it comes up here sometimes and is reversed. I think no one can say that the difficulty of stating in appropriate language the true nature of an invention is other than very great. In a patent cause also, when we try it, we have the advantage of seeing before us not only the plaintiff's machine, but various other machines. We have three or four concrete things from which we are to rise up to a statement of an abstract principle. When the patentee takes out a patent, he has not that. He has his own machine, but you know how extremely difficult it is from one single embodiment of a principle to state that principle in the abstract in such terms as to be exactly accurate, covering not too much and not too little.

There is a very good illustration of it which was supplied to me this morning by Mr. Smith, and that is Watt's condenser, his great invention of improvement in the steam-engine. Before his time it had been customary to introduce steam in the cylinder underneath the piston, and, when the steam had lifted the piston up, to squirt its jets of water, condensing the steam, and the partial vacuum created by the condensation let the piston down. The difficulty was, that every time you put the steam in you heated up the cylinder, and every time you squirted the water in you cooled it, and it produced very great loss, and the operation was very slow. He conceived the idea of doing the condensing in a separate chamber, continually kept cool by a stream of water squirting into it, and then opening a communication between the condensing-chamber and the cylinder at the proper moment, and letting the steam escape into the cylinder, to be condensed, and thus produce the vacuum. That was a very great improvement unquestionably. If he was going to describe that, he would have described it as a mode of condensing steam by providing a separate chamber into which the steam could escape, where it could be condensed by squirting water into it. He did patent it, but you will not find to-day a marine engine that will come within this claim; for by the present mode—and it has very many advantages which I need not stop to describe—instead of squirting in jets of water, you surround the condensing-chamber with cold water and keep the chamber cold, and there are tubes traversing it filled with cold water, circulating through them to get what is called a surface-condensation. It is almost inevitable, if Watt had described his invention according to any mode known to him, he would have described the principle of the invention technically to consist of a separate chamber, with a stream of water injected into it. There is a case where the builders of surface-condensers could certainly and clearly avail themselves of the most valuable features of the invention, and yet they probably would not have come in contact with the terms of his claim.

There is another illustration that has been suggested to me, which is a little more complicated, but more curious perhaps in its application. Some years ago a gentleman invented a machine for sewing the soles of boots and shoes to their uppers. It was a modification of the ordinary sewing-machine in this, that instead of the large table of the sewing-machine the plate on which the work is laid was dwarfed to a size about as big as my finger-nail, and it was mounted on the end of a long arm or horn, so that the shoe could be brought down upon it sole upward, and this horn or rest could be inserted in the leg of the boot or shoe, and that served as a table. Then the needle above was forced through the sole and upper and sewed them together, the needle carrying a heavy waxed thread. One thing had to be introduced into that which was not needed in the ordinary sewing-machine. If you ever observed an old shoemaker or cobbler at work, the most striking thing is that after he got hold of the thread he would jerk his elbows and arms out and draw the stitch tight. The reason of that is, that unless the stitch is drawn very tight indeed, the two thicknesses of leather which form the sole will work on each other as they are bent in walking, and will shear off the thread, and the shoe will rip open. To accomplish that result in the machine, they gave to the needle which drew the thread so great a power as to bring on each thread a strain of thirty or forty pounds. Presently they found difficulty in that. The sole of a shoe is not of uniform thickness all around, the front part of the shoe being quite heavy, the shank under the hollow of the foot being quite thin, while when it gets around to the heel the upper leather is folded over two or three times, and the thickness of the counter being added, there is a good deal more leather to sew through. They found if they gave a certain amount of thread to the needle at all times, that where the sole was very thick there would not be thread enough, and it would break; and where the sole was thin there would be too much thread and the stitch was not drawn entirely tight. So they had to devise some method by which they could feed down to the action of the machine exactly the amount of thread needed for the purpose of the work to be sewed together at that exact point, and they did it by this device. The shoe was placed sole upward on the end of that horn. A little instrument called a presser-foot came on the top or outside of the sole and worked up and down at each stitch. When that presser-foot was down on the work, the distance between the presser-foot resting on the outside of the sole and the horn which bore against the inside was exactly the thickness of the leather, and represented the length of thread required at that particular point. This presser-foot was connected by levers and other devices with an instrument which drew the thread off from a reel in just the length required; the higher up it was—that is, the thicker the leather was—the more thread it fed; and if lower down, less was drawn off the reel. That was a great improvement on the old machine. They patented that. By and by the same gentleman who owned that machine undertook to make a machine for fastening the soles of shoes by nailing, and they took a coil of wire and fed it down, seized it by a pair of pincers, and fed it down between a pair of nippers or shears which cut it, and that made the nail. Then they fed down a further length and cut it, and that made another nail. The distance it was fed down determined the length of the nail. If the wire was fed down more, they got a longer nail; and if fed down less, they got a shorter nail. They wanted to cut the nail to the exact length for each part of the shoe, so as not to stick through into the stocking. Whereupon, taking the device of the horn and the presser-foot from the sewing-machine and putting it on their nailer, they connected it with nippers, which drew the wire off the reel, and of course it drew off just the right amount each time. No doubt that machine perfectly utilized all the valuable principles of the invention embodied in the first. In point of fact, in that particular case, it did it so closely that the gentleman who built the second machine took the frame-work of the first, a great deal of the iron-work of one of the original machines to build it with, because his idea was to make merely the changes needed to adapt this principle to its real use; but that required great ingenuity and invention, and for what he so did he got a patent. Then, when they came to look at the specification of the sewing-machine improvement, they found it described as a sewing-machine improvement, and that it did not refer to a nailing-machine, because the thing was not thought of at the time the patent was issued. Therefore, in order to cover the principle of that invention embodied in the second machine, they had to reissue it. They did, and nobody made any objection.

Senator MORGAN. The same gentleman did not possess both machines?

Mr. STORROW. The same gentleman did not make both inventions, but the same people owned and controlled them. By and by, another person came along, a stranger, not interested in those machines, and he conceived the idea of fastening the sole on with screws, screwing it on.

It is on that process that all the shoes of the Army are made now, though on a slightly different machine. He took a coil of wire and cut a screw-thread on it, and fed that wire down by pincers until it came between the nippers, and was screwed into the shoe. When just enough had been screwed in to reach through the inner sole, the screwing stopped and the nippers came together and the wire was cut off. He used precisely the same device of the horn and the presser-foot that the first man used. When the first man went to stop him, and said he was using the principle of their invention, they found the first patent described a sewing-machine, and the reissue described also as a nail-machine, and neither described it in terms applicable to a screwing-machine, so they had to reissue it and state the principles in general terms which would cover that. Thereupon the owners of the first invention brought suits against the screw-machine, and, after consideration and examination, the defendants became convinced that the principle of the original invention covered their machine, and gave up the defense. The right of the first inventor, you understand, was to exclude others from using his invention, and the right of the others was to exclude him from using theirs. He could not use their improvements any more than they could use his devices; so they did what all sensible men do in such cases, joined together, built all the best machines, and divided the profits on terms which they agreed upon.

That is only one instance of many that illustrates the difficulty of, at the outset, stating every application which can be made of your invention.

There is another case which, if I had time enough, I should like to refer to, and which came before the Supreme Court, the case of *Morey* v. *Lockwood*, in 8 Wallace. The two pictures, perhaps, will describe it better than anything I can say. (Exhibiting.) There was the original invention, which was a syringe, consisting of an elastic India-rubber bulb with an induction-pipe at one end and a squirting or eduction pipe at the other. By squeezing it the water was forced out of one, and by relaxing the grasp the bulb expanded and the water was sucked in through the other. By and by a man infringed it by making that, (pointing.) He found that without any difficult change the bulb could be turned at right angles and both tubes could be made to enter it at one end, and by squeezing it as before, and with the same arrangement of the valves, the water was forced out through one, and when it expanded it was sucked in through the other. But the first man had described his invention in the only way known for using it, and it was thought to cover the principle of the invention. The court found that the description of the principle of the invention did cover the old arrangement, but did not cover the new. So the court defeated him in a suit, but said it was a proper case for reissue. Of course the court having said that, when he came to reissue it the defendant saw that he had no defense left.

Now, that case was very curious in another respect, illustrating one of the modes of reissue which we think ought to be practiced. It appears in that case that when the man first came to the Patent Office and stated his claim he stated it in such a way as to include this second principle, but the Commissioner or the examiners in their wisdom said that it was not a proper statement of the invention, and they obliged him, as they have the power and the right to do, to limit his description so as only to describe what was the original form of its application. When the court read the patent it found that it did not cover this second form; but the claim which he had asked for, and which the Commissioner refused, exactly did cover it, and they decided that he could reissue his patent accordingly. That is instructive in this way, because the courts have said two or three times that they will not allow a reissued patent to be valid unless they can see that it, or they will for the same invention as the first by comparing it with the original patent alone; but there was a case where they found themselves obliged, for the sake of justice, to say that the patent ought to be reissued, not in view of what the original patent contained on its face, but on what was contained in one of the papers which the applicant filed at the office, but which the Commissioner said contained matter which ought not to go into the patent.

Now, this being the nature of a reissue, what shall it be based on ? The applicant must bring to the Patent Office, when he comes there for the first time for his original patent, the information upon which a patent can be issued. He must tell the Commissioner what he has done. That is not all he must do. The statute peremptorily requires that he shall state his mode of using his invention, the nature of his invention, the principle of his invention, and what is new and what is old. The statute requires him to make the statement, not generally to the understanding of ordinary men, but to state it specifically in such clear, exact, precise, and certain terms, without prolixity, that everybody can understand it; that is substantially the phraseology of the statute. Now, our idea is that when the patentee has once come to the office, and has laid before the office information which, in the language of the court, in one case, and it is very happy language, substantially indicates rather than correctly defines or precisely states what his invention is; and when he has once substantially indicated that to the office by papers filed there, the government ought to give him a grant in proper terms to cover what he has substantially indicated. It may be the fault of the Commissioner, as in the case of Morey v. Lockwood, or the fault of his solicitor, that he does not get it stated in legal form in his patent; that is, the accident or mistake which he wishes to remedy. Our idea is that if amendment is allowed, it ought to be allowed in such a way that persons having occasion to amend can go back to a description of the invention which the applicant first deposited in the office and reissue his patent, so that its technical phraseology in compliance with the law shall set forth or cover the same, or nothing more than what was substantially indicated by this original application.

We think that the party ought not to be allowed to cover anything which is his own invention unless it was substantially indicated or shown by the papers which he originally filed. There are various theoretical reasons why he should not, but the practical one is that if you allow a man, after an invention has been used for years, to go back and prove by *ex parte* evidence, for these are *ex parte* hearings, and by evidence *aliunde*, generally his own testimony, what he has invented, you would open the door for frauds so monstrous that no legislature should entertain the project for an instant. We think, therefore, in reissuing the patent the party should go back to that information describing the invention which he deposited with the office at the outset. That information seems to us to be the written specification and drawings and not the model. The express requirements of the statute are that he should describe his invention by a specification and drawings, and then in certain cases that he should add a model to "exhibit advantageously" the invention. I think, therefore, the true office of the model under the statute is exactly what Mr. Commissioner Leggett explained the other day, not to define or describe the invention, but to exhibit one embodiment of it, so that it can be conveniently and advantageously seen. I think it is more in the natrue of a verbal explanation, if I may say so, a crystallized and permaneut verbal explanation, not to describe the invention but to enable any one reading the application to better understand it. There is another reason why I think models ought not to be resorted to upon reissues, and that is, considering the manner in which they are kept, the manner in which they are exhibited to every one who wishes to look at them, and the frequency and ease with which they may be tampered with, it would be a dangerous operation to permit a patent to be issued by any model in any important case. A great many models are made of mahogany or bay-wood glued together. For example, it may be very material to a machine whether a certain joint is a rigid joint, permitting no motion, or whether it is a movable joint. Suppose you have a wooden model, glued together, and it is broken, how are you going to tell whether that was a fixed joint incapable of doing certain work or a movable joint capable of doing it?

It is a perfectly familiar fact that there is a lot of rubbish, little fragments of models, gathered in each show-case in the Patent Office, swept up, taken away, and burned. Those are parts of models which are gone. If you were to reissue by models you would reissue by broken models, and have to supply the parts by conjecture or affidavits, and you would open the door to fraud. We think for that reason the word "model" should be stricken out.

Senator MORGAN. In the case of a reissue you would not prevent the Commissioner from looking at the model in connection with the papers?

Mr. STORROW. Not for the purpose of better understanding the thing. I think the true office of the model is to assist the understanding of the person studying the patent, and not to describe and show what the invention is.

Mr. SMITH. There are two places where the word "model" would want to be stricken out.

Mr. STORROW. I will come to the second one directly. Now, the original provision about reissues in the oldest statute on this subject declared that a reissued patent should be subject to the same defenses as the original patent; and although that clause has been left out of all the subsequent statutes, I suppose that, upon a proper construction of it, it is still law, because the defenses to an original patent are that the thing described in the patent was not invented by the patentee before any one else had invented it, or that it had been in public use too long. But that is not all that is necessary for a reissue. You do not reissue a patent to a man to enable him to claim everything that he has invented, or everything of which he was the first inventor. It is only such things as he was the inventor of and entitled to obtain a patent for as were substantially indicated by his original application. One trouble which now exists is that the courts have apparently laid down a rule which, to a certain extent, makes the act of the Commissioner conclusive or of considerable force. Therefore we have undertaken to provide that the Commissioner shall, under certain circumstances, make a reissue of a patent. That is the place where the word "model" first comes in, and may be stricken out. We have declared in the clause where the word comes in the second time that the court may revise that decision upon precisely the same elements that the Commissioner had to go upon. Under the present law there are certain classes of cases, where there are no models or drawings, where the Commissioner is allowed, and, indeed, required, to issue a patent to cover anything which was shown not only by the original papers, but by the affidavits of the inventor, by *ex parte* testimony, *aliunde*, as part of his original invention. Patents have been reissued under that provision; and in

one very important case it is said a patent was very improperly issued.
I do not know how it was about that case, but one can readily see it is
a power liable to gross abuse if the Commissioner may reissue a patent
upon evidence *aliunde* or *ex parte* affidavits without the hearing of other
persons interested, and his decision is to be conclusive. You not only
open the law to gross abuse, but you shut the door against any attempt
to remedy that abuse. We have thought it best to shut the door to
that particular abuse entirely, but leave it open to the courts to see in
all cases that what the Commissioner did was legal and rightful, and
what he ought to have done in reissuing the patent.

Senator MORGAN. In the case you put of the three different applications of an invention, one applying to sewing, one to nailing, and another to screwing a shoe together, is it not a rule of practice in the Patent Office, for instance, to issue the second patent subject to the first,
and the third subject to the first and second?

Mr. STORROW. It is not a rule of practice. As a matter of law it is
subject to such patents as exist. The fact that a machine is described
in a patent, or contains a certain device shown in the patent, does not
exempt it and is not a defense to the charge of infringement of a prior
patent. One of the early cases was a case in Washington's Circuit Court
Reports, where the patent in question happened to be a nail-machine too.
A man had made a nail-machine, and another man had made an improvement on it, and the question was whether the maker of the machine should use it with all the improvements, or whether the maker of
the improvements could use the improved machine as he had built it.
The court said "No; one man owns one thing, and another man owns
another thing, and neither can use what the other owns." Of course the
practical way in such cases is for the two parties to join and make the
same machine, or for the second one, holding the improvement, to wait
until the patent of the former expires.

Senator MORGAN. I put the question with a view to get information
as to whether there is any chance to remedy that difficulty by legislation.

Mr. STORROW. I think not. I do not think any is needed. It is a
matter of law, and the courts remedy it. It was suggested that in issuing a subsequent patent, the use of which involved, or might involve,
the use of any prior invention, the Commissioner of Patents should be
required to state everything that had been done or patented on that
subject, and which prevents the improver from using the machine to
which he wished to attach the improvement. The answer to that is that
it would be perfectly impossible to do it.

Mr. HATCH. I think there is a proposition of that kind before the
House now.

Mr. STORROW. I was not aware that there was. I think if we could
get a Commissioner and about one hundred and fifty examiners, and
give them unlimited time and resources, with attending counsel on both
sides, we might sometimes possibly accomplish it.

Senator WADLEIGH. If they got $25,000 a year apiece?

Mr. STORROW. Yes; when you compare the character of men who
can be paid as examiners, and the character of men who can be paid as
counsel and experts, you must say that you must make some allowance
and difference between the two.

Senator MORGAN. It looks to me as if it was very liberal to give the
inventor of the machine you spoke of as sewing the thread the benefit
of an application about which he did not know anything when he obtained his patent.

Mr. STORROW. It is not that. He gets the benefit of the use of his invention; that is all. If he had sued the subsequent user, the man who made the screwing-machine, he would not get the profits of that whole machine. He would get under the law now so much of the profits as would be due to the use of his invention.

Senator MORGAN. I understood you to say he could get a reissue.

Mr. STORROW. In this way, sir. In this first claim he had described the device as part of a sewing-machine. That device might form part of a great many other machines, and what he got by a reissue was not the right to use an improvement, but the use of that device in any machine to which it is applicable. In French law there are or were certain rights given to the original inventor of a machine to appropriate to himself, or to have some superior right to improvements which anybody else subsequently makes on his machine. We have never adopted that principle. I do not think it is wise or just. I think each man should stand on his own invention.

A good deal of opprobrium has been heaped upon the right of reissue, and I think without due reflection. There is no reason why a man's invention should not be fully protected; if it is introduced into extensive use, it would be grossly unjust to allow a rival in business to substantially appropriate it and escape through a defect in the phraseology of the patent, which yet was clear enough to instruct the infringer how to avail himself of its benefits. In the nailing-machine case that I spoke of, the screw-machine was a direct rival, and owed its existence to the invention appropriated. The hardship comes when a patent has lain dormant, neglected, unworked till the original invention of another has constructed a machine some one feature of which infringes, and then the old patent, which gave rise to no industry of itself, which was incapable of giving rise to any, which was virtually abandoned by its owners without further expenditure of time or thought, turns up to stop the new industry due to another's genius; these are what we sometimes call obstructive patents. Now the annoyance—I may say the public injury—from these patents results from the inherent worthlessness of the inventions, and does not depend upon whether they are correctly set forth in the original or require a reissue; it is because such patents are generally reissued that the outcry is made about reissues. The true remedy is to extinguish such patents altogether, and it is for that purpose that we have introduced the periodical fee of section 11. We believe that this fee will accomplish the desired result, and we see no other way to do it. A more strict insistance by the Patent Office that the invention should be valuable as well as capable of some use would not do, because the mistakes of the office whenever it has attempted to apply such a rule are notorious; it takes several years' experience to determine the value of most inventions. Ericsson's caloric-engine is a good example. He invented it originally as a motor for sea-going vessels. Skilled men insisted and proved that it would not work; still the office granted the patent. It proved worthless for the purpose for which it was especially designed; the skilled men were right; but, with some improvements, the invention was adapted to small engines of one-horse power or thereabouts, and there are thousands of them in use.

The first revision of the patent law, which was made in 1836, was made by your predecessors, the committee of the Senate, and I think it is appropriate and reasonable that this second revision which, 1 think, is the only real revision of substance which has been made since, should be made by a similar committee. We do not think that anything can be changed to advantage in the principles of the law of 1836; I mean the gen-

eral abstract principles. I do not think experience has shown that any
changes in the principle of that law are required. What we have undertaken to do was not to make abstract and theoretical changes in the
law, but to find where, in the administration of that law, certain hardships had crept in which I do not think were part of the principles of
that law, but which I think were opposed to the principles laid down in
it. We have undertaken, where we have found that hardships have
arisen in the administration of the law, to put our finger on that particular thing and apply a remedy to it, and without undertaking to arrange
a whole system and recast the whole of that system or rechange the language of that system in particulars where it had not been found to work
practically bad, although on paper it looks as though it might work
badly. That is one reason why we have put in this bill some phraseology which is not very apt in some instances, not very good English,
not, I think, so good as some of the suggestions which have been made
in the memorandum which I handed to the chairman, but we have been
very loath to change the old language.

Forty years of litigation have settled the meaning of almost every
clause of the statute of 1836; and we are very loath, in order to please
our ears with better English, to change a word of that which has been
settled at so much cost and by so much experience.

A few years ago the English Government undertook to examine the
workings of the patent system. They had a commission which sat for
a good while, and produced the usual large blue-book full of testimony
bearing on the subject. The result of that commission was, that there
were few things so valuable in the laws of England as the patent system; and there is now a bill pending before Parliament, or was last
winter, to correct that system, particularly by establishing patent-office
examinations, making that system conform more to ours. You have not
had the advantage in one sense of a commission and that kind of an examination, but it seems to me you have had what is equivalent, I am not
sure but what it is better.

This proposed law which is now come to you is the result of an amount
of conference among men skilled in it, such as I think never has been
brought before to bear on any subject for legislation. We have had in
our conferences, and you have had before you, gentlemen representing
different, hostile, and opposing interests, special interests, and I think
they presented themselves in such a way as to bring to the notice of us
and of this committee pretty much everything that could be brought
to notice, and that has been extremely useful. I think I may say also
of those gentlemen, and of all others who have assisted in our conferences, that, although when they first came together they thought each
had special grievances to be redressed or special remedies to be applied,
they have brought to our discussion here, as certainly they did to that
in Chicago, which lasted seven days, a spirit of candor, a true professional desire, apart from any interest of a special kind, to make what
they honestly and in their hearts believe to be a real improvement in
the law.

I think I may say properly that what you gentlemen have had before
you at this meeting and upon this bill is not the argument of counsel
debating for any special interest, desiring to aid any special client, but
it is the testimony of men most skilled in this matter as to what they
really, upon their professional honor and consciences, believe to be just
and proper and desirable recommendations of changes in the law, and
you have their testimony that they do not think of anything else which
ought to be added to or changed in the law.

You have had all this work done for you during the summer, and in the manner which has been stated, and you have had it all done under the judicious, the zealous, and the conscientious care of a gentleman whom we in New England delight to acknowledge as the head of our patent bar. I think very few commissions that could be got up, very few examinations of parties interested and skilled in the work, would be of as much weight as what you have had presented in the discussion, and summed up in the bill presented to you. I could thank you, on behalf of myself and my associates, more earnestly than common, for the manner in which you have listened to us; but I think it not so much an occasion for thanks of counsel as it is for congratulations to the friends of the patent system, that you have shown your appreciation of the importance of the subject by the attention you have given to it, and I am sure will continue to give to it till the work is completed.

Judge Abbott, of Boston, senior counsel for the Eastern Railroads Association, has had our amendments for several weeks, has conferred with his clients about them, and he and they approve them and hope that they may become law. He intended to come here to-day to signify so much to the committe; and charged me to say it for him, if he found himself unable to reach here.

AMENDMENT OF J. E. HATCH.

Mr. HATCH. I desire to submit an amendment to take the place of the second section as to profits and damages. My amendment is to strike out the clause providing that the court may increase the amount three times, and to add at the close of the section the following:

On the rendition of any verdict finding damages, or on the confirmation of a master's report in a suit in equity founded upon a patent, the court shall have power to increase or diminish the amount found by the verdict or the master's report, so as to meet the ends of substantial justice between the parties, and may, in its discretion, award to the prevailing party as costs a sum sufficient to compensate the said party for the entire expense of the litigation, or such part of the entire expense as the court may deem proper.

The object of the amendment, in just one word, is simply this, not to change the statute which has existed now substantially since 1836, and every word of which, as Mr. Storrow said, has been determined by judicial decisions, but to add at the close of the section a discretion to the court to increase or diminish, as it may see fit, to meet the ends of substantial justice in a case of peculiar hardship; and certainly those cases do arise and ought to be provided for by some means. Also, to give the court power to award as costs an amount that may compensate the party for an unjust prosecution. It seems to me the amendment would meet everything that it is necessary to meet, and be far better than to add a clause like the second section, which covers a page, nearly, of closely printed matter, with such complicated provisos, that no one knows what it means, for the gentlemen who have presented it have not agreed as to the meaning, and it would require ten years of judicial decisions to determine what it is.

Mr. STORROW. I merely wish to say that, upon the question of an extra allowance of cost, it should not be done in every case at the will of the party, but it should be done where the claim is vexatious or frivolous.

Mr. HATCH. My amendment provides that it shall be done in the discretion of the court.

Mr. STORROW. I should like to have the discretion controlled, for I think in many cases in New York such discretion would be dangerous.

GENERAL SUGGESTIONS.

Senator MORGAN. I think the gentlemen who have appeared before the committee are entitled to great respect for the ability which they have displayed. I wish to say to them that my mind is strongly impressed with the necessity of confining the jurisdiction to one court—the court of equity. If there are objections existing in the statute, or in the proper administration of the patent law, which would militate against that view and show that it would be improper, I would be obliged to any of the gentlemen to address me personally by note or otherwise, or to address the committee, and to suggest those objections. My mind is impressed with the idea that there is no necessity to have a double tribunal, and that the court of equity furnishes plenary jurisdiction of the very best kind for the disposal of every question relating to patents.

Mr. STORROW. It is only a question between law and equity whether the judge is sitting on one end of the bench or the same judge is sitting on the other end.

Mr. BLANCHARD. I should like to ask whether this is to be regarded as the close of the hearing before the committee.

The CHAIRMAN. No, sir; it is not the closing, but the committee propose to adjourn for a week.

Mr. BLANCHARD. I should like to make a few remarks in reference to the matter of reissuing patents upon models. I feel that I ought to say now, with all due deference to what has been said by gentlemen here, that they are leaving out the most important feature upon which a patent can be reissued, and that the committee is asked to pass a law which shall substitute for the most important feature the thing more likely to be correct, more likely to embody the views of the inventor, than anything else can possibly embody them. The committee are asked to leave that out and pass a law which shall compel an inventor to reissue his patent, if he reissues it at all, upon those features which are much less likely to be correct than the model itself.

I should be very glad to have an opportunity to say a few words on this subject.

The committee adjourned until Monday, November 26, at 10 o'clock a. m.

MONDAY, *November* 26, 1877.

The committee met at 10 o'clock a. m., pursuant to adjournment.

In addition to the gentlemen heretofore present, A. J. Todd, esq., ot New York, appeared.

ARGUMENT OF W. WHEELER HUBBELL.

Mr. HUBBELL. Mr. Chairman and gentlemen, I will endeavor to present my views in a brief way to a practical end. Your honors must have observed in the preparation of this bill and in the arguments that the inventors of this country have not been represented here. I suppose there are thirty or forty thousand inventors in this country, for whose benefit, as well as the public generally, in regard to the progress of the useful arts, that provision exists in the Constitution, and you are here in a measure as their guardians and as the executors of that Constitution. It is a right and a power vested in the United States and denied to the States to secure to authors and inventors, " for limited time or times, the exclusive right to their respective writings and discoveries," the declared object being to promote the progress of the useful arts. Inasmuch as the power is denied to the States, and is not concur-

rent in them, the words "exclusive right" must be allowed to have their
full potency and meaning. They mean an absolute right; do not mean
a conditional right; not a defeasible right; but a right absolute in its
nature and exclusive as to the person, limited only by the provision of
limitation expressed in the Constitution, and that is as to time. To
secure that, remedial laws are needed. Without a remedial statute, of
course a naked right has no effect as law. The remedial laws must be
coextensive with that right. You cannot grant the right, on the one
hand, under the semblance of conforming to the Constitution, and then
provide a remedy, on the other, which detracts from the right. That is
well settled by the Supreme Court of the United States. The whole
tenor of this bill is in favor of infringers and in denial of the right which
the Constitution professes to secure, and which, inasmuch as it is denied
to the States, it becomes a duty in Congress to secure; for I hold that
where a power is vested in Congress by the Constitution, and is not a
concurrent right with the States, but is denied to the States, it becomes
a power which it is the duty of Congress to execute. Congress cannot
say that it will pass no patent laws. It has no right to refuse to
execute the duties imposed upon it and denied to the States. It cannot
say that it will pass a patent law that is not commensurate with that
provision of the Constitution. It cannot say that it will deny a remedy
coextensive with the right intended to be secured by the Constitution.
If it is not the true principle that when a power is vested in Congress
and denied to the States it becomes the duty of Congress to execute it,
then this ceases to be a government *de facto* with duties and obligations,
and becomes a mere institution depending upon the will, for the time
being, of Congress. Congress has its duties, therefore. Now, I would
ask you, as the guardians of the inventors of this country, and as the
executors of that instrument, to consider that it is a duty to execute
that patent law and the Constitution to its fullest extent. ·

Laying that down as the fundamental principle, how does this bill
apply to it? Let me read the first section :

> That from and after the passage of this act no profits or damages in any suit at law or in
> equity for the infringement of a patent shall be recovered which shall have accrued more
> than four years next preceding the commencement of such suit.

You have said by the law that the time, which is the only limitation
that should have been authorized to be put upon this grant, shall be seventeen years. You have issued these grants, and the law is now that
they shall be issued for that time ; yet, when it comes to the remedy, you
say substantially, so far as the practical working is concerned, it shall
be restricted to four years. Do you mean to say that a patentee, with
poverty imposed upon him to develop his invention, with the unalter-
able maxim applied to him as to every one, that " necessity is the mother
of invention "—for most of these inventions grow out of the necessities
of the inventors and their poverty in a struggle to benefit themselves
as well as to benefit the world—do you mean to say that he shall have
imposed upon him the duty of bringing a suit every four years? That
would be five suits in the term of that patent against the same infringer.
He would have to bring five suits, provided the infringer commenced
soon after the patent issued.

You cannot reconcile any principle of limitation with the terms of the
grant unless the litigation begins, as it would under the law of 1870,
with the expiration of the patent. The very moment you come to apply
the statute of limitations you detract from the grant you have made,
you deny a remedy coextensive with that grant; and inasmuch as the
infringement is a tort, you do what is not recognized in law, you under-

take to separate that tort into sections. A tort is a continuous act. The law does not recognize any separation in a suit. You may bring a suit in equity. I have had that question tried on a bill which I drew against the Philadelphia and Trenton and Camden and Amboy Railroad Companies. I did not set out whether I sued them jointly or severally. They demurred. That question came up. My answer to the court was that they are in a tort, and they are both jointly and severally liable. The court sustained the bill and ordered them to answer. You cannot separate it; you cannot divide a tort; it is not divisible in law either as to time or as to parties, and it should not be divisible as to any statute of limitations.

The old law of 1870 proceeded upon the correct basis that the statute of limitation should not run during the term of the patent, but should commence to run at the expiration of it; and then it proceeded as other statutes of limitation do, upon a presumption that if the inventor, within six years, did not bring his suit, he either remitted it or was paid. You could not have a statute of limitations run against a note before the note became due. Neither could you properly have the statute of limitations run in a case where the infringement and use would be a tort, for that is not separable in its nature and not divisible. You could not do it upon any known principle of law, and any such statute as that, which has no precedent in a case of this kind, is in clear violation of every principle of law, and is an encroachment upon the term of the grant.

Now, I am not in favor of denying a statute of limitations, but my idea is that it should be consistent with the principles of that law recognized in regard to statutes of limitations, and it should be consistent with the nature of the grant, and consistent with the duty of Congress to protect the inventor during the term of his grant. It should read, therefore, to give the greatest advantage:

That from and after the passage of this act no profits or damages in any suit, at law or in equity, for the infringement of a patent shall be recovered which shall have accrued more than six years next preceding the expiration of the term of such patent, nor upon any suit unless brought within six years after such expiration.

Senator MORGAN. Do you think, if a man had an estate for a term of years in a tract of land, that he ought not to be compelled to sue in an action of trespass *quare clausum fregit*, or any action of that kind, until six years after the expiration of the term?

Mr. HUBBELL. No; because that is a common-law right.

Senator MORGAN. Is not the remedy growing out of or connected with the grant?

Mr. HUBBELL. Yes; the right of remedy must depend upon the grant, but if he sits idly by and sees another person trespass, the law supposes him to acquiesce.

Senator MORGAN. That is what I understood was the decision in patent cases; that acquiescence would be presumed in a case of that sort.

Mr. HUBBELL. There it is a continuous tort. You cannot begin to make the division. Acquiescence could not be presumed, for that reason. In the case of land, the person is supposed to have a personal supervision over the land; he is supposed to be in actual possession of that land, and its nature is such that he can see and determine whether there is a trespass upon it; but it is not so in relation to a patent. The law, in the first place, presumes that every one knows that a patent is granted, because it is a matter of public record, and the government gives notice by publication; but it does not presume that a man knows his patent is infringed, because that would be a physical impossibility.

A man cannot be personally present all over the vast landed territory of this United States to see what is being made of his invention in all the workshops, which he has no right to enter. Furthermore, it does not presume that he is personally present in these places. Why should a man go to New Orleans and look around in all the shops there to see whether his patent is infringed, or why should he go to the State of Maine for that purpose? He cannot do it; the law does not presume it; but in the case of land, where the person has acquired it by contract, and it is limited, of such a character that possession is a part of the title, the presumption is if a trespass is continued for any length of time he knows of it, or he ought to know of it. That is not the case with a patent. You cannot apply that principle to an infringement.

Senator MORGAN. The question I had in my mind was this: You were making an argument to the effect that the constitutional qualities of the grant forbid any statute of limitations in reference to it until after the expiration of the grant.

Mr. HUBBELL. Yes, I think so. You cannot make a grant of a certain power and then provide a remedy which encroaches on that grant on a presumption, which presumption does not exist in fact; because it never has been presumed that an inventor knows of all the infringements, or that he can know of all the infringements that are going on all over this vast country. How in the world can he know it? Suppose he owned all the land in the United States. In such a case as that, would the law presume that he was personally cognizant of every trespass? I do not think it would in that case, but the law has established through custom and from statute law, that a man owns only so much land, which he acquires as he is able to have the personal supervision over it, and therefore, if a trespass goes on for any continued length of time, and if he sees it, or his agent sees it, or there is a reasonable presumption that he does see it, such as improvements going up, he is barred from setting up any defense. But you cannot apply it in the case of a patent; the country is too vast; the infringement is too vast; you cannot get any foothold for its application; and the only safe rule, therefore, is to have the limitation commence from the expiration of the term. That was the old law; and if that is altered so as to encroach upon the time, you are only offering a premium to men to infringe and pirate in secret—an infringement and piracy which they can readily do. You cannot get at it in any way. You could not even have an order. I have seen that tried, where a bill in equity has been brought against a party upon slight proof that he was infringing a patent; but there was no such proof as would establish it in a court. After the bill was filed, the patentee has had to go into court and ask for an order for inspecting those premises. You cannot go in without an order; you cannot go in without permission. The court grants an order, and appoints a master to go and inspect and examine. That is the only way you can get an examination before an action.

The nature of the case is peculiar, and, therefore, it would be exceedingly unfair, and a practical and a clear violation of the nature of the grant, to have any statute of limitation to run during the term of the patent. It would not answer at all, any way. The easiest thing in the world for parties who are always ready to infringe patents is work in some remote place, or in a shut-up place, and say "no admission here," and go on and pirate to any extent, and the patentee would be helpless.

Such a provision would multiply suits also. It is not the policy of the law, where you grant an exclusive right to an inventor, to pursue a course that would overwhelm him with suits. This bill is calculated to overwhelm an inventor with suits. The man had better bury his invention than bring it out and then have imposed upon him the burden of suits that he would have to carry on, if he could. He could not carry them on under the bill; it would be utterly impossible. If he even says a man infringes his invention he is to be sued everywhere over the United States, where any captious man chooses to file a bill against his patent, and how is he to defend them all without money? It may be that all his property is invested in the development of that invention; it is the hope of his life; and here it is attacked on all sides by suits to declare that patent void. It is enough when he brings his suit for the defendant to have the privilege of overturning, if he can, the *prima facie* title which the government has granted on an invention, and to declare the patent inoperative so far as he is concerned. That is enough without subjecting the inventor to suits in all directions which he can not possibly defend, neither in time, nor in extent, nor money, in order to protect his patent from being declared void.

It is all wrong. This whole thing is got up to facilitate the infringement of patents, and it is got up by infringers. They say able counsel have been employed. I have no doubt able counsel have been employed, but they have been employed in the interest of infringers. Now, I am an inventor. I have numerous patents. I am also a lawyer. Therefore I speak here for myself and for the inventors of this country, as they have sent nobody especially here. I heard it suggested that they thought of appointing somebody; I do not know but it was merely a casual suggestion. I feel it my duty to try and protect myself and protect them. That is the reason why I am opposing the bill in the form in which it is presented. I am willing for fair litigation in every respect. Inventors never suffer by fair litigation; it is only by oppressive litigation, which takes advantage of the fact that they cannot be in numerous places at the same time to defend suits, and because they are limited in means. They are required also, if they bring a suit, to give a bond for security for costs, which I will ask you to do away with, and require in lieu of that to file an affidavit that their patent is infringed. I shall take the course here to try to facilitate the carrying into execution of that provision of the Constitution of the United States which Congress is intrusted with as a duty to carry into execution. It is not a privilege, not a power conferred which may be exercised at option, but I say it is a duty, because this is a stable, permanent government, to be kept in existence with all the functions of the government in that Constitution, and expressed as powers. When there is not a concurrent jurisdiction in the States, so that there may be an alternative remedy, and there is not in this case, then that power of government must be exercised. I would ask the modification I have indicated at the beginning of the first section. Then the bill goes on:

Provided, That where a party, in order to preserve his right of recovery, finds it necessary to institute a number of suits involving the same issues, and he is proceeding with good faith and with reasonable diligence to bring one of them to final judgment, any court in which any of them are pending may, in its discretion, grant a stay of proceedings from time to time in any such other cases pending before it.

That recognizes the very difficulty I have just stated, an inability to carry on all these suits coextensively at the same time. That is right. That is done now in equity. I do not know that it is necessary to state it in a statute. However, it does no harm. The section proceeds:

Provided, also, That rights of action existing at the passage of this act may be enforced by suits brought within four years—

I say six years—

thereafter, if not previously barred by laws already existing.

Then I propose to add these words:

And, on the plaintiff filing an affidavit that the defendant infringes his patent, no security for costs shall be exacted from him.

Gentlemen, I have seen this actually occur. These railroad companies infringed a patent beyond all question, and they knew the inventor was poor and could not bring suits all over the United States against these different railroad companies, and they have taken a rule upon him for security for costs, and he, in his inability to furnish it, has been barred and thrown out of court. They have resorted to that expedient. I say that is wrong, and if he will file an affidavit that his patent is infringed, no security for costs should be exacted from him. I think that is fair under the circumstances, because the current costs in the case they have to pay in advance, the fees to the clerk, and so on, and the cost of taking testimony, need not be incurred at all by the defendant until the plaintiff has first taken testimony to make a *prima facie* case, and then they may take the risk for costs, just as they do in other cases, and not where they use a man's invention, and knowing that he is unable to sue for infringements all over the country, take a rule on him for costs and throw him out of court. This was done over here in Baltimore. The Baltimore and Ohio Railroad Company did that, to my knowledge, where they infringed a patent.

Senator MORGAN. What is the extent of the security for costs—the costs incurred by plaintiff?

Mr. HUBBELL. The court exacts security for $200, generally.

Senator MORGAN. It is not limited?

Mr. HUBBELL. It is not limited.

Mr. STORROW. It is only in a case where the plaintiff is a non-resident of the district.

Senator MORGAN. That is on the motion of the defendant.

Mr. STORROW. If the plaintiff does not reside in the district the court may order bonds in such sum as it may require, $200 ordinarily.

Mr. HUBBELL. They grant the rule where the plaintiff is a non-resident, of course; but the patentee cannot be a resident in all the districts of the United States, from the very nature of the case, and he would be liable to have a rule against him for costs.

Mr. STORROW. But if he goes into court and shows that he is unable to comply with it, in the discretion of the court the sum would be remitted.

Mr. HUBBELL. He must either deposit the money, or give security within that district satisfactory to the court.

Mr. STORROW. If the court want it.

Mr. HUBBELL. The inventors cannot do it always.

Senator MORGAN. There is no use of protecting the business in one particular district with security for costs. They might have suits, as the gentleman suggests, in every district of the United States. I do not think there ought to be any security for costs required in such cases.

Mr. HUBBELL. The inventor cannot make a case unless he first submits evidence. He has to pay the clerk and the costs to get his writs in the court, and therefore the court should not exact this bond.

Senator MORGAN. You would allow him to go into equity and file a bill, and swear to this bill?

Mr. HUBBELL. Yes; he has to state that in equity.

Senator CHAFFEE. Do I understand your position exactly? You say it is the duty of Congress to grant these exclusive rights?

Mr. HUBBELL. I say it is the duty of Congress to carry into execution that provision of the Constitution by the enactment of a law which enables the grant of these exclusive rights for a limited time or times, just as the Constitution states.

Senator CHAFFEE. Why do you say it is a duty?

Mr. HUBBELL. Because it is a right which the States and the people, in the formation of the Constitution, have vested in the United States exclusively, and denied to the States. Now, they did it for what purpose? They did it that it might be exercised, not to be neglected.

Senator CHAFFEE. Is it not based upon the public welfare and general polity of the country that these rights should be given or not given?

Mr. HUBBELL. What is the fundamental object? To promote the progress of the useful arts.

Senator CHAFFEE. There is no duty about it. Congress is not compelled; it need not grant any patent for any invention.

Mr. HUBBELL. I think they are compelled by the terms and nature of the Constitution.

Senator CHAFFEE. I do not see why they should be compelled.

Mr. HUBBELL. You might say, upon the same principle, that the Congress of the United States should never pass any law to carry the Constitution into effect.

Senator CHAFFEE. I do not think you take the right ground. Congress shall have power to do so and so; among other things, to borrow money. Now, if the government does not need any money, because Congress has that power to borrow money it should not be compelled to borrow money.

Mr. HUBBELL. But they have power as to taxation. To borrow is simply an alternative power in relation to obtaining money by taxation; but there is no alternative power in relation to this exclusive right in Congress to promote the progress of the useful arts.

Senator CHAFFEE. Congress shall have power to maintain a navy. If they do not think it is for the benefit of the country to maintain a navy, they are not compelled to do so. They shall have power to do all these various things.

Mr. HUBBELL. I think they are compelled to do so, because the framers of this Constitution knew that this country had a sea-coast, that it had a commerce, and they knew that that sea-coast and that commerce, under the ordinary rules of national law, and under the duties of the nation, required protection by a navy. If they think differently they can amend the Constitution and take that out. If this had been an inland territory, so that a navy was not essential, that clause would not have been in the Constitution, the framers would not said, "Congress shall have power to maintain a navy"; but inasmuch as this country had a sea-coast and had a commerce, and it was the ordinary course of nations and national law to protect it by a navy, and as other nations do the same thing, the power is granted by the Constitution, and it is denied to the States. Therefore I say it is the duty of Congress to maintain a navy. As to the extent of the navy, that is a matter of discretion. They may say that "we will have but one vessel, and that is a sufficient navy." I take it that this is a government *de facto*, and that it cannot perish by neglect, and that the powers which are conferred upon Congress and denied to the States, where there is no concurrent jurisdiction in the States, become duties in the Federal Government.

Senator CHAFFEE. It does not appear that way to me.

Mr. HUBBELL. That must be the logical conclusion of law.

Senator CHAFFEE. Perhaps it is; but it does not appear that way to me. These powers are defined here for various purposes. Congress shall have power to do so and so under various circumstances and on various matters. This is one of those powers. Now, then, if it should not appear to Congress to be for the public good and for the benefit of the country to grant these exclusive rights, I do not think they are compelled, or that there is any duty in Congress to do so.

Mr. HUBBELL. I think they are compelled unless it is remitted in some way to the States, so that they may exercise their original jurisdiction and discretion if Congress does not do it. I do not think the States ever gave the power to Congress and denied it to themselves that it should be neglected, because the purpose is set out in the Constitution. Those who framed the Constitution thought that it ought to promote the progress of the useful arts, and after that conclusion and that grant of power Congress has no right to turn around and say it will not promote the progress of the useful arts. Congress is a mere instrument of that Constitution, and it has no right to say, "We will ride above the Constitution and deny the object and purpose for which those powers were granted."

Senator CHAFFEE. I do not think they would ride above the Constitution. If Congress decided it was not for the public welfare, then there would be no violation of the Constitution.

Mr. HUBBELL. The Constitution first and primarily says that to promote the progress of the useful arts Congress shall have power to do this thing. The jurisdiction of that question is not given to Congress, because it is a power accompanied with a conclusion as to the purpose and effect as to the useful arts vested in that Constitution, coextensive with the power which created Congress, and it is not in the power of Congress to turn around and say, "We will conclude it does not promote the progress of the useful arts." The instrument says it does promote the progress of the useful arts.

Senator CHAFFEE. Let me put another case. Suppose Congress thought it was not for the public welfare, or for the benefit of the public, to declare war, would they be compelled under the authority given in the Constitution to declare war?

Mr. HUBBELL. No; because the Constitution does not say it is for the public benefit to declare war. That is left as a matter of discretion. Congress has the power to declare war for cause.

Senator CHAFFEE. Yes; and it has the power also to grant these exclusive rights.

Mr. HUBBELL. Ay, for cause stated. In the one case the cause is stated, and in the other it is not. The power to declare war is a power resting entirely in the discretion of Congress.

Senator CHAFFEE. Certainly.

Mr. HUBBELL. It is not upon any cause stated. If the Constitution had said that for any cause stated, defining the specific cause, then when that cause arose Congress would be compelled to declare war; but that is left entirely in the discretion of Congress.

Senator CHAFFEE. I think it is all in the discretion of Congress.

Mr. HUBBELL. I will put this case. Suppose another nation declares war against the United States, or there is what is recognized amongst nations as a cause for war. Suppose there are ships seized at sea and destroyed by another nation; under the law of nations, there being no redress obtained by this government in the way of compensation, or by any arbitration or negotiation, and this thing goes on, and *per se* it is an act of war, is it not the duty of the Congress of the United States to declare war?

Senator CHAFFEE. I should think probably it would be under such circumstances. Congress would be the judge there themselves.

Mr. HUBBELL. They would be the judge; but in this case it has been predecided by the Constitution that the granting of these rights does promote the progress of the useful arts.

Senator CHAFFEE. I do not suppose that any inventor could compel the issuance of a patent. If there was not any patent law he could not get a *mandamus* against Congress and obtain a patent under the Constitution.

Mr. HUBBELL. No; he could not. The presumption of law is that Congress will do its duty; but, nevertheless, if it does not do its duty, the only redress the people have is to put in another Congress. But that does not make it any the less a duty because Congress neglects it. I say it is a duty to have a patent law, and to grant a patent for time or times. As to the limitation of time, that is in the discretion of Congress. The Constitution does not say anything about that.

Senator CHAFFEE. Then if a member of Congress should vote against the passage of any law granting these exclusive privileges he would be violating his oath under the Constitution?

Mr. HUBBELL. I think he would, for he has sworn to sustain the Constitution, which has that express provision in it for that purpose.

Senator MORGAN. He would certainly be allowed to wait until he got a law that suited him.

Mr. HUBBELL. Yes, sir; he is sent here to make a law to suit him; but I understand the gentleman's question to be that if he voted against any law because he thought there should be no law, he would violate his oath. That is what I understood you to mean by that proposition.

Senator CHAFFEE. No, sir; I do not think that under the Constitution Congress is compelled to pass any law.

Mr. HUBBELL. You cannot compel Congress to do anything.

Senator CHAFFEE. I think it is not a duty of Congress that they are bound to perform.

Mr. HUBBELL. I think it is a Constitutional duty.

Senator MORGAN. The right to the invention does not become a vested right until Congress has passed a law under which and in pursuance of which it may take that form. The Constitution itself does not create the vested right. That is done by act of Congress.

Mr. HUBBELL. No; it is an inchoate right. It is not a common-law right. You cannot say that a man has an alternative common-law right. If you could, then, of course, there would be grounds for your position. It is purely a Constitutional right, derived from the Constitution, through a law to be made by Congress, and, unless that is done, there is no right, as Senator Morgan says.

Senator CHAFFEE. Your argument proceeds upon this basis, that it is the duty of Congress to grant these exclusive rights?

Mr. HUBBELL. It is the duty of Congress to pass a law in accordance with that clause of the Constitution under which these exclusive rights for a limited time or times, taking the words of the Constitution, " can be granted," and become a right or franchise, or property.

Senator CHAFFEE. Then you argue that any limitation of course would be equally unconstitutional?

Mr. HUBBELL. I say that the remedy must be coextensive with the nature of the grant, and that it is unconstitutional, and it has been so decided by the Supreme Court, to deny a remedy or to so hamper and encumber it that it denies the exercise of the grant. The remedy must be coextensive with the nature of the grant, and not an abridgment of it, and not granted in such a way as to be practically impossible to exercise it. That is laid down in Howard's Reports, and it is unanimously conceded by the judiciary. I had a memorandum here.

Mr. STORROW. That is the case I read the other day, the case of Bronson *vs.* Kinzie.

Mr. HUBBELL. It is an elementary principle of law. It was more elaborate than you read, but the whole principle is laid down in 1 Howard, 316.

Mr. STORROW. The principle is laid down. I do not say, however, that your principle is laid down as you state it.

Mr. HUBBELL. It is the same principle. There is no difference. I know you trembled a little in regard to it when you said it could not be considered so and so, but it can be considered so and so. The whole of it is exactly in that case, and the Supreme Court had no doubt about the principle; they were unanimous in regard to it. Blackstone lays it down. Then this section proceeds:

But nothing in this section contained shall revive any right of action already barred, nor prolong the right to sue on any cause of action already existing.

With those modifications which I have suggested, I see no objection to the first section. As to the second section I would strike the whole of it out except the proviso. I will state my objection to that section. It never has been the practice of any government, and I hope it never will be the practice of this government, to undertake to legislate specially for the courts; to put cases stated, and say that, on the cases stated, the law shall be so and so. That is an encroachment upon the judicial power, and it never should be done. If you begin in patent cases to say the law shall be so and so in cases stated, where will the end of it be? You would almost have to frame a new section for every different case that came up here every year. There would be some special case stated, and a special law would be passed in relation to it. I am in favor of leaving that, as it always has been left, to the judiciary. All these are special subjects of legislation encroaching upon the judicial power. I will read the second section:

In all cases where the patentee has elected to license other persons generally to use his invention, in like manner to that in which it was used by the defendant—

Now, how could it be "in like manner to that in which it was used by the defendant," to begin with? The patentee, under the exercise of his exclusive right, elects to give certain persons a license for reasons which apply to him. They may be relations; there may be some obligation during life which induces him to do it; there may be obligations executory, family obligations, by which a party is induced to invest money. These are not all to be paraded out before the public; they are the exercise of the functions within his exclusive right. It is simply the exercise of a right vested in him for reasons which he chooses to keep to himself. Now, how could it be "in like manner to that in which it was used by the defendant"? The defendant is a tortfeasor, an infringer. It is predicated upon perhaps an impossibility. At all events, it is predicated upon a state of things which is not likely to exist at all. In effect it would be simply a license to a defendant to go on and pirate a patent and be subjected to no greater license-fee than was paid by the most favored parties of the patentee, who had risked their capital and everything they had, perhaps, to demonstrate whether or not it was a success. If it is not a success they would lose all they ventured in it. If it is a success, and the business turns out to be profitable, then a tortfeasor, an infringer, is to be allowed to come in and break up that business by setting up an opposition, because it is successful in the hands of those who first ventured their capital in it. Is that right? Is it equity? Is it justice? Is that the exercise of an exclusive right upon any principles that are pertinent to an exclusive right? What right has Congress, when a man has an éxclusive right granted, to come in and say, "If you demonstrate through capital, through any of your friends, through any influences which will enable you to carry it into execution, that it is a successful business matter, therefore any pirate may come in and take away your profits or participate in them by setting up an infringement, and you shall only hold him to the same measure of license-fee." That is denying the terms and the exercise of the right in the grant. It is denying equity; it is contrary to public policy. No patentee would ever be able to get any one to invest any money in the development of his invention if such a law as that existed. Instead of promoting the progress of the useful arts, it would stop it and prevent it and lock it up.

The second section proceeds:

Or where it appears to the court or jury that, from the nature of the invention, it is for the interest of the patentee that other persons generally should use the same in like manner, and pay him a license-fee therefor—

Now, in making laws, you do not always make them for railroad companies. This bill is written from a railroad standpoint. Here is an invention useful on railroads. It is to the advantage of the patentee to use it on all railroads. But this bill is not confined to railroads. You are making a general law here that refers to all cases; and how are you going to make it refer to all cases and not merely to the railroads? Very few men can build a railroad and get a franchise and the stock for the purpose of carrying the patented invention into execution. It becomes a mere incident of the railroad; but it is not so with all inventions.

Where it appears to the court or jury that, from the nature of the invention, it is for the interest of the patentee that other persons generally should use the same in like manner, and pay him a license-fee therefor, the just measure of the plaintiff's damages shall be the same, both at law and in equity, and no account of profits or savings shall be allowed.

That is specious legislation. It is in entire contravention of the judicial power, and would break up a man's opportunities of introducing an invention where the profit or benefit of it was not of that character where its use depended upon personal enterprise, which is the case with ninety-nine in a hundred almost of inventions. Very few inventions relate to these public works, such as railroads. This section was written by a railroad lawyer to suit the railroads. You cannot legislate here for railroads by general laws which are inimical to the interests of patentees in relation to all other matters.

If a license-fee has already been established by a reasonable number of transactions of a character applicable to the case at bar—

That would refer to railroads—

that shall be adopted as the measure of said damages; but if not, then the court or jury shall determine the same from all the evidence in the case.

That is, if a man has an invention applicable to a railroad and they pay him a license-fee, which generally is the case, then other railroads may go on and not pay a license-fee, and if he sues them and obtains a verdict he can only recover the same license-fee that he received from the other roads. That is, they have the privilege of going on and destroying him if they can; and if they cannot, they are only to pay what they would have had to pay if they had taken a license. That would be the grossest injustice. If they choose to set his patent at defiance let them take the consequences. They have the right with other roads in cases of that kind to buy a license. If they can prove that he denied them a license the court shall say, "If you denied them a license upon the same terms that you granted a license to others, then you shall only recover the same amount"; but where it appears that they might have obtained a license upon the same terms and did not, but chose to set themselves to work to destroy his patent, and set the law, the grant, and the Constitution, at defiance, to say that they shall only come in and pay the license-fee is monstrous.

Senator MORGAN. The great danger about that, it seems to me, would arise from the fact that the inventor is compelled oftentimes, perhaps always, to permit a railroad corporation for instance, or any manufacturing establishment, to have the enjoyment of his invention at a very low rate in order to get it introduced.

Mr. HUBBELL. That is often done.

Senator MORGAN. It seems to me it would be a hardship upon him to compel him to abide by that rule after the invention had been developed and proved to be one of great value to himself or the public.

Mr. STORROW. The only question would be whether the transaction, such as you speak of, would be a transaction of a character applicable to the case at bar. The object of putting in these words was to prevent inferences from cases not justly applicable to the case at bar.

Senator MORGAN. That idea was considered?

Mr. STORROW. Yes, sir; and those words were put in exactly for that purpose. The courts have considered precisely that matter, and in cases where they now apply the law the license-fee is the rule, if it is of a character applicable to the case before the court. It may be that the license-fee formerly established ought to be increased, or it may be that it ought to be diminished, according as the circumstances of the case at bar differ from the circumstances under which the license-fee had been granted.

Senator MORGAN. The whole purport of that section is to allow the court to fix what are reasonable damages.

Mr. STORROW. Exactly.

Mr. HUBBELL. The words of the section are—

But if not, then the court or jury shall determine the same from all the evidence in the case.

If you could prove he refused to grant a license, then, of course, you could fall back on the prior license-fee; but the motives of the inventor are not always subject to proof. Therefore you cannot, by specific legislation, lay down any rule in regard to it. Let the judiciary take care of that part of the section, which, perhaps, covers the ground as far as the Constitution recognizes any such ground in relation to common-law rights of property. Continuing with the language of the section, at line 14—

In taking an account of profits in any case, the defendant shall not be charged with any saving he may have made, unless it has enabled him to realize an actual profit in that part of his business connected with the use of the invention.

Suppose he uses the invention in a disadvantageous manner, to the injury of the patentee and to the injury of the character and reputation of the invention, then, of course, he is to be allowed to take advantage of that. The law could not recognize any such thing as that. The law would simply say what in all probability that invention produced as a matter of profit incident to the invention by the use of it with ordinary care and skill.

Mr. STORROW. In Dean *vs.* Mason the Supreme Court decided it just the other way, and that decision has been followed ever since. It is not a question of what the man would have probably made, using the invention with diligence.

Mr. HUBBELL. What the defendant would probably have made by the use of ordinary care and skill.

Mr. STORROW. The court, in Dean *vs.* Mason, decided that was not the law.

Senator MORGAN. The defendant might be so poor that he could not handle the invention at all.

Mr. STORROW. He might be so careless and so ignorant as to be incompetent to handle it. The question is what he did make.

Mr. HUBBELL. By the use of ordinary care and skill. Perhaps the case was not prepared to bring all the points before the court. I never had any difficulty of this kind in these cases before 1857. The second section proceeds:

And the court shall determine what proportion of such profit is due to the use of said invention, and what proportion to the other elements from which such profit was derived, capital and personal services excepted; and the proportion of actual profit so found to be derived from the use of the invention shall be the measure of the profits to be recovered. But if, in any case, it shall appear to the court that the damages or profits, ascertained as above, shall be inadequate to give the plaintiff a just compensation for the injury done by the infringement, or shall be in excess of such injury, the court shall have power to increase or diminish the amount to such an extent as may be just and reasonable.

What is the use, then, in all this special legislation, if that principle is to be adopted? I propose to adopt that principle of law, and not to have all this special legislation in regard to it. The Constitution says that private property shall not be taken for public use without just compensation, and that is as far as those who framed it thought the legislative power ought to go. As to the mode of arriving at a just compensation, that is a judicial question, always depending upon the testimony in the particular case. Therefore, I propose in one section to embrace Senator Morgan's idea about an equity suit in this way:

In all suits in equity the letters patent shall be *prima-facie* evidence of their validity, and be evidence of possession of the invention, and the right to proceed by suit in equity shall not be denied.

I think you cannot take away a man's right to proceed at law or before a jury under the Constitution where the amount is over $20. You cannot deny him the right, but you may put equity upon the same footing and say that the letters patent, having undergone an examination by the court, shall be evidence of possession of the invention. He must show evidence of possession of the invention in some way or other in equity before his bill shall lie, but Congress may declare that the *prima-facie* character of the patient is sufficient for that purpose, and then it will sustain a suit in equity. That, I take it, will be the proper way to put it. I propose to insert:

In the estimation of damages or profits under a patent, the owner shall have a right only to recover a just compensation for his invention used, and his time, ingenuity, and expense bestowed upon the same.

That covers the whole ground. Leave it to the judicial power to determine, not as profits, not as damages actually, but what is a just compensation, under all the circumstances of the case, for the invention used; not for his invention as covered by his patent, not for the whole invention. When I put the question to that old gentleman here, what objection there would be to that, he said it would be very hard on the infringer if the defendant would have to pay for the whole invention under a patent. That is not the meaning of it. The court would not say the man was liable for the whole of an invention, but only liable for the invention used, and I put in the word "used," so that there is no doubt about that. But the judiciary would settle that, of course. A man cannot be sued for the use of a whole patent exclusively, when he uses only one machine infringing the patent.

And his time, ingenuity, and expense bestowed upon the same.

That is the same language now expressed in the act of Congress, to be considered in determining compensation on the question of an extension. They are to take all those elements into consideration.

With a right to a penalty not exceeding three times the amount in all, in the discretion of the court; and due allowance shall be made for the capital, labor, and circumstances under which the invention has been used in the estimation of damages or compensation.

It strikes me that it is perfectly right and fair that due allowance should be made for the capital, labor, and circumstances under which the invention has been used in the estimation of damages or compensation. I will put a case. Suppose an invention is applicable exclusively to a railroad. The inventor not owning any railroad, not being able to organize and put one in operation, cannot derive any beneficial use from his invention. There is the franchise, there is the capital, the engines, the cars, and all the appurtenances and machinery of the road, and this invention is only incidental to all that. It would be very unfair because that invention seemed to work to their great advantage in the saving of expense by its use on that road that no allowance should be made for capital, labor, and the circumstances under which the invention has been used. If it saved the employment of one brakeman, for instance, as in the case of brakes, it does not follow in the estimation of damages that the entire service of that brakeman would be applicable to the use of brakes. He might be useful in many other ways on that road. In the estimation therefore of the damages or of the compensation, they must confine themselves to the nature of the invention, the result that it produces, and all the other inventions or machinery that have to be used in connection with it, so as to make it useful, and to which it is only incidental, and what amounts to "just compensation." You cannot lay down any special law, any general rule, that is going to apply to all cases. That is the function of the judiciary, with all the machinery of the court and the evidence that may be brought forward in a particular case to determine it. They shall not say that this thing is to be estimated on profits as such, nor on damages as such, but taking all these facts, what appears as profits, what it appears that the man has suffered in damages, what his invention appears to be worth in the relation that it occupies in the mechanical world or in relation to other matters in connection with which it has to be applied, what would be a proper proportion of the particular use in relation to the general use; all those are questions for the court, to be summed up and to be made to appear in the one expression "a just compensation," which this section, after winding around all through this special legislation, seems compelled to recognize in these words as an essential principle, and it is the only essential principle. I am in favor of leaving that which belongs to the judiciary, and have the legislative functions expressed in the brief expression as the Constitution recognizes it, "a just compensation," and confine the invention as incidental to capital, labor, and circumstances under which it is used, which I think is fair. Then let the proviso come in :

Provided, That the provisions of this section shall not apply in any case in which a decree for an account or assessment of damages has, at the date of the passage of this act, already been pronounced.

The object of this would be not to disturb a judicial determination.

Nothing contained in this section shall affect the right of the plaintiff to an injunction.

That would be in accord with the right to bring a suit in relation to which the invention is incidental. That is as far as, I think, as Congress ought to go. I do not think you can find that any government, and you cannot find that this Congress, has ever gone into this special legislation in relation to any matters or any rights arising under the Constitution. It is always left, where it properly belongs, to that branch of the government which the Constitution itself creates and recognizes coextensively with Congress, that is the judiciary. We all know the Supreme Court has jurisdiction both of the law and fact, not simply of the law. In all these suits in equity, the Supreme Court has just as much jurisdiction over the facts as it has over the law. Then comes the third section:

In all patent causes, after a decree has been made upon the merits of the case, in favor of the complainant, establishing the validity of a patent finding an infringement thereof by the defendant, and ordering an account or an assessment of damages, the court in which the cause is pending may, if it shall see fit, authorize the defendant to appeal forthwith from such decree; and thereupon, if such an appeal shall be taken and perfected within such time as the court shall prescribe, it shall be competent for the court to stay proceedings in whole or in part during the pendency of such appeal, and to require from the defendant a bond, with sureties, to answer the final decree in the cause, or to dispense with such bond, as it shall see fit.

The meaning of that, I take it, is that, before that account comes in, the case may go to the Supreme Court; that is, you may divide it. I propose to add:

Provided, That the Supreme Court may order an account before finally disposing of the case.

You see the position which it would put the Supreme Court in without such a proviso. The determination of the amount of the decree is within the jurisdiction of the Supreme Court. They take jurisdiction of both the fact and the law. Suppose when the case went up, where the decree of the lower court had been in favor of the patent, and they had ordered an account, but the account did not go up with the record, and the Supreme Court sustained that patent, the case goes back again to the court below with the patent sustained. It has, therefore, to go up to the Supreme Court again on the account for damages. That is not right.

Senator MORGAN. Where would you find the original jurisdiction of the Supreme Court to pass upon that after the account had been ordered? It would be the exercise of original jurisdiction necessarily if the Supreme Court, after decreeing that the patent was valid and the parties were entitled to recover, should order an account to be taken by the master in the court below, or by its own clerk, or by a special master. Whenever that report came back to the Supreme Court, in acting upon that, it would be necessarily exercising original and not appellate jurisdiction, and it has no such original jurisdiction, as I understand it, under the Constitution.

Mr. HUBBELL. When it comes from the master, it goes to the court below. That court make upon the report of the master a decree of damages. Now, if either one on the other parties appeal from that, you would have two appeals in one case. The Supreme Court would not like to submit to a thing of that kind. That would go up to the Supreme Court, and they might increase or reduce the damages. It would go up as a second appeal in the same case, which is never done. The Supreme Court will not entertain a case at all now, until it is finally and totally disposed of in the court below.

Mr. STORROW. That is the reason of the section, so as to meet precisely that thing.

Mr. HUBBELL. Exactly; but what right have you, when the Supreme Court has established a practice which they are able to conform to, to say to the Supreme Court, "We will appeal half of this case up, and, if it is necessary to bring the other half at another time, we will bring up the other half"? I say this, that you cannot require them to pass finally upon the case unless the account comes up; so that they may order it, "provided the Supreme Court may order an account before finally disposing of the case." I say that you should not legislate for the Supreme Court of the United States in that way, but should leave it to their discretion to order up the account; and when they make a judicial decision, let them make it upon the whole case, as they do now. If they say upon any preliminary hearing that they may order, or upon the record that this patent is invalid, and that it ought not to be sustained, that this decree must be reversed, it is unnecessary to send an account; let them make that interlocutory decree and send the case back again, but do not compel them to have two decrees in one case before they can get to the end of it. That does not exist in any practice of the Supreme Court of the United States, and I do not think it is right for Congress to impose any such obligation as that upon a co-ordinate department of this government. It is never done.

Mr. STORROW. Cases not infrequently come up twice in the Supreme Court on an appeal from the decision of the court below, declaring that the patent is invalid and no account ought to be taken, or in a partnership case declaring that an account shall be taken; and, when that question comes up on an appeal, the Supreme Court says an account ought to be taken, and then the case goes back for the account to be taken; or an appeal may be taken where the account was not taken on the principles enunciated in the mandate. The case may come up two or three times.

Mr. HUBBELL. The whole case may come up two or three times, but not half a case.

Senator MORGAN. In the case of the Galveston Railroad Company vs. Cowdry the case came up twice; first on the question of the priority of mortgages, and second on the account.

Mr. STORROW. It not infrequently happens. The established practice of the Supreme Court is—and I do not think anybody ought to change that—that when a question is once deliberately passed upon and settled it cannot be reopened, and it is only new questions which arise subsequently that can be reopened.

Senator MORGAN. I made that suggestion because, as I understood it, Mr. Hubbell proposed an amendment by which the Supreme Court would order an account to be taken pending a cause in the Supreme Court.

Mr. HUBBELL. Yes; that the Supreme Court may order an account before finally disposing of the case. For instance, suppose the decision of the court below is adverse to the patent; of course there is no account, and it comes up as an entire case to the Supreme Court. The Supreme Court reverses that decree and says the patent is valid, and then the case goes for an account, and then it may come up again; but each time it comes up as an entire case; it does not come up divided into sections. This section applies only to cases where a patent is sustained and an account ordered, and before that account comes up they may take an appeal to the Supreme Court, so that you cannot take up the account. There is no such practice as that in the Supreme Court, I say.

Senator MORGAN. I think there is. I think the case of the Galveston Railroad Company *vs.* Cowdry has settled that practice.

Mr. STORROW. The court have held in some cases that where the great question in dispute is the priority or validity of mortgages, and there is a decision below determining that priority, then it cannot decide finally the cause, because there has been no foreclosure by sale; yet so far is it conclusive of the rights of the parties below, that they allow an appeal to be taken as though the decision were final. This is in conformity to that theory.

Senator MORGAN. I understand you are trying to remedy a difficulty of this kind which has existed in patent causes where the rule you refer to does not apply.

Mr. STORROW. Yes, sir.

Mr. HUBBELL. It does not apply at all, because mortgages are fixed sums.

Mr. STORROW. Not fixed sums.

Mr. HUBBELL. There is a valuation under sale, but in the case of damages that is a matter under appeal. They will only pass upon the points in dispute. The Supreme Court does not take any account. The Supreme Court issues its order to the court below, and that makes a reference to a master, who takes the account. That is the business of the court below.

ARGUMENT OF A. J. TODD.

Mr. TODD. I should like to say, on this occasion, a word or two. I have read this whole bill with great pleasure, and, as a practitioner in these cases, it has met with my approval, with one or two exceptions. One, I think, was an inadvertence on the part of the parties who drew the bill, and it leaves a portion of the matter unprovided for. In a certain contingency, the section has provided where there is a stay of proceeding a case may go up; and, in that case, the account may be held in abeyance. Now, I do not see any necessity for that, except that it is optional, if the party defendant desires it; that is to say, it makes it his option. There should be, in my judgment, added to the 4th section this clause:

The defendant may, in all cases, appeal before an accounting without a stay of proceedings; and, if the account has been taken before the hearing of such appeal, the proceedings on such accounting, if appeal is also made therefrom, shall be added to the record of the case in the court below.

As you gentlemen are all aware, it takes two or three years before a cause is determined in the Supreme Court of the United States; and there is no reason whatever why the accounting should not proceed, and by the time that the appeal is reached, the accounting proceedings will be ready to go up to be annexed to the record; and the labor of the

Supreme Court may be saved to the extent of one-half and the delay to the extent of one-half.

Mr. HUBBELL. Under this proviso it is not necessary to have any legislation.

Mr. TODD. The object of this, as I understand it, is, in one case, the hardship of the injunction pending the taking of the account.

Mr. STORROW. It is not so much that as it is the great delay, when what the parties really want to get at is a decision as to the validity of the patent.

Mr. TODD. Certainly; but while staying the order at one end you are letting it out at the other. Why not let the account proceed?

Mr. STORROW. It may in these cases. It shall be competent for the court to stay proceedings.

Mr. TODD. But there is not any express clause providing that, if it is desirable to have the accounting go on, the plaintiff may not cause delay.

Mr. STORROW. It provides now that it may go on. The third section provides :

"If such an appeal shall be taken and perfected within such time as the court shall prescribe, it shall be competent for the court to stay proceedings in whole or in part during the pendency of such appeal," or they may allow them to go on accounting.

Mr. TODD. Suppose, in the interest of a defendant (and a patent is in the hands of one man generally in these cases, and he has great interest at stake), the judge be so satisfied as to the patent being valid that he may say, "We grant a stay;" but he may say in the interest of the defendant also, "The accounting must also be stayed; let the whole thing stand." Now we want to provide against just such a contingency, and I think in drawing the bill and endeavoring to make it perfect we should make it as near perfect as possible.

Mr. HUBBELL. I am opposed to all that special legislation. As I said before, all that it is necessary to provide is this:

Provided, That the Supreme Court may order an account before finally disposing of the case.

If it is necessary for either party, on Friday they can go and make a motion in the Supreme Court, and have an order to take the account and send it up. All this legislation about it one way or the other is not necessary. Leave it to the judiciary. The only proceeding would be to make a motion for an order.

Mr. TODD. An order in what court?

Mr. HUBBELL. An order in the Supreme Court. The moment you have docketed the case there you can get a motion made the next Friday, showing cause, and they issue an order to the court below to send up the account, and that disposes of the whole matter. There is no necessity for any legislation in Congress about it.

Mr. TODD. Have not the statutes a right to say that no time shall be lost?

Mr. HUBBELL. They need not lose any time. Either party may do it. You may docket the case on Monday and make the motion on Friday in the Supreme Court of the United States, or you may make the motion before a judge of the court in chambers.

Mr. TODD. That was the objection I was met with the other day when I desired to amend section 4 by an application to the Supreme Court. Senator Morgan said that the Supreme Court did not want to be troubled with motions in these cases, because it was necessary to some extent at least to look into the merits before issuing the order.

Mr. HUBBELL. In a motion of that kind, the merits are stated in an affidavit which is filed, on which you make the motion, just as you do in any other case. It is a common thing to make motions there to send up the record in some other form. It is a common practice in the Supreme Court. You do not want any special legislation about it, but simply to settle that power in the court which they now exercise in other cases. Section 4 provides—

The several courts vested with jurisdiction to cases arising under the patent law may at any time during the pendency of any patent cause grant or suspend the issuing or operation of an injunction upon such terms as the court may impose, and shall have like power after an appeal of said cause, and while the same is pending in the Supreme Court.

Senator MORGAN. Under the patent laws the district courts of the United States are vested with jurisdiction, I understand.

Mr. TODD. The judges of the district courts sit also as circuit judges.

Mr. STORROW. There are one or two districts where they have circuit court powers.

Senator MORGAN. There is a great number of them, and I have been confused a little about those instances. I am very much impressed with the necessity, or at least the propriety, of confining the jurisdiction of the court in equity to particular methods of procedure. Is there any constitutional objection to taking from the circuit court what is called their common-law power to assess damages?

Mr. STORROW. Either now or some time I should like to state the result we have come to on that question.

Senator MORGAN. I do not want to interrupt the argument.

Mr. HUBBELL. Do you mean to take the whole jurisdiction away?

Senator MORGAN. Yes, sir; and confer it upon the equity side of the same court.

Mr. HUBBELL. How does that article in the Constitution read?

Senator MORGAN. The third article of the Constitution first relates to the judicial power of the United States, which " shall be vested in one Supreme Court, and in such inferior courts as the Congress may from time to time ordain and establish."

Mr. HUBBELL. I refer to the right of trial by jury.

Senator MORGAN. That is one of the amendments of the Constitution.

Mr. HUBBELL. Does it not read that no person shall be deprived of the right of trial by jury, where the amount in controversy exceeds $20?

Senator MORGAN. But that was in cases where they had the right of trial by jury, at the time of the adoption of the Constitution, by common law.

Mr. HUBBELL. In any case arising under the Constitution, I think; not at the common law only.

Senator MORGAN. That was held in Josiah Morris's cotton case to mean this: that was a lawful proceeding to confiscate cotton, and the proceeding was instituted after the forms of admiralty; and it was understood by the judge who presided in the district court and tried the cause, that all the admiralty jurisdiction and all these methods of procedure applied to cases like that, and, therefore, the party was not entitled to jury trial. The Supreme Court held that the party was entitled to jury trial because it involved the right of property, and was such a right as would have been tried by a jury because it was a right triable only in a common-law court at the time of the adoption of the Constitution. But where the right of trial by jury did not exist at common law in that particular case, or in reference to that particular matter, at the time of the adoption of the Constitution, it was perfectly competent for Congress to pass a law by which the right of jury-trial should be taken from the party.

Mr. STORROW. Was that decided in admiralty cases?

Senator MORGAN. Yes; and that has been the decision of the courts of the States, so far as I have taken occasion to follow out the principle. I know that, in a case which arose in my own State, where three justices of the peace were empowered by statute to try a slave for his life, and condemn him to death—and they did try slaves for their lives and condemn them to death—the right of trial by jury was insisted upon as being one of the constitutional rights guaranteed to every human being. The supreme court of Alabama held, after great deliberation and debate, that that was true in reference to all rights that obtained at the time of the adoption of the Constitution of the United States, but that at the time of the adoption of the Constitution of the United States these people were slaves, and were not provided for in that instrument; and the consequence was they could not say there was a constitutional guarantee in favor of such people, or the right of trial by jury; and therefore these three magistrates had the right to sit in final judgment upon the life of a human being. That was a case, you see, in which the very extreme view of the question was presented, and I think it has been firmly established. It was so considered by the supreme court of Alabama, when they tried hard to get rid of it, but under the compulsion of a line of authorities which was unbroken, they were compelled to hold that those constitutional provisions applied only to this right which existed at common law at the time of the adoption of the Federal Constitution. Now, this right, under the patent law, did not exist then. That is a right given by the Constitution in part, but really conferred by act of Congress; and it seems to me that Congress have the power to regulate the trial of the right without reference to a jury at all.

Mr. HUBBELL. You are right about that. The right is restricted to the common law in the Constitution.

Mr. TODD. Do you think it right to restrict it in any court and not give the alternative remedy?

Senator MORGAN. It is my judgment that we ought to restrict these cases to the equity side of the court.

Mr. TODD. You know the present Revised Statutes do give the defendant the right of trial by jury where all property is concerned.

Senator MORGAN. I know, but practically the whole profession resort to the law side of the court, and to suits in damages merely in reference to patent causes, and I think that this remedy belongs to the equity side of the court and ought to be applied to all cases.

Mr. TODD. It may cost a man $50 to litigate a case on the equity side, where it would not cost $5 on the law side. Although he has on the law side the minds of thirteen men to satisfy as to the validity of the patent, in many instances the poor man is driven to the law side of the court because he cannot stand the expense of examiners' fees and counsel-fees, and the preparation of elaborate arguments, and the printing of records for an equity hearing.

Mr. STORROW. The equity hearing is more expensive from the necessity of taking testimony.

Mr. TODD. I would be sorry to see anything of that kind in the bill, with all deference to the views of the Senator.

Mr. HUBBELL. This provision of the Constitution is limited to common-law actions; there is no doubt about that; but, then, in framing this modification here I have worded it so as to leave it optional with

the patentee.   I have framed it so as to give him, on the faith of his
patent, a standing in equity without the necessity of going into a trial
at law, or without the necessity first of inducing parties to take licenses
so as to establish the possession.

Mr. STORROW. No such rule exists now.   A man may sue in equity
on his patent at once.

Mr. HUBBELL. I beg your pardon.

Senator MORGAN. It is presumptive evidence of his right.

Mr. STORROW. It is so far evidence as that a court will grant a preliminary injunction on the faith of the patent only.

Mr. HUBBELL. That is interlocutory only, and then they send it to a
jury.

Mr. TODD. That is the English practice, not the American practice.

Mr. HUBBELL. I know what the practice is.   I have drawn many a
bill.   What I mean is this, that he may go on to a final decree without
the intervention of a jury, or without reference to a master to ascertain
any facts.   He may go on on the faith of his patent in this way :

In all suits in equity the letters patent shall be *prima-facie* evidence of their validity.

They may be contested in equity.

And be evidence of the possession of the invention.

They cannot contest that.   That is, he is free of these reference cases
that may be made subsequent to an interlocutory injunction.

And the right to proceed by suit in equity shall not be denied.

That leaves it optional with him to bring a suit at law if he prefers to
do so, but you cannot compel him to bring a suit at law.   That is the
point.

Mr. TODD. There is nothing now to compel a man to bring a suit at
law in the present practice of the law.

Mr. HUBBELL. He may be compelled to bring a suit at law in order
to sustain the possession of the patent.   He must show the possession
in some way.   He must show it by acquiescence or license.

Mr. TODD. There is no power in the chancellor to order a jury.

Mr. HUBBELL. Then he may dismiss his bill or refuse to grant relief.
That is not the point.   The point is this, that he shall have a standing
in equity on the faith of his patent.   If you can show its invalidity,
then it falls; but you shall not drive him first by obtaining an interlocutory order suspending proceedings in equity and turning him over to
the law side, or by suspending proceedings until he shows possession or
requiring him then to go into proof to show it.   I say you should not
do that.   Let him go on upon the faith of his patent, but do not deny
him his right to proceed at law if he elects and finds it is better for him
to do so.   For instance, these judges are very capricious sometimes.
Some of these judges are good patent lawyers, and some detest patent
cases and kick them out of court every chance they get.   Suppose he is
in a district where he has to proceed in equity before a judge of the
latter kind.   Some of these judges say they cannot understand these
patent matters; they cannot comprehend machinery and inventions, and
they are glad to get rid of these cases as speedily as they can; and
they send a case to a jury when they can.   Let the man elect in a case
like that to go before a jury.   He may say that he would rather go before a jury than go before a judge.   Give the man the right of election
in cases of that kind and let him choose which forum he will take.

Mr. TODD. Does he not have that now, Mr. Storrow ?   I understand
he has.

Mr. STORROW. He has now. Mr. Senator Morgan's suggestion is to take that right of election away from him and try the suits in equity in all cases.

Mr. HUBBELL. I think it would be rather dangerous to take it away from him. By the way, I wish to meet Senator Morgan's view in this, to enlarge the power in equity by putting him in such a position that he can proceed with as much safety and certainty as he can at law; that he cannot be thrown out of court because he has no verdict of a jury to sustain him, or no evidence of acquiescence or possession, or he may work the machine himself and show possession by that. If he is allowed to stand upon his patent alone, then he can go on in equity on that, if he chooses, and you cannot throw him out of court. He may go on and get a final decree of damages on that.

Mr. STORROW. You want the patent to be conclusive evidence?

Mr. HUBBELL. *Prima facie* evidence of validity, conclusive evidence of possession, not of validity. It is now *prima facie* evidence of validity, but it is not now *prima facie* evidence of possession, and you may drive the man out into the law side now. I say arrange it so that he may stand as firm on the equity side as he does on the law side.

Senator MORGAN. I suppose the equity jurisdiction in regard to patents arose originally from the idea of getting an account of profits in the hands of an infringer.

Mr. STORROW. The origin of the equity jurisdiction was in the statute, which allowed them to go into equity chiefly to get an injunction.

Senator MORGAN. An injunction first.

Mr. STORROW. An injunction after a hearing, and then an account of profits.

Senator MORGAN. You go into a court of equity with a bill for an account of profits, and you add to it the damages which might have been given by a jury at law, and you add also penalties at the discretion of the court.

Mr. STORROW. Counsel fees.

Senator MORGAN. Really penalties; the power to increase the damages arbitrarily. That is a penalty imposed upon the defendant.

Mr. HUBBELL. That is done on the law side.

Senator MORGAN. On either side.

Mr. STORROW. It comes under the purpose of the statute to give him a just compensation.

Senator MORGAN. It is something resting in the discretion of the court, which the judge may impose upon the defendant, because he has in some way outraged the rights of the plaintiff, or does some great wrong to him. It seems to me that there ought not to be two tribunals, one to judge of the damages in a man's case by one rule of procedure, and another court or another side of the same court to judge of it by a different rule of procedure; one side of the court possessing power to take the whole subject into consideration, damages, penalty, compensation, and everything connected with it; the other limited to the consideration of the damages merely according to the form in which the plaintiff may bring his suit. It is said it is much more expensive on the equity side than on the law side, and yet clients and counsel are resorting all the time to the equity side, notwithstanding it is expensive.

Mr. TODD. In equity there is but one mind to satisfy instead of thirteen, and in a jury of twelve there is apt to be disagreement.

Senator MORGAN. And you incur additional expense in order to avoid that difficulty.

Mr. TODD. There is a statute providing that on the trial at law he can waive the jury, and therefore get a *viva voce* hearing, and it is a very speedy mode of trial. The complainant always wants to waive the jury trial. What I want to do is to avoid taking testimony before commis-sioners, in order to save the expense which attends a cause on the equity side.

Senator MORGAN. Can you not take testimony also by a commissioner?

Mr. TODD. They are commissioners in chancery.

Senator MORGAN. There is a little difference. One is the commis-sioner appointed in a particular case to hear all the evidence, the other is a commissioner to whom the parties go and examine witnesses.

Mr. STORROW. Practically there is no distinction between them.

Mr. TODD. They are considered commissioners.

Senator MORGAN. Of course these gentlemen know better than I do about the expense of different forms of procedure, but it seems to me the matter could be regulated so as to be cheaper.

Mr. HUBBELL. I have tried patent cases that cost $125,000.

Mr. TODD. Only about one case out of a hundred is now tried before a jury, but still sometimes you do have a poor man for a client, and you want to get his case through cheap.

Mr. HUBBELL. If you do not take the depositions, you have to pay the expense of carrying witnesses, and keeping them, and feeing them.

Mr. TODD. Mr. Hubbell referred to section 15. The other day I asked to present an amendment providing leave to apply to the Supreme Court to sustain the operation of an invention. As I say, in many cases that I have met with, it has been a great annoyance and expense to my clients where you had to deal with a judge so prejudiced in favor of the complainant that you could not get him to budge from his decision in the case. Now I say there should be this added:

Such application may be made to any of the judges of, or to the associate justice for, the circuit in which the case has been heard.

The object is to give leave to apply to any judge of that circuit or the associate justice. That is sometimes an advantage, because when the case is appealed, there is at least one member of the Supreme Court bench who has knowledge of the facts to a certain extent. The section, as it now reads, implies that you must go before the same judge who issued the mandate of the court or the decree.

Mr. HUBBELL. You can make any proposition after I get through.

The committee adjourned until Friday, November 30, at 10 o'clock a. m.

FRIDAY, *November* 30, 1877.

The committee met pursuant to adjournment.

SUGGESTIONS OF W. WHEELER HUBBELL.

Mr. HUBBELL. In view, if your honors please, of some remarks which fell from Senator Morgan in the examination of the law, as he stated it, I have modified this section, which I have marked "Letter A," to take the place of section 2, so as to embody his idea, as far as I think it is proper to go, in relation to trial by jury. I cannot stand here and say that a man shall be denied entirely the right of trial by jury. I think in view of Magna Charta and the practice in this country that would be going too far, but the practice under the patent law can be regulated so that the party may have the benefit of that trial if, in the opinion of the court, it is necessary. I modify that section in this way, so as to read:

In all suits in equity the letters patent shall be *prima-facie* evidence of their validity, and be evidence of possession of the invention, and the right to proceed by suit in equity shall not be denied. The right of action at law is abolished, and the court may, in its discretion, send any issues of fact to a jury for trial.

That is in accordance with the English practice.

Mr. STORROW. There is an express statute on that point already, giving that power to the court of chancery.

Mr. HUBBELL. I know that, but then that provision does not abolish the right.

Mr. STORROW. I does abolish the right.

Mr. HUBBELL. No, sir.

Mr. STORROW. They send issues out of chancery to be tried by a jury under the act of February, 1875.

Mr. HUBBELL. Yes; but when we confer a power, if we would make it exclusive, the entire power should be stated in the act itself, so that there may be no mistake about it. It is not intended under all circumstances to take away the right of trial by jury. I proceed with the section as I propose it:

" In the estimation of damages or profits, or the amount of recovery, under the patent, the owner shall have the right only to recover just compensation for his invention used, and for his time, ingenuity, and expense bestowed upon the same, with the right to a penalty not exceeding three times the amount of compensation in all, including expenses of suit in the discretion of the court; and due allowance shall be made for actual labor and circumstances under which the invention has been used in the estimation of damages or compensation, if any penalty be allowed ;" that is, if a penalty is allowed, that penalty shall include the expenses of the suit, but it cannot, under any circumstances, including everything, exceed three times the amount of the compensation in all. That would be twice the amount of the compensation added. The words " in all," would restrict it, and it would not be three times in addition, of course.

In regard to the principles of law upon which I wish to have these sections placed, the bill, as it is drawn, has been based, to my mind, upon the erroneous idea that patents are granted in this country, under this government, in the exercise of a prerogative right, as they are granted under the monarchical governments of Europe. If patents were granted as a prerogative right of the Crown, they would have a right to impose all these restrictions and conditions and defeasances and litigations upon the patentee; but patents in this country are granted not upon any prerogative right; they are granted simply in accordance with that express declaration in the Constitution which determines the nature of the right in all particulars, both as to its character and as to its time, except that extent of time is left as matter of discretion to Congress. That being the case, the grant, I will say, must be in accordance with that. It cannot be a conditional grant. The word " exclusive" relates to the grant, and not exclusively to the person. It cannot be a grant conditioned upon some subsequent payment of a fee. The grant must be perfect in all particulars when it is made, as it is now and always has been in this country. The fee must be paid at the time or before the grant is made, and when the grant goes out it is perfect in all respects in accordance with the Constitution. It is not conditional and it is not defeasible ; it terminates by lapse of time solely. That being the principle, all remedial laws in relation to it must be coextensive with the nature of that grant to carry it into effect, and not detract in any way from it.

Senator CHAFFEE. Do you mean that when Congress gives a grant of this kind, it has no power to impose a condition ?

Mr. HUBBELL. No; the grant must not be a conditional grant. It must be an exclusive grant. That means an absolute grant ; that is, it should not be a grant to run for five and then to run for ten years, if a fee is paid at the expiration of the five years, and then to run for fifteen years if a fee is paid at the expiration of the ten years. That would be a conditional grant, a defeasible grant, and not an exclusive grant, abso·lutely for a certain time.

Senator CHAFFEE. Does not "exclusive" mean that no other person shall have the right?

Mr. HUBBELL. Yes; and "exclusive" means more than that; it means absolute; it relates to the grant as well as the person of the inventor.

Senator CHAFFEE. Without any conditions whatever?

Mr. HUBBELL. Without any conditions whatever. It means an exclu·sive grant for a certain time. That is what the Constitution says. The phrase "time or times" gives the right of extension. "Time or times," says the Constitution. There is where the Congress gets the right to extend the patent, but there is no right accruing out of those words which gives a right to defeat it, or to make it conditional or defeasible. It never has been the practice. Now, the English law is that way, be·cause it is the exercise of a prerogative right, and there is no form pre·scribed whatever. The English law has always been restrictive upon the original prerogative right exercised by the Crown. They used to grant patents for making bread, and for all sorts of things. The object of these conditional fees is to derive revenue for the Crown. The pat·ents were originally granted in England in order to derive revenue for the Crown; but that is not the case in this country. The object of this government is not to derive revenue for the government. The patent system is a self-sustaining institution. It would be, besides, an extreme hardship upon inventors, and contrary to the policy of the government heretofore, where it has been found that even fourteen years often is too little. They cannot make, perhaps, the expenses which they have un·dergone in that time. It would be an extreme hardship to impose an additional duty of paying $100 or $500 when a man wants his patent extended, provided it has been granted only on a conditional grant. You would defeat some of the best inventions and ruin some of the best inventors in the country. They often do not realize anything until near the expiration of the term of the patent, when it has been granted for fourteen years; and then sometimes they do not realize anything, and Congress extended the term for seven years more. Now it is made sev·enteen years absolutely on the original grant.

Senator CHAFFEE. When Congress makes a grant, that includes every·thing necessary to carry out the object for which the grant was given, either express or implied; but then it does seem to me that Congress, having the power to make this grant, has the power to impose a regula·tion.

Mr. HUBBELL. Exactly; a regulation in the nature of a remedy; but here comes in the principle of law, and I ask particular attention to this case, the case of Bronson vs. Kinzie, laid down by the Supreme Court of the United States:

The remedy must be consistent with the nature of the original grant, and not in any way interfere with it.

This whole matter hangs on this decision of the Supreme Court of the United States, and the principles laid down here always have been the law. I will read a few of the passages which bear very strongly upon the principle in regard to remedies. I will commence in the middle of a paragraph; I will not read the whole of it; it is entirely too long:

Regulations of this description have always been considered in every civilized commu·nity—

That is in relation to exemptions—

as properly belonging to the remedy, to be exercised or not by every sovereignty according to its own views of policy and humanity, It must reside in every State to enable it to secure its citizens from unjust and harassing litigation, and to protect them in those pursuits which are necessary to the existence and well-being of every community. And, although a new remedy may be deemed less convenient than the old one, and may in some degre e render the recovery of debts more tardy and difficult, yet it will not follow that the law is unconstitutional. Whatever belongs merely to the remedy may be altered according to the will of the State, provided the alteration does not impair the obligation of the contract.

Now, the Constitution of the United States directs a specific contract. It is [a contract, and it has always been considered so. It is founded upon contract between the government and the patentee. Then it goes on :

But if that effect is produced, it is immaterial whether it is done by acting on the remedy or directly on the contract itself.

Senator CHAFFEE. You say it is a contract between the government and the patentee?

Mr. HUBBELL. Yes; it is so considered.

Senator CHAFFEE. According to your theory, one of the parties to this contract has no power at all, but by the Constitution is directed and compelled to make this grant.

Mr. HUBBELL. Yes; a grant of a specific nature.

Senator CHAFFEE. Having no power to make any conditions or regulations except as to time?

Mr. HUBBELL. Except as to time. Congress may include conditions precedent to the granting of a contract; and so it does.

Senator CHAFFEE. Certainly.

Mr. HUBBELL. That is, it may require the performance of certain conditions-precedent to the granting of a contract.

Senator CHAFFEE. It requires the invention, of course.

Mr. HUBBELL. It requires the invention, it requires the petition, it requires an oath, and certainly forms, witnesses' signatures, drawings, models, the payment of certain fees of money into the Treasury on certain installments prior to the issue of the contract. It requires all those conditions.

Senator CHAFFEE. Those are all incidents to the invention. They establish the invention.

Mr. HUBBELL. No; some of those are conditions and considerations precedent; and those are perfectly legitimate. Congress can do that. It can establish any conditions precedent; but when they are all matured and the contract becomes complete and the patent is issued, that patent must be an "exclusive right" or an absolute grant limited only by time, exclusive in its nature. It has to be absolute to be exclusive, and not conditional, and not defeasible.

Senator CHAFFEE. It has to be exclusive as to others, of course.

Mr. HUBBELL. It is the "exclusive right" in the individual, provided he is the inventor, and the right itself is also exclusive or absolute, and *prima facie* he is the inventor under this action of the government; but if others can show that he is not, then, of course, he loses his right, because the Constitution makes that a condition precedent, and if there is a mistake as to that it is his misfortune.

But if that effect is produced—

That is, the impairment of the obligation of the contract—

it is immaterial whether it is done by acting on the remedy or directly on the contract itself. In either case it is prohibited by the Constitution.

That is, your remedy must be coextensive with the nature of the grant.

Senator CHAFFEE. I would not dispute that. I think it is perfectly sound that the remedy has to be according to the nature of the contract, but the only doubt I had was in regard to the power of Congress to direct the nature of this contract; that is, to impose conditions and regulations.

Mr. HUBBELL. I do not think there can be any conditions subsequent. The conditions must be all precedent, because the Constitution prescribes the nature of the contract, and the only limitation or condition about it is the time or times. Congress can extend the patent under that phrase " time or times."

The court further say :

In deciding the point, the court say: "It is no answer that the acts of Kentucky now in question are regulations of the remedy, and not of the right to the lands. If these acts so change the nature and extent of existing remedies as materially to impair the rights and interests of the owner, they are just as much a violation of the compact as if they directly overturned his rights and interests." And in the opinion delivered by the court after the second argument, the same rule is reiterated in language equally strong. (See pages 75° 76, and 84.) This judgment of the court is entitled to the more weight because the opinion is stated in the report of the case to have been unanimous, and Judge Washington, who was the only member of the court absent at the first argument, delivered the opinion of the second.

Then in a note at the bottom this is found :

Nothing, in short, can be more clear, upon the principles of law and reason, than that a law which denies to the owner of land a remedy to recover the possession of it when withheld by any person, however innocently he may have obtained it, or to recover the profits received from it by the occupant, or which clogs his recovery of such possession and profits by conditions and restrictions tending to diminish the value and amount of the thing recovered, impairs his right to and interest in the property. If there be no remedy to recover the possession, the law necessarily presumes a want of right to it. If the remedy afforded be qualified and restrained by conditions of any kind, the right of the owner may indeed subsist and be acknowledged, but it is impaired and rendered insecure according to the nature and extent of such restrictions.

Now, the whole of that is derived from the principle laid down in the English law by Blackstone, which I will ask you to keep in your minds, in relation to this subject, because the whole of this bill has been written in adverse interests to those principles. I ask that a great part of it be stricken out, and that other parts be modified in the manner in which I have made memoranda here. Blackstone, in his Commentaries, lays down these principles, and the law is founded upon the maintenance of them :

The remedial part of the law is so necessary a consequence of the former two, that laws must be very vague and imperfect without it.

That is as to the rights and to the maintenance of the contract.

For, in vain would rights be declared, in vain directed to be observed, if there were no method of recovering and asserting those rights when wrongfully withheld or invaded.

It applies directly to patents, it will be seen, as well as to other rights.

That is what we mean properly when we speak of the protection of the law. When, for instance, the declaratory part of the law has said that the field or inheritance which belonged to Titius's father is vested by his death in Titius, and the directory part has forbidden any one to enter on another's property without the leave of the owner; if Gaius, after this, will presume to take possession of the land, the remedial part of the law will then interpose its office, will make Gaius restore the possession to Titius, and also pay him damages for the invasion.

That language is just as applicable to patents and just as applicable to the nature of the grant under patents. I will not read any more of this decision, because what I have read shows clearly that the whole principle was discussed there and determined by the Supreme Court of the United States, and is an elementary part of the English law.

Senator CHAFFEE. From what do you read?

Mr. HUBBELL. I read from Bronson *vs.* Kinzie, 1 Howard, 316, 317. The principle is elaborated in other parts of the decision. But I would ask you to make yourselves familiar, and I have no doubt some of you are already, with the principles of that case, in refreshment of your memory upon the subject. Upon those principles, as I have heretofore stated, I have modified the bill as regards the limitations so that it shall not operate at all during the term of the patent. That is in regard to the second section that I have just read, and I have given a memorandum of it.

Senator CHAFFEE. On your theory any other limitation would be unconstitutional?

Mr. HUBBELL. I think there is no right to enforce a limitation during the term of the patent, because you sanction the man to infringe the patent and only hold him responsible in a portion of the damages by doing so. That, I think, you will have no right to do. You will find that the case falls directly in the principles of this case. It is denying them damages. But if the patentee has neglected, or from any inability after the patent has expired has not brought suit during the term of the patent, you may say then, "You shall recover only for six years, and you may have six years to bring your suit in"—just as in a case of assumpsit on a note or in the case of contracts.

As to section 5, in relation to the preservation of the records of patents, some gentlemen objected to the model being used. I think there is nothing in that objection. You have no right to presume that the government does not take proper care of the records, the models, and the drawings. There is only one word I suggest to be inserted here, and that is the word "original" before model.

Senator CHAFFEE. I did not object to the model.

Mr. HUBBELL. No; but some gentlemen who addressed the committee objected to the use of the model, and said that the model could be altered. I would insert the word "original" before "model," because then if the model was altered, and it could be proved, it would defeat the patent and throw it out of the case. As the section now reads it might be assumed that the model was absolute evidence, but by inserting the word "original" it precludes any possibility of an alteration of the model without being subject to proof. That is all the alteration I would make in section 5. In other respects it is very much like the practice now, I believe.

In regard to section 6, it was urged that it would be extremely hard for a man who built a machine which did not infringe the original patent, on account of some technical defect in the claim to be stopped by an injunction. I admit that is so, and I would alter the section to read in this way:

No machine or other article made prior to the surrender of a patent and the issue there-upon of a new patent, which, or the use of which, did not infringe such surrendered patent, and held to be an infringement of any of the claims of the new patent not existing when such machine or article was made, shall be stopped by injunction.

That is, that no machine built and held to be an infringement of the reissued patent, and not of the surrendered patent, shall be stopped by an injunction. That, I think, is perfectly fair, but the patentee should be entitled to reasonable compensation for the use of the machine after the patent had been reissued, but he should not be put in a position to stop that machine. It would be merely a question of the ascertainment of compensation that the man should receive. I would strike out the proviso. A proviso that will not apply to past as well as to future patents must be inequitable. We do not need the proviso with that alteration. That removes the only objection which I really see to that section.

Sections 7 and 8 I have no objection to. Those are merely administrative matters in relation to the preservation of testimony. But section 9 I do object to. Section 10 I object to. Section 11 I object to. My reasons for objecting to section 9 are that it tends to plunge a patentee into endless litigation. If, when a man has a valuable patent, every person is to be allowed to take it, and put him on the defense all over the United States, where he may be involved in a hundred suits at once, the poor patentee who has made a valuable invention is put into a position where he cannot carry on the defense of these suits; he is at the mercy of a parcel of pirates who are seeking to get it away from him, and they may force him into such terms as they please. All they have to do is to begin these suits against him, and the more valuable the patent is that he may have the more he will be harassed by litigation. Now, that is entirely contrary to the spirit and intent of the Constitution of the United States. The intention is, as expressed in the Constitution, to "secure" him, that is, that your legislation must be directed to making him "secure" for a short time, and allow him to exercise that as an "exclusive right," not to burden him down with litigation which may be brought into existence at the caprice and motion of other parties, who, from their own interests, may be adverse to him, and desirous to break him down by litigation, which would be a very easy thing for them to do. Patentees are poor. There is great truth in the adage that "necessity is the mother of invention." Often their poverty induces them to make these inventions, and they are not able to carry on these suits against every pirate and every man who may want to take away from the inventor this right, under any sort of process that they can bring against him. Therefore, I am opposed to all this plan of allowing parties to bring suits against the patentee to declare the patent void. If his patent is void or voidable he cannot sustain it.

Senator CHAFFEE. The necessity referred to in that adage I do not think is the necessity of the individual to invent for means of subsistence; it is necessity for the use of the invention.

Mr. HUBBELL. Both. The expression covers the whole. How often do you find poor men making inventions for the purpose of realizing reward or compensation? It is ninety times in a hundred.

Senator CHAFFEE. It is necessity which compels him to do anything of any kind for compensation.

Mr. HUBBELL. Very often it is. Sometimes men think, although they are wealthy, that they cannot live without something to do, and they keep on in business; but there is universal truth in the adage, both as to the individual inventor and as to the wants of the community. Of course unless the inventor invents something that has not been known before, and that there is necessity for among the community, he cannot derive the profit he is seeking. So that it applies both ways.

I will not elaborate on this section, it is so manifestly wrong and unjust, and in violation of the spirit and intent of the Constitution, as comprehended by the word "secured." It would make him unsecured or insecure in the most extreme way. Then section 10 provides—

Whenever any person shall be injured by a claim by the owners of any patent, or the parties entitled to sue thereon.

I need go no further. If he is injured by a claim of that kind he has a right in an action on the case at common law for damages, and there is no necessity for Congress to establish any legislation upon the subject by which he may bring a bill. It is simply in keeping with the other section to plunge a patentee into litigation. There is no necessity for Congress to have any litigation on that subject. A man who thinks he is injured in that way or in any other way has a right to an action at common law for damages. That is another pretext for breaking down inventors and patentees with suits.

Section eleven contemplates additional fees. I said at the outset this morning that that is the exercise of a prerogative right and not in accordance with our Constitution. That is done by the crowned heads to derive revenue. It never has been done in this country, and I hope Congress never will attempt it. I need not elaborate on that point. Senator Morgan was not here at the time I touched upon that, but he will see at once that under the Constitution the grant must be perfect at the time, and must not be a defeasible grant, and must not be a contingent grant. He can see what I have said upon that subject in print.

Section 9 I have no objection to. It simply is doing as in other conveyances, to put the evidence of transfers, &c., on record.

Section 13 I have stricken out entirely. My reasons for striking out section 13 are these: where there are joint owners it proposes to give either one a power to convey the exclusive right. That is giving a man power to do what he does not possess.

Mr. STORROW. You understand that is the law now.

Mr. HUBBELL. One of the joint owners cannot grant a right under the law now which will prevent an account.

Mr. STORROW. Certainly.

Mr. HUBBELL. No, sir; the other party is entitled to an account. The object of this section is to do away with that, so that the party taking a license shall not account. If it is the law now, why put it in here? You might as well say that where two hold a piece of land jointly, one of them could lease it and that the other should have none of the profits. You cannot divest him of his right without his consent in some way.

Section 14 I have no objection to, nor to 15, nor to 16, nor to 17, nor to 18, nor to 19. Section 20 I object to entirely. The law now is that the Commissioner, under certain circumstances, has a discretion. The object of the section is to forfeit a man's invention entirely if it has laid unacted upon for two years in the Patent Office. That is contrary entirely to the spirit of the patent law. That is another process of stealing a man's invention. That is all it comes to in the end, and that I detest. Inventors often have to let their inventions lie there for many causes. They may be in extreme sickness; they may be unfortunate in pecuniary matters; many troubles incident to life may overtake them, so that they cannot go on and finish this, as required by this section, within the two years. Now there is a limited discretion left with the Commissioner, a very small discretion in relation to the matter, and the object of this section is to take that away and make it an absolute forfeiture, for what purpose? But that some other man may come in and get a patent for his invention, when the record shows that the former is the original inventor in reality, under a sort of presumption that it is not perfected, or that he has abandoned it, and therefore somebody else has a right to a patent for it.

Senator MORGAN. Could a man get a patent under such circumstances?

Mr. HUBBELL. Yes, sir.

Senator MORGAN. How could the applicant say it was a new invention, when it was not a new invention?

Mr. HUBBELL. He could not under the Constitution, and I say it is inconsistent with the Constitution, and that the whole thing is wrong. It is only a process of stealing another man's invention. The Constitution intended that the man who has first put it there shall have the right to it if he is the first inventor.

Senator MORGAN. Does this section or any law now in force permit the patenting of an invention which has been forfeited for the non-payment of the tax?

Mr. HUBBELL. Yes, sir. They never look at in the examination at all. Another man can go out and take a patent, and its original invention will be regarded as experimental, not perfected, and it will not be looked at.

Senator KERNAN. How is it held in court, where they find that the testimony had been published or filed? Do they not hold that the new man is not the original and true inventor, and that the invention has been described and its description filed in the Patent Office? I speak of the matter in the way it is considered by the courts.

Mr. HUBBELL. If that matter was to come before a court, I think they would decide (and for that reason I ask to have this section stricken out) that if the invention was shown in those original papers, and became a matter of public record; if it was shown so clearly that a mechanic, or one skilled in the art, of ordinary ability, could construct it, it would be a defense against the patent. I think a court would be bound to so hold.

Mr. DODGE. I will answer the question raised by Senator Morgan. When the bill was before our association we wanted to add at the end of it the words, "it shall become the property of the public"; but there was raised this objection to it, that that would necessitate the publication of the rejected application in the office, which would be so burdensome that it could not be done. Mr. Hubbell is right. The case has been passed upon by the Supreme Court in the last two years, and it did lay down the rule that no matter how many rejected applications were in the office or how perfectly they may describe the invention, it is not a bar to a patent subsequently granted, unless it is proved that the thing had been put on public sale or in use; and the practice of the office since that decision has been changed entirely in that particular. Formerly they would reject a new applicant upon any former application which showed the invention, but the Commissioner thought he was bound by that decision of the court, which I think was a great mistake, because he would be able to distinguish between the grounds of possession in a case where the patent had been granted and the inchoate right which exists simply in the application for a patent. Therefore they now hold that any rejected application cannot be cited at all as against another party who comes in subsequently and claims the same thing, and they are every month granting patents for things which their own records show were invented by other parties ten years ago perhaps, who complied with every requirement of law, paid their fee, and made as full and complete drawings and model as this last had been.

Senator KERNAN. If it is a vested right, the court will hold that the man was the true and original inventor according to the record which had been published.

Mr. DODGE. The court has abandoned the experiment, unless it was put into public use.

Senator MORGAN. A man must be the true and original inventor, and not the first inventor.

Mr. DODGE. Yes, sir, that is the practical condition of things. I think it is all wrong. I do not see how we are to remedy it unless Congress provide for the publication of those rejected applications.

Senator KERNAN. As it reads, it would be forfeited to somebody if he files the application and does not do anything in two years.

Mr. DODGE. That application would be forfeited, but he could come in and make a new application at any time in the future.

Senator MORGAN. He might, but not another.

Mr. HUBBELL. Yes, another. It simply says the application shall be regarded as abandoned by the parties thereto. I think the whole thing is wrong. I do not think there ought to be any such law. I do not think you have any right to take away a man's invention because through some mistake which was not within his control, through an act of Providence, or something of the kind, he was not able to go on for two years. I do not think you have any right to do it, and there is where the trouble arises.

Senator CHAFFEE. The inchoate right becomes vested when the patent is granted.

Mr. HUBBELL. They will not allow him to take the patent under that application; they say it is abandoned.

Senator CHAFFEE. And the right of the patentee is inchoate.

Mr. HUBBELL. But some other man may take a patent for the same thing; he may derive information from that same thing, and come in and get out a patent for that man's invention, and then undertake to turn around and say that the first invention was merely on experimental thing; and if the first inventor has not the money to go on, and perhaps that is the very reason why he had not got the invention into use, it is yet accessible to the public in some way or other. The very man who applies for the second patent may have got it through the record, or through his agent, and the original inventor be deprived of all right. That is not right. You are creating the constructive abandonment of a thing which has been never abandoned. Under the act of 1836 the principle of abandonment was correct; and there was more law and justice in that act than there is in these modified and tinkered-up patent laws that they have here lately, and which they are trying to force upon Congress all the time. The law there was, that to abandon an invention it must be in public use for more than two years with the inventor's consent and allowance. That was the law, and that is reasonable. That ought to be the law now; but of course these alterations make business; they make business for the office, but the true, original inventors suffer, and Congress is made to do things inequitable and unjust and wrong. The opponents in this case, those who advocate this bill (I say the proposers of the bill), say the Constitution is all right, but the law is wrong. I say the Constitution is all right; there is no doubt about it. The only thing is to administer it as it was meant to be administered. I ask that section 20 be stricken out entirely. The object of it is to take away even the little discretion left in the Commissioner. The fact is that the original section, section 4894, ought to be stricken out from the statutes. It is only a legalized system of piracy and robbery upon the true and original first inventors, who put their inventions into the custody of the government, then, through misfortune of their own, they are not able to go on and take out patents.

Section 21 I have no objection to. There was one suggestion made to me by one of the committee, to examine whether there was any such thing in the bill, which leads me to think it is something of the same character as these other sections which I have just objected to, in re-

lation to abandonment, and that is this : section 11 requires additional
fees. One of the reasons for urging that was, that a great many
worthless patents would be got out of the way. When a patent is
issued by this government it is issued upon the ground that it is for a
useful invention. A worthy invention may not for some years appear
to be of practical use ; yet the truth is, in the advance of science there
is not an invention ever made but what has some place entitled to
merit in the general advance. It may not appear how it may be developed ; it may require some combination ; but each one is a link in the
great chain of progress. That is the truth of the matter. Take, for
instance, Benjamin Franklin, with his kite at one end and his key at
the other, the string intermediate. He was playfully experimenting
with electricity, showing that the silken kite would attract electricity,
the string would conduct it, and the key would be charged. It was not
then applied to any useful purpose. You might have said it was a worthless discovery, a worthless invention, but how is it now ? The same
principle girdles the world with intelligence ; and all over this continent
that identical principle is the means of communication, simply by inventing an alphabet to measure the length of these sparks of electricity, and
by the use of metallic conductors instead of a string. It is the same
principle ; there is an illustration of it ; and yet they want you to say
that these worthless patents, as they call them, these mistaken grants
of the government, shall be pushed out of the way, unless the inventor
has happened to be able to pay additional fees, and for what ? To allow
some other persons to say that they will obtain patents for substantially
the same inventions with some little trivial alterations, claiming that
they perfected the inventions, and these worthless inventions are now
rendered useless, and so they will go on. You only open the door to a
robbery of the original inventors by some trifling modifications represented by the subsequent patentees. That is all wrong.

There should be no additional fees. When the grant of the government is made on the ground of a new and useful invention it should
stand until the court overturned it. There should be no alleged granting of worthless patents in order to fix fees upon the poor inventors who
are struggling to make something. Many of them are struggling through
misfortune ; and, owing to the fact that their link of invention has not
reached its full development, they cannot realize perhaps the expense
that they paid to the government on their patent. Now, I am an
inventor. I have seen the bearings of these things. I am a lawyer.
How was it with my inventions first, when I, a young man only nineteen
years of age, began to invent war-powers which carried this government
to victory in every battle, which sunk the Alabama with her picked
English crew and best of English guns, which reduced every fort, and
which defeated every army brought against them in the late war ? How
was I met ? I was met with the declaration that I had undertaken to accomplish impossibilities. That is how I was met ; but I did not believe
it. Through seven long years I struggled with all kinds of adversities—pecuniary, experiments left in a maze—but I struggled to success,
and this government had to take them in the hour of its extremity to
maintain itself; and it did maintain itself in every contest where it used
them. I had to struggle with poverty. I had to earn every dollar that
I invested in building targets, in moving guns, and preparing shells and
fuses. I was met with all kinds of adversities, and I feel the wrong such
a bill as this would inflict upon the inventor. For thirty years I have
had to wait to receive recompense, and then what ? I was visited, by
order of Congress, with a seven years' suit, and confronted by all the

evils that human nature develops, jealousy, pretension, adversaries, competitors; and finally when I obtained the finding of a court that there is $200,000 reasonable royalty due to me from the United States, and that I am the first inventor, I have been paid as yet only fifty cents on the dollar by this government, and the balance is due to me. There is an illustration of what an inventor has to go through with. I ask you in the execution of that provision in the Constitution to have sympathy with inventors, in the spirit in which it was framed, and not to break them down with litigation, and with assessment of fees and forfeitures in the Patent Office, and every trouble that perverted ingenuity hostile to the spirit of invention can suggest.

Senator MORGAN. While I have no doubt that I felt the force of your inventions, I am ignorant of the precise inventions you speak of.

Mr. HUBBELL. I invented what is called the Navy fuse for explosive shells; and I invented the percussion-exploders for rifle-shells of the Army of the United States. Both inventions were used, the former in all the smooth-bore shell-guns, and the latter in all the rifle guns of the United States.

CLOSING ARGUMENT OF J. J. STORROW.

Mr. STORROW. Mr. Chairman and gentlemen of the committee, I will speak first of the suggestion which Mr. Senator Morgan made the other day with regard to giving up the common-law right of action for the infringement of patents. That involves giving up the right of trial by jury in such cases, because although a court of equity in patent causes may send issues to a jury, and by act of February, 1875, may summon in a jury to try them, yet it is at the discretion of the court whether it will or not, and the parties have no right to have issues sent to the jury in any cause in equity. The ground upon which it is suggested that Congress has the power so to modify the law as to take away the right of trial by jury in patent causes is that as Congress created the right of the patentee it has power to mold the remedies. The fact that Congress creates the right does seem to me to give it the power to modify the right itself. I think the right under the Constitution, so long as it exists, must be exclusive, but the duration of the right undoubtedly may be fixed by Congress. They may make it for fourteen years or for seventeen years; they may make it for five years, extendible by the payment of a fee; they may make it for seventeen years, defeasible if the fee is not paid. I do not find any difficulty in that. When we come, however, to the question of how far they may mold the remedy, there are other interests that come in. It does not seem to me true as a general statement that because Congress creates the right they can mold the remedy in any way they please. For example, I think no one would say that Congress could provide that if a patent was infringed the remedy should be by applying to the Representative in Congress for the district in which the patentee lived. One reason why that would not be lawful would be, that that would be conferring judicial power upon a person who was not a member of the judiciary.

Senator MORGAN. It would be trenching upon the powers of one of the co-ordinate departments of the government.

Mr. STORROW. The technical difficulty would be that although Congress in one sense did create this right, and might in one sense, and to a certain extent, mold the remedy, it must do so subject to the other

provisions of the Constitution which relate to the remedy, and one of
those provisions is that the remedy shall be given through the judiciary
and not through members of the legislature or any one else. Take an
instance. If Congress should grant the right for seventeen years to
mine minerals, to search for, raise to the surface, and take away minerals from a certain tract of government land, that would be a right
created by act of Congress, molded and formed by act of Congress;
its terms and conditions would be learned only from the act of Congress;
and yet I think no one would say that a right like that could have a
remedy attached to it that for a trespass upon it no jury should be sum-
moned; that neither plaintiff nor defendant should have a right to trial
by jury to ascertain the damages caused by trespass upon that incorporeal right. Take the case of a ferry franchise, a franchise to maintain
a bridge over navigable waters, a franchise to build a railroad, a franchise to become a national bank—all these are rights created by acts of
Congress. In the great case of the United States Bank the Supreme
Court held that inasmuch as the bank was created by Congress it could
give exclusive jurisdiction to the United States courts not only in matters
involving the existence of the bank, but in all rights connected with the
exercise of its powers; that that power to give the remedy in the United
States courts extended to an ordinary action on a promissory note,
because all the rights connected with that bank grew out of the act of
Congress which created it; and yet no one, I think, would say that Congress should declare that no action which touched the interest of a
national bank should be tried except in a court of chancery, and that
no jury trial should be had upon it.

Mr. HUBBELL. The common-law rights of property are prohibited
from a denial of jury-trial by the Constitution; but this is not a common-law right of property in any way; it is simply a statutory right, in
accordance with an express provision of the Constitution. There is the
difference. You deny trial by jury at law, but I say you may give a
judge discretion, and I would modify it in that way, so as to send special issues to a jury.

Mr. STORROW. That is taking away the right. It seems to me clear,
therefore, that to say because a right is created by Congress we may
take away the trial by jury, is too broad a statement, and it does not
rise to the accuracy of a definition of the power of Congress on that
subject. One reason why limitations must be put upon that power
is that the remedy for the infringement of a patent right does not concern the patentee merely. Inasmuch as the patentee asserts his right
under the act of Congress, he may possibly be said to submit to everything which Congress annexes to the grant; but the defendant does
not have his right under the act of Congress. If the patentee has an
exclusive right and it is infringed, and he says to the defendant, " Pay
me a thousand dollars out of your pocket; transfer it from your pocket
to my pocket; not because it was my money when it was in your pocket,
but because, being your money, it ought to be paid to me to afford compensation for the injury you have done me"; that is a case where the defendant does not hold his thousand dollars under any act of Congress.
It is a case where the power of the law comes in and takes from him that
which was his own, because he has inflicted an injury upon another or
because he has destroyed the property of another.

In every case, therefore, the remedy for the infringement of a patent
involves the right of a defendant who does not claim under the act of
Congress, as much as of the patentee who does claim under it; and
that is where the limitation begins to come in. I stated the other day

the distinction between the right of the patentee to the exclusive use o his invention and the remedy which the law gives him for an invasion of that right. I want to make another distinction in regard to the remedy, and that is between the character of the relief which is given to the man and the mode of procedure by which or the forum in which that relief is sought. For example, Congress may say to the inventor, "You shall have an injunction." It says to him, "You shall have damages for the invasion of your right." That is the kind of relief which may be given. When we come to the mode by which that relief is to be sought, the tribunal which is to measure the extent of it, then we come to a somewhat different class of questions.

To state exactly the position, if I can, of the parties, I will say Congress has established a legal right in the patentee. His right is a right, I mean, which can be recognized by a court of law, and not merely by a court of equity. It is transmissible; it is assignable; it may pass by devise or inheritance. Congress has recognized in him (and this bill proposes emphatically to recognize in him) the right to have damages for the invasion of his exclusive right. That right to damages, in whatever forum it may be sought, is in its nature a legal right as distinguished from an equitable right; that is to say, it is a right which, according to the course of law at the time the Constitution was adopted, was a remedy given him by courts of law and not by courts of equity. The Constitution recognizes the distinction between claims which at the time the Constitution was adopted were the subject of common-law actions, and claims which could be enforced in equity or admiralty. It undertook to say that with respect to all those matters which at that time were proper subjects of suits at law, the right of trial by jury should not be taken away. It seems to me, in the first place, that this claim for damages was in its nature a claim given by the common law, and was intended to be enforced in the courts of law. It is entirely true that the right which is created is one which was not in one sense a right at common law; but the claim of the party for the damages for which he brings his suit is a claim which was recognized by the common law; it is a right to maintain an action of trespass on the case for the invasion of an incorporeal right; and whenever Congress created an incorporeal right in the patentee, without any provisions in the statute giving jurisdiction to any court to enforce those rights, without any provision giving remedies for their violation, the law and equity jurisprudence of the country would have taken hold of those rights and furnished that remedy. The law of England, long ago—long before the adoption of the Constitution—furnished a legal remedy for the invasion of patent rights by an action of trespass on the case for damages, or an equitable remedy in which profits or an injunction could be obtained.

Senator MORGAN. We call this a right of property. There is great force in the reasoning; but, after all, it is more of a privilege than a right.

Senator CHAFFEE. It is a franchise.

Mr. STORROW. What is the right to build and maintain a railroad?

Senator MORGAN. That is a franchise.

Mr. STORROW. What is the right to be a corporation?

Senator MORGAN. That is a franchise.

Mr. STORROW. What is the right to mine and take away ore from land of the United States?

Senator MORGAN. You get into a different element there. One is a pure franchise granted by the government; the other is a privilege granted upon some basis of right, resulting from the discovery, or something like that. It is something like the mine you spoke of. You take elements of nature and combine them into the discovery of some new combination of forces or principles, so as to produce a certain result in a convenient way. Now, that combination, though said to be a discovery by you, is not created by you by any means at all. There is not an element of it that the man creates who makes the discovery. The government, the world, mankind at large, possessed these elements before in free use, and another man had a perfect right before you became the patentee, if he could do it, to discover and combine the same things and use them freely. You have done so, and the law of the land gives you a privilege in connection with that thing, not because it is absolutely property of yours, but because it was simply made so by the acquiescence of the government, that you should have the exclusive right to enjoy it for a certain length of time.

Mr. STORROW. Is that a franchise ?

Senator MORGAN. No, it is not a franchise in strict terms.

Mr. STORROW. It is an incorporeal right.

Senator MORGAN. The mere thought or idea is in the nature of an incorporeal essence granted by the government out of its own powers. The use is a privilege granted in connection with something which exists independently of the government as a privilege to mine lands.

Mr. STORROW. It is based on something which the inventor has in the most just sense created: a new and useful art not before known, or a new and useful improvement. It is not something which he has subtracted—self-appropriated—from the world's possessions, as in the case of the old monopolies. The whole world has become, and forever after his patent has expired will continue to be, stronger or richer for what he has done, for the new use he has taught it to make of the forces of, nature; this is the highest creation open to human power.

But to take even what seems to me to be the lower class you mention. Suppose the government said to a man, "If you discover a gold mine in such a tract you shall have the exclusive right to dig out the gold for one year" ?

Senator MORGAN. That is a mere incorporeal right, not a franchise.

Mr. STORROW. That is an incorporeal right, and I have no doubt that is a right which is within the purview of the clause of the Constitution which provides for trial by jury. Let me go a step further to meet exactly the suggestion you make. Suppose we concede, as was laid down distinctly in the case of Parsons vs. Bedford, 3 Peters, 447, that the provisions in the 5th and 7th amendments to the Constitution apply to only those claims and causes of action which, at the time of their adoption, were recognized by the laws of this country.

Senator MORGAN. At common law.

Mr. STORROW. Not simply by the common law.

Senator MORGAN. I mean the laws of the country.

Mr. STORROW. You will find that decision expressly says that those provisions apply not only to those rights recognized by what is popularly called the common law of England, the unwritten law, but to those rights which existed at that time under the statutes and practices of this country. Of course the court in saying that did not mean to say that if the claim existed under a statute, Congress, by repealing that statute and the next week re-enacting it in the same terms, would so change the right that they could take away the trial by jury; but they referred to the nature of the right in itself, the character of the right, as distinguished from the precise language of the statute which created it.

Now, you will find it true, if you look at the dates, that the first pat ent law of this country was passed in April, 1790. That law gave to the patentee, for the invasion of his right, the right to damages, to be assessed by a jury. That was the law of this country before the 5th and 7th amendments were adopted; so that upon precisely that question you have the fact that when those two amendments were adopted not only the law of England recognized the common-law right of action of trespass on the case for the invasion of a patent right, and gave a jury to assess damages, but the laws of this country had created it and recognized it.

It seems to me it would be very bold to say that a right of that sort, which existed at the time of the adoption of these amendments to the Constitution—for they were not adopted by all the States until 1791 — could be so modified by Congress as to take away the right of trial by jury, which those amendments were intended to preserve inviolate, because, if you should take that construction, I hardly know any right at all which is created by statutes from which the right of trial by jury cannot be taken away by simply repealing the statute and re-enacting it in different terms.

I have stated the argument against the power of Congress to authorize a court of equity to find damages, But the argument in favor of that power is very difficult to answer. When a court has acquired jurisdiction in equity, by reason of the peculiar relief asked, or for any other reason, it can go on and give entire relief to avoid two sets of actions for the same wrong, even though a court of law would be competent to give part of that relief; at least this is true as a general principle. It is true, also, that a court of equity can, in some cases at least, include unliquidated damages in its decree, ascertaining them either by a master or by an issue; so the Supreme Court declared, through Chief-Justice Taney, in Kelsey *vs.* Hobby, 16 Pet., 279 ; so, also, the supreme court of Massachusetts, in Milkman *vs.* Ordway, 106 Mass., 242. Is it not, therefore, true that where a court of equity, in a patent cause, as one part of its relief, gives damages assessed by a master, it exercises only that jurisdiction and power which was in courts of equity at the adoption of the Constitution, and which the VIIth amendment left to them ?

If this question should ever come before the Supreme Court, I am sure that the extreme convenience of the practice would be pressed upon them, and they would feel that convenience; it ought to weigh with them on a close and doubtful question. This is not all that should weigh with them. The VIIth amendment provides that the verdict of a jury in the cases to which the amendment applies shall not be re-examined otherwise than according to the course of the common law. The patent-act of 1790 was repealed by the act of February, 1793, and I believe that since that repeal there has never been a time when the recovery in an action at law on a patent was limited to the amount found by the verdict of a jury. During part of the time it was three times the usual license-fee; during part of the time it was three times the damages; during more than half the time the court has had the power to increase the verdict up to three-fold, at its own discretion. Certainly this departure from the simple damages found by the jury is not according to the course of the common law; it is not obedient to the VIIth amendment; and it has been universally acquiesced in by Congress, the community, the courts. Upon the question whether damages for the infringement of patents came within the VIIth amendment, a long line of honored authorities would justify, perhaps would require, the court to say that this construction (upon whatever theory it arose), contemporaneous with the Constitution, ratified by the consent of all men, at all times, in all places, has become too firmly a part of the established jurisprudence of the country to be overturned by abstract reasoning.

We must not forget, also, that the power of the chancellor to pass upon questions of title, of validity, of infringement, has been established, and the only question open is the comparatively subsidiary one of damages, and, perhaps, even if reasoning cannot solve that difficulty, the armory of the law can furnish means to cut it when it arises.

▶ I confess the question is one of considerable difficulty. It was first suggested to us several months ago by some gentlemen who were of opinion that the right to assess damages was in its nature a common-law right to be tried by jury, and ought not to be given to courts of chancery; though when the suggestion was first made to us, it was not made in the view which Senator Morgan suggested, but upon general principles.

When the suggestion was first made I will say I thought there was nothing in it, because it seemed to me that if Congress created the right they could mould the remedy, but the more I have studied it and thought of it since, the more difficulty I find in taking that view and the more strongly it seems to me that the nature and form of the procedure is something which is regulated by the Constitution; that Congress may mould the remedy so long as they do not violate other provisions of the Constitution; and those other provisions apply, for the various reasons I have mentioned, to these cases. The case has never been passed upon by the Supreme Court, and I cannot bring myself to say that I can have an opinion definitely as to how the court would decide it when they come to pass upon it. In that condition of mind, it seems to me that, inasmuch as by this bill we have restricted a certain class of patentees to damages alone, and taken away from them the right to recover profits, we ought not to embarrass them by taking away from them the only forum or court in which, possibly, they can recover damages. I think we ought not, also, to take away from any suitor the right of trial by jury in a class of cases where it has existed from a time anterior to the provisions of the Constitution, unless it be clear that we have a right to take it away, in the first place, and perfectly clear, in the second place, that we can give him another forum in which to reach the same relief; and also that it be perfectly clear that there is an overwhelming necessity for taking away that right; for, as was said by the court in the case I have referred to in 3d Peters, the right of trial by jury is justly dear to the American people. I think upon such a question, particularly, as the assessment of damages, the jury tribunal is worth a great deal in a great many cases, for there is no tyranny that the citizens of a free country can suffer under so grievous as the whims or fancies or peculiar turn of mind of a judge who is too good and too honest to be removed, and yet whose turn of mind inflicts great hardship upon suitors before him. Although I believe it to be true that very few cases will be tried at law, yet the right to go to law when you want, the right to require a jury when you want, I think is a good corrective against that kind of injury and that sort of abuse.

I think, therefore, if it is not entirely clear what the law is on the subject of trial by jury as applied to patent causes, the right ought not to be taken away, because the existence of that right and the use of that right has involved no hardship and no evil which it particularly demands remedy.

Senator MORGAN. Allow me to ask you for information, if under the patent laws as they now exist a chancellor upon a bill filed on the equity side of the court has not the right to award damages to the complainant ?

Mr. STORROW. Under the law of 1870 he has. A great many gentlemen have doubted whether that law is constitutional, but the question has never been passed upon.

Senator MORGAN. Still they award damages.

Mr. STORROW. It has been done since that law was passed, but never before.

Senator MORGAN. Then is that a violation of the right of the defendant ?

Mr. STORROW. That is just the question which I have endeavored to discuss. It never has been settled. I understand there is a case pending in which that question has arisen, and is likely to be decided by the Supreme Court, unless the case goes off, as it may, on some other point.

Senator MORGAN. The constitutionality of that grant of power is doubted.

Mr. STORROW. Yes, sir. Of course, it is the defendant who raises these objections. The plaintiff might prefer to go on. I happen to have a case now where I am counsel where there is no question at all about the infringement; it is admitted; the right of the plaintiff is admitted, and the sole question in the case is the amount of damages. That is peculiarly a case for a jury.

Senator MORGAN. Neither the plaintiff nor the defendant can elect to avoid the law side of the court, if we have no power to deprive either of the parties of a jury-trial. They are obliged to go to the law side of the court if either party desires it as the statutes now are.

Mr. STORROW. Either can compel the other to go on the law side of the court if the right of trial by jury exists, though there is another way out of it, I suppose, under the act of February, 1875. The circuit court sitting in equity in a patent cause has a right, instead of sending an issue to a jury, to summon a jury of not less than five nor more than twelve, to whom the issue is transferred. It is a very convenient way. I suppose, if the defendant made the objection that the case ought to go to a jury the court could call one, but still that does not give it to him as a matter of right; it is a matter of discretion on the part of the court, unless indeed the court should determine that the seventh amendment required them to give him a jury.

Senator MORGAN. How would it strike you to transfer the whole jurisdiction to the equity side of the court and let him proceed by a bill in equity, and preserve the right of trial by jury, by permitting either party upon a demand made in a certain form to have a jury ?

Mr. STORROW. Limiting that right to the question of damages, I think that would get rid of a constitutional objection.

Senator CHAFFEE. Let me inquire in a case of that kind, suppose a plaintiff commences on the law side of the court and the defendant prefers to have a decision by a judge ?

Mr. STORROW. He cannot help himself. A suggestion of the opposite kind was made in the old case of Goodyear v. Day. The objection to taking away the common-law right of trial by jury applies only to a claim for damages, because that is the only one which the common-law recognizes. It does not apply to the question as to the validity of the patent, or infringement, or profits, or an injunction.

Senator MORGAN. I do not see how a right of trial by jury can apply to one point in the case when there are five other points to which it does not apply.

Mr. STORROW. Suppose the case was one where the courts at law and in equity had a concurrent jurisdiction. There is one remedy in a court of law and one remedy in equity. Now, the Constitution says as regards the relief which you at that time had a right to obtain in a court of law, the right of trial by jury shall not be taken away; but as regards the relief which at that time you had a right to obtain in a court of equity, the ordinary forms of procedure of courts of equity shall be afforded.

Senator MORGAN. Here is a case involving five or six different propositions of law and fact, and it turns out that the judge will have a right to decide four of these propositions, and the fifth must be decided by a jury. Then you have to go through a jury trial and exhaust the jurisdiction of the law court before you can get at a decision which will affect the equitable rights of the parties.

Mr. STORROW. Not entirely. If we allow the plaintiff to have the same remedy that he had before the act of 1870, he might elect to take no damages and go into equity and get his injunction and his profits. That was the course before the law of 1870. The plaintiff went into equity, but got no damages; he got profits and an injunction. The call for a jury only arises when there is a claim made for damages, *eo nomine*.

Senator MORGAN. That is your view of the Constitutional obligation resting upon Congress to furnish a jury, that a jury is demandable as a Constitutional right where there are damages to be given in a case ?

Mr. STORROW. It is my view that the question is doubtful, and we have no power in this room to settle it.

Senator MORGAN. And where there are no damages claimed the jury is not needed ?

Mr. STORROW. Yes, sir; that is, if the right is one that the courts of equity can, in their nature, take hold of, and the party can go there and get equitable relief, profits, and an injunction; but if the right is one which the courts of law, in their nature, take hold of, then the party can go there and get a trial by jury and his relief in damages; and trial by jury is secured to him under the seventh amendment.

Senator MORGAN. Unless there is some plain Constitutional objection to it, I should like to see the difficulty removed.

Mr. STORROW. Is it a difficulty ? No one has found it so; no one at any of our conferences or before this committee has complained of any evil from the right to bring actions at law. Should you not put it the other way, and say you ought not to take away or embarrass the power of the plaintiff to get damages, when by this bill you provide that in certain cases he shall recover nothing except damages, unless it is clear he has got a remedy to collect those damages which the Supreme Court would not declare nugatory ?

Senator MORGAN. Of course I have seen few patent causes tried, because patentees generally live in the Northern States, and send their inventions down South. We use the inventions made here, and if you go before a jury in my country as a foreign patentee, you are just as apt to get no damages as otherwise, whatever the nature of your case may be.

Senator KERNAN. The parties in that country elect to take the profits.

Mr. STORROW. I think there is a little of that feeling at the West. I have no doubt that there are fifty equity suits tried for one at law, and that there will be, because the chancellor can understand a complicated machine better than the jury can.

There are only one or two points in Mr. Hubbell's argument that I wish to refer to; the rest, I think, are sufficiently answered by what has already been said by the friends of the bill. Section 9, to which he referred, the section allowing patents to be repealed, does not introduce any new feature into the law. It is, I think, clear beyond much doubt that the proceeding to annul a patent can now be brought in the name of the United States, first getting the permission of the Attorney-General to use that name. The grant of a patent is not a grant by the United States of something that belonged to it. It is an *ex-parte* grant, affecting the private rights of other persons; and any person who is aggrieved, if his grievance is of a suitable nature, upon applying to the Attorney-General, can get leave to bring a bill in the name of the United States to annul that grant. (See act 1793, § 10; op. Atty. Genl., Nov. 19, 1874, Pat. Off. Gazette, vol. 6, p. 723; Atty. Genl. *vs.* Rumford Works, 9 *ib.*, 1062.)

Senator MORGAN. A bill in equity or a *quo warranto?*

Mr. STORROW. It has been an information in equity when it has been tried. In England I understand it is by a *scire facias.* I think a bill in equity is the form. The change introduced by this section is that instead of lobbying the Attorney-General, if I may use that expression, to get that right, you shall ask the court when you may be allowed to do it, and that the court shall decide. Certainly that is a great deal better. I will say in regard to all those sections—the 8th, 9th, and 10th, to which Mr. Hubbell objected so much—that every one of them is guarded in this way, that the proceedings therein contemplated cannot be set on foot unless on application to the court, and after the hearing they find, in their discretion, there is good cause for having it done.

Section 20, to which he referred, is one which, I confess, as it stands, does not exactly suit my mind. Mr. Dodge, Mr. Raymond, and myself all thought that it ought to be changed a little; but I find a majority of the patent bar here, who are more familiar with that precise subject than I am, do not wish the change made. I do not know what the Commissioner's views are on the subject. It seemed to Mr. Raymond, Mr. Dodge, and myself that when the application was abandoned the invention should be abandoned, and abandoned to the public, so that it would become open to the world after that time, and not be put in such a position that some one else could come in afterward and take the benefit of it and get a patent for it. It does seem to be, I should say if the Supreme Court had not expressed a *dictum* on the subject, incomprehensible that when one man has made a proper application to the Patent Office and it has been rejected for want of invention, another subsequent claimant can come in and file a duplicate of that application and get a patent. Yet that seems to be the law, and such things have happened.

Senator MORGAN. The practice, you mean.

Mr. STORROW. I do not know whether it is the law; it is the practice, because the Commissioner is of opinion that the Supreme Court has so decided. I do not think that if it were presented to the Supreme Court, and argued on that question, they would decide so; yet the tendency of their decisions has been in the direction of not allowing a patent to be anticipated by anything except a printed publication or the actual use of the device. Two or three ways have been suggested to get rid of that difficulty. One is, that all rejected applications should be printed; and I do not see any reason why it should not be done. here. The expense would not be very great; and then they would become printed publications; the public knows what is in them; and that of itself is a sufficient defense. Another way would be to put into the section a provision that, upon the rejection of any application or upon failure to prosecute the application under that section, the invention should be abandoned to the public, not merely the application. For my own part, I rather prefer the method of publishing the rejected applications themselves, after they have been six months or three months rejected. The expense would not be very great.

Senator MORGAN. This applies to a matter of practice in the office. Is not every patented invention numbered and published?

Mr. STORROW. Every one that is patented is published.

Senator MORGAN. This applies to patented inventions that have been forfeited by the non-payment of fees?

Mr. STORROW. I beg your pardon. It is the application for a patent on which the patent has not yet issued which this section applies to.

Senator KERNAN. What is the object of this part of the clause?

Or upon failure of the applicant to prosecute the same within two years after any action therein, of which notice shall have been sent to the applicant or his agent, they shall be regarded as abandoned by the parties thereto.

Mr. STORROW. The intention of that is, that after a man has got his application in the office he shall not sleep on it more than two years. Suppose the Commissioner or examiner rejects the application or requires an examination to be made, suggesting some amendment which ought to be made——

Mr. DODGE. They write an official letter.

Mr. STORROW. They write an official letter, and send notice in that way.

Senator CHAFFEE. Suppose the party dies and the estate is not settled up in two years, what would become of his application?

Mr. STORROW. The application may be prosecuted by his executor within the time. He must attend to it. One difficulty arising in those cases is when a man makes an invention and puts in an application he sometimes lets it sleep for three years, and by and by he gets out a patent, and that prolongs the monopoly longer than the law allows.

Senator MORGAN. Then he files a caveat, which will keep everybody else away.

Mr. STORROW. A caveat only lasts for a year.

Mr. DODGE. It may be renewed from year to year. Morse's patent was preserved thirteen years by caveat.

Senator MORGAN. Then you can delay your application as long as you choose, and after you get it you have two years to enjoy it before the patent need be be granted.

Mr. STORROW. It must not be used for more than two years before your application.

Mr. Senator Morgan suggested the other day something about dispensing with security for the costs on the part of the plaintiff in patent cases. That is not a provision peculiar to the patent law at all. It is not a part of the patent law. In United States courts all suits must be between residents of different districts, and they must be brought in the district where the defendant lives; and therefore the plaintiff is almost always a non-resident, except in patent and bankruptcy cases, where by reason of the nature of the controversy jurisdiction attaches without regard to the fact of the residence of the defendant in the district in which the action is brought.

If there is to be any change on that subject, it seems to me the amendment ought to be of the judiciary act and not merely of the patent law. I should not like to see a patent act loaded down with things which belong to other matters.

In accordance with Mr. Senator Morgan's suggestion, it was understood that a clause should be inserted in the latter part of section 2, authorizing the court at its discretion to award against the defeated party in patent causes such sum as it saw fit to cover counsel fees and expenses of suit, if the claims set up by the plaintiff, or defenses or infringements of the defendant have been vexatious or upon frivolous grounds. Perhaps those phrases restrict the power to cases of malice. I would, therefore, use the words " without probable cause," instead of " upon frivolous grounds." These words have an established legal meaning in the revenue laws, and in the law of prize, and are there used to distinguish between acts which the court thinks are not deserving of censure, though not justifiable as matter of law, and cases where the party offending has shown a lack of a proper respect for the rights of others.

The answer to the rest of Mr. Hubbell's remarks is found in the views which have already been presented to the committee. There is one great beauty of the constitutional provision about patents which he seems to lose sight of and which I think cannot too often be insisted upon. Government does not collect taxes from the people and pay them to the inventor in the way of reimbursement for his time and expenses. It gives him the exclusive right to his discovery—the right to use, to sell, and to license others. His reward, therefore, not only is a part of the general gain of which the public have all the rest, but it is directly based upon, dependent upon the money value of his invention, irrespective of the cost to him ; it is exactly what, under the operation of the inexorable laws of trade, he can sell his rights for. The remedies should be based on the same theory. He should have the profits which come for the use of it or the damage he suffers from interference with his enjoyment of it, and they are to be based on the commercial value of his invention, its market-value, just as his gains would be if he were left alone. Otherwise dull, wasteful, expensive, tedious, and useless mediocrity will get overpaid and the brilliant genius that invented the cotton-gin will get little or nothing.

I had one or two verbal amendments which I thought of suggesting, but I can as well leave them with the reporter. I will say with regard to the longer amendment suggested to section 8, it is one that I have been asked to hand to the committee.

It seems to me to be proper. Without it the section is one-sided. The public have always the patentee to notify under this section, but there is no one to be called the public and notified by the patentee. Practically the patentee cannot avail himself of this section. It is therefore quite reasonable that when the petitioner starts an inquiry upon a particular subject and puts in all the evidence on one side, the patentee may, in the same proceeding, and on the spot (always under the direction of the court), put in the evidence on the other side and thus, so to speak, complete the record ; and when any one opens that record to avail himself of it, the whole may be used if part is. I ought to say that I have not conferred with all my associates about it enough to say that all of them approve it, though I do not know of any disapproval. One of the other amendments is intended to prevent the depositions from being destroyed by technical or formal objections when it is too late to remedy them.

I did want to say one word on another subject. Mr. Hubbell says the inventors are not represented. I beg leave to say that Mr. Smith, Mr. Livermore, and myself have undertaken to work upon this bill partly at the request of some inventors and patent-owners, who are far-sighted enough to see and to believe that a bill which is best for everybody is best for their own interests ; and between us and other gentlemen, I think that not only inventors, but both sides have been fully represented, and probably as large interests on both sides as were ever collected in this room before.

The arguments upon the bill having been concluded, the committee adjourned.

APPENDIX.

The amendments suggested November 30, 1877, by Mr. Storrow to Senate bill 300 are

SECTION 8.

Line 12. After " examined " insert " and the facts proposed to be proved by each."
Line 15. After " may " insert " if it deems it just and reasonable so to do."
Line 16. After " directing " insert " before whom and."
Line 19. At end, after " and," insert " the petitioners may."
Line 20. Strike out " which " and insert " relating to the facts set forth in the petition ; and thereupon, in relation to or in rebuttal or avoidance of the matters put in evidence by the petitioners, the respondents may introduce the legal testimony of such witnesses as they or any of them may see fit to call, and as the court, upon application, in the same proceeding may permit. All said."
Line 21. After " shall be " insert " certified by the person or persons taking the same, and by him or them, respectively, returned to the court and."
Line 28. After " party " insert " No testimony taken hereunder shall be rejected by reason of failure to comply with this act in respect of the form of the petition or the manner of taking the testimony, or upon the ground that it relates to matters not set forth in the petition, application, or orders, unless, upon objection duly made, and upon motion filed in court, not later than one calendar month after the return of the testimony objected to, the court, in said proceeding, shall sustain such objection."
Line 52. At end of section add : " But whenever testimony taken hereunder by the petitioners shall be used, testimony taken in the same proceeding, by the respondents, in relation to or in rebuttal or avoidance of the matters referred to by said evidence of the petitioners, may be used by the party against whom said evidence of the petitioners is used."

SECTION 10.

Line 5. After " shall " insert " within a reasonable time."

SECTION 11.

Add at end of section :
" It shall be the duty of the Commissioner to keep a record of said payments, and a receipt therefor, or a certificate that the payment has been made, sealed and executed in the manner required by law for certified copies, shall be conclusive evidence of the payment ; and upon request it shall be the duty of the Commissioner to cause such a certificate to be indorsed upon or annexed to the letters patent."
Line 5 *and line* 8. Before " patent " insert " original."

Suggestions of Mr. Dodge as to section 1 *of Senate bill* 300.

1. This is not a statute of limitations of the ordinary kind. It does not limit the *time within which an action must be brought,* but it limits the *time for which a recovery can be had ;* hence it is a limitation of the *amount to be recovered.*
2. It will work a great wrong in certain cases, because it will *cut off the right of recovery* in cases where patents are infringed *without the knowledge of the owner of the patent,* and such cases are numerous.
All *process* patents, and a large proportion of mechanical patents, can be infringed secretly, because no one can tell from an examination of the article whether it is made by a patented process or machine. All such may be shut up in a room and worked for years and the patentee know nothing about it. In nearly all manufacturing establishments the public are shut out—not admitted ; hence can't find out. Besides, the owner has no reason to suppose his patent is being infringed, is no way put on his guard, and how, then, can he know it ?
Again, this is a very large country, and in order to spread himself all over it at once,

a party must be spread out exceedingly thin ; in short, *it is a physical impossibility* for him to know what is being done all over this vast country.

As a prominent law-writer has said : "Patent property *is the most difficult of all property to defend.* It cannot, like real or personal property, be defended by possession or force, *because it is intangible ; and a thousand different persons may infringe it in a thousand different places at the same moment.*"

Why, then, should the owner be cut off for damages that accrued in a distant part of the country, or by *a secret use,* when in the nature of things *he could not know of the infringement?* It is clearly unjust. It would be like a law prohibiting a citizen from recovering his horse or other property that had been stolen, because, being from home, he did not know *when* it was stolen.

Hence the section should be so amended as not to let the limitation run against a party before he had knowledge of the infringement.

3. On the other hand, it does sometimes happen, though not often, that a party innocently infringes a patent, or some claim of a patent, and the owner of the patent has knowledge of it, and *purposely keeps still, in order to let the infringement go on, so as to pile up the damages.*

This is all wrong; and therefore the law should be so amended as to compel the owner of a patent to give notice in writing, or bring suit, say within *one year* after he has knowledge of the infringement, or be barred from recovery.

These two amendments would obviate the wrong or hardship on both sides, and make the operation of the statute just to all parties.

I do think the committee will see the force and reason of these suggestions, and hope they will draw or amend the bill accordingly.

Respectfully submitted by

W. C. DODGE.

As to jury-trials in patent causes, they are very seldom resorted to, and generally only in cases where the party hopes to secure, by the sympathies or prejudices of the jury (generally his neighbors and friends), that which he feels assured a court of equity would not give him.

I would as soon have a patent cause of my own, if I had one, decided by a toss of dice, as by an ordinary jury ; not because they are dishonest, but because they are utterly incompetent to understand the various inventions involved in the consideration of the case. Hence I would give courts of equity exclusive jurisdiction of these cases.

What we ought to have is *special courts for the trial of patent causes,* as is proposed in England, with judges who have such a knowledge of mechanics and the arts as to enable them to dispense with the services of "experts," as a general rule. This would relieve the present overburdened courts, secure early decisions, and greatly lessen the expense and delay of litigation, which is becoming something appalling. But I suppose this cannot be had at present, though it certainly ought to be.

W. C. DODGE.

UNITED STATES PATENT ASSOCIATION.

Mr. DODGE presented a series of resolutions adopted by the United States Patent Association, composed of manufacturers and others interested in patents, and residing in various sections of the country, with the remark that they related to certain changes of the law, some of which are provided for in the present bill.

At the annual meeting of the United States Patent Association, at Philadelphia, September 7, 1876, the following resolutions were adopted:

Resolved, That in the opinion of this association the best interests of the public and the Patent Office demand that the law be amended to provide as follows :

First. That the Patent Office be separated from the Interior Department, and organized as a separate bureau, on a basis similar to the Agricultural Bureau.

Second. That the tenure of the Patent Office officials, from the Commissioner to and including the principal examiners, should be for life, or during competency and good behavior; and that their appointments be made with especial reference to their qualifications for the duties to be performed, regardless of politics, under a proper civil-service reform.

Third. That the entire receipts of the Patent Office, under proper safeguards, should be used for securing increased facilities for the transaction of its business with promptness and efficiency.

Fourth. That before any one shall be permitted to practice as a patent solicitor he must first have passed such an examination, before a board approved by the Commissioner, as shall satisfy him that he is of proper character and has sufficient capacity and education to properly conduct applications before the Patent Office.

Fifth. That all transfers of any rights under a patent, of whatsoever kind or nature, including licenses, should be recorded in the Patent Office within sixty days from their execution, so that the record shall show how and in whom the title stands.

Sixth. That the law should be so amended that when a patent is reissued the owner thereof shall not be deprived of his right of recovery for infringements that occurred prior to the reissue; but that such right shall be preserved notwithstanding the reissue, and so that machines or articles made prior to such reissue shall not be held liable for infringement of any new claim made in such reissue.

Seventh. That in the case of an application for the reissue of any patent the application and oath may be made, and the corrected specification signed by the assignee or assignees of the entire interest.

Eighth. That the examination system of the United States Patent Office, although it may be in some particulars defective, and may admit of improvements, is based on just principles, and is to the best interests of inventors and the public.

Ninth. That whereas, in a recent decision by the circuit court of the United States, the doubt has been expressed whether there is any authority in law for direct proceedings in the name of the United States or of any officer of the United States, for the repeal of letters patent for inventions : Therefore,

Resolved, That an amendment to the existing statutes to provide for such direct proceedings for the vacation of letters patent for inventions, on the ground of fraud or improvidence in the grant thereof, is desirable.

Suggestions filed by John E. Hatch upon proposed amendments to the patent laws before the Senate committee.

SECTION 1.

Some statute of limitations upon suits under the patent law is desirable, but especial care is necessary to so frame it as to avoid any features which may facilitate powerful corporations or combinations in their efforts to thwart or crush out struggling patentees whose resources are comparatively limited. We respectfully suggest two modifications of the proposed section :

First. The four years' limitation should apply only where the infringement is public and open. Where it is a secret or concealed manufacture or use, the statute should begin to run from the time when it becomes public, or is brought to the knowledge of the patentee or assignee of the patent. Infringements are often carried on stealthily for years. This is especially true where the invention relates to a process, as, for instance, a chemical process. Infringers should not be protected by law in such infringements so long as they can successfully evade detection. The analogy of other statutes of limitation should be observed in this respect.

Second. Where the patentee is prosecuting in good faith one suit in which the validity and construction of his patent is to be tested, he should not be obliged to increase the expense by commencing a large number of other suits which may be scattered through many districts in which only the same issues can be raised.

Such a suit often consumes, from the time of service unto the entering of the interlocutory decree of the circuit court, more than the time allowed by the proposed statute of limitations, when the patentee is pushing it with all possible diligence, It is not uncommon for the circuit court to hold the case under advisement more than half that time, after it is submitted on argument, before rendering its opinion, and probably all lawyers of any considerable experience in this branch of practice will recall cases which, after argument, the court has held under consideration much longer than this. There may be scores of similar infringements within the same district, and many more scattered over the country. It is neither considerate toward the patentee nor in the interest of a wise public policy to compel the owner of the patent, under pain of forfeiture, to institute a large number of suits involving the same issues. The court costs alone, irrespective of attorneys' fees and other expenses, would, in many instances, consume a fortune. The courts are already behind their dockets and overcrowded with business. Such suits, whether commenced to be immediately prosecuted or to be stayed by order of the court, would clog the dockets and greatly increase the labor of the chancellor and all officers of the court. Even under the provisions for granting a stay of proceedings, the difficulty is but partially remedied. The costs of commencing the suit alone usually amount to from one to three hundred dollars in each suit. The moving party is often required to give bonds in a considerable amount. Under the provision of this section he might repeatedly be compelled to appear before the courts by his counsel in remote districts to attend upon motions made by defendants. The defendants are also put to the cost of employing counsel and appearing in court. Nothing is gained by either party by all this expensive proceeding beyond a notice of the claims of the owner of the patent and a suspension of the statute of limitations.

A powerful combination could soon multiply expenses upon a patentee to, such an extent that he must surrender in despair.

We suggest the following amendments as accomplishing all that is necessary in the way of protecting alleged infringers from delay and bringing the issues before the court, and at the same time as far as possible restricting the expense and labor to which the owner of the patent is put in preserving his rights:

"*Provided*, That where a party has commenced, and is prosecuting in good faith, and with reasonable diligence, a suit in which the validity or construction of the patent sued upon is in issue, he may serve upon any infringers of such patent notices that they are infringing, and of the pending of said suit, stating the court in which and parties between which the same is pending; and in any suit upon said patent against any party so served with notice, commenced within ninety days after the entry of the decree or judgment of the court of original jurisdiction in said first-mentioned suit, determining the issues therein raised affecting the validity and construction of said patent, such notice, if pleaded in the declaration, petition, or bill of complaint therein, shall have the same effect in preserving the right of recovery as such declaration, petition, or bill of complaint would have if filed at the time of service of said notice: *Provided, however*, That if any party so served with notice shall at any time make it appear unto the court in which said first suit is pending that the same is not being prosecuted in good faith and with reasonable diligence, such court shall have power, by its order, to limit the time thereafter within which said notice shall continue to preserve the rights of recovery against the party moving for such order. And in any suit against said party, commenced after the expiration of the time so limited by court, said notice shall be of no effect for the purposes hereinbefore recited."

Under this provision, court-costs and counsel-fees in commencing suits to be subsequently stayed are saved. The alleged infringers themselves are relieved from considerable expense; they suffer nothing from the notice. Patentees will be deterred from serving notices unnecessarily by the fact that they by so doing invite co-operation in defense. The courts will be relieved from a large number of unnecessary suits. The alleged infringers will be enabled, upon notice, to examine the scope and validity of the patent, and to determine their action accordingly, without the expense of appearing or obtaining any orders of court in suits against them. They will also, if they prefer, be enabled to avail themselves of their remedy, under section 9 or 10, by a suit in equity against any party who serves them with such notice.

Perhaps, instead of this provision, it would be quite as well to so frame the section that it shall read as follows: "That from and after the passage of this act no profits or damages in any suit at law or equity for infringement of a patent shall be recovered which shall have accrued more than four years next proceeding the service of notice of the alleged infringement upon the defendant;" and strike out all that follows the seventh line. This would leave persons who served with notice to seek their remedy under the ninth or tenth section, if they do not choose to wait the commencement of suit by the patentee.

SECTION 2.

The latter part of this section, from the twenty-seventh to the thirty-ninth line inclusive, is desirable as an amendment to the law as it now stands. The first part of this section would not, in most instances, vary the operation of the law as contained in the Revised Statutes. Wherever an established license-fee seems to afford any measure of the damages actually suffered by the plaintiff, the courts would, under the present statute, invariably adopt it as the measure of damages. It is only in the absence of such a license-fee, where the plaintiff has chosen some other method of obtaining the benefit of his franchise, or where some peculiar equity arises which cannot be satisfied by a license-fee, that the court adopts a different measure. In such cases it would be unwise to limit the discretion of the court. Suppose, under this section as now proposed, an exclusive license had been granted to certain parties, who are the sole manufacturers under the patent, the territory within which they have the exclusive license is invaded by infringers; all their profits, which might otherwise be large, are destroyed. The license-fee would be the measure of recovery for the owner of the patent under whom they were licensed, but it would leave nothing for the exclusive licensees, who have perhaps suffered several times the injury inflicted upon the owner. Under the present statute the courts would be authorized to give actual damages or the profits acquired by the infringers by reason of the wrongful use of the invention. Under the statute proposed there would seem to be no relief for the exclusive licensees.

There are also instances where the owner of the patent finds it extremely important to limit the licenses granted to certain localities, which will not affect the profits of his own manufacture. Infringers coming directly into his market may inflict upon him an injury manifold greater than the amount of the license-fee which he has established in reference to the remoteness of his licensees. In all such cases latitude is allowed, the courts under the law as it now stands to look into the actual damages suffered, adopting as their measure either the license-fee or such other evidence as may under the circumstances of the case seem to afford a more just and accurate means of determining the actual injury.

In cases where the license-fee is the proper measure of damages, the proposed amendment would not change the operation of the law as it now stands; in cases where this is not the proper measure of damages, it is better that no change should be made.

The question as to in what way it is for the interest of the patentee to use his franchise, whether by license or otherwise, is not a proper one to be determined by either court or jury. This property, so long as it exists, should be treated, like other property, as belonging to the owner, to be used by him as he may see fit, provided by so doing he inflicts no injury upon others. The theory of the patent law is that he has a right for a limited period of time to retain for himself the benefit of his invention. The inexpediency and injustice of submitting to a court or jury to determine how a person shall use other property than that secured under letters patent would be at once evident. The public have an interest in having all property wisely used. It is for the interest of certain communities that certain crops be cultivated to the exclusion of others, and it would be as reasonable to empower courts and juries to determine how a land-owner shall cultivate his fields, and what produce he should bring into the market, as to submit to the same authority the question as to whether the patentee should reap the advantage of his franchise by manufacturing and selling the article covered by it himself in person or through his agents or by licensing the public at large to manufacture and sell it upon a license-fee. It is as proper for courts and juries to determine whether a man ought to sell his timber and fix a price upon it, when he chooses to preserve his forests undisturbed, as for the same tribunal to determine that he should grant licences under his patent and fix the price on such licenses, when he chooses to reserve the rights to himself. It is a fundamental rule of law, not in any way peculiar to this subject-matter, that any person who has been wronged by another is entitled to such compensation as shall indemnify him, so far as pecuniary damages can, for the injury inflicted upon him, and that no person who has availed himself of the property of another wrongfully shall be permitted to retain any profits made through his own wrong. The peculiarity of the present statute is not that it entitles a patentee, in seeking his remedy, to either rely upon indemnity for the injury inflicted upon him, or upon the profits made by reason of the wrongful appropriation of his property by a wrong-doer; it is in the fact that it enables the same court, and that a court peculiarly adapted to the purpose by its mode of procedure, to apply either remedy, as the equities of the case may demand. In this provision the statute is peculiarly fortunate. There is no reason why patentees should be deprived of both these remedies any more than why they should be withheld in cases where the rights pertaining to other classes of property are involved. There are difficulties in the application of these rules to all classes of property; none that are peculiar to property existing under the patent law.

As the law now stands, the patentee, in an account of profits, is only entitled to such savings as are shown to be due to the use of his invention, except, possibly, where the law in regard to confusion of property might apply. The only substantial change introduced by the portion of the proposed section, from line 16 to 26 inclusive, is that under this section, if a defendant could show that by reason of mismanagement or misfortune in any part of the business in which he had wrongfully used the invention he had recovered little or no profits, this would be so far a bar to recover, although it might be that through the use of the invention he had actually saved a very large amount. For illustration: A railroad company might wantonly use an improved brake for years, saving to itself many thousands of dollars; but if by mismanagement in some of its departments the company had squandered the profits so saved, and was able to say that, as a whole, it had accumulated no profits through its business, the owner of the patent upon this brake could make no recovery. The proper rule is the one adopted by the Supreme Court under the present statute, by which the actual savings by reason of the use of the invention is the measure of the recovery. We suggest that the present law, that is section 4921 of the Revised Statutes, amended by substituting for its last clause the portion of this section extending from the 27th to the 39th line inclusive, would be preferable to the entire section as proposed.

If the first part of the section proposed is to be retained, the license-fee should be made a measure of damages only as against a party who has established such fee. It would be unfair for a territorial assignee of a valuable patent to be precluded from recovering substantial damages by reason of the fact that the owner of the same patent for other territory had some time granted licenses for a trivial sum.

The 4th, 5th, 6th, and 7th lines of this section and the 14th and 15th seem somewhat at variance. Would it not be better to have the 14th and 15th read: "But if not, then the court or jury shall determine from the evidence in the case what is an adequate remuneration for the damages sustained by reason of the infringement," striking out what precedes the middle of the 10th line?

SECTION 3.

This section is needed, and seems to be in all respects free from objection.

SECTION 4.

Query, whether this amendment has not the effect of lessening the importance that should be attached to a final decree in the court of original jurisdiction, and of encouraging a dilatory preparation for the trial upon the assumption that, if it should go against the defendants, they will still have an opportunity of looking up and presenting new defenses. The practice in some of the circuit courts has become such already that in many cases the final decree is but the beginning of litigation, to be followed by motions for rehearing and petitions for review almost indefinitely. It is on many accounts desirable that when a patentee has fought through a suit to final judgment, that final judgment should, so far as a judgment of the court in which it is entered can, set the question between the parties at rest. The parties should be made to feel that in preparing for trial they are preparing for a final adjudication of the issues between them, and while there may be exceptional instances where justice might be furthered by this statute, it is probable that the advantages obtained in this way would be more than counterbalanced many times over by the embarrassments and hardships that would be inflicted upon the patentee. If such a statute is passed, should it not be with the provision that the courts should have power, whenever motion is made for the relief therein provided for, to award to the plaintiff in the original cause, costs sufficient to compensate him for the labor and expense occasioned by the same?

SECTION 5.

This section appears to be an improvement upon the law as it now stands. Should not the reissue be confined to that which is suggested in the original specification as novel with the patentee? Models showing entire machines are often filed where the invention relates to a subordinate feature. Where the patentee does not suggest that he has originated anything more than a particular feature of the machine, should he, after evidence that other features were old has disappeared, be permitted to reissue and claim all that is shown in the model? As the section stands, a patent which suggests no novelty in anything beyond the wheel or axle of a carriage, may be reissued ten years after to cover the carriage-seat that happens to be shown in the model. The fact that a feature appears in a model is not even presumptive evidence of novelty.

SECTION 6.

This is also an improvement. We suggest that there should be inserted in the twelfth line of this section, after the words "and no suit shall be barred or abated by such surrender," the words, "except as to claims not retained in the reissued patent." The provision at the end of this section as it now reads, would seem to exclude subsequent reissues of letters patent that have once been reissued prior to the date of the passage of this act, from the operation of the act. This probably is not intended, and the language should be so changed as to avoid this construction. We suggest that instead of reading "shall apply to letters patent reissued prior to the date of the passage of this act," it should read, "shall apply to reissues granted prior to the date of the passage of this act." Letters patent reissued prior to the date of the passage of this act should, so far as all subsequent reissues are concerned, be under the operation of the amendments.

SECTION 7.

This is an improvement much called for. It is possible that there should be some provision by which either of several persons who had by mistake joined in the application as joint inventors, might, upon a proper showing to the Commissioner, and upon indemnifying the other nominal joint inventors against any costs to which they might be put in the proceedings, be entitled to have the patent corrected. Otherwise, one obstinate party might exact unreasonable terms of those joined with him, or prevent their obtaining the relief to which they were in equity entitled.

SECTION 8.

We think there are some objections to this section, and that its purposes are better answered by sections 9 and 10. Under section 8, as it now stands, it would be possible for powerful combinations, by serving notices of taking testimony in remote portions of the country, and perhaps contemporaneously, to inflict enormous expense and hardship upon patentees, and virtually to prevent their attending upon the taking of all the evidence that was to be used against them. The statute would often be abused, and made the instrument for crushing out patentees whose resources would soon be exhausted. If this section is to pass, it should be with such limitations as will enable the courts, by their order, to indemnify the patentee or owner of the patent for all reasonable costs and expenses, as well as for his time.

It would seem, however, that sections 9 and 10 answer all the reasonable uses for which section 8 is intended, while not exposing the patentee to the expense of attending upon testimony that is not to be used in a case actually pending and to be prosecuted to determination.

SECTIONS 9 AND 10.

These are both much-needed amendments, and appear to be properly drawn.

SECTIONS 12

and following, appear to be substantially correct.

JOHN E. HATCH.
ROBT. H. PARKINSON.

SECTION 11.

This section could not be justified upon the score of increasing the revenue of the Patent Office, for this avowedly is not the object of our patent-system, as it is of some European systems. It would probably hardly be within the scope of the authority conferred upon Congress by the clause of the Constitution relating to this subject, to impose an additional taxation upon inventors simply for the purpose of increasing the national revenues. This clause would be justified, if at all, upon the theory that it would serve to eliminate the worthless patents after a limited period. The practical difficulty is, that it is oftener the most valuable inventions than the most frivolous that only begin to pay for themselves after a period of years, during which they have been the source of both labor and expense. The statute would operate quite as strongly and probably more strongly against the most meritorious inventions. The more novel an invention is, the wider departure it makes from established usages, the more opposition it encounters in the market. The history of the most valuable patents would show that few of them have remunerated the patentee for actual cash expenses during the first five years, while many have fallen far short of such remuneration during the first ten years. Fifty or one hundred dollars is, to many inventors, who are struggling against the difficulties of introducing a new manufacture, and exhausting all their resources in the effort, a very considerable sum, sufficient in many cases, when added to the difficulties they are encountering, to complete their discouragement. The more frivolous patents often bring a speedy remuneration, and are quite as likely, if not more likely, to be continued under the provisions of this act than those of greater originality and scope. If a patent is worthless it does no harm to have it still nominally in force. It is sometimes said that it serves to deter subsequent invention. If it covers nothing that is really essential and valuable in subsequent inventions it cannot do this; if it simply shows some feature which is inoperative and invalid in the mechanism which it covers, the patent would itself be invalid, so far as this feature is concerned, and could not be the means of preventing its use in combinations where it is operative. If it covers some improvement which is found to be essential in subsequent inventions, it is but fair that so far as this improvement has contributed to the public by the original inventor, he should have the right of property in it during the term for which patents are usually granted. Moreover, if at the end of four years, the only purpose which a patent serves is to restrain subsequent invention, the fee is quite as likely to be paid for the purpose of continuing the patent in use and obtaining royalties from the owners of subsequent patents involving this invention as it is for any other purpose; in any case the statute would not seem to discriminate between frivolous and meritorious inventions, to the advantage of the latter.

ROBT. H. PARKINSON.

We agree as to the suggestions above made, except as to the eleventh section. If, at the end of four years, a patent has not shown sufficient utility to justify an expenditure of fifty dollars to keep it alive, should it not expire, so as to leave the field open for subsequent inventors of really valuable improvements?

JOHN E. HATCH.

STATEMENT OF THE ASSISTANT COMMISSIONER OF PATENTS.

DEPARTMENT OF THE INTERIOR,
Washington, D. C., December 10, 1877.

SIR : In compliance with the request of the Assistant Commissioner of Patents, I have the honor to transmit herewith, for the consideration of your committee, a communication embodying his views on section 24, Senate bill No. 300, for amending the statutes in relation to patents.

Very respectfully,

A. BELL,
Acting Secretary.

HON. NEWTON BOOTH,
Chairman Committee on Patents, U. S. S.

___

PATENT OFFICE, *Washington, December* 7, 1877.

SIR : I desire to submit, as briefly as possible, some remarks on the last proviso in section 24 of Senate bill No. 300 for amending the statutes in relation to patents.

The proviso referred to reads as follows:

"*And provided further,* That in the case of reissues no interference shall be declared with any patent of later date than that sought to be reissued, except when the original application for such subsequent patent is shown by the office records to have been of prior date to the application of the patent sought to be reissued, nor with any application for a patent filed subsequent to the date of the patent sought to be reissued ; but, if desired by such subsequent applicant or patentee, on an application for reissue, an interference may be had with the reissued patent, after the same shall have been issued."

An interference is a proceeding to determine which of two or more parties is the first and original inventor.

The scope of a reissue and the power of the Commissioner in granting the same is thus set forth by the United States Supreme Court:

Power is unquestionably conferred upon the Commissioner to allow the specification to be amended, if the patent is inoperative or invalid, and in that event to issue a new patent in proper form, and he may doubtless, under that authority, allow the patentee to redescribe his invention, and to include in the description and claims of the patent not only what was well described before, but whatever else was suggested or substantially indicated in the specification, drawing, or Patent Office model which properly belonged to the invention as actually made or perfected. Seymour *v.* Osborn, 11 Wall., 514.

The act relating to patents of February 21, 1793 (sec. 9), first authorized the proceeding known as an interference. It provided that in case of interfering applications the same should be submitted to the arbitration of three persons, one of whom to be chosen by each of the applicants and the third person to be appointed by the Secretary of State ; the decision or award of such arbitrators in writing was final as far as respected the granting of the patent.

The reissue of a patent was first provided for by section 3 of the act of July 3, 1832 (4 Stat. at Large, 559). The ground for such reissue as there expressed was, that the original patent was invalid or inoperative, by reason that any of the terms or conditions prescribed in the third section of the act of February 21, 1793, had not by inadvertence, accident, or mistake, and without any fraudulent or deceptive intention,

S. Mis. 50——14

been complied with on the part of the said inventor; and the Secretary of State was therein authorized, upon the surrender to him of such defective patent, "to cause a new patent to be granted to the said inventor for the same invention for the residue of the period then unexpired, for which the original patent was granted, *upon his compliance with the terms and conditions prescribed in the said third section of the said act.*"

The conditions of the third section of the act of 1793 were that the applicant should swear or affirm that he was the true inventor or discoverer of that for which he solicited a patent; that he should deliver a written description of his invention in full, clear, and concise terms; explain the principle thereof, distinguish the invention from others known before, furnish drawings, &c.

Just prior to the passage of the act of 1832 the United States Supreme Court (Chief-Justice Marshall delivering the opinion) had, in the absence of any statutory regulation, upheld the Secretary of State in reissuing patents to correct inadvertent omissions or other accidents in the description of the original patent. (Grant *vs.* Raymond, 6 Peters, 218.)

Section 8 of the act of July 4, 1836 (5 Stat. at L., 117), gave to the Commissioner of Patents the power to determine "the question of priority of right or invention" between pending applications and between the latter and any unexpired patent; and section 13 of the same act the power to reissue patents.

Section 8 of the act of March 3, 1837 (5 S. L., 191), provided that "whenever a patent shall be returned for correction and reissue, the specification of claim annexed to every such patent shall be subject to revision and restriction in the same manner as are original applications for patents," and further required that the Commissioner should not grant the reissue until the applicant shall have "altered his specification of claim in accordance with the decision of the Commissioner; and in all such cases the applicant, if dissatisfied with such decision, shall have the same remedy and be entitled to the benefit of the same privileges and proceedings as are provided by law in the case of original applications for patents."

The laws relating to interferences and reissues remained as thus prescribed by the acts of 1836 and 1837 until the passage of the act of July 8, 1870. (16 S. L., 198.) Section 42 of this act, which is precisely the same in terms as section 4904 Rev. Stat., provides:

Whenever an application is made for a patent which, in the opinion of the Commissioner, would interfere with any pending application, or with any unexpired patent, he shall give notice thereof to the applicants, or applicant and patentee, as the case may be, and shall direct the primary examiner to proceed to determine the question of priority of invention. And the Commissioner may issue a patent to the party who is adjudged the prior inventor, unless the adverse party appeals from the decision of the primary examiner, or of the board of examiners-in-chief, as the case may be, within such time, not less than twenty days, as the Commissioner shall prescribe.

Section 53 of this act (sec. 4916 R. S.), relating to reissues, continues the restriction placed upon their grant by section 8 of the act of 1837, above cited, viz: "The specification and claim in every such case shall be subject to revision and restriction in the same manner as original applications are."

From the time of the passage of the act of 1837 until nearly the present date the Patent Office and the courts, so far as the matter came before them, held that these provisions requiring reissue applications to be revised and restricted in the same manner as original applications are, authorized the Commissioner of Patents to declare interferences with reissue applications and original applications and unexpired patents to determine the question of priority whenever the reissue applicant claimed that to which another applicant or patentee asserted title. December 20, 1859, in the sewing-machine case of Wilson (assignee of Aikens & Felthousen) *vs.* Singer, the circuit court of this District, on appeal from the Commissioner, held, in affirmance of the Commissioner on that point, that under the 8th section of the act of 1837, on a reissue "the question of joint invention is open, as is also priority of invention, laches, or any other legal cause, which on an original would lead the Commissioner to refuse a patent. * * * It is not only competent for, but the duty of the Commissioner, to declare an interference if there is an existing claimant asserting right as original first inventor, and so the office has properly decided in this very case. * * * The duty of the Commissioner to the public calls him to decide these questions when they arise and appear in the evidence before him, before he issues the patent applied for. Mr. Wilson, the applicant for the reissue, must meet the questions not only of priority, as to Singer, but the right to a joint patent of Aikens & Felthousen, his assignors in the original patent granted to them August 5, 1851." (3 *Book of Appeals, Patent Office,* 334.)

The same reissue application of Atkins & Felthousen was made subsequently the subject of a second interference with another party, and in sustaining the right of the Commissioner to declare such second interference, Mr. Justice Nelson, in the case of Potter *vs.* Dixon, 2 Fisher, 381, remarked that section 8 of the act of March 3, 1837, conferred on the Commissioner the same power on a reissue, over the question of granting it, which he possessed in the case of an original application for a patent.

The rightfulness of declaring interferences with reissue applications was reaffirmed by the circuit court of this District, in the cases of Hicks *vs.* Shaver, 3 Book of Appeals, Pat. Off., 439, and Snowden *vs.* Pearce, *Ib.*, 468.

In June, 1868, however, a decision was rendered by his honor Judge Fisher, of the supreme court of this District, in the matter of the appeal of Merrill and Carlton, assignees for reissue of patent issued to C. Reichman in 1858 for improvement in lamp-burners, in which it was held that the Commissioner's power over a reissue application was a limited one, to "revise and restrict" the same as original applications were restricted as to form, and to confine the same to the invention set forth in the original patent, *and that was all.* " He has no right," the court observed, "to review and revise prior decisions of the office made upon the original application, but only to restrict the specification proposed for reissue, so as to limit it to the original invention." The court, therefore, ordered the interference in that case to be dissolved. The effect of this decision would have been, if observed, to have prevented not only the declaration of an interference with a reissue application, but all inquiry on the part of the office as to the *novelty* of the invention at the date of the original patent. This narrow construction of the law as to the power of the Commissioner over reissues had never before been advocated, and was not followed by the same court, as the records of this office show.

But in two recent cases the supreme court of this District orally held that the Commissioner of Patents had no authority of law to declare interferences with reissue applications. Mayall *ex parte*, June, 1875; Mayall and Williams *ex parte*, May 21, 1877. The decree in the case last named was amended June 19, 1877, to read that the reissue application should not be withheld " by reason of interference with any *junior* application."

The practice of this office was modified in accordance with these decrees.

The views of the Acting Commissioner of Patents on this subject were set forth as follows in the case of Carroll vs. Morse, 9 Off. Gaz., 453 :

In the case of Grant vs. Raymond (6 Peters, p. 218), which was decided before the statute relating to reissues was incorporated in the law, it was held, that "the new patent and the proceedings on which it issues have relation to the original transaction. The time of the privilege still runs from the date of the original patent. The application may be considered as appended to the original application."

So in Shaw vs. Cooper (7 Peters, p. 314), "the new patent has relation to the original transaction, and the application may be considered as appended to the original application." If the application may be considered as appended to the original application, I see no reason why it should not be revised and restricted precisely as the original application was, not only for the purpose of considering whether or not the claim and the description are the same as those set forth in the original application, but whether or not the thing claimed was new and original with the applicant. The purpose of the reissue is not to enable the applicant to set up any claims which he may choose, regardless of the state of the art, but for the purpose of enabling him to give a more perfect description of his invention. (O'Reilly vs. Morse, 15 How., p. 112.)

The terms of the act relating to reissues appear to me to clearly point out the duty of the Commissioner in respect to this matter. He is directed to subject the specifications and claims in every case of reissues to revision and restriction in the same manner as original applications are.

Now, the duty of the Commissioner in respect to the examination of original applications is not simply to see that no matter is introduced by way of amendment subsequent to the filing, which was not shown at the time of filing the application, for this would be a small matter, and of very infrequent occurrence ; but he must distinguish between what is old and what is new in the application, judging it by comparison with the state of the art existing at that time. It must follow, therefore, that the revision and restriction of reissue applications, in order to be the same, as in case of original applications, must cover the same ground. Any other view of the matter appears to me a departure from the plain sense of the words—a departure not required by the spirit of the law, or to harmonize any conflicting sections, and with no other result than a wholly mischievous one.

When an application, then, is made for the reissue of a patent, the duty of the examiner is first to determine what the invention of applicant is. Whatever existed prior to his invention, in any patent or printed publication, is not his invention ; and both he and the office are required to make a distinction between what is new, and of which a monopoly may be granted him, and what is old and must be denied him. In addition to this, the office must decide whether this new invention, which so far as appears from an examination into the state of the art may be conceded to him, was in any way shown in his original application. An examination into the state of the art is the very basis on which must be determined what his invention is, and without which nobody can know, not even the applicant himself. What a man invents is not necessarily his invention in a patentable sense. It may be the invention of a former generation, and any examination of an application for reissue which would leave out of sight the state of the art would not half fulfill the plain requirement of the law. This was the view of Judge Dunlop, in Wilson vs. Singer (MS. Appeal Cases, D. C., 60).

And as follows by the Commissioner and Acting Commissioner in the case of Sargent and Burge, 10 O. G., 285 :

In the case of Brooks vs. Fiske (15 How., 212), the court, in passing upon a reissued patent in controversy, said:

"It is deemed proper to remark that the fact of procuring a patent for a new and useful machine in 1845, under the assumption of a reissue, which was not useful as patented in 1828, for want of feed and pressure rollers, now used, as alleged in defense, would present a question of fraud, committed on the public by the patentee, by giving his reissued patent of 1845 date as an original discovery made in 1828, and thereby overreaching similar inventions made between 1828 and 1845."

In Burr vs. Duryee (1 Wall., 531), the court, after stating clearly and explicitly the fact that the invention embraced by the original patent in controversy was entirely new at the time of the filing of the original application, proceeded to say, however, that the purpose of the patentee was clearly transparent, by the means of elastic and equivocal claims and description, to cover up inventions subsequently made.

The court not only condemned this practice, but indicated the duty of the Patent Office in the premises in the following language:

"The Patent Bureau in this country is composed of men of scientific attainments, who examine the merits of every claimant of a patent, and decide whether, in their opinion, it attempts to claim a monopoly of things before known or invented. They are not expected, as formerly, to grant a patent, without inquiring, to every applicant who is ready to pay the fees. Such a course of conduct would be highly injurious to the public, by furnishing means to impose on the public by false pretenses, and with threats of expensive and ruinous litigation.

"The surrender of valid patents, and the granting of reissued patents thereon, with expanded or equivocal claims, where the original was clearly neither 'inoperative nor invalid,' and whose specifications is neither 'defective nor insufficient,' is a great abuse of the privilege granted by the statute, and productive of great injury to the public. This privilege was not given to the patentee or his assignees, in order that the patent may be rendered more elastic or expensive, and therefore more 'available' for the suppression of all other inventions."

Again the same court, in Carlton vs. Bokee (17 Wall., 471), remarked:

"We think it proper to reiterate our disapprobation of these ingenious attempts to expand a simple invention of a distinct device into an all-embracing claim, calculated by its wide generalizations and ambiguous language to discourage further invention in the same department of industry and to cover antecedent inventions."

*   *   *   *   *   *

It being the duty of the office, then, to restrict reissue applications, in view of the state of the art, in the same manner as original applications are restricted, it remains only to inquire whether an interference is a necessary part of such restriction. The only evidence, in many cases, which the office has of the state of the art, as opposed to a particular patent or application, is the fact that the same invention is claimed by a different party.

Whenever a claim is made, of which the office has jurisdiction, it becomes its first duty under the law to ascertain whether the claimant is the first and original inventor. In the case of a patent opposed by an application, it is necessary to settle this question, in order to ascertain whether a patent shall also be granted to the applicant; and jurisdiction is given to the office over the patent, not for the purpose of correcting, restricting, or invalidating it, but for the purpose of ascertaining the rights of the opposing parties to the subject-matter thereof. So, in exercising the jurisdiction the law gives over a reissue application, no attempt is made, or lawfully can be made, by the office to invalidate the original patent. The surrender of that is not effected until a new one issues in its place. But the applicant for reissue having come within its jurisdiction, and the question being whether to him or to another party belongs the title of first and original inventor of the precise matter on which the government is asked to extend further and fuller protection, the office cannot avoid the determination of that question without violating the first and paramount duty required of it by the law. That question cannot be settled without an interference, or some other similar proceeding, by which the rights of the respective parties to this species of property can be judicially investigated and determined.

Whether a patent is valid or not is a question for the courts; but whether the patentee is the first inventor is a question for the office whenever the protection of the office to a particular invention is asked by one who opposes the claims of the patentee to that title.

It is said that reissue applicants, under the practice of declaring interferences therewith, are subject to the embarrassment of having their patents frequently held up in the Patent Office, while the life of the same is running out, to determine the question of priority between such reissue applicant and another subsequent patentee or applicant who may have intentionally incorporated into his patent or application matter found but not claimed in the original patent of the reissue applicant. In such cases, too, it is urged, the right of the reissue applicant to sue in the courts is so greatly delayed, that often, by the time the applicant has succeeded in correcting his original patent, no sufficient time remains to bring suit before the patent expires.

Without now contending that, without any exception, reissue applications should be put in interference whenever, upon coming into the office, they are confronted by patentees who have already claimed and applicants who are claiming the same invention, now for the first time perhaps claimed by the reissue applicant, it may be well to state that between six and seven hundred patents are now yearly reissued, and it is submitted that the power of the Commissioner to revise and restrict

reissue applications should not be curtailed or hampered to the detriment of other patentees and applicants and to that of the general public.
I am, very respectfully, your obedient servant,

W. H. DOOLITTLE,
Assistant Commissioner of Patents.

Hon. NEWTON BOOTH,
Chairman Senate Committee on Patents.

Amendments proposed and transmitted by the honorable COMMISSIONER OF PATENTS to "A bill to amend the statutes in relation to patents, and for other purposes." (Senate 300.)

Page 4, section 5, line 10, strike out all after the word " invention" to and including the word " entitled," in line 14.

Page 5, section 5, line 30, after the word " act" insert *"but no new matter shall be introduced into the specification not shown, contained, or substantially indicated in the specification or drawings of the original application or its amendments."*

Line 25, after " restriction" insert " and rejection."

Line 37, strike out from " shown" to end of section, and insert " contained or substantially indicated in the specification or drawings of the original application or its amendments, and to which he would have been entitled."

Section 5 will then read as follows:

SEC. 5. Section forty-nine hundred and sixteen of the Revised Statutes is hereby amended so as to read as follows: Whenever any patent is inoperative or invalid, by reason of a defective or insufficient specification, or by reason of the patentee claiming as his own invention or discovery more or less than he had a right to claim as new, if the error has arisen by inadvertence, accident, or mistake, and without any fraudulent or deceptive intention, the Commissioner shall, on the surrender of such patent and the payment of the duty required by law, cause a new patent for the same invention, and in accordance with the corrected specification, to be issued to the patentee, or in the case of his death or of an assignment of the whole or any undivided part of the original patent, then to his executors, administrators, or assigns, for the unexpired part of the term of the original patent. Such surrender shall take effect upon the issue of the amended patent. The Commissioner may, in his discretion, cause several patents to be issued for distinct and separate parts of the things so shown or described upon demand of the applicant, and upon payment of the required fee for a reissue for each of such reissued letters patent. The specifications and claim in every such case shall be subject to revision, restriction, and rejection in the same manner as original applications are. Every patent so reissued, together with the corrected specification, shall have the same effect and operation in law, on the trial of all actions for causes thereafter arising, as if the same had been originally filed in such corrected form, except as otherwise provided in this act; but no new matter shall be introduced into the specification not shown, contained, or substantially indicated in the specification or drawings of the original application or its amendments. In any suit at law or in equity upon a patent hereafter reissued, the defendant, having given notice or pleaded the same in the manner set forth in the forty-nine hundred and twentieth section of the Revised Statutes, may prove in defense to the whole patent, or any of the claims thereof, that the new patent, or any claim thereof, is not for the same invention shown, contained, or substantially indicated in the specification or drawings of the original application or its amendments, and to which he would have been entitled.

Page 15, section 16, line 7, after the word " price" insert "*for uncertified manuscript copies, the reasonable cost of making the same.*"

Page 17, strike out all of section 20.

Page 18, strike out all of section 22 and insert, "*Any person who has an interest in an invention or discovery, whether as inventor, discoverer, or as signee, for which a patent was ordered to issue upon the payment of the final fee, but who fails to make payment thereof within six months from the time at which it was passed and allowed and notice thereof was sent to the applicant or his agent, shall have a right to make an application for a patent tor such invention or discovery the same as in the case of an original application. But such second application, in order to be a continuation of the original application, must be made within two years after the allowance thereof. But no person shall be held responsible in damages for the manufacture or use of any article or thing for which a patent was ordered to issue under such renewed application prior to the issue of the patent. And upon the hearing of renewed applications preferred under this section, abandonment shall be considered as a question of fact.*"

Page 19, section 24, line 7, strike out the words "as the case may be." Also, line 12, strike out all after the word "chief" to and including the word " be."

Also, line 27, strike out the words " application of the."

REVISED STATUTES, section 483, is amended to read as follows:

The Commissioner of Patents shall cause to be classified and arranged in suitable cases, in the rooms and galleries provided for that purpose, models, specimens of composition, fabrics, manufactures, works of art, and designs which have been or shall be deposited in the Patent Office; and the rooms and galleries shall be kept open during suitable hours for public inspection.

The Commissioner may also receive such working models of patented machines or specimens of patented articles of suitable size as parties interested therein may desire to furnish and as will illustrate the progress of the arts. Such models and specimens shall remain in the custody of the Commissioner.

REVISED STATUTES, section 4891, is amended to read as follows:

In any case which admits of representation by model, if the drawings filed be deemed insufficient, or there be doubt whether the machine or device forming the subject of the application will operate in the manner set forth in the specification, or if in an interference or on appeal a model be deemed desirable for more ready illustration, the applicant, if required by the Commissioner, shall furnish a working model of convenient size to exhibit advantageously the several parts of the invention or discovery. Such models may, in the discretion of the Commissioner, be retained in the office or returned to the applicant. All such models, together with exhibits in interference cases, not deemed suitable to be retained in the office, and not removed after due notice, may be sold by the Commissioner, and the proceeds paid into the Treasury, as other patent moneys are directed to be paid.

STATEMENT OF THE COMMISSIONER OF PATENTS.

DEPARTMENT OF THE INTERIOR,
OFFICE OF THE SECRETARY,
December 11, 1877.

SIR: I have the honor to transmit herewith a communication from the Commissioner of Patents, relating to amendments of the patent law.

Very respectfully,

C. SCHURZ,
Secretary.

Hon. NEWTON BOOTH,
Chairman Senate Committee on Patents.

DEPARTMENT OF THE INTERIOR,
UNITED STATES PATENT OFFICE,
Washington, D. C., December 11, 1877.

SIR: I beg leave to submit, through you, to the Senate Committee on Patents, some suggestions touching the proposed amendments to the law relating to patents, now under consideration by the honorable committee, together with some further amendments in relation thereto.

Sections 1, 2, 3, 4, 6, 8, 9, 10, 13, 14, and 24 of the bill (Senate bill 300) relate to matters pertaining more to the courts, and not directly to the organization of the office or the conduct of business therein, and I have left the discussion of these sections to the learned counsel who have heretofore presented this matter to the committee. I desire, however, simply to add that the sections specified have my hearty approval.

Of the other sections, a part were suggested by myself, and the rest were given definite form after I had been consulted in regard to them. With some less important exceptions, particularly specified in a paper accompanying this, entitled "Amendments proposed by the Commissioner of Patents to Senate bill 300," it seems highly important to me that the amendments offered in the bill should be incorporated in the law.

I suggest, in amendment to section 5 of the bill referred to, that all reference to the model in reissue applications be erased from the section. Under the present law, following the decisions of the courts, it has been the practice of the office to permit parties to amend their specifications and drawings in reissue patents by the model, and this although the model forms no part of the patent itself. This proceeding is objectionable, first, because it introduces into the patent matternot necessarily covered by the original oath, not described nor illustrated in the drawing, and not attested in any way by the applicant's original signature or that of his witnesses. It affords opportunity, therefore, for the introduction of matter of which the public could have no previous notice except by inspection of the model deposited in the Patent Office. The part shown in the model, not described or illustrated in the specification and drawing of the original application, would not appear in any copies which might be ordered of those original papers. Further, the amendment of the specification on reissue by the model gives opportunity for and suspicion of fraud in many cases. These models occupy large space, and it is not practicable to keep them in such close and faithful custody as not to give sometimes the opportunity to change a model by adding or subtracting some part so as to materially change the invention, a very slight change in some instances amounting to a very substantial difference. At the present time, it should also be stated, nearly half of the models in patented cases have been consumed, and to that extent patentees have been deprived of the opportunity to amend by models under the law as it now stands, so that the proposed amendment would simply place all patents now existing on the same basis. I think the amendment, whether considered in relation to patents already granted or hereafter to be granted, imposes no serious hardship, and is necessary for the protection of the public. The section, as amended, also omits the provision of the present law, authorizing the Commissioner in reissue cases, where there is neither model nor drawing, to allow an amendment of a specification upon proof, outside of the record, that the matter sought to be introduced by the amendment was a part of the original invention. The only evidence which can be produced in such cases consists of voluntary and *ex-parte* affidavits. The opportunity for fraud is so great and the temptation in some cases so strong, that it seems wise to omit the provision. If any case of hardship should arise under the law amended as proposed, it would be due to the patentee's own inadvertence in not originally describing his invention, and the probable damage to individuals in particular cases would be less than that likely to be inflicted on the public by a reissue of patents improperly enlarged.

The seventh section explains itself. Such cases have arisen from manifestly honest mistake, and the department has held that there was no authority under the law to justify the Secretary of the Interior in affixing his signature to a certificate of correction. The issue of a new patent seems unwise, and would not avail in case the invention had been in use more than two years before the mistake was discovered.

The eleventh section provides for the payment of certain fees during the life-time of the patent, at fixed periods, in default of which payment the patent shall expire. The object of this section is to abridge the life of patents which may be useless for the legitimate purposes for which patents are granted. It is to be presumed that any patents covering an invention brought into use, or which the patentee is endeavoring to bring into use, will be worth the payment of the small fee specified in the section, and patents not having such value may as well be allowed to expire. Included among such patents are those granted for inventions which contain some elements of useful machines, but which are not, in themselves, organized so as to be of commercial value, and are never made or used. Such patents sometimes lie dormant, and are revived and reissued after improvements have been made which render the machine of value. There have been many instances of hardship in this respect; and many of these old patents, unthought of, unappreciated, and worthless in themselves, have been reissued to cover inventions subsequently made and of great value, but which contain some elements shown in these prior but, in themselves, useless patents.

The amendment in section 15 makes provision for the filing of a bond by the assistant commissioner. It seems proper; but as the assistant commissioner is liable to be in charge of the office for only short periods, I have suggested that the amount of bond for that office be fixed at $5,000.

Section 16 is intended to give the Commissioner enlarged discretion in the sale of printed copies, specifications, and drawings. The law now fixes the price of copies of specifications and drawings of patents at ten cents per copy as the minimum. This is a fair price for single copies, covering the expense of the copy and the attendance necessary for the prompt delivery of single copies. Applications are frequently made, however, for large numbers of copies, including a whole class. In such case the price is deemed to be exorbitant, and, in fact, is greatly in excess of the cost of the material added to the expense attending the selection and delivery of the same.

Section 17 simply adds models to the list of those matters in the custody of the office, certified copies of which may be furnished by the office and used as evidence, and provides that copies may be certified to by the assistant commissioner. The amendment appears to me just and convenient for the public and office.

The change contemplated in section 18 is simply for convenience in the transaction of business in the office. Under the law as it now stands the final fee must be paid within six months after the allowance of the application, but the issue of patents is made upon a certain day of each week. The proper conduct of the business requires that the issue should be closed upon a certain day. In case the final fee is paid on the last day of the six months, occurring before the date of issue, it is impossible to give the patent the date of issue next preceding the date of payment of the fee, and the patent must be issued upon the regular day of the week following. In order to come within the terms of the law, which requires the issue of the patent within six months after the allowance, the office has been compelled to resort to the fiction of issuing a new letter of allowance of a later date than that originally issued. Further than this, the patent takes date and begins its term of seventeen years prescribed by law on the day on which it is signed. The present arrangement requires that these patents shall be signed in blank, and that afterward the specifications shall be printed, the drawing photolithographed, the patent made up, and the seal affixed thereto, the whole business for each week's issue requiring about two weeks after the date of signing, and after the commencement of a life-time of the patent. The present section will permit the Commissioner to have the papers all prepared and ready for delivery on the day when the term of the patent begins. It seems also necessary in connection with this that the proviso should be added, that after the allowance of a claim, and the payment of the fee, which completes all the duties required by law of the applicant, the patent should not be withheld by reason of any interference with an application filed after the payment and allowance as aforesaid.

Section 19 is intended to remove the restriction placed upon patents in this country by reason of the prior issue of foreign patents for the same invention in foreign countries. Under the existing law the lifetime of an American patent is abridged if the inventor has taken out a foreign patent prior to the issue of the American patent, when the foreign patent expires before the termination of the seventeen years which, otherwise, the American patent would run. The simple effect of the present law is to tend to discourage American inventors from taking out foreign patents. I know of no advantage whatever arising from this provision of the law. In the case of American inventions which the parties desire to patent abroad there arises this dilemma: if the inventor takes out a foreign patent first, he is liable to have his American term abridged thereby. If he apply first for an American patent, and that be issued, and he desires also to make application for an English patent, he is compelled to exercise extraordinary diligence in order to anticipate the arrival in England of the printed publication of his

American patent, which would defeat his English patent. In order to prevent (what might be, perhaps, considered some disadvantage) the enjoyment of an invention abroad by a foreign patentee during any considerable part of the life-time of his foreign patent, and the subsequent taking out of the patent for the same invention in this country, a provision has been added to the section requiring such foreign patentees to make application in this country within two years after the date of their foreign patent.

The twentieth section of the bill under consideration, in connection with the twenty-second section of the same, contemplated simply putting applications allowed and forfeited by reason of the non-payment of the final fee upon the same standing as applications abandoned by non-action for more than two years. Under the existing law and practice, an application abandoned after rejection and inaction over two years does not debar the same applicant from commencing *de novo ;* but if the same application had been allowed and not renewed within two years, he could not make a new application, but is forever barred from receiving the patent for that invention, notwithstanding that the invention may not have gone into public use or been known except to the applicant and to the office. No reason appears for this discrimination, and I propose to remedy it without any other change in the statute than simply by inserting in section 4897 the words, "in order to be the continuation of the original application." This renders unnecessary the amendment of section 4894, and the repeal of section 4897, some of the provisions of which should stand.

Section 21 is a modification of the act of 1870, so as to restore the law in this respect to the form in which it existed prior to the act of 1870. It permits the owner or owners of the entire interest in a patent to make application for a reissue, and sign and swear to the corrected specification. I know of no reason why this should not be done. The amendments introduced must be substantially covered by the original oath of the inventor, or they could not be properly introduced on reissue, and there is no good ground for referring to him when the invention has gone wholly out of his hands. The law, as it now exists, gives an inventor control over a patent after he has sold the entire interest therein, and compels the purchaser to resort to him for aid in amending the patent in which he has no more right of property than any other party whatever.

The twenty-fourth section of the bill referred to provides that the application of the successful party to an interference shall not be put into a second interference with any application filed subsequent to the closing of the testimony taken on his behalf in the pending interference. Cases have arisen in which parties defeated in one interference have appeared in the office as assignees of some other inventor before the issue of a patent to the successful party, and put him to the expense and delay of a second interference. It is frequently alleged in such cases that the second interference is merely for the purpose of delay, and it is a matter of complaint that in such cases the defeated parties have the benefit in the second interference of knowledge of their opponent's case obtained in the first interference. The section excludes from interference with the application only such parties as file their applications after the closing of the testimony of the successful party. An interference may then be declared, but it must be with the patent, the successful party having that presumption and advantage in his favor. The second proviso relates to interferences in case of reissues. The present practice of the office, following the decisions of the supreme court of the District of Columbia, is not to declare interferences between applications for reissues of patents and any application for a patent, or with any patent, whose date of filing in the office is later than the date of the patent sought to be reissued. The ruling of the court has been that the application for a reissue should be revised and restricted precisely in the same manner as it would have been had the claim made in the reissue application been made in the original application. The practice of the office has varied somewhat under different Commissioners. The provision referred to simply embodies in the statute what is understood to have been held by the courts, and what appears to be wise and just.

I have added an amendment to section 4891 not contained in the bill referred to. The amendment contemplates dispensing with models in a very large number, perhaps a large majority, of cases. The practice hitherto has been almost uniformly to require models in all cases which admit of illustration by model or drawing. The result has been an immense accumulation of models; so great that before the destruction of one-half of them by the recent fire the collection had already become to some extent unwieldy. They required an immense space for such storage as would allow the exhibition of them and ready access. They are accumulating by the addition of from twelve to fifteen thousand per year. It would become a matter of serious embarrassment to provide room for those belonging to cases already patented, and have them properly arranged for exhibition, as the law requires. These models constitute no part of the patent. They are not referred to in the specification or drawing, and the law requires that the specification and drawing of the patent shall be complete in themselves, and shall disclose the invention so clearly that any one skilled in the art shall be able therefrom to make the invention, in order that the patent may be valid. The present model system tends rather to the issue of patents with imperfect drawings and imperfect description. The model illustrates more readily the machine. In the examination of applications for patents, the examiner, having before him the model and the drawing, derives his knowledge of the invention most readily from the former. It may easily escape his notice that the knowledge which he has of the invention may have been conveyed in some respect solely by the model and that the drawing may be defective. But in any event the specification and drawing should disclose to him fully the invention, if they are sufficiently clear and full to disclose it to the public. In case there be any doubt as to the sufficiency of the drawings, or capability of the machine to operate, the section proposed contemplates that a working model may be required. It also contemplates the requirement of such models in interference cases and upon appeals, where the ready illustration of an invention may be particularly necessary. In all these cases, however, working models are required. Where they are furnished and retained in the office, they illustrate to some purpose the state of the art. If not deemed worthy, they need not, under the proposed section, be retained. Under the present system, a very large proportion of the models are not practically working models; not half of them are of practical value as illustrations of the arts to which they pertain, and often the really valuable are obscured in the crowd of comparatively worthless models. Under the section proposed, it will be practicable to retain all the advantages that can be derived from models, and at the same time the large bulk of models in cases hereafter patented may be dispensed with, thereby relieving inventors of a heavy expense, and also relieving the government of the expense attending the storage and custody of the models which are of no material benefit to the public, or to any one, after the patent has been issued.

In connection with this matter, I have suggested in the paper referred to an amendment to section 484, which provides for the reception and custody by the Commissioner of Patents of working models of patented machines, and specimens of patented articles and the like. These models and specimens, it is contemplated, will be only such as parties are manufacturing or using. A gallery filled with such specimens of articles of practical value will be an object of great interest, and will show in a substantial manner the manufactures of the conutry. If the proposed amendments are incorporated in the law, it will be practicable to fill the halls made vacant by the recent fire, with models of machines used in various parts of the country and of practical value, or with specimens of American manufactures, and without any intermixture of material practically valueless for the purpose of illustration or exhibition.

I have the honor to be, very respectfully, your obedient servant,

ELLIS SPEAR,
Commissioner of Patents.

Hon. CARL SCHURZ,
Secretary of the Interior.

ARGUMENTS

BEFORE THE

COMMITTEE ON PATENTS

OF THE

HOUSE OF REPRESENTATIVES,

ON

HOUSE BILL No. 1612, TO AMEND THE LAWS RELATING TO PATENTS
(*Which is identical with S.* 300, *printed on pp.* 1-9, *supra*).

A bill to amend the statutes in relation to patents, and for other purposes.

Argument of J. H. Raymond, attorney, &c., representing Western Railroad Association, Chicago.

Mr. Chairman and gentlemen of the committee:

The subjects to be presented to the committee this morning are so manifold, and depend so largely upon peculiar facts, that, to cover the ground I desire to go over within reasonable limits, I have found it necessary to severely condense my remarks. I may have done so at the expense of perspicuity. If so, I will be obliged if any of the committee should interrupt me and ask an explanation of any statement I may make.

In discussing general amendments to the law and questions of public policy, no man can entirely divest himself of the prejudices which naturally grow out of his peculiar experience and business relations. I therefore deem it necessary, as well as advantageous to my argument, to frankly explain, on this my first appearance before this committee, the business in which I am and have been engaged. And it would materially assist the committee in weighing the arguments to be presented if you should require a similar explanation from all those who may appear before you upon this bill, which proposes a revision of many of the general provisions of the patent law.

You are aware that the patent statutes form the basis of a distinct department of the law, in which no solicitor, however able, is competent to advise in the simplest matters, unless he has given it particular attention. As an illustration, we are continually forced to rebuy licenses under patents, costing in the aggregate many thousand dollars, because the first licenses taken, though drawn by the ablest general solicitors in the country—and drawn, too, with care, and intended at the time to convey full protection—still have some loop-hole, through which the sharks with whom we are forced to deal can drag us into court and technically mulct us in damages. For instance: A grants a license, including any possible extension, to two connecting railroads, B and C, which interchange cars. Because the respective licenses did not in terms give to B and C the right to run the other's cars, having the patented improvement, over its road, or to run its cars, so equipped, over the other's road, the assignee of the patent claims and recovers additional compensation. This department of law, also, has this peculiarity, that each case, to a greater extent than in any other department, is *sui generis.* There is so little of logical, consistent sequence running through the system, and so few general principles which govern in all cases, that the patent counselor must have his eye upon the whole field of statutory provisions and adjudicated cases in order to give competent advice in any single case.

Accordingly, in January, 1867, the railroad companies centering in Chicago, having common interests in a very large and fraudulent patent claim, put all their defenses into the hands of a gentleman who had had some experience in that particular matter, and for that purpose organized the Western Railroad Association, of which I have the honor to be

226   MR. J. H. RAYMOND.

an executive officer. The smaller claims followed that larger one, and we soon found that it was not safe to experiment with or to introduce any improvement, although bought from the owner of a patent, without a full investigation by experts and attorneys of its patent relations, on account of various and intricate questions of infringement involved, of which I shall speak more fully hereafter. The business, service, and membership grew, till now the association acts in the matters I have referred to, and in similar matters, as the general solicitor of eighty-one railroad companies, operating about thirty-two thousand miles of road, running from a line drawn through Buffalo, N. Y., and Knoxville, Tenn., north to Saint Paul, west to San Francisco, south to Georgia and Texas. It would be gratifying to me to inform the committee as to the manner of our doing business and of the results thereof, but I will content myself with citing the opinion of the attorneys who appear before us, that the association is of as much real benefit to the honest inventor as it is to the railroad companies. So fair and so full are our investigations, that of the hundreds of claims which we have rejected during the last five years, only *three* are now in litigation.

As the members of the committee, solicitous only for the public interest, represent more largely the users of patents, and also the small portion of people comprising inventors, so the railroad companies represent, primarily, the business interest which is the largest user of patents, and secondarily the small number of railroad officers and employers comprising the inventors of the more valuable of the improvements we use. So far forth as it is consonant with the public interest to grant monopolies in inventions for the purpose of encouraging progress in science and the useful arts, it is for the interest of the railroad companies that inventors in their department should be so encouraged.

Plainly, the duty and, without doubt, the intention of the committee is to consider the questions presented by this bill from the single standpoint of the public good, the greatest good to the greatest number, being mindful of the interests of the inventor only as to resulting benefits. There is no other foundation for any action by Congress. The Constitutional provision is a limitation as well as a conferment of power, and confines Congress in the purpose of any and all legislation upon this subject to "promoting progress in science and the useful arts." May I insist that this rule, which cannot be gainsaid, shall be kept in mind throughout this discussion, that all the arguments shall be made by counsel and weighed by the committee from the single selfish and arbitrary stand-point of the "general welfare and progress of the public"? Arguments, specious and plausible in appearance, will be presented in objection to the provisions of the bill, and amendments will be proposed which would keep from the public benefits which are proposed to be conferred by the bill, and which are proposed simply and cunningly in the interests of particular patents and private interests.

I shall leave it for my friend and senior, Mr. Chauncey Smith, of Boston, to give you the history of this bill and to inform you as to the care and time, the ability and experience which were bestowed in its preparation; only remarking that a bill embodying its more important provisions in a modified form was first presented to Congress by our association in December, 1875; and, after a thorough *ex-parte* consideration before the Judiciary Committee, was passed by the House of Representatives.

Nor need I dwell upon the importance of the patent system as affecting all branches of trade and industry, or upon the necessity of its immediate and radical revision. A simple illustration is that of a loaf of bread which is produced by the use of and pays tribute to twenty-one

classes of patents, in each of which classes many patents are now alive.
The plowshare, point, handles, and tackle; the harrower, the seed-sower,
the cultivator, the harvester, the thrasher, and the separator; the bolts,
the hopper, the stones, and the gearing of the mill; the bag, the holder
of the bag, and the strap or string with which it is tied; the yeast or
baking powder, the oven, the extension table, and the dishes are each
the subjects of patents to which tribute is paid. Everything visible in
this room has at one time been the subject of a patent monopoly; and a
fact important to me is covered in the extravagant expression of another,
"that you can't drive a nail into a railroad-car without driving it through
one or more patents."

The number and importunity of the requests which are coming to
Congress from the people for such amendments as are now proposed are
sufficient evidence of their necessity, to which I will only add the resolution adopted by that able and conservative body of business men, the
National Board of Trade, at its annual meeting in August last, "that,
in the opinion of this board, Congress should take action upon the subject of the revision of the patent laws."

The nature of the provisions proposed require a general consideration
of, 1, the utility of the patent system; 2, its present defects; 3, the nature of the grant conferred upon the patentee and of the title held by
him; 4, the specific provisions of the bill under consideration; and, 5,
the Constitutional powers of Congress in the premises; for which I beg
your indulgence, promising to be as brief as possible, and confining
myself, as to the specific provisions of the bill, to the sections relating
to patent litigation, and leaving it for my brothers, Whitman and
Dodge, of the Patent Office Bar Association, to explain those provisions, which relate more intimately to the administration and practice
of the Patent Office.

UTILITY OF PATENT SYSTEM.

Article I of the national Constitution confers upon Congress a discretionary power "to promote the progress of science and useful arts
by securing for limited times, to authors and inventors, the exclusive
right to their respective writings and discoveries." We are confronted
at the outset of any general discussion arising under this provision with
the question whether the practical results of existing statutes for the
enforcement of this Constitutional provision and of the judicial rules
which govern in the administration of the statutes demonstrate the
wisdom of the provision and the statutes. The cry of the utilitarians,
Cui bono? has here peculiar propriety and force. I answer that the
wisdom of the Constitutional provision cannot be doubted. A wise
patent system does encourage invention, and therefore promote public
progress in science and the useful arts. The difficulty to be guarded
against, but which, in my opinion, the public have been pushed head-
long into by the statutes and judicial rules which have obtained for the
past seventeen years, is that the system should not cost the public more
than the necessity or justice of the case requires; and I unhesitatingly
answer the question as to these statutes and rules in the negative.

We are usually treated, upon occasions like the present, and frequently in the courts, to eloquent panegyrics upon the patent system by able
men, in which it is held up as the primary agent in the attainment of
the civilization which we enjoy; as one of the principal guarantees of
the permanence of our government; as the incentive upon which invention solely depends; as the great cheapener of the articles of common

·consumption ; as the enticer and protector of capital, and the promoter of competition in trades and manufactures.

I have not been in the habit of so considering it. The consideration of the elements which have caused the wonderful progress, patriotism, and peace which have characterized the last twelve years of American history and the guarantees given for the permanence of our principles of government form a favorite theme of my feeble thought. Of these elements the first is the Christianity which gives us an eternal and an immutable foundation by which to measure and on which to base our civil and social laws. Then follow the general principles of our government, involving, among others, the sovereignty of the individual and the perfect enjoyment of the inalienable rights ; then the institutions of our civil liberty, with its freedom of the press, of public assemblage and discussion, its trial by jury, and its common schools; and the *last* element is the statutory provisions punishing wrong, protecting property, and encouraging development in character, knowledge, and, indeed, in invention. Nor does the inventive genius of the people, which seems to be indigenous to the very soil, depend for its further development or exercise solely, or even primarily, upon the incentive and inducements of the patent law. The true, natural inventor invents for the same reason that the preacher preaches, the philosopher studies, the statesman educates and guides, and the attorney advocates—I speak not of those who are in those professions by accident or mistake—because he can't help it. If you will pardon the homeliness of the illustration, the inventive genius making improvements is like the hen laying eggs, and she, unlike a few others of the female persuasion, knows well the sphere for which from all eternity she has been destined, and with commendable modesty and faithfulness sticks to it.

1 will not detain you to demonstrate the falsity of the theory that granting a *monopoly* upon any improvement in an art cheapens the price of the product of the art or creates competition therein. It, however, is to be remarked in this connection that, while the improvement itself cheapens ultimately the price of the product of any art, it is equaled, if not surpassed, by some other of the many elements which forever tend toward this result.

I am not one of those who share the growing belief that there is no necessity for or commensurate benefit from a patent system, and who favor its entire repeal (which class of persons is much larger than is generally supposed), nor do I sympathize with those other extremists who attribute all progress in science and the useful arts to the patents issued upon improvements and the law permitting and regulating the same. At the risk of being unjustly classed as an extremist of the first kind, and of being characterized as inimical to a just and equitable patent system, I unhesitatingly and confidently assert that that part of the progress of recent years, during which the genius of the people has been exclusively directed to the arts of peace, which is directly the result of the patent system which has obtained during same period, when put into the scales with the tax, the annoyance, the burden, the "scarecrowing" of capital, the unnatural strifes, the unhealthy speculations, the inflated values, the exorbitant prices, the black-mailing, the tedious and expensive chancery litigation, and the other unholy practices which the patent law has of late hatched and fostered, the progress which it has brought about receives a shock which throws it up into the thin air. The complaint, I repeat, is not against the Constitution and any patent system, but against the rules and provisions which now obtain, which seem to have been piled one upon another with the sole purpose of benefiting the speculator in patents, who for years now has been treated with the same consideration as married women used to be and as fools and minors still are.

With these general considerations bearing upon the question how, much of a reward the interests of the public dictate should be given to inventors, some of the

EXISTING DEFECTS

to which the provisions of the pending bill are directed will be noticed:

1. The practices of black-mailing which have been described to the committee in the consideration of another bill are not limited to the two cases then cited, but characterize some of the patents in each of the numerous classes we find in the indexes of the Commissioner's report. The practice consists of threatening suit to individuals unused to litigation, or living in the country, or away from the seats of Federal courts.

2. To meet this and other evils, bills have been proposed which, in my opinion, are clearly unconstitutional, for the protection of innocent purchasers in open market. If constitutional, such provisions meet but a small part of the difficulty; for while it is perfectly safe to say that from eighty to ninety per cent. of the infringements of patents are, on account of ignorance, innocent, in my opinion not more than twenty per cent. are caused by the purchase of devices in open market in such a way that an implied license to use the device does not go with it. This illustration, which I shall have occasion again to refer to, is in point. Some time ago, say five years, a compound, of which Paris green was the base, was so made that it could be used to kill the cotton-worm without affecting the cotton, and was patented. Mr. Smith and Mr. Brown, in North Carolina, bought the right to use the compound from the inventor. It was not six months before the compound, traveling from mouth to mouth, from plantation to plantation, was being put up at a drug-store for Mr. Jones in a village on the Gulf.

The question in the practices and facts already noticed is, How to prevent the threatening of suits, and how to protect not only the innocent purchaser, but generally the innocent infringer, having a just regard for the rights of the patentee.

3. The association which I represent is defending fifty-seven suits, which were not commenced until after the patents had run for their original term of fourteen years, had exhausted their extension of seven years, and until the statute of limitation of 1870, of six years (making about twenty-seven years), had nearly run out. When I refer to the scores of suits now pending under the "middlings purifier" patent, "the Paris-green compound for killing the cotton-worm," "the conductory patent for mills," and hundreds of other suits that are now threatened, the evils resulting from the want of an arbitrary, short statute of limitations need not be enlarged upon.

4. There are many patents that are void and fraudulent, the parties to whom the patents were issued not having been the inventors of the devices claimed, or who, if they were the inventors, were not the first inventors, and therefore have no legal or equitable rights in the matter. The testimony, however, necessary to show the illegal or fraudulent character of these patents depends upon witnesses of advanced years. These patents have several years yet to run, and the parties who own them are simply waiting for these witnesses to die, when suit will be commenced and the defendant will be remediless. A statute of limitations does not reach this difficulty, and the defendant should be allowed to perpetuate.

testimony in this as in the protection of other kinds of property. If it be objected that the general provision of the Revised Statutes concerning the perpetuation of testimony is sufficient, the reply is, first, that it is the opinion of a considerable number of able patent counsellors that that provision has no application in such cases; and, second, if it had, it does not allow any number of manufacturers, farmers, planters, tradesmen, or railroad companies, having merely a general community of interest, to join in such proceedings, and therefore reap the benefit, by a single proceeding, of the perpetuation of such testimony.

5. There is a considerable number of patents issued annually from the Patent Office which are of no force or value except for black-mailing and for interfering with the business of parties competing with their owners. I am glad to say that the present Commissioner of Patents appreciates this fact, and is doing all he can to correct the practice; yet from the nature of the case this fact is unavoidable, and must continue to a greater or less extent. These patents should be repealed and annulled. The only mode now available for doing so is by a bill brought in the name of the United States, by and with the advice and consent of the Attorney-General. Individuals, as well as the government, should have the privilege, under proper restrictions. to commence proceedings upon their own motion and in their own right for the annulling of invalid patents.

6. Another useless and pernicious class of patents is what I call the considerable number of accidental patents issued annually to ignorant and officious meddlers in arts in which they are not skilled.

An Irshman from the backwoods, while taking his biennial trip along the railroad track " to town," sees that some of the nuts attaching the fish-plates of the rail are loose, and having heard of " the squire" who got rich out of somebody's patent, proceeds to invent a nut-lock. The only benefit which ever arises from such an invention is to some New York patent agency, whose sole object in business is to get as many patents as they can, no matter how narrow and frivolous they are, and as many fees as possible out of the people who are attracted to their office by extensive advertising.

7. Another great evil is the interfering with settled branches of trade and art by the granting of extensions and reissues. Many extensions have been granted, both by the Commissioner and by Congress, which were due and compatible with the public interest. Many more have been granted that had not these characteristics. If a digression from the subjects presented by this bill be excusable, it is proper to suggest that the determinative consideration in any application for an extension which may come before the committee is, how much would progress in sciences and the useful arts be promoted by granting the application, and what would it cost? There is no privity in such matters between Congress and any particular inventor.

The present practice of granting reissues, while based upon a sound theory of giving opportunity for the correction of accidents and mistakes, is an unmitigated fraud. That it constitutes a great evil is admitted by all. A very large majority of such reissues are taken out for the sole purpose of incorporating into the patent some element that the inventor had not even dreamed of at the date of the original invention, and for the sole purpose of either covering or interfering with some part or all of an improvement subsequently made. I am free to say that I was overruled by the able attorneys with whom I was associated in draw-ing up this bill in this matter, adding only that my solution of the diffi culty would be to enact that no reissue should be allowed after three years from the date of the patent.

8. One of the greatest, if not the greatest embarrassment under which the public labor by reason of the patent laws, is on account of the many and very intricate questions of infringement and equivalents which attach to almost every patent issued. The first and simplest of these questions affords an illustration. Having to deal largely with inventors of but a single improvement, and with business men whose attention is almost exclusively directed to other matters, I have found great difficulty in satisfactorily explaining how one patent may be valid and yet infringe another.

This illustration, although the plainest one I have met with, I have used unsuccessfully. A invents a watch with but an hour-hand, B improves it by adding a minute-hand, and C adds a second-hand. These inventions are made very near each other in point of time. C's patent is the one operated under. It shows all the parts of the watch with the three hands, and the public buys of him upon his exhibiting his specifications and drawings bearing the great seal, not knowing that sooner or later they must account to B and also to A. In the case supposed, A, B, and C have each valid patents, but B's cannot be used without paying A, and C's cannot be used without paying both A and B. Add to this simple case the thousand and one questions of mechanical equivalents which determine questions of infringement, and the difficulty is apparent. The ingenuity of the profession has not been able to devise any direct, practicable, and just solution thereof. This matter has not escaped the appreciation of the present Commissioner of Patents, and I am at liberty to incorporate in my remarks the following circular in point recently issued by him:

DEPARTMENT OF THE INTERIOR,
UNITED STATES PATENT OFFICE,
Washington, D. C., January 15, 1878.

[CIRCULAR No. 4.]

In the present condition of the patent system, with great numbers of patents issuing every year, I am impressed with the conviction that more and more care ought to be exercised by examiners in requiring applications for mere improvements to be distinctly defined from generic inventions, and that applicants should discriminate between what they claim as new and what they deem to be old.

The remarks of the United States Supreme Court in the recent cases of Merrill *vs.* Yoemans, 11 O. G., 970, and Keystone Bridge Company *vs.* Phœnix Iron Company, 12 O. G., 980, plainly indicate the duty of the office in this regard.

It is doubtless a matter of common observation with the Examining Corps that the tendency on the part of the applicants for patents is to avoid or neglect reference to prior patents upon which their invention is an improvement.

I think much of the odium attached to patents, and much of the injustice and vexation arising from patents with narrow claims would be obviated were the applicant compelled to state specifically, where it can be done, on what his patent is an improvement, and define accurately the state of the art prior to his invention, so that any one reading his patent, even if unskilled in patent matters, would see not only what is claimed, but would see set forth clearly the state of the art upon which his invention was based.

At this time, when patents have been brought into disrepute, principally on account of those of a trivial nature which are used to embarrass persons not able to determine the scope of such a grant, it seems especially necessary that the office should exercise great caution in this respect.

I think the practice of the office has hitherto been lax on this point, and I desire earnestly to call the attention of the Examining Corps thereto, and to urge the exercise of care and more rigid requirement in the examination of cases which may hereafter be brought before them.

ELLIS SPEAR,
Commissioner of Patents.

9. I come now to the greatest injustice now being perpetrated in the name of law, namely, the rules which obtain in ascertaining the measure of damages in patent litigation. Its importance will be appreciated when it is remembered how manifold are the ramifications of patents, and that their value depends primarily upon the amount that can be recovered for their infringement.

A fair average estimate of the living expenses of every inhabitant of our country is $100 per annum. That equals $4,500,000,000. Those ignorant of this subject will not, but those versed in it will admit that ten per cent. of this amount is a fair average for the amount paid annually as patent royalties, which equals the annual amount of $450,000,000. In short, it thus appears that the amounts paid on account of patent royalty would, in five years, more than pay the whole amount of the national debt.

The law of 1790 gave such damages as the jury might assess and the forfeiture of the thing made. This was changed in 1793 to three times the license fee, and again, in 1800, to three times the actual damages. In 1836 the jury were to find the actual damages, and the court to treble : em in its discretion. This was at law. In the mean time the courts ave establised the rule, *without seeing where it led*, that in equity, the efendant's *profits or savings* should be the rule, and under this rule it has been recently solemnly declared, by judicial decisions, that a single patent may be worth ten, twenty, thirty, fifty, and, in one case, sixty millions of dollars. It would seem as if such results ought to satisfy the most grasping. In 1870, however, a new provision was added to the law, by which, in addition to the profits, the plaintiff is to have the damages he may have sustained by reason of infringement.

These profits and savings are proved up in equity largely by expert testimony, which, to use a familiar phrase, "can be bought by the cord," and as a sole basis of ascertaining the damages for an infringment is capable of being justly applied in very few, if any, cases.

I shall return to this subject of damages in a few minutes.

We have seen how that it is impossible to remedy some of the defects in the system by direct, positive, and effective amendments to the law. This bill which I present to you as the result of the mature and laborious consideration and consultation of many of the ablest attorneys from all sections of the country, while conservative in its character, provides great relief and goes as far in amending the law as we deemed it prudent to go at this time.

A few brief considerations as to the

NATURE OF THE GRANT

conferred upon the patentee, and of the title held by him, will aid to a full understanding of the specific provisions of the bill.

The Constitution and the law grant to the inventor "the exclusive right" to his invention for seventeen years. It is a close monopoly which, in my opinion, should be given in no case. While the law grants to the inventor the exclusive right to practice his invention for seventeen years, there is no process by which he can be forced to practice it, and, at his discretion, he can lock it up in a closet and deprive the public of its benefits for the period named. This is especially onerous in view of the fact that almost every important invention is made simultaneously in different parts of the country by different persons. All patent litigation proves this fact. I know of but one case—the English case of Smith *vs.* Davidson [1857], 19 C. S., 697—in which it has been impossible to ascertain with reasonable certainty which of two original inventors was the first to perfect his invention, yet in almost every case in the books a prior invention by another is set up and contended for.

In the second place, the sole object of the grant being the public good *pro tanto*, its very object is defeated by the provision depriving the public for any period of the benefits of the improvement.

This is especially true, if, as I claim in the third place, that an inventor has *not* a natural right to the exclusive enjoyment of his invention, and that while the granting of exclusive monopolies forms a part of the common law of England, it has no natural place among the institutions of our government, but is flatly opposed to its general principles. [Vide Web. Pat. Cases, I, IV, and V.]

You will be told that the highest title that man can have to property is the title of creation and discovery and possession. So in tangible property, less so in intangible property, and not at all " so by natural right" in the creations, discoveries, and possessions of the mind, which were intended by Him after whose likeness mind was made to be given freely and fully, as through the air itself, to all men for their progress toward that which is to come. If, perchance, there be a single thought in these remarks which is new and useful it is not and was not mine by natural right, but was given me by Infinite intelligence to be by me given again. So of every operation and result of the mind. And the most arbitrary, unnatural, and dangerous right that can be conferred upon man is to say that he shall have the power to prevent others from enjoying the results of his intellectual creations and discoveries.

Time does not suffice to discuss the hardships which result from the conferment of this exclusive right, but in my closing remarks I shall attempt to show that the substitution for this exclusive right, of a right of property which would not be exclusive would be constitutional, and I would like an opportunity to argue that such a substitution would be of benefit to the inventor.

THE SECTIONS OF THE BILL

which relate especially to patent litigation and require any explanation, are, the 1st, 2d, 3d, 8th, and 9th, and, adding the 11th, I shall briefly explain them in the reverse order.

Section 11, providing for a tax upon patents of fifty dollars at the expiration of four years, and one hundred dollars at the expiration of nine years after the date of the patent, under penalty of forfeiture, is copied, except in the amounts of the tax and the dates of its maturing, from the English law. The evils resulting from trivial, impracticable, and invalid patents, and from those which become of value late in their existence, and then only for the purpose of infringement suits and speculations, have been noticed. It has also appeared that it has been impossible to prevent the issuance of such patents in the first instance. The remedy lies in this provision, which, in the English law, where the tax is more frequent and of greater amount, results in annulling seventy-five per cent. of all the patents issued. The provision of this section has been criticised somewhat, because the tax was too great and too frequent. It has been criticised more as being too small and not frequent enough. In my opinion, if changed at all, it should be increased both in amount and frequency. The grant, in any case, is a tax upon, or a deprivation to the public, and should not be perpetuated unless it is worth a good fee.

Section 9 allows suits to be brought for repealing and annulling patents. I have already alluded to the necessity for this provision, to which need only be added a citation to an opinion of the Attorney-General of 19th November, 1874, printed in volume 6 of the Patent-Office Gazette, at page 723. I have full confidence that without any further explanation or discussion you will find the provision to be sufficiently guarded to protect the owners of patents against vexations and malicious proceedings of this character.

Section 8 is a provision for taking testimony *in perpetuam* in patent cases, introduced because the general law applicable to all cases is not adequate in patent causes, as has already appeared. My reading of the section will sufficiently show that the onus of this proceeding is upon him who wishes to perpetuate testimony, and that the interests of the owner of patents are sufficiently protected in this regard.

Section 3. In patent suits in equity, the court first determines the validity of the patent and the question of infringement; it then orders an account. An appeal cannot be taken unless the account has been completed. The accounting is very expensive, and consumes much time, and if the decision as to validity or infringement is reversed, or even modified, on appeal, it becomes useless. This section authorizes the court in such cases to permit the appeal to be taken at once. I predict confidently that where an interlocutory decree has been given sustaining the validity of the patent and the infringement, and an appeal is taken to the Supreme Court before a reference to the master for an account is had, and the proceedings of the court below are sustained in the Supreme Court, in nine cases out of ten no accounting will be had, but the case will be settled, and this the most expensive and the most unsatisfactory part of and the greatest delay in patent litigation will be thus entirely avoided.

I come now to the first two sections of the bill, which at once form its most important features, and would afford the greatest relief to the public. With your permission I will consider the first section first. It provides:—

That from and after the passage of this act no profits or damages in any suit at law or in equity for the infringement of a patent shall be recovered which shall have accrued more than four years next preceding the commencement of such suit: *Provided*, That where a party, in order to preserve his right of recovery, finds it necessary to institute a number of suits involving the same issues, and he is proceeding with good faith and with reasonable diligence to bring one of them to final judgment, any court in which any of them are pending may, in its discretion, grant a stay of proceedings from time to time in any other cases pending before it: *Provided also*, That rights of action existing at the passage of this act may be enforced by suits brought within four years thereafter, if not previously barred by laws already existing; but nothing in this section contained shall revive any right of action already barred, nor prolong the right to sue on any cause of action already existing.

There is now no statute of limitations applicable to patent causes. This proposes that no recovery shall be had for an infringement more than four years old, leaving the right to sue for what has been done within four years where the infringement has continued. It allows the court, where many suits are brought on one patent, to have one brought to trial, and meanwhile to stay proceedings in the others.

It is proper that I should remark that in explaining these provisions I have quoted somewhat from a "memorandum of the principal changes" made by the bill, which was prepared by Mr. J. J. Storrow, of Boston, to whom you will have the pleasure of listening during the progress of the discussion.

In support of the unquestionable doctrine that statutes of limitation should be considered statutes of repose, and are *strictissimi juris*, I read from Cooley's Constitutional Limitations (*vide ibid.*, p. 364 and note):

It is evidence of the mildness of this section that it is not a limitation upon the right to commence a suit, but upon the extent of the damages that may be therein recovered, and bears in character a perfect analogy to State limitations upon the recovery of mesne profits in actions of eject-ment, which limitation in the State statutes varies from one to three years. Under this section, the plaintiff must delay bringing this suit for more than four years after the defendant has ceased to infringe, in order to have his right to recover barred.

Referring again to the fact that so large a proportion of the infringe-ment of patents are innocent infringements. He who doubts that the policy of the government and the policy of the patent law is to give no-tice of these monopolies to the public, certainly has not read the stat-utes with intelligence. The government goes as far as it is practicable to go, in my opinion, in this direction, in publishing the printed copies of patents, and in requiring the stamping of patented articles. And yet the people are supposed to know (they are bound to know the law) the full force and effect of the fifteen thousand patents granted annually, whereas in fact they know very little about it.

The bill which passed the House by a large majority last year con-tained a limitation upon the recovery of one year prior to notice of in-fringement. While the raising in such a provision of the vexatious question of actual and constructive notice is objectionable, there is no so cheap, satisfactory, and complete way of giving notice as by the fil-ing of a bill.

The term of four years is named, because in contested patents it takes about three years to carry the contest to an interlocutory decree, and de-fine the validity, force, and effect of the patent.

It has been objected that this section should not apply to cases of will-ful and secret infringement, to which there are two satisfactory answers: First, such cases are very rare—so rare as not to deserve notice in a gen-eral enactment; and, second, it is well established to be bad practice to incorporate such exceptions in a statute of limitations. As evidence of the second statement, I refer to all the statutes of limitation which have had any permanence, and especially to those pertaining to bankruptcy matters, which, while not having any such exception, are not applied by the courts to claims which, through fraud, accident, or mistake, are barred by the general provision of the statute. In other words, the courts will make all the exceptions which justice requires in these and similar cases.

It has been suggested that an amendment should be added eliminat-ing from the operation of the section cases of willful or concealed infringe-ment, to which there are two satisfactory answers:

First, such cases are very rare—so rare as not to deserve notice in a general enactment; and, second, it is well established to be bad prac-tice to incorporate such exceptions in a statute of limitations. As evi-dence of the second statement, I refer to all the statutes of limitations which have had any permanence, and especially to those pertaining to bankruptcy proceedings. The court will make all the exceptions which justice requires in these and similar cases.

I desire, however, to call your attention to the second proviso of the section. The first part thereof reads as follows: "*Provided, also*, That rights of action existing at the passage of this act may be enforced by suits brought within four years thereafter." * * * It is a general rule of all statutes of limitation that a reasonable time should be given after the passage of the enactment within which to commence suits to recover for rights of action already existing. That provision is put into almost all laws of limitation, and varies from ten days to (in this case) four years, the longest case I know of. This had escaped my attention, and I want to demur to that proviso. It was put into this section because the limitation in the body of the section was made four years; and we drifted along, I suppose, thinking the one provision was just hitting on it as a compromise between six years and a shorter time, and, therefore, adding the other provision of the same length.

In the second place, that question of how long a time should be granted to escape the operation of any statute of limitations, is wholly and entirely within the discretion of Congress, and cannot, except in very extreme cases, be reviewed by the courts. In my opinion, six months is all the time that should be allowed for the commencement of suits that will not be subject to this provision. And this is because of a good many reasons, which are apparent on the face of the matter. Whether or not the statute of limitations of 1870 has any force or effect at all; whether the repeal of the Revised Statutes (if, indeed, it was repealed) wipes out its effect entirely, is a mooted question. If it did, then we have no such recourse against patents that were granted twenty-seven years ago; more than that, we have no recourse at all for any patent that has ever been granted by the government. Any hour they may trump up a case where we infringed forty years ago, unless we have relief very soon from this bill.

A MEMBER OF THE COMMITTEE. Do I understand this provision to cut off suits absolutely?

Mr. RAYMOND. Never, except in the case I supposed, where I infringed your patent six years ago, and continued infringing six months, and then stopped, and you delayed suing until to-day; in such a case it would. There is a bill pending before the committee, introduced by Mr. Lathrop, of Illinois, which provides for a limitation against the commencement of suits unless it is done within two years (I think it is) of the commencement of the accruing of the right of action.

The pending bill was put in the condition in which it now is as the result of a modification of the bill that was before Congress two years ago, and to avoid the intricate questioning of notice which was therein involved. The evil of this matter is, that ninety per cent. of the infringements that occur are innocent infringements; and the patentee should be obliged to give the public notice. The government is doing all it can in this direction by scattering its volumes of reports. It is the theory of the law that the parties shall give notice, and the public should not be mulcted in damages unless they have notice. The theory started out with was to make the statute of limitations apply one year prior to the notice; they could recover for one year prior to the notice. To obviate the difficulties of that notice, it was changed to this form.

A MEMBER OF THE COMMITTEE. Why does not the general statute of limitations with reference to actions apply?

Mr. RAYMOND. There is no general statute of limitations in the Revised Statutes.

A MEMBER OF THE COMMITTEE. Why don't the statutes of the States where the court is held apply?

Mr. STORROW. It has been held that rights created by the United States authorities are not subject to State limitations, because it would allow the States to interfere with Congress. It was supposed for a long time that the State statutes would apply, but it has been decided that they would not, for this reason, that every State could put a six months' limitation on the right given by Congress.

Mr. RAYMOND. I would like to make this suggestion to the committee: There is hardly a word in this bill that has not been thoroughly considered by the best talent in the country and very thoroughly discussed. Everything in it means something——

A MEMBER. Was it discussed by parties representing both interests?

Mr. RAYMOND. Yes, sir; by parties representing both interests and *all* interests—the interests of the patentee and the interests of the user of the patent. It has received the attention of all the gentlemen present who have participated in the discussion, and who met in Chicago and Boston during the summer, from time to time, to consider the provisions of this bill. A thousand copies of the first draught of the bill were sent from my office to the patent attorneys of the country, requesting them to make suggestions as to the revision, and a committee met in Boston afterward and considered the objections and suggestions made by the patent attorneys of the country; and they made such modifications and as they could before presenting it to Congress. Mr. Storrow and Mr. Smith will give you the history of the bill, however, if you desire it. Allow me to say that, unless there are some radical objections to the provisions of the bill, I hope the committee will be a little jealous about making amendments to it, so that we may get through without a difference of action in the two branches of Congress, which causes delay, and which prevented the passage of any bill at the last Congress.

The two things that I insist upon that the committee shall consider in the way of amendments to the bill are, first, as to the matters of reissues; whether the provision abolishing all reissues from three years after the issuing of a patent is not preferable; and, second, reducing the time within which the parties may bring suits on existing causes of action after the passage of this act.

I come now to the second section of the bill, which is the most important provision in it. [Reading the section.]

A MEMBER. What rule does the court adopt as a measure of damages now?

Mr. RAYMOND. If a party sues now at law before a jury, he recovers damages. His damages are measured by his license-fee, if one is established. The question arises, What is the license-fee? It is hinted at in a phrase used in the section, and is determined "by a reasonable number of transactions applicable to the case at bar." If I have just received a patent and want to introduce it, and I go to a railroad company and say, "I want the prestige of having it introduced by your company, and I will give it to you for $500," that has no effect at all upon the license-fee. If I am in straitened circumstances and obliged to sell the thing for much less than it is worth, to keep myself from starvation, that has no effect at all on the establishment of the license-fee. But a reasonable number of transactions, varying from three to three hundred, according to the nature of the case, to be judged of by the court—a reasonable number of commercial transactions, free from restraint or duress, establishing in practice the patentee's estimate of the value of his patent, and fixing the value as between the buyer and the seller of the thing which is the subject of the controversy, will constitute the license-fee, and limit, in an action at law, the plaintiff to that recovery. There is now a one-sided provision that the court may increase this three times. "It is a poor rule which will not work both ways," so this bill gives to the court full discretion to increase or decrease. As a matter of fact all patent litigation is now brought on the equity side of the court, but that provision, which applies both to law and equity, allowing the court to increase three times, has never yet been used in a single instance. The reason is that the recoveries which have been obtained in patent cases were so ridiculously high, that the court has never dared to use that provision, or the advantage of that discretionary power. That being the rule of damages which now obtains at law, the amcunt of damage is ascertained in equity largely by expert testimony as to what the defendant has made or saved, or what he might have made or saved, and what the patentee (if that is the basis he wants to go on) would have made or saved, or both, and they award that amount to the patentee. Of course we don't find any such statement as that in the adjudicated cases, but that is the fact about it: the damage is ascertained in equity largely, if not entirely, by the theoretical profits, or savings, or both, of the user; that is the rule of damage in patent cases, and the practice of the courts.

Mr. Blanchard requested an opportunity of saying a few words as a mechanic and inventor, and not as a lawyer. He said all the speakers before the committee were lawyers, so far as he knew.

Mr. RAYMOND. I would be glad if the rule would be established by the committee that anybody who has a material amendment to present to the bill can be heard, so that the friends of the bill may be present and have an opportunity of answering any objection that may be raised to it.

Adjourned until Saturday, February 2, 1878, at 10 a. m.

HOUSE COMMITTEE ON PATENTS,
Ten o'clock a. m., February 2, 1878.

Mr. RAYMOND continued. Mr. Chairman and gentlemen of the committee: I would like to give the committee some additional illustrations and arguments on the point submitted yesterday, but can only indulge, and that very briefly, in two particulars:

And, first, as to the character of the grant giving to the patentees, and the exclusive monopoly which he enjoys. I refer again to this because I believe the principles set forth in the pending bill, and the pending public agitation, constitute the first step in the abolition of this kind of a grant; and I think it may be added, the first step in the abolition of the rule of profits or savings as having any consideration in the measure of damages to be recovered. But as to the exclusive grant, I take this illustration of the only case in which it is possible that such a grant should be the real objective desire of the patentee. If a half-dozen or more manufacturers through the country are now making pins by hand, and a machine is invented by which the whole market can be supplied from a room not the size of this room, the inventor wants a monopoly of that market; what his selfish interests require and demand is, that he have a perfect monopoly, so that he can control the market, being able, through making these pins by machinery, to make them much cheaper than by hand, and thus control the market at a little less than the usual price and at a greatly enlarged profit. That and similar cases are the only ones in which it is the true interest of the patentee, even, to say nothing of the public interest or questions of public policy, that he should have a close monopoly upon the things granted. All such classes of cases, in which close monopolies are desired, must result, of course, in hardship to the people, which I need not delay the committee to enumerate. Secondly, they defeat, as I have already shown, *pro tanto*, for the term for which the grant was made, the object and the sole purpose of the grant under the Constitution, and without any commensurate and without any immediate advancement of the interests of the people. In the third place, such a grant, on such terms, is directly contrary to public policy.

The second point in the argument yesterday, to which your attention is again called, was that concerning reissues; and the proposition was submitted to abolish the right of reissue after three years after the date of the patent. I desire to add an illustration given by a member of the present House of Representatives, who is president of a sewing-machine company and a large manipulator of large manufacturing patent interests, who is in full sympathy with this bill, and in full sympathy with this provision concerning reissues. In fact, the provision is proposed by him. In his sewing-machine business they are manufacturing rufflers—an article which every lady in the land uses—which picks up the cloth, makes a tuck, and holds it until the needle passes through and takes the stitches. It is one of the simplest combinations in the world, requiring simply the stamping out of a piece of metal in the proper form. It costs him to make it, twenty cents. For seventeen years, and I think longer than that, he made it without paying anybody any royalty on it, being advised that there was no patent claimed on that trifling machine or device. At least, until after seventeen years after the grant of three patents (the original grant and their extensions), there was no patent claim upon this device, and no royalty paid. But they were then so reissued that he now pays upon this device, the cost of which is twenty cents, *twenty-seven* cents as patent royalties. That royalty must be, of course, a small amount per machine, on account of the number of them being made. That royalty is paid to men who are not entitled at all to it, and never were, but got it by the reissue of old patents. No claim was made until after the seventeen years had run.

Mr. CLARK. After he had found it an article of such utility, why did he not patent it?

Mr. RAYMOND. I think he had a patent on it.

The CHAIRMAN. And then did he have to pay a royalty on all he had made previously?

Mr. RAYMOND. No, sir; that is the only salvation or palliating circumstance about this question of reissues. Heretofore, when a man surrendered a patent to have it reissued, he surrendered all rights under it. There is one clause in this bill which I leave others to advocate to the committee. It is that clause which saves to the patentee any right of action under the original patent, even though he surrenders it for a reissue; but does not continue any such right of action unless it is continued in the reissued patent.

I pass now to explain the provisions of the second section of the bill, having yesterday stated the rules which now govern in ascertaining the damages through profits or savings, both at law and in equity.

I am well aware that this provision of the bill amounts to a little less than a revolution in equity jurisprudence in patent cases; but it is a revolution such as is demanded, in my opinion, not only by the principles and the purposes of the patent law, but by the prevailing economy of the times and by the unmistakable demand which comes from the people in this regard.

The provision is as to the measure of damages in patent cases, establishing the same rule for both law and equity that now obtains in law, and says what this shall be—being, as to cases at law, simply declaratory.

If the committee will pardon me, I have made statements which contain the provisions of this section, though not in the order in which the provisions are found there, but which, I think, will serve to a better understanding of them than if the provisions were read again.

The section abolishes, in the first place, the distinction in these matters between law and equity, the reasons for which distinction no man within the past two years has been able to give. That distinction is abolished, and the rule is made—subject to the provisions which I shall further notice—the same in equity as it is in law.

- Second. The section abolishes profits and savings in all cases " where it is for the interest of the patentee that other people generally should use " his device. I have referred to the pin-machine. That would not come under this provision which I am now citing.

The controlling clause is in the fourth, fifth, and sixth lines, which read: "Where it appears to the court or jury that, from the nature of the invention, it is for the interest of the patentee that other persons generally should use the same in like manner, and pay him a license-fee therefor."

In such cases the license-fee, and not profits or savings, shall govern the measure of recovery, with the provision at the end of the section, which applies not only to profits and savings, but also to the license-fees—allowing the court to increase or decrease the amount of recovery so found, at its discretion. The proviso reads: "But if, in any case, it shall appear to the court that the damages or profits, ascertained as above, shall be inadequate to give the plaintiff a just compensation for the injury done by the infringement, or shall be in excess of such injury, the court shall have power to increase or diminish the amount to such an extent as may be just and reasonable."

I noticed on yesterday the provision of the present law, allowing the court to increase the damages three times, and said if it was right to give *that* discretion to increase, they should also have the discretion which the courts wish they had, to decrease the damages in cases where they were excessive. We thought it better not to direct the court to increase or decrease threefold, but give in this matter, as in similar matters, the widest discretion. It should be a proper discretion to either increase or decrease the damages, according as the justice of the case may require.

The CHAIRMAN. Why should not the court, if this power be given to increase or diminish the verdict of the jury—if it is proper for the court to do that—why should we have any trial by jury at all? As I understand this provision, it gives the court discretionary power to increase or decrease.

Mr. RAYMOND. There are a great many reasons for that. I will simply say this, that the present provisions of the statutes allowing courts to increase the damages have been found to be of advantage, and reasonable in their operation in actions before a jury. In a law case, it is well known that a jury know little or nothing about patent law. They go by their prejudices in such matter, very largely, and if we have a jury made up of a certain class of men, whose business interests are on a certain side of the matter, the minds of the jury will be molded thereby; whereas if this discretion, which should be double, to increase and decrease, and that discretion, too, being the subject of review in the higher court, be given, no injustice follows it; it is a relief from injustice which might otherwise follow, and require an additional trial of the case.

Mr. TOWNSEND. What would be the use of a jury trial at all, then ?

Mr. RAYMOND. We are bound to open the case to be passed upon by a jury on account of the fifth amendment of the Constitution, which preserves inviolate the trial by jury. The proposition was argued before the Senate committee, under a suggestion to give the trial of patent causes only to equity. That was clearly in the face of the Constitution, and was abandoned.

Mr. TOWNSEND. But you propose to abrogate the trial by jury indirectly, if not directly. Why not directly ?

Mr. RAYMOND. If it would amount to abrogation of trials by jury, I think it would be unconstitutional. We can reach it by indirection, and not directly, and thus save the violation. It saves setting aside the trial and granting a new trial, which power is given to the court in many cases, and has been sustained as a proper provision.

Mr. WARD. I wish to call attention to one expression of yours, that this reduction or increase is a subject of review by a superior court. Don't you think the affirmative power to increase or diminish, is a question of discretion, and not a question of review by a superior court?

Mr. RAYMOND. It can be reviewed in equity cases, where all questions are considered on appeal, but in a case of law, where the basis of the action in the superior court was on a writ of error, where questions of law simply were reviewed, probably it could not; but in an equity cause the questions of fact are reviewed, as well as the questions of law.

I defined, I think, yesterday, what a license fee is sufficiently to show that it, as a measure of damages, would not be unjust in any sense. You will see that where it is for the interest of the patentee that other people generally should use his device, then the license fee obtains.

The remaining portion of the provision is directed to what I consider to be a prostitution, by the courts, of the doctrine of trusteeship, and no matter how much we may differ as to what the rule now is as to recoveries in equity courts, the Supreme Court has held that a man may be decreed to pay to the plaintiff, say $50,000, where it appears from the *expert* testimony in the case that he *saved* $50,000 by use of the device, although in his business he has not actually made a cent. In other words, to make myself plainer, if he had not used the device he would not have lost as much as he did lose into $50,000; under which circumstances the court holds that he is bound to pay that amount although he has not got fifty cents in the world. One becomes a trustee for the conversion of property only where he has had that property in his possession, or for damages from the use of a patented device where he has had that money in his pocket, and there is no justice to require him to pay that which he has saved when the use of the patent resulted in no profit to him. The remedy is contained in lines 14 to 24 of the bill, as follows:

In taking an account of profits in any case, the defendant shall not be charged with any saving he may have made, unless it has enabled him to realize an actual profit in that part of his business connected with the use of the invention. And the court shall determine what proportion of such profit is due to said invention, and what proportion to the other elements from which such profit was derived, capital and personal services excepted ; and the proportion of actual profit so found to be derived from the use of the invention shall be the measure of the profits to be recovered.

I will say, in passing, that it is my opinion that "capital and personal services" should not be excepted, but I do not wish to call your attention specially to that point.

I would like to review this explanation of the section again, but time does not allow.

The closing sentence in the section reserves and maintains inviolate the writ of injunction, as it now exists, so as to protect that right which is the utmost conferred under the Constitution, viz, the exclusive right. The first, principal, and practical remedy—that by injunction—is still retained to the patentee, without any alteration.

It has been objected on former occasions that this section in question very largely reduces the amount of damages to be received in any suit at law or in equity by a patentee, and for that reason amounts to a premium upon torts. No comparison can be made between a tort which is committed in an infringement of a patent and the other torts known to the law, such other torts being, in almost every case, a wrongful conversion of property, without any palliation. The value of patents, except those referred to under the illustration of a pin-machine, depends upon their being generally used and infringed; so that, while the infringement is technically a tort, it is only technically so. If, in answer to this, some one should say it is necessary for his interest that the public should pay the owner of the patent first and use afterward, the answer is plain. I refer again to the illustrations used as to the compound for killing cotton-worms. It was for the interest of the patentee that it should travel from mouth to mouth, from plantation to plantation, and that in the mean time every farmer should be using it, and that he should take a reasonable time to collect the damages. There is not the least semblance between this kind of a tort and any other known to the law. Infringements, also, are necessary on the part of common carriers. Take, for instance, the operations of the laws under which they are suffering. Being obliged, far the protection of persons and property, to use the very best devices known, whether patented or not, if the railroad company sets a man's house or barn or hay-stack on fire through a smoke-stack which has not the latest improvement in smoke-stacks patented—if this patented improvement is not used the railroad company is mulcted in damages for accidental burning; and if it is used, the company is mulcted in heavier damages for infringement. Then, again, refer to the laws of trade, which are just as inexorable and absolute. It is an absolute necessity in almost all the branches of trade that patents should be infringed by merchants, farmers, tailors, carpenters, masons, &c. The idea that the infringer is, in any degree or manner, guilty of a tort in any other sense than a mere technicality, is absurd. If the present rule of damages is wrong, is iniquitous, and a burden upon the people, and Congress can change that rule and make it a reasonable one, it is for the interests of the patentee that it should be done.

I met, a year since, a gentleman engaged largely in the manufacture of machines in the West, and he gave me these figures as indicating how men in the West engage in the manufacture of reapers, mowers, &c., who own patents and have to account to men who own patents that antedate theirs. He gave me one instance of where the whole cost of a machine, estimating the money invested in the manufacture, the amount of the wages of the men employed, the cost of timber and time for the sale of the machine, was $40, and yet he had to sell it at $150, in order to make himself whole, and to enable him to receive twenty per cent. from the business to cover profits and depreciation. The great difference between what the machine ought to sell for and what he is compelled to ask for it in the market, is paid to these speculators who own the patents which his patents and productions infringe.

The CHAIRMAN. Do you know what machine that was, Mr. Raymond?

Mr. RAYMOND. It was either a reaper or mower, or harvester, something of that sort.

The CHAIRMAN. Where was it made?

Mr. RAYMOND. In Illinois. It was an Illinois man who told me, but I cannot tell his name. It would not, perhaps, be proper for me to do so. I am quoting from an argument that I made before the Senate Committee on Patents last year, during the last Congress.

Another machine so costing $80, he tells me, is for like reasons sold for $280. Another one again, costing $250, he is obliged to sell for $650. It is the farmers who are paying these prices. Referring, again, to the rule I spoke of a few moments ago, that the basis of recovery in litigation determines the basis of settlement under these patents with these speculators; you, gentlemen of the committee, are simply asked to modify this rule which requires the people to pay these enormous royalties. Before the Patent Committee of the House of Representatives of last Congress, an application was made for the extension of a sewing-machine patent. The chairman of the committee, in a unanimous and lengthy report to the House, stated this fact as proven by testimony taken before his committee, viz, that the cost to the public of extending this patent for seven years would, under these rules, and under the practice, be more than *one hundred and fifty-nine million dollars*. It has been a fact, until recently, that you could send to England and buy a sewing-machine and transport it to this country cheaper than you could buy one here.

Another illustration from the railroads shows the absurdity of this rule of profits and savings under a patent. A man will commence to figure, for instance, how much fuel his device will save—it being something pertaining to the furnace-box—and he will demonstrate, upon the theory of his figures, so that the ablest mechanical experts on the railroad cannot show a flaw—cannot tell where there is a mistake—that 33 per cent. can be saved by its use. Well, experimentation shows that it saves something, but exactly how much cannot be estimated, on account of the difficulty of the problem. Pretty soon another man will come on with a device pertaining to the cylinder—a balance and relief valve—and show that it will utterly prevent any equilibrium of the piston in the cylinder, by which another 33 per cent. in the fuel is saved, the power formerly used to destroy the small degree of equilibrium which existed being now applied to the ultimate purpose of locomotion; and then another man will come in with a device for the exhaust-chamber, a petticoat-pipe, or a set of blinds, and he will demonstrate a saving of another 33 per cent. Put them all on to the locomotive and it is the old story of the Irishman "eating his cake and saving it too." While that is ridiculous, still it is a fact that, if we go into the courts to defend infringements of these patents, we will, under the pending rules, be charged with every pound of coal we have ever used.

I beg to again refer to the cotton-worm compound. Under this rule the inventor of that compound may start from the Ohio River and go South, and by employing able counsel can recover from the planters from one-fifth to one-third of all the crops of cotton cultivated there for the years during which his device has been in use, every particle of cotton that has ever been saved by the use of that compound. If they had saved one-third of the cotton crop which otherwise would have been destroyed by the worm, the whole of that third belongs to the patentee and not to the farmer. I need not multiply these illustrations.

I desire to call the attention of the committee to a general principle concerning this rule of profits and savings. It is a mistaken idea which has been controlling iu the courts for the last ten years, aud as well among the people, that a patentee is to be *compensated* for his invention. It is entirely wrong. The theory is simply to give him a reasouable reward, not a compensation.

Every part of a locomotive has at one time or another been subject to a patent, and it is fair to consider the whole thing as a simple patent. There are no figures that can convey the benefits which have accrued from its use. Take as well the utilization of electricity for conveying intelligence between distant points; there is not money enough in the country to *compensate* the inventors for the benefits which have been conferred upon the public thereby. The public cannot afford to compensate, they can only reward. The grant is a gratuitous grant; it is for the purpose of promoting the progress of science and the useful arts, in order that the public may reap the benefits of it; and all that is ever intended, or even practicable or possible to give to the invention, is a sure, a certain, a reasonable reward, which shall be an incentive to him, through getting a return for a class of labor which no other man gets a similar return for. The rewards given to patentees are not in any true proportion to the allowances made to others for similar labor, where property is created or protected, or a reward given by operation of law; and in this respect it is fair to compare the reward of the patentee with the salaries of the legislative, executive, and judicial officers.

The operation of this second section sends us to the courts and jury to ascertaiu the measure of the recovery. It is *strictissimi juris*, a right which the people have. The courts are constantly estimating the value of all kinds of property, acquired in all kinds of ways; and why this should be any exception to the rules which obtain in other kinds of property in this respect, I do not know. It might result in a possible injury, in one case out of a thousand, to a patentee; but that is unavoidable in every general statute. While this is true, I have no doubt that the patentee would be perfectly satisfied, in ninety-nine cases out of a hundred, with what the courts would do for him; and there is no doubt that the settlements would be more prompt than under the present rule, and the burden of tax and annoyance of chancery litigation thus be gotten rid of. If you make the measure of recovery reasouable and easy of application, the number of suits and the number of patent speculators will be decreased, the rights of patentees will be more easily ascertained, more patents will be used, and the inventor will get his recompense easier, quicker, and oftener. The public are afraid of these patents. They won't use them now, if they can avoid them.

The people of this country are under very great obligations to inventors. I do not underestimate their value. I agree with every other man who has construed the Constitution rightly, that what the inventor wants and should have *is a certain and reasonable reward.*

By making this reward just and reasonable the public will be better satisfied; the growing hostility to patents will be allayed; the users of patented inventions will be more numerous, and will pay for such use far more willingly; and the temptation to buy patents for the purposes of speculation be in a great measure done away with.

What, then, shall be the measure of value of a patented invention?

There is probably none that would be entirely free from objection; but we believe that a fair and reasonable license-fee will come nearer to accomplishing the desired end than any other, especially if you leave, in addition, the rule of profits and savings in cases where it is not for the interest of the patentee that the people should generally use his devices.

As the closing part of my argument, I desire to anticipate some very important objections to the first and second sections, which will be made during the argument, as to the constitutional powers of Congress in the premises, and the argument that the bill as it now stands will result in the taking away of any right of property, and therefore would be in contravention of some constitutional provision; and that, therefore, provisions should be attached to these sections of the bill making them only applicable to the extent of the constitutional provisions. The purpose for which these amendments are proposed is to protect certain speculative private interests, and with the object that the public agitation of the present may be allayed, and that these amendments to the law, to be enacted by this Congress, may be repealed during the time that these sections are inoperative by virtue of amendments to the bill to be proposed.

And, first, as the power of Congress to grant to the patentee less than an exclusive right, the Constitution providing that "Congress shall have power to promote the progress of science and of the useful arts, by giving to inventors for a limited period *the exclusive right* to their respective inventions."

I quote the following from Cooley's Constitutional Limitations, page 187, as bearing on this question:

Every positive direction contains an implication against everything contrary to it, or which would frustrate or disappoint the purpose of that provision.

I am utterly mistaken if it does frustrate the very and sole object for which the constitutional provision was enacted, to give to inventors an exclusive monopoly for any considerable period.

I quote again from the same volume, page 129:

Taxes should only be levied for those purposes which properly constitute a public burden. But what is for the public good and what are public purposes, and what does properly constitute a public burden, are questions which the legislature must decide upon its own judgment, and in respect to which it is vested with a large discretion, which cannot be controlled by the courts, except, perhaps, where its action is clearly evasive, and where, under pretense of a lawful authority, it has assumed to exercise one that is unlawful. Where the power which is exercised is legislative in its character, the courts can enforce only those limitations which the Constitution imposes, and not those implied restrictions which, resting in theory only, the people have been satisfied to leave to the judgment, patriotism, and sense of justice of their representatives.

The last authority seems a sufficient answer to the theory which contends that Congress cannot grant to the patentee a right of property that shall not be an exclusive right.

Just about as hopeless is the argument that the Constitution, containing a limitation as well as a conferment of power, and providing its single and sole purpose, also provides *the single and sole means*, namely, "an *exclusive* right," by which the purpose can be carried out. To suggest that the less includes the greater; that the discretion is one that is proper to confer upon the legislature; that such an iron-clad provision would be almost useless under the Constitution, and not in accordance with the established construction of other provisions of the Constitution; that the affirmation of that power implies the discretion for which I am contending, and that it was manifestly intended that that discretion should be left in the hands of Congress, simply foreshadows the argument, which is conclusive upon the subject.

The Constitution provides that an exclusive right may now be granted, and the natural, the first, and, if forcibly administered, a sufficient means therefor is the operation of the writ of injunction. No other statutory provision is necessary to embody the provisions of the Constitution. Congress, however, has wisely granted additiona remedies to enforce this right, and to compensate authors and inventors for the infringement of this right.

The provisions of this bill relating to litigation—those to which I am directing my attention—do not change the right of property in the patent itself, except remotely and indirectly, but are directed solely to the manner and extent and mode of recovery.

A modification by Congress of these additional remedies, having a retrospective application, can only be objected to as being *ex post facto;* as impairing the obligations of contracts; as infringing vested rights, or as being in contravention of some limitation of the Constitution. For it has been repeatedly held that retrospective laws, when not of a criminal nature, do not come in conflict with the national Constitution unless obnoxious to its provisions on other grounds than their retrospective character. (Cooley's Const. Lim., 264.)

Though the infringement of a patent is technically a tort, plainly the regulation of the damages therefor by *any* enactment cannot be classed as *ex post facto,* there being nothing of a criminal nature involved.

Proceedings to recover such damages are not *ex contractu,* but are *ex delicto.* Certainly there is no shadow of a contract between the owner of a patent and a tort feasor, and I am relieved from sustaining a denial of any contract between the government and the owner of a chose in action to recover these additional remedies, for there is no inhibition upon Congress, though there is upon the States, not to impair the obligation of contracts. I will, however, add in this connection:

A patent is not based upon a contract between the patentee and the Crown, in which the patentee, by communicating the secrets of the invention to the public, gives a valuable consideration for the grant, but is simply an exercise of the royal prerogative. (Feather *rs.* Queen [1865], 8 B. and S., 285.)

If I had time I would answer that there is no contract between the government and the patentee, from the fact that there is no sufficient consideration for which the public should enter into such a contract. The contract cannot be sustained for want of an adequate compensation.

I have heretofore demonstrated that the United States patent system is based upon a gratuitous grant (and in no sense a contract) made for the purpose of public progress.

There are few laws which concern the general policy of the State, or the government of its citizens, which may not affect contracts made both before and after their enactment. "For what are laws of evidence, or those which concern remedies, frauds, * * * or *acts of limitation,* * * * but laws which affect the validity, construction, or duration, or discharge of contracts?" (Vide Ogden *vs.* Saunders, 12 Wheat, 259.) "Whatever merely belongs to the remedy may be altered at will, provided the alteration does not impair the obligation of the contract, and it does not impair it provided it leaves the parties a substantial remedy." (Vide Bronson *vs.* Kinzie, 1 How., 316; and 3 Grant's cases, 243.) "Without impairing the obligation of the contract, the remedy may certainly be modified as the wisdom of the nation may direct." (4 Wheat., 122, per Marshall, Ch. J.) Whether or not an infringement of a patent extending over ten years is considered a continuous infringement or a succession of daily infringements, certainly none will contend that there is any *contract* between any of the parties to the patent, or to the infringement thereof, that a *certain amount* should be recovered for such infringement, or that the damages thereof should be computed upon any particular basis of duration.

The only remaining objections are that the proposed provisions, if

SEC. 2 IS UNCONSTITUTIONAL.

made retroactive, would infringe vested rights, and be in contravention of the fifth amendment to the Constitution, prohibiting the appropriation of private property without "due process of law."

Probably a sufficient answer to that objection is the fact that, while "due process of law" is generally not satisfied by mere legislative enactment, but must include judicial action, still in a number of cases it is satisfied by mere legislative enactments, and in such cases as this.

I am not able to give a full and satisfactory review from the decisions as to the meaning of this term, "due process of law." The Supreme Court has, however, held that it does not necessarily imply judicial proceedings. Nor have I been able to review the cases to demonstrate that the present case is one in which judicial proceedings would not be required, and in which legislative action is final.

Mr. POLLARD. The Supreme Court has given, within a few days, a full definition of the term "due process of law."

Mr. RAYMOND. I have not had access to the opinion.

The answer to the objection which I am now considering is twofold. In the first place, I think that the provision of the Constitution is avoided entirely by the character of the provisions which are now pending before the committee.

But, secondly, the question is, what vested right of property has the owner of a patent in the damages to be recovered for an infringement thereof? It is a general and familiar rule that "there is no vested right in a particular remedy." Any rule or regulation in regard to the remedy, which does not, under the pretense of modifying or regulating it, take away or impair the right itself, cannot be regarded as beyond the proper province of legislation. The utmost of the rights under consideration—the utmost of the rights which Congress, pursuant to the Constitution, can confer upon authors and inventors—is "the exclusive right to their respective writings and discoveries." The "particular remedy" and the "right itself," as above, in the patent law, is the "exclusive right" of the Constitution, and *the* remedy is by injunction. Congress has added other remedies, but they are so founded and of such a character that no right can so vest therein as to take them out from Congressional control. A right of action itself (here we are considering only the method and extent of the *remedy* attaching to the action) is undoubtedly property, which may in some cases become vested. But it is competent for the legislature to take away the right of action itself, unless it springs from contract or from the principles of the common law. (7 Johns., 477; 12 N. Y., 211, *et al.*) "It has been held that the legislature may even take away a common-law remedy altogether, without substituting any in its place, if another and efficient remedy remains." (Cooley's Const. Lim., 288.)

The case of McClurg *vs.* Kingsland, 1 Howard, 570, seems to me determinative of the questions now at issue. In this case the question was as to the validity of a patent granted under the patent acts of 1793 and 1800, those acts having been repealed, subsequent to the commencement of the suit, by the act of 1836; and the Supreme Court therein said, speaking of the right of property in the patent itself, *i. e.*, its validity, "This repeal, therefore, can have no effect to impair the right of property then existing in a patentee or his assignee, according to the well-established principles of this court in 8 Wheaton, 493. The patent must therefore stand, as if the acts of 1793 and 1800 remained in force; *in other respects, the 14th and 15th sections of the act of 1836 prescribe the rules which must govern on the trial of actions for the violation of patented rights, whether granted before or after its passage.*"

I continue quoting from the same case :

The power of Congress to legislate upon the subject of patents is plenary ; and as there is no restraint upon its exercise, there can be no limitation to the right to modify at pleasure the laws respecting patents, so that they do not take away the right of property in existing patents.

It is no objection to the validity of the laws respecting patents that such laws are retrospective in their operation. (McClurg vs. Kingsland, 1 Howard, 206; Sup. Ct., 1843)

Referring now to the particular sections (1 and 2) under consideration :

The limitation of section 1 does not take away any right either of action or recovery. It simply directs the court, in decreeing the remedy, to ascertain the same, with reference to the general principles of stale claims and laches in a definite manner herein provided. If the infringement sued for had continued but for four years, the statute would not apply at all. If it had continued for five years, the extent of the remedy would be modified accordingly, but not denied. So of the second section : in certain cases it simply provides that the courts shall not be governed, as now, solely by certain rules in ascertaining the remedy, but for the purpose of equity and justice shall broaden their vision beyond the horizon of profits and saving.

It has been the habit and the *animus* of the bench, and of the members of the bar representing patents, to erroneously consider the rights of which we are speaking as more sacred than vested rights in real estate and other kinds of property, which, after being vested, are constantly being affected in their values and titles by legislative acts *in præsenti*. It is because this incorporeal right, inhering merely in the effusions of genius and in letters-patent which give expression thereto, depends, on account of public necessary practices of infringement which are beyond legislative control, not for its existence, but for its speculative value upon these rules of recovery, that my brothers of the bar are so tenacious and jealous of such enactments by Congress.

I had intended, Mr. Chairman, to refer the committee to some considerations as to the public policy of making these acts *in præsenti*. I will indulge myself in one of them, though I feel that I have already occupied too much time.

However much the gentlemen of the committee may differ from the views that I have expressed, they will allow me to say I think that is our right, and the right of all those I represent to present these views in the forum which the Constitution has given us, namely, the courts of the country. We do desire that, so far as possible, the provisions of this bill shall be provisions *in præsenti*, and apply to existing causes of action, to existing patents, and to any evils which now exist where no risk is run of losing their benefits entirely by having them held unconstitutional as illegally retroactive. Where there is any such danger we have obviated it by making the sections apply only to subsequent rights.

[A general conversational consideration of facts followed, in which the members of the committee and others present took part.]

J. H. RAYMOND.

NOTE.

In the printing of this argument, I take the liberty of adding to the general notice of the many untruths and misstatements of A. H. Walker's arguments, which appear immediately after the same in this record.

This which I mean to be an unqualified denial of the truth and fairness of almost every allusion made by him to either Mr. Payson, the Western Railroad Association, or myself, and especially the statements made in his brief dated March 4, 1878, as to Mr. Payson's opinion of the constitutionality of the second section, as evinced by the telegrams appended. And I call the attention of the committee to the manifest unfairness and bad faith in the manner in which the statements of this, his last effusion, is made up.

J. H. RAYMOND.

WASHINGTON, March 5, 1878.

To GEORGE PAYSON, Esq., Chicago :

Walker is reprinting the falsehoods with which he regaled his argument, and alleging, that because undenied, they are admitted.

Telegraph me immediately a denial for print of his statement that you told Mr. Kales second section was unconstitutional, because made applicable to existing causes of action.

J. H. RAYMOND.

CHICAGO, ILL., March 5, 1878.

Mr. J. H. RAYMOND, Washington, D. C.:

I never told Kales any such thing. It is absolutely false.

GEORGE PAYSON.

CHICAGO, ILL., March 5, 1878.

To J. H. RAYMOND, Washington, D. C.:

Kales says must be a misunderstanding, that he never had any conversation with me on the subject.

GEORGE PAYSON.

ARGUMENT OF MR. G. H. CHRISTY.

Mr. CHRISTY. I will take up the question under discussion right where my brother Raymond left it off—on this question of profits and losses. The suggestions made by one of the committee are exactly in point. I fail to see the injustice as regards purchasers and users as to gains and profits on business carried on *ex delicto ;* and I take a case in point, in which I brought a suit for infringement of a patent on a horse-rake. It involved litigation running through some years, and I got a final decree, sustaining the validity of the patent, awarding an injunction, and ordering an account. I put the defendant on the stand, in order to get the number and the amount of his sales, to ascertain his gains and profits; and, to my utter dismay, he produced his books, showing the sale of two thousand machines and an actual loss of some $2,000 in the business. The sole value of the rake depended on his using the patented device. It was the only thing that gave it market value. There, I could not recover profits under the law of 1836 and 1839. Now, then, that man was a man of wealth; he carried on other branches of business, and he was able to respond in damages or profits. He had carried on his business in such a negligent manner, he built these rakes so poorly in respect to mechanical workmanship, using green wood for wheels, that they were all returned to him, and, as a matter of fact, he did not make anything. I had to settle the suit the best way I could, and my client got little or nothing. In that case the rule of license-fee could apply; but now I submit a case in which the rule of license-fee would not apply. I presume the committee have noticed the quality of sheet-iron used for locomotive jackets—a dark-blue sheet-metal. That metal is made by a client of mine, who is the only manufacturer of it in the United States. He and his father, and grandfather before them, have been in that business now for over half a century. They have built up the business and made it pay by putting into it their own capital—the best years of their lives; and a fourth descendant is coming onto the stand. They have put into it the best work of their brains, and have got an article of sheet iron which is superior to any sheet-iron in the world, and vastly better than the best Russian sheet-iron. Now, he has a manufactory established which is able to supply the entire demand. Suppose this bill passes, and under it it shall be held that a reasonable license-fee shall be the measure of recovery. His neighbor says, as I am only responsible for that reasonable license-fee, which will run about so much a pound, I will put my money into that business; I will go into that trade and undersell the business, and I will crush him, and account to him for a cent or two or three cents a pound on what I make, instead of 20 per cent. profit which my friend spoke of as being a fair manufacturing profit on reaping-machine manufacture. Now, there is a case of gross, rank injustice, which this law would authorize by virtue of abolishing the rules of damages *ex delicto*, and allowing them a license-fee to measure the injury done after a long operation in taking testimony.

My brother Raymond has made, I think, some very rash statements, and I only wish I had time to follow them all. He has done it not through any intention, but through failure or forgetfulness to weigh words. The committee will remember that on one point he claimed that the action for infringement was only in the most remote degree an action technically *ex delicto*, and also that the issue of a patent by the government and the public is not one *ex contractu*, but merely a gratuitous grant; and thus he argues that the injury done is one in the nature of an act *ex delicto*. I call attention to the inconsistency of the entire argument, where in one case he claims it is an action *ex delicto*, and that in another case it is *ex contractu*.

I wish to state one word on the cotton-worm question. That worm was hatched up before the Senate. I am surprised that as much weight has been attached to it as has. The argument that a man who has invented a compound of Paris green and flour is therefore entitled to all the benefits of the cotton crop which results from the killing of the cotton-worm, is the most absurd theory I ever heard in connection with a patent law. Suppose I should patent a remedy which was a sure cure for *cholera infantum;* on the same plan I could say every child has got to account to me for the value of its life during the ordinary term of human existence. I would not like any softer thing than that. The measure of the damages resulting from the killing of the cotton-worm must be simply the gain or profit on the sale of the mixture, or a reasonable license-fee. The effects derived from it do not come from the Paris green and the flour; they come from the wind and the weather and the sun. You kill the worm; there is the end of the invention. Whether or not you get a good crop depends on the wind and weather, for they are alone the sole cause, and to charge the results to the remedial agency of the compound is absurd.

When a case was called for and our friend responded with the Tanner-brake case, it is sufficient to say that that was a mechanical and not a chemical device. A question of mechanics involves the using of machinery, and every time that machinery runs it is an infringement. You use your medical remedy once, and that is the end of it. The profit or gain in reference to chemical mixtures—Paris green and flour—ends when you have made the mixture and sold it. In reply to the question raised by one of the committee, in reference to a purchaser in a drug-store, I will say that if the compound is made by the patentee and put ou sale, the right of the patentee has gone when the sale is established; the sale carries with it a license to use. But I apprehend the question arises in a case of this kind: where the cotton-grower goes to the drug-store and buys his Paris green, and then goes to his flour-barrel and mixes it and puts it on the crop. The only liability of the party then is for the gains and profits he has made by the mixing, or a reasonable license on the mixture. Now, in answer to the query, I say I do not think that question has ever been passed upon in any court, and the Tanner-brake case is not a similar one.

Mr. AIKEN. You know that there is a great monopoly in cotton-ties—the iron bands used by the manufacturers of cotton in baling their goods, and also in baling the raw cotton. Now, you also know that there are a great many methods of tying this band, all of which are claimed to be infringements of what is known as the "English arrow" tie. Suppose, as a private individual and planter, I am using one of the other devices, am I responsible for damages to the cotton-tie company?

Mr. CHRISTY. I suppose you are.

Mr. AIKEN. Even though I buy that tie from the manufacturer himself, who publishes to the world that he manufactures it?

Mr. CHRISTY. If you purchase from any person who is authorized to make it by the owners of the patents——

Mr. AIKEN. Suppose I know a man in Pittsburgh, or in some other city, who makes a tie, and I go to Pittsburgh and buy this tie in the stores or on the market, the representative of the English Arrow Cotton-tie Company follows me to my farm and sees me using it, am I liable to him for an infringement? Remember, I have bought from this manufacturer in Pittsburgh, who has advertised that he is manufacturing these ties.

Mr. CHRISTY. As the law stands you are, and that is what the Baker bill is intended to correct. That is one of the principal objections sometimes alleged to the patent law as it now exists. You are put, by virtue of this, on your guard, in reference to where and of whom you shall buy your ties; and you are required, as all men are required, to look to the article you purchase, just as you are in other matters. You go to a horse-broker to buy a horse, and you are expected to use caution to find out whether the man has a right to sell it. Supposing a stranger comes along and says, "I have got a good horse here, worth $150, which I will sell for $75," the presumption or suspicion will at least arise in that case that the man did not come honestly by that horse.

Mr. AIKEN. Suppose he asks $150; he wants to get the money that the horse is worth; there is no means of determining, in the first case, except by the offer below market price.

Mr. CHRISTY. I can only say the vendee must look out for his title, and as to the right of the party from whom he purchases, the same as

in real estate. You have got to make sure in real estate that the vendor has a good title to transfer to you, and the same rule prevails in
patents. You are put on your guard in that respect.

Mr. TOWNSHEND. It would be impossible for a man to discover whether
the vendor of a title was entitled to sell it. How can he ever ascertain,
by any record anywhere, that the person has a license?

Mr. CHRISTY. It is one of the necessary evils of the system.

Mr. TOWNSHEND. It is one, however, that cannot be possibly avoided
by an innocent purchaser.

Mr. CHRISTY. I do not know that. I may say in reference, for instance, to reaping machines, that the way for the farmer to protect himself is by purchasing from responsible parties. He is technically liable
for infringement for the use of that machine, and every time he uses it
he commits a new act of infringement; but the cautious farmer will
look well to the party from whom he purchases. If he purchases a Mc-
Cormick, or a Marsh, or a Wood mowing-machine, he knows that, on
ordinary business principles, the maker will protect him. I know a
party in Ohio who brought two hundred suits against the users of a
harpoon hay-fork, used to hoist off a load of hay and dump it into a
hay-mow. He did it to compel the manufacturer to go there and defend
the suits, which the manufacturer did. The farmer was not hurt a dollar. It was simply a little sharp practice, in order to get the infringing
manufacturer away from the forum where he lived, and where he wanted
the cases to be tried, and compelling him to go where the patentee lived;
and the suits were brought simply to put the manufacturer in such a
position that he had to defend his interest. The same applies in reference to this cotton-tie question; and I may say here that in three suits
I am retained against the American Cotton-tie Company. It is for the
interest of the parties in Pittsburgh from whom you purchased—and I
presume they are my clients, though I don't know whether you were
referring to any particular case or not—it is for their interest to protect
you, because if they don't you tell your next neighbor, "I can't buy that
tie, because I was sued;" but if the party from whom you purchased
comes forward and defends that suit, and the fact is known that you
will be protected, why you have no hesitancy in purchasing, and the
suits don't hurt you. And this is almost always the result, and is intended to be the result, when individual users are sued. The suits
against single users alone wouldn't pay the patentee.

Now, a word on this reaper question. The figures that Mr. Raymond
gave were that the machine costs $40; that after allowing a manufac-
turer's profit, amounting to twenty per cent., he sold it for $150. Take
off one-fifth from these as the manufacturer's profit, and that is only the
beginning. Brother Raymond forgot to tell *us*, or the reaper men forgot
to tell *him*, that there is an additional profit that has to go to the re-
tailer of that machine, who sells it to the farmer—the middleman. You
take off, then, twenty-five or thirty-three per cent. more from that. Now,
take off the losses from bad debts.

Mr. RAYMOND. The prices he gave me were the prices of the manufacturers to the middlemen. The figures I get are from representatives
of the company, from the machine company, and they are large manufacturers in Northern Illinois, at whose request Mr. Lathrop introduced
his bill to make the limitation short, and to repeal this profit and savings principle entirely.

Mr. CHRISTY. The Marsh Harvester Company you refer to. I know
them perfectly well; they are clients of mine, and I know those figures
are not true. I fought against the extension of those patents, and tried

to show how large license-fees they had received, and it was only a small fraction of what you name. I have since been counsel for the patents, and I know from personal knowledge that he did not state the facts correctly, or else you did not understand him correctly. One great allowance of the profit is a large sum which has to be paid out in insurance, transportation, and bad debts; and there is one villianous part of this business: they take notes—McCormick has got a safe full of them—with mortgages to secure the debt; and the costs of collecting, and various other things of that kind, and the carrying all your sales for three years in these long notes, bearing very little interest, and then taking out your $40 cost (they cost more, I am sure), and you have not a very large margin left for royalties for machines. I simply want to present this to show that this royalty is nothing like what Mr. Raymond would endeavor to make it appear.

Another rash statement is, that the value of a patented device results from the infringement of it. That is very much like the old theory of doing wrong that good may come of it. The reverse is true: the value of a device depends upon the honest use of it, the lawful use of it, and there is no patentee from one end of the land to the other, unless he is a speculator, who wants his patent to go into use by infringement; but he wants that the parties who desire to make use of it shall come to him and pay a lawful price.

A number of other statements were made, that I have not time to refer to. I wanted, also, to refer to other sections which I consider either good, bad, or indifferent; but I only propose to refer to those which I consider positively bad; and my opinions upon the others are divided between the good and indifferent.

The provision for taxing patents is one which meets my highest approbation, and I sincerely hope it will be reported, as the result will be undoubtedly to remedy a large portion of the evils which brother Raymond has set forth, such as speculations in patents, &c.

Again, after a patent has got established and become successful, it is a common thing to hunt up similar prior issues, purchase the patents, and, under the facilities afforded by law, on reissues obtain a reissued patent, covering what somebody else has invented, and then sue the real inventor. This will wipe out at least seventy-five per cent. of that class, and then we will have a great deal less trouble from that law.

I turn to sections 8, 9, and 10, and will refer to them, premising, however, under the law as it now stands, that we have but one remedy, and that is at suit for infringement at law or by bill in equity. This bill, as I understand, proposes now to provide for three remedies in the hands of the infringer; and I think my brother Raymond remarked in the Senate committee that this was a bill in the interests of infringers. In the first place the law makes provision in section 8 for testimony, that a party or a number of parties—for instance, the association of railroads which my brother Raymond represents—may associate together, and by certain proceedings in court lay up testimony to be used at some future time.

In the second place, by section 9, they may file a bill in the circuit court in order to repeal the patent, abolish it, wipe it out of existence.

In the third place, if they do not wish to resort to either of these remedies, they may go into court in case of the patentee's threatening to bring suit, and require him to proceed in an action of infringement.
. Now, it is a very rare thing to put three remedies in the hand of one man, and that man presumably the wrong-doer. I submit, now, that sec-

tions 9 and 10 give abundant remedy, and that section 8 gives a remedy that is very dangerous.

Section 9 I approve of fully. In case it appears that a patent is unjustly granted, or that it is informal, the parties may proceed under that section in equity and wipe it out of existence.

I have no particular objection to section 10, though I think it is needless. That is one under which the patentee or owner of the patent may be required to proceed by suit. I think two remedies certainly are enough, or ought to be enough, for one wrong. But now these parties come here represented by their attorney, and want an additional provision for testimony. I think the statement made yesterday was wise and sufficient, that the law at present gives sufficient remedy. I think, further, that it is a dangerous remedy to put into the hands of a wrongdoer, particularly if he is a wealthy party or corporation, and I use the word corporation not in any ill sense, for it is one of the most honest and legitimate ways of carrying on business; but it is specially dangerous to give the power to seventy or eighty wealthy corporations to pounce down on an inventor and snatch from him all his just rights, as was the case with Goodyear, and reduce him to absolute beggary ; and as was the case with Pullman when he was jacking up houses in Chicago; or as with Westinghaus, who was not able to pay me his first fee for his first *caveat*. Now, if it is good to put in the hands of an associated power representing such a consolidated amount of wealth, and with the unscrupulous character for which railroads are noted (I speak of it only as an entity, and not in regard to its officers)—I say it is a very dangerous thing to put such a grant of power into the hands of such an organization, in order that they may sit down on and squelch an inventor without any money to fight them.

There is another way in which they may squelch him by virtue of section 8. Suppose the bill passes in its present form. A patent is issued which I should like to kill on sight. It don't make any difference why. I serve notice to take testimony, and begin by calling the patentee on the witness-stand and asking him, "When did you make this invention ?" I interrogate him by a vigorous examination—and any lawyer knows how to conduct one who has had any experience of that kind—in reference to the very foundation of the grant of his rights, when he is off his guard, when he has not his papers to protect himself as against me, and when I am trying to get the worst record against him I can. I put him on record as to the date of his invention. I do it when he has not an opportunity to put his best record in shape. Having established the record against him as to the date of his invention, I proceed now to antedate him.

Mr. WARD. Does not the section provide that he shall receive due notice ?

Mr. CHRISTY. No, I am not bound to give him notice of what question I am going to ask him on the line of my investigation. I will take him off his guard and make him answer these questions. Now, then, if I have got seventy or eighty railroad companies at the back of me with their capital and their employés, it is a very singular circumstance if I cannot cook up some testimony among them. I do not say that brother Raymond would, but I do not know who his successor might be. Now, what do I do with this testimony ? I can bring in any testimony I please, bearing no relation to the subject, and a master in chancery has no control over the admission or rejection of it. I will put in hearsay testimony ; I will put in a story—that of garrulous old women ; I will make extracts from an old newspaper; I will lumber all that into the record. Now, if this came to a decision before a judge he would throw out all this refuse, and, knowing it, I would not then put it in.

This bill does not provide for any adjudication. There is no means by which the defendant can force it into a trial. I can put in anything I like, and put it all in. I make the worst case against him I can, without his having any opportunity to go before the court and expunge the irrelevant testimony. It is all put in, and put on record in the Patent Office, and there is a cloud at once put on the title. Now, what man here would like such an action taken in relation to his real estate? For instance, I buy a farm of sixty acres; I have a rich neighbor, who pounces down on me and says: "I don't think I want you here. I will file a bill to perpetuate testimony, showing that John Smith, squatter, or Bill Jones, or Jack Thompson, or somebody else, came and squatted on the property under the homestead act, and that his title is superior to yours. I will put that testimony on the records, and it has got to stay there, and you can't have any adjudication." And it becomes a cloud on your title as long as you remain there, thus allowing gross injustice to be done. It is putting a dangerous remedy in the hands of a most dangerous class—the wealthy part of our country, who want to use an invention without paying for it—in order that they may use it if they want to. I do not think they will; but I say it is a dangerous experiment to grant a power which they may use against a class of men who cannot defend themselves.

Mr. TOWNSHEND. Would this affect the inventor, unless he was a party to the proceeding?

Mr. CHRISTY. The bill proposes to make him a party.

Mr. TOWNSHEND. Then the bill proposes to give notice to him of any proceeding, does it not?

Mr. CHRISTY. He does not know what will be the direction of the examination.

Mr. TOWNSHEND. The bill must set forth " the date, number, and subject of the patent, and the name of the patentee, the names and residences of the several parties interested in said patent, so far as known to him, the names of witnesses proposed to be examined."

Mr. POLLARD. There is no issue made up beforehand ; nothing as to the direction or scope of the examination?

Mr. SMITH. The first clause provides that it shall set forth, &c.

Mr. CHRISTY. There may be no issue, and no suit; and worse than that, it is followed by no adjudication. It is the maxim of the law that there should be an end of litigation. I am utterly opposed to any such provision as will allow any litigation to be carried on unless followed by adjudication. I think it is a dangerous thing.

Mr. WARD. How much more notice, on the contrary, would come from the patentee as plaintiff?

Mr. POLLARD. But there is an issue there.

Mr. WARD. Anything more than a formal issue? Does it give any more light to the cause of action than a formal declaration does—and that does not give any.

Mr. CHRISTY. Well, it involves certain questions, but you do not know what the power to perpetuate testimony involves, nor does it render it necessary that the bill filed should state that.

Mr. SMITH. Your difficulty would be remedied by requiring a very particular description of the suit.

Mr. CHRISTY. It would be remedied in part; but it would enable testimony to be introduced to affect the title of a party who has a *prima-*

facie title, and would not be followed by any adjudication; in other words, you and I do not want any cloud thrown on the title of a patent we own.

The CHAIRMAN. Is there not in every State in the Union a law for perpetuating testimony, and cannot the same objection be made with the same force and effect in all those cases that you make now, and has any such evil ever arisen from that law by which testimony is perpetuated, as you suggest?

Mr. BRIGGS. Does the statute in any State for perpetuating testimony require the testimony to be recorded in any court where the titles are recorded?

Mr. STORROW. It does in Massachusetts.

Mr. WILLITS. There is nothing in my State that has the effect of *lis pendens*.

I think there is something in the suggestion I made yesterday about what is the extent and effect proposed in this notice by filing in the Patent Office. Now, they say this cannot be used as testimony, except between the parties. Well, if that is the case, what is the use of filing it in the Patent Office? It is to be a notice, and if that is the notice, is it to be a notice for the benefit of other than parties to the petition? And if it is notice to all parties, won't it be something in the nature of an estoppel? Don't it affect parties outside of the petition and outside of the proceeding? In taking this testimony, of course I have not looked it through. It looks as if the very fact of filing it in the Patent Office is intended to reach beyond the parties that are really involved.

Mr. BRIGGS. It does, by the terms of the bill, reach all *subsequent* purchasers.

Mr. CHRISTY. The exact purport and object is to crush the patentee, or to prevent his making any sales. For example, I take out a patent for tooth-picks; my neighbor, or friend, or enemy wants to make use of my mode of making tooth-picks, and without paying me anything for it. He says, "I will infringe"; or, "I will buy a license." Or I will change the illustration: He is making tooth-picks in some other way. Now, he says, "This mode of yours is better than mine, and I want to crush you in the business." He files a bill to perpetuate testimony. He throws out his drag-net (lawyers have always heard of fishing suits)—he throws out his drag-net in order to drag in testimony to affect the validity of my patent. He puts that on record in the Patent Office, in order that any manufacturer of tooth-picks who might be disposed to buy a license from me might have access to it, and through him find out some serious question as to the validity of my patent; and, if so, he may be dissuaded from buying a license from me. That is the object of it. It does not appear on the record what it is for; but that is the practical effect.

Mr. TOWNSHEND. Is the evil here any greater than the evil growing up under the law of the different States?

Mr. WILLITS. I think you will find this statute a great deal broader than anything of that kind.

Mr. TOWNSHEND. I use the question of land-titles as a parallel case for illustration. There is no Federal law authorizing the perpetuation of testimony.

Mr. CHRISTY. Unless it be the present provision in the Revised Statutes. My opinion of the point, now, is just this, that the present act covers all the remedy that is needed. It is such that, when an extreme case arises, an exceptional case, one associated with a vast amount of fraud, it will enable the courts to take jurisdiction on presentation of proper facts, and provide for the perpetuation of testimony; and that is all the remedy they need.

The CHAIRMAN. Is not the same objection tenable against the general statute for the perpetuation of testimony?

Mr. CHRISTY. No, sir; for this reason: Under the general statute, as it is now, the whole responsibility must devolve upon the judge. He has to be on his guard, so to speak. Now, the manner in which that authority is to be exercised is a matter devolving upon him; but you pass this law, and the judge then will say, " Why, I am relieved of a vast responsibility in relation to this by the legislative enactment, and as long as I follow the act it will be the fault of the legislative enactment if any wrong is done." The master in chancery in United States courts has no authority to pass on what is legal testimony. He is bound to take down everything that is offered. Who is going to say what is legal testimony?

Mr. TOWNSHEND. Could not the court always decide that in reviewing the testimony?

Mr. WILLITS. But the evil is done.

Mr. CHRISTY. Suppose I file in New York a petition for taking testimony in Chicago. I drag my fish-net through the shops of the railroad companies. I gather testimony, good, bad, and indifferent, and put it on the record. The master in chancery has taken down the testimony, and cannot pass upon the sufficiency of it. The law makes no provision for making issue, and how are you going to expunge what is immaterial? I can put in anything I please. I am five hundred or a thousand miles away, and I will carry on the examination just as I please, and you cannot stop me. I have already stated that I think section 9 is a wise one. Section 10 I have no serious objection to.

Mr. TOWNSHEND. Why do you say this testimony will be necessarily taken by a court commissioner?

Mr. CHRISTY. I do not know any other way.

Mr. TOWNSHEND. I think it is to be taken by the circuit judge.

Mr. CHRISTY. If you can get a circuit judge to sit for that, you can do more than any one else can do. They will do just as Judge Blodgett did, and as he is doing to-day. I went out there and entered a motion that the time be extended in a case. Judge Blodgett said, " I refer you to Mr. Bishop, master; he will decide it." There is the answer that you get before the judge.

Mr. TOWNSHEND. It does seem to me if the counsel on the other side brought out the fact that the evidence is not proper testimony before the case is presented, that, upon exception being filed to the report of the master, the court would strike out such testimony.

Mr. WILLETS. The case might not be tried for ten years.

Mr. TOWNSHEND. But if all the parties are there in issue, no matter whether the case is tried or not, the court will have the power to exclude the irrelevant and improper testimony.

Mr. BRIGGS. The objection is not that it is improper testimony, or that there is no discretion given the master or examiner, but that it must be put upon the proper record in the Patent Office, and thus cast a cloud on the title.

Mr. CHRISTY. They do not intend to bring the suit to trial, but intend to crush the patentee.

Mr. TOWNSHEND. And, supposing the testimony was taken before the commissioner, and he should make his report to the court, as has been suggested, would not the court order that the irrelevancy be stricken out before they would allow the case to be tried?

Mr. CHRISTY. There is no trial.

Mr. RAYMOND. There is a trial provided for, and this question has all come up, allowing the party appealing to take testimony.

Mr. TOWNSHEND. If we should provide a way by which the trial could be had, perpetuating this testimony—in other words, provide a way by which the court could sit upon a case, and expunge from the report of the master such testimony as he deemed proper—would not that avoid the difficulty?

Mr. CHRISTY. It would avoid a portion of the difficulty. There are many kinds of improper testimony. One is hearsay testimony, which is inadmissible for any purpose. Another is secondary testimony, which may become admissible, in case you lay the ground by proof of the loss of the original testimony. So, in reference to a loss of assignment, you may prove the contents of the assignment when you prove the original is lost. There is a great deal of testimony which may be competent under certain circumstances, though not generally. The courts are rather free in proceedings as to the order of taking testimony, and a party can generally put in secondary proof of the state of facts, without proving the facts, and render that secondary testimony admissible; but the court would not strike it out, because, when the case comes up for trial, the parties may lay their ground for that testimony. They undoubtedly would strike out any testimony inadmissible for *any* purpose, but not testimony which was conditionally admissible, or possibly dmissible under any circumstances, for any purpose, because, when a case comes to be tried, there may be ground laid for the admission. But it does not remedy my objection, which is, that it is not followed by an adjudication. It does not remedy my objection, that it is throwing a cloud unjustly on what seems to be a sufficient title; and also the additional objection, that if even you could, after a long job of taking testimony of that kind, go into court with your motion to expunge, it compels the patentee to employ the very best talent he can get in the patent profession, and, such counsel not being cheap, a poor inventor cannot pay them. Thus it would have been in the power of the railroad companies to have crushed Pullman effectually, and so with many others.

Mr. POLLARD. I understand you to say that the present act requires the deposition to be taken and the testimony perpetuated by a judge.

Mr. CHRISTY. I say the judge cannot do it. The judges have already more than they can do.

Mr. POLLARD. You said one reason why the depositions taken under the proposed law would be more in violation of the principles governing the introduction of testimony than under this law was because, under the statutes, the testimony had to be taken by a judge. I say it does not.

Mr. CHRISTY. That is Mr. Eldredge's suggestion.

Mr. ELDREDGE. My suggestion relates to section 8: "He may file a bill or petition in the circuit court of any district in which the parties," &c.

Mr. CHRISTY. A man may file his bill in equity or in the circuit court, but that don't compel the judge to take the testimony.

Mr. POLLARD. This clearly means to be taken in the usual way.

Mr. CHRISTY. And it does not give the officer taking it any right to pass upon the sufficiency.

Mr. WARD. Now, follow that one step further, and give the patentee the right to bring this matter immediately to issue.

Mr. CHRISTY. Then you have the 9th section, and this 8th section is superfluous.

Mr. POLLARD. No; give the patentee the right to call upon the party interfering.

Mr. CHRISTY. That is the 10th section.

Mr. POLLARD. Whenever this railroad association, which you seem to fear, commences steps to trouble the patentee, by clouding his title with these bills to perpetuate testimony, why not give the patentee the right to call upon the party interfering with him to meet him at issue? Now, that is analogous to the proceeding in some of the States where the party who files a mechanic's lien may be called upon by an owner of property to proceed and have the question tried under the laws, so that the owner of the freehold shall not be troubled.

Mr. CHRISTY. That is still further complicating the litigation.

Mr. RAYMOND. He has that right now. He can file his bill in equity or under this very section, and the section is as much a benefit to the patentee himself as to the infringer—not only in that case, but in the other case. I have now, I think, at least a thousand cases—claims made against railroad companies—in my office, where I have given the patentee a reference to a prior use or invention, and in some instances he is not satisfied with it. I am perfectly satisfied when the case comes to trial that I can defeat that patent, as it is utterly invalid, and I there-fore refuse to pay anything. In a great many instances the patentee himself wants to perpetuate the evidence on a particular reference.

Mr. CHRISTY. Supposing the railroad companies say: "Well, I guess we won't use that patent now; we will perpetuate the testimony and put a cloud on the title, and we will prevent him from selling to any-body, but we will not ourselves infringe the patent. He cannot throw us into court, because we don't infringe; but we effectually prevent him from selling to anybody else, and sooner or later he will have to come to terms."

Mr. RAYMOND. Cannot he perpetuate testimony to show that it is ma-licious, and will the court permit such proceeding unless the petitioners have an interest at stake?

Mr. CHRISTY. Why, you can allege, as the interest you have, that you want to use the invention and don't know whether it is safe. I say my whole point is this—that it is dangerous; that it is unexampled in the history of our legislation—looking to the administration of rights and the prevention of wrongs—in our whole system of jurisprudence, to al-low a cloud to be put on a title by putting this weapon in the hands of powerful parties without being followed by any adjudication, and where under some circumstances no adjudication may be possible or probable.

Mr. WARD. I say make it possible, then, to have the adjudication, if you can.

Mr. CHRISTY. Very well; then you remove a large part of my objec-' tion. Then, when you have got that, you have the present remedy, which enables the patentee to bring suit for recovery. You have then got the present law, or sections 9 and 10, in substance, and that is enough; and so there is no need for section 8.

Mr. STORROW. I desire to call your attention to the amendment in-troduced by you and proposed by M'r Hatch, which is found on page 80 of the Senate proceedings, and which reads as follows: "That no depo-sitions taken under this section shall be used except as against persons who were parties to such proceedings *and were served personally with notice*, or those claiming under them," &c. There is also the following amendment proposed. (See Senate appendix, page 190.) It will be seen by these amendments that the respondent may take testimony to rebut the facts in the same proceeding, and put them together, and they all go in the same lot; wherever one part is used the other can be.

Mr. RAYMOND. So that the petitioner may be made to pay the cost.

Mr. POLLARD. In my State the petitioner has to go into a court of record and make affidavit that the testimony which he is about to take is or will be needed, in all human probability, or that he expects to prove some facts concerning property in which he is interested. If you make these railroad companies come into court, and, before they get this commission to take testimony, swear that they are using the patent now, and that they believe it is necessary to protect themselves that this decree for testimony should be made, would it not cure the defect?

Mr. CHRISTY. That simply develops another point of danger. My whole point is, that it is dangerous. It is giving them that which they are not entitled to, and which is not their right; and that to strip it of its objectionable features will leave you nothing more than the law as it now stands, and the other two sections. Of course, if you strip it of all its objectionable features, by putting it in the power of the court to pass upon the sufficiency of the testimony and expunge any portion of it which may be deemed improper, and then follow it up with the suggestion that an adjudication may be at once had on it, then you have so far turned it into something else that it is something else.

Mr. RAYMOND. Except you do not allow the parties to join.

Mr. CHRISTY. I think it is provided for in the present law that parties having conjunction of interest can unite in the same suit. The court, to prevent a multiplicity of suits, will allow suits to be joined, and if your whole eighty railroads are each of them using the patented device they are interested jointly, and then they may join as interested parties in the proceeding, and in case the court is of opinion that such a dangerous state of facts arises as justifies it.

Mr. STORROW. At least the court will have all the cases tried together, or will hear one and let the others abide the result.

Mr. RAYMOND. We have no Federal statutes saying that thing is to be done. The reason is that the English chancery proceedings, which govern in Federal equity courts, do not permit any such proceeding.

Mr. CHRISTY. We have the English chancery practice in full force as it existed prior to the adoption of our Constitution.

Mr. RAYMOND. That practice does not permit of such proceeding.

Mr. CHRISTY. My impression is, that in chancery practice you can unite all parties that have a common interest, and save a multiplicity of suits. Leaving out the question of any law, the judge would permit, and the defendant would not object, because to object would result in eighty suits being brought against him instead of one.

Mr. POLLARD. We could make a provision to remedy the difficulty on that subject.

Mr. TOWNSHEND. As I understand you, the old statute can be made available.

Mr. CHRISTY. But the court will be very slow about using it, and will only allow it in an extreme case, and *only* then. I never heard of its being used, in my practice.

Mr. TOWNSHEND. It was stated that the present law was not applicable.

Mr. STORROW. It is legally applicable, but, owing to the peculiarity of the subject-matter and the relations of parties who may be interested, it is not adequate.

Mr. CHRISTY. Then the section that is now pending (section 8) is clearly objectionable, because it defines just what the court may do, and the court will say " We are relieved from any discretion in the matter by the direct provisions of law. A general power, under which the court may exercise equity powers, will enable it to exercise them so as to reach the evils complained of.

I want to talk about reissues and the amendment as provided in section 5. The law as it now stands requires the filing ——

Mr. STORROW. If you will take the form of section 5 on page 202 of the Senate document, the revision which the Commissioner of Patents made, and which is generally conceded to be better than the one in the bill.

Mr. CHRISTY. The point I was going to speak of was the authority the present pending bill gives with reference to the use of the model in a reissue.

Mr. STORROW. The change made by the Commissioner strikes out the reference to the model as a basis for reissue.

Mr. CHRISTY. The present law requires the filing of a specification or description, a drawing showing it, and a model—three things—and allows, in case of any errors, the drawing to be corrected by the model, on a subsequent application for reissue, the model by the drawing, and the specification by either of the other two, but not outside of them—not by any matter *aliunde*. Now, in administering that law, the Supreme Court have laid down this, if I rightly apprehend their meaning : that when a suit is brought on a reissued patent, and the defense is taken that the reissued patent is not for the same invention as that described in the original patent, that that question must be determined solely by a comparison of the specifications and drawings. You have got to compare the two documents, and you cannot get outside these two documents, in order to ascertain the identity, except by reference to the model, and the Patent Office is permitted to go to that extent.

The purport of this section, to amend the description or the drawings, either by reference to any written records contained in the Patent Office, or in the files of that office, gives them the right to use anything they find there. Now, the objection comes, and it comes with great force, from parties in the West; from the railroad associations; from the Grangers; from the South, and from the East, of the injustice of allowing patents to be unduly expanded by virtue of a reissue, so as to cover things not contemplated by the original inventor.

Now, it is this provision which enables an examination to be made of the description attached to the original patent, in case of reissue, so that whatever descriptive matter the inventor may have put in his old original case, or his attorney may have put in for him, may be a basis for a new issue. In my opinion, we should, instead of reopening those doors, and making these fraudulent reissue cases possible, shut them a little tighter. I think that it is unduly expanding a right which is too broad now. Now, you may amend your reissue by reference to original patents entirely, and the models and drawings under this section, and they say that is too broad and encourages the perpetrating of frauds in consequence. In this section you can proceed not only to amend by reference to the models and drawings, but by reference to any matters of record which were put into the old file, and which have been lying there in concealment for five or ten years.

Mr. WILLITS. Put in what?

Mr. CHRISTY. Put in what can be found in the old original application.

Take the case in 3 Sawyer, and it illustrates my point. A man named

Nobell, I think, applied for a patent covering the utilization of nitro-glycerine as an explosive. In that patent, he described some four or five inventions—over in England you can put in half a dozen inventions in the same patent. He filed it, and afterwards put in a new specifica-tion, striking out, say, four or five of the inventions, and took the pat-ent on the one, the original specifications remaining on file in the office, describing the five inventions. I am not accurate as to numbers, but just use them as pertinent to my point.

In the case of the Giant Powder Company against the California Powder Works (3 Sawyer), the patentee came to my partner and myself, and, under a practice then prevailing and still prevailing, I surrendered that patent on the one invention, and took out four or five patents based on the description which the man had put into the Patent Office five years before. Now, this case came up before Judge Sawyer, of Califor-nia, and he said it could not be done; that it was, under the present law, without authority of law, and he sustained the reissue, which was based on the surrender of the patent which we had taken, and set aside those claims of the reissue which were based on the descriptive matter put in with the old description five years before. Now, this section will sanction that practice, and as it is a very dangerous practice—I felt at the time it was—it was the practice, and there had been no decision on it, and the courts will not allow it; and without further knowledge I am satis-fied that the law should remain in this respect as it is. If you will turn to section 5, lines 10, 11, and 12, which read as follows: "The Com-missioner shall, on the surrender of such patent and the payment of the duty required by law, cause a new patent for the same invention shown in the model or drawings, or described in the original specification or its amendments,"—you will see it goes back to the old description, which has been lying in secret in the Patent Office for five, ten, or twelve years, of which the public have no notice whatever, and pertaining to inventions which other manufacturers have commenced using. You can go back and revive an old secret document, making that a basis for re-issue, and shut down on some of the largest manufacturing interests, as has been done.

Mr. WILLITS. Does not section six obviate that difficulty?

Mr. CHRISTY. It does as to infringements previously made; but sup-pose a man has invested $100,000 in business, it does not cover subse-quent infringements.

Mr. RAYMOND. I would like to hear about the proposition to abolish reissues after three years.

Mr. CHRISTY. It is clearly unjust. Under our old Federal procedure, before we had the present patent laws, the Secretary of State issued all patents. He issued a patent which came up in Grant v. Raymond, 8 Peters, which for some reason or other contained an error. Before there was any law whatever on the subject of reissues, the patentee goes back to the Secretary of State, who at that time granted patents, and says: "My patent has a mistake in it." The Secretary says, "Surrender your patent and I will give you a new one," and he did so without any law whatever. That case went up to the Supreme Court and they said it was proper, that he had the right to correct mistakes, and that it was the business of the government to correct its own errors, and that mode was one to which no objection could be taken. Now, if you prohibit all reissues, you are going to prevent the government from correcting its own mistakes, and you are also going to deprive the party of correcting innocent mistakes made by himself—a thing never tolerated or allowed.

Mr. RAYMOND. The proposition is to limit it; to give it three years from the time the patent runs.

Mr. CHRISTY. I do not know why it should be limited to three or five years. You made a remark to that effect in your argument. My opinion is that the value of the patent, or merit of the invention, would not be discovered until long after the patent is granted, and your restriction of three years simply compels the man to find out within a short time the actual value and the precise scope of his patent. I do not know why it should be limited to one or five years, nor why it should be three years instead of seventeen.

Mr. ELDREDGE. Would not that be a reasonable limitation—three years?

Mr. CHRISTY. There is no fixed time which is reasonable. Now, there are some patents taken out away in advance of the progress of the art, and it takes five, ten, or fifteen years to grow up to a point where a patent can be used. I recall a case of that kind. A patent was taken out a number of years ago for putting a carburetter in a railroad-car so as to light up the car. Theoretically that is very nice, but that could not be done for apparent reasons. It could not be utilized for practical purposes until the Westinghouse air-brake, which furnished a supply of air through the trains continuously, was invented. Then the invention became practicable. Now, in that case the patentee had all the elements, say, five years before the thing became practical, simply because the air-brake had not arrived at the proper perfection. Now the public have the benefit of his invention. Where it depends on the growth of the art we cannot fix the limitation, because one art may grow in a year. The Westinghouse air-brake reached its present state in three or four years, whereas those experimenters had been working for forty years in order to do the same thing. It may develop itself in one year or in twenty years. You cannot so fix the period of limitation as to affect justly all patents.

Mr. STORROW. I was concerned in a case where the owners of a patented device put it into a machine which went largely into use; after fifteen years a man made a machine of a different form, but having the same invention for its basis. This was the first infringement, and when the owner prepared to bring a suit, he found that the infringer, fully availing himself of the invention, had made a machine which was just outside of the claims. Often, also, the necessity of a reissue is known only when the court has passed upon the patent when it is ten years old. Merrill v. Yeomans, 94 U. S., is such a case.

Mr. CHRISTY. On the argument of a suit last November on an extension of the patent—the patent was originally granted in 1858 and extended in 1872; it will run out next year—the first suit ever brought on it was after the extended term. In that patent there was an erroneous reference to another patent as a matter of description. The effect of that error had not been found out until eighteen years after the patent was granted, and until that suit was brought they had never discovered an error, and it had been extended; the Commissioner of Patents had revised it; it had been extended, and the defect was not discovered until in the course of the suit. I say that in such a case as that the limitation is not fair.

I have one word further to say, which is with reference to the complaints which come up from different parts of the country about patents. I am aware of the hue-and cry which comes from the Grangers of the West, the manufacturers of the East, and I may say from the South (in reference to this same matter of paris-green). It is a characteristic of human nature, of you, and I, and everybody else, that we grumble most about paying for the necessities of our existence. I doubt if there is anything which excites more grumbling than the paying of gas-bills, unless it be butchers' bills, and it simply results from the fact that we have got to have the gas and pay that bill. As long as it was merely optional, we were willing to burn tallow-dips, or gas; but when in the change of our social relations and the progress of society we have got to buy gas, we immediately begin to say it is too high, and ought to be lower. When the sleeping-cars were first started, we did not mind paying two dollars or two dollars and a half for a seat; but when the change in business habits it brought about first enabled us, and afterwards practically compelled us, to travel all night, and we were then brought into such relationship with the sleeping-car that we have got to have it, grumbling commences. It is the same way with water, &c.

Now, when in the progress of the arts the farmer, instead of swinging his scythe as he could a few years ago; when, in consequence of the progress of arts, and the scarcity of labor, or a low price of crops, he is compelled to make the purchase of a reaping and mowing machine, he begins to grumble right off; and it is simply carrying out a characteristic of human nature.

The necessity of the thing arises from the perfection of the invention. It is not necessary for a farmer to buy a reaping-machine until the machine is so far perfected that it is largely preferable to swinging his scythe, and thereupon he goes and buys one. Now, the necessity has been created largely by the brains of the inventor that have gone into that machine, and the farmer makes use of the fact of its being necessary as a reason why the patent which created the necessity should be abolished; and in that respect I must take the liberty of criticising my friend Raymond's argument. A great many of his reasons, while tending to support the bill, go to show that the patent system ought to be abolished altogether; but I will do him the credit to say that he has repeatedly disclaimed any such object. Now, I do not mean to say that there is no good ground for a great many of these complaints. My point is this: that it is proper to make allowances for a great many of these complaints, simply because of the characteristics of humanity—because we complain of what we want most to buy.

The committee, on motion, adjourned to Tuesday, February 5, 1878, at 10 a. m.

ARGUMENT OF MR. STORROW.

[Feb. 5, 1878.]

MR. CHAIRMAN AND GENTLEMEN OF THE COMMITTEE:

House bill 1612 (the same as Senate 300) grew out of a hearing which took place before the Senate Committee on Patents about a year ago, on a bill that had passed the House without debate, without any hearing before you, and had been referred to the Senate by its committee. That bill contained a great many clauses, which, the moment they became known to parties interested in patents—rather by accident, for it had gone through the House very quietly—seemed to them to be destructive of the patent law; seemed substantially to take away all protection and all rights of inventors and patentees. It was opposed upon that ground. In the course of the discussion in the Senate, which was had just at the end of the session, so that no action took place afterwards, it was suggested that the gentlemen who were present and were largely interested—inventors, representatives of railroads, and others—should endeavor to frame some amendments to the patent law which would meet the necessities of the case, and which would not impair the efficiency of our patent system. In that view a draught was made, and a large number of copies printed and distributed to gentlemen who were likely to be interested in it and familiar with the subject. After that there was a meeting at Chicago, in the early autumn, of a dozen or fifteen gentlemen, representing a great many diverse interests. That meeting lasted seven days, and at it there was a very long and able discussion of many amendments which were suggested to the patent law. The result of that was a revision of the first draught of the bill, a thousand copies of which were printed and distributed throughout the country, to persons known to the framers as likely to be interested, and likely to have opinions worth considering on this subject. That revision was again revised at two subsequent meetings at other cities. Various sections were added to the bill relating to proceedings in the office, specially drawn by gentlemen here in Washington, who were familiar with the practice of the office. The whole bill was communicated to the Commissioner of Patents before being presented to Congress. It was that bill which was presented to the Senate and to the House, and it is upon that bill, so framed, that the hearing took place before the Senate Committee on Patents, and upon which the hearing is now being had before this committee.

The object of the framers of that bill was to guard against the abuses which had crept into the administration of the law by reason of the great extension of the patent system; and by reason, we think, of misapprehension on the part of the courts, to say the least, of the true · principles which should govern them in administering the law.

Before we consider the details of the bill, it is right that our attention should be called to the practical workings of the patent system, its effect on the inventor and the public, and the manner in which it comes in contact with various interests, in order that we may know where to apply a corrective, and what kind of a corrective to apply, because the patent law is not a proper subject for theoretical legislation simply.

The origin of the patent law is generally supposed to be the English statute of James I (1625), which in terms destroyed all monopolies, but allowed the crown to grant to inventors patents for new inventions and new processes of manufacture. I think that is very properly considered the origin of the law, because up to that time the obtaining a patent had not been a matter of right—it had been a mere matter of grace on the part of the crown. By the statute of James I, the law stepped in and regulated this matter. It gave, so to speak, to the inventor a right to obtain a patent, and thus converted the system from a mere arbitrary reward for past merit when it might be discovered, or might clamorously make itself known, to a promise of protection held out to all inventors—changing it thus into an incentive to obtain the reward which he knew they could obtain if he was successful. That statute did not in terms, and no English statute has since in terms declared the absolute right of the inventor to have a patent as ours does. In language, the statutes leave it, at least until quite recently, as a grace from the crown; but, according to the English theory of government, the regulation of the right by Parliament practically required the sovereign to grant it when the inventor had complied with the necessary formalities.

In this country, of course, before the adoption of the Constitution, we knew of this English system; moreover, the different States had repeatedly and to a considerable extent granted patents for inventions. This practice of the different States was stated, and a good many illustrations of it given in the Patent Office Report for 1850; and was referred to in one of our earliest statutes, that of 1793, in which Congress enacted that no one should take the benefit of that law unless he first surrendered the patent which he had obtained under the State authority.

The system of this country was started by that clause in the Constitution which has been read to you so often in the last few days, giving to Congress the "power to promote the progress of science and useful arts, by securing for limited times to authors and inventors the exclusive right to their respective writings and discoveries."

One of the first laws passed by the new Congress was that of 1790, which was amended in 1793, and again in 1800, and, with some minor amendments of detail, which did not essentially change its character, it remained until 1836. At that time the law was changed in this respect; previous to that, the officers charged with the duty of issuing patents (i. e., the Secretary of State and Attorney-General, copied in that respect from the English system) examined inventions and determined whether they were to be patented or not, but very inefficiently. The act of 1836 created the Patent Office and put an officer at the head of it, and charged him with the duty of examining all applications in order to ascertain their novelty and utility. That system—the American system—has existed in this country ever since, and it does not exist to any practical and useful extent in any other country. In 1860 the term of a patent was changed from fourteen years to seventeen years, and the power of the Commissioner to grant an extension was taken away. It was again revised in 1870, and by the Revised Statutes; but with those exceptions it has continued substantially as it was before, with exceptions of the proceedings in the Patent Office, which have been quite frequently changed in some particulars.

Our law originally was for fourteen years, and that is pretty conclusive proof that it came from the English statute, for the statute of James I provides fourteen years as the life of a patent, and under or subsequent to that statute the practice grew up of extending our patents for seven years more. From the fact that the term for which the patent existed by our first law was fourteen years, it is obvious that our law-makers had before them and had in mind the English patent system.

In pursuance of these laws, an inventor, in the first place, gets the idea of his invention, and when he has so far perfected it as to have put it into practical shape, he applies for a patent. That application, by the terms of the statute, must set forth the nature of his invention, and, in the case of a machine, the principle thereof, and the best mode in which he has, up to that time, contemplated applying the principle, all stated in such full, clear, exact, and concise terms as to enable any one skilled in the art to which the invention belongs to practice it.

Then, in the application, he must distinguish between what is new and what is old; that is, he must put into the application what are technically called the claims, declaring what it is that he claims as new, and pointing out precisely what it is. The application is then referred, under our system of classification, to an examiner having this class of matter particularly in charge, and whose supposed familiarity with the subject enables him to ascertain whether the matters are new or old. If the applicant is not satisfied with the decision of this examiner, there is a method of appealing from his decision to other officers in the office, and finally to the supreme court of the District of Columbia. If the applicant is referred to the patent or application of another person as anticipating him in the invention, and he thinks that other person is posterior to him in time, he can then raise a contest in the office, called an interference, between himself and the other person, to determine who, in the eye of the law, is the prior inventor. In this contest evidence is taken on both sides by depositions, and the case argued ; and it may be twice appealed. If he is successful in all this, the patent finally issues.

The next legal step is where the patent is infringed, and in the ordinary course of events a patent that is valuable is very apt to be infringed. To meet that difficulty the law has provided remedies for infringement. The right of the patentee is different from the right which any other property-owner has. The invention is not a physical thing which he may stand over and watch. His own care and strength will not help him in the least. The right exists only in the law itself, and, therefore, it is to the law only that he can look for protection. If the right is to be exclusive, is to be worth anything, as the Constitution intends it shall be, the law must protect him ; it must afford the means for his protection against injury, and recompense in case of his injury by its invasion. The right absolutely has no existence except by force of the remedies which protect it, and unless Congress provides efficient protection, it has not done what the Constitution contemplates, viz, " *secured* " to the inventor an exclusive right. That, speaking generally and leaving out the question of reissues—which I will come to in another connection—is the legal part of the system.

In the course of the practical part, the first step of the inventor is to arrive at what is sometimes called an inchoate invention. He has conceived in his mind the idea that certain things can be done in a certain way. The patent may be for a mechanical invention. It may be for an entirely new kind of machine to do something which had hitherto been done entirely by hand—a generic invention, as it is sometimes called. It may be for an improvement in an existing machine to enable it to work better or turn out a more perfect product. It may be a process, which can be a mechanical process, such as was described the other day in the well case, where the invention consisted in making a well and getting water from the earth by driving down through the upper strata into the water-bearing strata a tube with a sharp plug at the end and holes near the bottom for the water to come in, and then applying a suction-pump, creating a partial vacuum, and drawing the water first into the tube and then to the surface. It may be a chemical process. Such would be a new process for making sulphuric acid. It may be, and very often is, a patent for a product. Such was Goodyear's vulcanized rubber, and that rubber is a good illustration of what generally happens with patents for product or process in the case of chemical patents; it generally implies the invention of both process and product. In Goodyear's case, he invented a new process of treating rubber by mixing it with sulphur, plaster of Paris, lead, and lampblack, and exposing it for a definite length of time to a ce tain heat, and by that new process way he brought out a new product. So, since the driven well was first invented and made with common, unpatented tubes and a sledge hammer, there have been many improvements in the tubes, and particularly in the strainers which are used in this process.

In what I have to say, I will confine myself more particularly to the mechanical patents, because they are the most common, and, in some respects, the easiest to consider. When the inventor of the mechanical contrivance has got his inchoate idea, has determined that he can take the raw material and, by means of certain devices, manipulate it in a certain way, the next thing for him to do is to embody that idea in wood or metal. He has not done enough to make progress in the useful arts, he has not made an invention within the meaning of the patent law when he has only got the idea that the thing can be done and the general notion of how he will devise his machine and manipulate his materials. He must go further. He must embody his invention in some particular form; and, therefore, the next thing he has to do is to build a machine which shall embody it. It need not be the best possible form. It should be the best form that he knows of; but it is conceivable that the idea of the inventor may be embodied in a great many different forms. When he has embodied it in some form which is capable of work, then he goes to the Patent Office to take out the patent.

It may be that after he has got his inchoate idea he thinks it best to expend a great deal of time in perfecting it. In that case he files what is called a *caveat*—that is, a statement of how far he has gone, and what he intends to do—and that serves to prove at what time he arrived at certain points in his invention, and also serves to give him a certain standing in the office against subsequent applicants, or against anybody who attempts to steal his invention.

When he has obtained his patent, he has by no means got through the work which the public demands of him. He has his invention embodied in some useful form, but probably not the best. If it is a generic one, it is perfectly certain that the best form for using the invention will not be discovered until there has been a great deal of practice with the machine; because it is not enough, as you understand, in order to benefit the public, and therefore to make them demand the invention and desire to use it, and therefore bring to the inventor the profit he is working for—it is not enough that the invention should be made and put into some machine capable of work. It is not truly successful, in the broad sense, until it is financially successful—until it works so thoroughly, with so little trouble, with such results of product, as to make men desire it above everything else which has ever been used for the same purpose. In the most important inventions, it is necessary, therefore, immediately after the inventor has got his patent, to build experimental machines, and try them in actual use.

This is a matter oftentimes, and I think generally, of great difficulty and expense. The machine, as he first built it, subsequently requires improvements before it is brought to a suitable state, and every one of these improvements may require invention, and be itself the subject of a patent. The inventor must make experimental machines for use, and gentlemen familiar with the subject are very well aware that it is very easy to run away with five, ten, fifteen, or twenty thousand dollars in building experimental machines which, when perfected, will sell for a couple of hundred. To do this will require the employment of the skill and labor of the inventor or of some other inventor, and the most skillful mechanics, and the most excellent practical mechanical judgment, in order to bring the machine to the point at which the public will derive the most benefit from the invention. It is only when the machine has been built and used, and proved itself to be so perfect that the public desire to use it in preference to any other, that the inventor gets his reward. Therefore, there is a very great pressure on him to bring his machine to the point which the public good requires it to be brought to.

Now, it generally happens that the men who have the ingenuity to make these generic inventions have no capital to develop them, and the first thing an inventor has to do is to induce some capitalist to take a share in the patent, or to go in with him in some manner and advance money to the inventor to build the machine. After it is developed it has to be introduced, and that of itself is a work of great difficulty. It might seem that a manufacturer would be anxious to have a machine which would do his work more cheaply than it would be done by old processes, and would buy the machine immediately, but it is not so. He says to the inventor, "I have got a hundred thousand dollars invested in my machines now at work, and they work quite well, and even if you should say that your machine will do more and will work perfectly well and cheaper, still I don't want to throw away my existing machines." The consequence is, that it is a work of great difficulty to introduce the new machine. The only way to get at it, often, is for the inventor and his friends to put in capital and build the machine themselves, in order to convince manufacturers that they must use it, or be left behind in the price of their product. It is for that reason—because of the labor and expenditure required to perfect machines and introduce them into public use—that I think the right which the statute gives to an inventor to assign his interest in whole or in part, and the protection which the statute gives to the assignee as well as to the inventor, is as important a part of a patent law as the original grant of the patent itself. It is that which enables the public to get the benefit of the invention at the earliest possible date, because you will understand that it is not merely a question whether the public is some time or other going to get the benefit of the invention; whether a saving of $100,000 a year to the public is to come to-day or five years hence is a matter of national importance. The life of the patent is limited, and so the system necessarily presents a very strong stimulus to its beneficial introduction. The patent does not run from its introduction to use; it runs from the time of the original grant, and all the time that intervenes between the grant and its introduction to use is lost to the patentee and to his assignee; and therefore they have every possible stimulus to hurry as much as possible.

I said, in speaking of the legal part of the system, that it was essential that remedies to prevent infringement and measures to redress injuries done by infringers should be prompt, thorough, and efficient. It is necessary, also, that, while they should be prompt and efficient, they should not be hard, harsh, and unreasonable. They should not be oppressive. What is harsh, unreasonable, and oppressive is a question upon which gentlemen will not agree. But the remedies should be far from that character, and nobody is so much interested that they should be so as inventors themselves. For I suppose it happens, in nine cases out of ten—certainly in four out of five—that in lawsuits some patentee is defendant as well as plaintiff. It is a contest between two patents. Two men have devised two different machines to make an article in common use, and the question arises whether the later one infringes the first. The question is, whether the machine the second has constructed is generically a new machine, or a mere improvement upon the machine of his predecessor. Because, the man who invents the machine in the first place, and who has obtained a patent for it, is entitled to have the exclusive use of what he has invented, and nothing more. If another man comes along and adds another device, or takes away one device of that machine and substitutes for it another which performs the same functions in a better manner, or takes away two or three of the devices and substitutes one which performs the work in a a simpler and better manner, he is entitled to the exclusive use of that improvement, just the same as the man who invented the original ma-

chine is entitled to the exclusive use of what he invented. The man
who invented the original machine cannot use the improvement without
a license from the patentee of the improvement, nor can the patentee of
the improvement use the invention of the original man without a license
from him.

There are a great many more questions of this kind that necessarily
make the inventor and patentee a defendant, because the work of the
dealer in or manufacturer of the newest and most improved machinery
is always on that border-line which separates the known in the arts from
the unknown. He of all others is the man who comes in contact with
those who are inventors and creators of what was unknown, who acquire for themselves parts of that territory by right of discovery, and
therefore you will readily understand that certainly in four-fifths of the
patent cases there is a patentee who is carrying on the defense as well
as the attack. That is the reason why I say that it is just as much for
the interest of inventors as any one else, as much for the interest of
owners of patents as any one else, that, while the law must be efficient
to protect each man's right, it should not be any more oppressive than is
necessary to afford efficient protection. It is for their interest that the
best possible means should be employed in ascertaining exactly what
one patent means and covers and what another means and covers.

I want to call your attention a little to the growth of the patent system
of this country, as shown by the number of patents granted. From
1790 to 1836, forty-six years, there were 10,020 granted. Since 1836 to
the present time, forty-two years, there have been not far from 200,000.
In 1876, there were between fourteen and fifteen thousand patents for
new inventions, besides trade-marks and designs, and about 20,000 applications received. The fees received were $757,987.65, showing at the
end of the year, after taking out the expenses of the office, a surplus of
$105,445.05; so that the administration of patent law does not cost the
country anything in that respect. That is, it does not cost the tax-pay-
ers anything. Fees from patentees more than make up the expense.

There were recorded last year about fourteen thousand assignments
of patents. I don't know how many patents that refers to, because a
great many assignments cover five or ten, and sometimes twenty or
thirty patents each; but I think there cannot be less than twenty or
twenty-five thousand patents that have been assigned during the year.
These are largely transfers of interests from the inventor to the capitalist, who takes an interest with him in order to have a basis upon which
he may spend money to perfect the machine and introduce it to the
public.

The progress of patents in our country has been rather curious. Of
course, in the earlier years patents were mostly granted to the citizens
of the seaboard States, but that is quite changed at the present time. For
many years New England received more patents than any other six
States (except New York). That is changed now. In 1870, for the first
time, the six States of Ohio, Indiana, Illinois, Iowa, Wisconsin, and
Missouri took out more patents than the six New England States—2,915
for the West, against 2,757 for those Eastern States. During the last
year, 1877, the three States of Ohio, Indiana, and Illinois took out, for
the first time, more patents than the whole of the New England States—
2,579 for those three States, against 2,479 for New England. And in
comparing the proportion of the total number of patents granted in
each year in those Western States, I find that it has grown up amaz-
ingly within the last twenty years.

The CHAIRMAN. How did you find it in the Southern States ?

Mr. STORROW. They have been growing in that respect very considerably within the last few years. Of course, there was a series of years before that when no applications for patents came from the South. There have been quite a number of patents for improvements in cotton-gins and various things of that sort from Texas. The Paris green patent, which I don't believe is valid as a broad patent, is from the South. There have been more from Tennessee, Kentucky, and Texas than from the other Southern States; over a hundred each for several years. New Orleans is a place that takes out a good many patents—I think 79 from Louisiana last year. There were 51 from North Carolina, 34 from South Carolina, and 63 from Georgia last year (1877).

Mr. BOND. I have noticed a good many from Tennessee.

Mr. STORROW. Yes; there are a good many from Tennessee. New York is the largest State for patents, and Pennsylvania next; and they always have been, as far back as I have looked; now they are falling back in proportion to the West and the South, though New York for twenty-five years has taken more than all New England.

In 1851 those six Western States took one-half as many patents as New England; in 1877 they took fifty per cent. more.

One cannot help noticing this fact in connection with the manufacturing industries of those great Western States, which within the last ten years have grown enormously—out of all proportion to the manufactures of the Eastern States.

In that connection, if the committee will allow me, I want to lay before you some facts with relation to the growth of the industries of this country that are directly affected by patents, especially in the Western States, where the growth has been most rapid. I want to do that for two reasons. I want you to perceive the enormous growth of the industries of the country, and not only the growth of the industries, but the increase of capacity in the operative—the manner in which a man nowadays can produce more, and is worth more to the community, by reason of these patented improvements, than he ever was before, and the manner in which the products of his labor have been cheapened to consumers. And another reason is, that I want you, as these different industries are detailed to you, to notice the connection between our patent system and the industries themselves; the direct effect it has had upon them; how they have been created by it, localized by it, in the homes of the inventors, and have grown up under it.

If the committee will allow me, at this point I wish to ask Mr. Coffin, who is present, and who has spent a good many months traveling about the country with a view to procure this information, and who has collated the information that he has procured at the establishments themselves with information procured from the Patent Office from statistics, and from many other sources—I want to ask him to state to us something that he has learned bearing upon these points; and when he has done that, I will call your attention to the lessons which I think are to be drawn therefrom.

ARGUMENT OF MR. COFFIN.

Mr. CHAIRMAN AND GENTLEMEN OF THE COMMITTEE:

Some months since I was requested by gentlemen who are largely engaged in manufactures under patents, and who were aware that there were some proposed changes to be made in the law, to take a tour of observation, with a view of studying the industries of the country. They requested me to omit no industry that I could find, and to direct my inquiries to various points—such as what benefit has accrued to an inventor from a patent; what benefit to the public; what royalties have been paid for the use of a patent; how much of time, labor, and expense an invention has cost; what it costs to introduce an invention to the public; what grounds of complaint there were against the present law; and what modifications of the law were desired. These and various other points I was requested to direct my inquiries to, and also in regard to the building up of communities under patents. I was instructed to omit no point of inquiry which would enable me to lay before the committee, when these bearings came on, a full exhibition of the growth of the country under the present system.

I began my inquiries at Albany, taking in the stove and wood manufacturing industries of that section. I passed on through Central New York, stopping at Rochester, where there is a large variety of industries; then going on to Cleveland and taking the industries of that city; thence to Toledo. I was fortunate enough to find a gentleman at Toledo who was familiar with the industries of Detroit, and therefore I was not compelled to go to that city. I visited South Bend, Chicago, Rockford, Beloit, Janesville, Saint Paul, Minneapolis, Freeport; and Decatur, in Central Illinois; and then, turning my steps eastward, as I was somewhat limited in time, I took the industries through Central Indiana and Ohio to Cincinnati, and on to Pittsburgh. After that I visited quite a large number of industries in New England, so that I might be able to present to the committee, from this mass of information, something which would enable them, perhaps, to arrive at a proper conclusion as to what improvements were needed in the present law.

It has been said, Mr. Chairman, that the plow is the implement which is at the foundation of all wealth and the basis of all civilization; for without the plow there can be no successful cultivation of the soil. The most exhaustive treatise on the plow is to be found in the transactions of the New York State Agricultural Society for 1867, part I. And as the plow is the first implement that I shall take up, I will refer to that volume and present two or three passages which will show you the condition of the plow at different periods of the history of the country. You remember, perhaps, Mr. Chairman, the plows that were in use in your boyhood. I remember the plow my father used. I think it was about twelve feet long. I know that it required eight to ten oxen to draw it, one man to ride upon the beam to keep it in the ground, and a man to follow behind with a heavy iron hoe to dig up the "banks." We have a description, in the transactions of the New York Agricultural Society for 1856, how this plow was made:

A winding tree was cut down, and a mold-board hewed from it, with the grain of the timber running so nearly along its shape as it could well be obtained. Upon this mold-board, to prevent its wearing out too rapidly, were nailed the blade of an old hoe, thin straps of iron, or worn-out horseshoes. The land-side was of wood, its base and sides shod with thin plates of iron. The share was of iron with a hardened steel point. The coulter was tolerably well made of iron, steel-edged, and locked into the share nearly as it does in the improved lock-coulter plow of the present day. The beam was usually a straight stick. The handles, like the mold-board, split from the crooked trunk of a tree, or as often cut from its branches; the crooked roots of the white-ash were the most favorite timber for plow-handles in the Northern States. The beam was set at any pitch that fancy might dictate, with the handles fastened on almost at right angles with it, thus leaving the plowman little control over his implement, which did its work in a very slow and most imperfect manner.

But there is a little more graphic description of the plow, which appeared in 1820 in the Rhode Island American, where a writer describes the plow that was in use in the Eastern States at that time, especially in Massachusetts, known as the Old-Colony plow. He says:

It had a ten-foot beam and four-foot land-side; and the Sutton plows are not fit to plow any land that has sod on it; your furrows stand up like the ribs of a lean horse in the month of March. A lazy plowman may sit on the beam and count every bout of his day's work; besides, the great objection to all these plows is that they do not perform the work well and that the expense is enormous for blacksmith work. Six of these plows cost me on an average, last year, $5 each to keep the shares and coulters fit for work, and the wear of the other parts could not be less than $1 more—$6 per year for each plow.

Now, with this description of the plow which was in use in my boy-hood, I will present in a very brief statement the advance of invention.

Thomas Jefferson was one of the first to make suggestions in regard to the improvement of the implement, but his plow was exceedingly cumbersome. The first patent taken out in this country was in 1797, by Charles Newbold, who set himself to work to improve Mr. Jefferson's plow. Mr. Newbold resided in the town of Chesterfield, Burlington County, New Jersey, and made the first cast-iron plow ever made in this country. Here is his description of it:

The subscriber, Charles Newbold, of Burlington County, and the State of New Jersey, has invented an improvement in the art of plow-making, as follows, viz: The plow to be, excepting the handles and beam, of solid cast iron, consisting of a bar, sheath, and mold-plate. The sheath serves a double purpose of coulter and sheath, and the mold-plate serves for share and mold-board—that is, to cut and turn the furrow.

This was dated at Philadelphia, 17th June, 1797. Mr. Newbold was a progressive man. He found, after he had obtained a patent for his plow, that he could not introduce it in the country. There was a great objection to it. The farmers in those times entertained great prejudice against it. There was a universal idea throughout the country that a cast-iron plow would poison the land. I can remember myself when the same prejudice was entertained by the farmers. It was in the year 1837 that my father obtained the first cast-iron plow that was used in the vicinity of his farm in New Hampshire, and I remember very well, sir, of the farmers gathering to see it work, and the remarks that were made. They had the same objection—that they would not have it on their farms because it would poison the land.

I will not go over the inventions that were made between 1797 and 1842. There had been great improvement up to 1813, but from 1813 to 1842 there was very little improvement in plows. In that year, Mr. Nourse, of Boston, improved upon the Jethro Woods plow, and brought out what was known as the Eagle plow number 2, which was a great advance upon any other implement that had been used in this country for stirring the soil. You will read in this volume, that the lines of draught adopted in that plow were essentially the same lines of draught which you find in the best plows of to-day. It required from 1797 to 1842 for the inventive genius of this country, together with the obser-vations of farmers and mechanics, to arrive at any just conclusion of what would be the best form for the plow.

A MEMBER OF THE COMMITTEE. Was this man Newbold a practical farmer?

Mr. COFFIN. I do not think he was a practical farmer. I will read what it says here in this book:

Charles Newbold, the inventor of the first cast-iron plow ever made in America, was born in the township of Chesterfield, Burlington County, New Jersey, about the year 1780, and in 1804 married Hope, the daughter of David Sands, who lived a few miles south of New-burg, New York. He was endowed with a large share of energy and genius, which devel-oped themselves so rapidly in his teeming brain that he had no time to carry any one of them into successful operation. He had a graud scheme for founding three cities on the Hudson River to be called Faith, Hope, and Charity. These were to be the centers, respectively, of trades, manufactures, and commerce. They were to be connected together by the best possible roads, as well as water communication, and from the central city a grand road across the continent, similar to the Cumberland, was to connect the Hudson River with the Pacific Ocean.

I think he was not a practical farmer; I think he was a mechanic.

Mr. SMITH. Will you give me the date of the publication of that book?

Mr. COFFIN. It is the proceedings of the New York State Agricultural Society for 1867, part 1. I will say here that this is the most exhaustive treatise on the plow that has ever been published.

As I have said, in 1842 the Nourse plow was brought out. Prior to that time Governor Holbrook, of Vermont, had given some application to the manufacturing of plows, and about that time he gave his whole attention, I think, to their improvement. You will fiud in this volume the part which he took in the improvement of that implement. I will not stop to detail it.

In 1850 the New York State Agricultural Society, feeling that the time had come when the country should have the best possible information that could be obtained, instituted a grand trial of plows. The basis of their calculation as to what saving had been made in plows in economy of power, the difference between the kinds of plows that were then in use, is here given, and the rule by which they arrived at their conclusions. They say:

We have shown in a subsequent chapter that there is a difference of power required to perform the same amount of work by different plows, amounting to 46 per cent., as shown by careful trials in England, and to 42 per cent. according to the trials instituted by the society in 1850.

It follows from this, that if the plow having the least draught was brought into universal use to the exclusion of those which require a greater power, it would reduce the cost of plowing in the United States 42 per cent., or it would reduce it from twenty million dollars to eleven million six hundred thousand dollars, leaving eight million four hundred thousand in the pockets of the farmers as a fund to be applied to the payment of taxes or the improvement of their farms.

If we suppose that the same number of men and teams were employed as heretofore, then they would be enabled to cultivate an area 42 per ceut. greater, with the same expenditure of power that they now employ—that is, they would cultivate an area of one hundred and thirteen millions of acres without any more expenditure of power than they now do eighty millions of acres. * * *

We do not mean to assert that this sum would represent the actual increase of the annual value of the products of agriculture; but, allowing each reader to make the deductions which he may think necessary for the increased cost of cultivating this increased area (such as seed, planting, after-culture, and gathering), it will be seen that the use of the best form of the plow will increase the aggregate profits of agriculture to an extent equal to the auuual, national, internal taxation of the United States.

I have taken this, Mr. Chairman and gentlemen, as the basis of my investigation in regard to the improvements of plows from 1850 to the present time. I shall not have time, nor would you have time to listen to me, to go over all the improvements which have taken place since then. Many of you are aware that the plows largely in use in the western part of the country to-day are the John Dere, the Avery (manufactured at Louisville and largely used in the Southern States), and the Oliver chilled plow, manufactured at South Bend, and a great many others. They all have essentially the same lines of draught, because the point as to what are the best lines has been settled, and there probably can be very little improvement in that direction. It therefore follows that the best plow at this time is the one which shall enable the farmer to turn up his soil at the cheapest possible cost, and in that is involved economy of manufacture as well as economy of use. I shall have time only to refer to the last invention in this line, and I refer to

it not to say anything in regard to this plow above any other, but because it shows a new line of departure in manufacture. I refer to the
Oliver chilled plow. Mr. Oliver was a manufacturer of common plows
in Michigan. He began at South Bend in 1855. He saw that the demand of the farmers was for the plow that would have a mold-board
of hard finish—something much harder than iron, because iron was almost worthless in many of the western soils; something that should be
cheaper than cast-steel. Therefore he turned his attention to the production of a chilled mold-board. It was nothing new; it had been attempted for twenty-five years, and every time had resulted in utter failure—for this reason : it was found that when you attempted to enlarge
the surface of the mold-board beyond 36 superficial inches, you could
not produce a perfect piece of iron. There would be soft spots in it and
cavities called "blow-holes." Those who had attempted the production
of chilled iron said that these resulted from the gases in the metals.
Mr. Oliver came to a different conclusion after a great deal of investigation—that it was from some other cause. I will not detail the amount
of money he spent, or the difficulties he encountered. People called
him a lunatic, and his friends deserted him. His shop was burned down
and he had no means, but he held on to the idea that there was a possibility of obtaining a piece of chilled iron which he could use for a
mold-board. He finally concluded that these soft spots and blow-holes,
as they are called, were the result of moisture in the molding-sand, and
therefore he invented a mold with an iron pipe through it, through
which he could pour hot water and thus dry out the moisture from the
sand after the mold was made. After a great many trials he succeeded
in producing his mold-board in two pieces. That was the first step.
Then he discovered that there were some gases in the metals. He
started upon another line of invention, to have some holes connected
with the mold by which the gases should escape. Through those two
inventions he has produced the present chilled plow. He uses Lake
Superior iron, and, when he can obtain the Saulsbury ore, he makes a,
mixture of that with the Lake Superior iron, and thus obtains an exceedingly hard and tenacious metal, one which will resist the wearing,
and one which will also not be easily broken. Through those two inventions he has been enabled to produce this mold-board much more
cheaply than the cast-steel plow can be produced, and he has reduced
the price about $2. Instead of raising his price above all other plows
in use, when he made his inventions, he said to himself, "I will put
these plows so cheaply that they shall come into universal use." His
patent was the first one that was ever issued from the Patent Office for
the manufacture of chilled plows. There never had been a claim put in
before him. He has taken out eighteen patents as the improvement
has gone on. He brought out his first plow in 1870. He had been
studying upon it for many years, but only after a long period of time
(not actively engaged in experiment all the while, but he had been turning it over in his mind for a quarter of a century) was he enabled to
bring out this plow. If you were to visit his works you would find five
hundred men employed in the manufacture. He sent out fifty thousand
year before last, and sixty thousand last year. There are one hundred
and seventy-five thousand in use. His orders thus far indicate, he
stated to me, about seventy-five thousand to be called for the present
year. He sent out one train the other day of thirty car-loads of these
plows. And he has reduced the price about $2 from the plows which
were formerly in use—a plow not any better in its line of draught per-

haps, but better in the mold-board which he has produced by his process. He charges no royalty.

The CHAIRMAN. What does he charge for two-horse plows?

Mr. COFFIN. He has different sizes and different prices. I think from $10 to $12 is the price; I think that is the minimum and maximum. Now, taking that basis of the New York State Agricultural Society—and according to the report of the Commissioner of Agriculture there were 108,000,000 acres under the plow in this country last year—if we estimate the cost of plowing at only one dollar an acre, and take the basis, as given by the New York Agricultural Society, brought about by this invention, we shall have a saving of $45,000,000.

The CHAIRMAN. What is the difference between the Mohawk Valley plow and this chilled plow?

Mr. COFFIN. I put that question to other manufacturers. Of course, the answer which I obtained from the manufacturers of the cast-steel plow was, that Mr. Oliver had got a little thing of his own that he was trying to make something out of, but that it would not amount to much. Mr. Oliver himself informed me that he thinks his plow will outlast two to three cast-steel plows. I suppose the line of truth lies somewhere between the two statements. Any one who is familiar with metals will know that a mixture of Lake Superior and Saulsbury ores, with this process of chilling, must effect a great saving. Perhaps other inventors have made or are making equally good improvements. I do not pretend to pass upon that question.

Now, Mr. Chairman, I will refer to steam plows. This is the great want of the country to-day. I have met several gentlemen in my investigation who were manufacturers, who had no patents of their own, but who, perhaps, would like to obtain some now in use, who favored the utter abolishing of the patent laws. They say that necessity would compel invention; that, when there was a demand for an article, there would be somebody that would produce it. Let us consider the steam plow. It is the great want of the American community at this moment, and the country demands it.

In 1856, in Illinois, I saw a steam plow. It ran one day and then was thrown out by the side of the fence, and I think that was the last the world ever heard of it. I happened to be in California in 1868. I saw a steam plow, upon which more than $40,000 had been expended, brought out for trial on one of those large farms. It ran once across the field, and then it went into the junk-shop. Last year I was in Northwestern Minnesota, in the valley of Red River, where I saw a third steam plow, upon which $25,000, as I learned, had been expended. It was tried two or three days. A considerable amount of money was spent in endeavoring to improve it. If you were to go up to the little village of Glydon, where I happened to be when I saw the implement, you would see that the weeds had grown over it; it is entirely covered with rust; and that is the end of that steam plow.

Here is a machine which the country demands, and yet the inventive genius of the country has not conquered the problem. So that there is an answer to that objection of those who think that the demand always brings a supply. In England I saw a steam plow which is moved by a stationary engine. The plow is drawn across the field by a wire rope. You will find in the English agricultural reports that the steam plow does not make any saving in the cost of plowing. There are, however, two or three advantages which result from its use—a larger amount of acreage of grain can be put in; the trampling of the horses does not press down the soil. The soil is lighter, and therefore is in better condition for the crop. These are the two advantages of the steam plow. But I will state here that a great many efforts have been made in England to produce a steam plow which should travel across the lands. One gentleman testified before the committee of the House of Parliament, that he had spent £50,000 ($250,000) upon steam plowing, and had not achieved any success. Another gentleman did not state the amount that he had expended, but said, "I have spent an enormous sum of money in my endeavors to produce a steam plow."

Now I pass, in the cultivation of corn, to the corn-planter. The raising of corn is the greatest single agricultural interest in this country. The Commissioner of Agriculture estimates the crop of 1877 as the largest that has ever been produced in this country, at 1,300,000,000 bushels. I remember, Mr. Chairman, when I dropped corn, a boy, by hand, five kernels in a hill and a pumpkin seed in every other hill— that was the rule.

The CHAIRMAN. And sometimes a bean.

Mr. COFFIN. Six hundred and forty-seven patents for corn-droppers have been issued up to 1873. One of the first inventions in this line, which you will find in the Patent Office, was a box about the size of this book, not quite so wide, that was placed on the shank of a hoe, and there was a spring connecting with a slide that covered a small hole. The farmer would strike his hoe in the ground and make the place for depositing the grains, and then reverse the hoe and give another stroke, and that would let the corn out of the box, and he again reversing the hoe would cover it.

Then came an improvement upon that, a hollow hoe-handle with a spring running along the handle; the farmer could jerk the spring, and that would let out the corn.

Then we had the hand dropper or planter. First a man would take one in each hand and walk along the rows and strike them down, and each blow would make a planting, thus enabling him to plant two rows at the same time.

The next step was the horse-drill or planter, being a planter drawn by a horse.

But these methods of planting corn admitted only of cultivation between the rows in one direction. Then came the idea of cultivating in both directions with a drag. A long beam with pins in it was dragged both ways across the field by the horses, and then the farmer would go along with the hand-planter and plant the corn at the intersection of the rows, and thus he was enabled to save something in cultivation.

The next step was the corn-planter, which planted two rows at one time, with the rows running in both directions. A man sat on the machine, and at every point where the drag had crossed at right-angles he moved a lever that dropped the corn, which was covered by wheels that turned and pressed down the soil upon the seed. This was the invention of Mr. Brown, and came into almost universal use.

The last idea in this direction was the check-rower. That is an invention which has come into use within a very few years. It is a very simple implement, consisting of a wire chain, or knotted rope, stretched across the field. It is anchored at both ends, and it runs through the machine. As you drive across the field, every time that a knot goes through a little slot in the machine it touches a spring and drops the corn. All you have to do is to anchor this rope on both sides of the field and drive backward and forward all day long, until your acres are planted; and then you can cultivate in both directions. This was a great step. I will not attempt to detail its advantages. You can see at a glance that great advantages would accrue from such a machine. Those machines are now largely manufactured at Decatur, Illinois, there being two establishments there which I visited, and from which I obtained the details. The saving, you can see, would be very great in planting and in cultivation. Under the old way the man with a hand-planter could plant three or four acres per day. With a two-horse check-rower planter, twenty acres can be planted in a day. You see that by this process the farmer of Illinois is enabled to increase his acreage—the planting season lasting about ten days—from forty acres to two hundred acres by this simple process. This simple invention, therefore, enables a small farmer to become a large one. I say nothing of the saving in labor, nor the ability of the farmer to put in his crop on a few fair days.

The next implement is the cultivator. I remember very well, Mr. Chairman, when the cultivation of corn was carried on wholly by the plow. The farmer used a common small plow. We plowed twice between the rows, turning the soil against both. That was the process in my boyhood, and was the process down to about the year 1845, I think. There have been improvements over that process. First, harrow-teeth were put into a triangular frame, which was drawn through, and you had to pass but one way between the rows. Another form of the cultivator was a series of small double plowshares, which were put into a triangular frame; but since then there have been one thousand six hundred and seventeen patents taken out for cultivators.

One form of cultivator was called the "double shovel." I think it came into use about 1848. It had a very large sale. It was what was called a walking cultivator, and was used with a man walking behind it. Men now ride their cultivators.

I have here the experience of an Ohio farmer, who resided near Springfield, in regard to the use of this old double-shovel cultivator, and with one of the cultivators now manufactured in that town. He kept an exact account of the cost of producing his corn for three years. The highest cost was 12 cents a bushel by the double-shovel cultivators, and the lowest was 9 cents. He obtained one of the improved cultivators, and then kept an account for three years, and found that his highest cost was 8½ cents and his lowest 7 cents. Here the greatest saving was 3½ cents a bushel and the lowest 2 cents. Now, what is the saving at the rate of 3½ cents per bushel on the crop of last year? $45,500,000. And the saving at the rate of 2 cents would amount to $26,000,000. What is it that produces this saving? It is in the thorough cultivation brought about by stirring the soil by this implement. It cuts out all the grasses. The entire surface of the ground to any desired depth may be stirred. You may have it cut deep or shallow, according to the nature of your soil; obtain a thorough pulverization of the soil; the roots will run down and get the moisture and fertilizing qualities; and therefore you get this increase of your crop. That is the secret of it; nothing else—simply the thorough pulverization of the soil. And this was brought about only by long study, which could come only from years of observation and experiment.

The next thing which is to be considered, in the cultivation of corn, is the corn-husker. And yet it is the same with that as it is with the steam plow—the world waits for it. There have been a large number of inventions taken out for corn-huskers, and yet there is not one in use to-day in the country that commends itself to the farmers. The inventive genius of the country has not yet grappled with that problem. One hundred and fifty patents have been issued since 1858 for huskers, and a man who will make the successful husker has an immense fortune before him if he is protected by a patent law.

The next machine is the corn-sheller. Perhaps you remember, Mr. Chairman and gentlemen, the shelling of corn in your neighborhood. I remember very well sitting astride the handle of a frying-pan or the barn-shovel and scraping the ears against them, or using the cob of one ear to shell the corn from another, and often shelling the skin from my hands. About five bushels in ten hours a man could shell by hand.

Then came the first machine for shelling corn, which was a cylinder turned by a crank, by which a man might shell about forty bushels in a day. There have been three hundred and seventy-eight patents issued for corn-shellers. Now, if you will go to Illinois, you will see shellers by which two men, with a machine driven by steam or horse power, will shell one thousand five hundred bushels a day, the cobs being carried off into a pile by themselves or into a wagon, and the corn run into sacks or wagons, to be drawn off in bulk. Only two men are required to run the machine. Here, then, invention has carried us from the time of our boyhood, when one man could shell four or five bushels a day, to the present, when two men with a machine can shell one thousand five hundred bushels a day. What farmer in the West would be without the use of one of these corn-shellers?

The six great corn States of the Union are, I think, Illinois, Iowa, Missouri, Indiana, Ohio, and Kansas. They produce more than half the corn raised in the country. Now, of what inestimable value is that one machine, the corn-sheller, to those communities! Those States, by the census of 1870, had 1,775,000 persons engaged in agriculture. It would require the entire farming community of those States to sit astride barn-shovels and handles of frying-pans one hundred days out of the three hundred and sixty-five to shell their corn by the old process. Take the crop of last year, 1,300,000,000 bushels of corn. The entire population of the United States—every man, woman, and child, every individual of the 40,000,000 of us—would be obliged to spend the entire six working days of the week and till noon of Sunday to shell the crop by the old process. I do not know what would become of the country, Mr. Chairman, if we had to go back to those old times.

A MEMBER OF THE COMMITTEE. Do you contend that this improvement is the result of necessity or the result of the present law?

Mr. COFFIN. I put it down as the result of the present law.

Mr. RAYMOND. I would like you to show the connection before you get through with your argument.

Mr. COFFIN. I will endeavor to show the connection.

Mr. STORROW. We propose to show it, I hope convincingly.

Mr. COFFIN. Of course all the corn that is raised is not shelled. There are 1,300,000,000 bushels raised, but a large portion is fed from the ears, but if shelled by hand I do not know what it would cost in these days. A man used to shell for one-tenth of the corn.

The CHAIRMAN. What do the owners of machines charge for shelling?

Mr. COFFIN. I was not able to obtain that.

Mr. WILLETS. Half a cent per bushel in our country.

The CHAIRMAN. In your experience, Mr. Coffin, does the use of the separator—or, take another case, does the planing machine reduce the cost of the work performed to the people?

Mr. COFFIN. Yes, sir; and I will show that before I get through.

The CHAIRMAN. For instance, in building a house, formerly we used the old-fashioned plane. You have been along there, and so have I. Now, does the improved machine reduce the cost of building a house to the man that has it built?

Mr. COFFIN. Yes, sir; I will show that to you before I get through. There is a great reduction in the cost, and a great improvement in the house.

I now turn to the cultivation of wheat. From the time of Adam up to within a comparatively recent period the only method of sowing wheat was to throw it into the air by the hand. Those of you who have had experience in sowing know that if the wind blows with any great force it is impossible to sow it evenly; and if you sow clover with your wheat you have to go over the ground the second time. And if you put in phosphates or any fertilizers, it must be gone over a third time. Then in the sowing of wheat broadcast you do not sow evenly, because no man, no matter how deft he may be, can always throw out his hand at exactly the same interval every time. He must calculate his steps as he passes over the ground—calculate the gusts of wind that may come to him. No man can sow his ground evenly by that process. Then some of the grain will fall in the hollows, and some upon the ridges. Then when the harrow comes in some of the grains are buried too deep to come up; others are left under such shallow covering that they do not get moisture enough, and therefore do not sprout. Therefore, under the old broadcast sowing, you do not obtain the best possible results. Under that system you could not harrow till you had been over with your clover—if you sowed clover with the wheat. I will not go over the catalogue of the different drill and broadcast seeders which have been invented. About six hundred patents have been issued for seeders.

Now, what are the advantages of these seeders, as you find them to-day in use, over this broadcast sowing? The seeder covers the soil to a uniform depth. It sows evenly, and sows a specific quantity. You may graduate it so that, after a little experience, you can determine the amount per acre even to a quart of wheat. They sow all kinds of grain— wheat, clover, and superphosphate, if need be—at once. They harrow at the same time. They make the crop more certain. It is the united testimony of manufacturers and farmers alike that the crop is increased from one-eighth to one-fourth, especially in the winter wheat. Winter wheat, you are aware, in the freezing and thawing season, is apt to heave out. It is desirable to bury the seed a uniform and proper depth and to throw over the young plant such an amount of soil that it shall not heave with the freezing and thawing. Of the 360,000,000 bushels of wheat raised last year, I suppose more than 300,000,000 was winter wheat. One-eighth of this is 37,700,000 bushels.

Now, here is not merely a saving, but an absolute increase in the crop, representing that number of dollars. I give the testimony of a manufacturer of seeders at Springfield, Ohio, in regard to what it has cost him to bring his seeder up to its present point:

We have spent $20,000 in purchasing patents, besides an immense amount expended by ourselves in experiments and patterns which, after all our labor and expense, we have had to abandon. Yet, since 1857, notwithstanding the many improvements we have made, the prices of seeders to the farmers have been reduced 50 per cent., while at the same time we give them a far better machine. Every improvement we have made has inured to the benefit of the farmer. No farmer can afford to use to-day the machine that we made twenty years ago, even if he could have it as a gift. In 1857, the price was $75; in 1877, the price was $40 for a far better machine,

It would not have been possible for the farmers to have produced the crop of 1877 without the seeder. It is estimated that about 800,000 seeders have been made since 1858.— (See statements and pictures in The Cornplanter Patent, 23 Wall., 181.)

I pass now to the reapers. In 1794 a man in Scotland invented what was described as a most marvelous and wonderful machine for cutting grain—doing as much in one day as seven men could do with the sickle. This marvelous machine was the cradle.

The report of the Scottish Highland Agricultural Society says that—

With a common sickle seven men in ten hours reaped one and one-half acres of wheat—about one-quarter of an acre each. With the new machine a man can cut one and one-half acres in ten hours, to be raked, bound, and stacked by two others.

From this basis we begin our exhibit of what difficulties the inventors of reapers and mowers had to encounter, the successive steps of their labors, and the value of the invention to the world. In 1833 Obed Hussey took out the first patent. In 1834 Cyrus McCormick took out a patent, but the world heard little of a reaping machine until 1845, when McCormick built 150 at Cincinnati. In 1846 he had 300 built at Brockport, New York. In 1852 there was a general trial of reapers and mowers at Geneva, New York. Nine machines contested, for other inventors had taken out patents. Nineteen years had passed since the first patent had been issued. Out of the nine machines exhibited not one could start in the grain without backing to get up speed. There was a heavy side drift; they were clumsy; they could not turn easily. In 1855 about 10,000 machines had been built by the different makers, nearly all of which were one-wheeled machines. About this time Mr. Wheeler, of Auburn; Ball, of Canton, Ohio; and Miller, of the same town, began to manufacture two-wheeled machines. These manufacturers combined and bought more than a hundred patents. In 1855 there was an exhibition of reapers at the French Exposition: one English, one French, and one American—McCormick's. The French machine did its allotted work in 72, the English in 66, and McCormick's in 22 minutes. McCormick won the first victory at London over Bell in 1852, and now for the second time the American's invention achieved a triumph. Two years later, in 1857, there was a trial at Syracuse, New York, at which nineteen machines were exhibited. Mark the progress that had been made in five years. Of these, all, except three, could start in the grain without backing to get up speed. A great variety of machines were invented; some to prove utter failures, and others that were purchased, and what was valuable in them incorporated into some other machine. About 1860 the Wood machine made its appearance; and the Dorsey, Seymour, and Morgan machines were combined. These were great improvements. Twenty-seven years had passed since Hussey took out his first patent, and the inventors were then making their greatest improvements. The business attained such proportions that in 1864 not less than one hundred and eighty-seven establishments had been started to manufacture reapers, wholly or in part, turning out one hundred thousand per annum. There was a great trial at Auburn in 1866, at which forty-four different machines were entered. Of these, forty-two did their work well. All were much lighter, simpler, less noisy, and worked easier.

Some sworn testimony at the Patent Office gives the following history of the invention and growth of one type:

In 1852 Lewis Miller and his partners were engaged at Canton, Ohio, in working threshers and harvesters of the Hussey patent. He devoted a large portion of his time to getting up a combined machine which would both mow and reap. He first adopted the Hussey form of machine as a basis for his combination, and in the same year, 1852, they built about twenty-five of these combined machines. Most of them failed to mow. In 1853 they tried to improve upon the reaper, so as to adapt it to a combined machine for mowing also. After numerous experiments, they built twenty-five machines of this kind, which failed to work. The inventor also tried to get up a single mower in that year, and about twelve were built, which also failed. In 1854 he continued his experiments, and lost in them about $1,000 more. In 1855 the experiments were put an end to, in the month of June, by the burning down of the whole establishment. In 1856 they borrowed money and built five hundred single mowers, with two wheels and a flexible finger-bar; but most of them failed. They thus lost nearly $12,000 of money paid out, besides the labor of the firm. In the early part of 1856 the inventor and one of his partners got up another form of machine, and tried it, and patented it. In 1857 the inventor set about remedying the defects of and developing and improving the patented machine of 1856; and the result was the successful machine. It worked well, and was the commencement of that form of construction now known as the Buckeye machine. No profit had been made by the firm in manufacturing the flexible finger-bar machine prior to the year 1858.

The inventor says that he had no money of his own, and his inventive capacity was all that he contributed to the firm, in which he had an equal interest with the others. He continued in partnership with them, with some change of partners, up to 1865. In 1858 and since that time they have granted various licenses under all their patents for $10 a machine for the regular size and $7.50 for the smaller size; and they built up to 1865 over 24,000 machines. In that year the business was taken by two corporations, and they paid joint owners of the patent, as a license-fee, $10 for the large machines and $7.50 for the smaller ones. In the six years from 1866 to 1871, inclusive, these corporations built 30,000 large machines and 20,000 smaller ones. In addition to this, there were built at various times by licensees over 16,000 of the large machines, at $10 royalty. There had been built up to 1872 and gone into use in the United States over 90,000 Buckeye machines of which the inventor has direct knowledge. In addition to this, Adriance and Platt and other licensees had built 60,000 more of the same machines. In addition to that, those built under other licenses and by infringers amount to 100,000 more.

I pass now over the intermediate improvements and come to the last improvement—self-binders. There was still another step to be taken. The demand of the farmers was for a machine that would bind as well as reap. The farmer for ten to fifteen days during harvest was a slave, at the mercy of a set of men who made his necessity their opportunity, who demanded and obtained $2, $3, and sometimes $4 a day for binding, besides their board. They began in the southern section of the wheat-producing States, and moved northward with the advance of the season. They demanded good fare and made themselves at home in the farmers' kitchens. The extravagant wages demanded materially reduced the profits of the crop.

Since 1865 large sums of money have been spent in experiments on self-binders; but not until 1870 was the self-binder in any sense a mechanical success. Thus far only three types have been produced for general use—McCormick's, Gordon's, and Lock's. The first began to be used in 1874.

The inventor of one of these types was a jeweler. After a number of years' work, and using up $15 000, all he had, he became connected with a reaping-machine manufacturer, who caused machines to be built and improved till about $100,000 had been spent. There are three other concerns who have spent as much in their endeavors to produce a machine, and some of the manufacturers say that the problem is not well solved yet. In order to bring out a machine of this class it is necessary to make a great deal of observation. The harvest season is very short. Therefore they sent men to Texas, where the harvest commences early, and those men followed northward with the harvest season until it ends in Minnesota. And, more than that, they have sent a man to New Zealand, where the harvest season occurs during our winter, so that they may occupy as much time as possible during the year in observation, because from trials of machines in the harvest field only can they arrive at the data from which to make new improvements.

I will further remark that all the inventors and the manufacturers that I have visited, who manufactured these machines, say that the business is yet in its infancy. It was only in 1870 that it began, and time enough has not yet elapsed to bring out the best form of machine.

The best sources give the number of reapers and mowers manufactured in each State in 1875 as follows: In New England 2,500, New Jersey 750, New York 53,225, Pennsylvania 4,635, Ohio 47,850, Indiana 2,500, Illinois 8,150, Wisconsin 2,150, Minnesota 1,750, in Illinois 15,500, in other States 7,150 machines—(of harvesters, a machine upon which two men ride and do the binding, 4,000 are manufactured)—making a total of, say, 159,410 machines.

A MEMBER OF THE COMMITTEE. Why do they call one a harvester and the other a reaper?

Mr. STORROW. The harvester has a place for a man to ride on and bind the grain, or else binds the grain itself; whereas what is commonly called the reaper simply cuts the grain, and leaves it upon the ground to be bound afterwards.

A MEMBER OF THE COMMITTEE. McCormick's is a reaper, and he has attached to it a binder.

Mr. COFFIN. The harvester is the machine upon which two men ride and do the binding.

Mr. STORROW. The self-binder goes a step beyond that. They put an extra attachment on it, which takes the place of those two men, and does the work of those two men.

Mr. COFFIN. The amount of capital invested in the manufacture of these machines is about thirty million dollars. Almost every manufacturer of the machines now in use is a patentee. Over five thousand patents have been issued on reapers and mowers, and machines and devices connected with them. This indicates the amount of thought and labor, but it does not show the amount of money expended. I am assured by the McCormick Company that more than one million dollars has been spent by that company in experiments. I will also state that the Champion Reaper Company, of Springfield, Ohio, give similar testimony in regard to the amount spent by that company. Mr. McCormick granted few or no licenses to manufacturers. His facilities were very large, and he supplied the market himself. Hussey granted licenses at $2.50 on his scalloped cutter. This was adopted by nearly all the makers of other machines, yet, in 1858, so discouraging was the outlook that Hussey offered his patent for sale for $5,000. The party who declined the purchase subsequently paid $10,000 royalty for back damages, and $25,000 more for license fees. The patent ran 21 years, and his invention of the slotted guard and scalloped cutter are in use to-day, nor have they been radically improved. The Dorsey patent was offered at $10,000, and refused. The McCormick, Hussey, Seymour, Morgan, Dorsey, and hinge-joint patents have expired, and the license-fees paid to-day are very small on machines.

Mr. TOWNSHEND. Are Mr. McCormick's profits stated?

Mr. COFFIN. No, sir; manufacturers are reticent on that point. The machines have been so much improved that manufacturers who have all of these old patents free to-day say that they cannot afford to manufacture under them alone. They prefer to pay whatever royalty is asked for on the later improvements. The improvements on these machines have increased the capacities of men for labor to such an extent that farmers cannot afford to use a machine that was thought almost perfect in 1865. The highest license-fee paid on the ordinary machines has been about $10. On new and expensive machines, like the automatic binder, it has not exceeded $20 or $25. There are three self-binding machines in the market—the Lock, McCormick, and Gordon.

Every attempt to create a close monopoly in the manufacture of reapers has failed. I stated that in 1866 there were about one hundred and eighty establishments in the country engaged in making reapers and mowers, or parts of them. How many are there to-day? Less than twenty. The others have disappeared, mostly in bankruptcy. Within the last twelve months four of the largest establishments have gone down.

As to the amount of capital required to carry on the manufacture, it is not capital required in the plant, but in the amount of stock that has to be accumulated. Millions of feet of lumber must be used, that requires from two to three years in seasoning; and large amounts must be paid out before any returns are received. The machines are sent out to local agents in the months of May and June. Few farmers pay cash. The manufacturer thinks himself quite fortunate if he gets his pay at the end of the second or third season. The statement of the manufacturers, without exception, is that "we are compelled to carry the farmers."

The ignorance of farmers, many of whom know nothing of mechanics, is another element of cost which necessitates the sending out of men to set up the machines for them. This expense, of course, must be added to the cost of the machine.

A great expense is in experimenting. Every establishment has its inventors and mechanics constantly employed in devising something new and making new models to improve their machines. No manufacturer, however good his machine, can rest where he is. In invention, it is the survival of the fittest. The self-raking reaper of the past ten years is to-day being pushed aside by the self-binder.

Mr. Chairman and gentlemen, if you could have taken a little trip with me last fall on the line of the Northern Pacific Railroad, in the valley of the Red River of the North, you would have seen twenty self-binders, one morning, all starting together to reap a field containing seven thousand acres. That entire crop, which amounted to one hundred and fifty-four thousand bushels of wheat, which loaded five hundred freight cars, was not touched by a human hand until it passed into the thresher! No binder, demanding his three or four dollars a day, appeared upon that field. And there, sir, in the valley of the Red River of the North, and in Texas, and in California, is the great future of the self-binder. No man can measure what its capacities are—cutting its fifteen or twenty acres a day with a boy driving two horses, reducing the cost of the cultivation of wheat to its lowest terms. The reaper and self-binder have already exhibited a capacity to save a hundred million dollars per annum to this country, giving us that credit on the right side of the ledger. It is this that inventors are doing to-day. It is not the farmer who has given that $100,000,000 to the country on the right side of the balance-sheet, but it is the inventor behind the farmer.

It is Hussey in 1833, McCormick in 1844, and the great host of men of like genius who have spent their nights, and their money, and everything that they could get, to develop these machines, which have become a blessing to the world.

At this point the committee adjourned.

FEBRUARY 8, 1878—10 a. m.

The committee met pursuant to adjournment, and Mr. Coffin continued :

Mr. Chairman and gentlemen : At the close of my remarks on Tuesday, I had finished giving, in a very brief condensation, the agricultural implements of the country. I propose this morning to occupy a very short time in giving some other industries, and will commence with

HORSESHOES.

I have taken some pains to ascertain the exact difference in cost between hand-made and machine-made horseshoes. At a blacksmith's shop on F street, in this city, near the Patent Office, I found two men engaged in making horseshoes day before yesterday, making them by contract, seven dozen (eighty-four) shoes a day, costing $5 for the labor alone, without including the iron or the coal.

In contrast, I point you to a new horseshoe machine at Cleveland, Ohio, just going into operation, which is attended by two men and manufactures 7,000 a day. In both cases the labor costs $5. Making still further inquiries, I have ascertained that the gentleman who, with his sweeping-machines, keeps the streets of Washington free from dirt, and who employs a large number of horses, figures the cost of a set of machine-made shoes at seventy-three cents, and of hand-made shoes at ninety-eight cents. Thus, by the use of the machine-made shoes he makes a saving of twenty-five cents on each set—that is, four shoes. He has his horses reshod every three weeks, or sixteen times during the year. The difference for the year is, therefore, $4 for each horse. One of the leading blacksmiths of this city, near the Patent Office, informs me that city horses, upon an average, require shoeing twelve times a year, and country horses six times a year. He thinks that the average shoeing of all horses would be nine times a year. Now, figuring the gain of twenty-five cents on each pair of shoes by the use of the machine-made shoes, the total annual amount of saving on each horse is $2.25.

Mr. ELDREDGE. Do you take into account the fact that he uses the same shoes several times?

Mr. COFFIN. I inquired in regard to that, and am informed by the blacksmith and by the gentleman who sweeps the streets here (Colonel Wright) that they do not use the old shoes, and that it is cheaper to use new shoes every time.

By the census of 1870, there were between eight and nine million horses in the country. Eliminating two million that, for various reasons, are not shod, and calling the number six million, the saving per annum would be, if all were to use the machine-made shoes, $13,000,000.

Mr. SMITH. Does that include the mules?

Mr. COFFIN. I don't know in regard to that. I take my statistics from the census report, under the head of horses.

Machine-made horseshoes have been before the public many years ; but the blacksmiths of this city inform me that many persons are so prejudiced against them that, though they are afforded at twenty-five cents less per set, they are not yet regarded with favor by many of the

hucksters and teamsters. The blacksmiths prefer the machine-made
shoes, because the profits are relatively larger in setting them than on
hand-made shoes. The prejudice is wholly unreasoning, but time and
use are dissipating it, and the blacksmiths predict that a few years
hence hand-made shoes will be a thing of the past.

The CHAIRMAN. In making those shoes by machinery, do you not
break somewhat into a manual industry? Don't you deprive the blacksmith of a portion of his work—his proper employment?

Mr. COFFIN. I think not, sir. It is the testimony of the blacksmiths
that they can make more money by using the machine-made shoes.

Another industry is that of

HORSESHOE NAILS.

The horseshoe nail is a simple affair. The blacksmith will make two
at a heat; but after he has forged them he has to point them before
they can be used.

The first, or nearly the first, attempt at making horseshoe nails by
machinery was by the Putnam Company, which did not make a complete
nail, but one that required pointing. The cost of pointed nails made
by hand before this invention of the Putnam machine was seventy-five
cents per pound.

About 1862 or 1863 Mr. Whipple, of Massachusetts, an inventor who
had devoted much attention to working irregular shapes of iron by
machinery, invented a machine intended to make a pointed nail. He
patented it in 1864, and got a capitalist to help perfect and build it.
After spending a couple of years or more and several thousand dollars,
the machine would not work satisfactorily. The capitalist thought the
problem could be solved, and with profit; and so he employed two other
inventors, at different times, to work upon the machine.

Eight years of time and more than $60,000 were expended before the
first nail was completed by the Globe Company, and it is said that
nearly $200,000 were expended on the Putnam and Globe machines be-
fore the present pointed nail could be put upon the market, and then the
prejudice was so great that it was with much difficulty they were introduced at all. At first the nails were given away.

No longer ago than last summer, while taking my vacation in New
Hampshire, being in a blacksmith's shop, an old farmer came in to have
his horse shod, and he informed the blacksmith that he must have hand-
made nails used, because he didn't consider a machine-made nail fit to
use. The old gentleman said, "I want the good old-fashioned hand-
made nail; none of your new-fangled things for me." The blacksmith
gave me a sly wink, and, after the old man had gone out of the shop, he
used the machine-made nails in shoeing the horse.

The present price of horse-shoe nails—and I quote from the last
Journal of Commerce, of Boston—is as follows:

Putnam's pointed, No. 5, per lb................................. $0 26
    "   "   No. 10,   "   18
Globe pointed, No. 5,   "   26
    "   "   No. 10,   "   17

And other companies at about the same rate. That is the wholesale
price.

I inquired from the blacksmiths in this city what they paid for their
nails, and they told me about thirty cents a pound on an average, taking
all sizes.

Now, sir, why has it cost so much to produce that nail? If you will examine the nail you will see that, in the first place, it is produced by the cutting of what is called a blank from a piece of cold metal. The nail must be hammered, or subjected to some equivalent treatment, to give it toughness. It must also be shaped in the process of hammering, and if you will examine the nail you will see that, in its elongation, there is required a change in the form of the nail to produce the regular tapering, the curving, and the pointing at the end; you will see that to accomplish even such little insignificant things as these, must require long and careful study of machinery and long experimenting, and a great expenditure of money in producing this machinery. [Mr. Coffin here exhibited some machine-made horseshoe nails.]

At the hearing on Tuesday, Mr. Chairman, you inquired if labor-saving machinery reduced the cost of the manufactured article to the consumer, and instanced the building of a house and the use of the old jack-plane against the Woodruff planing-machine at present in use.

Here, in this horseshoe-nail machine, we have an illustration in point so plain that it will need no elucidation. The price of hand-made nails when the Putnam machine first started was seventy-five cents a pound; to-day a better nail is furnished to the blacksmith for thirty cents a pound. Nor could a blacksmith now make them for less than seventy-five cents a pound, furnishing the iron and pointing them. And he uses them to fasten machine-made shoes that cost twenty-five cents a pair less than old hand-made shoes. To come to this point has required the invention embodied in about one hundred horseshoe machines and over one hundred horseshoe-nail machines, and the inventive labor of over twenty-five years.

And now a word on clothing. Of our clothing, Mr. Chairman,

STOCKINGS

are considered essential. The time was when all hosiery was knit by hand, but that day has passed. I very much doubt if any considerable number of women of the next generation will know how to knit. Machines have almost wholly superseded knitting-needles; till within a few months, however, the stocking-machines in use did not wholly complete a stocking; there was still a seam to be sewed at the heel, or toe, or at the side, or bottom of the foot; but invention has conquered the last difficulty, and now if you will go into a chamber in an unpretending establishment in the town of Rockford, Ill., you will see twelve automatic stocking-machines at work—the invention of a hard-working, modest mechanic.

The CHAIRMAN. Is that the Lamb knitting-machine?

Mr. COFFIN. No, sir; it is the Nelson machine. There are only twelve machines in existence, and they are knitting a total of 5,600 pairs a week. The twelve machines are tended by a boy fifteen years old, who is paid $4 a week—making the cost of the knitting a pair of stockings one-sixth of a mill. And that you may see what the machine is doing, I have a pair of the stockings, which I lay before the committee.

The CHAIRMAN. I am afraid you are going to deprive the old ladies of a great deal of pleasure which they have had in knitting in the evening.

Mr. COFFIN. Now, sir, a machine commences at the top, and it knits down, widening and narrowing, changes the stitch as it goes on to the heel, where it shapes the heel, and finishes at the end of the toe with one thread; and then it goes on to the next one, and so on to another and another. It knits fancy stockings, and I saw some being knit with three or four colors; and it will go on, sir, and knit a mile of stockings, if your yarn will hold out, and no person need touch it. I exhibited that stocking to some of our Eastern manufacturers, and they acknowledged it was far ahead of anything that had ever been before produced.

Mr. BRIGGS. What did you say was the cost of knitting these stockings; less than a cent?

Mr. COFFIN. One-sixth of a mill.

Mr. BRIGGS. What does the whole machine cost?

Mr. COFFIN. I do not remember the price, but I think they are held at $200. They are patented machines. I don't know the name under which the patent was issued, but the firm is Burson & Nelson—Mr. Burson furnishing the capital, I presume, and Mr. Nelson inventing the machine.

Another article which the world cannot get along without is

WOOD-SCREWS.

In this connection I will give you a statement condensed from a paper furnished me by Mr. Biddle, of Cleveland, Ohio:

In 1840 he was a maker of screws. By the process then in use, the machines for cutting, slotting, shaving, threading, and heading enabled twenty men and boys to manufacture twenty thousand screws in a day. If you will go into the screw-works at Cleveland, Ohio, you will see two girls tending two machines which manufacture two hundred and forty thousand screws a day. So great is the consumption of screws that it would be utterly impossible to supply the demand by the old process.

The CHAIRMAN. They are made of iron, are they not? You mean by wood-screws that they go into wood?

Mr. COFFIN. Yes, sir.

We all of us like to ride in our carriages. See what a machine for finishing carriage-shafts has accomplished. Formerly it cost $18 a dozen to finish them; now, 75 cents. Foreign carriage-builders at the Centennial saw the shafts of Messrs. Russell & Snydon, of Toledo, and the result is large orders from England, Australia, and Germany. The cheap hand-labor of those countries cannot compete with this machine. It is converting every year nearly two million feet of oak and hickory into carriage-shafts.

I now come to the

ROCK-DRILL.

This machine has revolutionized the methods of blasting. When the Hoosac Tunnel was begun, many efforts were made to facilitate and cheapen blasting. I remember a large machine that was to bore its way through the mountain. It cost many thousands of dollars—probably from $50,000 to $100,000. It proved an utter failure. Drills were invented by Brooks, Gates, and Burleigh. They were tried and failed. There was the diamond drill and the French drill of Sommeillier. You will find abundant testimony in regard to those in the report of the Commissioner of Mines and Mining for 1870. While these machines, one after the other, were being tried, Mr. Charles Burleigh, of Fitchburg, Mass., was studying the great question. He began in 1865, and spent $30,000 before he put his drill in operation. It was brought into use in 1868 in the Hoosac Tunnel.

Walter Shauley, the contractor, testified before the committee of the Massachusetts legislature January 9, 1874:

"Since commencing work on this drill we have tunneled three miles in solid rock, besides doing a great deal of other drilling for the enlargement of the heading. To have done this work by hand drilling would have taken not less than twelve years, and the expense of labor of drilling would have been, I think, fully three times the cost of machine-drilling. In my opinion, works will now be undertaken which, under the system of hand-drilling, would have been considered impracticable. I have had a machine work three months without needing repairs, and in that time it drilled upwards of a mile of ground."

In addition, I will state that in Saxony, where hand-labor is exceedingly cheap, this is the only machine that has as yet wholly superseded it.

Mr. AIKEN. How long did it take him?

Mr. COFFIN. He does not state the time—how many years—but of course it was less than six years. In the reports of the Massachusetts legislature of 1874 you will find it stated that this machine in the construction of that tunnel saved over $3,000,000. It bored out Hell Gate, saving an immense amount to the government.

Mr. STORROW. The machine was not put at work until many years' work had been done on the tunnel.

Mr. COFFN. In the *Scientific American* for January 25, 1873, you will find a comparison between the work done at Hell Gate by the Burleigh drill and by the diamond drill, the next best machine.

As it is a matter of public record, I may properly allude to it; but I think you will bear me witness, Mr. Chairman and gentlemen, that in the presentation of what labor-saving machinery is doing I have carefully refrained from making any comparison of different machines, in justice to all parties. It is stated in the paper alluded to that during a period of four months the diamond drill removed $14\frac{4}{10}$ feet in a shift of eight hours, at a cost of $1.16 per linear foot; the Burleigh drill removed 26 feet at a cost of 43 cents per linear foot. The cost of repairs on the diamond drill for a single week was $700, while the repairs to the Burleigh drill were $27 per month.

The Sutro Tunnel was begun in 1869. For four years it was carried on by hand-blasting, making a progress of 5,200 linear feet of a tunnel $4\frac{1}{2}$ by 6 feet. The Burleigh was employed, and the size of the tunnel was increased, and it made 4,278 feet in thirteen months. The monthly expense, including pumping, by the former process of blasting, was from $34,000 to $50,000; but when the Burleigh drill was introduced it was reduced from $14,000 to $16,000. It is this drill which is in use in the silver mines of the country to-day, and if we are to have cheap silver, we regard the Burleigh drill as being very largely at the bottom of it. The cheapening of the cost of blasting and the reduction of the ore are the two main factors.

So, when that Fitchburg mechanic set himself to work and spent his $30,000 in expectation of reaping a reward under the protection of the patent laws, he produced a machine which to-day is affecting the transportation, the commerce, and the finances of the world. How great has been this personal reward for such an invention? Less than one thousand machines have been built. It is not a machine which is to be made in great numbers. He has received thus far not much more than enough to reimburse him for his expenses and a reasonable compensation for his time.

Mr. STORROW. It appeared in some proceedings in England a few years ago that up to 1872, before the diamond drill had got into suc-

cessful operation, the English engineers had spent over $100,000 in ex-
perimenting with it and perfecting it.

Mr. CHAUNCEY SMITH. I would say the first attempt, so far as I
know, to invent a machine-drill was in this country, by Mr. Fowle, about
1862; and I think more inventors have been engaged on that problem
than almost any other mechanical problem during the inventing period.
Until Mr. Burleigh produced his drill, I am quite certain that more than
seventy patents were taken out in this country (over two hundred before 1874) and a good many abroad; and the amount of thought and
labor expended on that machine to make it successful was, I think,
quite equal to that expended on any other machine which accomplishes
what that has done, and the problem passed through the hands of as
large a number of persons before any success was achieved.

Mr. COFFIN. When in Chicago, Mr. Chairman, I visited the large
manufactory of Adams & Westlake, who manufacture a great variety of
articles, and where I discovered that the invention of what we call little
things is sometimes of great moment. For instance, they manufacture
a sieve, the rim of which is tin. By a machine which they have invented, they have so cheapened the price that a sieve can now be purchased for 25 or 30 cents, far better than those formerly retailed for 40
or 50 cents. The old sieves had wooden rims, and a nest occupied considerable space in a railroad-car in transportation. It has been discovered that a rest of tin sieves occupies so much less space that the reduction of freight alone is almost a sufficient margin for profit.

Mr. ELDREDGE. Are they not heavier than the wooden sieve?

Mr. COFFIN. I think not, sir; but the space occupied in the car is the
i portant matter.

Mr. ELDREDGE. Were not the wooden sieves put up in the same way?

Mr. COFFIN. They were packed together.

The CHAIRMAN. Then where is the difference in the occupation of
space?

Mr. COFFIN. A nest of sieves with wooden rims will occupy about
four feet, but this kind with iron rims will occupy only one foot.

While in that establishment I saw some dozens of barrels filled with
tin

BABY-RATTLES

about to be shipped to England. It is a point worthy of notice that
labor is cheaper in England than in the United States; that our tin
comes from England; and yet this manufacturing company, by this patented machinery, is able to send these baby-rattles to that country. So
these gentlemen of Chicago are amusing the infantile community of
England, and putting money in their pockets by the operation.

While upon toys, I recall what I saw in the old town of Nuremberg,
in Germany—the center of the toy-trade of the world. I saw flour-
barrels in a large toy warehouse that seemed to be of American manufacture, and I discovered that they were filled with little brass and iron
wheels, pinions, and such sets of tea-furniture as your little girl perhaps
has stored away in the cupboards of her doll's apartment.

"Do you make these here?" I asked. "O, no; they come from Con-
necticut, in the United States."

It is the patent machinery of this country that is turning the parts
out by the barrel, and which are put together by the women and children of Germany, who can use their fingers, but who have not yet been
able to make iron and steel and steam do the work of human hands,
as have the inventors of the United States. I will pass to the,

WOOLEN INDUSTRY.

A young man (Arthur Scholfield), a machinist, came from England to America and settled in Pittsfield, Massachusetts, in the year 1800. England at that time was intent upon building up her manufacturing industries, and she had a law prohibiting the carrying of machinists' tools out of the country, so Arthur Scholfield came without his tools; but he had a retentive memory and mathematical mind, and set himself to work to construct machinery which would card wool more perfectly and economically than the farmers' wives could do it by hand.

The Pittsfield Sun of November 2, 1801, contains an advertisement of this, the first carding-machine in America:

"Arthur Scholfield respectfully informs the inhabitants of Pittsfield, and the neighboring towns, that he has a carding-machine, half a mile west of the meeting-house, where they may have their wool carded into rolls for twelve and a half cents per pound; mixed, fifteen cents per pound. If they find the grease, and pick the grease in, it will be ten cents per pound, and twelve cents and a half for mixed."

The first broadcloths manufactured in this country were by Scholfield, in 1804; the wool was carded in his carding-machine, the cloth woven by hand. It was gray-mixed, and when finished was shown to the different merchants of Pittsfield, and offered for sale; but no one would purchase it. He took it to New York, and left it with a merchant there. A few weeks later Isaiah Bissoll, a leading merchant of the village, went to New York to purchase goods. He bought a stock of woolens,. and upon his return asked Scholfield to examine them.

" I have seen some of these goods before," said Scholfield.

" You have seen them before—where ? when ?"

" I made them, and that is my private mark," said Scholfield. The merchant had purchased what he had once rejected; and yet so strong was prejudice against the article which he turned out that it was impossible for him to sell these cloths except by this surreptitious way. In other things the prejudice has been equally strong against articles made at home, and in like manner it has been often conquered.

In 1808 Scholfield manufactured thirteen yards of black broadcloth, which was presented to James Madison, and from which his inaugural suit was made. A few merino sheep had been introduced from France, and Scholfield, obtaining their wool and mixing it with the common wool of the country, manufactured the cloth. This was hand-woven. The wool was carded in his carding-machine, but spun and woven by hand.

In the Pittsfield Sun of January 4, 1809, in an account of a meeting of some citizens of that town to take measures for the advancement of manufactures, they passed this resolution: "*Resolved,* That the introduction of spinning-jennies, as is practiced in England, into private families is strongly recommended, since one person can manage by hand the operation of a crank that turns twenty-four spindles."

That was the beginning of spinning in this country. Spinning was all done by hand. The first spinning-wheel was invented by a Frenchman, about 1510. From the creation of the world down to that time, the only method of spinning was by the hand distaff and spindle. Homer drew a picture of it when he portrayed the virtuous Penelope spinning for Ulysses. I, myself, saw this method of spinning practiced in the Orient a few years ago. You will find in many a garret of the seaboard States the old-fashioned spinning-wheel. I took pains to ascertain just how much a woman could spin on one of those household wheels. The lady, my informant, who did the spinning, though beyond middle life, was an expert spinner in her younger years. The threads as drawn out from the spindle are about six feet long, forty of which make a knot, seven knots one skein. The spinning was continued long enough to show that she could spin twelve skeins in ten hours, or $3\frac{8}{100}$ miles of thread. This was about a usual day's work for a woman. In spinning, the spinner walks twice over the floor to spin and wind up the thread—not the entire distance of six feet, but about four feet each way, or eight feet of walking to spin one thread six feet in length, making a distance of more than twenty-six thousand feet, or about five miles, that was walked to spin the twelve skeins. I have been somewhat minute in this, because I want to show what invention has accomplished. I give the work of a girl who tends a spinning-machine of the latest type. One girl attends to six hundred and sometimes eight hundred spindles, each of which spins five thousand yards a day, or for the eight hundred spindles four million yards, or nearly twenty-one hundred miles during the day! The thread would reach from the capital of the country nearly to the Sierra Nevadas, and the girl does not walk at all. I would qualify this by saying that such is the capacity of machinery.

In 1811 Elijah Smith, of Walpole, Mass., invented a card-clothing machine for dressing cloth, which was patented. The next year the Jacquard loom made its appearance in France and England, and gave a great impetus to the manufacture of cloth.

In 1812 the largest manufactory of these cloths was at Middletown, Conn., which turned out forty yards of broadcloth a day, which was sold at nine to ten dollars per yard, in the piece—not at retail.

In 1838 Mr. Crompton, who had invented a power-loom for the weaving of cotton, adapted it to weaving of fancy woolens, and I have here, Mr. Chairman, a piece of the first fancy woolen cloth that was ever woven in this country. In 1838 Mr. Crompton, who is now living in Worcester, was then weaving cotton at Taunton, Mass. [Mr. Coffin here exhibited a piece of cloth manufactured on Crompton's original loom at the Middlesex Mills, in Lowell, in 1838.]

Mr. WILLETS. What is that used for?

Mr. COFFIN. It is used for coats, or any kind of fancy clothing, or for ladies' clothing. It is a fancy pattern. I will say here that on that loom, or looms based upon it, are woven every yard of fancy cloth in the world.

Mr. WILLETS. Do I understand that that was invented here?

Mr. COFFIN. Invented here and sent all over the world.

Mr. STORROW. The man who invented it is still a manufacturer of looms, or rather it is his son who actually carries on the business,

Mr. SMITH. Looms which are sent to all parts of the world to-day.

Mr. WILLETS. Do you know the price of this when it was manufactured?

Mr. STORROW. No; I do not.

BIGELOW CARPET-LOOM.

In 1848 Mr. E. B. Bigelow, of Massachusetts, invented a power carpet-loom. He was a manufacturer of coach-lace at Clinton, Mass. At London, in 1851, at the Exhibition, he astonished the world by exhibiting carpets superior to any woven by hand. Improvements have been since made, until to-day the American Bigelow carpet-loom can turn out as high as seventy-five yards of carpeting in one day. He sold his patent for England to the Crossleys, who have not kept pace with him in his improvements; they, with their improvements, now only weave about thirty-five yards a day of Brussels.

I have here the report of the committee of the judges in the Exhibition of 1871. In a supplement to their report the jury state: "The specimens of Brussels carpeting exhibited by Mr. E. B. Bigelow are woven by a power-loom invented and patented by him, and are better, more perfectly woven, than any band-loom goods that have come under the notice of the jury. This, however, is a very small part of their merit, or rather that of Mr. Bigelow, who has completely triumphed over the numerous obstacles that presented themselves, and succeeded in substituting steam-power for manual labor in the manufacture of five-frame Brussels carpets. Several patents have been taken out by different inventors in this country for effecting the same object, but as yet none of them have been brought into successful operation; and the honor of this achievement—one of great practical difficulty as well as of great commercial value—must be awarded to a native of the United States."

The London Morning Chronicle, in noticing the exhibit, says:

At the eleventh hour, power-loom manufactured Brussels was deposited in the American division, the merit of the invention and application of this important discovery being due to Mr. E. B. Bigelow, of the United States. The evidence of the successful application of a much-wished-for invention is all that could be desired. Although various attempts have been made to adapt the power-loom to carpet-weaving in this country, there is not, we believe, at this moment, any machinery perfected for that object. Our American brethren have, therefore, gained another step ahead of us, and have won another laurel on this well-contested field of the industrial arts.

Mr. WILLETS. How much will a man do by hand in a day?

Mr. COFFIN. About five yards, I think. I will say here, sir, that this carpet-loom of Mr. Bigelow's has driven out the foreign production of carpets from the markets of the United States, and we are now sending them abroad.

COTTON.

I have time only to allude to the cultivation and manufacture of the great staple of the Southern States—cotton. It was the inventive genius of Eli Whitney, in 1793, which produced the cotton-gin, patented in 1794. It was considered a wonderful machine then—a contrivance of four posts, two cylinders, and a crank. A man could gin seventy pounds a day, whereas he could do only about four and a half by hand. What can be done now? The latest gin of to-day turns out four hundred pounds an hour, or four thousand pounds a day. And now a word as to the

COTTON-LOOM.

In 1806 Edmund Cartwright, of England, invented a loom for weaving cotton, which was propelled by water.

In 1814 the first power-loom in America was set up at Waltham, Mass.

In 1836 George Crompton invented a new loom, which he put into operation at Taunton—the same loom that two years later he adapted to the weaving of fancy woolens.

In 1850 he had made so many improvements that the loom threw the shuttle fifty times a minute—nearly once a second—across a web thirty-six inches wide.

How rapidly is the shuttle thrown to-day? ONE HUNDRED AND
EIGHTY TIMES A MINUTE, THREE TIMES A SECOND!
The agent of the mill where Crompton's first fancy-woolen loom was
used says: "With the improved loom of 1876 over that of 1850 there is
an increase of sixty per cent. in production, which is accomplished with
greater ease to the weaver, with also a saving of fifty per cent. in labor.
In addition, there is a saving of more than one hundred per cent. in
repairs."
"Since 1860," says the agent of the Amoskeag Company at Manchester,
N. H., "there has been an entire revolution in the cotton manufacture.
Machines in use ten years ago, to-day are obsolete, and no manufacturers could afford to take some of them as a gift."
"Has the power-loom reached its ultimate capacity?" was the question I put to Mr. Crompton, a few days ago.
"It is in its infancy," was the reply.
Whitney, McCartney, and the Remington Company have carried the
ginning of cotton from 70 pounds to 4,000 pounds a day. The Bigelow
carpet-loom, the Crompton loom in use in England and America, the
equally rapid Knowles loom, which is a marvel of ingenuity and mechanical skill and perfection, are all the inventions of Americans, all
patented under our laws. They are the machines that to-day enable
the manufacturer to purchase his cotton in South Carolina, or even in
Texas, transporting it to Boston and Fall River, or even to Manchester,
N H., fifty miles inland, manufacture it into cloth and calico, and sell
it for 3⅛ cents a yard.
By the genius of these inventors, the poorest woman who walks our
streets may appear in a dress of calico of recent and tasteful design,
which shall not exceed sixty cents in the cost of all the material. Men
who can accomplish such results are certainly benefactors to their
race.
Now a word as to the future.
Mr. Chairman, you are considering not a law to govern the past, but
the future. And what is the outlook for the future? What the prospect for American industry, American invention, American manufactures and commerce in the marts of the world? The time was when a
large percentage of cotton goods in our shops were manufactured in
the mills of Great Britain, but that time has nearly passed.
Allow me to read an advertisement which you will see standing in
the London papers. I quote from the Boston Journal of Commerce. It
is headed

AMERICAN CALICOES ADVERTISED IN LONDON.

It is consoling to read the following advertisement which is inserted in the London
papers: "American calicoes. The Wamsutta shirtings and sheetings. This is the
leading and most popular brand in America, being admitted by all classes of consumers,
shirt-makers, ladies' and children's outfitters, and the trade generally, to stand unsurpassed
for regularity of make, quality of cotton, and general usefulness. Wamsutta Mills long-
cloth brands, Wamsutta, Tuscarora, and Seaside, in 30-in., 33-in., and 36-in. Wamsutta sheetings—plain, twilled, and double-warp, in 72-in., 81 in., 90-in., and 99-in. wide.
Wamsutta, 36-in. double warp, nightgown cotton, and 36-in. fine twill. Note.—Every piece measures fully the width stated, and has upon it a ticket bearing a picture of the
mills and the words, 'The Wamsutta Mills, New Bedford, Mass.' These goods can be
had from any wholesale house. Ellet, Glover & Co., 15 George street, Manchester; 9
Goldsmith street, London, E. C., and 22 Well street, Bradford, are the sole agents for the
mills, and only supply the wholesale."

We have reached a point, Mr. Chairman, where the capital employed
is sufficient to produce enough for our own wants and a little more.

We have just begun to send a few goods to South America, a few yards to China, a few to Turkey. In China there are 400,000,000 people, the great majority of whom must wear the cheapest possible clothing. We send out about 11,000,000 yards, England 263,000,000 yards; but this only gives twenty yards of cloth per annum to one out of every seventeen inhabitants of that land. There are 600,000,000 people on the earth (it is estimated) that now do not use cotton goods, except what they manufacture by their own rude hand-machinery, who, sooner or later, will be reached by the labor-saving machinery of Great Britain and the United States.

Upon this point I will give the views of a manufacturer of cotton, Mr. Edward Atkinson:

> Leaving to our competitors the share in the supply of the world's need of cotton goods which they have already secured, there yet remain outside of Europe and the United States, in Asia, Africa, and South America, from five to eight hundred million of people whose clothing consists mainly of cotton cloth. It must now be spun and woven by the slow process of hand-work. Can we obtain our share in this unworked field? Four hundred million persons, at five pounds per head, would require from our Southern States 4,000,000 additional bales of cotton, and would call for 40,000,000 more cotton spindles in Europe or America to work them up. Who will raise this cotton, and where shall these spindles be constructed?

You will observe, Mr. Chairman, that the area of cotton culture in the Southern States now under the plow is only about two per cent. of the land. If you will take the report of the British Commission to Parliament, giving a statement of where they obtain their cotton supply, you will see that America has usually, except during the war, supplied from sixty to seventy per cent. of the total amount. To-day the cotton manufactories of the world are supplying only twenty yards of cloth to each of about 170,000,000 people. The remaining millions, as yet, are not purchasers.

The annual consumption of cotton throughout the world is about 6,000,000 bales, of which the United States produces from sixty to seventy per cent. Double consumption, and you double your production. The States of Georgia and South Carolina have already begun to solve this great problem of the future. I have here a little item, cut from a paper this very week, which reads as follows:

> The new cotton mill at Atlanta, Ga., is now in operation. Steam was turned on last Monday, 10,000 spindles were set in motion, and the work of carding, spinning, and cloth-making was begun. The superintendent is George B. Harris, a graduate of Harvard, and a Massachusetts Yankee. Although he is only in his twenty-eighth year, he has been in charge of large cotton mills for eight years, and therefore speaks from experience when he predicts not only the success of this factory, but the rapid development of manufacturing enterprises in the South. When the mill is in full operation, as many as 600 factory hands will be employed. A Palmetto planter, who supplied the first ten bales of cotton used in the factory, instead of receiving cash in payment, preferred to take stock in the company, and agreed to send more cotton on the same conditions. The opening of this mill, and the anxiety of this planter to become financially interested in it, are good signs.

The future of this country lies, in a great degree, in our ability to produce and manufacture cotton and send the product about at the cheapest possible rate. There are in the problem four elements—

First. Cheapness of the raw material.

Second. Cheapness of manufacture—not the reduction of wages, but the employment of machinery to do the work of human hands; the manufacture has been brought to such a point that a saving of half a cent a pound, one-eighth of a cent a yard will carry the day.

Third. Cheapness of transportation.

Fourth. Our ability to receive the products of other lands which we cannot ourselves produce, or which we receive and manufacture at a profit in exchange.

In this presentation, Mr. Chairman, you have doubt'ess noticed some of the points elucidated : that labor-saving machinery is a growth ; that years of use are required before a complete and perfect mechanism can be developed; that inventions become superseded, or rather so super-added to, that the competitor in the race of industries must use the last ; that few inventors are reimbursed for their time and expense; therefore great rewards must be held out to the successful ; that the genius of American inventors has already enabled American industries to compete successfully with those of other lands; that the value of such machines as the inventors of the United States have produced under our patent laws is beyond all calculation.

If American inventors have accomplished this in the past, what may we not expect in the future? Having been through foreign lands—through Syria, Turkey, Palestine, Egypt, India, Japan, to the heart of China ; knowing that there are six hundred million of people in those lands who will reach out their hands for our products if their production can be sufficiently cheapened—knowing this, I look with confidence upon the future of our industries; such a future as no other country ever has had. In the light of that future, I behold a vast area of our country white with the opening bolls of the cotton-plant. I behold the majestic rivers arrested in their courses to the sea, and put to work for the benefit of the human race, giving to the millions of the Orient, of South America, and the islands of the sea the products of the loom which they do not and cannot now receive. It is in the power of the United States to lay her hand upon a goodly portion of the trade of the world through our ability to manufacture, by our improved and ever-improving machinery, this great staple more cheaply than it can be manufactured by any other country. We have reached that point in invention where we are just ready to enter as a people upon our great career, and it rests with this committee, with you, Mr. Chairman and gentlemen, by giving proper protection to inventors, to take the initiative which will bring about this great and immeasurable consummation of the future.

MR. HYDE'S ARGUMENT.

MR. CHAIRMAN AND GENTLEMEN OF THE COMMITTEE: I have been requested to appear before you to represent the Shoe and Leather Association of Boston, which to-day represents our largest industry; and whatever progress in manufacturing may have been made in other directions, to-day the largest industry that we have is included within the limits of this association. Mr. Coolidge, as a member of the association, and representing it, has also been directed to appear before you; but finding that your time is limited, he has asked me to speak in his behalf, as well as for the association.

I desire to explain briefly the position that we occupy in coming here. We are not the owners of patents, and in asking your consideration of the views that will be presented, it is from the stand point of the users and those who pay royalties.

The points that I shall direct my remarks to will be these :

First. What advantage has accrued to this one business by the inventions of the past twenty years;

Second. The abuses which we have suffered as users of patents; and *Third.* The remedy which it is desired to have incorporated in this bill.

As I said before the committee of the Senate, when appearing there, it is pretty safe to trust to inventors and those who own patents that they will be represented before a committee of this kind. The individual interests of such men are so large that they are sure to be heard and sure to be represented. It is very probable, however, that there will be overlooked a very large class, extending over the whole land, who are individual users of patents but who have no facilities for appearing here, and that you will not hear from them as fully as you will from those men who are inventors or the owners of inventions.

Now, in the first instance—and I shall talk of no interests except this one—we say emphatically (although we have suffered at the hands of inventors in various ways, as I shall state later) that we are indebted to the patent system to an extent that has surprised us when we have endeavored to gather our facts together. Some gentlemen of the association at first were in sympathy with the movement which originated at the West for the suspension or repeal of the patent law; but when all the facts were gathered together, with a view of having them presented here, they unanimously said, " We desire a patent law, because we are benefited thereby."

To go back twenty years, there were scattered all over New England many towns known as shoe-towns, where in shops the leather was cut by hand, then was parceled out to makers or bottomers, as they were called, who for a portion of the year labored upon the land and a portion of the year were fishermen, but at odd times made boots and shoes. These boots and shoes were taken home from the shop, and brought back finished, varying in time of completion from a week to six months, or even a year ; they were returned to the shop, examined, packed in cases, and sent to the market for sale. The result was that to accumulate for a season sufficient shoes to meet the demands of the market required six months of time.

About twenty years ago was the first introduction of machinery in the manufacture of boots and shoes, which consisted of two machines—the pegging-machine and the sole-sewing machine; these two machines came gradually into use, and, while they were adopted, there was for some time a prejudice that the machine-work was not as good as hand-work ; but this prejudice proved to be without foundation.

The result is that invention has gone forward, and manufacturers have called for other machines to keep pace with the pegging and sewing machines. Formerly the work done by machinery consisted of pegging and sewing. Now the pegger and sewer have made such progress that they have necessitated other inventions to do the remaining work pertaining to the manufacture of shoes. The result is that, even within the last year, the statistics show—and the means of obtaining them are very correct—that there were sewed on one class of machines 45,000,000 pairs of shoes; there were pegged upon the pegging-machine 55,000,000 pairs last year. And these machines have entirely revolutionized the business. Where before small shops existed throughout New England, now our shops have become large, labor has been brought together and classified and receives a larger compensation, wages have advanced 50 to 100 per cent. to the laborer, and the shoe in quality is 25 per cent. better than twenty-five years ago. And this great change has come about by invention, and is due to patented machinery.

Allow me to say a word in regard to making the shoe, of the
operations that are gone through, and how they are performed by machinery.

Take an ordinary shoe that is to be pegged. In the first place, the
upper leather is cut up by hand, but the sole leather is cut by machinery. Now, this cutting of sole leather by machinery not only saves
labor, but stock, because the soles are cut out by dies, so that there is
very little waste of material. The upper leather, as before stated, is
still cut by hand because the quality of upper leather changes so much
in the different parts of the skin, and it is the principal labor that now
is done by hand. The stitching is done by a machine; the lasting is
done by a machine; the pegging of the sole is done by a machine, or it
is sewed by a machine.

The edge of the sole is first chamfered and channeled by a machine,
when sewed by a machine. And let me state here that a gang of ten men,
with modern machinery, can make 600 pairs of pegged shoes in a day.
Then there is a beating-out machine, for beating out the soles; the bottoms are sand-papered by a machine. The heels are made by machinery; they are nailed on and burnished by machines. The result is, that
eighty-five per cent. of the labor necessary to make a shoe is now
done by machinery; and, to show you how a business can be revolutionized by a single invention, I have brought here an article which,
perhaps, has done more, as a single invention, to revolutionize pegging
work than anything else—the peg-strip of Mr. B. F. Sturtevant. There
were a great many inventions for pegging boots and shoes. They all
failed for lack of this. This was invented by a poor man, and by the
use of it in a pegging-machine 900 pegs are driven per minute. The
result is, that this and the sewing-machine have entirely revolutionized
the work of making boots and shoes. You see, the peg is in a long strip
and in a dry condition. It is a much better peg than the loose peg, and
is prepared with more care, the moisture being taken out. Now, when
that is driven into a shoe, the moisture having been taken out, the peg
is compressed, and the moment the moisture enters it it swells and becomes tight in the shoe, and consequently holds the sole firmer, and it
is admitted that it holds better than an ordinary peg driven by hand.
[Mr. Hyde showed the committee a strip or ribbon of peg-wood cut
across the grain and of a width just equal to the length of peg.]

Now, to show how much business there is in making pegs, let me say
there are 450,000 bushels of loose pegs made in New England, and those
pegs sell for from sixty-five to seventy-five cents per bushel; yet this
patented peg-wood has so superseded the loose pegs that last year there
were 55,000,000 pairs of boots and shoes pegged with it. The whole expense of this peg-wood averages about one-fourth of a cent per pair.
Thus one cent's worth of this material pegs four pairs of shoes.

A MEMBER OF THE COMMITTEE. I want to ask you about the operation of driving these pegs.

Mr. HYDE. First, there is an awl that punches a hole in the sole;
then this machine cuts off a single peg, and then a blow drives the peg;
and the operation is done so rapidly that 900 are driven into the shoe
in a minute.

Mr. WILLETS. How many pegs are there in one shoe?

Mr. CLARENCE SMITH. About four to six pegs to an inch—according
to the size.

Mr. HYDE. There is a great variety of sizes of peg-wood for different
shoes, and some shoes are pegged in double rows.

Mr. WILLETS. How long is this strip of pegging?

Mr. HYDE. That is about 100 feet long.

Mr. SMITH. On an average, there are about 22 inches of pegging to a shoe.

Mr. HYDE. Now, you see what a revolution patented inventions have wrought in this business. They have brought our labor together, organized it, advanced wages about 50 to 100 per cent. to the laboring class, and instead of the manufacturers accumulating a year's or six months' stock of goods, a great portion of the work is now done upon orders. Now, a merchant comes and buys a few cases of assorted stock, and finds which will sell best, and telegraphs on for more. In two or three days the order is filled, and the shoes sent to him. The factories are kept working right up to the orders, and the business of both manufacturer and merchant has entirely changed.

Mr. ———. Has it enabled the manufacturers to make shoes any cheaper?

Mr. HYDE. The advance of labor has been about 50 to 100 per cent. The advance on stock has also been about 20 per cent.

Mr. STORROW. Fifty per cent. advance in stock on the better class of work.

Mr. HYDE. The result has been that our advance in wages and stock, all matters that we cannot control, has nearly kept pace with our savings in pegged work. The profit per shoe has been brought down to a very small figure indeed, and the advantage is in the very large number that the manufacturer is enabled to turn out, thus allowing a small profit on a large number to equal a large profit on a smaller number.

To give another illustration of what is possible, allow me to relate an incident which occurred recently in Massachusetts. A large shoe-factory, turning out 2,400 pairs of shoes per day, was destroyed by fire on a Wednesday night, with contents valued at $75,000. It was at a busy season, with plenty of orders on hand. On Thursday the manufacturer hired a neighboring building, and set carpenters to fitting it up; on Friday he ordered his machinery from Boston; on Saturday the machinery arrived and the men set it up; on Monday work was started, and Tuesday he was filling orders, turning out the full amount of 2,400 pairs. Now, had that occurred twenty-four years ago, the season's market would have been entirely lost to the manufacturer. As it was, his customers never knew, by the want of goods, of the fire; and what is true of that man is true of others. It is a great thing to save to a manufacturer both his orders and customers—the saving of one season's profits.

Now, to illustrate further, for I am not going into details upon this, I chanced to pick up the catalogue of one of the dealers in shoe-machinery, and I will leave it here, as showing the great variety of machinery that is used in the manufacture of shoes. You will see that there are over two hundred varieties now made and sold by this man, and he is only one of the manufacturers; and all or nearly all of these machines are or have been patented. I think every one of them at some time, unless it may be the original leather-roller, which was not patented, but that is now very much improved by a patent bed. They are not all covered by patents now, as some patents have expired; still, most of those even have had patented improvements added.

We exported about $8,000,000 worth of leather in 1876 and about the same quantity in 1877. There are used in tanning sixteen different processes, in all of which patented machinery is used. There are hundreds of different kinds of machines used in tanning, of which very many have been patented.

Mr. SMITH. The recent improvements made a saving in the tanning material to a very considerable exent—say 81 per cent.

Mr. HYDE. If you will look at the list of patents issued, you will see that there are some three hundred patents granted under the head of tanning in this country. These include bark-mills, pumps, splitting-machines, &c. Then take another industry which has grown up in connection with shoe-machinery—that is, the making of lasts. Two million are now made in this country in a year, and they are made by machinery, the result of the Blanchard invention for turning out irregular forms. But the machines actually in use, for the most part, embrace later improvements. That invention, which was patented, and which was originally suggested for the manufacture of gun stocks, is now used in the manufacture of lasts.

Now, I have tried to be entirely just in admitting the great blessing which has come to us from the use of inventions, nearly all of which have been patented. The total amount of royalties paid per pair on fine goods is $3\frac{1}{4}$ cents upon sewed work; upon pegged work the total is about 2 cents per pair. This covers all the machines that go into the best-equipped factories. Of course we pay them royalties, but we don't grumble at it. The royalties are very small compared with the saving to the manufacturer, to the consumer, and the general gain to the public.

Mr. ———. You spoke about manufacturing fifty-five or forty-five million pairs. Do you export any shoes?

Mr. HYDE. I was coming to that a little later. We have just commenced to export boots and shoes. It is believed that there is a larger field of industry in exporting shoes than in any other article of manufacture that we have in this country. We have commenced to work on boots and shoes to send abroad. Large consignments have gone to South America within the past year. Of course the shoes of the East are different in kind, and it takes longer to create a demand. Men are in Japan trying to induce orders. Orders are being received, and shoes are going out; but the difficulty that we have to contend with is the fact that they wear a different kind of shoes, and they are a little longer in adopting ours. The Peruvian Government has sent large orders, which have been filled, for shoes for their troops; and it is believed that in the next few years the export trade to that point will greatly increase.

Mr. STORROW. Quite an amount goes to Germany now.

Mr. HYDE. Men have recently been in this country from Switzerland, where they are about to purchase our machinery, to employ it in their manufactories, where labor is very cheap. A gentleman was recently in Boston, and stated that unless he could get his people to buy our improved machinery, and to use it as well as we did and improve it as fast as we do, he could not compete with American work, and that he must have it. Now, as I said, the gentlemen we represent are not the owners of patents; they are not the owners of inventions; but they have desired, and do desire, to be just to these men who originated these inventions. We must admit that they have generally been made by persons outside of the business, who had a genius or spirit of invention, and they have been adopted by manufacturers after being brought to their attention. Now, it is but just and due to the inventors, and we desire frankly to acknowledge our great indebtedness; certainly we should not now occupy our present position in business were it not for these inventions, and these inventions would not exist unless patented by some patent law.

Mr. RAYMOND. I thought you were going to give us the estimate of how much the patent law helped to foster invention.

Mr. HYDE. Of course that is a difficult question, to say how much is due to the patent law. So far as my personal observation has gone, I believe the greater portion of inventions are made by men who have not much thrift in the way of business—men without much business tact—and who are always looking forward to the protection of the patent law for their reward.

Those men don't look to days' wages, but are always thinking of the great reward a successful invention will bring them under the patent law; th.'y always believe that they will succeed sooner or later, and are that kind of men that are ready to work and wait for a great future. But they wouldn't do it if they didn't see that at the end.

The patentee has a spirit of invention born within him, and the patent law is a sort of a foster-mother. If I had the time or opportunity, I could give some instances which are known to me personally. For example, if you will allow, take this pegging-machine and peg-wood. The man who invented both these was very poor. He was at work trying to get a living in bottoming shoes, and he believed that a better way could be devised. He was so poor that he could hardly keep body and soul together; that is, he would work a few days in bottoming shoes, and then he would go to work upon his invention. He finally brought out the idea successfully; but, owing to his poverty, he was not able to build his pegging-machine or introduce his invention. Now, this peg-wood, which went with the other machines, he was unable alone to hold without assistance. He borrowed about $700, to enable him to perfect his invention and pay the fees of the solicitor and the Patent Office. As security for the loan, he assigned a portion of his invention. He afterward paid the $700 and interest, and, besides, paid the lender over $33,000 for the loan.

It was the only way possible for him to bring out his invention. He obtained a similar loan, from another man, to enable him to patent his machine making the peg-wood, and paid, in addition to both loans, over $60,000.

Mr. AIKEN. If invention is a labor of love, and of little profit, I would ask you if invention would not be stimulated without a patent law?

Mr. HYDE. Take this case just cited. Suppose there had been no patent law; the lenders never would have advanced him the money, as he had no security to give except the assignment of a portion of the patent. The money never would have been obtained on the credit of the man himself. No, sir; these men never would have loaned that money unless they felt, if the thing was successful, enough would come back to pay them handsomely. Invention, to be successful, must always have at its back capital to assist. The inventor sometimes fails to reap the reward, but the public gets the machine. In this particular case the inventor was not a manufacturer trying to increase his profit by improving his factory. He looked to nothing but the actual money-value of his invention, which the patent would secure to him. He did, as inventors are very apt to do, impress some one else with his idea of value, and raised the required money by a pledge or sale of part. He worked on, and worked on, continually inventing and improving; he has got rich, and the public has got the machinery. It would not be easy to tell how many inventors of shoe-machinery have been set to work by his example and his success; but the crop of improvements that grew up after him, and have changed the business, and all of them patented as soon as made, is pretty strong proof on this point.

Mr. AIKEN. Suppose there was no patent law at all, would not invention be as rapid and great as it is at the present time?

Mr. HYDE. I do not believe it would. There is no doubt in my mind that the inventor has a spirit of invention in him, but he is always a man of expectation. He always believes that his ship is coming in some day, and it is very amusing to notice how those men cling to a patent. I knew a man once who made a valuable invention for warfare—a torpedo, I think. He made it a good many years before the war, and of course there could be no consumer for it except the government. The department declined to do anything about it, and there was no one to buy the things, and so a patent wouldn't have brought him any money. So he didn't patent it, and didn't disclose it, and there was an end of his invention. So, you see, in his case it wasn't the desire to invent, or the glory of having invented, that touched him, but the desire to make money by it.

Mr. RAYMOND. I think your description of patentees is perfectly just, if the description is that the foundation upon which the patentee can base his air-castles will give as strong an impetus to his labors as any patent law would give him.

Mr. HYDE. His castles are built on the hope of money the patent will give him. My observation is, that men would not perfect their inventions, and they never could obtain capital to assist them, without some patent law.

Mr. BRIGGS. Then they have just as much pride in their patent as a college-boy has in his diploma.

Mr. HYDE. It is wonderful the way these men will take to secure their patents, and also the passion they have for their inventions, and their belief in their success.

Now, as I say, I have desired to be perfectly fair to inventors and inventions; but the people I represent are those who pay royalties and do not own inventions; and we have at times suffered very severely at the hands of patentees in connection with the use of patents. To give you one illustration—although they have not always occurred to such an exaggerated degree as this, but many times in minor forms: The pegging-machines now used are of three kinds, known as the Champion, the New Era, and the Varney. They are the only ones that to any considerable extent are used. After these had been in use generally in our community fifteen years, and some of them even longer, there came along a man who said that all these pegging-machines infringed three old patents which he owned or represented, and he demanded that all the people who used pegging-machines in the manufacture of boots and shoes should settle with him for back damages and profits, or if not he would commence suit. The manufacturers believed that they did not infringe these patents which had lain dormant for fifteen years; that they had used the machines openly and in good faith; but he commenced suits—over one hundred and fifty in number—against the manufacturers, and made attachments and placed keepers in the shops, under the law for mesne attachments which we have in Massachusetts. Now, there was not one of these manufacturers who had violated any patent rights intentionally, but they were subjected to this injury; and except that some wealthy men in the trade had come forward with bonds to protect the weak manufacturers, many of them would have been compelled to settle the demands.

This litigation cost the shoe-manufacturers $35,000 in one year in defending the suits, which have never prevailed. Now, I say, we believe there should be a remedy furnished against such abuses; there should be in the patent law—which we believe is a wise law, properly enacted—a protection against these abuses, and therefore I have been instructed to call your attention specially to two features of the proposed bill. The rest of the bill we have carefully examined, and we believe it is a great improvement upon the law as it now stands; but as to the other portions of the bill we are not particularly interested. We desire simply to call your attention to the first and eleventh sections. These give the great remedy and great relief which the users in our part of the country consider necessary to them. The first section of the bill provides a statute of limitation. I quote the first clause of the section:

That from and after the passage of this act no profits or damages in any suit at law or in equity for the infringement of a patent shall be recovered which shall have accrued more than four years next preceding the commencement of such suit.

There is no statute of limitation at the present time; at least, the patentee can take the full length of the patent, and six years longer, in which to bring suit. The statute to-day allows not less than twenty-three years in which to bring suit. Now we want a brief statute of limitation. The limitation which is put in the bill is four years; we desire to have it shorter than that. The ordinary statute for torts is two years; but four years is a great deal better than nothing. We should prefer one year, and we feel compelled to urge this substantial relief. This provision, we believe, will protect us so far as suits brought to annoy, and under it we will be protected from those classes of patents which are known as reissued, and which are sprung upon manufacturers when other inventions have become successful, and a large business has been built up in obtaining the reissue of old patents which antedate an invention in use. If notice is given of a man's invention, there is no objection to paying a royalty; but the practice is very common for men to lie by for a series of years, and then make large claims and put users to enormous expense to protect their rights, when, by proper notice in advance, the users might have protected themselves without litigation.

Mr. RAYMOND. The second proviso of the section provides, "That rights of action existing at the passage of this act may be enforced by suits brought within four years thereafter, if not previously barred by laws already existing, but nothing in this section contained shall revive any right of action already barred, nor prolong the right to sue on any cause of action already existing." There is no doubt but what some provision ought to be made. The question is, what your opinion is as to the length of that time.

Mr. HYDE. I should say that the length of time of four years in the proviso corresponds with the four years in the first clause of the section, which I consider right; but we should much prefer a shorter limitation. The users of patents I represent have talked this matter over, and they have instructed me to say what I have said in relation to the clause of limitation. Their result and conclusion is for one year, and they have so passed and voted in their association, that they think one year is better than any longer period of time. If parties who own these patents come forward primarily and assert their rights, we know how to meet them; but it is to protect us from those who come forward years after and claim damages larger than the entire profits made on the goods sold, that we desire this change in the law.

Now, the eleventh section of the bill is a section taken substantially from the English laws, and reads as follows:

SEC. 11. On each and every patent for an invention issued after the passage of this act, there shall be paid to the Commissioner a duty as follows, namely, fifty dollars to be paid on or before the first day of January occurring next after the expiration of four years from the date of the patent, and one hundred dollars on or before the first day of January occurring next after the expiration of nine years from the date of the patent; and in default of any such payment, the patent shall expire on the first day of April next thereafter. But the Commissioner, for good cause shown, may allow the payment to be made at any time before such first day of April, in which case the patent shall not become void. The Commissioner shall annually, in the month of April, publish a list of the patents which have expired for non-payment of duties. Patents issued under this law shall contain a notification of the annual duties to be paid and the time of such payments.

We believe that it is a wise provision, for there are a great many patents which are taken out, and which lie dormant and are not put into active use.

Mr. SMITH. The pegging-machine.

Mr. HYDE. Yes; that is an illustration. These patents remain in the archives of the office and are not brought into use; but, after many years, when some subsequent patent has gone into successful operation then old patents are hunted up, reissued, and suits commenced against parties using the later patent.

There is now growing up a class of men in the country who, when they find an invention in successful use, go to the Patent Office and rake over all the patent files to see if they can find an old patent which will supersede the later successful one, and then buy it up for a mere nominal sum. After obtaining a reissue, if needed, they commence an onslaught on legitimate business. Now, by the provisions of this section, these patents will not be kept in existence, because people will not be found to pay the continuing fees at the end of four and nine years, and in this way it is estimated that 75 per cent. of the patents issued from which the community does not derive any money benefit, will be wiped out. The remaining one-fourth, probably, secure some useful invention which is likely to benefit the community, and men will be found to pay the continuing fee. Those that are worthless, that are only lying about for speculators to pick up, will be weeded out, and this section will furnish, as we believe, substantial relief.

The rest of the bill we have looked over, and do not advocate or oppose it. We believe it is better than the present law. We simply appear here to urge upon you the two sections to which I have alluded, and we earnestly hope that in some form they will substantially be embodied in a bill to be reported; for we believe that by the enforcement of these provisions we shall be protected from worthless patents, litigation, and oppression in the future.

Mr. WILLETS. Do I understand you that this is a copy of the English law?

Mr. HYDE. I think they have three payments—three, five, ten.

Mr. WILLETS. I see the German law makes an annual payment.

Mr. STORROW. The German is annual; the French is annual; but the English law runs for fourteen years instead of seventeen, and has two payments, but, of course, nearer together than ours. The English payments are £50 and £100.

Mr. HYDE. What we have felt upon that question was that we were willing to give every man a fair time and opportunity to introduce and try his invention. If it is a success, he should have the benefit of it. Having that opportunity, if he does not bring it into actual use it should not be kept alive to trouble subsequent inventions.

Mr. WARD. You were speaking of this pegging-machine infringement. Did not the man in that case go to the Patent Office and get out his patent for the same article?

Mr. HYDE. Yes; I believe it was for portions of a pegging-machine.

The pegging-machines in use include a jack, a knife, and a gauge. The claim was that in these three particulars the machines in use infringed prior patents, which, however, had never been embodied by the inventor in any practical working machine. There were a good many years of time between the alleged inventions.

Take this case of the pegging-machine. If the eleventh section had been in force, nobody would have kept the patents alive; they would have been wiped out, and our community would have been saved from a very large annoyance.

Mr. WARD. That man applied for a pegging-machine.

Mr. HYDE. Yes; but he didn't have a pegging-machine that would operate. He had practically abandoned it, and sold it for a song to the men who reissued it. If you should take his patent and construct a machine as devised, you would have a machine, but it would not operate successfully. He claimed that in the construction of the machines in use there were certain *portions* that infringed his patents which he never put into use. It is fair to say that Judge Woodruff sustained his claim as to one of his patents. That the machine we used did not infringe those patents, we fully believe.

These suits were a very serious interruption to business, and perhaps for that reason, as far as possible, our people avoid litigation, and try in some way to settle, if it is possible to do so. But these two sections furnish us the remedy, and we most earnestly urge their adoption. We believe that there are other portions of the bill that help in the same direction; but we feel if we have these two we shall have the protection and remedy we need.

MR. STORROW'S ARGUMENT.

(Continued from page 271.)

MR. CHAIRMAN AND GENTLEMEN OF THE COMMITTEE:

I am going to speak particularly of the connection between the patent system and the growth of industries that are affected by it. I shall endeavor to show you, as a matter of fact, how the granting of patents does encourage the progress of the arts; but before I begin on that subject I want to call attention to one or two points in addition to the remarks of Mr. Hyde.

Mr. Hyde spoke about the shoe business, and in particular of the manufacture of pegged shoes. There are also a large number of shoes made in which the soles are sewed on. The improvements that went into use in that one branch were principally between 1858 and 1864. Very much greater improvements, requiring more ingenious machinery, were found necessary in sewed than in pegged work, and they have consequently had a more marked effect on the trade. An ordinary kind of shoe—the women's shoe—which is made in the largest numbers, is sold by the manufacturer at about $1.50 a pair, on the average; these are women's gaiter-boots, and comprise the great majority of sewed shoes. Shoes of the same class, from 1850 to 1855 sold for about $2.25 a pair; they now sell for $1.50. The materials which are used in the manufacture of them during this time have gone up 40 to 50 per cent., and wages have more than doubled. For example, along in 1852 and 1853, before machinery was introduced, the women who sewed the uppers together got 50 cents a day; now they get $1.33. Men got $1.12 per day, varying according to their skill, but a fair workman got about that; now they get $2.50—some rather less, many a good deal more.

I went, not long ago, through a Lynn shoe-factory, which turned out a couple of thousand pairs a day. In the bottoming room, as it is called, where the shoe is lasted, the sole and heel put on, trimmed and finished, mostly by men operatives, though there were quite a number of women and boys, the average pay of every individual was $2 a day.

Now, the result of this machinery in that business is, that the shoes are made with more regularity and better sewing. The operative has had his wages doubled, and the hours of labor have been shortened; while the shoe is sold to the public, in the face of the 50 per cent. increase in the cost of material, at $1.50, instead of $2.25, as formerly. And if the work had to be done by hand, in the old way, and the operatives receive their present rate of wages, the shoe would cost at least $1.75 more than now. There are 45,000,000 sewed boots and shoes sold in a year; and you can easily see the gain. I do not mean to say they are sold to consumers for that price, in either case, as there is an addition, probably, of 75 cents on each pair, before they reach the foot of the wearer.

A MEMBER OF THE COMMITTEE. Since what time has material gone up?

Mr. STORROW. Since 1855 the uppers have gone up about 70 per cent., and the sole leather and bottoms have gone up 40 per cent.

Now, on that whole class of machinery used in those factories on those shoes, the entire royalty that is paid on all their machinery—taking it right through everything, and reckoning the extra cost of every machine beyond an ordinary machinist's price for unpatented machines—amounts to about three to three and a quarter cents a pair. I asked a manufacturer, who was using a particular machine, how much he considered was the real cost to him of the use of that patent, and he said the royalty which is included in the cost of that machine is a great deal less than the rent of the additional room which the men would occupy if they did the work by hand. He said that in that sense the royalty did not cost him anything, because the extra rent that he would have to pay to get room for these workmen would more than equal it. In one particular machine alone, that sews on the soles, a single operative does ordinarily about 500 pairs a day, and they have run as high as 1,000 pairs in that time. It was an extremely skillful workman who could by hand sew six pairs a day. How plainly does this illustrate the change!

Take, again, another branch in the same business. I have here some pieces of leather which are fastened together by a machine that has just come into use within a year or two. It fastens the sole to the upper by screwing in a brass or iron wire, which cuts its own hole in the leather, and so securely does it fasten itself that nothing can rip it apart. That machine consists of three principal devices. One is a support that holds the work, another is a rapidly-revolving spindle which screws the wire in, and the third is a device that cuts off the wire. As you all know, a sole varies in thickness in its different parts—in the tap it is thick, and along the shank thinner, and unless the wire should be cut off at the proper time it would stick through the inner sole. That was a difficulty encountered, and it was ingeniously provided for, so that the wire will go through, or almost through the sole accordingly as you adjust the machine, and then, when the machine is once adjusted for the thickness of the leather at any one part of the sole, it varies the length of the screw automatically just as the thickness of the leather varies. That was the result, however, of separate lines of invention.

In this machine the wire is screwed in, but there is another machine which drives it in.

The first machine, which was made in 1858, was very poor and imperfect. Then some other persons, building a different kind of machine, invented for it a support, upon which the shoes could be held. In 1865, some one else devised a nailing machine with the device for cutting the wire at an automatically variable length. It was not until all three of these separate inventions had been put together and combined in one machine with some other inventions, about three years ago, that it became practically and financially successful. Inventors had worked many years in perfecting each; on one since 1858, on another since 1862, on the last since 1865. Each one of these lines of invention has cost over $100,000 in experiments, and, therefore, the combined machine, before it became successful, cost, in experimental expenses, over $300,000. Now, I think you will say that no manufacturer would have spent $300,000 in building one little machine, besides all the time and labor required, unless he knew and was satisfied that when he had completed it he would have the exclusive use of it for a certain term of years. If he had known that at the moment he completed it every one of his neighbors could compete with him, and use it without being burdened with a large outlay of money in experiments, the machine would not be in existence.

Allow me to take another case, which, perhaps, illustrates another point under the patent law. It is sometimes said that a generic invention, the invention of an entirely new class of machines, is of great importance, but that the little improvements are not worthy of patents; that the public do not gain from the use of the latter. That is a very mistaken notion. It is these little improvements that make the machine a practical financial success, and valuable to the public; for the great generic invention often is not of very great value to the public, unless it creates a desire in other practical minds to spend time and money in its perfection. Take the case of the Crompton loom, that Mr. Coffin spoke of. That was a generic invention, and was successful at an early day. At the Middlesex mills, at the present time, they make nearly two or three times as much in quantity, with a corresponding saving in price, as on the original loom. There has been no radical change in the loom, but the continued series of improvements, a little added here and there, largely by Mr. Crompton and his son who succeeded him in carrying on the business, have developed its powers and capacity.

Take another case—the manufacture of plain cotton sheetings since 1838 or 1835, when the business began to assume large proportions. There has been no radical change in the process of manufacture. Almost the only generic change has been in the substitution of what is called ring-spinning for the old-fashioned mule-spinning and flyer-frames. The gain has been by adding a little improvement here and there, which prevented the machines from breaking down, made them run quicker, or did a little better work, with less waste, &c. And yet the result is perfectly enormous. A year or two ago, one of the most competent men in the country made a report to the association of cotton manufacturers about it. He took two mills, one in Massachusetts and one in New Hampshire, which had been since 1835 manufacturing, the one chiefly drillings, and the other sheeting, weighing about $2\frac{9}{10}$ lbs. to the yard. In one of those mills, 90 hands, working 60 hours a week, in 1875 turned out as much cloth as 231 hands, working $76\frac{1}{2}$ hours per week, in 1838; in the other they turned out 23,300 yards per year per operative instead of 9,574 in 1835. Each loom now turns out 12,191 yards a year against 7,766 in 1835, and the cost of labor has been reduced about from 4.8 to 2.85.

The improvement in the condition of the operative is not merely in the shortening of the hours of labor, but his wages have been raised. Comparing the period of 1838 with this present month, when wages are lower than they have been for years, the gain in the wages of the operative in one mill is 22 per cent. in the females and 46 per cent. in the males, and more in the other.

The operatives of these large establishments live mostly in boarding houses, and pay a rate of board regulated by the corporation; the boarding-house keeper is allowed to charge just enough to make a fair profit, but no more. Deducting from their weekly pay, the weekly board which they paid then and now (and that gets out of the way all questions of living), the net gain in the remainder is 40 per cent.; and everybody knows that what has to be bought by the operative out of the remainder of his wages, cotton and woolen cloth, and more particularly ready-made clothing, is a great deal cheaper now than then.

A MEMBER OF THE COMMITTEE. Can you apply that question of clothing to families?

Mr. STORROW. I imagine what is true of one person is true of twenty persons.

The committee here adjourned to Saturday, February 9, 1878, at 10 o'clock a. m.

FEBRUARY 9, 1878—10 a. m.

Mr. STORROW resumes:

Mr. Coffin and Mr. Hyde told you something yesterday of the growth of the industries of the country. I now want to compare the growth of these industries with the growth of the patent system itself, and endeavor, if I can, to trace the connection between the two.

Take the case of the shoe machinery that Mr. Hyde spoke of. There have been granted over 2,000 patents on shoe machinery, shoe tools, lasts, &c. That industry has grown up within twenty years, and it is probable that one-half or two-thirds of these patents are still in existence. I think you can say that, if an industry can ever be ridden to death by patents, it would seem to be this one; and yet the unanimous admission of users or those who pay royalty is, that the patents have created the industry—that it could never have grown and been fostered as under the patent system and by the improvements which the patents embody. Take the case of the Sturtevant pegger, that he spoke of. It is a very good illustration of the practical effect of the system on the industry.

About 1832 the first patent was taken out for peggers, but nothing was accomplished and no very great amount of attention was given to it until about 1848 or 1850, when the patents began to come along pretty rapidly; but no successful pegger was put on the market until Mr. Sturtevant built his machine and brought it out, in about 1857. That machine, although it cost him several years' work and some money, was only the beginning of the enterprise. The next thing that he had to do, in order to make that pegger a practical success, was to make pegs specially adapted to that machine. It took two years to do that. Having discovered that wood in long strips, instead of separate pegs, was essential, he next found it necessary to have a machine to make the peg-wood, cutting it not with the grain, but by taking a round log and, through the use of a peculiar lathe, cutting it off in a spiral ribbon. This is the manner by which you get in one strip the great length that was shown you yesterday. He then had to make another machine, because this ribbon is very tender and delicate when first cut, to wind it up; he had to dry and season it, and that required a peculiar process; and then another machine was required to point it and sharpen the edge—to bevel the edge—so as to make the pegs pointed; and at one time he had a machine in use which would notch the wood, so as to point the pegs on all sides. He found that it was essential to have the bevel always at a certain angle, and he had therefore to construct a machine to grind the knives of the sharpener so as to keep the same angle on the knives, that they might always cut the same way. Then he afterwards devised a machine for compressing these pegs, making the pegs better and the work better. So you see it was not the happy thought of a moment to produce this system of making pegged shoes, but was the result of a long series of inventions, extending over ten years; and I may say, in passing, that the time frequently required to perfect an invention is three to ten or more years.

Mr. Coffin spoke to you about the great number of patents there are on that very little article of pegs. I find there were 276 patents granted on peggers, and that, as near as I can ascertain, about 200 are in existence; there are 2,000 patents on shoe machinery, and I think probably 1,200 or 1,500 are still in existence.

Mr. WILLITS. There are a very small percentage of practical use.

Mr. STORROW. At the present time I suppose there are about ten per cent. that are actually in use. A good many have expired, while a good many others have been superseded, and a good many of these machines embody many patents each. Mr. Sturtevant's, for instance, embodies thirty or forty improvements in its present condition, and I know quite a number of machines embodying a dozen or twenty patents.

Mr. WILLITS. Were those all his patents, or did he buy some of them?

Mr. STORROW. Nearly all his improvements, I think, are his invention; some of them were bought, and some were made by men whom he employed to improve and perfect his machinery. All the patents on the machine expired a year or two ago, but a good many of the auxiliary improvement patents and the patents on the peg-wood remain.

I have referred to the manufacture of boots and shoes, because it affords a good illustration of the effects of the patent system. It may surprise you, but it is the fact, that it is almost the largest industry in the United States. By the census of 1870, the annual product of the business was $181,644,090, and the only products that exceeded it were in the following order: Flouring-mill products, iron in its various forms, and lumber. In the amount of wages paid ($52,000,000 from shoe shops only, besides individual cobblers), iron alone exceeds it. Five-sixths of the work is done in factories, and all this has been the growth of the last twenty years. Hardly a machine is in use that is not subject to a patent; long before the patents expire on a machine, such new improvements are made that the factories find it for their advantage to throw away the old and buy the new. The result of this to the operative and the consumer you have seen; the total royalties are only about two per cent. of the savings due to the inventions, and the amount is so small that its payment or non-payment cannot be felt in the price paid by the ultimate purchaser and consumer. The manufacturers have had their share of annoyance from patents, though it is significative to observe that here, as in many other cases, those annoyances came from legal provisions (in this case attachment by mesne process), which are no part of the patent law, and that the attack was virtually defeated by what will always defeat such attacks—courage, mutual assistance in defense, discretion, and a sense of justice in a judge who would not permit the process of his court to be abused. It is there- fore instructive to see that these men who use this patented machinery have formally met, deliberated upon the matter, and sent their commit- tee and counsel to say to you that they so fully appreciate the benefits of the patent law, that while they want it improved in two particulars which this bill covers, they who feel what some men think its burden, but what they are enlightened enough to see is the real source of its benefits, desire that nothing shall be done to diminish the encourage- ment which it holds out to the inventors, the improvers, the introducers of improved machinery.

Take the case of the horseshoe, which Mr. Coffin described, and note the gain in cheapness. There are over one hundred patents on machines intended for their manufacture. The first was taken out in 1843, and they have been going on from that time, and it was fifteen years after the first one was taken out before the manufacture got perfected so as to make satisfactory work and take its place among the industries of the country. The first horseshoe-nail machine patent was taken out in 1851, and since that time over a hundred patents have been granted in that class.

I described the growth that had taken place in the matter of spinning and weaving cottons. There have been over twelve hundred patents on looms (cotton and woolen), one thousand on spinning machines, three hundred and fifty on carding, and many more on machines for other parts of the process, such as dressing, and so on. One happy thought, matured at a moment, coming into place just at the instant some one wanted it, has not done this. It has required a long period of time and the labor of many men to perfect and make practical labor-saving ma- chinery.

There is one fact which may be noted by examining the Patent Office reports, and that is, that the same name occurs again and again; that is, a man who has made one invention is very apt to continue along and be continually making machines of the same class, or of classes to which his early inventions have directed his attention. A successful invention has given him the means, and has taught him those habits of concen- trated thought which are essential for an inventor.

I want now to trace, by figures taken from the census, and other sources, the correspondence between the patent system and the growth of the industries of the country. I do not believe that the gentlemen of this committee are aware of the importance of the manufacturing indus- tries of this country. We sometimes speak of ours as an agricultural nation, raising raw products with great advantage. I do not know the figures that exist to day, but by the census of 1870, the mechanical and manufacturing products of this country were almost twice the agricul- tural products. By the census of 1870, the agricultural products of the country were $2,447,538,658, and the manufactured products $4,232,- 325,442; wages of farm laborers, including board, $310,286,285; wages of operatives, $775,584,343. The growth has been altogether out of propor- tion to the population. Between 1850 and 1870, our population increased 65 per cent., while our manufacturing industries increased in value 322 per cent. Part of this is owing to general rise in values; but, after making all the allowances suggested by the able discussion in the quarto vol- ume of the census, our manufactures have increased three times as fast as our population in the last twenty years; so that we are not only grow ing in manufactures as we grow as a nation, but we are growing to be come a great manufacturing nation, and the manufactures of the country are throwing the agricultural interests into the shade. Take the single article of cotton: since 1830, our population has increased between three-fold and fourfold; the amount of cotton manufactured in this country has increased thirteen-fold.

I think you will be surprised to see how these industries are distributed at the present time. Taking the census of 1850, 1860, and 1870 as a basis (and I take these three because, although I have not entire faith in all the results set forth in or directly obtained from the census-table, without allowing for other elements not shown therein,* yet as the census for these three years were taken under the same law, that of 1850, upon the same schedules, and by the same organization) the results which those three years present will be a tolerably fair basis for comparison.

In 1850 the mechanical industries of the six great Western States were considerably less than half that of the New England States—45 per cent. of the New England industries; 135 million dollars for the Western States and 283 millions for New England. In 1870 it was 91 per cent., or 914 millions for those States against 1,009 millions for New England; and at the present time there is every reason to believe that they exceed the industries of the New England States, although I have not been able to get at any figures to show exactly what they are at the present time. The last report of the Board of Trade of Chicago says that in spite of the present depression of business, there are to day 1,664 more workmen employed in the manufacturing establishments of Chicago alone than a year ago.

In 1870 the manufacturing industries of Ohio, Indiana, Illinois, Missouri, Iowa, Wisconsin, and Minnesota gave a product of $937,000,000, while the agricultural industries of the same States brought only $861,000,000.

In Illinois, which has been looked on as a great agricultural State, the agricultural product was $210,860,000 and the manufactured product $205,620,000. In Missouri the agricultural product was $103,000,000 and the manufactured $206,200,000. Even in Wisconsin the manufactured product was $77,200,000, while the agricultural was only $78,-000,000; and in Ohio the manufactures were far ahead, and so through those States.

Mr. HURLBUT. In that $77,000,000 manufactured product of Wisconsin, do they not include the lumber?

Mr. STORROW. Yes, sir; I think they do, and I think they should; its

---

*An attempt was made some years ago to show an enormous profit in the manufacture of patented articles from the figures given in the census, by adding together the cost of materials and labor of operatives, subtracting their sum from the value of the product, calling the difference the profit, and comparing it with the sum reported as capital employed. The fallacy of this is seen at a glance. The Superintendent of the Census reports that the capital employed is at least twice that shown by the tables, and that those figures are totally unreliable. This mode of computation takes no note of general expenses, depreciation, repairs, advertising, and bad debts, which often amount to two or three times the cost of labor. It takes no note, in the case of patented articles, of the actual expense even of inventing, improving, experimenting, and perfecting. Mr. J. S. Perry, of Albany, has shown that the same rule applied to unpatented industries discloses, in large groups of manufactures of unpatented articles, much larger profits; i. e., on one group, covering a product of several hundred millions, 99¼ per cent. profit.

He might have added many instances. The same rule applied to the tables would show that both in 1860 and 1870 the average profit on all manufactures was 45 to 50 per cent. a year on the capital; that in Missouri, in 1870, the average profit of all industries was 74 per cent., and on the manufacture of tobacco 102 per cent. Of course every one knows that no such profit is realized; and the application of the assumed rule shows that though "there are millions in it," there is not one word of truth.

value consists in the labor put upon it. I think they also include flour;
but in the export tables I shall refer to presently neither flour nor lumber is included.

Mr. ELDREDGE. The grain would be included in the agricultural product?

Mr. STORROW. Certainly wheat would be included in the agricultural
products, and the timber would be, I suppose. There is another way to
get at the relative importance of the two, which I think is better still,
and that is in the wages paid. These States show as follows:

States.	AGRICULTURE.		MANUFACTURES.	
	Products.	Wages.	Products.	Wages.
Ohio	$198,256,907	$16,480,778	$269,713,610	$49,066,488
Indiana	122,914,302	9,675,348	108,617,278	18,366,780
Illinois	210,860,585	22,338,767	205,620,672	31,100,244
Missouri	103,035,759	8,797,487	206,213,429	31,055,445
Iowa	114,386,441	9,377,878	46,534,322	6,893,292
Wisconsin	78,027,032	8,186,110	77,214,326	13,575,642
Minnesota	33,446,400	4,459,201	23,110,700	4,052,837
Total of States	860,927,426	79,315,569	937,124,337	153,110,728
Whole United States	2,447,538,658	310,286,285	4,232,325,442	775,584,343

In these census tables the value of the board of the farm-hands is
added to the cash wages paid, and included in the tables as part of the
wages stated, and the sum given for agricultural products includes not
merely salable products, but the value of all farm improvements. Whatever allowance be made for mechanics and small manufacturers working
for themselves, and for farmers working on their own farms, it is clear
that within the last twenty-five years maunfactures, and not agriculture,
have come to be the great interest of the nation. Indeed, the census of
1870 shows that the *net* value added to the raw material by the process
of manufacture—that is, the difference between cost of raw material and
value of product—is undoubtedly more than the *gross* value of salable
agricultural products.

Now, I find, by comparing industries given in the census tables with
the business of the Patent Office, a remarkable coincidence in the growth
of the two. In 1850 the manufactured product was 1,000 million dollars;
in 1860 it was 1,800 million dollars, while in 1870 it was 4,200 million
dollars. The growth in the Patent Office took place chiefly at two stages.
One great jump was in 1854. For the four years before that the average issue had been 961 a year, while for the six years after that the average was 2,931 a year. And a still greater jump took place between
1860 and 1870—about 1865, when the average ran up from 3,000 to over
7,000. It is now 12,000 to 13,000 patents for new inventions. In the
same way, as I told you the other day, the patents taken out in the Western States have run up. In 1850 about one-half as many patents were
taken out in those six Western States (113) as in New England (221),
and a great many less than in New York (235). In 1870, for the first
time, these six Western States took out more than New England (3,528
for those States against 3,188 for New England), and at the present
time they take out 50 per cent. more (in 1877, 3,677 for those six States
against 2,479 for New England). Now, you cannot help seeing that the
industries of the whole country have grown with the patent system, and
if you take different localities, or compare different localities, you will

find that those places have gained most rapidly in industries which have grown most rapidly in the number of patents they have taken out.

I tried, from the census, to see if I could find out how much the improvements in machinery had increased the power of human labor, and I have sought to get at it in this way: If we take $100,000 of raw material to a factory and find that at the end of the year the manufactured product is worth $150,000, we know that $50,000 has been added by the operatives of that factory; and if there are 1,000 men, they have added $50 each; if 500 men, they have added $100 apiece. Now, applying that rule to the census, I find that in 1850, the value of the labor of an operative in a manufacturing establishment was $483. In 1870 it was $870, taking skilled and unskilled laborers together. At the same time his wages have been increased. The average yearly wages of mechanics, comparing 1850 with 1870, was $247 in the former and $377 in the latter year; and, as I showed you yesterday, the net result of gain to the operative would be something like 40 per cent. now as compared with thirty or forty years ago.

The following table includes only those establishments which produce over $500 a year; that is, it does not include the mechanics so common in the villages, who employ no men, but only live from the labor of their own hands. The first four columns are taken from "Compendium of the Ninth Census" (pp. 796–'9), and the last two columns are formed from them in the manner described (*i. e.*), e, power of labor, $= \frac{d-c}{a}$; f wages per hand per year $= \frac{b}{a}$. The population has been—1850, 23,191,876; 1860, 31,443,321; 1870, 38,558,371; and you will notice how much greater the increase in the hands employed, the total wages paid, and the total product is than the increase in population:

	(*a*) Hands employed.	(*b*) Wages per annum.	(*c*) Material used.	(*d*) Value of product.	*e.*	*f.*
1850...............	957,059	$236,765,446	$555,123,822	$1,019,106,616	$483	$247
1860...............	1,311,264	387,878,966	1,031,605,092	1,885,861,676	651	296
1870...............	2,053,996	775,584,343	2,446,427,242	4,232,325,442	870	377

For some other facts connected with the growth of industries, see page 130, *infra*.

I tried in another way to get at the effect of these improvements on the industries of our country. I considered the question of supplying our own market with the manufactured articles, and more particularly the question of supplying the neutral foreign markets—the supplying of which latter class depends upon the cheapness with which products can be offered. To be sure, commercial facilities, steamship lines, geographical position, and other causes have a good deal to do with it, but still, in the long run, every one will buy of the manufacturers who manufacture the cheapest. It appears from the exports and imports of this country that we have been steadily gaining on England in this respect. For the ten years ending in 1830, our average exports of manufactured articles and industrial products were $6,550,000, out of a total export of $53,221,241; for the ten years ending 1850, they were $15,750,000, out of a total of $112,000,000; while last year they were $152,000,000, out of a total of $632,000,000. But the mere growth in amount is not all that I wish you to notice. Since 1850 the manufactured articles have increased faster than the raw materials in our exports, and it is matter of common knowledge among those engaged in industrial pursuits that, unless loaded by duties on raw materials, we have now come to the point where we can compete with England in large classes of our manufactured products; and the movement for export trade, which has become so active within a few years, testifies to this. The figures given are taken from report of Bureau of Statistics for April, 1875, and No. 4 for 1877. The classification (manufactured and unmanufactured) adopted in the former paper is followed, except that I have placed among manufactured articles cheese, now mostly made in factories; refined oil, 20 per cent. of the value of which is added at the refineries, mostly by patented processes and patented apparatus, while the wells are drilled and pumped by patented machinery, cleared out and enlarged by patented torpedoes, and the product is transported in patented packages. I have not included dressed lumber or flour among the manufactured articles. I might, however, with propriety, for the purposes for which I am using these figures (though I have not), have included breadstuffs among our industrial products, for without the machinery which inventions (still patented) have given us, the crop could be neither sowed nor harvested, nor thrashed, nor shelled. If we had men enough to do it, they could not compete with the cheaper labor of the basin of the Danube and the Black Sea.

Now, in this same way, within the last few years, we have succeeded in diminishing our imports; and the great diminution has come, not in the raw materials to be worked up and used in this country, but in the manufactured articles.

The quarterly report, No. 4, for 1877, of the Bureau of Statistics, p. 251, shows our imports:

	1875.	1876.	1877.
Manufactured articles	$318,292,024	$254,934,784	$256,790,875
Crude or partly manufactured	200,554,801	191,003,982	181,737,255
Totals	518,846,825	435,938,766	438,528,130

That is, the falling-off has not been chiefly in the import of raw materials, but of manufactured articles.

Our exports have been as follows:

	1875.	1876.	1877.
Unmanufactured and partly manufactured	$451,496,479	$469,140,489	$481,044,111
Industrial products	107,741,159	125,676,382	151,935,969
Totals	559,237,638	594,816,971	632,980,098

With England and France, it has been just the other way. Their exports of manufactured articles have decreased; their imports of manufactured articles have increased. The tables on page 568 of the same report give the following figures for the first six months of each of the following years:

ENGLAND.

	1875.	1876.	1877.
Total imports	$887,047,686	$893,156,715	$943,038,530
Total exports	529,994,212	476,392,743	451,765,329

Articles other than raw materials and food.

	1875.	1876.	1877.
Imports	$269,147,764	$271,274,624	$284,710,319
Exports	353,177,069	318,587,837	296,394,925

FRANCE.

	1875.	1876.	1877.
Total imports	$316,613,412	$349,227,903	$349,839,134
Total exports	362,489,126	343,291,802	320,954,368

Articles other than raw materials and food.

Imports	$103,299,969	$107,842,610	$109,168,327
Exports	167,208,831	150,595,391	136,545,956

It is tolerably clear, therefore, that in the markets of the world we are gaining ground, because we can give the purchasers more value for less money. We can afford to sell many manufactured articles cheaper; and when you ask how that is, turn right back to the table of the census, and you find that, by the use of the improved machinery, the operative can produce two, three, and four times as much in different branches of industry as he did twenty years ago. Undoubtedly improved machinery is not the only cause of our growth as compared with England in the exportation and importation of manufactured products since 1850; but cheapness is the *sine qua non* of this; not absolute cheapness merely, but a continued cheapening, greater than has been accomplished in England.

Now, this directly bears on the patent system in this way: The improvements of our machinery have been effected by our patent system out of all proportion to the manner in which the patent system of England has affected their industries. Our patent system has been made cheap and popular, and has reached every workman of inventive mind, for the number of patents granted shows that it reaches almost every workshop in the land. Up to 1855, England granted about the same number of patents that we did. In 1855, she granted 2,044 patents, and we granted 2,024. But in the next year our great patent growth took place, while hers went along with a slow increase, till now we grant perhaps 10,000 a year more than England; say, 13,500 against 3,500.

The increased growth in industrial progress which I have shown you in this country, and as compared with England, has coincided with the period during which we have surpassed her in the granting of patents.

Belgium is looked upon as one of the most prosperous manufacturing states in the world. Her territory is only one-fifth as large as the State of Illinois; she grants about 2,500 patents a year.

If we take a few branches of our export business that have shown themselves particularly flourishing, we shall find how patented improvements help instead of hurting them.

Cheese is one of our large exports at the present time, and it is made almost entirely in factories. About 1851 or 1852 the factory system of making cheese was first started. About 1855 it grew to a substantial industry. Its great growth was about 1864 and 1865. We consume in this country not far from a hundred million pounds in a year. In 1855 we exported five million pounds, though that was rather a small year; last year we exported a hundred and seven million, and so far this year the exports are twenty per cent. greater than last year. All of this great industrial work has grown up under the patent system. Up to and during the time when we exported but a small amount of it, say from 1790 to 1849, inclusive, we had granted about one patent a year on appliances for cheese-making, but from 1850 to 1859 we granted about four patents a year, and from 1860 to the present time we are granting about thirteen a year; so that a large part of the appliances used are still subject to existing patents. I suppose hardly one can be found that is not; and yet the growth and progress of the art applied to that industry (relatively, if not absolutely, for all animal food has about doubled in cost throughout the populous part of the civilized world in the last fifteen years), just as in the case of all the others, has cheapened the product, enabling us, not by a fall in the price of milk,

but by lessening the cost of manufacture, to surpass other nations that
have not grown in patented inventions applied to this industry.
Now take the saw business. There is a large manufactory in Philadelphia that makes saws—Disston & Sons. Saws have been a subject
of patents from a pretty early date, and over 2,300 patents have been
issued on saws and saw-mills. Mr. Disston and his associates have
taken out a very large number of patents, so that there is not a thing
done in their manufactory that is not the subject of their patent, and
yet within the last fifteen years the capacity of each operative has increased fivefold, his wages have increased one-third, and they have so
cheapened their product that they have not only nearly succeeded in
driving out English saws from our market, but have created a large
export business to England, France, and all over the civilized world
where saws are used. In that way America is driving out English
saws, because they can lay them down cheaper and better in every respect.

Lobdell & Co., of Wilmington, Del., are manufacturing patented
car-wheels and chilled rollers under patents taken out by them. Their
car-wheels, I think, have some improvements in the manner of chilling
the metal and of forming and bracing the web; these features and
pretty much all their work are covered by their patents, but they have
so improved and cheapened their product that they can compete with
England abroad. They are supplying nearly all the street-railroads of
England and France with car-wheels made in Delaware. They were
also sending to South America car-wheels for steam-roads and street-
railroads; sending calender-rolls for paper, for rolling India rubber,
and for rolling sheet-metal, to England, to a large extent. They have
recently obtained a large contract for a set of rolling-machinery for
Japan, in competition with English makers.

Baeder, Adamson & Co., of Philadelphia, are another concern that
are having a similar experience, and a pretty interesting one in some
respects. Their business is the utilization of what may be termed waste
materials. They take all those portions of animals that are not good
for food, and from them manufacture tallow, glue, horn, bone, curled
hair, and so on. Their business is covered with patents based chiefly
upon inventions of Mr. Adamson. They now have an enormous export
business of sand-paper and emery-paper, and are driving out the English articles almost entirely. They export rawhide whips and curled
hair to Germany, England, and other countries in large quantities.

A gentleman of Philadelphia, who has accurate knowledge on the
subject, reports to me that the exports of articles manufactured under
patents or by patented machinery from Philadelphia alone, last year,
were eleven and a half million dollars, not including furs, breadstuffs,
articles of diet, or fresh beef. The export of fresh beef, due to several
American inventions, was more than a million dollars from Philadelphia
alone.

From the establishment of Adams & Westlake, in Chicago, locomotive head-lights made by patented machinery go to England and South
America.

Wheels and carriage-trimmings and hardware go to England, as Mr.
Coffin has told you; and all this can be done only because our manufacturers can lay down their goods in those countries cheaper than foreign manufacturers can make them with their cheaper labor, because
the patent law has stimulated the inventions under which and by which
they are manufactured.

Messrs. Baeder, Adamson & Co. are now engaged in perfecting an invention which is to be of enormous value, an account of which was given in a paper read before the Cotton Manufacturers' Association last fall, and from that and other sources I derive my information. They are endeavoring to perfect a process of utilizing cotton-seed by making oil from it. Of course we all know that this oil is made and used to a very considerable extent now, but still the manufacture is in its infancy. If I understand the figures, for every pound of cotton there are about two and a quarter pounds of cotton seed.

Mr. AIKEN. There are twenty-four bushels of cotton-seed to every four hundred pounds of lint, and a bushel of cotton-seed weighs thirty-two pounds.

Mr. STORROW. Two and a quarter pounds of seed they call it. Thirteen hundred pounds of cotton, as it is picked, make four hundred pounds of lint.

Mr. AIKEN. One-third is generally considered to be the result of clean cotton—thirty-three per cent.

Mr. STORROW. Yes, that is about it. Nine hundred pounds of seed out of thirteen hundred pounds of the material as picked; nine hundred pounds of seed to four hundred pounds of baled cotton.

Now, the cotton-seed oil, when properly prepared and purified and refined, is one of the most valuable oils known to commerce, and is taking the place very largely of olive oil for the purposes of salad and table uses, and for burning, and a very large export business has grown up in sending it to Italy and the Mediterranean, to be made into olive-oil soap.

Mr. Adamson is a large manufacturer, and by the process which he thinks he has nearly completed he will be enabled, in the first place, to take the cotton-seed and remove from it the lint which the gin cannot take away. This lint is about ten per cent. of the whole yield, and that he makes into paper stock. Then he removes the hull or husk of the seed, which has some valuable ingredients—phosphates—and then presses the farinaceous matter which is left for the oil. He then refines the oil. Now, if he succeeds, as he thinks he has about done, the estimate which he makes—and it is a very low one—is that the cotton-seed will be worth from $30 to $40 a ton; and a very few figures will show you that it will add thirty to forty per cent. to the value of the cotton product of the South. That there is a market for the oil, and that this business is growing, is shown by the export figures. In 1876 the export of cotton-seed oil was $146,135, and in 1877 it was $842,248, and there appears to me to be no limit to the amount that can be used. It will supplant olive oil certainly in the arts, and will take the place of a great many other kinds of oil.

Now, Mr. Adamson is not going to spend years in experiment—his money, time, years of labor—if the moment he has completed his process his neighbor can step in and take the invention in its perfected condition, thus depriving him of the whole fruits of his exertions. He is doing it, as he has made all his improvements, for the sake of taking out patents and reaping his reward. Improvement after improvement he has taken out patents for—I do not know how many; but his name is constantly met with on the index of the Patent-Office reports.

I speak of these particular instances, because I happen to know about them, but they are only examples; other branches of industry show as many.

We have got within the last year some very interesting testimony from foreign sources as to the value of the patent system. In England their system, though theoretically perhaps not bad, yet practically it

318 MR. J. J. STORROW.

has not been what we consider a good patent system. That is to say, the expense of taking out patents is great, the expenses of litigating are enormous, and, more than that, the system has not become popularized so as to reach the working class. The habit and tone of mind among the large manufacturers, with some notable exceptions, has been to discourage their workmen from taking out patents, and the consequence is that, with a manufacturing population larger than ours, they take out about 3,500 instead 13,000 patents; and they find, as a consequence, that they do not get inventions and improvements as we do. Recently they have been agitating various modifications of the patent law, though I think without a great deal of wisdom. In 1875, after a long inquiry, government introduced a bill to amend the patent system; it was obvious upon inspection of it that it was not the work of practical men, but the work of theorists; they were continually afraid of chimerical dangers. It bore the marks of being the work of men who had no extended knowledge of the actual operation of the system on manufacturing industries. It hung along, and after it had been debated more or less in the House of Lords and in the House of Commons, it was withdrawn and a new one brought in, in 1876, I think; but this also was objected to by the best men for similar reasons.

Sir William Thomson went home from our Centennial Exhibition, and just as he had got home he appeared before the British Association, before the section of steam-engineering, of which he is the president; and, in giving them an account of what he had seen in this country, he called their attention very sharply to the effect of patent laws on the improvement of labor-saving machinery. He told them that unless the countries of Europe speedily amended their patent laws, and unless they amended them in a contrary direction to the bill pending in Parliament, they must understand that they would lose their manufacturing supremacy, and that America would take it from them. Another gentleman (Mr. St. John V. Day), discussing the pending patent bill quite in detail at the same meeting, declared that, unless they improved their system so as to give more general encouragement to inventors, they would lose their manufacturing supremacy, and with that would give up their commercial supremacy, for that depended on their ability to cheaply supply neutral markets; and, after an interesting discussion, the association resolved that a committee be appointed to procure changes in the law, so that it might be more favorable to inventors. The consequence has been, that only last June (1877) government withdrew their pending bill.

Mr. Hulse, the English judge of textile machinery at the Centennial, says of our patent system, and the appreciation of inventions by the people generally:

As regards extent of invention and ingenuity, the United States was far ahead of other nations. I do not remember an exhibitor who had not some features of novelty and ingenuity to claim in the machines he exhibited, and as regards consummateness of invention and arrangement of mechanism (due to an older experience) the palm was, in my judgment, earned for Great Britain. The extraordinary extent of ingenuity and invention existing in the United States, and manifested throughout the exhibition, I attribute to the natural aptitude of the people, fostered and stimulated by an admirable patent law and system, and to the appreciation of inventions by the people generally.

Mr. WILLITS. As I understand, they do not have the model system there. Before you get through, will you say something about it?

Mr. STORROW. No, sir; I shall not. The change proposed in the model system does not come within the scope of the bill now before you; but I will give you a copy of a brief prepared by Mr. Howson of Philadelphia, a gentleman of high standing and very long experience in his profession; he knows much more about it than I do, but I will say his views have a great deal of force. I think I like them.

In Prussia, in 1868, Prince Bismarck sent a communication to the Parliament, in which he spoke very harshly of the patent laws, and asserted that they did not promote the progress of the useful arts, rather intimating that they had better be abolished. I don't wonder much at it, from his experience. Their law exposed the public to sufficient annoyance, and it was neither framed nor administered so as to reach or encourage inventive talent everywhere. It was not, in effect, a patent system, as we understand it. But the result of the Vienna and Philadelphia expositions was to wake them up to a necessity of improving their machines, and, as a proper method of bringing that about, they came to believe that they must improve their patent laws, so as to really offer encouragement to inventors, and last May they passed a very fair patent law, based very largely on our system.

Switzerland never had any patent law, and it has been held up, time and time again, as a country the people of which were shrewd enough to avoid patent laws, which objectors said might impose a tax on her citizens, while the absence of such laws would leave them free to adopt whatever might be useful in the patented inventions of other nations. It was a country very well situated for that purpose. The people are industrious, intelligent, cultivated, educated, and free; they have been long trained in some of the nicest of mechanical industries, and one would think that if the experiment could be made to ever succeed, it would be in such a country and with such a people. Well, the Swiss sent over here two commissioners of more than ordinary intelligence, Mr. Favre-Perret and Mr. Bally. Mr. Favre-Perret was a watchmaker of prominence, and is the author of the report, which I suppose you you know of—the report made on English and Swiss watches, comparing the American machine watches with, not the cheap, but the very best English and Swiss products—and finding the superiority in favor of the Waltham watches. That report has been published by Robbins & Appleton, the agents in New York of the American Watch Company of Waltham, and it is interesting reading. When he went home he made a speech to his constituents (published in the same pamphlet of Robbins & Appleton), and told them plainly that unless they went to work to improve their methods and modes of making watches, the superiority which Switzerland had for fifty or a hundred years retained in watchmaking was gone. The other commissioner, Mr. Bally, is a man who had peculiar advantages in maturing his judgment with regard to our industries. He is the largest shoe manufacturer in Europe. He has an enormous establishment at Schoenenwerth, between Basle and Zurich. He has been in this country several times. His factory is fitted with American machines, set up for him by American mechanics, and he has been here often enough to know our method of organizing labor, and he is not at all lacking in capacity. He is, therefore, a most favorable example of the Swiss idea of adopting the inventions of others, and relying on the ordinary stimulus of manufacturing competition for domestic improvements. He declares that plan a total failure. He went home in despair at the results of our machinery. Within six months after his return, shoes made in Massachusetts were laid down in Switzerland, freight all paid, at a price less than he could produce them at.

He has written a pamphlet to arouse his countrymen. He tells them that when he has filled his factory with imported American machinery, the Americans, paying three times as much per day for labor, can beat him in quality and cost of product—the Americans improve the machines so much faster than he can; they use them so much better, so much quicker than he can teach his men to do. To make progress in industrial arts, to improve the construction of machinery and the use of it, the inventions cannot be imported; they must be the growth of the soil. The nation that originates will always be ahead of the nation that copies, and the same causes that educate one workman up to the point of inventing will educate his fellows up to the point of skillfully using, and nothing else will do it. He said this, and he told his countrymen that, among other things, and as one of the first means to the end, they must adopt a patent system. His pamphlet has been published in French at Neufchatel, with an appendix by Mr. Dubied, further enforcing the same lessons. And both these writers apply their remarks not only to watches and shoes, but to leather, ribbons, cotton tape, cheese, and other articles. The pamphlet is so interesting that in the course of a week or so I shall endeavor to send a translation of it to the gentlemen of the committee.

All these results show the connection between the growth of industry, the cheapening of the product, and the growth of the patent system better than any theoretical argument. It cannot be true that the growth of the patent system injures the progress of the useful arts, when we find that the growth of the one has accompanied the growth of the other in this country and in each particular section of this country; that the inventive skill of the West, within the last ten or fifteen years (recorded on the files of the Patent Office), has created industries and localized them there; built up industries at home; that we have been surpassing other nations in the cheapness of the products furnished to neutral markets. We must recognize these good effects of the system, and must act upon it, as the best minds of other countries are recognizing it and acting upon it; and all the more so because we have profited by it and practically originated it.

Sometimes it is said, Mr. Chairman and gentlemen, that the demand for inventions and the demand for improvements in machinery will create the supply. What does that mean? Certainly it is a law that political economists have delighted in, have acted upon, have relied upon, and with good reason, from experience—that the demand will create the supply. What does the law mean when you analyze it? Does it mean, if one hundred thousand men want bread, that the fact that they want it will bring it if they have got no money to pay for it? Does it mean that the supply will come *when the demand comes from men ready to pay for the supply when they receive it?* Now, that law will create inventions. If the inventor is rewarded, if he is going to supply a demand that will pay him, that demand will bring the supply. That is what the law of supply and demand means, and it is precisely on that that our patent system is founded.

Mr. TOWNSHEND. I wish to ask you this question: You stated that the improvements in agricultural labor-saving machinery and manufacturing machinery had reduced the demand for labor.

Mr. STORROW. Not at all, sir. I did not say that, I think. I said they had increased the power of labor, the productiveness, the capacity of the workman.

Mr. TOWNSHEND. Let me state a case. I know a farm of over 1,800 acres which is operated almost entirely by machinery. Before these improvements in agricultural implements, that farm was covered to a great extent with tenants, and also a large number of men were employed to harvest, &c. Since the introduction of labor-saving machinery, the farm is run by one-tenth the labor, and there are no tenants. I ask you if the introduction of labor-saving machinery has not decreased the demand for labor?

Mr. STORROW. Do you know where those tenants are now?

Mr. TOWNSHEND. It is asserted that a great number of them are now out of employment.

Mr. STORROW. Isn't it a fact that they have employment elsewhere? Are they not in Minnesota, or Wisconsin, or Nebraska, farming by machinery at twice the wages they used to get? The experience of the whole world has been that the introduction of labor-saving machinery for the first year or two in a particular industry undoubtedly throws men out of employment; but the cheapening of the product in consequence of its use increases the demand for the product, so that there is a continually increasing field for the employment of a larger number of men.

Mr. TOWNSHEND. Take, for instance, the shoe-manufacturing business of Massachusetts.

Mr. STORROW. There is a great deal more employment in that business now than formerly.

Mr. TOWNSHEND. I do not so understand it. I understand that one man now does the average work of what formerly required the labor of ten men.

Mr. STORROW. Of about four, on an average; but in certain classes they do the work of about ten men.

Mr. TOWNSHEND. What has become of the other nine?

Mr. STORROW. They are making more shoes, or they are doing something else. There are twice as many used now as formerly.

Mr. TOWNSHEND. As I understood you, you said that under the old system the material was distributed to the people, who took it to their homes and made it up.

Mr. STORROW. Yes, sir; quite largely. Now they are collected in factories. Lynn and Haverhill and Brockton and Marlborough have grown enormously since the introduction of machinery.

Mr. TOWNSHEND. You say that these men have found employment elsewhere?

Mr. STORROW. Undoubtedly. Let me give you an illustration. I myself remember when railroads were very new in our section of the country. When I first knew railroads, the conductors were the old stage-drivers who had been driven off their lines. The fear which was expressed then—expressed also in England—was, that these miserable railroads would destroy the necessity for horses; that the stage-lines would be all taken off, and there would be no more market for oats to be raised. Well, the result has been that there is no country in the world so covered with railroads as England, and there is no country where horse-flesh is in such demand. Why, the number of horses required to take people to the depots is far larger than the old stage-routes required. I heard of a case in New Hampshire of an old farmer who was very much disturbed by the introduction of a railroad through his place. He said there would be no more market for his oats; but what was the result? Why, in three years his oats had doubled in value, because there was a bigger demand for them and facilities for marketing. Now, if you take the introduction of these patented improvements, you will find that just at that spot where they are introduced there is sometimes a diminution of the demand for labor in that particular industry for a few years, but you will also find that the demand for the product is so increased that the amount of labor required is increased. Let me see if I cannot give you some figures that directly show it.

In speaking of the great improvement of labor-saving machinery between 1850 and 1870, I told you of the increase in the wages paid, which certainly does not show any diminution in the demand for labor. Take the case of the sewing machines, where one operator does the work of I don't know how many women; I suppose there are twenty times as many workwomen employed now as twenty-five years ago. The whole business of making clothing has gone on increasing, and many more stitches are taken in everything, and the demand for labor has gone on and kept pace with it. In fitting (sewing) uppers of shoes women used to earn half a dollar a day by hand. Now they do it by sewing-machines run by power, and they earn $1.33 a day.

Mr. TOWNSHEND. You don't think the number of tramps has been increased?

Mr. STORROW. Very likely it has been; but one reason is that we are growing to be an older country, and we have more of that peculiar population that makes tramps. Beside, in the past year or two, there has been great depression in everything, which has thrown people out of employment.

Mr. TOWNSHEND. Does not depression mean that men cannot get work?

Mr. STORROW. I do not think it means that altogether. That is one thing it means. You will remember that the men were thrown out of work by stoppage of establishments ruined by the panic. The want of work did not precede, but followed, the financial troubles, though it has undoubtedly increased and prolonged them—perhaps I should rather say formed a part of them.

Mr. AIKEN. It means they don't work, because a heap of them won't work.

Mr. STORROW. One way to get out of that difficulty—that depression —is by improving our labor-saving machines, and trying very hard first to export our products, by making them cheap enough to compete with other nations, to export to China and South America. We export from America cotton cloth enough to supply about five million people. There are three hundred and fifty million people in China who want machine-made cloth, and one-half as many in South America, and that is the way to overcome this depression; and we have just about got to that point where we can export. And exporting manufactured articles means that all the world comes here to give employment to our workmen.

Mr. TOWNSHEND. If I understand you, then, you concede that, at the present time, at least, the present improvements of labor-saving machinery does throw men out of employment?

Mr. STORROW. I do not concede that. The introduction of one particular machine will undoubtedly throw men out of employment in that particular branch, at one particular moment, but after awhile the demand will increase, and more men will be continually employed. Mr. Coffin gave an instance where the demand increased so fast that more men were employed almost from the start.

Now, all labor-saving machines are not made and introduced in one day; the change is continual, and therefore continually at different stages; and when one machine does for the moment at one factory diminish the demand for labor in one branch of the work, the cheapening of the product as the result of an invention of a previous year, the mere supply of the new and useful thing in perhaps some other industry is that day calling for more labor. Of course, there are other temporary causes; a financial crisis or other disturbance paralyzes industry or agriculture, and throws men out of work; but that has happened just as often and quite as severely at periods and in industries not affected by the recent introduction of labor-saving machines.

Our people consume more than twelve times as much cotton cloth as they did in 1830, though the population has only increased about three-fold. And this results from the increased product and the diminished cost of it which increases the demand; and in this not only has the demand for labor kept up, but the wages have increased.

I think this is the best possible proof, in the long run, that labor is not less in demand than formerly.

Mr. TOWNSHEND. Since 1860 you have largely increased the amount of labor that you had in the manufacturing establishments in the East?

Mr. STORROW. It has been very largely increased.

Mr. TOWNSHEND. Now, what is the effect of these improvements in machinery in the West and South and the agricultural section of the continent?

Mr. STORROW. Well, sir, the effect on the West is that their manufactories in those Western States have grown up to be as large as ours in the East, and have grown a great deal faster, and that absorbs some of the labor. More wheat is raised, and that absorbs labor.

A large market is made for raw cotton, for example, because it can be spun to a greater advantage, more cheaply, and a greater demand is created for cloth, and consequently for cotton to make it of. A farmer can raise more crops, his crops can be better utilized, and can be better sold to other people, because they are comparatively cheaper when he has got them raised; and if you look through the census you will see that the agricultural laborers have steadily increased in number, just as operatives in manufactories have.

The suggestions made by the honorable member of the committee are directed to the increase of labor-saving machinery, and are not affected by the fact that that machinery is or is not patented; but the pertinency of those suggestions is that they assume, and, I am sure, correctly assume, that the invention and introduction of that improved machinery is due to the patent system; and they go upon the ground that a patent system does promote the progress of the useful arts, not only by creating and introducing improved machinery, but by, at once, so cheapening the product that the old system of labor cannot compete with the new; and the inquiry is, whether the progress of the useful arts is helpful or hurtful to the State, improving or injurious to those workmen who are engaged in the arts. The direct effect upon the moral and intellectual condition of the workmen I hope my associate and senior, Mr. Smith, will speak about. The inquiry put relates directly to their employment.

The argument that would reject all labor-saving inventions as contrary to public policy, is answered by the spirit of the age. The railroads will not make it, for those inventions have created them as a means of surpassing the old method of foot and horse, and no one will say that they are a curse. All other interests of this country are in the same position. If such an argument were made, I should not waste time in replying to it. I have only wanted to answer directly the specific question put, because the facts stated indicate the reply that society makes to the whole question.

The question is an interesting one, but it is not new, and experience has answered it. When Lee invented the stocking-frame, in 1589, Elizabeth, and afterwards James, would not patent it (it was before the statute of monopolies, so called, the statute which abolished monopolies and allowed patents), because, they said, it would throw the hand-knitters out of employment. Yet there are probably a hundred times as many hosierymakers now as there were then. The inventions of Watt and Arkwright, the introduction of cotton spinning by machinery, led, in England, to the Luddite or machine-breaking riots of 1812 and subsequent years. Yet there are now employed in the English textile factories over one million people (1,005,685 in 1874), one-tenth of what the whole population was when those riots took place. In this country there has been very little of that feeling. Mr. Coffin read you an account of the manner in which our citizens encouraged the introduction of those same spinning-jennies. Our working population is more intelligent than the English, and, moreover, is ready to turn from one occupation to another.

·Let me give you some figures from the census. No reliable figures exist for the boot and shoe business, because the work was formerly done to a considerable extent by farmers and farm laborers and fishermen, who took the materials home and worked at odd times, so that one person in the census-taker's list would represent, perhaps, only two months' work. Still, I find that, by the table, the increase has been:

	1850.	1860.	187
Hands	105,254	123,026	135,889
Wages	$21,622,608	$30,938,080	$51,972,712
Product	53,967,408	91,889,298	181,644,090

The textile industries have been carried on in factories for so many years that the returns from them, collected under similar conditions at the three periods, afford a better basis. I take the figures from Table X, p. 596, of quarto volume on industry, of the census of 1870:

The textile industries of cotton goods, woolens, worsted goods, carpets, and hosiery.

	1860.	1870.
Hands	181,550	255,328
Wages	$37,301,710	$79,401,367
Product	196,416,400	395,158,565

This table only shows the progress in old-established industries. To get the whole effect, we must take those that have been newly created by patented nventions (e. g., vulcanized rubber, agricultural implements, and a host of others); and outside of the great factories, they form a great part of our industries. We must take all our manufactures together. The figures from the census, given in the table on p. 112, *supra*, show that while our population has gained an addition of only 67 per cent. since 1850 (from 23,200,000 to 38,500,000), the hands employed in manufacturing have more than doubled.

The case is the same with farm-labor. Agricultural machinery, as an important element, dates from about 1850; it was 1855 to 1858 before sowers, reapers, mowers, harvesters, and thrashers became so distributed as to have any decided general effect, and the result will be most shown in the great grain and hay raising States. Now, look at the following figures from the census:

Farmers and agricultural laborers in the principal reaper and mower using States.

	1850.	60.	1870.
California		31,257	47,863
Illinois	141,099	200,862	376,441
Indiana	163,229	199,641	266,777
Iowa	32,779	115,824	210,263
Michigan	65,815	124,541	187,211
Minnesota	563	27,921	75,157
Missouri	65,561	264,385	263,918
Nebraska		4,437	23,115
New York	313,980	370,514	374,323
Ohio	270,362	309,969	397,024
Pennsylvania	207,495	249,717	260,051
Wisconsin	40,980	125,331	159,687
Total	1,301,863	2,024,399	2,641,830

Bushels of wheat, rye, oats, and barley in United States	266,425,951	382,675,387	616,532,883
Tons of hay in United States	13,838,642	19,083,896	27,316,048
Hops in United States, pounds	2,497,029	10,991,996	25,456,669
Flaxseed, bushels	562,312	566,867	1,730,444
Wool, pounds		60,264,913	100,102,387

I have put the amount of various agricultural products in this table because they are chiefly produced in the grain-raising and reaper-using States, and they tend to show where some of the labor not absorbed by the greatly-increased grain and grass crop has gone. Many new agricultural industries, so to speak, have grown up—wine-making, for example.

The raising of small fruits and peaches on a large scale and the canning of fruits and vegetables are the growth of late years, and employ a great deal of labor.

The table of laborers is interesting in other respects. Missouri had in 1870 a few hundred less agriculturists than in 1860, and perhaps the war is partly accountable for this. New York and Pennsylvania have grown very slightly during those years in that respect; but the natural growth of that class has partly emigrated to the fast-growing States of the same latitude, and to a greater extent changed its occupation, for the tables of manufacturers show that there are employed in industrial establishments:

	1850.	1860.	1870.
Missouri	15,808	19,681	69,777
New York	199,349	230,112	351,800
Pennsylvania	146,766	222,132	319,487

I will add the number of operatives from the tables found in the quarto volume on Industry of the Ninth Census, page 393. The tables for 1850 and 1860 include mining and quarrying, and I have added miners to that of 1870. I omit California, where the operatives are chiefly miners, and the change to new gold-fields has been great.

Operatives.	1850.	1860.	1870.
Illinois	11,559	22,963	90,483
Indiana	14,440	21,295	60,575
Iowa	1,707	6,307	26,660
Michigan	9,344	23,190	70,075
Minnesota	63	2,123	11,341
Missouri	15,808	19,681	68,777
Nebraska		336	2,703
New York	199,349	230,112	356,977
Ohio	51,491	75,602	148,443
Pennsylvania	146,766	222,132	400,702
Wisconsin	6,089	15,414	44,611
Total	456,616	639,160	1,281,347

It is pretty clear that, wherever those men spoken of by the honorable
member may have gone, the progress in agricultural machinery between
those years did not diminish the demand for labor.

Mr. Coffin has told you of the cotton-gin, of which one of the latest
forms, tended by, I suppose, half a dozen men, can do 4,000 pounds a day,
instead of four or five pounds a day, which one man could do before
Whitney's time. Instead of diminishing the demand for labor in the
cotton States, it has created those States and all the demand for labor
that exists in them. No one doubts that the greatest boon to those
States would be machinery which should do for their agriculture what
machinery has done for the grain-raising States; if the crop could be
raised and gathered at one-third the present amount of labor, there can
be no question about the enormously-increased demand for American
cotton that would follow; and, I think, no doubt not only of the increased
demand for labor that would spring up there, as it has in the grain-raising States, but in the improved quality of the labor. Whoever works
alongside of a machine is driven to be industrious and intelligent to
keep up with it.

In truth, it is a law of political economy that society tends to employ
all useful labor; and thus the more valuable the labor the more fully it
is employed. This is as true of communities as of individuals. The
England of to-day is busier than the England of five hundred years ago.
For idle hands you do not go to England, or Belgium, or Northern
France. You go perhaps to Ireland, where there is little invention and
little labor-saving machinery; or to Spain, or to Southern Russia. In
Italy the beggars are not in the industrial cities of Turin and Milan
and Florence. The busiest parts are where a day's labor is worth the
most. In the existing condition of the world, increased capacity means
increased employment and increased wages. And this increased capacity, due to labor-saving patented inventions, cheapens the cost of the
product to the consumer; he spends as much, probably more, but *he gets
more for his money*, and he earns more by his labor.

Mr. CLARKE. I don't see how it can be that patented inventions
cheapen cost to the consumer. I mean by what I say, that when we
buy, we buy with all the entailed expense of the royalties; all this is
added upon it; and is it not exhaustive to the West and South, especially to the South?

Mr. STORROW. It is not exhaustive to the West, because they manufacture for themselves.

Mr. CLARKE. But not as largely.

Mr. STORROW. At the present time they manufacture more largely than New England. I spoke of 1870 in my former remarks. At present they are undoubtedly far ahead.

It affects the South in this way: The result of these labor-saving machines, in spite of the higher cost of labor that is used with them, as shown by our competition with England and by a great many other ways, is that the article is produced cheaper, or comparatively cheaper, than twenty years ago. You get now an article for seventy-five cents or fifty cents which formerly cost $1; and that is the net result of the system. You must remember the distinction between patents for inventions and patents for monopolies. When the English Sovereign gave to a man the sole right to import salt, he acquired the monopoly of a business which before that time had been the free right of all; he gained the power to exclude others from what they had freely done before, and consequently he had the power to increase the price of an existing article. Nay, the very object and intent of the patent was to enable him to make money by increasing the price, and this was the natural effect. But a patent for an invention forbids no man to carry on the industry and business he has always carried on. It cannot raise the price, for people may manufacture in the old way; the patentee only has the sole right to use the new method he has invented. He cannot make any money by his patent unless he can manufacture cheaper than any one else can by the old method. His temptation, and the inevitable and invariable result, is that he undersells the old manufacturers, so as to absorb all the trade, unless they take licenses, and so become able to reduce the price also; that is, he at once reduces the cost to the purchaser. Indeed, whether he desires it or not, he cannot help it; an increased supply, capable of being produced at a lower cost, so acts upon the market as to diminish the price by the inexorable laws of trade. So the patent cannot add to the price. It necessarily and invariably cheapens. I said at the former hearing that the patent is based on—is for that which the inventor has in the most just sense created—a new and useful art or improvement or composition of matter. It is not something which his patent enables him to subtract, to self-appropriate, from the world's possessions, as in the case of the old monopolies. The whole world has become, and forever after his patent has expired will continue to be, stronger or richer for the new use he has taught it to make of the powers of nature; that is the highest creation open to human power. If you could have got all this labor-saving machinery and all these improvements invented, perfected, and introduced without paying for them, then you would have undoubtedly gained as much as I could gain if I could buy a barrel of flour without paying for it; but I should hardly expect to do that a second time.

Mr. CLARKE. I want to give you one particular character of patents —sewing-machines. I have seen wagons, till I was sick of them, peddling sewing-machines all through my country, that cost probably $10 to $16, and they were retailing them to our people at $75, $85, and $125. I think the average cost of those sewing-machines was not over $20.

Mr. STORROW. No, sir; you are wrong about the figures. There is a book printed which gives the figures and the reason for the large cost. Undoubtedly, in the case of sewing-machines, there was a handsome royalty, though nothing like what was generally supposed. I think those patents were not judiciously managed, but the question is, whether you would have gotten the machine in fifty years, as at present improved, without the encouragement of patents. It was not simply the original Howe machine; all these original patents are run out, and nobody would build a machine on them alone. There have been several thousand patents on them since, covering improvements.

Mr. WILLITS. They use the same needle.

Mr. STORROW. Yes, sir; but that is only a small part of the machine. The present machine, for which you pay whatever the price may be, has got in it the inventions of hundreds and thousands of men, who have been laboring and spending money to bring it to that point. Now, at the present time all the bottom patents have expired, and all the more important patents have expired; there remain only a comparatively few accessory later patents in existence. You get them as cheap as the manufacturer can make them. Whether the community would have obtained the benefit of these things without a patent, or anything like as soon, if there had not been patents, is a question upon which theoretical reasoning is worth little; but the actual fact of the growth of our industry, the cheapening of our products, our growth, as regards England and other countries, the fact that our growth in all respects has kept pace with the patent system, shows that it does encourage invention, and foster cheapness by encouraging the invention of labor-saving machinery.

Mr. AIKEN. Isn't there a great deal of truth in what the gentleman said yesterday, that the men who invented the patents are hardly ever the recipients of the profits?

Mr. STORROW. I don't think that McCormick would say that. I will speak of that again presently. But one of the great advantages of the old system of patents for fourteen years, with a chance for one extension by the Commissioner, was that the inventor of a meritorious improvement always had a chance for a reward by an extension for his benefit, while, as only about five per cent. of the patents were extended, the average life of a patent was shorter than under the present system. It was much better than the present law.

We speak sometimes of the reward which the patent system gives to the inventor. I don't think that the proper term to apply. I think the profit he receives is not so much a reward as a necessary prerequisite to the existence of the invention—to the existence of the machine.

Take the occasional case which happens where a man is full of invention, and wants to invent—has got it in him so he can hardly be repressed in spite of disappointment. These are precious men, and ought to be encouraged. They make generic inventions, valuable particularly in that they will lead others to improve and perfect. These men are extremely rare, and yet I think you cannot rely on those men to keep up the progress of the arts. I think you can no more rely on those men to keep up the progress of the arts than you can rely upon spontaneous combustion to cook your dinner every day. Now, if you meet one of these men, or men who think they are of that character, you will find that the one thing paramount in his mind is his right in his invention. Talk with one of these men, and he won't tell you much about the ingenuity of his machine; he will speak most about the wonderful results which it will accomplish when he gets it completed, and what a fortune he will make out of it. Unthrifty such men are, sometimes, in not taking good care of their money; but no one thinks more of their prospects or is more lured on by hope of reward than they. You will find that these men do take out patents, and that seems pretty tolerable proof that they are affected by the desire to take them out. The large body of inventors, however, are the men who improve machines; not the great geniuses, but the men who go on improving and improving the machines. These men are sometimes employed by the manufacturer at very high wages. I know a man who works in his shirt-sleeves, a mechanic, employed at about $6,000 a year inventing improvements. There is not a large reaper manufactory or sewing-machine manufactory, or manufactory of any kind, making patented articles or machinery, that does not employ men at from $3,000 to $10,000 a year continually inventing and improving machines. Then there are a great many people who improve and invent, and sell their inventions at a round price as soon as made, and the assignee may make upon the patent five times as much as he paid, or he may spend a large sum improving and then lose the whole. These men very wisely sell out to avoid the risk and to enable them to turn their mind to inventing something new—and the risk is very great. Any one familiar with the subject will tell you that time and again a man will take an invention which he thinks promises well and sell it and the assignee spend thousands on it and get nothing in the end. I happened to know of two cases quite interesting in that respect. One was that of a gentleman who was a patent solicitor, as skillful a mechanical expert as, I think, I recollect. He had a large interest in an invention on which he had worked professionally for many years, and which had been brought to completion. Another invention sprang up for accomplishing the same result in a different way, and he was afraid it would supersede the first. He sold out his interest in the first and bought the whole of the second, and the result was, that after he had spent a large sum on the second he became convinced that it was perfectly worthless, and the old one went on and multiplied about tenfold in value.

Another case was that of an extremely skillful mechanical engineer, who bought some patents and paid $50,000; he spent $25,000 more in improving them, and they turned out to be—financially—perfectly worthless to the end. A man not only has to put his money in, but spend his time in the first place in inventing, then pay his money in perfecting and introducing, and all this with the uncertainty that, with the best skill and knowledge, he may never get his money back. Thousands and millions have been spent in machines which led to nothing at all.

One was the case of the horse shoe-nail, which Mr. Coffin spoke of. The first set of patents, on which one of the companies spent a great many thousand dollars (I think about $60,000), they had to give up as worthless. The owner then took up another inventor, and began all over again in a different way, before he got a successful machine. Now they have got a good machine, but at one time they all thought they were ruined, and would have been glad to get rid of it and throw it away if they could have got clear.

Take the case of a man like Goodyear, who certainly showed the greatest persistence in invention. Can any one imagine he would work on as he did, a dozen or fifteen years, in those experiments to vulcanize rubber, without expecting to be repaid? The best proof is that every stage of progress he made he patented as soon as he made it. His personal history is that he persevered because he believed a fortune would come with success. So it was with McCormick and all those men. They would not have gone on and perfected their machines, and put them into public use, unless they had had the stimulus of the further results to look to. Men have to be of a peculiar turn of mind to persevere under discouragements, but inventors are generally sanguine, and sanguine not only of mechanical success, but of the pecuniary results of it. One of the most interesting cases is that of Mr. Bessemer, the inventor of the process of making steel—and substantially all the steel of the world is made by his process; all the steel rails and larger articles. It consists, as some of you know very well, in driving atmospheric air through a mass of about five tons of melted cast iron. The air is introduced through the iron from underneath, and, passing through the iron, burns out the carbon and silicon in the iron and leaves in it just enough carbon to make steel, and after blowing about twenty minutes through the crucible and putting in a little manganese iron the whole of the contents of the crucible are converted into melted cast steel. Now, Mr. Bessemer was a bronze-worker in London, a man of some means, apparently, and he was endeavoring to devise some method of improving metal for ordnance. He wanted to get it to an intense heat, and in the course of two or three years of experiments, costing a great deal of money, he came upon this method, and found out he could burn out the carbon and produce an intense heat by driving the air through the melted metal. He disclosed this to Mr. Nasmyth, the great iron-worker, and that gentleman told him at once it was the greatest progress made in the art of iron-working in a century; certainly since the invention of the hot blast and the use of anthracite coal. Mr. Bessemer was doubtful about the ability to handle the metal, but after consulting the iron-masters, they said it could be done without any trouble, any engineer could do it. Mr. Bessemer then sold licenses to one leading iron-master in each iron district.

Mr. BRIGGS. He patented it, did he?

Mr. STORROW. Yes, sir; he patented it at once, but he put the fee at a very low rate, in order to get them to introduce it and get it into use; and these men went to work and put up works, spent a great deal of money in building their works—the Bessemer-plant for a rail-mill at the present time costs not far from a million dollars—but after trying it thoroughly, every one of them found they could not handle the iron. The process could not be worked. Mr. Bessemer thought that that was about the time for an inventor to come in, and he went to work devising an apparatus to overcome the difficulty. He worked for two or three years, and spent about $100,000; and finally, even after he had succeeded, these iron-masters who had already bought and paid for their licenses would not go on. They said it was a very good thing in theory, but it was a chimera, and would not work, even with his new apparatus. So he was obliged to actually construct works and start as a steel-maker, but only got orders at first for lots of 56 pounds and other small quantities.

By and by it dawned on the minds of the iron-masters that there was Mr. Bessemer making for $75 to $100 a ton steel which cost them $200, and then they were glad enough to come in; but the patent was six years old before it became profitable. The consequence was, that in 1872 and 1873 there were made in England about 250,000 tons of steel rails, sold at a price of about $55 a ton at the particular time this testimony was taken, whereas before the invention of this process it cost $200 a ton, and its large manufacture was not practicable. The price now is between $30 and $35 a ton in England, I think. Well, it is perfectly obvious in that case——

Mr. TOWNSHEND. What is the price of iron now?

Mr. STORROW. Iron rails are about $10 a ton less than steel, and steel rails in this country are about $45 a ton, or less.

Mr. WARD. They have come down considerably in price.

Mr. STORROW. They have been, I think, at $42, and iron rails at about $30; the steel rails sold first at about $125 here. Now we have eleven mills capable of turning out 450,000 tons of steel rails in all. This invention has made steel rails possible, and is a good illustration of the way in which an invention both cheapens the product and increases the demand. Mr. Bessemer granted licenses freely to everybody who would put up works and use them properly; the highest royalty required on this great process, which reduced the price of steel from $200 to $55— that is to say, $150 a ton—was one pound sterling, or $5 a ton; that is, but little over three per cent. of the saving. The patent on the Bessemer process has now run out. He has, however, a patent still existing on the apparatus, and the royalty on that is 2s. 6d. a ton, or 75 cents a ton in this country. You see what portion of the saving the public got, and how small a part he was satisfied with, even during the life of his patent, and wisely, for the low price made a great demand. Mr. Bessemer was asked what he would have done if there had been no patent system; he replied, "I never would have spent a dollar of my money or an hour of my time." "Would you not have worked in secret?" "How could I work in secret an invention requiring a plant costing a million, and requiring a great many hundred men to run it?" And then he gave them an illustration. His father was a type-worker, and had devised two processes which he kept secret, and which perished with him. One was undoubtedly the process of electrotyping—depositing metal from a solution by electricity. It was not until thirty or forty years after that it was rediscovered, and the Elkingtons carried it on with great profit to themselves and the country. Now, if that old man had felt the impetus of a patent system, the first thing would have been to patent his discovery, and even if he had never used it, and locked it up for the whole life of his patent, or taken all the profit to himself, still the public would have got it twenty-five years sooner. It certainly was not true in this case that if he had not invented it some one else would have the next week, for the world waited forty years for it. Mr. Bessemer had a secret process of his own, which he worked many years, and no one else discovered it. No improvements were made on it, because he did not dare to have any one around, except a few people. He doubted very much whether the public had ever received substantial benefit from it, because he made so little of the article that he kept the price up, and did not lower it very much, and because he had no competition which obliged him to lower it. Very different this from the immediate public gain from his steel.

The hosiery business in England is very interesting, because within the last thirty years it has been turned from hand to machine work. It is mostly carried on in Nottingham; and one of the largest manufacturers is Mr. Mundella, who has been in Parliament. It has been the practice in that industry, different from most other branches, for the manufacturers to encourage the workmen to make inventions; and the consequence is that the inventions which have revolutionized this branch of industry have been mostly made by the superintendents and foremen—the skilled workmen of the establishment. Mr. Mundella said he asked one of his men, who had made a good invention, and who had worked on it a good many years, as to what he would have done if he could not have got a patent. "I should have gone to America pretty quick," said the workman. Mr. Mundella said he had received the same answer from at least fifty men.

They reduced the cost of certain undershirts, hosiery, drawers, and so on, I think, from ten or twelve shillings a dozen to 2s. 6d., and the highest royalty, Mr. Mundella said, that was charged for any of the machines used in any branch was threepence a dozen; so you see the mere little proportion of saving in that case which the patent receives—3d. royalty for a saving of 8s.—say three per cent. Mr. Mundella was asked whether a great deal of money was not spent on unsuccessful machines. He said there certainly was, but the machines could not be perfected without trials; if they were not patented the expense and loss would be just as great, only with a patent a man was willing to incur it, because he would get his money back if he succeeded; or if he didn't get it back out of one invention, he might out of another; and the result of this work was a great public saving.

Mr. Coffin told you about the Bigelow carpet-loom, but that is only one of Mr. E. B. Bigelow's inventions. He is still an active man, but I may, nevertheless, say that his career is a good illustration of the patent system. He began as an inventor very early in life. While a clerk in a store he conceived of a machine for weaving coach-lace, and his first thought was to patent it and better his condition by his inventive skill. He was without means, but he walked boldly into the store of a large importer of this lace, and the proprietor having become interested by the young man's examination of his goods, entered into conversation with him, and Mr. Bigelow said he had invented a machine for making the article, and wanted to borrow $100 to build his model, &c. He imparted to the capitalist some of his own confidence in the pecuniary success which he felt sure of for his invention, the requisite money was advanced, the machine perfected, and the industry for the first time established in this country by means of it.

He was the original designer of the Lancaster mills, at Lancaster (now Clinton), the first manufacturers of ginghams in this country. From an account written by him in 1851, and vouched for by the officers, I condense the following:

The project of a mill for weaving cotton checks and ginghams by power-looms was started in 1844. It found immediate favor, and stock, to the amount then supposed necessary, was immediately subscribed. For more than two years a large part of his time and attention was devoted to this object. The system in use for manufacturing ginghams in England required too much manual labor to be carried on at the high rate of wages current in this country. So he had before him the problem of how to reduce the cost of the product and at the same time pay much higher wages than in England; or, as he stated the case, "it is a generally-admitted fact that in the manufacture of cotton goods our competition with the foreign article is more or less successful according to the ratio which the cost of labor in the fabric bears to the raw material," and as we could not or could hardly compete on even terms in plain cottons, it was apparent that some new force must be brought to bear to enable us to compete in ginghams, which required about twice as much labor per yard. The work was done in England on hand-looms, by weavers working at home. Obviously the end was to be attained by labor-saving machinery to be invented.

" By the improved machinery and methods of the Lancaster mills the gingham manufacture is placed, notwithstanding the high percentage required for labor and a comparatively short experience (this was written in 1851), on as good footing in regard to foreign competition as are plain cottons and calicoes. The amount of labor saved in this establishment over any other system of methods for producing the goods is equivalent to at least a cent and a half per yard. In other words, no machinery or methods known before the erection of the Lancaster mills, and operated at such rates of wages as are paid in New England, could produce the same goods at a cost so low by a cent and a half per yard.

The product of the establishment at this time (1851) is at the rate of 4,400,000 yards per year." Up to the end of 1846 only 34,000 yards were produced. In 1875 the mills produced 11,560,000 yards, from 1,115 looms, employing 1,041 hands (560 males, 481 females). The town of Clinton, which contains this gingham-mill, the Bigelow carpet-mill, and the mill for weaving wire-cloth on looms invented by Mr. Bigelow for the purpose, and numbers 7,000 inhabitants, owes its existence to his inventive skill; and each one of these industries has been created by his patented inventions. He was not a manufacturer improving his business, but a poor man seeking fortune by that use of his brains for which Nature had best fitted him. The patent law held out this stimulus to him, and he responded to it; and he has attained the reward, but his country has gained a hundred-fold as much.

We hear sometimes of the great fortunes made by the owners of patents. Where are those men? If we look for wealth, we go among the railroad builders or owners, among the mine owners, among those who speculate in grain or stocks; not among patent owners. Here and there is one who has grown rich from patents, but their number is few. Why should they not? All their money must be got back within a few years or not at all. No business is so full of risk; and in such a class, where fortune rewards only the few successful, you must not limit their gains by the sure and certain payments that are sufficient in the steadier walks of life. You must average the great gains of the few cases among the many men who work to improve the arts by new inventions, before you talk of the profits of inventors as a class. And if you examine the case of any of the successful patent owners, you will find yourself in doubt whether his wealth is due to the protection of the patent law much more than it is to the business capacity which would have made a fortune in any walk of life. And you must remember, while in the case of the few who have grown rich, and the very many inventors who have bettered their condition by the use of their brains, that the primary condition of their success is that they furnish to the world some supply better or cheaper than it ever had before.

People talk about men having a desire to make inventions, and even compare it with the writing of a poem. They say a man does not need to be encouraged to write a poem; but there is no comparison between the two things, and if there were, I think the encouragement given to invention, over and above that given to literature—the encouragement given by the pecuniary reward and the improvement it has led to—would be a good illustration of the benefits of the system.

Tennyson is as much the product of the culture of two thousand years—of the genius of his time—as Homer was the product of his age; and yet no one would say that Tennyson surpasses Homer as the spinning frame—where a girl of fifteen will make three million yards a day—surpasses the distaff of Penelope. If you go to the museum at the other end of the avenue you will not see such progress in excellence between the Greek Slave of Powers and the Venus of Milo as exists between the galleys of Greece and the modern iron-clad. Will this building (though I think it externally the handsomest parliament house in the world) differ in merit from the Parthenon as much as the latest harvester differs from the sickles after which Ruth gleaned? The truth is, mechanical invention and literary invention are different things; they are inspired by different causes; they aim at different results. In industrial invention we look to nothing—nothing is considered invention, within the meaning of the patent law, unless the thing is useful—unless it produces something better, cheaper than we have had before. But

you do not refuse to see a play or read a poem because it is inferior to
a tragedy of Sophocles, any more than you will refuse to eat a peach
next autumn because it is not as good as the one you ate a year ago.
They are entirely different kinds of things, and you cannot compare
them.

It was stated the other day that the patent system was not in accordance with the genius of a free country. It seems to me that that is a
great mistake in fact; a great mistake historically. The peculiarity of
the system in this country is, that it is not for the capitalist, it is not
for a class already selected and favored, but it is for everybody. It
realizes the great boast of Napoleon : it opens a career and a future to
whoever has talents to seize it. Our patent system is made for everybody, and everybody can, if they have the capacity, reap the reward.
Historically, the patent system arose in England by the statute of
James the First. It is called the statute of monopolies, not because it
created, but because it destroyed monopolies. The rising spirit of in-
dependence in Parliament had protested against monopolies of trade
which Elizabeth had granted, and extorted from Elizabeth a promise
" to examine all patents, and to abide the touchstone of the law." But
she broke her promise, and James did the like; and so, in spite of the
strenuous defense of royal prerogative which was made by the court
party in the debates, the House of Commons took away the power to
grant those patents which would not "abide the touchstone of the law."
The patents they put an end to were patents to cover existing trade and
commerce; the patents they retained were those that touched *new*
manufactures ; and they did this not by a grant conferring a new power,
but by an act in terms *declaring that this was the law*, and forbidding the
King to go beyond it. It was as much part of the English Constitution
as trial by jury, which rests on a not dissimilar protesting declaration
and extorted consent of the King, and from thence, first our States
and then our Constitution adopted it.

In France the patent system came in a year after ours did, in 1791,
as one of the first fruits of the free ideas of the Revolution. In this
country, it had existed, as I told you, under grants from the States,
long before our Constitution, and was put into our Constitution as one
of the provisions, and, I think, justly, because it encouraged men to
exercise the right of pursuing their own welfare in a manner helpful to
the State.

I look upon it as a mark of the highest civilization that a country
shall recognize by its fundamental law the utilitarian effects of pure
brain power; as a mark both of the highest civilization and of the
highest reaches of the law that a nation recognizes as property to be
protected, because helpful to the State and to all its people, the pure
creations of the intellect; a species of property not inherent in or attached to any particular portion of matter, but which depends for its
recognition on the appreciative intellect of the community, and for its
protection—that is, for its existence as property—upon the national deference for law and order.

Mr. RAYMOND. Do you mean the patent system was created by First
James?

Mr. STORROW. The patent system was substantially created by that
statute. It was changed from a grant, at the mere grace of the sovereign, to something which could abide the touchstone of the law, to a
system which held out to the inventor—that is the great thing (it is not
to reward him, *if* the King pleased)—which held out to the inventor
the *promise* of a reward if he should deserve it; and, as I said the other

day, the English patent system rested on that statute when our Constitution was adopted and until the statute of William IV.

An invention which was contemporaneous with the statute of monopolies well illustrates the effect of the system. Lee invented his stocking-frame in 1589—before that statute. Elizabeth would not give him a patent; James would not. So, instead of setting up his frames in England, he went to France, where the King gave him a privilege and he set up his frames. It was not until thirty or forty years afterwards that they were used in England, brought back by an apprentice of his, and then they, or the workers on them, were made the subjects of special privileges. So he did just as Mr. Mundella's hosiery inventors said they would do—carried his invention from his native country, that would give him no patent, to another that would.

It is said, sometimes, that inventions come whenever they are wanted. The history of invention directly disproves that. We have wanted a steam-plow for I do not know how many years. We wanted a binder for I do not know how many years; and the same with reapers. You may look through the long lists of inventions, and it is not the declaration of a want and the meeting of it. You find hundreds of patents, and years of labor of hundreds of inventors, and hundreds of thousands of dollars of money expended before the want is met, even where the want precedes the invention. You will find, in a large number of cases, that the invention creates the want, instead of meeting it. It is the invention of the thing which makes the public desire it: vulcanized rubber is such an instance. There are many wants not supplied. For thirty years we have wanted paper-pulp made of something besides rags. It is only within ten years—hardly so long—that the problem has been successfully solved. Twenty years of invention, a large number of patents, and an enormous expenditure of money have been made to supply that want; and I know of two establishments that, in improving one process, spent over $300,000. I know of one company that put in a capital of a million dollars, and spent all the earnings for seven years in experiments. They wanted it badly enough, but it took them all that time to come to the result; and now mechanical pulp can be made for 2½ cents, while rag pulp costs 6 cents, and it has kept down the price of rag pulp in addition. Why, if there is anything wanted in this country, it is a cotton-picker to pick cotton in the South. They have been at work for many years on it, and only week before last there was a patent issued for a cotton-picker; but the demand has not brought it yet. I cut the following from a newspaper:

A SHEEP-SHEARING MACHINE.

[From a South Wales paper.]

Many efforts have been made to produce a machine for shearing sheep that should enable the work to be done as well as by hand, and with greater rapidity. Some inventive mechanic in England, some time ago, made a machine for this purpose, which was tried in Australia, but we had recently to record its failure there. Now we have a machine made by an American mechanic, who has spent eight years in perfecting it, and which seems to be perfectly adapted to the work required. We have tested the machine, and feel satisfied that a sheep can be sheared in five minutes much better than could be done by hand. The fleece is cut off very evenly and closely with this machine, the sheep cannot possibly be cut by it, and there can be no cutting through and injuring the staple. The cutters, made precisely upon the principle of the mowing-machine knives, are of chilled steel, and self-sharpening. The motion is communicated by means of compressed air, and three thousand revolutions per minute can be easily given to it, although one thousand five hundred are sufficient for a working speed. The air-pump is worked by a crank, and one man can produce sufficient power to work twenty-five machines. The air is forced from the pump through a flexible rubber tube, which allows ample freedom of movement. The working pressure of the pump is five pounds per square inch, but it may be worked up to forty-five pounds by using an engine or a windmill. One pump is sufficient to work twenty-five of the machines, and these may all be attached to a supply pipe, from which the compressed air may be let off or on to the machine, as needed, by taps. One pump will supply power for twenty-five shearers. These, having merely to hold and direct the machine, which barely fills the hand, and requires no muscular force to work it, are not exhausted, or required to stoop over the sheep, if benches are used, and may, therefore, work more quickly and certainly than with the or dinary shears. The cost of shearing will be much reduced; and, as the cost of the apparatus is very moderate, almost every person owning a flock of sheep would find it advantageous to use it. We should, however, recommend the use of a shearing-bench or chair, by which the necessity for stooping and bending over the work would be obviated.

That American mechanic would not have worked eight years out of pure pleasure nor pure philanthropy. If the cotton-picker is to come, it will come as the harvester came, and as perhaps the sheep-shearer has come, under the stimulus of a patent system.

It is said that many inventions are simultaneous; that different men in different places make the same invention at the same time. That is not the fact. Undoubtedly it has happened from time to time that several men, striving in the same branch, hit upon substantially the same devices; but the cases are comparatively rare. Why, the best proof of that is, that in not one of these industries will you find any one man at one time inventing a complete thing. If the invention to be made was a single, distinct thing, I could conceive of simultaneous inventors; but not where the perfected machine—the thing accomplished—is the result of years of work and many inventions.

We have a way of ascertaining some proof about this from the Patent Office. There are filed in the Patent Office about 20,000 applications a year; and I think I rather understate it in saying that each one of the patents contains three claims, on an average, for three different things—separate devices. If that be so, there are something like 60,000 claims filed in that office in the course of a year by men who swear that they are the original and first inventors thereof. Now, there is a process by which, if one man overlaps other claimants, an "interference" is declared; and how many out of this large number are put into interference in the course of a year? Last year was the highest number, and that was 614.

Now, that is pretty good proof that simultaneous inventions are by no means common. But if they were, what does it show? Because men, when stimulated by the patent system to study the same problem, sometimes hit upon the same solution, it does not tend to show that they would have found any solution or bestowed any study if they had not been encouraged to do so.

Mr. AIKEN. Please explain that again.

Mr. STORROW. There are about 20,000 patents, and each application contains, on an average, as many as three distinct claims. I mean to say that each patent granted may have three or four or five features, all combined in one machine, but so connected that they may all be put into one patent, in different claims.

The CHAIRMAN. Do you know of any cases in interference where the parties live a considerable distance apart?

Mr. ———. That is repeatedly the case. I know one in Tennessee and another in New York, and it occurs very frequently.

Mr. RAYMOND. What proportion of these cases get into the Patent Office?

Mr. STORROW. Pretty nearly every man who makes an invention himself—I mean if he made the invention and has not copied it—applies for a patent, unless he finds some one so far ahead of him that it is obviously useless; and so the office files undoubtedly disclose all cases that are near enough in date to be fairly called simultaneous, and most of them get into "interference."

Mr. RAYMOND. Should you not take the number of patents not issued—that are not followed up, for the reason of prior use?

Mr. STORROW. No; for if they are so apart as that, they cannot be called simultaneous. But I am glad of the suggestion, for it bears on another point. If you find the same invention made by different men, many years apart, that shows that it is not a mere question of supply and demand; and we ought to be grateful to the system under which the first man made, and perfected, and published his invention—the system which gave us early what was not found out for many years by any one else.

I have stated sufficiently the manner in which a stimulus is created to induce men to put in their time and their money; let me endeavor to state a little more fully another effect of it, and that is, that the impetus it gives to further invention. Take the case of Mr. Bessemer's secret process: it did not lead to any further invention, because it was not known. On the other hand, the moment any process is made public it leads some one else to improvement, and that is the way it gives the public the greatest results. It does not incite any one as much as it does the owner or patentee himself. Improvements do not come from the general public, the general user, or general manufacturer of machinery; they come from the man who builds improved patent machines, whose attention is fixed upon new inventions. And he has two reasons why he seeks improvement: one is, he wants to extend his exclusive manufacture, for he knows that when his patent is run out his business is gone, unless he shall so improve his machine or product that the people are ready to come and pay a good price for his new machine. Take the case of the reapers. Men to-day will go and buy the highest-priced machine, and won't take the machine which made the reputation of American makers in 1858. It is not worth anything.

Mr. WARD. Did you ever hear of the McCaffey cast steel? It is not a patented cast steel—it is a secret process.

Mr. STORROW. I never heard of it, perhaps because it is secret.

Mr. WARD. I know of two establishments that are running on it.

Mr. STORROW. Do they manufacture very much of it?

Mr. WARD. No; it is used for small parts that are required for heavy straining. I remember it in connection with your remark about the Bessemer process.

Mr. McCaffey came over from England, having the secret. It was not patented, but the idea was that nobody could ever discover it. He started his works at Chester three or four years ago, and a man who worked in the establishment, and who was not the depositary of the secret, nevertheless discovered it, and other works have now started, and they are both running.

Mr. STORROW. Secret use does not seem to be very encouraging to a man who wants to rely on a reward to induce labor and expenditure. One English manufacturer said he was not sure that a pot of beer would disclose any secret process; but he knew that two pots would.

Mr. COFFIN spoke to you about the opinion of Governor Straw, of New Hampshire, the great cotton manufacturer, as to the effect of modern machinery upon cotton manufacture. He said that the cotton-mills could not afford to take as a gift the machinery in existence in 1860. I could not help thinking that that was exactly the machinery upon which the patents had expired. No, Mr. Chairman; a man had better take the most expensive patented machinery of to-day than attempt to use machines so old that all patents on them have expired.

Mr. BRIGGS. Those large mills break up their machinery and sell it for old iron—thousands of dollars' worth.

Mr. STORROW. I want to speak more particularly of the prices of patented articles, the saving made by the invention, and the manner in which the saving is divided between the patentee and the public.

You have had laid before you a number of instances of improved machinery whose immediate as well as ultimate effect has been to cheapen the product of the art to which it belongs. I call to mind the horse-shoe, the horseshoe nail, the common cut-nail, the wood-screw, the pegged or sewed boot or shoe, pulp for paper-making, hosiery, steel, and others. These were cases where the product is old, but the process or machine is improved. Let me add a few more. In a report to Congress on the extension of the Marshall knitting-machine, chiefly used for Shaker socks and cardigan jackets, the committee said that there were made about 3,600,000 pairs of these socks per year. By hand, a woman could knit four pairs a day, for which she received 33 cents; by the machine she could make twenty pairs, and earn $1.33 per day. Cardigan jackets, made on the English hand-frames, could be produced at the rate of about five per day per man, and cost for labor 58 cents each. By this machine a girl can make four dozen a day, at a cost for labor of about 3 cents each; and about 2,400,000 a year are made.

The committee doubtless know of the aniline dyes, obtained some years ago from coal-tar, which produced such a change in the arts. Their success, and the value of patents based on such inventions, has led to further analogous discoveries. The most important material in calico printing and dyeing cottons is extracted from the root of the madder plant, which grows in Europe, but is best found in Asia Minor. The principal substance in it, which contains the coloring properties, is known as alizarine. It was ascertained that this substance, after a very subtle analysis, yielded anthracine as one of its elements. Now, this anthracine is found in coal-tar. So two industrial chemists, Graebe and Liebermann, set to work, and finally succeeded in obtaining the constituents which made up alizarine, and then in combining them together, till they had built up an artificial alizarine as good as the natural, or perhaps better, for it contained some newly-discovered ingredients. Of course they patented it, and their patent has recently been sustained; and when I say that their process consists in first preparing bibroman-thrakinon or bicloranthrakinon and then converting them into alizarine, and that their alizarine contains the newly-discovered bodies, anthra-purpurine and isopurpurine, you will readily believe that invention was required, at least to find language in which to describe their invention. Their factory makes, if I have not mistaken the figures, 168 cwt. a day, and they sell the product at such a price that the natural madder, its competitor, has been forced to come down from 12 and 16 cents to 3 and 4 cents.

You see what a saving to the public this represents, over and above all the patentees' profits.

When the invention is of an entirely new thing, the saving to the public is perhaps best shown by the readiness with which the public buy it.

These instances could be multiplied indefinitely. You can find none to the contrary. The new machine or process or product goes into use because the user or consumer finds a gain in using it over anything known before. If the patentee charges more than the gain, of course no one buys it; so he is continually led to put down his price, in order to extend his sales, as low as he conveniently can. Thus, in effect, the paten-tee divides the benefit with the public, even during the term of his ex-clusive use; and the public have no idea of how large a proportion of those savings they get, and how small a proportion the patentee gets, in the case of inventions which go into general use.

Mr. Raymond spoke the other day of the Marsh Harvester Company as an example of it, and their counsel, Mr. Christy, corrected the state-ment. I have here a letter from Mr. Bond, of Chicago, one of the gen-tlemen who framed this bill, and who for twelve years has been the local counsel for the Marsh people; he knows their business, and he says the highest royalty ever paid on these machines was $9.50, and this, together with the cost of another patent they bought up, makes the total royalty to all patentees not to exceed $10 per machine.

The testimony of a large number of manufacturers is, that $10 is the highest royalty charged on the ordinary classes of machines. I have be-fore me a list of patents owned by an association which was organized and attempted to buy a great number of patents and monopolize the business, or one class of it. They bought up the one hundred reaper and mowing-machine patents, and told everybody they must take out licenses, and the highest they asked for the license fee for all their pat-ents, and they covered an excellent class of machines and all that were needed to make those machines, was $10, and they often took less. Then on the Buckeye machines—I take the sworn testimony from the files of the Patent Office—the license fee was $10 for the large and $7.50 for the small machine, and more were made by licenses at these prices than by the owners of the patent at their own factory.

Mr. RAYMOND. Do these figures which you give include the money paid on account of litigation, &c. ?

Mr. STORROW. These figures covered all the fees paid to and received by the owners of all the patents on these machines; it was only such part of it as remained, after paying expenses of litigation and other ex-penses, that the patentee had for his profit. The day those patents ex-pired $10 was all that was taken off the machine. What some manufac-turers may have spent in defending themselves from ill-advised attempts to use the patents without paying even that small license, I do not know, but a great many took the license without contest. All the patentee's expenses were included in this fee.

In some cases of very valuable machines, when new (as, for instance, the self-binder), the royalty has run up to $20 or $25; but the tendency is always to go down. I have taken all these figures not from hearsay, but from careful examination, and inquiries from factories and gentle-men who, from professional relation to these large establishments, had occasion to know. One was counsel for one of the largest manufactories, and is probably more familiar with the reaping-machine patents and their history, and has been for twenty years, than any one in this country.

Take the saving of labor on the harvester for a year (the larger ma-chine with the royalty of $10, and the lighter machines with a royalty $7.50), and you will find the total royalty to-day on these machines is not over 2 or 3 per cent. of the saving to the public. You see what it was in the case of the Bessemer patent, only $5 royalty against a saving of $150 per ton on steel. You heard what Mr. Hyde told you yesterday, that in certain classes of the shoe business—in the one that I spoke of particularly, where the actual saving with labor at the present prices would be about $1.75, and the actual cheapening was 75 cents, although the material had gone up 50 per cent. and the labor 100 per cent., the highest royalty was from $2\frac{1}{4}$ to $3\frac{1}{4}$ cents per pair, say 2 per cent. on the saving. So with the English hosiery trade. Take it all the way through and you will find that 5 per cent. is as high a proportion of the saving as the patentee generally gets, except with certain peculiar patented goods, where the demand is small, or with others while the invention is new, where, in order to get back his expense and the proper profit, a large per cent. is charged; but in the articles and products generally used by the public it will not exceed 5, or sometimes 10 per cent.

Take the royalties on looms in weaving cloth. A loom will weave, I think, 12,000 yards a year, or some such number, and it will last ten years. Suppose the loom costs $200 or $300 more than an unpatented one, that would amount to nothing on the aggregate amount of cloth manufactured, and really nothing on the saving, if it was worth using at all; it would be a fraction so small that you could not figure it.

Now, even if the patentee realized as high as 10 per cent. a year, what would be the result to the public? Why, if all the patent system did was to introduce the invention into use two years or a year and a half sooner than it otherwise would have been accomplished, the public cold afford to pay the per cent. and be the gainer by it. It takes a certain number of years to perfect the machine and to introduce it, and I think twelve or fourteen years is as long as a patentee receives a royalty under our law. If it was 10 per cent., which is twice what he generally gets, then the gain from getting the invention into general use eighteen months earlier would amount to more than all the royalties paid during the whole life of the patent; and can any one doubt that the effect of the patent law is at least to advance invention many times eighteen months?

Most of the objections to a patent system resolve themselves into ignorance of what the patents are and of what the system is. The cases of hardship which you hear of, nine times out of ten are submitted to because the party does not know enough to defend himself, or does not know enough to refuse to buy a patent which is not worth what he gives for it. If you have an excellent machine and your operative cannot work it successfully, you do not destroy it; you teach him about it; and the remedy here largely is to disseminate education on this branch in the community, and that is being done very fast.

The Patent-Office Gazette, which has a very large circulation, and, if the price be reduced, as the Commissioner desires, will have a still larger, has disseminated a great deal of knowledge. The Commissioner tells me that last year alone he sent out over 200,000 copies of patents or drawings, and if he is allowed to reduce the price of the copies to about. cost he will double that number. Those copies of course do not reach every man in the land, but they go into the centers of industry, into the hands of lawyers, into the manufacturing community, and by that means a general knowledge about patents gets spread through the community.

In my section of the country they are already tolerably well informed; and in the West, after a few more years, probably the people will have a general understanding of the subject.

Nevertheless the law is not what it should be. In some important details, and still more in some parts of its administration, departing from the true principles of the law of 1836, hardships and annoyances have come to be felt. But these can be in large part removed without in the least impairing the efficiency of the system, and it is the aim of the bill before you so to remove them. That this bill will leave the law so that it will never bear hardly on any one would be too much to expect. Legislation never accomplished that. We do not ask it in other matters. We want government, though it entails disagreeable taxation and abuses in its administration. We must have courts of justice though they sometimes decide wrong. But we believe that this bill is not only efficient, but that it goes as far as it is prudent to go; that no other bill is needed; that it is drawn in what I hope you are satisfied is the proper spirit—a conviction that the patent law, on the whole, is of great benefit to the community.

That the bill as drawn is perfect would be almost too much to expect. We want that it shall be, and therefore I am glad that it will receive intelligent criticism at your hands. Its present form is the result of much criticism from many sources, and we should consider it a favor if we might hear the suggestions of the committee—not to argue against them, but to bring before you the special considerations bearing on them or the practical results of changes, better than can be done in a general argument, and to enlighten our own minds by the result of your reflections. I am not sure that too many heads are always best in framing a law, but I am sure that those who have to enact it, and those who want it enacted in its best form, cannot be too ready to invite and to submit to the body that is to pass upon it the sharpest comments of those who are willing to carefully study it, for this will disclose the latent defects which may escape a single draughtsman.

ARGUMENT OF MR. STORROW—Continued.

I want to speak now somewhat of the legal questions involved in this bill, and I have handed to each member of the committee a brief upon that subject.

The bill before the committee consists of twenty-five sections.

SECTION 1.—*Limitations*. There is now no statute of limitations applicable to patent causes. That one should be provided for actions on patents as well as for every other form of action cannot be doubted. This section proposes that no recovery shall be had for an infringement more than four years old, leaving the right to sue for what has been done within four years where the infringement has continued. It allows the court, where many suits are brought on one patent, to have one brought to trial, and meanwhile stay proceedings in the others.

A continuous infringement is a continuing cause of action. If the plaintiff can prove an infringement within four years, he can recover damages for four years before suit brought, but he cannot inquire into profits or damages before that time, nor rely on an infringement before that time. This is analogous to the ordinary statutes of limitation about *mesne* profits in ejectment; a long adverse use, generally twenty years, is required to bar the *right*, and this section does not allow the right to be barred by adverse use; a short period, as here, bars the time for which *mesne* profits or damages can be recovered.

The limitation should not be too short. The owner of the patent cannot have the same physical oversight and care over it that he can over a piece of real estate or a specific chattel. It may be infringed in every town in the United States, and in secret. The rules laid down by courts will, of themselves, except from the operation of the limitation cases where the defendant fraudulently conceals the cause of action. (*Bailey* v. *Glover*, 21 Wall., 342; Senate Arg., pp. 124–7.) It is impracticable to make any other distinction between defendants as to the application of the law, without making it a statute of contention, instead of a statute of repose.

We fixed on four years partly because it is for the interest of the community that the patentee should have time to carry one test case to the conclusion, at least in the circuit court, before he needs to bring many suits to preserve his rights, and four years will generally enable him to do this. It has been suggested that in this *proviso* in line 15 the term of four years within which the bar shall not apply to causes of action now existing be changed to two years. I have no objection to this, but the language of the *proviso* in that case would require considerable remodeling.

SECTION 2.—*Damages and profits.* It is sometimes said that the law gives to the patentee better remedies than to an.y other property owner. Nothing can be further from the truth. The great protection of property—the strong arm of the law, the power of the police and of the criminal courts, the right of every man to defend his own by force—is utterly denied to the patentee in this country. For one who steals the machine of the infringer there is the summary arrest and the prison, but for the infringer who has wantonly stolen my invention, there is no policeman, no prosecution at government expense, no terror of punishment. That aid from physical force in protecting one's possessions which belongs to all corporeal property, and to those incorporeal hereditaments which inhere in or attach to specific property, cannot be had from the nature of the case. But that does not necessarily exclude the aid of the criminal law. Forgery, or counterfeiting, or libel are punishable offenses, and the European systems generally punish infringements of patents by criminal proceedings, as well as by civil remedies. We do not here, and, I think, wisely, for a criminal court is a poor tribunal to try patent questions. But, if you had no protection, physical or legal, from the burglar, the libeler, the counterfeiter, the forger, except a civil action, you would say that all the power of the law should be concentrated to make those civil remedies more prompt and more efficient to recompense you—more terrible towards the tort-feasor than ever civil remedies were before. And yet the patentee has no civil remedy except such as the ordinary principles of law and equity give him. Those remedies are three: an injunction, which a court of equity allows, because his right is exclusive, is limited in time, and an invasion causes irreparable damage; an action on the case for damages; the right, in a suit in equity, to recover profits, such as equity always gives in a suit of equitable cognizance, such as the law gives in the action for mesne profits, such as equity delights to give when it allows a plaintiff to convert a wrong-doer into a *quasi* trustee.

In an action at law, the plaintiff recovers "actual damages." (R. S., sec. 4919.) And the court may increase this threefold, though this power has rarely been exercised, and only in cases where, without the limitation of the word "actual," the law would give punitive damages. According to the existing rule of *damages*, if the plaintiff has been in the habit of granting licenses at a certain price, and a market-value has thus been attached to the use of the invention, that license-fee is the primary basis for measuring *damages;* not conclusive that the damages shall be the same in amount as the license-fee, for it may have been established with reference to a different class of cases, but, generally speaking, it is the basis to start from. (*Seymour* v. *McCormick*, 16 How., 489 ; *Burdell* v. *Denig*, 92 U. S., 720; *Packet Company* v. *Sickles*, 19 Wall., 618; *Birdsall* v. *Coolidge*, 93 U. S., 70.)

Our section adopts the same rule with the same flexibility. The license-fee is to be the measure, only when the licenses have been " to use the invention in like manner to that in which it was used by the defendaut," and it must be a fee "established by a reasonable number of transactions of *a character applicable to the case at bar*"; if the case furnishes no measure for damages, the court or jury are to "determine the same from all the evidence in the case."

In *Seymour* v. *McCormick*, 16 How., 489, the court explained the evil of the old method before 1836, which was that the infringer should pay three times the damages. Of course this was in the nature of a penalty *in terrorem*, but Congress determined, and justly, in the opinion of the court, that the only proper rule was to give actual damages, to be first ascertained in all cases, and then to commit to the discretion and judgment of the court the power to inflict vindictive or punitive damages, in cases that called for such an infliction. The court then made some remarks about the impossibility of applying one rule of damages to all cases. It said, however, that "where an inventor finds it profitable to exercise his monopoly by selling licenses to make or use his improvement, he has himself fixed the average of his actual damage when his invention has been used without his license. If he claims anything above that amount, he is bound to substantiate his claim by clear and distinct evidence."

Besides his right to recover damages, and inasmuch as the nature of his patent-right and the kind of remedy he is entitled to give him a right to maintain a bill in equity, he may waive the tort, and a court of equity has long been in the habit of considering, in such cases, that the defendant has, by the wrongful use of the plaintiff's invention, realized gains and *profits*, and treating him as a trustee thereof for the benefit of the plaintiff, and ordering him to account for them. (*Burdell* v. *Denig*, 92 U. S., 720.)

Courts of equity do not treat as trustees those only who assumed to act as such, or who deliberately and intentionally entered into relations of trust with the plaintiff. They will, for the sake of the remedy, treat as trustee of gains and profits actually realized, one who acted either as a wanton wrongdoer, or in the belief of a right, and without any intention of acting for or becoming accountable to another; and it is this same principle which is applied to patent cases, for an account of profits was never given by any statute, but decreed by the courts, as part of their ordinary equity jurisprudence. (*Stevens* v. *Gladding*, 17 How., 455.)

In *Birdsall* v. *Coolidge*, 93 U. S., 68 (action at law), the court explained the rule about damages and profits, and the distinction between them; the object of the first being to give to the plaintiff what he had lost—" to compensate him for the injury sustained by the unlawful violation of the exclusive right secured to him by the patent—without regard to the question whether the defendant had gained or lost by his unlawful acts"; as to the second, the patentee may "proceed in equity and recover the gains and profits which the infringer has made by the unlawful use of his invention, the infringer in such a suit being regarded as the trustee of the owner of the patent, as respects such gains and profits."

In cases where it is proper to give profits, the courts—unadvisedly, we think—have been led into a rule which they have since declared to often work injustice, and the error of which is easy now to point out.

The rule for ascertaining profits is not laid down by statute, but is to be arrived at by a court of equity upon its own principles.

In *Livingston* v. *Woodworth*, 15 How., 559, and more pointedly in *Dean* v. *Mason*, 20 How., 198, the question was presented in a suit in equity whether the defendant was to be treated as trustee in respect of the *invention*, and therefore bound to use it with the diligence required of a trustee, and to account not merely for profits actually made but for such as he ought to have made, or whether his *quasi* trusteeship extended only to *profits actually realized.* The court took the latter view, and held that he was trustee of the profits realized, and not trustee to use the invention, and therefore that he was accountable only for "profits received," and not for profits which he might have received. Or, to state it in another form, the plaintiff who waives the tort is entitled to take from the defendant what has actually come to his hands, and no more. In *Goodyear* v. *Providence Rubber Company,* 9 Wall., 788, the report of the master allowed for bad debts, and held the defendants liable, in the language of the court, only for "ultimate profits." The Supreme Court approved this, and said : "The calculation is to be made as a manufacturer calculates the profits of his business. 'Profit' is the gain made upon any business or investment when both the receipts and payments are taken into account. (*People* v. *Super. Niag.,* 2 Hill, 23.) The rule is founded in reason and justice. It compensates one party and punishes the other. It makes the wrong-doer liable for actual, not possible gains. The controlling consideration is, that he shall not profit by his wrong. A more favorable rule would offer a premium to dishonesty and invite to aggression."

In *Mowry* v. *Whitney,* 14 Wall., 620, the patent was for a new mode of treating car-wheels after they were cast, and consisted in cooling them in such a slow and peculiar manner that the "chill" or temper of the rim was not injured, while the inherent strains of the metal, due to the uncompensated contraction which takes place when the wheels are allowed to cool in the open air, were avoided, and the wheels made stronger. The defendant made wheels according to this process, and the plaintiff insisted that he should be held accountable for all the profits actually realized in the manufacture, about $90,000. It appeared that this cooling was only one step in the whole manufacture; that there were other modes of cooling which made merchantable wheels, and that the advantage to the manufacturer from using the Whitney process over any other in this step was about $5,000. Thereupon the court held that the $5,000, and not the $90,000, was the gain or profit made by the defendant from the use of the plaintiff's invention.

The decision was undoubtedly correct. But that part of the reasoning which was intended to limit the result arrived at by the master was caught up by the courts as if it was a complete and exhaustive rule, to be applied without regard to results or to the other facts of the case. The idea arose that the defendant was always to be held liable for the difference in cost between the plaintiff's process and any other process open to him ; that is, that he was to be held liable for "savings," neglecting entirely the old rule laid down in *Dean* v. *Mason* and *Goodyear* v. *Providence Rubber Company,* and assumed and acted upon without discussion in *Mowry* v. *Whitney*—that the defendant was only liable to pay over "profits actually realized." And, finally, in *Mevs* v. *Conover,* 11 Official Gazette, 1111, where it appeared that it cost half a dollar a cord less to split wood by the plaintiff's machine than by hand, but the business was such that the defendant made a loss and no profit, the Supreme Court held him liable for the half dollar under guise of profits, because they said the machine saved him from the greater loss of the half dollar, which he would have suffered *if* he had carried on the business by hand-labor.

This mode of reasoning not only assumes that he would have carried on the business by hand-labor, but it further assumes that the ordinary result of the ownership or use of a patent is, that the patentee or user receives *all* the gain arising from the saving in cost. He never does;

his right is for a limited time; his object is to create the largest possible demand at once, as the best way of getting a profit. In actual practice this is invariably the case: either he sells the machine and licenses its use at a price far less than the cost of the labor it saves, or the benefit it confers, or he makes the article and sells it at a price far below the old price. The more widely-extended use the article is capable of, the more he strives to popularize it by a low price. A case often put is that of the inventor of printing. He sold a whole edition of Bibles at the cost, perhaps, of two or three manuscript copies. If the process had been patented, and an infringer the next year had done the same, and had been held answerable for the difference between the cost of a thousand printed copies and a thousand manuscript copies, no treasury in Europe could have responded; he would have been held liable for a profit which he did not make, and which neither he nor the patentee would have made in the ordinary course of events. We must not give the patentee the advantage of the large sale induced by the low price, and the high price incompatible with the large sale.

Take the case of the horseshoe nail, which has been spoken of; made by hand, they cost seventy-five cents a pound; the patentees make them by machine, and find a satisfactory profit in selling at twenty-five cents. Suppose to-day that all the patents were owned by one man, and that a stranger builds a machine which, after litigation, is held to infringe them, the rule of *Mevs* v. *Conover* (11 Official Gazette, 1111) would require him to pay seventy-five, less twenty or twenty-five, say fifty or fifty-five, cents a pound as *profits*, when he did not and would not sell the article for more than twenty-five cents, gross price. Now, this is the exact case which is presented, in a more or less complicated form, in every instance of infringement, by the use of a labor saving or cheapening machine or process. Why cling to a rule which, not accidentally nor in a few cases, but necessarily, and from the false assumption on which it is based, leads to injustice?

Livingstone v. *Woodworth* (15 How., 555) went upon the ground of "actual gains and profits." It was a bill in equity for the infringing use of a patented planer. The first report of the master found fifty cents per thousand feet as the profits realized; upon a recommittal he reckoned at one dollar per thousand feet as being "the amount of profits which may have been, or with due diligence and prudence might have been, realized by the defendants." The Supreme Court declared that it should be restricted to "the actual gains and profits of the appellants during the time their machine was in operation, and during no other period." The question of "savings" does not seem to have been discussed, but it is clear that the decision excluded that ground; for, of course, the actual saving by the use of the machine, over the old jack-plane, far exceeded fifty cents a thousand feet. The decision was, that the amount recoverable upon an accounting should not exceed the "actual gains and profits of the defendants," although their failure to make more was not due to the machine, but to their own want of "due diligence and prudence."

But with the remedies which now exist, and which will continue to exist if this bill becomes a law, profits are not the only recovery. A wanton infringer may sell cheap and depress the price, and not only make no profit himself, but prevent the patentee or a licensee, who has paid for a license, from getting any. In such a case "profits" are not a sufficient redress; an actual injury has been done for which damages should be recovered, in addition for profits, for the injury in excess of

346 MR. J. J. STORROW.

the amount recovered as profits; and if the ordinary remedies will not reach this, the discretionary clause of this section will.

It must not be supposed that because an account of profits gives an insufficient amount in any case, it is the whole recovery that can be had; in the same suit the plaintiff can claim damages. But the two kinds of recovery are different; if one does not give enough, it will be supplemented by the other under the present law and under this section; they are arrived at by different methods; they depend upon different principles; do not pervert one from its true character by making it do the work of the other, when you have the other ready to perform its proper function.

Since the statute of 1870, a court of equity may also give damages where the infringer has so conducted his business that the profits do not give adequate compensation. (§ 4921.) These recoveries are not cumulative; the plaintiff takes whichever sum is largest. (*Birdsall* v. *Coolidge*, 93 U. S., 70.) In England, the present statutes give to a court of law the power to award an account and an injunction in addition to damages. The great advantage of the equity jurisdiction lies in the difficulty of making a jury understand the intricate questions involved in a patent case, and the short time and imperfect means they have of studying them, even if they were competent.

Profits actually realized should, therefore, be the rule of profits as such (though never to the exclusion of damages); for any other assumes that which is not the fact, and which, in the ordinary course of human affairs, cannot be the fact. Such a rule so applied always leads to unjust results; but the court has felt itself so bound by previous decisions that it could not break away from them. In *Packet Company* v. *Sickles* (19 Wall., 618) it declared that, even with the corrective power of a chancellor, its rule of assuming profits had produced results calculated to excite distrust. The case has arisen, therefore, where the court, powerless to relieve itself, must be aided by the legislature.

The purport of the second portion of this section is to enable the court to escape from the mere and absolute rule of savings, and, so to speak, return to the true rule, viz, such portion of the profits actually found in the defendant's hands as are due to the use of the plaintiff's invention.

Cases may well arise where the defendant would have made a profit by the use of the invention, but afterwards lost it in some other part of his business. Such would be the case of a farmer who got his seed cheaply into the ground, but lost his crop from drought or fire or a hurricane. The inquiry as to profits should, therefore, be limited to that part of the business in which the invention is used.

The bill seeks to attain all these ends by that part of section 2 which begins in line 14:

In taking an account of profits in any case, the defendant shall not be charged with any saving he may have made, if he shall show that it has not enabled him to realize an actual profit in that part of his business connected with the use of the invention.

And the court shall determine what proportion of such profit is due to the use of such invention, and what proportion to the other elements from which such profit was derived, capital and personal services excepted ; and the proportion of actual profit so found to be derived from the use of the invention shall be the measure of the profits to be recovered.

The limitations contained in the second paragraph quoted are law to-day. (See *Rubber Co.* v. *Goodyear*, 9 Wall., 788, and *Mowry* v. *Whitney*, 14 Wall., 620.)

When we first undertook to draw this section we tried to state rules which should govern the accounting in all the important elements, but every draught we made we rejected upon examination. We came to the conclusion that it was unsafe to attempt this. We perceived that the cardinal error of the court was in departing from the doctrine of actual profits and adopting the doctrine of savings; or, to state it as the court did, in assuming that the actual profits were in all cases the savings. And so we thought it safest merely to relieve the courts from this rule; to indicate to them the road they must forsake and the direction they must pursue; and it will be readily seen that this is the plan and the purport of this part of the section.

The objection which has been made to the rule proposed is, that it will be difficult to take the account under it; the chief ground, I think, on which overworked judges have been disposed to adopt the rule of savings, is that they have thought it a cheap and easy method of getting at results. Certainly it is a poor argument that a court shall deliberately adopt injustice because it is easy to obtain, and refuse the labor necessary to do justice. A still easier way, and one in many cases tending to more just results, would be to refuse to allow any account at all. But I deny that the objection is well founded in fact. In the planer cases (*Livingston* v. *Woodworth* and *Dean* v. *Mason*)—in the great Providence rubber case, where profits of several hundred thousand dollars, actually realized, were found by the master and decreed by the court, no insuperable difficulty was found. In the Tanner brake cases and the swedge-block cases, where the account was taken on the rule of savings, the result so far reached, whether right or wrong, has been after some of the longest litigations on record. In the latter cases, the report was once revised, enormously cut down, and recommitted by the circuit court; and yet, when it came before the Supreme Court, in *The Cawood Patent* (94 U. S., 605), that court found that it was almost worthless, and hardly presented any data upon which they could find a just decree. Profits actually realized must still be ascertained in all cases where the infringement consists in making, and in many cases where it consists in using, a new product, or in using a machine or process which produces an article of better quality than before, though at no less cost.

The right to recover *profits* is extremely important. Nothing will better serve to check wanton infringements than a conviction on the part of the infringer that he cannot retain any profits due to his wrong-doing. But in practice serious difficulties have arisen with regard to the recovery of profits as now allowed by the courts.

How can you show by any system of accounting what a railroad gains by the use of a safety-switch, more expensive to make and to maintain than the old, but which may save the lives of passengers? or by an expensive spring or ventilator, which adds to their comfort? or how much a man gains in money from an artificial limb, or an improvement in it, or from a more comfortable shoe? or how much a city government gains from an electric fire-alarm? From the use of these and many other inventions the defendant derives a real advantage, which can be estimated by a jury or a master, but cannot be proved in figures by the technical process of accounting.

The attempt to reach justice in such cases—and there are very many of them—by the ordinary process of a debtor and creditor account must end in failure; or if a decree is for the balance of an account in such a case it will be mere chance whether it be right or wrong. The judgment of a court, or master, or a jury may arrive at a just result; but an account, where judgment and discretion can enter only indirectly and furtively, and theoretically not at all, is as incompetent to reach a conclusion in such a case as a jury is to state a partnership account.

Let us see if we can define the cases in which this difficulty, or, rather, this impossibility, arises.

Clearly, it will be only in cases where the essence of the infringement consists in the *use;* or, to state in another way, where the gain consists in the *use* in the course of the infringer's business, and not in making the patented thing, nor selling the patented thing, nor in selling the product of that which is patented, whether the patent be for a machine or for a process.

If the mill-owner makes a new implement, which exactly takes the place of the old, and he uses it in his mill instead of the old, and the only advantage is that it is cheaper to make, there is no insuperable difficulty in ascertaining his gain. If he uses the new machine or new process in producing an article for sale, there is no more difficulty than there would be if he had a quarrel with his partner and a court of equity took an account between them. If he makes and sells the patented machine or composition of matter, there is no difficulty.

The trouble arises whenever the effects of the element which belongs to the plaintiff are so interwoven with the effects of the far greater number belonging to the defendant, that the ultimate result of the whole business cannot be dissected, and a due proportion thereof attributed to each element with the certainty required in accounting. This case will arise chiefly, and perhaps entirely, where the invention can be used only in connection with, or as a part of, a business or industry of such a character that the patentee cannot carry on the whole of it himself, but must expect to derive profit from his invention by in some manner licensing the *use* of the thing by others. A patented railroad-switch was instanced in *Seymour* v. *McCormick* (16 How., 480), as an apparatus, the actual *use* of which no patentee could or would desire to confine to himself. A valve for marine engines would be another instance. On the other hand, certain patented machines may be such that, with one establishment stocked with them, the patentee can supply the market with the product, and, therefore, may well keep the machines for his own use.

The first part of this section attempts to deal with this acknowledged difficulty by providing that in the class of cases where it arises damages may be given, but no account of profits as such allowed, and I think that the only question for debate under this section, the only question upon which the section can reasonably be criticised, is whether the language we have used will include the class which ought to be included, and will include no more.

Within that class the section places, first, all those patents whose owner has declared their character by his course of dealing in licensing freely; it also places within the class those patents with relation to which such a course of dealing has not yet arisen, but which, from their nature, must obviously be so dealt with. It has been objected that it was dangerous to allow a court to say how the patentee is going to use his patent. There is force in the objection, abstractly considered, but it is thought that the provision is now so guarded that no injustice will arise in practice. Some of the most important of these safeguards were suggested by the course of discussion before the Senate Committee, and will doubtless appear in their report, which we shall lay before you.

Experience has shown that the variety of circumstances presented in patent cases is so great and so unexpected that, after the best rules are laid down, it is essential to give the court power to modify the result in exceptional cases, and the third clause has been introduced for that purpose, allowing the court to increase or diminish the amount of re-covery. It has been objected that this leaves the whole matter to the court; and, therefore, that the previous rules are useless. This objection is ill-founded. The previous parts are needed largely to enable the court to escape from the rules by which they now feel bound; and, moreover, it is common, especially in equity, to find judicially-established rules, which guide the discretion, though they do not bind it, as a statute would, in cases exceptional in their character. The patent law has almost always given to the court power to increase the damages. (R. S., 4919, re-enacted from the old statute.) The court has declared (*Rubber Co.* v. *Goodyear*, 9 Wall., 788) that in equity "the severity of the decree may be increased or mitigated, according to the complexion of the conduct of the offender"; and in *Packet Co.* v. *Sickles* (19 Wall., 618) it spoke of the "corrective powers in the hands of the chancellor." From this experience of judicial action, it is certain that the scope given by this section will be looked upon and used as a corrective power, to be availed of in exceptional cases after the rules have been applied, and not as an invitation to disregard all the rules which the previous part of the same section has laid down.

In accordance with suggestions made at the hearing before the Senate committee, it was understood that the following clause would be inserted near the end of the section, just before the proviso:

And whenever the court shall be of opinion that the claims of the plaintiff in the suit, or the defenses or infringements of the defendant are either vexatious or without probable cause, it may award in favor of the successful party such sums for counsel-fees and expenses of suit as may be just and reasonable."

This will very strongly tend to prevent vexatious claims or vexatious defenses, and will enable persons to refuse to pay claims sometimes made by speculators who will no longer be able to frighten a defendant into a payment to avoid the expense of litigation. (See, upon this point, Arguments before Senate Committee, pp. 126, 188, 189.)

This whole section was very much discussed before the Senate committee. (See passages referred to on p. 217.)

The present statutes relating to remedies are—R. S., 4919, 4921, taken without essential change from act 1819, c. 19, 3 Stat., 481; act 1836, c. 357, § 14, 5 Stat., 117; (see act 1800, c. 25, § 3, 2 Stat., 37;) act 1836, § 17.

Two other objections have been made to this section. One is, that it will, in some cases, diminish the amount the plaintiff is to recover, and it is said that, considering the great trouble and expense he is put to by the wrong-doer, the path of the latter ought not be smoothed. The objection is unsound. The normal rule of profits and damages as it now exists, and also as this section will leave it, applies alike to the wanton infringer, to the men who combine to break down the patentee, and to those who, in ignorance of the plaintiff's patent, or who, with entire good faith and upon the advice of the most competent men that they do not infringe, have embarked in the business which the court finally holds is against the plaintiff's right. All notion of punitive damages, or damages compensating for the expenses of litigation, must be banished from such a rule, as it is from all other rules of damages; certainly it has no place in a court of equity. We have not lost sight of the consideration, however, but have put in an express provision about expenses of suit, which will enable the court to reimburse the plaintiff his expenses when the character of the acts calls for such a decree.

The other objection is that this section retroacts on existing causes of action. For this see p. 185, *infra*.

I said that the plaintiff was not barred of recovery when there were
no profits; that he always had his claim for damages, and that great
sheet-anchor of the patentee—his right to an injunction. To guard
against any possible misapprehension on that score, we originally added
a clause expressly saving the right to an injunction, and I now ask you
to add a similar clause saving the right to damages in equity, as under
the statute of 1870. (R. S., 4921.) Add at end of section 2 the following:

Nor to recover in a suit in equity, in addition to the profits to be accounted for, the
damages the complainant has sustained by the infringements complained of.

SECTION 3.—In patent suits in equity, the court first determines the
validity of the patent and the question of infringement; it then orders
an account. An appeal cannot be taken unless the account has been
completed. The accounting is very expensive, and consumes much
time, and if the decision as to validity or infringement is reversed, or
even modified on appeal, it becomes useless. This section authorizes
the court to permit the appeal to be taken at once.

SECTION 4.—This preserves in the circuit court, pending an appeal,
the same power over the parties, with relation to the injunction, which
it had before the appeal. The Senate committee have proposed to add
after the word " and" in line 5, the words "subject to such rules and
regulations as the Supreme Court may establish"; the amendment is
good.

SECTION 5.—*Reissues.* This section was the subject of much discussion before the Senate committee; many verbal amendments were
suggested, but it is believed that the best are embodied in the communication of the honorable Commissioner of Patents, and that the
section should be adopted in the form approved by him and printed in
Senate Arg., p. 202. The committee are referred to all the passages in
the Senate Argument collected on p. 218 of the index, but especially to
pages 45, 136, 204, for a full statement of the reasons why a reissue is
required, and the manner in which it should be made.

On page 136 and subsequent pages I discussed the subject at considerable length, and gave a number of illustrations. I will not repeat
them, but will ask the committee to read them. The views of the Hon.
Commissioner are expressed on page 204, and should be studied.

It is not enough for the inventor to describe the machine which he
has constructed. He must show the public, " in full, clear, concise, and
exact terms," how to make it and how to use it. " He shall explain the
principle thereof, and the best mode in which he has contemplated applying that principle, so as to distinguish it from other inventions; and
he shall particularly point out and distinctly claim the part, improvement, or combination which he claims as his invention or discovery."
(R. S., 4888.) To comply with these statute requirements needs a perfect knowledge of all that has been done up to that moment—that is,
of the "state of the art," as it is called—which few inventors possess.
It requires a statement of and explanation of the "principle" of the invention, which is extremely difficult in many cases. (*v.* Senate Arg., p.
136.) For example, Mr. Bell has caused to be constructed a great many
telephones, in accordance with his invention. Scientific men have as
yet vainly endeavored to discover " the principle thereof." How could
Mr. Bell state it and explain it a year or two ago ? If, therefore, through
inadvertence, accident, or mistake, the inventor fails to comply with
these technical (but valuable) requirements of the statute, and makes
his patent invalid by inserting too broad a statement, or an erroneous
explanation, or restricts it by so narrow a statement that others can

avail themselves of it and yet keep outside of its letter, the law ought to allow him to correct his mistake. Indeed, for the same reason that it requires him to make the statement it should encourage him to correct it when he finds that it is wrong. Experience has shown that pleadings, even under our untechnical forms, must often be amended, and so the practice of the government, from the beginning of the patent system, was to permit such amendments. In *Grant* v. *Raymond* (6 Peters, 244) the Supreme Court (Marshall, C. J.) sanctioned this practice, and declared that they were "satisfied that it is required by justice and good faith." They held that it was proper "where the defect in the specification arose from inadvertence or mistake, and without any fraud or misconduct on the part of the patentee." The case of *Grant* v. *Raymond* was decided at the January term, 1832; and July 3, 1832, Congress recognized and regulated the practice, using language "inadvertence, accident, or mistake, and without any fraudulent or deceptive intention," evidently taken from the opinion of the court; and this has continued to be the statute law ever since.

The court said that one case where it was required was where the mistake arose from the fault of the government, because the Secretary of State exercised the power under the old act, and the Commissioner of Patents is required to exercise it under the act of 1836, of obliging the inventor to make his specification conform to their views. Such cases often arise, and one came before the Supreme Court in *Morey* v. *Lockwood* (8 Wall., 200).

The patent is to be amended so as to express what the inventor substantially disclosed to the office as his invention in the papers which he filed there, or (in the language of *Seymour* v. *Osborne*, 11 Wall., 644, 645) "whatever was described, suggested, or substantially indicated" as constituting "the same invention as that embraced and secured in the original patent;" *i. e.,* what he showed that he intended to secure, but failed to. Against the validity of a reissue two lines of defense should therefore be allowed, one the same as that allowed to original patents, that the patentee was not the first inventor; another, peculiar to reissues, that the amendments introduced go beyond the proper scope of amendments, and interpolate other inventions. The language of Marshall, C. J., in *Grant* v. *Raymond* (6 Pet., 242), shows that he considered both defenses open. The courts, however, first inclined to hold that the decision of the Commissioner was conclusive on the second question (*Allen* v. *Blunt*, 3 Story, 744), though perhaps they never came quite to that point. They have since nearly escaped from that doctrine, but by a process of reasoning which has involved them in other difficulties. They declare that if they could see, on comparison of the old patent and the new, that as matter of law they were not for the same invention, the new patent was void, because in granting it the Commissioner exceeded his jurisdiction. (*Seymour* v. *Osborne*, 11 Wall., 644.) Yet the same opinion declared that the reissue might embrace matter "substantially indicated in the * * * Patent-Office model" which forms no part of the original patent. In *Morey* v. *Lockwood* (8 Wall., 230) the court had no doubt but that the specification might be corrected by the original application. The reasoning of the court in *Seymour* v. *Osborne* shows that what they had in view was that the amendment should not go beyond the facts placed upon the files of the office before the original patent issued.

This section, as drawn and amended by the Hon. Commissioner, so limits the right of reissue, and clearly leaves all these essential questions open for judicial examination.

It is thought that the model ought not to be resorted to for reissues; it forms no part of the patent nor of the application; its whole function is to " exhibit advantageously " (R. S. 4891) what the application and the patent describe and claim. This new section is so amended. (See particularly Senate Arg., pp. 47, 57, 65, 78, 140, 195, 204, 218.)

The present statute allows *ex parte* oral evidence to be resorted to in certain cases. This section prevents that entirely.

The present law is R. S. 4916.

A MEMBER OF THE COMMITTEE. What is your idea of the propriety of a statute of limitations on that subject ?

Mr. STORROW. The objections to that are twofold. One is that the mistake should be corrected whenever it is discovered. Time and again a mistake is not discovered until the lapse of quite a length of time. If it is corrected in the proper way, it does no harm; it must be done with proper caution. The difficulty in limiting the time would be that you would practically destroy the right of reissue; for I think most patents are not reissued until they are more than three years old. The defect is not discovered until after that. If you limit it to three years, then when the court at a trial finds a verbal defect in the specification, which certainly will not be till the patent is more than three years old, you go back to the difficulty they had in England in the beginning, when for years the courts would find some flaw in the language, and patent after patent was overthrown forever, because the language of the specification did not aptly describe the invention. The courts were quite astute in finding that out, and patents were destroyed by them until inventors became discouraged and thought it useless to invent machines if they had also to invent a language to describe them.

These are the main reasons why I think the right of reissue should not be limited in time, but should be limited to what the parties have referred to in the papers that were on file in the office at the time the first patent was issued; and it should be re-examined to the fullest extent.

SECTION 6.—*Reissues not to retroact.* The law requires that patents should state what the inventor claims as new; all that is not so claimed the public may lawfully use. If the patentee amends his claims by a reissue, and these new claims cover a machine which was not covered by the claims in existence when it was made, the patentee may prevent the use of the same machine which the defendant lawfully built and invested his money in. (*Stimpson* v. *West Chester R. R. Co.*, 4 How., 402.)

In order to amend his patent, the law obliges the patentee to surrender it and take out a new one. The courts have held that the destruction of the patent by surrender destroys his existing right of action for past infringement.

The amendment takes away from the reissue its retroactive character in both respects.

The abstract justice of this change is apparent. Its practical utility will be very great. The severest annoyance from reissues comes in cases where a reissue for the first time brings under the claims of a patent some device which, until then uncovered, has gone into general use as a part of expensive machines. If it had been patented, the parties might have used something else in place of it; but it would now cost them so much to reconstruct their machines, that they are obliged to submit to some exaction to save that expense.

SECTION 7.—Provides that if a patent be issued to two on the invention of one, or to one on the invention of two, this mistake may be corrected as a clerical error, by the consent of all the inventors and owners.

SECTION 8.—A provision for taking testimony *in perpetuam* in patent cases, introduced because the general law applicable to all cases is not adequate in patent causes.

Various amendments to improve its practical working and prevent abuse were introduced before the Senate committee, and should be adopted. (See Senate Argument, pp. 80, 109.)

SECTION 9.—Allows suits to be brought to repeal and annul patents which are void.

Existing laws afford no adequate remedy. (See Opin. Attorney-General, of Nov. 19, 1874, Patent-Office Gazette, vol. 6, p. 723; Attorney-General *v.* Rumford Works, 9 ib., 1062.)

SECTION 10.—Supplies a remedy for cases where a person injures the business of another, by advertising that it infringes a patent, and yet refuses to bring a suit in which the validity of the patent or the question of infringement can be tried.

SECTION 11.—*Periodical fees.* According to the spirit of the Constitution, patents are granted to encourage such inventions as promote the progress of the useful arts. If the invention at once takes place in the arts as a practical thing, or if it so clearly embodies a great step forward that the inventor or others are incited to develop it to a practical and pecuniarily profitable application, it constitutes a progress, and purpose of the law is satisfied. But features are often patented which are afterward found neither to be useful nor to hold out hopes of usefulness enough to lead to attempts to improve them. A subsequent inventor, making a truly useful machine, unconsciously uses one of those features, and the patent stops him; it does not promote the progress of the useful arts that such a patent should live merely to hinder, and not to constitute, progress. It is impossible for the preliminary examination at the Patent Office to weed out such patents, for only several years' trial can demonstrate their failure. Attempts to do it in advance will generally end in mistakes. Patents were refused in Prussia for the Bessemer process of making steel and for the Siemens regenerative furnace. Virtual abandonment by the patentee is the only safe test; and this section, for this purpose, requires a fee of $50 at the end of four years, and $100 at the end of nine years; non-payment of either is to kill the patent. The system works well abroad. In England, the first payment of £50 leaves only about 25 per cent. alive, and the second of £100 leaves only about 10 per cent. Our fee is one-fifth as large, and our patents are much better sifted by a preliminary examination than the English, and therefore the system will not have so much effect here, but it will doubtless be extremely useful to meritorious inventors and to the public. (See Senate Arg., p. 143, and remarks of Hon. Commissioner of Patents, p. 205, and amendments which should be adopted, p. 190.)

The result in England has been that the average life of a patent has been shortened from fourteen to about four years; we think that this section will shorten it from seventeen to about eight years, and it will not diminish the stimulus to invention, because it will only cut off those which, after trial, have been practically abandoned as worthless.

SECTION 12.—This requires exclusive licenses to be recorded in the same manner as technical grants, because, practically, the two are equivalent. It shortens the time allowed for recording assignments from three months to one month; improvements in the mail-service since

1836 justify this. It allows all agreements about patents to be recorded, and makes certified copies from the record to be legal evidence.

SECTION 13.—The law now is, that each joint owner of a patent may grant licenses without the consent of the other. (*Clum* v. *Brewer*, 2 Curtis, 524). The object of this amendment is to give full effect to an agreement between them as to which shall exercise this power, if the agreement be in writing, signed by all the parties, and recorded.

SECTION 14.—This punishes, by not exceeding one year's imprisonment or $1,000 fine, whosoever sells as unencumbered a patent which he actually knows he has no power to sell and convey. This is new. To be amended by inserting in line 1, after " whoever," the words "with intent to defraud."

The following sections amend those which regulate proceedings in the Patent Office; and particular attention is invited to the comments of the honorable Commissioner upon them in Senate argument, p. 204 :

SECTION 15.—This requires the Assistant Commissioner of Patents to give the same bond as the Commissioner.

SECTION 16.—This establishes the price for Patent-Office copies—in no case to be less than actual cost.

SECTION 17.—The old statute allowed certified copies of papers to be used as evidence wherever the originals would be competent. The amendment extends the provision to models, and also allows the assistant commissioner to sign the certificate.

SECTIONS 18 AND 22.—R. S. 4885 and 4897 allow six months' grace for payment of the final fee, and then two years more, in addition, by means of a renewed application. This amendment consolidates the two sections and abolishes the two years' allowance.

The honorable Commissioner advises to strike out our section 22 and to adopt a different phraseology. (See Senate Arg., pp. 203, 207.) He also proposes to add a proviso to section 18 (v., p. 206). Both these changes should be adopted.

SECTION 19.—The law about granting patents in this country to those who have patented their inventions abroad has been changed several times, particularly by the act of March 2, 1861, in a manner which has caused considerable confusion. This section establishes what is believed to be a just and reasonable rule. It retains the provision that a foreign patentee cannot come here to get a patent for an invention that has been in use here for two years, and this part, down to the word "application" in line 10, is copied with merely one or two verbal changes from the present statute. The section then adds a new requirement, that if he makes it known, by patenting it abroad, he must apply it here within two years, or it can be used by the public.

SECTION 20.—This amends sec. 4794 by making two years' neglect to prosecute an application conclusively equivalent to an abandonment thereof. The honorable Commissioner of Patents proposes a modification of this which does not essentially change its character, and the modification should be adopted. (See Senate Arg., pp. 203, 207.)

SECTION 21.—At one time the surrender of a patent and the application for a reissue were required to be sworn to by the assignee and at another time by the inventor. This amendment leaves it to be sworn to by the assignee. The oath is of no importance, because the action of the Commissioner is to be based on the sworn statements filed by the inventor on his original application. To require his oath to the new application, is to enable him to extort money from the person who has already bought and paid him for the invention.

SECTION 23.—The law has always required the patentee to mark on the article the date of the patent. About 300 patents a week are now issued, all bearing the same date. This amendment requires him to add the number of his patent, in order that it may be identified.

SECTION 24.—This amends section 4904, about interference applications in the office, so as to include reissue applications, and make the law about them substantially conform to what the decisions have established about them, except that, in determining whether an interference contest shall be ordered, reference is to be had solely to the dates of the original applications. The subject-matter of this section and the history of the decisions bearing upon it are elaborately discussed and stated by the honorable assistant commissioner of patents (Senate Arg., p. 197) and the honorable Commissioner (p. 207), and the section as drawn is approved, with some verbal amendments. (See also Senate Arg., p. 71.)

The honorable Commissioner of Patents has added a new section, by way of amendment to R. S. 484 and 4891. These amendments look to the abolition of models, except in special cases, and also enable the Commissioner to require working-models in certain cases. His views (Senate Arg., pp. 203, 208) appear to be sound. For a discussion upon the subject of models, see Senate argument, pp. 79, 87.

SECTION 25.—Repeals all inconsistent laws. Careful provisions have been added to each section which relates to substantial rights as distinguished from the form of remedy, so that the changes introduced by this bill shall not be destructive of existing rights of property.

Under this last head, I propose to offer some remarks upon a question which received considerable discussion before the Senate Committee, viz: What is the right of a patentee, and do the retroactive clauses of this bill affect any vested interests—anything which is "property"—within the meaning of the Constitution or of those rules which should limit the exercise of legislative power?

Constitution of the United States, article 1, *section* 8: "The Congress shall have power * * * to promote the progress of science and useful arts, by securing for limited times to authors and inventors the exclusive right to their respective writings and discoveries."

This provision gives to Congress the power "to promote the progress of science and useful arts." It is for Congress to determine whether it will do this or not; but if it elects to do it, the Constitution provides only one means for doing it, and that is "by securing for limited times to authors and inventors the *exclusive right* to their respective writings and discoveries." It is for Congress to decide whether it will secure the right, and for how long it will secure it; but the nature of the right is fixed by the Constitution; it is to be "exclusive," just as much as the rules of naturalization and laws on the subject of bankruptcy are to be "uniform." As to these two, the Constitution does not say in terms that a law not uniform shall not be enacted; it is enough that it gives no power to enact any laws of bankruptcy or naturalization except "uniform" laws and rules, nor to secure any right to the inventor except an "exclusive" right.

It is not, however, very material for the purposes of the present inquiry what, under the Constitution, the right must be; it would be enough that the existing rights of existing patentees are exclusive; and we may readily agree that they are, because, for nearly ninety years, all the statutes have in terms given them the "exclusive right to make, use, and vend."

We shall not dispute, and, indeed, for my own part, I shall always strenuously insist that the right conferred by the patent is "property," within the meaning of the seventh amendment and of the rules which protect vested rights. The courts of the United States have put this question at rest.

In the case of *McClurg* v. *Kingsland* (1 How., U. S., 206), the question was whether certain defenses allowed by the acts of 1836 and 1839 could apply to a patent granted before 1836? It was argued that these acts only changed the remedy. But the court held that even Congress could not make such a change as to interpose new defenses which would destroy the validity of the patent; for, in effect, it would be to "take away the *rights of property* in existing patents." "This repeal, therefore, can have no effect to impair the *right of property* then existing in a patentee or his assignee, according to the well-established principles of this court in 8 Wheaton, 493."

This decision is entitled to peculiar weight, because at the same term the court had before them the very important case of *Bronson* v. *Kinzie*, which involved the fullest consideration of the doctrine of vested rights under our Constitution, and which is reported in the same volume. The two cases may fitly read together.

In *Seymour* v. *Osborne* (11 Wall., 533), they said: "Inventions secured by letters patent are property in the holder of the patent, and as such are as much entitled to protection as any other property consisting of a franchise during the term for which the franchise or the exclusive right is granted."

The grant of a patent for an invention is not a pure gift, but is, upon consideration, as much as a patent for land given upon payment. The Government has declared that if any one will invent, will deprive himself of the ability to work his invention in secret for an indefinite term, and will disclose it to the public, it will protect him in the exclusive enjoyment for a limited time; and when he has done his part, and the Government has granted its patent, the promise and the grant have all the elements of a contract upon consideration, and it has been so declared. (*Attorney.General* v. *Rumford Works*, 9 Gazette, 1062.)

On the other hand, it is equally well settled that the legislature may modify the remedy; and the only limitation upon this power—and it is a power which it may become their duty to exercise—is that it shall not be so exercised as to impair vested rights. And the distinction and the limitation are well laid down in *Bronson* v. *Kinzie*; and as both that case and the passages quoted from *McClurg* v. *Kingsland* rest professedly upon *Green* v. *Biddle* (8 Wheat., 493) those three cases will give us the law, and I think all the law, that bears upon the point.

Under a contract to pay money, the right of the creditor is to have the whole amount due on the day when it is due. He recovers against the debtor as a contractor, not as a tortfeasor. On the footing of the promise he recovers his debt, not damages, though he may also recover damages, as interest, for the wrongful detention of it. He recovers, in effect, the thing itself; and a law which declared that when he sued he should recover less than the amount promised, or should be delayed two years, would keep him out of his property, and so substantially impair his right, not to his judgment, but to his property, his contract.

But the patentee has no promise from the infringer. Whether his recovery be of damages *eo nomine*, or whether, at his request and for the sake of the remedy, a court of equity converts the infringer into a trustee *de son tort*, nevertheless the one recovers, not his property, but damages for an invasion of it; and the other is condemned, not to deliver what he has promised to deliver, but what the court considers compensation for a wrong done.

The right in one case is in the money promised; in the other it is in the exclusive use, not in the damages for its invasion. All that relates to the damages belongs to the remedy, and the legislature may change the remedy, so long as they afford one which is efficient, and which leaves no hope of profit to the infringer. That is my position. Neither of the three cases shakes this, but they rather support it.

Green v. *Biddle* (8 Wheat., 490) was a case which rested on a contract made by a State. The court established that the State which granted the land in question and another State which had contracted to respect that grant could not refuse to allow the grantee to recover his land from a trespasser without impairing the obligation of their contracts; and the question then was, whether the statute under discussion did impair the *right in the land*. It was in the nature of a betterment law. It declared that a trespasser should, under certain circumstances, be allowed the value of his improvements; not their value to the owner of the land, but, under the terms of the statute, there might be awarded in his favor an amount much greater than any gain the plaintiff could derive from them, and much greater than the mesne profits; and the plaintiff might be kept out of his land until he paid the sum so awarded. There was in the case some general talk about *any* alteration of the remedy, which the court subsequently retracted; but the ground of the decision was, that such a statute made it cost the true owner a sum, to be paid to the trespasser (over and above any benefit received), in order to obtain his property, and, therefore, substantially impaired his right in the land itself.

In *Bronson* v. *Kinzie* (1 How., 311); the State legislature had passed a law delaying for a certain length of time judicial sales under mortgages, and further providing that no sale should ever take place unless the land would bring such price as might be named by appraisers. The court held that, though in terms this affected the remedy, it substantially impaired the obligation of the contract, because it delayed its fulfillment.

The court (Taney, C. J.) said: " The existing laws of Illinois created and defined the legal and equitable obligations of the mortgage contract. If the laws of the State, passed afterwards, had done nothing more than change the remedy upon contracts of this description, they would be liable to no constitutional objection. For, undoubtedly, a State may regulate at pleasure the modes of proceeding in its courts in relation to past contracts as well as future. It may, for example, shorten the period of time within which claims shall be barred by the statute of limitations. * * * It must reside in every State, to enable it to secure its citizens from unjust and harassing litigation, and to protect them in those pursuits which are necessary to the existence and well-being of every community. And, although a new remedy may be deemed less convenient than the old one, and may, in some degree, render the recovery of debts more tardy and difficult, it will not follow that the law is unconstitutional. Whatever belongs merely to the remedy may be altered according to the will of the State, provided the alteration does not impair the obligation of the contract. But if that effect is produced, it is immaterial whether it is done by acting on the remedy or directly on the contract itself." The court then proceeded to rely on *Green* v. *Biddle*, and to quote from it as follows: "It is no answer that the acts of Kentucky now in question are regulations of the remedy and not of the right to the land. If these acts so change the nature and extent of existing remedies as *materially* to impair the rights and interests of the owner, they are just as much a violation of the compact as if they directly overturned his rights and interests."

The proposed section provides—

1. Against further infringement an injunction final or *pendente lite*, as heretofore.

2. Actual damages as heretofore.

3. All the profits which the infringer has actually realized by the tort in all cases where it is possible to ascertain them.

4. It gives a discretionary power to the court to increase the recovery so as to make it commensurate with the injury sustained.

5. It allows the court to require the wanton infringer to pay the plaintiff's expenses of litigation.

It cannot be pretended that it fails to furnish an efficient remedy or that it invites deliberate infringement by telling the infringer that he shall retain part of the profits of his wrong. And the objection that it ought not to retroact, assumes that it is just abstractly.

All the change which it effects is to modify a rule which the courts have declared to often work injustice; or, in the words by which the court, in *Bronson* v. *Kinzie*, described one of the powers of the State in relation to change of remedies, it " insures the citizen from unjust and harassing litigation."

It therefore affords a full and efficient remedy for any invasion of the patentee's rights, and it is not obnoxious to any objection, unless the *vested* right of the patentee suing for damages for a tort is not merely to *some* adequate remedy and adequate damages, but to exactly such damages as would have been recovered by the judicially-ascertained rule in force when the infringement took place.

Now, though I agree that a plaintiff has a vested right, if you please so to call it, to *adequate* damages, and that no recovery is adequate which allows the wrong-doer to profit by his wrong, yet no case can be found which decides or declares *that there is a vested right in any particular measure of damages*, in an action for tort. On the contrary, the rule, I think, is settled, that the measure of damages is of the remedy, and not of the right. Limitations of actions, rules of evidence, particular rules for the measure of damages, are universally considered to belong to the remedy, and not to the right. The diligent examination of the counsel who represents a special interest—the Tanner brake, so called—has been able to furnish no authority in point. That the patentee is entitled to *some* adequate remedy and an adequate measure, and that to deprive him of it substantially impairs and therefore takes from him his property, the authorities and sound reasoning show; but the right, the property which they affect, is his patent; the reasoning which would push it beyond that would deny to the State the power to change the remedy, for every such change affects the position of either plaintiff or defendant.

On the other hand, the distinction which I insist upon, between the right which is vested property and the damages for its invasion, which are of the remedy, has been pointedly established by the Supreme Court in a case which I used before the Senate committee, and the force of which has never been assailed.

Upon a promise to pay money and interest, the interest as well as the principal is recovered upon the footing of the contract; the contract right is to both; and if the promise is silent as to the rate of interest, the law puts into it the rate of the place of the contract. But if the promise be merely to pay a sum certain, on a day certain, then, whatever is recovered beyond that, in the nature of interest, is by way of damages, and not in the nature of the enforcement of a contract. The Supreme Court of the United States have decided (*Foster* v. *Goddard*, 17 Wall.,) that in such a case as that the rate of interest to be recovered by way of damages is to be governed by the law of the place of trial, and of the time of trial. I am unable to see, under that decision, why the amount to be recovered for the invasion of a patent right must not be settled by the law of the *forum*, and, consequontly, that it may be changed as any other remedy may be changed, by the law of the *forum*. Indeed, the right of the plaintiff is to such damages, such remedy as the law in existence at the time and place of trial will give him, subject only to the limitation that the remedy must be adequate.

But do we change the rule? *Livingston* v. *Woodworth* and *Dean* v. *Mason*, in their facts, presented precisely the cases which our section is supposed to affect; yet the decision in those cases was exactly in accordance with our rule, and was utterly wrong if the so-called rule of savings alone is to be followed. Which is law? Or, rather, which will the Supreme Court declare to be law when the question is carefully presented to them? Are you changing a rule which has become established as a rule of property, and on the faith of which rights have become vested? or are you establishing one upon a question which is yet unsettled, and where you are only striving to correct a tendency of the court to depart from what, up to *Moury* v. *Whitney*, was settled, and what was not disturbed by the *decision* in that case, however it may have been partly lost sight of by the learned judge who wrote the opinion? Could not the Supreme Court adhere to the earlier decisions the next time the question comes up, without being exposed to the charge of disturbing vested rights? Upon precisely that question I call your attention to *Olcott* v. *Supervisors* (16 Wall., 690), and cases cited, where the Supreme Court considered and declared when a judicial decision upon a question had so far ripened into a rule of property that it could not be changed without affecting vested rights; and the problem before you is entirely wanting in the elements upon which that case rested.

Whether it is wise to make the change is one question, and that is addressed to your discretion. That you have the constitutional right to make it, I cannot doubt.

That sections one and two ought to retroact, if you have the power to make them, seems to me clear. If the change is useful, the sooner it takes effect the better. Moreover, the argument of practical usefulness is very great; for if they do not apply to existing causes of action, then in a suit brought next year for a continued infringement, one rule of profits must be applied up to-day, and a different rule from to-day onward, and that in the same suit.

Let me repeat what I said before: No one can feel more deeply than I do the benefits the patent system with all its drawbacks has conferred on the community, and among the interests that I represent here are those who are inventors and owners of some extremely valuable and practically successful patents—men whose business is based on patents. I hope this bill will become a law, because I think it will improve the system, and improve it in the interest of the inventor as well as the user. It will not impair the protection which the patentee receives, but it will relieve the public from many annoyances which are felt from some rules which the courts have declared to work injustice. It is for the interest of the patentee that they should be removed; for a system which works injustice cannot work smoothly in this country, and is always in danger of destruction.

ARGUMENT OF GEO. PAYSON, ESQ., GENERAL COUNSEL WESTERN RAILROAD ASSOCIATION.

[*February 22, 1878.*]

Mr. PAYSON. Mr. Chairman and gentlemen of the committee: It is a matter of surprise to me to find myself here addressing you on this subject after all the argument that has been had upon it; but I take it for granted that as long as you are patient enough to listen, some one will be found to talk. I shall endeavor, for my own sake, as well as for your own, to be as brief as possible, and I shall confine what few suggestions I have to offer to those portions of this bill (H. of R., 1612) which seem to me the most important, and those which I understand are most likely to meet with opposition.

LIMITATION.

I wish to call your attention, first, to the first section, in regard to the statute of limitations; not so much with a view of insisting upon the importance of this amendment, because I consider that to be generally conceded; but to call your attention to what seems to me to furnish the fullest and most satisfactory explanation of the difficulties with which this whole subject has been attended from the beginning. Congress and the courts, and more particularly the courts, have dealt with this whole subject of patents and patentees as if it were something that lay entirely outside of the general course of judicial and legislative proceedings. They have dealt with the patentee very much as they have been in the habit of dealing with the Indian; partly as if he were a spoiled child, and partly as if he were a wild beast: only in the case of the patentee there is a great deal more of the spoiled child and less of the wild beast. In doing this they have disregarded what seems to me to be a fundamental maxim of the law, namely, that you shall make no discrimination, whether just or unjust, between one class of citizens, or between one species of property and another, unless it is absolutely necessary. In all the legislation upon this subject—I may call it "judicial legislation"—this distinction, I think, exists to a certain extent between patent property and other property, that whereas the other property owners throughout the length and breadth of the United States are subject to a certain set of rules, which are the same in all important respects, the law in regard to patents has an entirely separate set of rules. Of course, to a certain extent, this is unavoidable, but the mischief has not stopped there. Separate and different rules obtain in all the provisions of the patent law. No better illustration of this can be found than this statute of limitations.

You all know that in relation to all other species of property than patent property in every State of the Union we have what is known as the statute of limitations, and though the tendency some years ago was to regard the plea of these statutes as savoring of meanness, that has gone by. We look upon these statutes as statutes of repose, made just as much for the benefit of the creditor as for the debtor. It is perfectly fair here to apply the well-known maxim that "short credits make long friendships." By some strange fatality until the year 1870 no statute of limitations was passed by the American Congress. Whether the State statutes of limitations have any application to patent statutes may be questioned; but whether they apply or not, it is manifest that it is far better for all concerned that there should be but one statute common throughout the length and breadth of the land.

PERPETUATING TESTIMONY.

The length of these statutes of limitations varies in different States from six years, as the longest period, to one year. This bill provides for the general allowance of four years, and it not only thereby puts the patent owner on the same plane with the owners of other property, but I think it is equally an advantage to the patentee as well as to the so-called "dishonest" infringer.

It has been suggested that this amendment itself might well be amended, and that is my view of this matter. I say nothing as to the body of the section which provides for four years' statute of limitations, but the proviso at the end of it, which provides that "rights of action existing at the passage of this act may be enforced by suits brought within four years thereafter, if not previously barred by laws already existing," partakes a little of the character of the special legislation that I have been speaking about, and gives to the owner of patent property a period in which to bring his suits which is wholly unknown to the law in former times. Thirty days has been, in many cases, considered amply sufficient to enable the property owner to bring his suit after an act becomes a law. Here it is four years. I suggest to you the propriety of shortening the four years and bringing it within much more reasonable limits.

The next point to which I call your attention is that in regard to perpetuating testimony. It has been suggested in regart to that, first, that there is no need of it, because the general law on that subject already existing is sufficient; and, secondly, because it would work a prejudice to the patentee.

I have given considerable time and study to this matter, and I will say with the utmost confidence, that there is no existing statute on this subject which is at all able to meet the case. There are two defects in the general law—I mean the sections of the Revised Statutes now in force providing generally for the perpetuation of testimony. In the first place, under that act only one petitioner or one party interested can bring suit. If there are eighty or one hundred different parties all equally interested in the matter, they must go to the enormous expense of filing eighty or an hundred different petitions. This bill provides that all parties interested may join in one petition. This is equally advantageous to the petitioners and to the adverse party. I represent a large number of railroads; every one of whom, with but two exceptions, I think, is interested in resisting a pending claim. The claim is an old one; it took its origin in 1852. The lives of our witnesses are continually dropping out. If, under the existing law, I should file a petition for the sake of perpetuating testimony of the few witnesses who survive, the expense of that alone would probably restrain me.

In the second place, the act does not apply at all to any case of this character. The law on that subject is well laid down in Daniels on Chancery Pleadings and Practice. It is well shown that the party must be able to swear that his title or interest in the property in question is in the nature of a revision, not to take effect for years. It does not apply to property of this description, and there is no court in the country that will hold that it does so apply. I don't know how it is in other States, but in Illinois the statute is simply a declaration of the common law; it does not make it any broader, so that it has been precisely as if the common-law doctrine was the only law in force applicable to this subject. The principal objection made to this statute is that it enables the giving to the patentee what has been here called the "black eye."

Probably it does do that, but it enables the patentee to furnish the plaster. The same provision which enables the petitioner to come into court and establish proof of priority of invention, or to offer evidence going to show that the patentee was not the first inventor, also enables the patentee to come into court and remove that stigma and put in evidence that which he may be equally desirous of preserving—the showing of the date of the invention. I have, therefore, thought that there is no force in either of these objections, and, though I admit that in all probability this section will not be frequently used, yet the very fact of its being upon the statute-book will render it less necessary, and will compel patentees to bring their suits to a speedy issue.

This latest [Senate] copy of the bill is open to one objection, in the nature of a reply to what I have just stated, in that it provides, in an unfortunate use of phraseology, that the patentee may put in evidence for the purpose of "contradicting or impeaching" the witnesses of the petitioner. I suggest that it would be far better to recall the original word, and to allow the patentee to "rebut," which has a well-settled meaning, and a much broader meaning than the words "to contradict or impeach." I think with that changed back again, the revision of the section would be an improvement; and with the right to offer evidence by way of rebuttal, such a law would be equally advantageous to both parties, because the patentee as well as the infringer, and the witnesses upon which the rights of each depend, are liable to sudden death.

REISSUES.

The next section I notice is that concerning reissues. It is an old saying that "if you scratch a Russian you will find a Tartar." Scratch a reissue and you will find a fraud. In nine cases out of ten you will find a fraud upon the law, and in every instance a fraud in fact.

It becomes necessary for me to call you attention to what I must regard as the most extraordinary instance of judicial legislation which has ever come under my notice. The terms of the act are perfectly clear and unambiguous—the act in regard to reissues. The act provides that whenever a patent shall be found inoperative and invalid by reason of a defective specification, or by reason of the patentee claiming as his own that of which he was not the original inventor, if the error has arisen by accident or mistake, the Commissioner shall grant a reissue. It would be impossible for us to devise words more free from ambiguity; yet, gentlemen, with two solitary exceptions—the decision of Chief-Justice Taney in 1840 and of Judge Grier—the courts have from the beginning considered the words as if they meant "too little." And what is the consequence? Why, so often as one patent is surrendered and reissued for claiming too much, seventy patents are surrendered and reissued for claiming too little. There is no warranty for it in the law; there is no justification for it in the statute; and yet the courts, either by accident or from their constant leaning in favor of the patentee, have put upon it this marvelous construction. I never yet have seen, so far as my memory serves me, a single reissued patent according to the provisions of the act of Congress.

A MEMBER OF THE COMMITTEE. Do you mean that the reissues generally contain more than the original?

Mr. PAYSON. I mean just that. It never contains less. And yet the act of Congress says that it may be surrendered only because it contains too much. That is never done. I don't mean that there never was a single instance, but it is proper for me to say that it is never done. The object of obtaining a reissue is to expand the claim. Judge Taney in 1840 decided in strict compliance with the provision of Congress, that there were but two cases where the reissue may be obtained lawfully: 1. Where there was a defective description, where the patentee had failed so to describe his invention that the patent could stand in the courts; and 2. Where he was unfortunate enough to claim that of which he was not the inventor. But the other courts (except Judge Grier), from that day to this, have always proceeded on the other theory, as if ignorant of the terms of the statute, or on account of their favor toward the patentee. That is the history of nine reissues out of ten. This, in importance, is probably the second mischief arising out of the way the patent law has been administered. You notice it does not grow out of the law, but it grows out of the interpretation put upon that law by the courts.

Take an example: A has got out a patent. He has described in that patent precisely what he has invented. In describing what he has invented it must unavoidably happen that either in the drawings, or specifications, or model, some incidental device will present itself he has never thought of, or, if he had, only in a dream. To say he has invented it would be an abuse of language. B, some years later, makes an invention of this incidental device. He, of course, examines the records of the Patent Office. He finds A's patent, and finds that A has not claimed the invention B has made. He finds more than that. He finds that in law A has in fact disclaimed it, because the construction of law put upon that species of patent is that what is shown but not described is disclaimed. Relying upon that equitable doctrine, and taking for granted that A had not patented the invention, B builds expensive buildings, fills them with costly machines, puts into the investment the property of himself and others, and goes on for years manufacturing under his own patent in entire good faith. Finally A finds it out. "Here," says he, "this will never do in the world; my whole property is here injured. What right has this man to come here and get out this independent invention, and crowd me out into the cold?" He goes to a patent lawyer; he says to him: "Mr. C, just look at this. Here is my patent rendered entirely worthless. I must have it reissued. I want you to try to reissue it, and if you succeed I will give you five, ten, or seventy thousand dollars." The lawyer (I suppose with good conscience) says: "Very well; you may leave the papers with me, and I will attend to it." He gets out the reissue. He is aided therein by the remarkable elasticity of the English language; he is able by the cunning words so to expand that claim that it will cover the whole horizon. B then finds himself involved in a suit, or, it may be, a thousand suits, for this infringement committed, *as is alleged*, in fraud of the rights of this prior patentee. He is called in the courts a "thief" for having so manufactured; he is dragged through all this merciless litigation at an expense, it may be, so great that long before he reaches the end of it he has reached the end of his purse. He is, perhaps, unsuccessful; he is defeated; his buildings are rendered worthless; all the property which he has invested is taken from him; or, he is compelled to come down on his knees to the subsequent inventor (though prior in point of time) and yield to whatever terms he may demand.

The Supreme Court, though they were the first to get us into this difficulty, have again and again expressed their disapprobation of this practice. They have exhausted all the artillery of argument, rebuke, and sarcasm, and have been compelled to acknowledge that "though we may rebuke this practice, it is not in our power to prevent it." Congress can prevent it, however, if the courts cannot. The suggestion in this bill does a great deal to remedy that evil. The amendment does not go as far as I wish, but I have found out that we cannot have all we would like in this world, and I am here to lend my free and happy support to this bill. It does put a final stop to this practice of reissuing patents for the purpose of getting in contribution subsequent and maturer inventors, and it does that in a way all ought to be thankful for.

A MEMBER OF THE COMMITTEE. How does it cover the case you have suggested ?

Mr. PAYSON. It covers it in this way : it provides that when a patent is reissued nothing that was previously made, nothing that was then in existence, shall be considered an infringement ·so far as the specified machine is concerned. That is the sixth section. If I have built this manufactory and filled it full of this machinery, and the manufacture is subsequently patented, I cannot start out on a fresh infringement, but I am not compelled to withdraw from the work already started.

Let us take an actual fact; it came to my knowledge yesterday. In 1866 a man got out a patent for a " continuous brake." In describing his brake, as he had to do in his specifications and drawings, he showed, of course, the brake-beam. It is a bar of wood which goes across the front of the wheels to which the brake-blocks which check the motion of the car are attached. That brake-beam has been, for a great many years, hung up by a loop in the form of an oblong ring. The upper part of this loop is attached to the upper part of the truck, and the brake-beam hangs down a foot or two below it.

A patent says, " P is the loop." It is shown in the drawings. Of course, that is mere accident. It is not claimed in the patent, and at the date of the original issue undoubtedly formed no part, in the inventor's mind, of his invention. That patent was obtained in 1866. Now, there is not a railroad in the United States that does not use a brake-beam supported by this loop. Somebody happened to look at this patent in 1866, and noticed there this loop-hanger. Perhaps the patentee found it out. The patentee goes to the Patent-Office and gets a reissue, by which he claims this loop-hanger, and commences suit upon it against several of our leading railroads. The probability is that these suits will be thick as leaves in an autumn forest. The device, which the man never dreamed of patenting, and which he put in as a simple necessary adjunct to this continuous brake, without any idea of claiming it, at a day subsequent, forms the basis a patent claim.

A MEMBER OF THE COMMITTEE. How does the reissue affect that?

Mr. PAYSON. The only injury in this instance is that some timid railroad will pay, because they are very much afraid of the courts.

Mr. STORROW. The time of invention relates back to the original patent, and not to the date of the reissue ?

Mr. PAYSON. And I will supplement that by saying that it dates back farther than the original patent. It may date back many years, and that we can never find out until we get into court. This patent was granted in 1866, but this reissue will not simply relate back to the date of the original patent in 1866. It will go back to the date of the invention of the continuous brake, and we don't know anything about the date of the invention until we come into court, and then, it may be that the inventor will be able to carry back the date of his invention to a date long anterior to the period when the patent was granted. It would not make any difference at all if another party had come between and patented that loop. It would not prevent the original patentee from going back and obtaining his patent for the loop, and if he proved to be the first inventor he would prevail, notwithstanding the second party may have gotten out a patent for the identical thing.

A MEMBER OF THE COMMITTEE. Would not he be infringing upon the second patent?

Mr. PAYSON. No, sir ; there cannot be two patents for the same thing, and the rule is, the first in time of invention shall prevail. The second patent is entirely invalid. If the device was shown in the first patent, that is proof that the first patentee invented it ; it shows that he had it there, and as the law stands, there is nothing to prevent his getting a reissue covering it.

Mr. PAYSON. Yes, sir ; an infringer from the date of the reissue, and his own patent would be only waste paper.

This amendment will not prevent the retroactive effect of the reissue. It enables parties, however, who were manufacturing the device at the date of the reissue to keep on.

The Patent Office will make the same sort of a search when an application for a reissue comes up as in an original application ; and if they find that this loop was already in existence they will not allow a reissue, but in nine cases out of ten they have no means of ascertaining the fact. As I have shown, this 1866 patent was the first to show the loop, but it may have been in use, as I am told it was in use, for many years before the date of the patent. I may know that this loop-hanger was used by the Baltimore and Ohio Railroad many years prior to the date of the original patent of 1866, but I have got to prove it, and prove it in the only way known to the law, by living witnesses or by a printed publication. If there is a printed publication that is old enough I am all right. But the lives of men are limited, and if the only witness who has within his breast a knowledge of the prior use should be taken from me by death or accident, I am helpless. As the mere fact the thing was used before no longer avails me, and the man may come on and add fraud to fraud, he may have his reissue for what he may know was used long before his invention, and will lay every railroad in the country under contribution ; and though under the proposed amendment, the railroads may go on using the identical brakes they cannot add to them. If they build a new car and put this brake upon it they must pay for it, unless they are able to prove a want of novelty at the date of the original invention, which defeats a reissue in the same way it defeats an original patent.

If the reissue contains matter not in the original patent (I mean that which is not claimed and not shown in the drawings or specifications) the reissue is void upon its face. But the evil is not that. The thing introduced in the reissue is what is shown in the original patent, but is not claimed at the time. In this patent that I have been speaking about, all that the patentee claimed was the continuous brake, that is, the means of braking from one end of the train to the other. In the body of his specification he says, " P is the loop-hanger to hold up the break-beam "; but that is all. He declares in effect, " This is my invention (the continuous brake), but this loop-hanger is not a part of my invention "; and though saying that the courts have held this void as a disclaimer. He in effect says, " I don't invent this loop-hanger, but what I have claimed—the continuous brake." If the courts had held to the first construction, and said to the man when he wished a reissue, "That disclaimer shall still hold good," that would have been all right ; but they do not ; they have from the beginning allowed a patentee to incorporate in his reissue, and, too, in his claims, anything indicated or suggested in his original specifications or drawings, though he didn't claim it at the' time of the original patent.

A MEMBER OF THE COMMITTEE. Please state how far the decision of the Commissioner would be conclusive, or whether it would be conclusive at all upon the court.

Mr. PAYSON. The decision of the Commissioner is conclusive upon the court and the jury with regard to every question save one. The courts finding the difficulty into which they had been unwittingly led, sought the best way out of it which they could devise, and, though it is not a very good way, still it does answer the purpose. The courts have arrived at this conclusion; that though the decision of the Commissioner shall be conclusive upon every other question, the courts shall be at liberty to look into this question, namely: Is the reissue for the same invention as the original? and in determining whether the reissue is for the same invention as the original, they have decided that they can look at all the papers in the case, that is to say, they can compare the original specifications, and drawings, and model with· the reissue, and if they find that what is now claimed for the first time in the reissue, is shown, or described, or indicated, or suggested (whatever that word may mean), either in the original specifications, drawings, or model, they uphold the reissue. If they cannot find it in the original specifications, drawings, or model, they decide that the Commissioner has exceeded his jurisdiction, and, therefore, it is competent for them to reverse his decision; and in that case only have they found a reissue void, though I say they have again and again signified their utter disapprobation of the modern system of expanding the reissue of patents; and Judge Greer says " it is our duty always to rebuke it, but, unfortunately, we cannot prevent it."

I come now, gentlemen, unless there is some other question I have not made clear, because it is impossible for me to see all the difficulties attending this—

A MEMBER OF THE COMMITTEE. What is your opinion about the necessity or propriety of retaining models so as to prevent an improper reissuing?

Mr. PAYSON. The model, so far from preventing a reissue, is often made the most available means for obtaining it; and I will state to you here a case (on the favorite theory of mine, that an actual case is better than a mile of abstract reasoning): A man obtained a patent some years ago—no matter when or what for. He assigned that patent to another party. The assignee goes to the Commissioner and he obtains a reissue, claiming something shown in the model; and he make the necessary oath that the inventor invented that thing, but through inadvertence, accident, or mistake, he had left it out of his original patent. Now, the fact was that the original inventor had never invented it; the fact was it had been left out by express instruction to his solicitor, because he had not invented it. The assignee knew it, and the attorney who acted for the assignee knew that fact. Yet that attorney drew those papers, went before the Commissioner of Patents with a lie in his mouth, and because this device happened to be in the original model, and because his conscience was as elastic as the words in which the original specifications happened to be written, he did obtain from the Commissioner of Patents (who of course knew nothing about the facts) a reissued patent covering the device which the original patentee was too honest to demand. How often that may occur is known only to God! Oftener, I am afraid, a great many times than we have any idea of.

A. H. WALKER. How did he get that reissue without the oath of the inventor? I understand that an assignee cannot make the oath of actual invention.

Mr. PAYSON. Not under the present law, and it is sought in the present bill to get rid of the oath of the original inventor in an application by his assignee for a reissue. It is thought to be a hardship on the assignee that he should be compelled to get the oath of the original inventor. It is said that this oath is nothing but a form; "Why should not I take that oath as well as the inventor," says the assignee. Why should he not take it a great deal better than the original inventor, in the case I have suggested!!

A GENTLEMAN. Explain what is the difference between the oath of an assignee and the oath of an executor or administrator.

Mr. PAYSON. If I understand the question, when a man dies, that is the end of him; there are no commissioners known to us in either of the places to which he may have gone who can take his oath, and the executor or administrator has to make it. But, in the case of the assignee, the patentee, if he is still living, is within our reach and should take the oath, for he alone is the man who can know in his heart whether he really invented the device or not.

The evil cannot be prevented if the patentee be dead. There are a great many evils in this world which we can only complain about. If the inventor be living it is another case.

Same MEMBER. Why should a patent ever be reissued to an assignee?

Mr. PAYSON. You have got me now, sir. You must go to a wiser man than I.

SECTION TWO.

I come now to what I deem the very heart and soul of this bill. It is, undoubtedly, its most important part, and, as might be expected, is subjected to the most amount of obloquy and reproach. It is the second section. I will defy any gentleman, present or absent, to find for me a single instance where a rule of recovery for damages, for any species of injury, has ever been adopted in any court in any country in Christendom, civilized or uncivilized, that begins for enormity, for absurdity, for injustice, for tyranny, to furnish a parallel to the rule of recovery which has for many years prevailed in the courts of the United States in patent cases. I can find no words strong enough to express my utter abhorrence and detestation of this sort of judicial legislation. But I must add to that, that I do not conceive the courts are in any wise to blame. They went in at a door that promised fairly; they walked along a path that was smooth and even. No living soul could tell them the dangers and pitfalls that lurked in the path along which they were traveling so smoothly.

It was the inexorable logic of events which showed the fatal errors the courts have committed; and which they are in one sense powerless to prevent, because it is the rule of courts to take no steps backward. The rule in law gives to the patentee the price which he has put upon his invention. I want you to notice these words: it is the price which he himself has put upon his own invention. Of course there must be two to make a bargain, and he confers with those whom he finds disposed to use his invention. I have been a party to making these agreements myself, and no blow or the first hard word has ever passed between us. The roads I have represented and the patentees have never had the slightest difficulty in making up their minds what is the proper recompense to the inventor for the thing he is to sell. That is the rule in law where there is a license fee.

The rule in equity is that the defendant shall pay to the plaintiff the profits which he, the defendant, has made by the unlawful use of the invention. The argument by which that is supported or attempted to be supported is, that the infringer shall not profit by his wrong, and that the patentee shall not suffer by the infringer's wrong. I imagine you asking: "How can anything more equitable than that be devised? Why should this dishonest infringer, this thief, complain? Why should he complain because he is called upon to pay to the patentee the profits which he has derived from the unlawful use of the innocent patentee's invention?" Of course the patentee ought to have it, and the defendant ought to pay it. What is this rule which we are so ready to commend? The courts have taken it in hand. They found it misshaped, meaning nothing or everything; and after working upon it for a long time they finally arrived at this conclusion, namely: These profits which the defendant has made, and which he has got to pay over to the patentee, are represented by the savings which he has made, and these savings are to be got at by estimating the difference between how much it has cost the infringer to do what he has done by using the infringing device, and what it would have cost him to do it by any means free and open to the public at the time of the infringement. If by means of the patentee's device it cost the infringer a dollar, we will say, to make this box [exhibiting box], it being made by the patentee's machine, and if it had cost him before that to make it by hand five dollars, the amount which he has saved by making this box by the patentee's device is four dollars, and that is the profit which he has made, and which he has got to pay over to the plaintiff.

This is the rule which the Supreme Court, after long deliberation, arrived at in the famous case of *Mowry* vs. *Whitney* (14 Wallace). Up to the present time the value of this rule has not been very manifest. It has so happened that the cases that have been settled with that rule have fitted to it pretty well. When the rule has not fitted them the amounts in controversy have been so small that nobody was very much hurt.

This rule which the Supreme Court has laid down is what I referred to in saying that a harsher, a more anomalous rule never found its way into a court of justice or on the statute-books of a free and enlightened country.

First, the law is wholly anomalous. There is no law whatever in regard to any other property similar to it. I mean to say that there is not a single form of injury to any species of property, owner or person known to mankind where the courts have ruled that the converter of it shall pay the profit which he has made by its use over and above the use of some other device then open and free to the public.

In the great fire which devastated Chicago, a gentleman friend, by the help of a horse and cart belonging to somebody else, carried away $1,700,000 in government bonds and greenbacks. He had converted this horse and cart, and all that he could have carried on his body would have been but a small proportion of the amount; by this unlawful use of the plaintiff's horse and cart he is enabled to save the whole of the amount. What would you think of a rule of law which, when the owner of the horse and cart had brought his action of trover (it would be the same thing that is being done to-day in these patent cases in equity), if the court should say, "Here, Mr. Defendant, you have saved $1,700,000 by the use of this man's property; this property you have converted;

you thief, you have saved $1,700,000 by the unlawful use of this plaint-
iff's property, and the law declares that you should pay him the whole
amount." That is the law to-day in equity, in patent causes, and that
is the rule at law where there is no license fee.

This is what I refer to when I say that the courts have given to this
particular species of property this wonderful, extraordinary character.
They have hedged it about by remedies and definitions unknown to the
law, in every other branch of our jurisprudence. The law then is
anomalous.

But, in the next place, it is in every way unjust. The objection is
made here that when the plaintiff whose patent has been infringed
comes into equity, we seek by this bill to give to him the price which he
himself has fixed upon his invention. Now, I ask again, is that a hardship? If he has been satisfied to deal in that way with the public, is
there any hardship in putting upon the patent the price thus made?
Why should he complain? The courts say, "We must not do it; we must
not allow this poor, misguided patentee to be so limited; he is an Indian,
he is a spoiled child, he doesn't understand his own interests;" and they
will give to him an amount so much in excess of the amount he himself
has fixed, that when I state it to you I hardly expect to be believed.

There is a patent case now pending in the Supreme Court of the United
States, the invention of which cost in labor a few weeks, and a few hundred dollars of expense. If the alleged inventors were to be paid the
price which they expected, they would receive from $300,000 to $700,000.
Now I ask you, is not that enough? Do you know of any citizen who
ever came to bless this country, whose services would not be repaid by
either of those amounts? Do we need to give to the patentee more than
$300,000 for the patent, and for the good he has done to the public?
Do we need to offer greater prizes than that? Judge Drummond, under
this same patent, entered a decree, finding himself in the grasp of the
law—which he could not escape—a decree which, if applied to all railroads in this country, would give to the owner of the patent, in equity,
from fifty to a hundred millions of dollars.

A. H. WALKER. Is that the Tanner brake patent?

Mr. PAYSON. It is the Tanner brake patent of which you have all heard
so much. Lest I should be thought to be mistaken about it, I think it
is perfectly proper for me to say that the owner of the patent has himself stated to me when I put the amount at sixty millions, that he thought
I had underestimated the effect of the decree. I don't know what the
Supreme Court is going to do. That is what Judge Drummond has done
He has reviewed it two or three times. The first decree was for more
than that. After learning what it meant, he took off thirty per cent. or
so. But suppose they reduce it. Are we to pay them $5,000,000? Is
any one here willing to vote that the public should, by law, in advance
agree to pay for any patent $5,000,000?

This is an extended patent. It was issued in 1852, and it expired 21
years thereafter, in 1873.

A. H. WALKER. Isn't it a fact that the owner of the patent has offered
to settle?

Mr. PAYSON. The patentee some years ago went into a hotel in New
York, and he said to a friend of mine, "You needn't trouble yourself
any more about this matter, for I have about settled with the railroads
for twenty millions of dollars. They are to give me twenty millions, but
I am to allow them twenty-five per cent. for the trouble of collecting it.
I am to have fifteen millions of dollars, *and passes.*"

S. Mis. 50——24

A. H. WALKER. That's all very well for a joke; but isn't it within your knowledge——

Mr. PAYSON. How much of it is a joke and in earnest when we come into the courts? Is it any joke to pay thirty or forty millions of dollars? [A fuller explanation of this case, in reply to a question by Mr. A. H. Walker, followed, which, not being specially pertinent to the pending bill, is, by request, omitted from this record.]

Mr. PAYSON. If the law had been what we want to make it, namely, that the patentee shall have his license fee, this matter should have ended years ago. The roads would have paid the five or ten dollars a mile which the owners of this patent had declared to be a sufficient recompense, and there would have been peace; but in the mean time there came this chimera of the courts by which they are betrayed to their ruin.

A MEMBER OF THE COMMITTEE. How does the proposed law remedy the matter?

Mr. PAYSON. The remedy is that the measure of the plaintiff's recovery shall be a license fee—the price which he himself has put upon his commodity. In this very case, if that were the rule, the owner would recover from $350,000 to $700,000.

The proposed statute (section 2) may be divided into two or three separate clauses. The first clause obtains where the patentee has already established a license fee, and the second obtains where he ought to do so—where it is for his interest to do so.

In two cases reported in the 2d of Fisher, Judge Grier, some years ago, declared in express terms that in a case such as here provided for, that is, where it was manifestly for the interest of the patentee that everybody should use his invention, he has no right to come into equity; he has no need of an injunction; and where it is for his interest that everybody should use his invention, the whole damage he has sustained is the non-payment of a license fee.

A MEMBER OF THE COMMITTEE. This second part provides that where there is no established license fee, but where it would be for the interest of the patentee that other persons generally should use his patent, the court or jury shall determine the measure of damages. How is the court to determine what the measure of damages is?

Mr. PAYSON. The court and the jury are to determine that question precisely as they determine analogous questions at the present time. If A brings a suit for conversion of personal property, for slander or libel, or fraud, or injuries sustained in a collision, the court and jury are called upon to do precisely this same thing, and I cannot see any wrong in subjecting the owner of patent property to the same rule to which all the other owners of real or personal property are subjected. The danger is not that the court and jury will give too little, but that they will give too much. In the bill which I drew, and which passed the House of the last Congress, it was provided that the court and jury should take into consideration the time, labor, ingenuity, and experience involved in making the invention in assessing the damages in cases where there was no license fee. But I surrendered the point in draughting, with other gentlemen, the present bill, and left it in the form in which it now is, as the other gentlemen were afraid to hamper the court and jury.

A MEMBER. Did I understand you to say that Judge Grier had said that in cases where it was for the advantage of the patentee that his patent should go into general use, there was no necessity for an injunction?

Mr. PAYSON. Yes, sir; that was the point before him. He said expressly that where it is for the interest of the patentee that his patent should go into general use, the patentee has no reason to go into equity, and has no need of the extraordinary aid of an injunction. The only remedy is in damages, and the only injury to the patentee is the non-payment of the license fee. And, I add, if he is not satisfied with the price which he himself has put upon his invention, or not satisfied with the price the court and jury are disposed to put upon his invention, let him come into equity, and by this extraordinary remedy of injunction he can put a stop to the use of his device at a price he and the user cannot agree upon.

The next objection to the present rule in equity, and, in the absence of a license fee, in law, is that it is wholly impracticable. Here, gentlemen, is a whip [exhibiting it] that two or three years ago, in the exposition of Chicago, I saw being manufactured by a patented machine, and I bought it. The machine turned out these whips at a most rapid rate and at a very trifling expense. It is made out of cane or rubber, and is woven all over with fine strips of leather, and there is a piece of lead at the top of it. The manufacturers told me they made a profit of five cents. They sold them for 25 cents, and they cost 20 cents. Now, suppose the infringers of that machine were sued, having sold a hundred thousand of them. It would cost, say, fifty cents to make that whip by hand, consequently the infringer has saved 30 cents, and has got to pay 30 cents, although the gross amount of the sales was only 25 cents a whip. In other words, he has got to pay not only the miserable amount of profits he had made ($.05 × 100,000=$5,000) but pay 30 cents, or $30,000, when he received as the gross earnings from all his business 25 cents each, or $25,000. This is strictly in accordance with the rule of equity in the United States at the present time.

This is one of the very numerous class of cases which I have found. Although the manufacturer had sold his wares at a loss, he still would be compelled, under that rule, to pay the difference between the cost of manufacturing them by the patent process and what it would have cost him under a process open to him at the time of the infringement. You may look at almost any article of furniture in this room—the legs of this table, the arms of that chair; they can be made by machinery at a cost infinitely less than by hand; and if the infringer of the machine by which they were made were called upon to pay according to the present rule, he would have to pay many times the amount of the price he had received for the whole chair or table.

Gentlemen, I will close what I have to say, and the committee will please bear in mind this one closing suggestion: That this patent law was framed when the population of this country was probably not more than one-tenth what it is at this day. You must remember that the evils in regard to patent property have gone on increasing from that time to the present, not simply in proportion to the increase of population, but far in excess thereof. You will please to remember that the license fee, which forty or fifty years ago might have been a very inadequate reward to the inventor, will to-day enable him to live like a prince. Let me remind you that you are here legislating for posterity. That as the population of the United States has gone on increasing in the last fifty years, it will, in like proportion, go on increasing in the years to come. And I beg you to consider the importance, when this country shall contain a population of one or two hundred millions, of a patent which it is for the interest of the patentee that the public should generally use. Every year adds to the number of the population, and every year we live adds to the value of each patent. What to-day is possibly an inadequate reward to the patentee is sure, in the slow growth of years, to exceed one's wildest anticipations.

I am not here, Mr. Chairman, to advocate the repeal of the patent law. I could not if I would, and I would not if I could. At the same time, I am very far from sharing in the opinion of others, that the patent law is the principal element of our national prosperity. The most valuable inventions were made before the patent law was heard of, and they would continue to be made though the last vestige of the patent law were blotted off the statute-book. The patent law does not bring the invention out of the inventor. It is in his nature, and, though poverty and ruin and disgrace were staring him in the face, the genuine inventor would still go on, as Milton sang his song, not for the present time, or for the ten pounds paid him, but because he could not help it. It is a very great wrong to suppose that this class of the community are actuated by love of filthy lucre. They don't invent, Mr. Chairman, for money, but because God makes them invent. But still there is a larger class of so-called inventors that do need this petty stimulant. If I had the power, I would not repeal the patent law; I would amend it, and if I could not remedy the defects, I would repeal it altogether. Judge Drummond says the patent law ought to be radically amended or totally abolished.

The history of the world is but a history of inventions, made, many of them, before, as I say, a patent law ever was heard of——

A GENTLEMAN. But will the inventor develop and introduce his invention without the stimulus of the patent law?

Mr. PAYSON. You may as well ask me "will a mother forget her suckling child," as to ask whether an inventor will neglect or abandon the product of his brain. He loves it, cherishes it, and while life and being last he will follow it, although he sees his wife in rags and his children without bread to eat.

I am happy to say that we are acting in entire unison and concert with inventors all over the United States. I am happy to say that the most earnest advocates of the amendment which we are here seeking to have passed are those inventors that know, more than I know, the necessity of the law; and the only fault they find with this bill is that it does not go far enough. There are others, the representatives of inventors, and still others who are making their living by the manufacture of patent machines, who are heartily with us. And I wish to repel, with the utmost earnestness of which I am capable, the stigma sought to be cast upon us, that this is an attempt upon the part of a few infringers, men who have no interest in patent law, to get rid of the effects of their infringements.

We are aiming at the greatest good to the greatest number. I believe sincerely that what I have been doing here is as much for the interest of the patentee as it is for the interest of those who use his device. I do not understand this cry, "Great is Diana of the Ephesians." It is the same old cry that the world has heard for a thousand years, which, however, I confidently trust will have no manner of weight with this committee; but the rather that the manifold considerations already presented will commend at least these more important sections of this bill, which I have hurriedly discussed, to your hearty approval and cordial indorsement.

GEORGE PAYSON.

ARGUMENT OF MR. WHITMAN.

[FEBRUARY 22, 1878.]

Mr. WHITMAN, of Washington, addressed the committee.

Before calling your attention, gentlemen of the committee, to the sections of the bill before you, I want to take the liberty of answering a question put by the honorable chairman of this Committee.

During the discussion, in which I have taken a great deal of interest, the statement was made that more patents were taken out, according to the population, in certain Western States than in all the New England States. I was somewhat surprised at the time to hear such a statement, but I find upon examination that it is so. The honorable chairman of the committee inquired, "How was it with the South?" I have taken occasion, for I felt a deep interest in the matter, to examine the report of the Commissioner of Patents for the last year (1877) upon that point, and I find that in the adjoining State of Maryland, during the year 1877, one person in every 4,067 took out a patent; in New Hampshire, one person in every 4,080 took out a patent; in Maine, one in every 4,749; in Vermont, one in every 5,733; in Texas, one in every 7,117; and in Louisiana, one in every 9,073. It would appear from this statement that the State of Maryland has already left in her wake no less than three of the New England States, and that the remote State of Texas is only a little behind the State of Vermont.

Mr. ELDREDGE. That would not show precisely how many patents were taken out in the respective States.

Mr. WHITMAN. No, sir; it was not that; it was the estimate of the number of patents according to the population. I will read the statement again. The experience of every lawyer practicing before the Patent Office, in patent cases, is, that the number of patents taken out in the Southern country is wonderfully increasing. The gentleman has mistaken my statement, and I read to him again: "In Maryland, during the year 1877, one person in every 4,067 took out a patent"——

Mr. ELDREDGE. My question is this: Supposing one person to have taken out twenty patents?

Mr. WHITMAN. The estimate was not based upon the number of patents that any one particular person had taken out, of course.

The CHAIRMAN. Did I understand you to say that the ratio in Maryland was one in every 4,000?

Mr. WHITMAN. One in every 4,067. It would appear, then, gentlemen, that the Southern State of Maryland—that is, looking at the Southern States as those south of Mason and Dixon's line—has already left not less than three of the New England States in her wake, and that the remote State of Texas is only a little behind the New England States. I know that it has been a fashion among the members of Congress from the West and South—perhaps not of the South, but certainly of the West—it has been the fashion among members of Congress representing particularly agricultural constituencies in the West, to speak of patents as a New England institution. They look upon patents very much as they look upon codfish, or baked beans, or wooden nutmegs, as the gentleman suggests, as purely a Yankee institution; whereas, in the adjoining State of Maryland, they took out more patents, according to, the population, last year, than they did in several of the New England States.

But, Mr. Chairman, I will direct your attention to the bill pending before the committee. I have had time to consider only a few sections of this bill, and I shall therefore call your attention only to those sections that I have found time to examine.

Of these, the section relating to reissues seems to be the most important of those to which your attention has been directed. Now, in order to understand this matter of reissues, it is necessary, in the first place, to follow up the procedure of taking out a patent; for it is impossible to understand the theory of reissuing a patent without following up the steps incidental to taking one out in the first place. The first thing that the inventor does, when he has made an invention, is to embody it in some form. Sometimes he makes a machine which not only embodies the invention as the model would embody it, but shows an article capable of actual practice and actual results. Now, at the very instant that he has completed that machine he has an inchoate right of property established, for it is not the taking out of a patent that first vests in him rights recognized by law. That property-right was partially established as soon as he made the invention. He can assign it, he can sell it, and it is valuable to him. The very instant he has made that invention, under the laws, he may put an assignment on record, and perhaps obtain thousands of dollars for the child of his brain, although his rights become more distinctly defined when the invention is reduced to practice, or, in other words, when he has made the machine capable of actual and successful use.

A great deal of talk has been made before the committee about fraudulent reissues. Well, Mr. Chairman, it seems almost impossible to designate any instrumentality known to the law that may not, in the hands of bad men, be made the vehicle of fraud. Take the matter of conveyances. It is a matter of daily practice, as you who are lawyers well know, to file a bill in equity against a party who has taken property under a fraudulent conveyance; and we know that after taking out an execution, it is frequently necessary to file a creditor's bill, in order to follow the property of the judgment-debtor into the hands of fraudulent vendees. Now, how thoroughly absurd would it be to stand here and condemn the whole system of conveyancing throughout the country, and brand it as a fraud, because there are, now and then, fraudulent conveyances? And I venture to assert that where there is one fraudulent patent taken out there are hundreds of fraudulent conveyances made.

The main argument against reissues seems to be that the model may show what is not described in the original patent. In this connection, I am free to state that while I do not oppose the amendment that has been suggested by the Commissioner of Patents, to strike out the word "model" from this section, I think it would be well for you to investigate both sides of the question before making this important change. The argument against relying on the model in reissuing seems to be, that a man may deposit a model in the Patent Office, and leave it there for three or four or more years; that meanwhile devices which are shown in that model, but not in the patent, are introduced into use in the workshops of the country; and that therefore the parties who use the devices shown in the model had no opportunity of knowing that they were, or would be, patented after four or five years—say the objectors; the party comes back to the Patent Office; picks up his old model; prepares drawings to correspond with his model; writes a specification, describing what is shown in the drawings; claims certain features that are shown in the specification; and he goes before the public with the patent, claiming not what was described in his original patent, but what was shown in this model at the Patent Office. Supposing, what is not probable, that a reissue of this kind would be sustained by the courts, there is no doubt but that it would operate as a hardship, which would be remedied by the amendment.

But there is another point, which should be considered, that the gentlemen who have discussed this matter have not called your attention to. Now, in the case cited, instead of depositing a model in the Patent Office at the time the application was filed, suppose the inventor had quietly put the model away upon his shelf; suppose he made an operative machine, and did as Whitney, the inventor of the cotton-gin, who locked up his invention in his stable. Five years afterward he goes to the stable where this machine has been hidden from the public, transports it to the Patent Office, and takes out a patent, claiming broadly everything shown therein. Now, not one of these gentlemen who have argued against this use of a model in reissue cases would attempt for a moment to say that the party had not the right to take out a patent on the old machine that was hidden away, unless he had abandoned it to the public, or it had been for two years in public use.

Now, what difference would it make to a defendant whether a suit was brought upon the reissue founded on the model at the Patent Office, or on an original patent based on the secreted machine? So, after all, this matter of reissuing a patent upon the model is not so decided a hardship as the gentlemen would have us understand. At the same time, I can say that I am opposed myself to the word "model" in the law, and I am willing that it should be stricken out, though it has been the law in this country since the foundation of the patent system.

Here is another point: It seems to have been supposed by some of the gentlemen who have addressed the committee that the right to reissues comes by statute—by the act of 1832, in which reissues were first mentioned; that it is a boon or favor received from the Congress of that time. Now, as a matter of fact, the United States has been in the habit of correcting its own grants from the date of its foundation. As long ago as 1828, before this law of 1832 was passed, Henry Clay being then Secretary of State, some inventor came to him to take out a reissued patent. There was no authority under the law for doing it; there was no section providing for it; but that reissue was taken out and litigated, and carried to the Supreme Court of the United States. It was the case of *Grant* v. *Raymond*, that has been referred to by my brother Storrow. Upon the coming up of the case to the Supreme Court of the United States, most able counsel were engaged on both sides; the Hon. Daniel Webster, then in the Senate, representing the defendant. That gentleman took the ground that Henry Clay had no right to reissue that patent; that he had no authority by law; and that, in order to reissue that patent, he should have had some authority given directly from the statute. But Chief Justice Marshall, (and who shall question his decision?) then upon the bench, decided that he had such a right, and that it was right under the patent system. Therefore you are not repealing a boon that has been granted by Congress to the people of the United States, but, in denying the right to reissue a patent upon a model, you are taking away from the citizen a right which he has had since the foundation of the government; a right which was given to him, irrespective of the statute as it existed at that time, by such a man as Henry Clay; and a right that was declared to be valid by such a jurist as Marshall, after a most thorough argument at the bar by such an interpreter of the Constitution and laws as Daniel Webster.

Mr. HUBBELL. Is not a model deposited at the Patent Office open to the public inspection, and evidence to all the world that what it contains is the substance of the patent ?

Mr. WHITMAN. If it is deposited there, and the Commissioner puts it in the model cases.

Mr. HUBBELL. Are they not all arranged so the public can see them—cannot any one go there and see them ?

Mr. WHITMAN. He cannot, perhaps, find a model that represents some particular invention, unless it happened to be in the model case. It might be in the examiner's room; there is very considerable trouble in keeping models in the cases all the time, because the examiners are always engaged in examining new applications and require the models; and they are sent to their rooms, where they are frequently kept for days and weeks. If I am wrong in this, here is an examiner of the Patent Office, who will correct me.

Mr. HUBBELL. Cannot any one go in there and call for that model, and be either taken to it or it brought to him ?

Mr. WHITMAN. Yes, sir; he can. But I would also say, as the law now stands, a model is not required[to be produced when the application for letters patent is filed.

The CHAIRMAN. That is only a rule of practice at the Patent Office.

Mr. WHITMAN. That is only a rule of practice at the Patent Office. It is not necessary for the Commissioner to demand a model in any case without he chooses to do so.

Mr. ELDREDGE. And the model is not made notice by law to anybody.

Mr. WHITMAN. No, sir; not by the statute. It does not properly constitute a part of the record, as the statute now stands. Under the old law, as it existed prior to 1870, I think the model did constitute a part of the record. I see an ex-Commissioner of Patents present, and if I am incorrect he will inform me.

Mr. FOOTE. It is not part of the record; still, it was always referred to.

Mr. WARD. Is the model in any sense such notice to the world as the patent itself—legal notice to anybody ?

Mr. STORROW. It is nothing that a man is bound to take notice of.

Mr. ELDREDGE. The records are made notice.

Mr. STORROW. The public records are made notice.

Mr. ELDREDGE. I am not aware that the model is notice.

Mr. WHITMAN. I should not suppose that in the present condition of things it is. The Commissioner is not required by law to call for a model, but he is required to call for drawings, specification, and oath of inventor.

Mr. TOWNSHEND. There is another thing in regard to models in this bill.

Mr. WHITMAN. There is a section making models evidence in courts.

Mr. STORROW. Making certified copies as good as originals are.

Mr. WHITMAN. That is what it amounts to. Heretofore there seems to have been some doubt on the subject. Models have always been good in the courts as testimony, but some question on the point has been raised.

Mr. HUBBELL. Is it not the practice in courts to make models from those in the Patent Office, and have them certified and admitted in evidence in a case ?

Mr. WHITMAN. That is the practice.

Mr. HUBBELL. Does not the law require, also, the Commissioner to demand a model, where the nature of the case admits of a model ?

Mr. WHITMAN. It does not require, but allows him to do so; however, I shall be obliged to pass over this ground very rapidly.

As I said before, in order to understand this matter of reissue, it is necessary to follow up an application for a patent.

Now, in the first place, when the inventor has made an invention, he generally goes to the model-maker and employs him to make a model; but sometimes he makes it himself. That is what the inventor sees himself, and also what he makes himself. Certainly there can be no better evidence of what the man really does invent than that model. He makes it with his own hands, or it is made under his own eyes.

He sends that model on to Washington, or puts it in the hands of some local practitioner to prepare an application for the Patent Office. The next step is to prepare a drawing from that model. As a matter of fact, the inventor very frequently never sees that drawing, as the law now allows the drawing to be signed by the attorney. The model comes on here to Washington; the attorney prepares the drawing from the model, and signs it himself, as he has a right to do, by the express words of the statute. After the drawing is made, a specification is written, descriptive of the drawing. It is then sent back to the inventor, who reads it, and makes the oath of invention. It is not considered necessary for him, under the law and practice of the Patent Office, to see the drawing. Then the application is filed at the Patent Office for action. The different inventions filed at the Patent Office are divided into some twenty-two different classes, each being in charge of some one examiner. Suppose I file an application for an improvement in a sewing-machine. The application is referred to the examiner having charge of that particular class. The duty of the examiner, upon having an application referred to him, is to carry out the words of the statute, and make a thorough examination as to its novelty. In the first place, he makes an examination of all American patents which have been heretofore granted, which he can do with facility, because the drawings are arranged in the port-folios of the Patent Office, so that they can be easily reached. Having made a thorough examination of all the American patents, it is then his duty to examine foreign patents, and this examination is not so thorough, perhaps, as it might be or as it ought to be, which is occasioned from the fact that we do not receive at our Patent Office copies of all foreign patents; and to make a thorough examination, they should all be searched. However, there are very complete collections of French and English patents, through which the examination can be extended. Having made that search, he then goes to the encyclopedias, reference-books, digests, &c.

If he finds anything in the way, as in nine cases out of ten he does, he writes and informs the inventor his application has been rejected, or informs him it will be necessary to modify his specification; that there are other inventions before him; and usually reference is given to a number of prior inventions. This is particularly true in cases of sewing-machines, harvesters, plows, stoves, &c., classes of inventions in which there have been many patents granted.

Then it is necessary for the inventor to modify his application according to these references that are given. And here a point is made that I want to refer to. The objection has been made that specifications should not be corrected by an amendment filed at the Patent Office. Under the theory of the objector, it seems to be perfectly right that the inventor should go back to the original specification and correct his patent by that, but he should not correct it by any other amendment filed in the Patent Office. Now, you will observe from what I have stated, in nine cases out of ten—I do not know that it would be an exaggeration to say ninety-nine out of one hundred—the case is first rejected, and it is necessary for the inventor to rewrite it. Now, that rewritten specification is the specification that goes out with the patent. It is the amended specification, not the original specification. After the specification is amended, it is printed by the Patent Office, and the inventor has no right to see it while it is in progress of being printed. It is sent to the Government Printer for that purpose, and the Government Printer may perhaps make mistakes, or the proof-reader make mistakes. I have known cases where whole paragraphs have been left out, and this all without the fault of the inventor. The inventor then takes out the patent with the specifications and drawing, and upon examination he finds that the Government Printer may have left out portions of the specifications.

Mr. STORROW. I had a case last week in which the Government proof-reader changed the meaning of the sentence by altering the punctuation.

Mr. WHITMAN. He finds that error, for which there is no remedy except the right of reissue. He comes back to the Patent Office for a reissued patent, which is the only way in which the correction can be made, and the office, of course, corrects it for him. That shows how valuable this right of reissue is.

The CHAIRMAN. What is your opinion about the limit of that right?

Mr. WHITMAN. I should say, in regard to the right to limit reissues to three years, that, I believe, is the time which has been recommended——

Mr. RAYMOND. I think a long term——

Mr. WHITMAN. I will try to answer the question of the honorable chairman by citing a case (*Morey* against *Lockwood*) that went to the Supreme Court of the United States. One of the parties went to the Patent Office and applied for a patent. A party goes to the Patent Office (the party in this case) and makes application for a patent. His claims were rejected by the Commissioner of Patents—some of them. It was afterwards decided by the court that he had a right to those claims. Now, a man may not know that his patent is invalid till it goes into the courts, for if he takes it to the patent lawyers, there may be a dispute about it; one will tell him it is good and need not be reissued, and another that it is bad, and ought to be reissued. He may not actually find out this error until the case is litigated in the courts, and we all know what litigation is in courts. Why, I know a case, now on the docket of the court in the other end of this building in which I am one of the counsel, which has been there for over two years since the appeal was docketed. Now, follow up patent litigation; the man may be four or five or six or seven or eight years before his case reaches the Supreme Court of the United States, before he finds that his patent ought to be reissued. He makes the attempt, and finds a three years' limitation is on the statute-book. Now, there is no justice in that, I think. If the patentee has the right to the reissue of the grant at all, he should have the right during the whole term of the patent.

As I stated before, the government has always exercised the right to correct its own grant, and this correction often benefits the public more than it does the patentee. Now, here is my idea of a patent: The government says to me if I have made an invention (and I have made one or two, I think), "You have an invention and you have a right to keep it locked within your own breast; it may be valuable—it is valuable—and we want the right to use it. Now, the Constitution of the United

States and the acts of Congress authorize us to make a contract with you. You file an application at the Patent Office and give us a thorough description of your invention in such a manner as it may be understood by those skilled in the arts, and we will give you a patent." I comply with the agreement. I go to the great pains and expense of preparing specifications and drawings, and file them at the Patent Office. Now, the consideration that the government receives for the grant of the patent is that written description; for that written description, after the expiration of the patent, enables the public to make and use the invention forever. Take the case of Whitney, the cotton-gin inventor. Why, gentlemen, less than a century ago seven or eight bales of cotton were seized on the English docks, on the ground that so much cotton could not be produced in the United States market. Now our export of this most valuable staple is millions. It is scarcely necessary to go to history to find out the reason.

In the old time it took a negro woman a day to gin a pound of green-seed cotton. Now look at what the cotton-gin is doing. It built up that staple for the Southern country, it built up the great plantations of the planters of the Carolinas, and it has been of most inestimable benefit to our people. Take that case as an illustration. Whitney, the Georgia school-master, might have quietly locked that cotton-gin in the stable where he first put it, and kept it there. He might have quietly ginned the cotton for himself, and made a fortune in ginning cotton for the neighboring planters. But the government says : " You have made a great invention ; we want a right to use it. You shall have a patent if you will permit the planters to use it upon reasonable terms, and after the patent has expired allow the invention to become the property of the public. We therefore ask you to tell us all about it." The inventor assents to the arrangement, and writes a description and files it at the Patent Office. But suppose the description is defective; suppose he files there a defective drawing or specification and goes on secretly manufacturing his cotton, and at or before the end of the patent term dies or transfers the right to manufacture to another. The public has not received its consideration for the contract; it has not had the clear description of the invention to which it is entitled. In that case it would be necessary for the inventor to reissue the patent for the benefit of the public ; and it is not only so in that case, but more particularly is it the case in chemical manufactures and patents for processes and compounds, where a correct description is the only means of using the invention. Therefore, we must well understand before we abolish or limit the right, or attempt to do so, that we are using a sword that cuts in both directions.

I have not time, however, to go into this reissue matter at any length. It seems to me, however, that the present amendment of the law obviates all difficulties that arise now in reissues. The only objection, and the objection universally urged, is, that something may be introduced into the reissued patent which is not shown in the original patent, and thereby the public may suffer. Some gentlemen who have addressed the committee have spoken quite pathetically of the sufferings of our large manufacturers in this connection. I must say I have never known of such cases as some of those cited ; but I have known of inventors who, under bad advice, took out expanded reissues, litigated them at an enormous cost, and lost all their money for their pains. The taking out of these expanded reissues injures the person who procures them, in nineteen cases out of twenty, more than it injures anybody else.

Take one of the cases that has been cited, as an illustration. Here a

man, at a great expense, takes out a reissued patent. He may have
been advised to do so by some incompetent attorney, and goes through
the courts to the Supreme Court of the United States. He spends
thousands of dollars. The Supreme Court declares, as they should do,
that the reissue is invalid; and who has been injured? It strikes me
that the party who has taken out the reissue is the sufferer; and that
judicial investigation, which our fifth section requires, is the best safe-
guard against improper reissues.

Mr. RAYMOND. How many cases do you know of, that have gone to
the Supreme Court, where the accidental or fraudulent defect has been
found out by litigation more than five years after the date of the patent?
Could not all the instances that are in the books, of that kind, be count-
ed on your fingers?

Mr. WHITMAN. I think if you will take the trouble to look up the reports, you won't find that many cases reach the Supreme Court within
five years after the patent was issued.

Mr. MASON. In a case pending before this committee, for an extension, it is alleged that there were eight years lost, and the illustration
that Mr. Whitman made recalls it. In that case the specification was
filed, and the Commissioner granted a patent for only the portion of the
claim which he thought was not covered by prior invention, and rejected the other portion of his claim. It went along five years, and it went
into court, and they found that the specifications to the patent that had
actually been granted to him were an infringement. An attorney was
appointed and investigated the original patent, and went back long
enough and convinced the Commissioner that all the authority that had
been cited for throwing out a portion of the specification was wrongly
construed, and they granted a reissue on the original specifications.
That was more than eight years after the thing had happened. That is
one of the grounds that they claim an extension on; they claim that it
was an error on the part of the Commissioner, and the Patent Office
itself, in granting the original patent, and therefore they lost eight years
of their time. This question of reissue practically comes up in some
cases.

Mr. WHITMAN. Mr. Mason very justly observes that if any limitation
is made it should be after the time that the mistake is discovered. It
strikes me that a limitation of that kind would not be objectionable.
For instance, a man takes out a patent covering a combination of *five*
different elements, or *four*, and he sues a man who uses a machine having three of these elements; it goes to the courts, and on appeal to the
Supreme Court of the United States, which learned tribunal is in the
habit of deciding a patented combination covering *four* co-operating
parts is not infringed by a combination covering three. If, in this case,
the court construed the claim to be for a combination of four parts, of
course the only remedy is to go back and take out a patent covering
the combination of three parts. Now, if the limitation could be made
to run from the date of the decision of the Supreme Court, or the period
the knowledge has been brought home to him that his patent is invalid,
I do not know that the limitation would be altogether objectionable.

Mr. HUBBELL. Where is the legal or equitable right for any limitation at all, if he has the right to a reissue?

Mr. WHITMAN. I do not propose to defend any limitation whatever;
neither do I stand here to advocate one.

Mr. STORROW. There is no practical necessity for compelling a man
to take it out as soon as he needs it; they are quick enough to take out

a reissue if the original patent has been found bad. Our sixth section gives a sufficient motive.

Mr. WHITMAN. Then comes the following section, seven (7), and that seems to be a necessary amendment of the law, although I have not heard it alluded to at all before this committee. It provides as follows:

SEC. 7. Whenever a patent has been issued to one person for an invention actually made by him jointly with another, or others, or a patent has been issued to several persons for an invention made by only one or more of them, and such error has arisen through inadvertence, accident, or mistake, the Commissioner, upon the application and oath of the true inventor, or inventors, and with the written consent of all the owners of said patent, entered of record, may correct the mistake as a clerical error. No new patent shall be issued in such case, but the correction shall be entered upon the old patent, or the record thereof, or both, and said patent shall thereafter, for all purposes, be regarded as having been properly issued, in its corrected form, at the date of its original issue. Upon such correction, a fee of twenty dollars shall be paid, under such regulations as the Commissioner of Patents may from time to time prescribe.

The law now seems to be obviously defective on that point. For instance, suppose two men, A and B, mistakenly make application to the Patent Office as joint inventors. Afterward it turns out that they are not joint inventors, but the invention, instead of having been made by A and B, was in fact made by B. This may be a very common mistake, because persons taking out patents in different parts of the country are not skilled in the patent law; they do not know whether they are several or joint inventors, and they may honestly fall into that error. They come on to the Patent Office, four or five years afterward, for a reissue of the patent, and the Commissioner informs them that there is no authority in law for the reissue of the patent. I am somewhat doubtful upon the legal ground that has been taken by the Secretary of the Interior and the Commissioner of Patents upon that question, but I do not propose to question, at this time, such distinguished authority. The inventor is informed by the Commissioner of Patents that he has no right to take out a reissue. There is only one remedy in that case, and that is a rather expensive one, if there is any. The patent law provides for interferences. Therefore, in a case where two parties make application for a patent for the same invention, an interference is declared between them, and one of the parties has the right to prove that he was the prior inventor to the other party.

Well, now, in this case the only remedy would be for one of these parties, who was in fact a several inventor, to file an application of his own. An interference would then be declared between the several application and the joint application, and if he could prove that he was the original and first inventor, priority would legally be awarded for his invention. Then, however, the public would be burdened with two patents for the same thing, and it would probably be necessary for one of the parties to go into a court of equity and file a bill to have the other patent declared void. Well, now, this section of the law obviates all that trouble and difficulty by merely allowing the Commissioner to correct as a clerical error that mistake.

Section 8 I have not had time to consider, and section 9 has been pretty thoroughly discussed, I believe. I will pass over the other sections till we come to 13.

Some statements were made in regard to this section by some of the gentlemen who argued the case before the Senate committee, which seem to me ought to be answered. The ground seems to have been taken that one of two joint owners of a patent has no right to assign or license other parties in such a way that an action could not be maintained against them for an account by the other joint owner. Now, the courts have decided that point within the last ten years, and this section of the law merely legalizes or re-enacts the decision.

Mr. PAYSON. It has not been decided by the Supreme Court.

Mr. WHITMAN (to Mr. PAYSON). These cases to which I would call your attention are those of *Vose* v. *Singer*, by the supreme court of Massachusetts, and a decision of Mr. Justice Drummond, of your own circuit.

Mr. PAYSON. The Supreme Court never have decided it. That case in which Judge Drummond did decide it, I know all about; and I know there is a great deal of doubt about the correctness of that decision.

Mr. WHITMAN. That certainly is a railroad case, and one with which you are undoubtedly familiar. I think that Judge Drummond clearly decided that where a patent had been issued to two parties, or where the parties were tenants in common——

Mr. PAYSON. He did decide that precise question; but what the Supreme Court would do, we do not know.

Mr. WHITMAN. That precise question has been decided in that way by the circuit court of the United States, and after long and thorough argument by the supreme court of Massachusetts, in the case of Vose *v.* Singer.

We may go back of the decisions of the court, and go to common sense upon the question. There is a doctrine, based on the English statutes that have come down to us, that one of two tenants in common of real estate may compel the other to account for the profits, although at common law there was no such right for an account. It depends upon the statute of Anne, I think.

Mr. HUBBELL. I think my remark, made before the Senate committee, covers that point—that a man cannot sell what he did not own, and that Congress cannot give a man a right to sell what he did not own.

Mr. WHITMAN. A patent right bears no analogy to the ownership of real estate; it is not the same thing, by any means. Suppose I am one of the joint owners of a valuable patent for a sewing-machine. Now, if the other joint or part owner sells, say, one of these machines in every county seat in the country, he enhances the value of that patent by simply selling that number of machines, and he makes my rights as a tenant in common more valuable than it was before. Another analogy that might be drawn would be between the right of way over a piece of real estate and the right to use an invention. Suppose three or four parties possess the right of way over real estate, what lawyer here, or anywhere, would think of compelling the joint tenants who use a right of way to account to the one who did not use it? The courts have never held—at least, I have yet to see a recognized authority where they have held—that one or more tenants in common or joint owners of a patent could be compelled to account to the other for using the invention. Each one is an owner; each, as tenant in common, has a right to enjoy; and, by the statute, enjoyment of a patent consists in making, using, or vending, and in licensing others to do this; and each tenant may so enjoy it, because, from the nature of the right, it cannot be otherwise enjoyed. This section simply re-enact what has been decided by the courts. Moreover, it makes the law uniform all over the United States, and takes away from the State courts the power of establishing conflicting rules concerning property in invention.

I will omit several sections to which I had proposed to call the attention of the committee.

Section 19, in regard to the taking out of patents in foreign countries, and the taking out of patents in the United States, reads as follows:

SEC. 19. Section forty-eight hundred and eighty-seven of the Revised Statutes shall be, and hereby is, amended so as to read as follows : No person shall be debarred from receiving a patent for his invention or discovery, nor shall any patent issued subsequent to March 2d, be declared invalid, by reason of its having been first patented in a foreign country upon the invention of the same person, unless the same has been introduced into public use in the United States for more than two years prior to the application; but all applications hereafter to be made for patents for inventions which shall have been patented in a foreign country upon the invention of the same person shall be made within two years after the date of such foreign patent.

As the law now stands, if an invention or patent is taken out in a foreign country, the statutes limit the American patent to the term of the foreign patent, or to the one having the shortest term. That is to say, if I take out a patent in England, where patents are granted for fourteen years, and afterward come here and take out a patent, the law of the United States would limit me to a term of fourteen years from the grant of the English patent. On the other hand, if I should take out my patent here first, that patent is published by the United States Patent Office all over the world, and all over Europe. If I go to Chancery Lane, in London, to the British Patent Office, you can look at any American patent that you call for. It is publicly filed there a few weeks after it is issued from our office. That is a publication under the British law that renders a subsequently-issued patent void. If I take out a patent in the United States first, it is impossible for me to take out a valid patent abroad, in England, for instance, because it will be published there before I can file an application, after receiving my patent here.

Hon. Mr. VANCE. Could you file a caveat?

Mr. WHITMAN. Under the British law, a caveat cannot be filed.

If, under these circumstances, I filed an application in England, it is probable that the patent would be granted, because they grant all applications unless an opposition is filed. They do not make any preliminary examination, but grant you a patent and leave you to vindicate yourself in the courts afterward. So that the patent would be granted; but if I went into the English courts with that patent, I would be met by the unanswerable argument that the invention described and claimed had been published in England before I took out the patent, and therefore that my British patent was not worth the paper upon which it was written. Which horn of the dilemma is the inventor to take? If he takes out the invention in the United States, he is at the mercy of any pirate in Great Britain; for in Great Britain it is not necessary that the inventor should take out the patent—any party may take it out. If I take my patent out in the United States first, it is only necessary for some British sharper to go to the United States Patent Office and pick up the patent there, or pick up a copy of the American specifications, and take out a British patent as an importer—a man who had no right to the invention whatever; and he thus gets a valid patent—a patent recognized by the British laws and the courts of Westminster Hall. Afterwards, if I go to England and take out a patent, I am met with two defenses: first, that my invention was published abroad; and, secondly, if it had been patented by the English importer, that he is prior in point of time to me.

Now, there seems to be no sense in that provision whatever. As the law now stands, if I do not take out a foreign patent at all, but take out my patent first in the United States, Uncle Sam gives me a seventeen years' patent without question. That is, if I say to the whole civilized world, "Take my sewing-machine," or "Take that invention and use it the world over," but take out no foreign patent, I can come to the United States and take out the patent, and they give me without question a term of seventeen years. On the other hand, if I go abroad and take out foreign patents, and say to the foreigners that they shall not use my invention, Uncle Sam limits me to a patent the term of which is shortened, and which must correspond to that foreign patent. In other words, Uncle Sam says: "Let all foreign countries compete with the American manufacturers who use that invention in the markets of the world, and you may have a seventeen years' patent; or take out your foreign patent, and thus prevent them from having an advantage in competition, and your term of patent shall be shortened—if you prevent them from competing with us in the markets of the world, we will limit your right in the invention."

Mr. MASON. The United States would say, if you patent in Austria, you shall not have a patent of the United States but for five years.

Mr. WHITMAN. What sense is there in that?

But not only are American inventors affected in this way; the foreigners are also affected. In nine cases out of ten, foreign inventions introduced in this country are worked by American capital. A man takes out a British patent, and he corresponds with the people of the United States, but as the law now stands the American capitalist would hesitate or decline to invest in that foreign patent; for he may be met, after he has taken out his American patent for seventeen years, with the assertion that the patent has expired in some foreign country, and it is not worth the paper upon which it is written. How is anybody to know but that that patent has been taken out abroad? I defy the best patent lawyer to make an examination in this case which would satisfy the capitalist; he might say that the patent on its face was valid, but there may be a patent in Austria, Prussia, or Italy, which we know nothing about.

Mr. MASON. Or in Spain, where they do not publish them?

Mr. WHITMAN. Therefore we cannot give you an opinion as to the clearness of your title; in consequence, there is a cloud on every foreign patent, and it prevents American capital from being invested in foreign patents, and prevents thousands of operatives, now out of employment, from earning their bread. That seems to be a good argument, if there is one, for the repeal of that senseless proviso.

Hon. Mr. BRIGGS. If the United States Government issues a patent for seventeen years, and that is published abroad, and there is no effort made by the patentee to protect himself abroad, has a party in a foreign country the right to manufacture that article without asking for a patent from that government?

Mr. WHITMAN. He has, sir. As a matter of practice, British manufacturers to-day have their agents in the British Patent Office hunting up American patents.

Hon. Mr. BRIGGS. Can he send that production back here without infringement?

Mr. WHITMAN. No, sir; not if it was a patented machine. He might if it was the product of a patented machine, or a manufactured article which would pass into the hands of commerce and become undistinguishable from the patented article. If it was a patented machine that could be recognized—for instance, a sewing-machine—it could not be sold in this country without infringement.

This agent will find some new invention, for instance, in sewing-machines, and the English manufacturer will seize upon that description and go right to work and manufacture the machine; but if he sends that machine back to the United States for use, he will be met, of course, with the answer that he had no right to use the invention in the United States, for the right to patent covers the right "to make, vend, and use the invention." The right to make and vend may have been exercised in a foreign country, but the right to use in this country would remain in the patentee.

Mr. MASON. If you used the sewing-machine in making fabrics, and sent those fabrics to this country, it would be different. He could make the machines, but he could not send them to this country; but he could send the work done on them here. There are no means of protecting the patented machines, and the manufacturer can make as many machines as he pleases, without being charged with infringement, and use them in England or any other country.

Mr. WARD. This publication in Chancery Lane is notice?

Mr. WHITMAN. Yes, sir; that has been decided.

Mr. MASON. It has been so decided.

Mr. WHITMAN. They have made decisions in analogous cases; for instance, where publications had been forwarded to the city of London, and proved to have been put on sale on three different occasions in that city. That was considered in a case decided by the lord chancellor.

Mr. WARD. That would be a protection, to be afforded by the court upon an application by the American patentee, that would prevent the Englishman from using the patent.

Mr. WHITMAN. It would prevent him from patenting the machine at all. This publication of patents, for instance, in Chancery Lane is sufficient to prevent any one from taking out a patent in England—any foreigner or any American. It would be a publication that would forever invalidate a patent.

Mr. STORROW. After the copy of the American patent had been published there, no man can come afterward and take out a patent.

Mr. WHITMAN. It becomes public property, and no one can afterward patent it.

Mr. MASON. It has been decided, within the last year, that when our Patent Office sent a copy of our patent, as they always do, to the English Patent Office, after that no patent could issue for that invention in England that was valid.

Mr. WHITMAN. The objection to operating the invention would be that the English manufacturer could get his agent to watch the issue of patents as they come out, and as soon as a patent is issued these specifications are published all over the world. It is only necessary for this agent to take the printed specifications and drawings and send them to England, where, if he gets them before the publication—before the Patent Office sends its copy—he can take out a patent as an importer.

Mr. ———. Is that patent invalid?

Mr. WHITMAN. No, sir.

Mr. ———. Why cannot the American patentee do the same thing?

Mr. WHITMAN. The American patentee can do it; but the trouble is that his American patent would be limited to fourteen years as the statute now stands.

Mr. MASON. We punish an American inventor for attempt ng to restrict the use of his invention, by curtailing the term of his American patent. If he allows all the world to use it, he may have a valid patent here for seventeen years; but if he takes a foreign patent, then he is curtailed of his term here. If ever there was a senseless provision, it is that; and no one has been able to see how this ever got into the law.

Hon. Mr. BRIGGS. The sewing-machine has been of great public good, not only to the manufacturer, but to the entire public who use fabrics made from these machines. Now, suppose a patent taken out here, and an English manufacturer steals it, and they go into the manufacture and the sale and the use of the patented articles in Great Britain under no restrictions. Now, has it not been the fact, in the history of sewing-machines, that while people of this country have been paying $50, $60, or $70, you could go to England and buy a machine of the same quality for $20 or $25?

Mr. WHITMAN. Yes, sir; that was the very evil occasioned by not taking out a patent abroad, which it is the object of this amendment to remedy.

Hon. Mr. BRIGGS. Does not that give the English manufacturer so much the advantage in the manufacture of these articles?

Mr. WHITMAN. If I take out that patent, and do not patent it any-where else, they give me seventeen years. If I do take out a foreign patent on it, they only give me fourteen years under the American patent law.

Mr. WILLITS. Might not the explanation why this provision is in the law be, that in 1861 they were making a raid on the patent law? Now, they might say, we want to pay this patentee what the patent is really worth to him, and if he has patented it in England he gets some compensation thereby. There are two strings to the bow.

Mr. WHITMAN. Nine times out of ten it is a dead loss to him to patent in a foreign country.

Mr. WILLITS. Now he has got the two countries, and we will reduce it from seventeen to fourteen years if he sees fit to take his patent out in a foreign country.

Mr. STORROW. Those two changes in the law came nine years apart, one in 1861 and one in 1870.

Mr. MASON. And it was in view of this mischief that is here suggested, that after the expiration of an American patent, or if a thing was not patented abroad, there would be an unfair competition as against our manufacturers, and it was attempted to remedy it by this legislation, which only aggravates the evil.

Mr. WILLITS. Now, how does this provision of the bill help?

Mr. WHITMAN. The present section declares that all patents issued since March 2, 1861, shall have a term of seventeen years, and it provides further, in regard to future patents, that if they shall be taken out in this country within two years from the time they are patented abroad, they shall run for the full time. The party, therefore, would be obliged to make application within two years from the time of patenting the invention abroad.

There was still another objection, which strikes me now. It is that a law which it is impossible to put in force—a dead letter on the statute-book—ought to be repealed, if for no other reason. Now, I will attempt to prove why it is impossible to put the law in force. The foreign systems are entirely different from ours. The British system is entirely different from ours. In England, a man could take out a patent two or three years ago for two things—say a steam-engine and a hammer; or, to make a wider difference, he might take out a patent on an agricultural machine and a chemical compound in the same patent. The theory was, that the patent came directly from the Crown, and could cover everything that was incorporated in it. Now, suppose he takes out such a patent abroad, and comes here to obtain an American patent. If we are going to limit the term of his American patent, it would seem that we must make his American patent identical with his English patent; and how are we going to do it? · His English patent may cover a dozen different devices, and under our law it may be necessary for him to take out each one of these in a different patent. Again, under the

English system they do not file caveats. They take out one patent after another, upon inchoate inventions, upon mere speculative drawings. An idea strikes a man, and he gets up a drawing and files an application, and without any examination, a patent is granted him. In the course of years he may take out fifteen or twenty mere descriptions of inchoate, incomplete inventions. At last he embodies them all in one operative machine which is really valuable, and takes out a patent for that operative machine in this country; but he is met with the answer from the Commissioner of Patents that the machine is shown in some fifteen or sixteen English patents, and that the law requires the American patent to be limited according to the foreign patent, consequently, in order to answer the requirements of our laws, it would be necessary to issue one patent for a half-dozen different terms, a part of it running for five years, and another part for six, and still another for seven. It is impossible to execute such a law properly, and the Commissioner has found it impossible, and therefore he himself has recommended a repeal of this proviso.

I would have liked, also, to have spoken on several other subjects which had suggested themselves to me, but I have already occupied more time than was assigned me, and will not further trespass on the committee.

Mr. STORROW. The two years' clause at the end of the section is for the following purpose: Suppose an American manufacturer finds an invention patented abroad and not here, and he wants to use it, he cannot; for, after he has built his machinery, the foreigner can come over here and patent it and stop his machines. Under our proposed law, if it has been patented two years abroad he knows he can use it.

After some discussion, the committee adjourned until twelve o'clock, February 23.

ARGUMENT OF MR. WALKER.

[FEBRUARY 23, 1878.]

Mr. ALBRT H. WALKER, of Chicago, addressed the committee as follows :

MR. CHAIRMAN AND GENTLEMEN OF THE COMMITTEE:

I understand that you, together with your brethren of the House of Representatives, are sent by your constituents to this Capitol for the purpose of enacting such laws as, in your wisdom, seem to be fit and proper; but that it frequently happens that those laws take hold on subjects with which the members of the committees and of Congress have no special familiarity. I apprehend that it was on account of such considerations as these that patent lawyers, who make it their profession to master this branch of our jurisprudence, have been invited to appear here and explain, as well as they may be able, what they have learned about the philosophy of the patent system, about the laws as they now exist, and about the hardships arising thereunder; and what provisions, if any, are necessary to remedy such hardships as seem to call for removal. In following out such duty, I suppose it is the purpose and desire of those gentlemen who appear here to be frank, honest, and candid, and not to attempt to mislead the minds of the gentlemen of the committee who are so kindly listening to them.

Now, I presume it would not be a very difficult thing for me to quote authorities and statutes in such a way as to wrest them from their true meaning; and, unless the committee were to have before them all the books, to test the truth of my citations, they might obtain an erroneous opinion, and base some action upon it. I should, however consider it entirely improper in me to attempt to do anything to thus mislead you, with reference to the law as it now is, or with reference to its application to the facts, or in any other way.

In the course of my remarks, I am sorry to say, it will be necessary for me to correct some of the statements of some of those who have preceded me, which, if allowed to go uncontradicted, might tend to mislead the committee in reference to the laws and facts upon which you are called upon to act.

With this short preface, I will address myself to the bill; and I will begin by reading the first section, in order that we may be sure that our minds are refreshed as to the provisions:

☞ That from and after the passage of this act no profits or damages in any suit at law or in equity for the infringement of a patent shall be recovered which shall have accrued more than four years next preceding the commencement of such suit: *Provided*, That where a party, in order to preserve his right of recovery, finds it necessary to institute a number of suits involving the same issues, and he is proceding with good faith and with reasonable diligence to bring one of them to final judgment, any court in which any of them are pending may, in its discretion, grant a stay of proceedings from time to time in any such other cases pending before it: *Provided, also,* That rights of action existing at the passage of this act may be enforced by suits brought within four years thereafter, if not previously barred by laws already existing; but nothing in this section contained shall revive any right of action already barred, nor prolong the right to sue on any cause of action already existing.

That is a statute of limitation, with such provisos as sometimes are attached to such statutes, but which are frequently omitted, although it omitted they are generally construed by the courts as being within the intent of the framers of the statute. This is a four years' statute of limitation, and in discussing the question of statutes of limitation, and the necessity for enacting such a statute at the present time, the most light can be thrown on the law by a review of its history.

Congress had never felt called upon to enact such a statute pertaining to patents until the year 1870, when it passed an act that all actions under patents " shall be brought during the term for which the letters patent shall be granted or extended, or within six years after the expiration thereof." In 1874 that provision was, as I understand, *accidentally* omitted from the Revised Statutes. At any rate, it was omitted; and it was provided that all provisions that were in former statutes and omitted from the rev sion were thereby repealed; but there was a saving clause annexed to this repealing provision, which provides that rights of action then already existing *may* be enforced within the same length of time as though the repeal had not been made.

Up to the present time, nobody has ever been able to understand exactly what Congress meant by this repealing clause, taken in connection with the saving clause, and two views are held by lawyers who have given the matter attention. One view is, that the repeal of the statute wiped it wholly out of existence, as if it had never been. The other is, that it wiped it wholly out with reference only to rights of action accruing after the date of passage of the repealing act in July, 1874; and that with reference to rights then in existence, whether under patents that had expired or otherwise, it remained in full force, and does so remain up to this day.

Mr RAYMOND. Is the latter your position?

Mr. WALKER. No; it is not. I said that Congress never felt called upon to euact a statute of limitations on the subject of patents until the year 1870; and the occasion for so doing never seems to have been brought to the attention of that body. But actions were brought from 1812 down to 1870; and, curiously enough, during that time, although there was generally in the laws of the States a statute which provided that rights of action arising from torts must be vindicated by suits brought within five years of the commission of the tort, no such statute was invoked until forty years after patent suits began to be brought. I think it was in 1853 that a State statute of limitation was first invoked for the purpose; and up to the present time they have been invoked in seven suits only, as far as the reports of the cases in the circuit courts reveal, though possibly they have also been invoked in cases where no reports have been made. Indeed, I know they have been unsuccessfully set up against suits recently brought by me in four different circuits; but, as I have said, from 1812 to 1877 State statutes of limitation have, in the reported cases, been set up as a bar to patent suits but seven times. In three of these seven cases the courts held that they did apply, and in the other four that they did *not* apply, to actions under patents. Judge Leavitt, the district judge in Ohio, Judge McLean, who held the circuit court in Ohio, and Judge Hall, of the northern district of New York, decided that they did apply; while those who decided that they did not apply to rights of action arising under patent laws were McDonald of Indiana, Grier in Pennsylvania, Swayne in Ohio, and Shepley in Massachusetts.

Now, the argument I deduce from this is not an argument with reference to whether one of these classes of judges or the other was right, but it is this, that the necessity for any statute of limitations is not very pressing, in view of the fact that for sixty-five years, the presumably applicable State statutes were invoked only seven times, and in nearly half of these cases were invoked successfully. Therefore, I conclude that the world will continue to revolve on its axis in the absence of this statute of limitations. It is not one of the most overwhelming of necessities; although, while expressing this opinion, I am in favor of a clear and just statute of limitations, and think such a one should be enacted, because at the present time no one can say what is the exact status of the statute of 1870, and nobody can say what the Supreme Court will decide as to whether or not the State statutes of limitation apply. Everybody, however, agrees that if Congress should enact a statute of this kind, then the State laws could have no further effect; therefore, I say we ought to have a statute of limitations, in order that the obscurity should be cleared away, although there may not be any particular necessity for one in itself.

Mr. STORROW. Yet we have now got one or two hundred cases in my district where the statutes of limitation, of four or ten years, would be invoked if there was any such statute to resort to. I have no doubt there are very many cases where parties would be glad to have such a statute.

Mr. WALKER. My only point, thus far, is, that it is not such an overwhelming, pressing necessity as some suppose.

Mr. BRIGGS. Is it not the fact that there is no statute of limitations— is not that the reason?

Mr. WALKER. The contrary has been generally supposed. It has been the opinion of a large majority of the lawyers throughout the country, that the State statute of limitations did apply to patent cases.

Mr. HUBBELL. Is that not held only in the case of contracts?

Mr. WALKER. Oh, no; not at all. The leading opinion on that subject was Judge Leavitt's, and it has been the opinion of a large majority of the lawyers throughout the country; and the fact that the Supreme Court has never passed upon the point shows that nobody has cared enough about it to carry it up.

Granting, therefore, that there ought to be a statute of limitations, I wish to remark upon the length of this period. Four years is a very unusually short one. Rights of action arising under contracts throughout the United States are usually not barred under five to six or seven years; and with reference to torts, the almost universal rule is five years in which a party is permitted to bring his action.

Mr. POLLARD. The right of action in Missouri upon a written contract is limited to ten years.

Mr. BRIGGS. In New Hampshire it is two years, for torts.

Mr. WILLITS. In Michigan it is two years.

Mr. WALKER. Not with reference to torts, I think. I have taken pains to look through a large number, and have not found one in reference to torts of less than five years.

Mr. BRIGGS. There are different kinds of torts, on which the limitation is six in some cases, and two years in others.

Mr. WALKER. That may be; but it is entirely apart from the argument I am about to make. Rights of action under patents are peculiar things; and I will submit some reasons why I think the limitation should be more than under an ordinary tort. In the first place, the infringements out of which they arise are spread over a great length of time, instead of being committed at any one period. Another reason is, that there are often a multitude of cases under the same patent. There are cases where patents are infringed continually for twenty years, and it would be a great hardship for the patentee to comply with the provisions of the act under such circumstances, because if the four years' statute of limitations is enforced, he has got to bring five different suits in order to comply with its provisions, thus making a multiplicity of actions, and charging himself with great expense, and the defendants also. If he finally fails he has spent a great deal of money, and put the defendants at great cost in defending five suits; whereas, if it had not been for the statute of limitations, he never would have brought but one.

Mr. STORROW. Why should he bring five suits? In such a case as you have cited he recovers up to the date of the accounting, and not merely up to the date of bringing the suit.

Mr. WALKER. Even that is the case only in equity. At law, he can recover for no infringement committed after the declaration is filed.

Notice, also, the language of the bill, with regard to another state of facts: "That from and after the passage of this act no profits or damages, in any suit at law, &c., shall be recovered which shall have accrued more than four years next preceding the commencement of such suit."

Mr. RAYMOND. Then read the proviso in that connection.

Mr. WALKER. The proviso is immaterial in connection with the point I am about to make. Let me proceed in my own way, and I shall probably succeed in conveying my idea more clearly.

It happens frequently that the patentee is injured by a hundred different infringements continuously for a period of twenty years; and very frequently, as I have known, for ten years. It is improper practice, however, even if it were possible, for the patentee to sue all these hundred infringers while he is engaged in a fight to sustain the validity of the patent. The practice has been, under such circumstances, to make a test case, that shall not annoy and perplex all the infringers, where there are a large number.

Take the Tanner brake case, which is about to come before the Supreme Court for argument. This case was begun in Illinois, in 1861. Now, I understand, if that patent is valid, and if Judge Drummond has rendered a true decision, there are 500 infringers who have been infringing since 1861 and before. Now, suppose Mr. Sayles, the owner of that patent, had not sued all the 500, the result would have been that he would have lost his rights of action not sued upon, if this statute had been in existence. Suppose he had sued every one of the 500, what benefit would anybody have derived from the long litigation with 499 of these infringers? None whatever. There would have been 500 suits instituted to determine a question (the validity of a patent) that would have been as effectually determined by the one suit. But, under the provision of this section, in order to prevent rights from being barred absolutely, a patentee will have to sue every infringer within four years after the infringement began. Therefore, I say, in view of the fact that the validity of a great many valuable patents cannot be vindicated within four years, the period of limitation in this bill must be lengthened materially, or great evils will result. On the one hand, the inventor will be stripped of his rights and barred without any fault on his part; and, on the other hand, if he is able to bring his suits, he will merely bring a lot of vexatious actions, doing no good to himself or anybody else, except the attorneys. I think this provision is, without doubt, very good for attorneys, but very bad for inventors, and frequently hurtful to alleged infringers.

Now I will discuss the first proviso:

That where a party, in order to preserve his right of recovery, finds it necessary to institute a number of suits involving the same issues, and he is proceeding with good faith and with reasonable diligence to bring one of them to final judgment, any court in which any of them are pending may, in its discretion, grant a stay of proceedings from time to time in any such other cases pending before it.

I apprehend that there is a good deal of danger that when that proviso comes to be construed, it will be found to amount to this only: that if I have ten suits in one court in one district in the United States, I may apply to the judge for a stay of proceedings in nine of those cases if I prosecute the tenth case; and if I have got ten suits in another district, I can do the same thing. If, however, I have ten suits, each in a different district, I shall have to prosecute them all, because this proviso, in my opinion, does not confer authority to stay proceedings in one court on account of a suit in another. That provision would, therefore, be only a partial relief from the evils and inconvenience I have tried to describe.

I will now pass to the other proviso, which is:

That rights of action existing at the passage of this act may be enforced by suits brought within four years thereafter, if not previously barred by laws already existing; but nothing in this section contained shall revive any right of action already barred, nor prolong the right to sue on any cause of action already existing.

That proviso would have been construed into the act by the Supreme Court if it had not been there; for in the case of *Sohn* v. *Waterson*, 1 Wallace, 596, somewhat recently decided, Justice Bradley delivered the opinion of the court, to the effect that rights of action existing at the time such a statute is passed may be enforced by a suit brought within the same length of time after its passage as that within which it is provided subsequent rights of action may be sought to be enforced after they accrued. In other words, it was held in that case that statutes of limitation begin to run against rights of action existing at the time of their passage from the date of the statute, and not from the date such rights of action accrued; and that if they did the latter, they would, in that regard, be unconstitutional. Precisely this proviso has thus been held to be an equitable appendage to such a statute by the Supreme Court; and I therefore think that if the limitation is made for four years the proviso ought to correspond with it in length of time. In that regard I have no objection to the bill. Mr. Raymond, however, in his argument before you, said he was dissatisfied with the bill in that respect, although, as I understood, he had, after consultation with gentlemen of different views from himself, agreed to submit this section to Congress without amendment on either side. He has said that he wanted that changed so as to compel the vindication of existing rights of action by suits brought within six months after the bill becomes a law, or not at all. Now, that is a very harsh measure, because the statute, very likely, would not be published under six months; and if it was, a great many people holding rights of action would not know of it, or would not, in point of fact, be able to bring their suits within six months. But I can explain to the committee exactly Mr. Raymond's idea about that six months' statute of limitations, and that is, that it has reference to a large number of suits on the Tanner brake that are pending against the Western railroads. I am attorney for Mr. Sayles, the owner of that brake, as well as attorney for the Stevens brake, and other patents. Now, the Tanner patent expired on the 6th of July, 1873; and if it is held that the national statute of 1870 is in force, as to these rights of action, because all these rights accrued before the statute of 1870 was repealed, then the national statute will operate to bar these suits forever on the 6th day of July, 1879, whether Congress passes the statute of limitation or not. I am, indeed, of opinion that no suits under the Tanner brake patent can safely be brought after the 6th of July, 1879, under pending laws. Therefore, we have only about fifteen months, after our expected decision by the Supreme Court, to sue infringers throughout the United States. That litigation has been prosecuted by my client with extraordinary diligence, but we have never been able to bring it to the attention of the Supreme Court. Our suit has been pending since 1861. It has been most elaborately and expensively defended by the Western Railroad Association. There have been hearings and rehearings, and we have had decision after decision of Judge Drummond in our favor. The case will come before the Supreme Court for hearing this spring. We feel entirely confident of success, and I am ready to discuss it now and everywhere.

[Mr. Walker then went into a full explanation of the brake case, which, by request, is omitted.]

The bill is drawn in the first section with a good deal of fairness, in many respects, and in such a way as not to hurt us in the slightest degree; because it provides that " rights of action existing at the passage of the act may be brought within four years thereafter, if not previously barred by laws already existing." Now, this statute of 1870 is probably a law in existence as to rights, and will bar them in much less than four years. It will probably bar our rights in fifteen months from now.

Mr. RAYMOND. The statute of limitation, I understand you to say, will bar you in sixteen months.

Mr. WALKER. I do not object to the bill as drawn, in reference to our rights.

Mr. RAYMOND. It seems to be the amendment I proposed, in relation to limiting these particular rights of action to six months, that you object to. Now, to show you that I am willing to give all you claim you are entitled to, I am perfectly willing to have it changed to eighteen months, to let your cases out.

Mr. WALKER. The great part of my argument is not addressed to any hardships relating to my client's interests, but to those of all other patentees who find themselves in the same position. I do not come here, gentlemen of the committee, to argue simply such points as would be material to Thomas Sayles, further than these points coincide with the policy and requirements of the patent system.

I now turn to the consideration of the second section of the bill, which has to do with the money that shall be recovered in court for the infringement of a patent, and which reads as follows:

SEC. 2. In all cases where the patentee has elected to license other persons generally to use his invention, in like manner to that in which it was used by the defendant, or where it appears to the court or jury that, from the nature of the invention, it is for the interest of the patentee that other persons generally should use the same in like manner and pay him a license-fee therefor, the measure of the plaintiff's damages shall be the same, both at law and in equity, and no account of profits or savings shall be allowed. If a license-fee has already been established by a reasonable number of transactions of a character applicable to the case at bar, that shall be adopted as a measure of said damages; but if not, then the court or jury shall determine the same from all the evidence in the case. In taking an account of profits in any case, the defendant shall not be charged with any saving he may have made, unless it has enabled him to realize an actual profit in that part of his business connected with the use of the invention. And the court shall determine what proportion of such profit is due to the use of said invention, and what proportion to the other elements from which such profit was derived, capital and personal services excepted; and the proportion of actual profit so found to be derived from the use of the invention shall be the measure of the profits to be recovered. But if, in any case, it shall appear to the court that the damages or profits, ascertained as above, shall be inadequate to give the plaintiff a just compensation for the injury done by the infringement, or shall be in excess of such injury, the court shall have power to increase or diminish the amount to such an extent as may be just and reasonable : *Provided*, That the provisions of this section shall not apply in any case in which a decree for an account or assessment of damages has, at the date of the passage of this act, already been pronounced. Nothing contained in this section shall affect the right of the plaintiff to an injunction.

The rule in equity with reference to the money recoverable for the infringement of a patent, was laid down, as my brother Payson said yesterday, in the case of *Mowry* v. *Whitney*, in its most modern form. It is a decision of the Supreme Court, and will be found in 14 Wallace, page 620. There are two cases of that name in the book, and this is the later one of the two. The rule established there is the rule Mr. Payson complains of; and it is the rule which the Western Railroad Association, by means of this bill, seeks to have substantially abolished. I will give the rule as laid down in the case of which I speak : " The question is, what advantage did the infringer derive from using the invention over what he had in using other processes then open to the public, and adequate to enable him to obtain an equally beneficial result ? The fruits of that advantage are his profits, and that advantage is the measure of profits to be accounted for."

That is stated in concise language, but it is still more easily and readily understood, perhaps, by stating the case. The patent on which the suit was brought was for an improved process for the manufacture of car-wheels. Mowry used this improved process of Whitney's without license, and was sued in equity, and the master directed to take an account of profits. The master found from the evidence that Mowry had manufactured 19,819 car-wheels under that process, and he found out that the exact amount of profit that Mowry derived from the manufacture of those wheels was $91,501.86. The circuit court held that he should pay that amount of money over to the plaintiff, the man who owned the patent. The case came to the Supreme Court, and they said, not so; it appears from the evidence that this $91,000 was not due alone to the use of Whitney's patent, for other things had been done to these car-wheels besides subjecting them to this patented process; and it is not fair to give to the patentee—whose process covered a portion only of the things the infringer had to do—all the profits that the infringer derived from the entire proceeding; and it is therefore clear that Whitney was entitled only to the profits actually received by the use of his process over what would have been received from any other process open to the infringer, which, in this case, amounted to only $5,500. That is the additional advantage the defendant derived by the use of the improved process. Now, that is the decision in that case—that $5,500 belonged to the patentee, whose right had been infringed, on the principle that the $5,500 had been such a proportion of the $91,000 as the patented process bore to the entire process used in the manufacture of those wheels. Now, is there any very horrible outrage about that? I cannot see but what heaven and earth would stand if that infringer did pay $5,500 out of $91,000. But that is the rule that is denounced here, and that is the rule that, in ingenious language, is sought wholly to be abolished, and the infringer permitted not only to keep the $86,000, but pretty much all the $5,500 would practically remain in his pocket, in a great many cases.

The only plausible objection to the rule that I have ever heard of was that suggested in the argument of Mr. Payson on yesterday, by means of his whip illustration, which was a very ingenious and pointed presentation of one of the hardships that may possibly result in a supposable case, although no such hardship resulted in the case of Mowry v. Whitney.

Mr. BRIGGS. It would result in any invention where the whole article was manufactured complete, as in the case of piano-legs, for instance.

Mr. WALKER. I will speak of the whip illustration, as we have had our attention called to that by the other side.

Mr. Payson says: "Here is a whip that is bought for twenty-five cents, and I am told it cost twenty cents to make by a patented machine, and would have cost fifty by hand in the old way. Suppose now the patentee sues the infringer and recovers the difference between fifty cents, the cost by hand, and twenty cents, the cost by machine, which is more than the entire price he received for the whip. That means, then, that in such a case the rule would result in the infringer being obliged to pay over to the inventor more than he actually received for the entire thing. But what ought the infringer to have done? He had three courses open to him to obviate that loss. In the first place, he could have minded his own business and not made or sold the whips at all. Another course would have been to have honestly bought a license from the inventor, or, if he must needs make the whips and infringe the patent, he ought to have sold the whips for fifty cents. There was no law compelling him to sell them for twenty-five cents, and no necessity. The Supreme Court have said, in effect, that if an infringer profits by his tort, and then fools away those profits on a horse-race, it is no defense to the claim that he shall pay the amount over to the owner of the patent infringed. Suppose the man who owned the patent says, ' Here, I have got a good thing in whips, and the profit is very large. I will keep the whole thing in my hands, make the whips for twenty cents, and sell them for fifty cents, and I will make and sell all the whips I choose for the next seventeen years.' He proceeds to do so, but this infringer says, ' No ; I will block that plan very quick. I will make your whips and sell them for twenty-five cents, and that will prevent you from selling them for any more.' And then, if the inventor sues him for the difference, he says ' I haven't got it. I sold the whips for twenty-five cents each.' That defense was argued before Judge Nixon, and the judge put this homely illustration as an indication of its fallacy : " Suppose I keep a livery-stable, and I am away from home, and a man comes to the livery-stable and says, ' Give me a horse ; I must go twenty miles to visit a man on some important business.' The servant replies, ' The man who owns the livery-stable is not at home, and I don't let out horses myself.' ' O,' says the man, ' I will take the horse anyhow, and see the owner about it afterwards ;' and he takes the horse without permission and goes the twenty miles and returns. The livery man says, ' Pay me my regular rates.' ' O, no,' says the man, ' I didn't find the man I went after, and made no profits from the expedition, and, therefore, you can't expect me to pay for the team.' " That was Judge Nixon's illustration, and seems a sufficient answer to the claim that because I have fooled away the profits that I have made by the infringement of the inventor's patent, I shall not be called upon to respond to the inventor. I think that very effectually disposes of the whip illustration ; and the whip argument is the only one that has ever affected my mind with any degree of force in favor of the abolition of the rule of profits. As presented by Mr. Payson, it seemed to be a great hardship that he might be called upon to pay thirty cents when he only made five—robbed, as he said to you.

You doubtless remember the story of Troy, how, under the cover of a wooden horse, the armed men were taken in through the gates of the city, and when they got in they disturbed things a great deal more than was anticipated by the people who brought them in. Very much larger results attended the transaction than were anticipated. That is the case with what is attempted to be done in this bill. Mr. Payson comes and shows the supposed hardship, and then proposes to remedy it, and by a bill that goes a thousand times further than is necessary for the purpose. It reminds me of some of the surgeons that were sent to the war from the North. They thought that was their time for making a reputation for performing capital operations ; and they desired to be able to say that they had cut off a thousand legs in one year ; and, therefore, it was not at all infrequent that our Northern surgeons—I don't know as to the other side ; I hope they were more honest—if a man had a bullet imbedded in the fleshy part of the arm, and considerable blood came out, thought there was a chance for a capital operation ; while the poor soldier's interest was not much regarded. Now, this remedy and hardship are quite analogous to those surgical cases. The remedy is a thousand times stronger than the hardship to be remedied. It reminds me of an illustration that my father once used—it is like brushing a fly off a man's face with a crowbar. This supposed hardship is fully provided for by this portion of the bill :

> In taking an account of profits in any case, the defendant shall not be charged with any saving he may have made, unless it has enabled him to realize an actual profit in that part of his business connected with the use of the invention.

This clause is scientifically adapted to provide for the hardship so enlarged upon. It provides that the infringer shall not pay over any more than he actually made from the manufacture of this whip. And further than that, if it turns out that the five cents was not wholly due to the invention, the inventor cannot obtain even that miserable five cents. But Mr. Payson don't content himself with that provision ; but, under the guise of remedying that supposed hardship, be introduces the abolition of the recovery of profits, in cases wholly free from the pretended wrong. He accomplishes such abolition in the first two clauses of the section, which read as follows:

In all cases where the patentee has elected to license other persons generally to use his invention, in like manner to that in which it was used by the defendant, or where it appears to the court or jury that, from the nature of the invention, it is for the interest of the patentee that other persons generally should use the same in like manner and pay him a license-fee therefor, the measure of the plaintiff's damages shall be the same, both at law and in equity, and no account of profits or savings shall he allowed.

Now, take the illustration that I used before the Senate committee, with reference to a patent that is yet to be granted.

It is well known that water is the most combustible thing in the world; consisting of two gases, hydrogen and oxygen—hydrogen being very inflammable, and oxygen being the great sustainer of combustion. The two being separated, the water would be transformed into fuel. This has been done, but no process has been devised to do it with any degree of cheapness; so, in practice, nobody does it. But I have no doubt the time will come when the problem will be solved in a simpler manner, and somebody will hit upon a plan; and, of course, when that is done, that will be the cheapest fuel that can be conceived of.

Now, suppose that the chairman of this committee should make that invention or discovery, and gets a patent on it? That would be a process patent, not involving machinery. He spreads on the records of the Patent Office an exact description of what to do in order to accomplish that result, and, in consideration of his so doing, the United States gives him the monopoly of doing that thing for seventeen years, and then after that everybody can do it without hinderance. Now, suppose the Baltimore and Ohio Railroad Company see the wonderful invention, and think that is a good thing, and a good deal cheaper than coal, and say: "We will proceed to infringe Mr. Vance's patent, and we will fight him ten or fifteen years, if he sues us, with the probable result of his exhausting his means before he gets a decree." Such a course of defiant infringement is, in many cases, the deliberate purpose of railroad men. It was the avowed practice of H. E. Sargent, the superintendent for many years of the Michigan Central Railroad, and one of the members of the Western Railroad Association. He has avowed it as his universal principle never to pay anything voluntarily to a patentee. He says: "Whenever our attention is called to a patent of value, we use it, and in a few cases we are made to pay, by plucky inventors; but, in the aggregate, we pay much less than if we took licenses at first." I admit the railroad companies do not generally avow such a plan of action, but I know they entertain such ideas.

Mr. RAYMOND. Mr. Sargent settled under your patent, and paid the money years ago.

Mr. WALKER. It was ten or fifteen years before he was connected with that road that the settlement you speak of was made.

Now, suppose Mr. Vance finally vindicates his patent, notwithstanding eighty-one railroads—after the manner of the Western Railroad Association—combine to crush him. The courts are placed where the vast wealth of a litigant cannot be flaunted with success, and, therefore, sometimes the poor get their deserts. Mr. Vance has his patent confirmed; and then it is referred to a master, to take an account of the amount of money that he should have. Mr. Vance will make his claim on the theory that the infringer has made $500,000 during the years it has been enjoying the patent, and now it ought to pay the money over to the patentee. Says the railroad company: "O, no; we will take shelter under this law, which provides that, when you do finally beat us, you shall not recover the profits at all, but the sum which you show you were injured by our infringement." Now, how much was Mr. Vance technically injured by the use of that invention on that road? He was injured in the degree that he was deprived of someting by their infringement that he would otherwise have had. As he could in no event have used his invention himself on the defendant's road, the use of it by the defendant deprived him of nothing he would otherwise have had, and therefore no damages can be predicated on any idea that he was injured, in a legal sense, by their infringement. Consequently, the only ground of relief would be a license-fee; and, under this bill, a jury is to be brought in and say what, on the whole, Mr. Vance ought to have had twenty years ago as a license-fee, and that is not to be augmented in any degree by the great delay he has been obliged to suffer in vindicating his rights. The road can successfully say, under this bill: "We will not pay over to you what we have derived from the use of your invention, but what a jury says we ought to have paid you twenty years ago, and that without interest." I will show you how this second section will operate if it is made to apply to the Tanner-brake patent.

In the early days of the Tanner brake, Mr. Sayles, who became the owner of it in 1854, determined to vindicate his patent in the courts. He proceeded to do so, and got it declared valid, in a hotly-contested case, the same year he bought it. He then said to the railroad companies: "If you will pay me a license-fee, without litigation, I will allow you to use my invention for $10 per mile, of 200 miles for $2,000; and you can use as many brakes as you choose along the line of your road." A large number of roads purchased the rights thus offered. In 1861, Mr. Sayles called on the Northwestern road and offered them a license for $2,000, and they refused to pay the price, and said: "We will not give you a cent, and if you sue us we will beat you. You beat the Erie road seven years ago; but we will beat you now, for we will fight it stronger than they did." As the result of that defiance, Mr. Sayles has given one of the most persistent and courageous of lives to the litigation of that suit. He has done so in spite of the combination of eighty-one railroad corporations, each one of them without a soul; in spite of their ability to employ the ablest counsel, and among others Judge B. R. Curtis, who was undoubtedly the ablest patent counsel in the country, to defeat us; and in spite of the reckless testimony of certain railroad employés. He has won every issue in the courts below, and expects to win his issue in the Supreme Court. He has made some settlements; the Saint Paul Railroad paid him $20,000, and the Alton and other roads also paid smaller sums; and so, by means of these settlements, he has been able to prosecute his suit.

Now, suppose our decree is affirmed in the Supreme Court next April, as in every probability it will be, in view of the facts established below; then the Railroad Association says: "We will pay you the money we ought to have paid you twenty years ago, namely, the license-fee; but if you won't take that, we will get a bill passed in Congress to compel you to take it." Now, gentlemen of the committee, that is all that bill was drawn for in the first instance, and in the latter part of my speech I will give a history of the bill, as I am intimately acquainted with its progress for the last year.

I will call the attention of the committee, at this point, to the fact that the bill is retroactive, and applies as well to rights of action already accrued as to those hereafter to accrue, with the single excep tion that it does not apply to cases where at the time of the passage of the act a decree has been "pronounced"; in suits already begun, and that have thus been carried far enough to get into the master's hands, but suits which have been begun and not passed to a decree, are subject to the operation of this bill.

About one hundred years ago there were some of the wisest men in the United States that ever lived in the world; such men as George Washington, Benjamin Franklin, Alexander Hamilton, and several others. They met and framed a Constitution, and in a very few years after it was ratified it was amended, and among other amendments there was inserted into that Constitution what has been a principle of English law since Magna Charta, namely: "No person shall be deprived of property without due process of law." Rights of action are property, and patents are property. The Supreme Court has, indeed, recently remarked, in a decision given by Justice Clifford and reported in 4 Otio, that patents are property, and there are a great many other decisions to the same effect. It is a familiar and fundamental principle of law that *choses* in action upon which one has a right to sue are, as well as anything tangible is, vested property. The doctrine is laid down in Cooley on Constitutional Limitations, and is beyond all question sound law.

Now, we have a right under the present law to recover from the railroad companies the profits they have derived from infringing our patent ; but this bill comes in, and says you shall not have these profits, but have a license-fee only. Mr. Payson has said to the committee that the profits I speak of amount to $60,000,000, and the license-fee to only about $500,000; so he says the profits are more than a hundred times as much as the license-fee. As Mr. Payson committed himself to these figures, I am doing him no injustice in using them, though they are grossly exaggerated. Under the law as it now stands, Mr. Sayles, he says, will recover $60,000,000, and under the law laid down here $500,000. Now, is it not very clear that the bill, if enforced, would deprive Mr. Sayles of $59,500,000 of rights of action, according to Mr. Payson's own estimate? Therefore, I say that, as far as the bill refers to rights of action already accrued, it is obnoxious to the fifth amendment to the Constitution, which provides that no person shall be deprived of property without due process of law. I have shown that rights of action are property. Now, what is "due process of law"? It is stated by Chancellor Kent, in his Commentaries, to mean the proceedings, judgments, and decrees of courts, and does not include the acts of any legislative body whatever. And the same doctrine was held in the 4th Hill in the supreme court of New York, on page 147. It has also been so held very lately by Justice Miller, when delivering the opinion of the Supreme Court in the Louisiana assessment cases. He says that it is very clear that if the legislature enacts a law that A's property shall be taken away and given to B, that that is obnoxious to the fifth amendment, and is not due process of law; but, he says, that if the legislature provides for a proceeding by which real property may be assessed, and the owners of the property, in accordance with the provisions of the statute, are permitted to come in and have their objections passed upon in a quasi-judicial manner, it is due process of law, because the legislature did not in so doing take away the property, but provided a quasi-judicial tribunal which, after a hearing, should be permitted to assess taxes upon the land. He affirmed, however, the well-known doctrine that a mere enactment of the legislature is not due process of law within the meaning of the Constitution. It is very clear, therefore, that property cannot be taken away by act of Congress.

Mr. WILLITS. Then this clause would be declared unconstitutional, and would be inoperative ?

Mr. WALKER. Of course, that would be the result as to rights of action existing at its passage.

Mr. STORROW. That is, *if* it does take away the vested right of property. The general proposition is true; but the question arises on its application to this case.

Mr. WALKER. The only argument that can be made against my position with any sort of plausibility is, that the proposed bill goes only to the remedy, and not to the right, and therefore is not unconstitutional. This is urged in accordance with the common idea that the legislature may modify the remedy as much as it sees fit. The Supreme Court have said that this proposition is true, provided the new remedy they give produces substantially the same results as the old remedy did. But, under the guise of modifying the remedy, they have no power to diminish the right of recovery. In proof of this last proposition, I will cite Bronson *v.* Kinzie, 1 Howard, 317 ; Greene *v.* Biddle, 8 Wheaton, 75. I will read the exact language in the latter case:

Nothing, in short, can be more clear, upon principles of law and reason, than that a law which denies to the owner of land a *remedy* to recover possession of it when withheld by any person, however innocently he may have obtained it, or to recover the profits received from it by the occupant, or which clogs his recovery of such possession or profits, by conditions and restrictions tending to diminish the amount or value of the thing recovered, impairs his *right* to and interest in the property.

The idea of that decision is this : That if, under the guise of changing the remedy, you take away one remedy and enact another, and the aggregate result, in dollars and cents, by the last remedy is substantially smaller than it was under the older one, you have, under the guise of a change of remedy, impaired the right of property, and rendered your law obnoxious to the fifth amendment to the Constitution.

Now, here I have to intersperse some remarks reflecting upon the Western Railroad Association. In this attempted retroactive effect is precisely where another Ethiopian is found in the wood-pile. I never have heard a lawyer or layman, except Mr. Storrow and Raymond, intimate a doubt as to the soundness of my criticism upon the attempted retroactive effect of this amendment. Everybody else who has argued the matter is of opinion, as far as I know, that it would be held unconstitutional. I do not stand here to argue the case because there is any danger that my clients would be injured by the ultimate decision of the courts upon it, but because it simply puts another stumbling-block in the way of their speedily obtaining their rights.

Now, suppose that this bill is passed, and our case is affirmed in the Supreme Court next April. Mr. Raymond shows his friends this bill enacted into a law. The railroad men say: "That reads very straight." The railroad men are not constitutional lawyers, you know, so they say to us: "We will fight you another five or ten years if you dispute the validity of this law." · It would take the very utmost diligence that we could exercise for at least five years to get the Supreme Court to hold that the bill cannot apply to rights of action already accrued. The only thing that I object to, as far as my clients are concerned, is that the bill, as it now stands, is the proposed enactment of a law clearly unconstitutional, and which would never enable anybody to gain anything, except to longer prevent other people from getting their rights in the courts than they otherwise would be able to do

I will now dispose of a couple of arguments that Mr. Storrow made
n reply to my retroactive argument before the Senate committee.
It was suggested by Mr. Storrow, before the committee, in November,
that Congress probably *has* constitutional power to make the second
section of the bill apply to rights of action already accrued, inasmuch
as the retrospective operation of 14th section of the patent act of 1836
has never been questioned on constitutional grounds.

The point Mr. Storrow here made was this: He says that when a patent law was enacted, about 1800, one of its provisions was that in suits
at law the plaintiff should be entitled to recover threefold the amount
that he had been injured.   When the patent law was revised in 1836, in the
14th section of the act of that year it was provided that the jury should
find the actual amount of damages only in actions at law, and that it
should rest with the court to give a judgment for three times that
amount if, in its discretion, it thought fit to do so.   This new provision
was made retroactive by the express provision in the act of 1836, and
nobody found any fault.

Mr. STORROW. That was not my argument.   I didn't rest the point
upon what had been done before ; I——

Mr. WALKER. I will come to that.   I can answer but one argument
at a time.

The precedent, however, affords no indication of the constitutionality of this bill, because what Congress did in 1836 was only to take
away the right to recover a *penalty*, which it had the power to do, at
any time before judgment.   (See note 5, page 362, Cooley on Constitutional Limitations, and numerous cases there cited.)

This threefold recovery was a penalty as to two-thirds of it, and nothing else.   But now they seek to take away, not any penalty, but the
very money-recovery to which we are entitled, of right, on principles of
equity, and I submit that is a very different thing.

Mr. Storrow also said that Congress may have power at least to make
the section under review apply to existing rights of action, upon which
no *suit* has yet been brought, and referred, without naming it, to the
case of Dash *v.* Van Kleeck (7 Johnson's Reports, 500) as being one
wherein it was held that legislative power cannot divest rights *already
sought to be enforced by action*.   He seemed to be under the impression
that the courts have never gone beyond that point, in setting aside such
retrospective laws.

A careful reading of the case, however, will show that Chancellor
Kent, who decided it, went much further than the last-mentioned doctrine.   He approved the opinion of the Supreme Court, in 2 Cranch,
272, viz: "That the point is too clear for argument, that a statute cannot retrospect so as to take away a *vested* right"; and he made no distinction, in principle, between rights *already* sued upon, and those *ripe*
for suit.   Moreover, the right he then vindicated was the right to a particular *remedy*.

If the gentlemen of the committee desire to get, in the smallest space,
the whole history of the opinions of the courts on the subject of retroactive laws, they will find it in that masterly decision of Kent.   He re-
views Justinian, and Bracton, and Coke, and all the authorities up to
his day.   He takes occasion, in the most vigorous and convincing terms,
to deny the power of any legislative body to make any law apply to
rights of action already accrued, whether these rights of action were
already sued upon or not.   If the members of the committee, or the lawyers opposed to me, desire to read an eloquent speech in my favor, they
can read Chancellor Kent's decision, and find it there.

I have thus, gentlemen of the committee, discussed the first two sections of the bill. With reference to the other sections of the bill, there is no very important controversy. Many of them were added for the purpose of taking off the curse from these two sections; and others were considered as needed reforms of the patent law. If I were drawing them I should change some of them, to obviate some minor injustices; but the majority are, in my opinion, very needful and very proper provisions, and will remedy a great many evils under which patentees, inventors, and others have been laboring. The gentlemen who have proposed this bill to the committee, proposed twenty-two very good sections, but they have brought in with those twenty-two good sections these other two sections, that were conceived in iniquity, and were originally designed for special purposes and special ends, and not for the public good.

The CHAIRMAN. Do you think the first section should be stricken out entirely, or amended ?

Mr. WALKER. I do not object to the first section, with a reasonable length of limitations.

The CHAIRMAN. What is your opinion as to the time?

Mr. WALKER. I should say not less than seven years. I will now, as my time has not quite expired, in a somewhat fragmentary manner, take Mr. Raymond's speech, which he delivered in this room, in the presence of the committee, on the 1st and 2d of February last, and will comment on some of the statements that he therein made. He says:

As the members of the committee, solicitous only for the public interest, represent more largely the users of patents, and also the small portion of people comprising inventors, so the railroad companies represent primarily the business interest which is the largest user of patents, and secondarily the small number of railroad officers and employés comprising the inventors of the more valuable of the improvements we use.

Now, the intimate affection that exists between the railroad companies and their employés was finely illustrated in July last in the presence of this whole country, and the anxiety with which corporations foster the interests of their employés was as fully set forth as are object-lessons such as they have in Sunday-schools for the purpose of inculcating abstract ideas. Therefore, I say it has an air of thinness about it, for a man who represents an association of corporations that had to shut up shop because their employés rebelled against them by reason of their oppressions, to come here and claim that he represents those employés.

A MEMBER OF THE COMMITTEE. The majority of the corporations were not put in that strait. The argument does not apply to all corporations.

Mr. WALKER. Not to all corporations, of course; but it does to the principal ones he represents. He says, again, on page 8 of his speech:

In the mean time the courts have established the rule, *without seeing where it led*, that in equity the defendant's *profits or savings* should be the rule, and under this rule it has been recently solemnly declared by judicial decisions that a single patent may be worth ten, twenty, thirty, fifty, and in one case sixty million of dollars. It would seem as if such results ought to satisfy the most grasping. In 1870, however, a new provision was added to the law, by which, in addition to the profits, the plaintiff is to have the damages he may have sustained by reason of infringement.

I should not have been surprised if Mr. Raymond had said that in an extemporaneous speech, but I compared this, last evening, with a copy of the speech he made in advocacy of substantially this same bill before the Senate committee last year, and it is a *verbatim* copy of the language he used there, and as it is a total misrepresentation of the law on the subject, I say that he is to blame for it. It was done after due deliberation, as he made the same statement a year ago. There are misstatements, both of law and fact, in it. He says that "It has been recently solemnly declared by judicial decisions that a single patent may be worth ten, twenty, thirty, fifty, and in one case sixty million of dollars." I think it would trouble him very much to mention a patent which has been "recently solemnly declared" to be worth either of those sums. Now, with reference to his misstatement of the law. He says: "In 1870, however, a new provision was added to the law, by which, in addition to the profits, the plaintiff is to have the damages he may have sustained by reason of the infringement." Now, the law he refers to is section 4921 of the Revised Statutes, and is as follows:

And upon a decree being rendered in any such (equity) case for an infringement, the complainant shall be entitled to recover, in addition to the profits to be accounted for by the defendant, the damages the complainant has sustained thereby; and the court shall assess the same, or cause the same to be assessed, under its direction. And the court shall have the same power to increase such damages, in its discretion, as is given to increase the damages found by verdicts in actions upon the case.

Mr. Raymond's statement is a true enough representation of what the statute literally says, but he knew that the Supreme Court had construed that statute in the case of Birdsall against Coolidge, 3 Otto, 68, to mean that if it turned out in the accounting that the profits were smaller than the damages, the court of equity could add to the profits such proportion of the damages as would swell the entire amount to what the damages alone would have been. In other words, the court says the statute means that the patentee shall not have *both* damages and profits, but shall have whichever is *largest*. We do not know what the law is, except by the construction put upon it by the Supreme Court, and if Mr. Raymond conceals from the committee that construction he attempts to mislead it in regard to the law. Again he says:

The Constitution and the law grant to the inventor "the exclusive right" to his invention for seventeen years. It is a close monopoly, which, in my opinion, should be given in no case.

A Daniel come to judgment! Again I read:

This is specially true if, as I claim, in the third place, that an inventor has *not* a natural right to the exclusive enjoyment of his invention, and that while the granting of exclusive monopolies forms a part of the common law of England, it has no natural place among the institutions of our government, but is flatly opposed to the general principles.

Then he quotes Webster's patent cases (I, IV, and V), as showing what the principles of this government are. Do the committee know that those cases were all adjudicated in England, under the English patent system? This is another attempt to mislead the committee. Monopolies were granted, in the time of Queen Elizabeth, not only for inventions and discoveries, but for things in regard to which the person who took the monopoly had no meritorious right. But Mr. Raymond should have studied Curtis. Curtis on Patents lays down clearly the American doctrine to be, not that a patent for an invention or discovery is an odious monopoly, in the English sense of the term, granted as the result of arbitrary power in the government, but that it is merely a contract between the inventor and the government. The inventor is granted the exclusive right to make, vend, and use his invention for a limited term of years, in consideration of his having spread upon the records of the Patent Office a full description of the same, so that the public may at all times be advised thereof. Mr. Raymond, however, comes here and cites an English authority, and says that that illustrates the principles of the patent law of the United States. Gentlemen of the committee, he might as well say that the powers of Congress are regulated by the unwritten constitution of England.

A MEMBER OF THE COMMITTEE. Do you know any case where it has been decided in a United States court that these letters patent are contracts?

Mr. WALKER. No, sir; I do not.

Mr. STORROW. The case of the Attorney-General *v.* Rumford Chemical Works, 9 Gazette, 1062, so states.

Mr. WALKER. Curtis unfolds the philosophy of the matter very fully, and says that, unlike the English monopolist, the patentee in this country gives a *quid pro quo.* Here he confers upon the world the benefit of his invention and what he has accomplished in the arts by making it. Now, here is a piece of Websterian eloquence:

> You will be told that the highest title that a man can have to property is the title or creation, and discovery, and possession. So-so in tangible property, less so in intangible, and not at all so "by natural right," in the creations, discoveries, and possessions of the mind, which were intended by Him after whose likeness man was made, to be given freely and fully, as though the air itself, to all men for their progress toward that which is to come. If, perchance, there be a single thought in these remarks which is new and useful, it is not and was not mine by natural right, but was given me by infinite intelligence, to be by me given again.

I suppose Mr. Payson, Mr. Raymond, Mr. Eldredge, and Mr. Hurlbut are all equally inspired; but that don't prevent any of them from drawing large pay from the Western Railroad Association while filling this room with divine afflatus. In like manner, the inventor who confers upon the country a great benefit, is justly entitled to secure his pay for being the agent of the divine intelligence that works through him.

During his speech, Mr. Raymond said: "I would like to make this suggestion to the committee: There is hardly a word in this bill that has not been thoroughly considered by the best talent in the country, and very thoroughly discussed. Everything in it means something." At that point a member of the committee—I wish I knew who he was; I would like to congratulate him—asked this question: "Was it discussed by parties representing both interests?" Mr. Raymond replied: "Yes, sir; by parties representing *both* interests and *all* interests—the interests of the patentee and the interests of the user of the patent."

When Mr. Raymond made that statement he knew that I represented by far the largest portion of the rights of action that are sought to be enforced against the Western Railroad Association, and he knew that I appeared before the Senate committee in February, 1877, and opposed the passage of the bill that was then pending before that committee, which was substantially this bill. He knew that at that time I had the co-operation of Mr. Chauncey Smith, of Boston, who in the speech that he then made said relative to this section——

Mr. STORROW. That was a thoroughly and radically different section from this.

Mr. WALKER. Mr. Smith at this point was not discussing the section as a whole, but a feature common to that section and this, and he said:

> The second section of the bill also forbids a recovery of *profits* which the infringer realizes by his unlawful use of the invention. Yet it is one of the most equitable rules adopted by courts of equity, that such profits *belong,* and ought to be restored, to the owner of the property trespassed upon.

This particular feature was common to both of them, and Mr. Smith denounced it at the same time I did. Mr. Raymond knew these facts, and he knew that I was informed by Mr. Smith, last July, by letter, that a conference of patent lawyers was to be held at Chicago on the 20th of September, for the purpose of framing a compromise bill that should be brought here to Congress, with the sanction of those lawyers that were represented, and presented to Congress as being the result of the deliberation of parties, on all sides, of the interests concerned. He knew, also, that during the month of July, 1877, I published a pamphlet in

regard to the first and second sections of the bill then pending, com-
menting on some of the things contained in those sections, and that
therein I said the history of the bill is as follows:

It was introduced in its original form in the House of Representatives by Hon. S. A.
Hurlbut, of Illinois, early in 1876. Its principal promoter in the lobby is James H. Raymond, of Chicago, the secretary of the Western Railroad Association, which latter is a combination of about fifty railroad companies, the original purpose of which was to furnish legal
advice and assistance to its members in their patent litigation. Succeeding less fully than
it expected to do in the courts, it turned its attention. at the beginning of 1876, to Congress,
and has since that time hoped that by means of this bill, patents heretofore, or hereafter,
vindicated in the courts, might virtually be defeated by statute.

Mr. Raymond knew that I represented by far the larger proportion
of the rights of action against his association. He requested that I
should not be invited to the conference, but still he comes here and states
that that bill was discussed by both parties, when he knows that he took
special pains to have me excluded from all share in its preparation. I
have understood, from members of that conference, which resulted in
that compromise, that they were very much surprised that I was not
there.

In another place he quotes Dash v. Van Kleeck, in the 7 Johnson, in
which case Chancellor Kent denounced these retroactive laws in a wonderful outpouring of indignation; and yet Mr. Raymond quotes that
decision of Chancellor Kent as sustaining his proposition—that a legislature can take away a right of action itself, unless it springs from contract or the principles of the common law. No proposition could be more
diametrically opposite to Kent's than that. There is no such statement
in Chancellor Kent's decision. I know how he came to make the mistake. He got the language which he uses from Cooley on Constitutional
Limitations, by entirely misquoting it. What Cooley says is, that where
rights of action spring from contracts or the principles of the common
law, they cannot be taken away by the legislature. But Mr. Raymond
wrests him into saying that, unless they do spring from those sources,
they *may* be so taken away; and then cites Chancellor Kent in Dash v.
Van Kleeck, which is a decision exactly opposite in every respect.

Justinian also says, in reference to the subject of retrospective laws:

It is a principle of the civil law that a lawgiver cannot alter his mind to the prejudice
of a vested right.

And Puffendorf, a modern writer on the civil law, says:

A law may be repealed by the lawgiver, but the rights that the individual has acquired
under it while it was in force do not cease.

Mr. STORROW. I desire to ask you whether you have any authority
from the Supreme Court of the United States, or any other court of last
resort in this country, laying down the doctrine that a right of action
for unliquidated damages for a tort is a vested right?

Mr. WALKER. Not exactly in that form.

Mr. STORROW. Will you give us a case that comes the next thing
to it?

Mr. WALKER. If Mr. Storrow can find any authority in which any
such distinction is recognized between torts and contracts, as that his
question seems to imply, I shall be surprised. The general rule is that
rights of action are vested rights, and neither authority nor reason can
be adduced upon which to found a distinction in that respect between
those growing out of contracts and those arising out of torts.

The CHAIRMAN. The safety of vested rights rests at last with the Supreme Court, does it not?

Mr. WALKER. O, certainly.

The CHAIRMAN. If Congress, therefore, passes an act that is unconstitutional, the Supreme Court would set it aside?

Mr. WALKER. They are bound to, and they will set this aside. But the point I make is this: that the members of Congress, equally with the judges of the Supreme Court, take an oath to support the Constitution to the best of their ability.

The CHAIRMAN. Of course, that is true.

Mr. WALKER. I say, therefore, that when a bill is shown to be clearly unconstitutional—as members of the committee will certainly conclude this second section is, when they review the authorities to which I have called their attention—Congress has no right to pass such a bill, the only effect of which will be to put litigants to the expense of going to the Supreme Court to get it abrogated.

The CHAIRMAN. No; they have no right, if they know it.

Mr. WALKER. They are bound to use due diligence in finding it out.

The CHAIRMAN. It has been argued before us, in the discussion upon this bill and another, that we have a right to pass a bill that is retrospective.

Mr. WALKER. There are many retrospective acts that are not obnoxious to the Constitution, but this is not one of them. If a law is unconstitutional by reason of being retrospective, it must be so held by virtue of one of three provisions. It must be so, either under that clause of the Constitution which says that Congress shall pass no *ex-post-facto* law; or that clause which says that no law shall pass impairing the obligations of contracts; or, under the fifth amendment of the Constitution, which says that Congress shall not deprive any person of property without due process of law. This bill is not obnoxious to the *ex-post facto* clause, because the Supreme Court has decided that that clause applies only to criminal matters. It is not obnoxious to the provision which, in certain cases, forbids the passage of laws impairing the obligations of contracts, because that is a restraint only on State legislatures. If this bill is unconstitutional, it is so, not because it is retrospective, merely, or because that word in a descriptive sense may be applied to it, but because it takes property away from A and gives it to B, in contravention of the fifth amendment of the Constitution.

Mr. WARD. Would not this come within the class of legislating on the remedy as distinguished from the right?

Mr. WALKER. No, sir; I think not.

Mr. WARD. You know that State legislatures have passed a law which came very near the boundary-line of depriving a man of his property through the intervention of statutes of limitation, for example; and that those enactments of State legislatures have been upheld by the Supreme Court of the United States.

Mr. WALKER. I think I have reviewed every one of those cases, and I found several in the State courts that agreed with what you have stated.

Mr. WARD. Where that distinction is drawn between the right and the remedy?

Mr. WALKER. Certainly. If the proposed bill goes only to the remedy in its essence, it is not obnoxious to the fifth amendment, although it is retrospective. But in the case of Greene v. Biddle, 8 Wheaton, you will find the law laid down that you cannot take away a man's property by indirection, when the Constitution says you shall not do it directly. The law in that case is that you may change the remedy as much as you choose; but you must leave as good a remedy as you take away; if not, you have really taken away the right.

Mr. WARD. Suppose, to-day, I am entitled to the mesne profits of certain land for ten years back; suppose that I had recovered the land in an action of ejectment, and that I had still an action for mesne profits and was entitled to $1,000, for which I have brought action. Next year the legislature passes a law and says, in the first section, that no man shall recover for mesne profits more than six years past. Would that law be constitutional?

Mr. WALKER. I will tell you of a somewhat recent case, decided in the Supreme Court by Justice Bradley, reported in 14 Wallace, 596, which disposed of that point. The court there said they would construe the intention of the legislature to be that a man shall have the same number of years after the bill becomes a law in which to bring his action for all rights previously accrued, as the bill provides he shall have in which to bring his action for all rights after they accrue. I think when you came to the Supreme Court, that court would construe that statute so that it would not be unconstitutional, and so that you would have your right to bring your action within six years after the law was passed.

Mr. WARD. That is not the question. Suppose the first section of the law I propose says that hereafter in no action commenced in any court shall the plaintiff recover for more than six years of mesne profits?

Mr. WALKER. That is nothing but a statute of limitations, is it?

Mr. WARD. Nothing else. Now, the legislature says that hereafter no plaintiff shall recover, in any court, for more than six years, mesne profits, and I want to get back ten years' mesne profits. I want to know whether, under your interpretation, that law would be unconstitutional.

Mr. WALKER. No; for I think that though the court would say that is a singular way to draw a statute of limitations, it means nothing else than that rights of action must be vindicated by actions brought within six years from the time they accrued, and, after that saying, they would say this statute does not operate on your rights of action until the lapse of such a time after its passage, as the statute itself provides shall in prospective cases elapse after the rights sued upon accrue. I have reviewed all the law on that subject, and find that there have been three classes of decisions and three ways of treating that question. One is, to hold that the statute has no effect whatever upon rights of action which, according to its terms, would be barred the moment it was passed. Another is, that such rights of action must be vindicated, if at all, by actions brought within a reasonable time after the statute is enacted. The Supreme Court of the United States takes the middle ground, and says that such statutes of limitation cannot be otherwise construed than that the rights of action already in existence may be vindicated within the same length of time after the passage of the act, as is provided by the statute may elapse as to future rights after they accrue.

Mr. WARD. But that is a saving clause.

Mr. WALKER. The Supreme Court would construe that saving clause into the act, if it were wholly absent from the letter.

Mr. WARD. If the statute I propose had in it a saving clause, then of course my four years of mesne profits would be saved; but I am putting a case on the supposition that there is not any saving clause.

Mr. WALKER. Then the Supreme Court would construe the saving clause right into it. The whole subject is learnedly discussed by Justice Bradley in that case I have mentioned, and it is laid down as I have stated it, and it remedies two hardships that resulted from the former methods of treatment. One of the cases was that of a New York widow, in a suit to recover dower. Her husband had been dead twenty years before she brought her action. A year or two before she brought the action a statute was passed providing that dower could be recovered only in a suit brought within four years after the death of the husband. The court in that case held that the woman should have a reasonable time after the law was passed in which to bring her suit, and as she brought it within a year or two they said that was enough. But of course that was loose ruling. A great many courts would have said that that statute has no application to her suit at all, because, according to its letter, it instantly would take away all the rights of this widow, and therefore in that respect be unconstitutional. The Supreme Court take the middle ground, and will always simply construe precisely this saving clause into the statute.

Mr. WARD. And uphold the constitutionality of the enactment?

Mr. WALKER. Yes, sir. They say the bill is all right so construed; but if not so construed it would be unconstitutional. In regard to the second section, Mr. Smith and Mr. Storrow were willing to indorse it in November; but Mr. Smith told me, after the argument, that the result would be that the courts would construe it to refer only to rights of action hereafter to accrue.

Mr. STORROW. I never entertained that opinion.

Mr. WALKER. I did not say you did. I said Mr. Smith did. I think the committee do not misunderstand me. Mr. Smith, after he had urged the bill upon the Senate committee, gave me his opinion that it would not be held to be retroactive, because the courts would say that if it was retroactive it would be unconstitutional.

Mr. STORROW. Mr. Chauncey Smith is not in the habit of expressing one opinion before a committee and another one in private.

Mr. WALKER. That is what he did say to me, in Boston, in the presence of a witness. What he did before the Senate committee was to make such comments on the bill as he saw fit, and to steer very clear of the retroactive question, and to say that on the whole he hoped the bill would be passed.

Mr. RAYMOND. I should like permission to make a short reply to the personalities that have been indulged in by Mr. Walker. I think it is due to myself that the committee should give me two or three minutes for that purpose.

(No objection being made, Mr. Raymond proceeded as follows with a written statement:)

It would seem that personalities and special interests have already sufficiently engaged the attention of the committee, and I will not use the ample material at my command to show the animus of the argument to which you have just listened. It has sufficiently appeared that Mr. Walker has forgotten the equanimity of a counsellor, and descended to the plane of personal feeling against his opponents, which he has exhibited here to-day.

I think it has also appeared that the able counsel representing *all* kinds of interests under the patent law had sufficient reason for excluding the counsel of the Tanner-brake case from the conferences which resulted in this bill. I apprehend that the consideration of this bill by the committee will be confined to its intrinsic merits or demerits, as affecting only the good of the public. I do not deem it worth while, in the closing of the case before the committee next week, to waste any time in disproving the many and flagrant misstatements of fact made by Mr. Walker, and especially in the review of the Tanner-brake case, which alone forms the motive of his present argument. I simply assure the

committee, without reservation or hesitation, and upon my reputation
for veracity, that his entire argument is so colored by the most frequent
misstatement of facts, that from no stand-point whatever have the committee received anything like a fair, competent, or just presentation of
the case adduced.

I will only add, in explanation of this occurrence, and to sustain my
own confidence in the just *intentions* of Mr. Walker, that he is a son-in-
law of Mr. Thomas Sayles, whom I will politely, and with considerable
forbearance, designate a professional, though poor, patent speculator,
and was until quite recently a real-estate dealer, carrying on an u
successful land speculation for and with the family.

I have somewhere read of a Scotch family of nine daughters and one
son. The son was made a clergyman for the purpose of saving marriage
fees.

In this connection, I call the attention of the committee to the very
great force and truth of the old maxim, " He who argues his own case
has a fool for a client."

Mr. WALKER. I have only to remark to the committee, in reference
to Mr. Raymond's statement about my adopting the legal profession,
that it might well have arisen out of the fact that the railroad companies have beaten Mr. Sayles out of his money for so many years, that
he was no longer able to hire a lawyer, and so had to educate one. If
the arguments I have submitted to the committee impress them when
they come to consider them, I fancy that they will be as effective as if
they had been made by Mr. Raymond himself, because the law rests not
upon what the counsel says, but upon what he cites to sustain his
positions.

It is easy to deny my allegations, as Mr. Raymond has done. To
disprove them would not be easy, but would be impossible. I am, therefore, the reverse of surprised to hear him say that he will not attempt it.

I remind the committee that I have read from records and from reports as evidence of my statements, and they can all be sustained by
ample parole testimony, and by a vast amount of documentary proof,
so far as the history of the Tanner-brake is concerned.

I thank the members of the committee for the kind attention they
have shown me.

ARGUMENT OF MR. FOOTE.

(FEBRUARY 26, 1878.)

Hon. ELISHA FOOTE (Ex-Commissioner of Patents) addressed the
committee as follows:

I do not, Mr. Chairman, represent any corporation, nor, indeed, do I
speak in the interest of any particular patent. I have had much experience in the practical operation of patent laws, and it is my interest
in the subject solely that induces me to make a few remarks to the
committee.

There are many provisions in the bill before you which I think very
desirable. But to the second section I am much opposed. In my view,
it should be stricken out entirely, and the law left as it now stands. I
have no idea that you will be able to frame any section which would be
so well adapted to all the various circumstances which arise in patent
cases as the present common-law remedies, which have grown up with

experience, and which are adapted to all the various circumstances which arise.

If I correctly understand the second section, it divides all the cases into two classes. First, where no account of profits or savings shall be allowed; and, secondly, where it shall be allowed. In the first class there are two divisions: first, where the patentee has elected to license other persons generally to use his invention, in which case the license fee is to govern in the assessment of damages; and, in the second case, where it shall appear to the court and jury that it is for the interest of the patentee that other persons generally should use his invention and pay a license fee therefor, then the court and jury are to say what would be the proper license fee.

The first clause is, I suppose, designed to, and apparently does, make the law conform to the present law in regard to license fees. But practically, sir, the differences are very wide. Common-law remedies are flexible, and can be changed or adapted to circumstances; but a statute is rigid, and must be obeyed by the courts; they have no discretion upon the subject. The theory of the patent law is, that the inventor has an exclusive right to his invention. If a man makes a cart or a wagon, it is his exclusively, to do with it as he, in his judgment, thinks for his own interest; and if he makes a new invention that is of practical utility, and has never been known or used before, *that*, to the same extent and in the same manner, is his for a term of years, after which it becomes public property. If a man takes your horse without liberty and without right, you recover for his use. If you are a livery-stable keeper, and have a fixed price for letting horses, that would govern in the assessment of damages; if not, then you would recover what the use of the horse was worth under the circumstances of the case. And this is precisely the rule in patent cases. The same common-law remedies are applied in both cases and in the same manner. If your horse was used in rescuing bank-bills from a fire, you would not recover the value of the bills, as one gentleman has supposed; neither would you in a patent case. There never has been an instance of any such recovery. You get simply what the use is worth, under the circumstances of the case.

The CHAIRMAN. The judgment, you say, that the man recovers for the use of the horse, would be according to what the custom was for his hire?

Judge FOOTE. Yes, sir.

The CHAIRMAN. Then why should not that same rule apply to a patent?

Judge FOOTE. It does; precisely the same.

The CHAIRMAN. Perhaps I misunderstood you. I understood you to object to that clause which says that the amount of damages shall be measured according to the amount of royalty paid on the machine.

Judge FOOTE. Perhaps I did not make myself sufficiently explicit on the subject. The difference is that the statute (if you pass it) will be a rigid rule that the courts must observe. But the common-law rule is flexible, and may be adapted to the particular circumstances of the case. Now, the proposed statute would in some cases give entirely too much. I know the case of a stove patent, where the patentee had a uniform license fee of two dollars on each stove. The court gave him fifty cents instead of two dollars. It was because the defendant had very much extended the business, and the patentee recovered and received more than he would have done but for the infringement. And that is an instance of the flexibility of common-law rules. Under the proposed statute, the court would have been bound to give the two dollars. Take the case of this Tanner patent, of which so much has been said. It seems that the master found profits to the amount of sixty thousand dollars, if I recollect rightly, and the court reduced it to forty-five thousand. Why? The counsel were unable to inform us. But it was undoubtedly because the court thought the sum too much, and in the exercise of that discretion which they have in all suits founded on common-law remedies, they fixed the amount at what they thought was right under all the circumstances.

Now, sir, if you had had a statute, if the court were positively directed to give the license fee or the profit received, there could not have been any such reduction. Statutes are rigid, and must be obeyed.

In some cases the statute proposed would give entirely too little. There are very many cases in which a patentee is obliged to make very great sacrifices, in order to get his inventions introduced and made known to the public. When he has made his invention and received his patent, his work begins. It is often more difficult and more expensive to introduce it and make it known to the public than it is to make the invention; and the cases are not infrequent where very great sacrifices are made. They sometimes give half their patent to a manufacturer who will make their device and introduce it and make it known to the public. It is only then that the patent begins to be profitable to the inventor. Sometimes they receive a very small license-fee for a limited time or to a particular person, in order to get the thing started. And to adopt the same fee for an infringer, who has had none of the expense of introducing it, who had taken it without any right or authority, would be a manifest injustice; and in the common-law remedies such circumstances are taken into consideration. With the proposed statute, they would be unable to do so, but would have to follow the direction of the statute.

Now, Mr. Chairman, I beg leave to read to you from a decision of the Supreme Court, to show what the present law is upon this subject. It is the case of Seymour et al. v. McCormick. The opinion was delivered by Mr. Justice Grier. It is found in 16 Howard, page 489. The court say:

It must be apparent to the most superficial observer of the immense variety of patents issued every day that there cannot, in the nature of things, be any one rule of damages which will equally apply to all cases. The mode of ascertaining actual damages must necessarily depend on the peculiar nature of the monopoly granted. A man who invents or discovers a new composition of matter, such as vulcanized India rubber, or a valuable medicine, may find his profit to consist in a close monopoly, forbidding any one to compete with him in the market, the patentee being himself able to supply the whole demand at his own price. If he should grant licenses to all who might desire to manufacture his composition, mutual competition might destroy the value of each license. This may be the case, also, where the patentee is the inventor of an entire new machine. If any person could use the invention or discovery by paying what a jury might suppose to be the fair value of a license, it is plain that competition would destroy the whole value of the monopoly. In such cases the profit of the infringer may be the only criterion of the actual damage of the patentee. But one who invents some improvement in the machinery of a mill could not claim that the profits of the whole mill should be the measure of damages for the use of his improvement. And where the profit of the patentee consists neither in the exclusive use of the thing invented or discovered, nor in the monopoly of making it for others to use, it is evident that this rule could not apply. The case of Stimpson's patent for a turnout in a railroad may be cited as an example. It was the interest of the patentee that all railroads should use his invention, provided they paid him the price of his license. He could not make his profit by selling it as a complete and separate machine. An infringer of such a patent could not be liable to damages to the amount of the profits of his railroad, nor could the actual damages to the patentee be measured by any known ratio of the profits on the road. The only actual damage which the patentee has suffered in such a case is the non-payment of the price which he has put on his license, with interest, and no more. There may be cases, as where the thing has been used but for a short time, in which the jury should find less than that sum; and there may be cases where, from some peculiar circumstances, the patentee may show actual damage to a large amount. Of this a jury must judge from the evidence, under instructions from the court, that they can find only such damages as have actually been proved to have been sustained. Where an inventor finds it profitable to exercise his monopoly by selling licenses to make or use his improvement, he has himself fixed the average of his actual damage, when his invention has been used without his license. If he claims anything above that amount, he is bound to substantiate his claim by clear and distinct evidence. When he has himself established the market value of his improvement, as separate and distinct from the other machinery with which it is connected, he can have no claim, in justice or equity, to make the profits of the whole machine the measure of his demand. It is only where, from the peculiar circumstances of the case, no other rule can be found that the defendant's profits become the criterion of the plaintiff's loss. Actual damages must be actually proved, and cannot be assumed as a legal inference from any facts which amount not to actual proof of the fact. What a patentee would have made if the infringer had not interfered with his rights is a question of fact, and not a judgment of law. The question is not what, speculatively, he may have lost, but what actually he did lose.

It seems to me, sir, very unwise to substitute any rigid statutes for these flexible rules, which adapt themselves to the various circumstances that arise. They are the results of long experience by the ablest minds of the country. They are familiar to the profession and to the courts. They are elastic, and adapt themselves, in all cases, to what is right and just.

Mr. RAYMOND. The bill is elastic—the court is to judge. "If the license fee has already been established by a reasonable number of transactions of a character applicable to the case at bar, that shall be adopted as the measure of said damages," is the language of the bill. Take the case you suggested, that a person, in order to get his patent introduced, has made arrangements with the manufacturers for a small license-fee. That would be one transaction. It would not be "a reasonable number of cases." The court would take that into consideration in deciding what was a reasonable number.

Judge FOOTE. That, undoubtedly, would have its influence.

Mr. STORROW. And they must be "of a character applicable to the case at bar."

Judge FOOTE. Yes, sir; but suppose there is a sufficient number of licenses to establish a license fee just as the section provides. These licensees may have expended much money in introducing the invention, making it known to the public, and creating a demand—a market for it. Then comes in an infringer, and perhaps destroys their business. The injury to the patentee would be still greater. His licensees cannot afford to pay him the fee when others use the invention for nothing. His receipts stop, and remain suspended until the end of a long and ruinous litigation. Such circumstances are taken into consideration by courts under common-law remedies. Not so under the proposed statute. The license-fee would be the extent of the recovery. The fraudulent wrong-doer could not in any event fare worse than the honest licensee. The provision says, in effect, "Wait until others have established the business and then come in and take the profits. If it should be found out how many you have sold, you will at most have to pay no more than you would have had to pay if you honestly took a license."

Mr. STORROW. The bill leaves it to the court to say, just as the court does now, first, whether the use made by the defendant is "in like manner" to that made by the licensees; and, second, whether the former transactions are "applicable"—that is, afford a just rule for the case at bar, just as they must decide now.

Judge FOOTE. I proceed next, Mr. Chairman, to the second clause in the section, which provides that "where it appears to the court or jury that from the nature of the invention it is for the interest of the patentee that other persons generally should use the same in like manner and pay him a license fee therefor, * * no account of profits or savings shall be allowed"; and the court or jury shall determine the license fee.

Mr. STORROW. They do not determine any license fee at all; they determine damages "from all the evidence in the case."

Judge FOOTE. This introduces a new feature in patent law; and, I doubt not, it would be new to the jurisprudence of any civilized country. It supposes that a man is not the proper judge for himself as to the best mode of using his own property; but, after it has been taken from him, it submits it to a court or jury to say whether it would not be for his interest that other persons generally should use his invention in like manner that he uses it himself. Applying the same doctrine to other property, this would be its effect:

Suppose you have a valuable horse, which you choose to keep for your own use, and some of your neighbors would like very much to have him, and they take him without right or permission. Then it is to be submitted to the court or jury whether it would not be for your interest that other people generally should use the horse as well as yourself, and pay you a reasonable license fee for it, and that would be the extent of your recovery. Or, suppose you have a house larger than you really need to occupy, and somebody else wants it, and crowds himself into it, and then submits it to a court and jury to say whether, under all the circumstances of the case, it would not be more for your interest to let other people generally into your house, to occupy and pay a reasonable price, than that you should occupy it alone. You could not say you had an exclusive right to your property; you could not control its use—any one could take it from you with impunity, paying only an ordinary rent.

The Constitution provides that inventors shall have, for a limited term, an exclusive right in their inventions. It does not authorize any kind of right but an exclusive right. The idea is that none but the inventor shall have any right or interest in it, or any control over it.

There is a large class of inventions in which the exclusive use was the principal motive for their production. I refer to inventions made by manufacturers for their use, to cheapen the cost of their own productions, or to make a better article than their competitors, and so have an advantage in the markets. The competition between different manufacturers has led to a great number of such devices, and to wonderful improvements in our manufactories. We are now able to compete with cheaper labor in other countries.

It has been detailed to you that we send manufactured articles to Europe: watches to England and France; sewing-machines to all Europe; reapers and mowers to Germany and other countries, &c. Now, sir, if, under such a section as this, any competing manufacturer may take these improvements and use them in his business by simply paying a license-fee, the whole object of invention would be frustrated, and such improvements would never have been made. I have now in my mind a particular case. There was an invention of a machine for making horse-shoes, of very great value. The inventor spent above $70,000 before he got his machine into operation, and I suppose very much more since in perfecting and improving it, and he has sold his shoes in the market at the very same price that he sells iron for making shoes. Apparently he would sustain a loss, but really his profit consists in affording a market for his iron, of which he has a large manufactory. It makes the sale of a large quantity of iron and keeps his mills in operation, which otherwise, under the present depressed market, would have to be idle; and it is of very great value to him. Now, if anybody else could take his machines, and supply the market too, you can see that his invention would be perfectly profitless to him. He would not have incurred such expense to produce it, and we never should have had the invention.

But I proceed to the third clause, which provides that, "in taking an account of profits in any case, the defendant shall not be charged with any saving he may have made, unless it has enabled him to realize an actual profit in that part of his business connected with the use of the invention." That is to say, any patent may be seized or taken without right or authority, to any extent of damage to the owner, and you cannot recover anything unless the man who has robbed you has made money out of the operation. If a man should steal your horse, you could not recover or get anything of him unless he had a profitable operation. This is a most extraordinary provision. Take the case of the Pullman palace-cars. I understand the patentee does not sell his patent in any way, but makes the cars himself and puts them on the road; he receives nothing from the railroad companies, but makes his profit on the extra price he charges passengers for using his cars. Now, if he was to bring a suit for infringement there would be no license fee; you could not recover for that; there is no court or jury that could conscientiously say that it would be for his interest to have a license-fee, and that the public should enjoy it in the same way that he does himself. Then he would be reduced to this third clause to recover for the use and profits; and any railroad which was not making dividends could take his property and pay nothing for it. You might as well do directly what this section does indirectly, and pass an act that every railroad which is not making profits or dividends shall have the privilege of taking any patents they please with impunity; and, if you make the thing entirely consistent and rational, you should also say that they may enter upon any one's land and cut their ties, and go into rolling-mills and take their rails, or any other property they choose to take, and they shall have them without responsibility to anybody.

Take the case of this Westinghouse brake, which, I understand, the patentee manufactures himself and puts onto cars at a very reasonable price. Now, suppose any of these Chicago railroads, making no money, should think it desirable for them to take and use this brake without paying anything for it. This section would undoubtedly authorize them to do so without any compensation, and they could grab any amount of property with impunity.

There is another feature about this section which is the worst of all. That I now come to. It requires an investigation in all cases of taking an account into all the business connected with the use of the invention, to ascertain whether a profit has been made, and, if so, to determine what proportion is due to the invention and what to other elements. Such an inquiry is almost endless. It must depend much upon estimates and opinions, in which witnesses will vary. A case that illustrates this came within my own experience. The late Henry Burden invented a machine for making railroad spikes, which fastened down the T-rails. They had before been made by hand at great expense. He invented a machine which made them at the rate of about one a second, and supplied the railroads at a very reasonable rate. But he had a competitor, a little below him on the same stream, who had also a large iron-works, and who desired to share in the profits of this business. He took the invention without any right, and put eleven machines into constant operation day and night, and supplied the country with those spikes. The Supreme Court, after hearing the case, decided that the patent had been unlawfully infringed, and that an account should be taken; and it was referred to the late Chancellor Walworth, of New York, to take an account. He adopted the rule which is provided for here. He went into an investigation of all the extensive affairs of that iron-works to find out whether they had made any profit in their business by the infringement. He spent ten years in the inquiry, with counsel and witnesses. His proceedings are recorded in ten large volumes. His own fees which the parties paid him amounted to $60,000. The parties spent hundreds of thousands in that investigation; and the result of it all was that the master brought in that the defendants had lost $30,000 in their business by stealing the invention.

The CHAIRMAN. Let me ask you right there: Did he bring in a correct statement of the thing? Did they actually lose the $30,000? If so, the other man ought to have been very thankful.

Judge FOOTE. Well, of course the plaintiff thought it an outrage. The defendants kept on losing, in spite of all the plaintiff could do, and does to this day.

Mr. BRIGGS. Why didn't he get an injunction and stop them?

Judge FOOTE. He did get an injunction, and finally stopped them, but the patent had nearly run out. The courts are very unwilling to give an injunction un.il the case is finally heard and decided. They do it in extreme cases, but generally they want to have the matter fully investigated before they stop a manufacturing operation, for the damages would be very great if they should be wrong, and they do not feel at liberty to interfere until the case is finally decided.

The practice in the spike case, and others like it, has justly been regarded as an opprobrium in the administration of justice. An end was put to it by the Supreme Court in the important case of Mowry v. Whitney, and there never was a more just or valuable decision. They held that they had nothing to do with the profits of the business in which the patent improvement was used, and that the only proper inquiry was as to the advantages derived from the use of the invention over and above what they would have had in the use of other processes. And this was strictly in accordance with the law in regard to all other kinds of property. In cases of trespass on lands, taking of personal property, depriving others of their rights, the question always is as to the value of the property taken, and the benefits derived from its use; and no inquiry was ever entertained into the profitableness of the business in which the wrong was committed. Such an investigation would be a scandal to any court in this country.

It is a great mistake to suppose, as some gentlemen have done who have addressed the committee with much eloquence, that the same court that has adopted a rule may not vary from it when other circumstances require a variation, in order to do exact justice in the case. Such extreme cases under this rule, as some have imagined, have never occurred, and would not in any court of justice. Common-law rules always bend to the circumstances of each particular case.

In the whip case, which has been brought forward as one of extreme severity, we are not informed how much the inventor expended in labor and money to produce and perfect his machine—very likely it was all he had. It reduced the cost of manufacture from sixty to twenty cents. The infringer, who had had none of these expenses, makes the whips and sells them in the market at twenty-five cents. The five cents above cost is no more than a fair salesman's profit. Should the inventor manufacture the whips and send them to merchants to sell, they would charge him that for selling. It is manifest that the inventor has been robbed of his property, and, if the case should come before the courts, I doubt not the infringer would be made to pay well for the wrong and injury he has done; but that he would be required to pay any extravagant sum, any more than what was just and reasonable, any more than he would be required to pay in other cases of like turpitude, is what no one is authorized to presume.

The second section we are considering requires us to go back to the abuses in the spike case. In all cases of an account, there must be an investigation into all the operations of the business in which the invention was used. It is an indefinite, enormously expensive, and almost endless inquiry.

Take the case of this Tanner brake, which has been one cause, as I suppose, of bringing this bill before you. I know nothing about the merits of the case. I refer to it merely as an illustration. It seems that the parties have been in litigation sixteen years, and the case yet goes to the Supreme Court. Should a new accounting be ordered, it may, if this bill be passed, require an investigation of all the affairs of the Northwestern Railroad for a period of twenty years, to ascertain whether in this long period they have made or lost money in their business generally, and, if they have made money, then to ascertain what proportion of it arose from the use of the brake, and what proportion was derived from other elements. It would require an examination of all the expenses and receipts of that company during that long period—of the lands purchased, their improvement, and present value; of the increase and value of depots, engine-houses, and other structures; of the improvement and condition of rails, road-bed, ties, culverts, bridges, and cost of the same, and wear by use and time; and many difficult questions would arise and have to be decided. Should the inquiry be, whether a profit was made during the whole time, or during each year? If any of the moneys have been squandered by officials, would that be taken into the account? If they have given any president of the company $50,000 a year for merely nominal services, should that be counted? If they have engaged in profitless speculations in other roads and enterprises, should that be allowed? And then to ascertain what proportion of the salaries, rents, coal, iron, cars, locomotives, &c., should be charged to the brake, and what to other elements. This would be a matter of opinion and estimate upon which witnesses would differ, and would require a long investigation. It is plain to be seen that the $40,000 which the plaintiff has recovered would not pay half the expenses of this reference. What chance would the poor inventor have against these powerful corporations? None but a very wealthy person could enter into such a controversy. The roads would not need the other provisions of the bill. This would enable them to take and use any patent they pleased with impunity, and no one would dare to sue them.

The CHAIRMAN. How about this clause: "But if in any case it shall appear to the court that the damages or profits, ascertained as above, shall be inadequate to give the plaintiff a just compensation for the injury done by the infringement, or shall be in excess of such injury, the court shall have power to increase or diminish the amount to such an extent as may be just and reasonable." Does that modify the bill?

Judge FOOTE. That is the clause I was next coming to.

The court are to have power, in their discretion, to increase or diminish the amount of recovery to such an extent *as may be just and reasonable.* But what is just and reasonable? That is the very question that arises in every case, and upon which the parties differ. If you say that the license fee is the proper recovery, then that must be just and reasonable, or you would not make such a rule; and the discretion of the court is to increase and diminish the recovery, so as to make it conform to the standard of what is just and reasonable that you have established. If it be proper that a party shall recover only what a court or jury shall say is a proper license fee, then that, of course, must be just and reasonable. If it be right and proper that a party shall recover nothing unless a profit has been made in the business in which the invention has been used, then that must be just and reasonable; and a court would have no right to set up any other standard of their own of what is just and reasonable. Statutes must be so construed that every part, if possible, may have effect. The whole must harmonize. The discretion which is given to courts is not an arbitrary one, but must be exercised in accordance with principles that have been established.

But if a different view should be entertained, and that what is just and reasonable be regarded as referring to the value of the invention and the length of time it has been used, then the clause would direct the court to do just what they do now, and to disregard all the previous provisions. The complicated investigations would have*to be gone through, the enormous expenses incurred and then all disregarded, and the court do just what they do now—find out what was just and reasonable, having reference to the value of the improvement and the circumstances of the infringement. I suppose there would have to be two references—first, to ascertain whether a profit had been made in the business; and, secondly, to find out what was just and reasonable. The whole clause would be contradictory. It would direct to give the license fee, no more, no less; to give nothing in some cases; and then it would direct to do neither, but give what the law now allows as just and reasonable.

I have thus, Mr. Chairman, gone through with the whole section, and it is manifest that it has been gotten up in the interest of infringers—those who find it convenient to take other people's property, but not to pay for it.

Suppose, Mr. Chairman, we had a band of robbers amongst us of great wealth and power; that they were accustomed to enter people's houses and drive them from their homes; that they took their cattle and their horses—that the wheat, the corn, the cotton, that others by their labor and expense had produced, they should appropriate, and to meet such an emergency you should pass an act like this second section, to wit, that there should be no recovery against these robbers beyond the price in the market of the articles taken, or what a court or jury should say ought to be a market price; that in case of an accounting nothing should be recovered unless the robbery had been profitable, and that the court should determine what proportion of profits was due to the robbery, and what to other elements; and, finally, that you should make all legal proceedings against them so onerous and expensive that none but very rich men could contend with them—would it not be justly said that you had promoted fraud and wrong, and discouraged industry, and injured all the best interests of society? I cannot view this section in any better light, in reference to the rights and interests of patented property.

Some gentlemen have urged here that inventions do not need the protection of patents; that they come as a matter of course, from the natural promptings of the human mind, and will be made without reference to profits or personal advantages. Such persons, I apprehend, have never investigated the subject. It is within my remembrance when most of the women were employed in spinning and weaving just as they were in the times of Homer. I have, myself, reaped grain in the fields with a sickle, in the same way that it was reaped when Ruth gleaned after the reapers in the field of Boaz. It was pounded out upon the threshing floor, and winnowed by a current of wind, in the same way that it was done as described in the Bible. The plows we used were much like the plows of the ancient Egyptians. Indeed since the practical operation of patent laws, there has been more advance in all the practical arts of life than was made before in all preceding ages of the world taken together. Never before has been seen such progress as we, ourselves, have witnessed in our day. And such is the advance now making that we can form no conception, we cannot imagine what will be the state of society fifty years hence. And why is this? The minds of men have not changed. They have the same desires and feelings, and are actuated by the same motives as formerly. You can ascribe it to no other reason than that we now give a property in useful inventions. Would men clear off, fence in, and bring into cultivation lands that they were not to possess? Would any one build houses that were not to be their own? Would products be raised, manufactures made, or anything but the barest necessities of life be produced but for the right of personal property, and the protection in the enjoyment of these rights which society affords? The same is true in regard to patented improvements. Such is human nature, and the constitution of society, that men must devote their time and energies to the support of themselves and those who are dependent upon them. It is the rewards, and the hope of rewards, that have stimulated the whole country to the study of practical improvements.

The CHAIRMAN. Do you think the new state of things gives as many people employment as under the old system?

Judge FOOTE. Yes, sir; that is a subject which has excited a good deal of attention and interest. The first introduction of patented machines has always been met with strong opposition. The inventors of the modern spinning machines and of the weaving machines endangered their lives. And when the reaping machines were first introduced they met with great opposition. It was thought they would drive people out of employment. And I remember that when the sewing machines came out I, myself, with all the reflection I had had on the subject, really feared that a great many poor women would be deprived of their only means of employment. But, now, what has been the practical result? Sewing women were never so much in demand; they never have been so well paid; and there never have been so many employed as at the present day. There are more men employed in reaping and harvesting grain than there ever were when it was harvested with a sickle, or indeed with the cradle. The wages of spinners and weavers are far greater than when the work was done by hand. Such has been the practical result of every invention which has been introduced. It has led to a greatly-increased demand, and the number of persons employed has been increased rather than diminished. As you reduce the price, the consumption increases in much greater proportion. When cotton cloth was one dollar per yard, but few could afford to use it. Now that it is ten cents, or less, more than a thousand to one wear it daily, and the number of persons engaged in its production and manufacture is much greater than it was when it cost one dollar per yard; and that is the history of every invention. A single case cannot be pointed out where it has not increased the number of laborers rather than diminished it.

S. Mis. 50——27

I do not wish to occupy your time unnecessarily, but there are some other provisions in this bill which I think objectionable. That in regard to a statute of limitations has very serious difficulties. A patent suit is a very serious matter, and a very expensive one. There is no other litigation in the country that is half as expensive. Few men are able to commence more than one patent suit. Supposing one commenced for an improvement in railroad appliances. It would be in the power of any of these corporations, with the able counsel which they employ and keep in their employment, to extend that suit through the life of the patent, especially if you allow an appeal before an account is taken, which would occupy three or four years, and then another after the account is taken, which would occupy as many more. Although there may be many infringers, one suit has heretofore been regarded as enough for all of them. It is supposed that the rights of the patentee will be determined by one suit, and that all others will be governed by the result of that one. The consequence of the limitation would be, that as against all but the company sued the inventor would get but four years, instead of seventeen years' use of his patent. Or else, to avoid that result, he must commence a number of suits, and get into an extent of litigation that would be ruinous to any man who had not unlimited means.

It is from such considerations that a statute of limitations has not before been passed. If it be proper at all, it certainly should be for a very long time. I should say ten years. If you make it less, you really cut off half the value of all patents.

There is another section, the tenth, which is very harsh on patentees. It compels one, on notice, to commence a suit or lose his patent. Now, sir, that would be very hard. Suppose any of these wealthy corporations should call upon a poor inventor to commence a suit against them, and to encounter a big railroad combination with all their able and learned counsel in their employ? It would be impracticable; he would have to give up his patent.

You have already a provision that anybody may commence a suit to correct or annul a patent that has been improperly issued, or needs any correction. If no one will do that, and the patent remains in full force, the patentee should not be debarred from asserting his rights under it. Let these railroads commence their own suits, and not compel others to bring suits against them. I would strike out that provision entirely.

Considerable has been said with regard to models, and some would not refer to them in granting reissues. The model, I think, is the very best evidence. The object of a reissue is to give a man what he ought to have had when he made his application. It is to correct errors and mistakes. It is a rule in the Patent Office that a patentee shall not resort to extrinsic or parol evidence to show what he had invented. I recollect a very strong case that arose in the office. A man proved that an important feature of his invention had been left out at the request of his attorney. He had taken it out of his model and his drawings against his own judgment, and it turned out that the part omitted was the very essence of the invention, and he came to the office to have his patent reissued. But it was thought that the practice would lead to frauds and be dangerous, and his application was refused. The Supreme Court has since, I believe, adopted the same rule.

Well, then, how are we to ascertain what was really the invention? The model is the best evidence. The inventor makes the model, and takes it to his attorney, who from it makes drawings and specifications, showing not the whole machine, but only such parts of it as he thinks it important to claim. The rest is left out. And very great mistakes are made by attorneys. They sometimes entirely overlook the important parts of the invention. And then the Patent Office itself, I am sorry to say, makes a great many mistakes. They sometimes refuse the inventor things they ought to allow and allow him what they ought not to allow, and the inventor finds when he comes into court to enforce his patent, that he has to reissue it, and correct the mistakes that have been made. If you were to strike out either, I should say it ought to be the reference to specifications and drawings, for those are the works of the attorney. But not the model, which is the work of the patentee himself, and shows what he embodied in his invention.

I want to say one word more, and that in reference to the eleventh section, which requires payments at different periods.

The CHAIRMAN. The British system?

Judge FOOTE. Yes, sir; somewhat like it. The patent fees are now more than are necessary.

The CHAIRMAN. You think it a good plan to have the fees less?

Judge FOOTE. I would have the fees now paid on making the application and issuing the patent reduced to ten dollars. The office now is accumulating one hundred thousand dollars a year over and above its expenses, and if the object is to encourage patents and inventions, the fee shall be made as light as possible, though enough to pay the expenses of the office. And I think if a small sum was charged for the first fee, and then more for the subsequent one, it would be a judicious change. If I had drawn the section myself I would have made it different. I would give a kind of preliminary patent for a few years—say three or four years. The difficulty is, that when an inventor gets an idea and has revolved it over in his own mind, he rushes off to the Patent Office, for fear somebody else will steal it or will anticipate him, and he takes out a patent before he has perfected his invention. Then, when he comes to put it into use he finds difficulties that he did not anticipate. Perhaps the whole thing may be useless, or may require very material alterations or additions before it is made practicable. Now, if he had three or four years in which to make those corrections and try his machine, and then could come into the office and make his application anew, in its best shape, and the office should re-examine his whole case again very carefully, I think patents would be very much more perfect, and there would be very many less of them than under the present system.

ARGUMENT OF MR. CHAUNCEY SMITH.

[MARCH 1, 1878.]

MR. CHAIRMAN AND GENTLEMEN OF THE COMMITTEE:

I had the honor some time since to open the discussion before the Committee on Patents of the Senate in favor of the same amendments of the patent law which are the subject of the present hearing. I took occasion then, at the commencement of my remarks, to make some general statements as to the history of the patent law in this country, and to make some general observations upon the results which the country has secured from the law. It seemed to me important and necessary that the value of the patent system to the country, the benefits which flow from it, should be taken into account in any proposed legis-

lation. An alleged evil existing under the law might be of such importance as to demand legislation for its removal, if nothing else were to be
considered, but it would not be wise to legislate without inquiring how
the proposed legislation might affect the benefits which the country was
receiving from the existing law. It might appear that more would be
sacrificed by a remedy proposed for some admitted evil than would be
gained by the remedy, and that some new remedy should be devised or
the evil be submitted to.

It is an inconvenient thing to most of us to pay taxes, and their collection by the means prescribed by law is often embarrassing and an-
noying to delinquents; but few of us would be prepared to say that the
raising of revenues should be abandoned, or that it would be wise to so
change the mode of collecting taxes, in order to get rid of some alleged
evils, as to render it impossible to collect them at all.

There may be evils attending the collection of the taxes upon whisky
or tobacco, but I apprehend Congress would not change the law in relation to those sources of revenue in order to correct some alleged evils
attending their collection, without considering how much is at stake,
and to what extent the proposed remedy would affect the amount of the
revenue derived from those sources.

It seemed to me, therefore, not only legitimate and proper that a discussion of any important modification of the patent law should be accompanied with a presentation of the operations of the law upon the industries of the country and its value in promoting those industries, but that
it was absolutely essential to judicious legislation that the relation of
the patent law to the progress of the useful arts should be kept constantly in mind.

I think I had reason to believe that the Senate committee regarded
the course I adopted as a legitimate and proper one. Justified, as we
thought, by these considerations, and, as we believed, by the judgment
of the Senate committee, Mr. Storrow and myself thought that it was
not only right and proper for us to lay before this committee also some
portion of the evidence as to the value of the patent law which was accumulating on our hands, but that it was our duty to do so. We thought
so all the more because we found some persons who believed, or affected
to believe, that some alleged evils connected with the patent law were
of greater magnitde than all the good connected with it, and that Congress would be justified in sweeping away the law to correct the evils,
if they could not be corrected in any other way. We thought, therefore, that it is proper to offer such evidence as we have of the value of
the law to the country.

I think that for another reason it was necessary, or at least legitimate
and proper, that the value of the patent law to the country should be presented to this committee. Numerous propositions outside of this bill
have been brought forward for the amendment of the patent law and
referred to this committee. I think they have been generally conceived
solely with reference to some special hardship which has arisen under
the law, and without regard to their general effect upon the practical
working of the patent law. Viewed with reference only to the specific
evils or hardships which they are designed to affect, they might not be
open to serious objection, but when considered with reference to their
general effect upon interests of great magnitude, it might be obvious
that they would work much more harm than good. But this result will
not be seen by those who brought them forward, or are disposed to advocate them, until they are impressed with the conviction that the evil
they seek to remedy sinks into insignificance beside the vast benefits

the country reaps from the patent law. This evidence will, we think, be valuable to the committee in considering all such special propositions for the amendment of the law.

Our conclusive answer to many of the proposed remedies for alleged special evils is, that if the evils are such as is alleged, and if the proposed remedies would correct them, the country cannot afford to apply them. I submit, therefore, that it is legitimate and necessary that this committee, and Congress itself, and the country, should take into consideration the value of the patent law in all discussions relating to its amendments.

I shall, however, present to the committee no such detailed statements of facts as were presented by the gentlemen who preceded me. But I think there are certain great historical facts which should be taken into account, and which demonstrate the value of patent laws.

Few people can be found to deny the value of inventions, but fewer still, perhaps, have ever known and clearly apprehended the magnitude of the results which have been achieved. The steam-engine is generally spoken of as one of the greatest inventions of man, but few people know how much it has added to the power of man. It is stated in a life of James Watt, published in 1874, that the steam-power of Great Britain is equivalent to the power of 400 millions of men. The imagination staggers under such figures as these. But this is not all. By the improvements which have been made in machinery, this power is much more effective than it was formerly. Automatic machinery for spinning was invented about the same time that the steam-engine was. Before its invention, a woman spun a single thread upon a wheel. If we estimate the power of six women to be equal to a horse-power, then six spindles absorbed a horse-power. But now, in our spinning-frames, a horse power will drive from seventy-five to a hundred and ten spindles. The same amount of power which the woman furnished, when derived from a steam-engine or water-wheel, turns from twelve to eighteen times as many spindles, and one person will take charge of from 600 to 800 spindles.

In the census report of Massachusetts for the census of 1875, the following statement is made as to the manufacturing industries of the State:

Under the title "Steam and water-power by industries," power is classified according to the industries in which it is used. The total horse-power of steam-engines and water-wheels employed in the industries of the State is 318,768, equal to the hand-labor of 1,912,488 men. This labor is actually performed with the aid of the motive-power of the State by about 300,000 men, women, and children. In other words, the industries of Massachusetts, without the aid of her motive-power, would require a population of 7,400,000, or nearly four and a half times as great as it is now, to furnish the hand-labor necessary to carry them.

The CHAIRMAN. Let me ask you, Mr. Smith, if, in your opinion, anybody has been thrown out of employment by the introduction of these patented machines?

Mr. SMITH. I have never thought so. I hope the committee will pardon me for introducing this anecdote: I recollect one day hearing a very intelligent man in Massachusetts, who had devoted himself with humanitarian views to philanthropy, express the conviction that such must be the case, that a great number of men must have been thrown out of employment by the introduction of machinery. I said to him, "I have heard that statement a great many times, but I have never seen any proof advanced. Now, will you give me proof of that assertion?" "Well," he says, "I have not time to do it now; I cannot do it *now*." I said, "You cannot do it at this moment, of course, but will you, in a reasonable time, produce any evidence in support of that assertion?" Thereupon he said, "It *must* be so in the very nature of things; it must throw people out of employment." " Well, then," said I, " if it must be so, you *can* produce the proof within a reasonable time." He declined the challenge. I have always found it so. I have heard many people make the assertion who fully believed it, but I have never found one who could support his assertions by proof of actual cases. I think the fact is just the reverse. When an improved machine is invented, the requisite number of them must be built to perform the work required. This creates a demand for labor in that branch, as the first effect of the invention; and before the machines are built and introduced into their appropriate place the labor supplanted will adjust itself to the new conditions. And I believe that is the universal history of the introduction of labor-saving machinery.

It is not alone in countries where labor-saving machinery is employed that men are out of employment, by any means. It is not in those countries where people starve. The people of China to-day, with highly-developed industries, are starving by millions, while England, with her overcrowded population, does not suffer in any such way. The increased productiveness of labor by cheapening the products of labor brings those products within the reach of the means of thousands of consumers who could not otherwise have them, and this often greatly increases the amount of labor required, notwithstanding its increased efficiency. The introduction of the cotton-gin certainly did not diminish the number of persons employed in raising cotton. It did not even diminish the number required to separate the seed. I am confident that more men are employed in transporting people between New York and Boston than would be if the journey had to be performed in stage-coaches. There can be no doubt that the number of persons engaged in any manufacture is increased by the inventions which have so diminished its cost that it can be used for a multitude of purposes where it could not formerly be used on account of the expense attending its production.

The labor required for the production of paper, and in printing books and newspapers, has been so reduced and their use has so much increased, consequent upon the diminution in the cost of books and other printed matter, that the demand for them gives employment to a much greater number of laborers than at any time in the world's history.

It should not be forgotten, in considering the effect of invention upon the demand for labor, that many inventions open up new fields of labor; and, so far from supplanting labor, they create new demands for it. The telegraph gives employment to thousands where none were employed before its existence, not only directly in the transmission of messages, but in the production of wire, the manufacture of insulators and telegraph instruments, the collection, transportation, and erection of poles, and in the care and maintenance of the lines after they are erected. The art of photography furnishes another instance of the creation of new fields of labor by new inventions. Thousands are now engaged in the production of pictures who have been taken out of other occupations to supply a new demand. The vulcanization of rubber is another art which created a new demand for labor. Much of the treasure of the earth, its gold and silver and other metals, including coal and petroleum, is placed so deep in the earth that it could not be reached except for modern inventions. These inventions have not only given man the treasure which he could not otherwise have secured, but have given employment to a multitude of men.

But to return to the manufactures of Massachusetts. This estimate which I have given of the value of steam-power in Massachusetts did not embrace railroads. The returns for the railroads were collected by a special commission, and I therefore applied to a very competent engineer, Mr. Edward Appleton, of Boston, to give me an estimate of the value of the locomotives in Massachusetts as compared with horse-power used on common roads. According to the returns of last year we had 1,030 locomotives in the State; the year before there were 994, showing an increase of nearly 40 in the last year. I have received from him a most instructive and interesting paper upon that subject, which I beg leave to submit to the committee, and which I desire to append to the report of my argument. I will now only refer to the conclusions which are given by Mr. Appleton. The whole number of locomotives owned by the Massachusetts railroad companies is 1,030, but, as parts of their tracks lie in other States, Mr. Appleton estimates the proportion due to the miles of track in the State to be 757. From this number he deducts 10 per cent. to cover the number which may be undergoing repairs or lying idle for other reasons, leaving 682 as the number assumed to be actually at work. This number, he says, is capable of doing the work which 1,519,496 horses could do on a good common road. He then takes the returns of the work actually done on these roads in the transportation of freight and horses, and finds it to be equivalent to what could be done on good common roads by 913,545 horses. Of course it is impossible for horses to move either freight or passengers as the locomotives do it, and, therefore, the economy of time effected by the latter could not be secured at all by the use of horses. The work of these locomotives, according to the rule adopted in the report of the Massachusetts census, is equivalent to the labor of 5,481,270 men, or to that of a population of more than 20,000,000.

A MEMBER OF THE COMMITTEE. How many men do you estimate to a horse-power?

Mr. SMITH. Six. By the aid mainly of her steam-engines, including locomotives, Massachusetts has the command and benefit of power equal nearly to that of 8,000,000 laboring men.

The CHAIRMAN. Did Mr. Watt receive a patent for his invention?

Mr. SMITH. Yes, sir. Before I close I shall give you a history of that, because I think it is one of the most instructive histories which I know of in connection with the patent law.

But in respect to locomotives: If we consider the cost of the equipment in harnesses and vehicles required for a million horses, and the number of men which would be required to manage and take care of them, and to keep in repair the equipment and the roads over which the work was done, I think you will agree that the actual value of the locomotives of Massachusetts must be more than double what we reach by the simple estimate of their equivalent in horses.

The importance of this subject may be presented in another way. In 1870 the population of the country engaged in gainful occupations was estimated to be about 12,000,000 persons between the ages of fifteen and sixty. This excluded a large number of women housekeepers, estimated at 7,400,000. Add that number to the number given in the table, and about 20,000,000 would have been the actual population of the United States engaged in what are called gainful occupations. If the population has now increased—as I suppose it has—about one sixth, the number now engaged in gainful occupations must be about 24,000,000.

I do not know what this committee would consider a fair estimate of the average value of the labor of these 24,000,000, when taken to represent the whole labor of the country, for work done by this number of people. I think, however, $1.25 per day would not be an excessive estimate, for we exclude in this estimate all the labor done by children under fifteen and by men over sixty, which is not an inconsiderable amount. This would give $30,000,000 as the value per day of the labor of the country, and, reckoning 300 working-days for a year, we shall find that the value of this labor for a year would be $9,000,000,000. If you assume, as I think you safely may, in view of the evidence which has been presented, that the inventions increase the value of this labor as much, at least, as 2 per cent. annually, the actual value to the country of inventions, with reference to its labor alone, would amount to $180,000,000. That is the value to the laboring men of inventions—the increased value given to their labor, through and by which they live.

But inventions do not show their full value in saving labor. There are a great many important inventions which produce other effects, and are valuable because they save raw material or introduce new materials which are cheaper or better than what was in use before, such as wood-pulp for the manufacture of paper, and rubber for clothing and other uses. So that if you add to the value of inventions in the saving labor their value in divers other ways, I think this committee will be impressed with the conviction that no other committee of Congress has to deal with a subject involving such great interests as this; that no other committee is called upon to exercise its judgment and discretion with more care than this in dealing with a system which has been intimately blended with our industries for nearly a century, lest it should adversely affect those great interests to which I have referred.

I have presented a hasty statement of some important facts, showing the value of inventions. Does the patent law stimulate or promote such inventions? Is this the fruit of the patent system? I refer, in proof of this, to the great fact, that the countries which have done this work, which have produced these inventions, are the countries which have had patent laws the longest. England was the first country to try the effect of a patent law in promoting its industries. This was in 1623. But, owing to the manner in which the law was viewed by the courts, it did not, I suppose, have much effect upon the industries of the country for the first hundred years. For about one hundred and fifty years the courts have recognized the value of the patent system, and have been disposed to interpret and construe all patents favorably to the inventors and have done this upon the ground that the interests of the country demanded that the law should be so interpreted and administered as to promote the progress of the arts. What other country has made such progress during the time that this law has been in existence as England? What other country, unless it be our own, which copied this system from England? France followed immediately after our country, in the adoption of a patent law, and has kept it in force till the present time. In naming these three countries which first adopted the patent laws, I have named the three countries which have done more than all the rest of the world, in the last hundred years, for the advancement of the useful arts.

I need refer, in proof of this assertion, only to facts which are apparent to the world. I have hastily set down from memory certain important and generic inventions which have sprung up in those three countries, and notably in England and in this country. I did not intend to make the list exhaustive. I could not have done so in the time allotted to me here. I only intended to recall to mind those inventions which have been recognized as of great value, and the sources of which everybody knows.

In England, we have, for instance, the spinning frame, the power loom, the steam engine, steam hammer, screw propeller, locomotives and railroads, hot-air blasts in the production of iron and the puddling process, the electric telegraph in several important forms, power printing presses, Bessemer's processes for making steel, steam plow, and paper machine.

In our own country, I can name a large list, because I am more familiar with the industries of this country. We have the cotton-gin, the steamboat, planing machine, Blanchard's machine for turning irregular forms, sewing machine, the Morse electric telegraph, vulcanization of rubber, steam-drills, steam-pump, reaping machine, threshing machine, folding machine for paper, paper-bag machines, card-machines, nail-machines, screw-machines, shoe machinery, watch machinery, and gun machinery.

In France a fewer number of inventions of a generic kind occur to me, but I am quite sure I have not exhausted the list of their important inventions. That country, however, certainly has not contributed so largely to making great inventions as the two countries which I have already named. But France has given the world the Jacquard loom, Turbine water-wheel, Giffard's injector, the Fresnel lights for light-houses, and paper machine, and numerous important chemical inventions. The origin of the continuous paper-making machine was in France, although it was soon afterwards planted to England, and received its chief development there, and so it was with the daguerrotype.

What other countries can furnish any such list of important and radical inventions as these three countries?

In this connection I wish to state some interesting facts in relation to the improvements in the printing press. The art of printing was invented almost four hundred and fifty years ago in Germany. It spread slowly into other countries. The printing press received a little improvement about a hundred years after its invention, and then remained almost unchanged until about the commencement of the present century. Since that time the improvements have been marvellous, but they have nearly all been made in this country and England, and have been patented. France has contributed something to its improvement, but not nearly as much as the other two countries. It was not till the art of printing came under the influence of the patent laws of England and this country that its improvement commenced. One inventor in Saxony conceived some important improvements in the press, but he went to England to work out his improvements and put them into operation. Notwithstanding its German origin, the art of printing as it now exists may be fairly assigned to England and America.

England took the lead in time, and in her patent law gained much the start of this country and of France; yet this country, by the character of its law, which not only gave the most effectual protection to property in inventions, but placed the expense of obtaining patents so low that the poorest inventors could secure the protection of a patent, has reaped greater benefit relatively than England.

In France the patent-law was much less wisely framed, I believe, and therefore developed the industries of the country less and stimulated its inventive genius less. I think I may attribute the great superiority of this country and of England to the fact that England has been longer in the possession of a patent-law than any other, and that this country has had one which brought its benefits within the reach of the largest number of its people.

If there is any one thing in reference to which the poor man may be equal to, or superior to, the rich man, it is in the endowments of Nature. He may be possessed of mental qualities of the highest character, and it would be doing him a greater wrong, as I think, to deprive him of the opportunity to reap the fruits of his mental endowments than it would be to rob him of the fruits of his physical labor.

Our patent-law has been in operation about eighty-eight years. It is based upon a provision of the Constitution that Congress shall have power to promote the progress of science and the useful arts, by securing to authors and inventors, for limited terms, the exclusive right to their respective writings and discoveries.

Observe that the framers of the Constitution instinctively recognized the fact that if it was desirable to promote the progress of science and the useful arts, the means to do it is determined by the laws of human nature.

The law is based upon one of the most deeply-seated and widely-felt springs of human action—the love of gain. This is active, is instinctively felt, and is constantly assumed to be almost universally present and active in the human breast, and it is more frequently appealed to than any others of the desires we wish to gratify. To this motive men appeal when they offer a reward for the recovery of lost or stolen property; for the apprehension and conviction of criminals; for a remedy against the spread of pestilence, or the ravages of wild animals, or the still more destructive ravages of those insignificant insects that, through their numbers, eat up every green thing, and spread desolation over the most fertile lands. It is not necessary to claim that the love of gain is the only motive which prompts men to action, or even to make inventions. Happily for the world, men are influenced by many motives, and the progress of civilization is not dependent solely upon any one of them. I could not deny, if I would, that many important inventions have been made without the stimulus of patent laws; nor will I deny that they would continue to be made without it. To say nothing of the arts of the ancients, I can point to many important inventions, made within a few hundred years, where no patent laws existed. Italy gave the world the telescope and the galvanic circuit, and Germany contributed the art of printing by movable types, without the protection of any patent law. England gave the Newcomen engine, also, though she then had a patent system, but the inventor of that engine did not take out a patent. Many important contributions to chemistry have been made by men who prosecuted their researches from a simple love of science. Wonderful discoveries have also been made, and are still being made, by men who had no great hope of pecuniary gain from their labors. The sciences of geology and mathematics afford instances. Yet, notwithstanding all this, it remains true, that the love of gain is a powerful stimulus to the exercise of man's inventive genius, when all other motives fail.

The question is not whether we should have no inventions without a patent law, but whether we should have as many, and as good ones, as we now have under its stimulus.

The suggestion is made, indeed, that inventors are so possessed with the spirit of invention that they would make inventions whether rewarded for it or not. But I am satisfied, from my observation of the inventors with whom I have come in contact, that those who make this assertion know but little of inventors. I have met many of them, but I have never yet seen one who did not labor constantly and zealously in view of the reward which he hoped to reap as the result of his labor. The man whom I have in mind is a man who is possessed of the spirit of original research and invention, if ever a man was; yet I have known him, more than once, turn from an investigation or a line of thought which was absorbing his mind, when he perceived that no practical and useful immediate result was to follow from it; yet he is not a man void of gain. Probably no one in this country has pushed scientific research further in his special branch (electricity) than he, but the law has led him so to direct his studies as to give the world immediate results. It is to him that we owe the electric fire-alarm and many of the most valuable improvements in telegraphy and in the application of electricity in naval warfare. I refer to Mr. Moses G. Farmer.

The common popular notion that an inventor is different from other men, in the original constitution of his mind, is an entire mistake. He is ordinarily regarded as a rare and peculiar production of nature—a genius fitted for special kinds of work and occupied with special kinds of inventions, which unfit him for any other work. On the contrary, he is generally only a patient and skillful worker, trained to his work by observation and reflection, and stimulated by the common desire to better his condition by the use of his powers. Inventors are simply skillful workmen, who bring to their work the same faculties and powers which they carry into their every-day labor, and they have the same desire to reap a reward from their mental labor as from their physical labor.

Those who expect and, perhaps, believe that inventors would make inventions without the hope of reward as well as with, assume, I think, that invention consists wholly in mental labor—in the intellectual exercise of conceiving and devising new things, which may be described in words and represented by drawings, if the subject is of a nature to admit of drawings.

But in almost all cases a good invention involves a great deal more than this. It involves experiments and trials, a large amount of physical labor, and the expenditure for materials of more or less money, according to the nature of the invention. The reduction to practice of an invention is a very different thing from the speculations which give rise to it—from the planning and devising which are often thought to constitute the whole of invention. The latter is the intellectual part of invention, and, without doubt, occupies a large part of the time of some men, and would do so even if there was no hope of profit from it. But this does not of itself often result in practical inventions. It must be followed by experiments to test the correctness of the conception. This involves labor and expense. It requires the employment oftentimes of the most skillful and expensive labor and the most costly materials. Experiments often result in failure, and the prosecution of the invention calls for more and more expense, till many an inventor gives up in despair. It is this practical part of invention which few men could or would undertake unless the product of the labor and expense should become their own. Most of our inventors are men who live by their daily labor, and they are frequently compelled to sell a share of their proposed inventions in advance of their reduction to practice, in order to obtain the means to reduce them to practice. Contracts of this kind are common, but they could not be made if the law did not protect the invention in the hands of the inventor when completed.

This brings me, Mr. Chairman, to answer your question as to

James Watt. If ever there was an inventor who was possessed with the spirit of invention beyond his control, it was probably James Watt, the inventor of the steam-engine, the greatest invention the world has ever received. But no one can read his history without being convinced that but for the patent law of England James Watt never would have brought the steam-engine to perfection. At the very outset of his labors we find him contemplating his expected patent, and dealing with the expectation in order to raise money for prosecuting his work. He had not proceeded far before he exhausted his own means, about £1,000. He was then compelled to sell two-thirds of his invention in order to obtain the means with which to prosecute his experiments and also to secure his patent. Before he had reduced his invention to practice, the means of the person with whom he had associated himself were exhausted, and he was compelled to get his means to secure his patent from another source. After he had obtained his patent, six years elapsed before he was able to complete a working engine which gave satisfaction. He was then endeavoring to negotiate with Matthew Bolton to take an interest in the invention and furnish the means to bring it into use. Bolton was one of the rare men that England has produced. At that time he was the most skillful manufacturer in Great Britain, and had in his employ a body of the best trained workmen probably in the world. He was, too, a man of inventive genius, and yet a business man of great ability; he possessed very considerable means. He became acquainted with James Watt and his invention after the patent was taken out, but Watt was under a contract with the first party and could not make a satisfactory arrangement. Watt, after the lapse of about six years, became free to negotiate with Bolton. Mr. Bolton then entered into a new examination of the invention. He was enthusiastic. He foresaw with the prophet's eye what there was in store for England in that invention. But six years of the patent had then elapsed, and as a business man he decided not to touch it; he was convinced that it would be impossible to get a return of the money requisite to bring the invention to perfection and introduce it into use in the eight years which then remained of the patent. Mr. Watt was therefore compelled to go to Parliament and surrender that patent and ask for a new one for twenty-four years. His petition was granted. Upon the grant of the new patent, Mr. Bolton embarked his capital and his energies in it. I think it may well be said that the Parliament of Great Britain never passed a law which had so great an influence upon the destinies of England and the world as that law giving to James Watt an extension of his patent for twenty-four years. All that Mr. Bolton anticipated took place. The difficulties of introducing the invention were enormous. The difficulties of finding trained workmen skillful enough to build engines and take charge of them were great. A large capital was required, and infringers appeared to compete with them. It was not until nearly the expiration of the twenty-four years that they began to receive a return for the money and labor which had been expended. No other invention, perhaps, went through greater difficulties, before success was achieved, than the steam-engine.

A MEMBER OF THE COMMITTEE. What year was it that his invention was made?

Mr. SMITH. It was first patented in 1769. Watt began his labors upon the invention in 1763. The extension of the patent was granted in 1775, and Bolton and Watt became partners soon after.

In the history of the steam-engine we have the history of many important inventions. The capital and business talent required cannot be secured except upon the security afforded by the patent.

There is yet another most important result of the patent law not often thought of, and yet quite as important as anything else connected with it. The Patent Office exhibits the result of an enormous amount of labor and experimental research. It shows, however, only a fraction of the labor and research actually performed by our laboring population, for I suppose no one will question the correctness of the statement that the great mass of our inventions are made by the laboring men of the country. Many a workingman carefully watches and observes the mechanical operations and processes which are carried on around him with a desire to discover some chance for an improvement, and he experiments, and plans, and devises, in order to work out what he deems for the time to be an improvement; and though he often produces what are called fruitless or worthless inventions, yet the labor is not wholly a loss to him or to the country. He acquires by the effort a valuable experience and training. It is often through failures that men learn how to succeed. Watt said that it was a great thing to find out what could not be done; that it led up to a knowledge of that which could be done. I have often been astonished at the great amount of scientific and technical knowledge possessed by our mechanics; at the acuteness of their observations; the activity of their imaginations in forecasting results, and their fertility in expedients, and the soundness of their judgments in all things pertaining to the properties of matter and the laws and operations of nature. They carefully watch for the results of the labors of scientific men in their fields of research. They are familiar with what has been achieved in those fields, and are diligently laboring to turn their knowledge and acquirements to practical account. It is no unusual thing to have a common mechanic, in explaining some invention of his own, refer to the researches and discoveries of such men, for instance, as Tyndall and Sir William Thomson. It is to our patent law—which has given to such knowledge a practical value in the hands of these men—that we are indebted for the possession of the most intelligent and skillful body of laboring men in the world—a body of men who, having overcome the disadvantages to which this country was subjected by its want of capital and the cost of labor, has placed within our grasp, as I fully believe, a large share of the manufactures of the world. Our country has secured to the common laborer, as no other country has, the fruits of his inventions, and richly he has repaid the provision.

It is not alone to the actual inventions which have been made under the stimulus of the patent law that we must look for the fruits of that law; it is also to the power which has been acquired to make future inventions, to the patience, and skill, and intelligence which have been developed.

Not long since, one of our most intelligent manufacturers—Mr. Angell, of Providence, who spent last summer in Europe, and took special pains to inquire into the condition of manufacturing industries abroad, particularly in England—expressed to me emphatically his conviction that it was only a question of time, and of no long time, when we should, to a large extent, supplant those countries in the markets of the world in supplying the demand for manufactured goods. " From what advantage possessed by us do you expect this result?" I inquired; " from our superior machinery and inventions?" " Not from those altogether, or even chiefly," he replied, " for those can be obtained by other countries; but from the superior intelligence of our labor, which makes it more productive with the same means in hand."

Invention involves a close and accurate study of the properties of things, and the laws and operations of nature, and a discovery of something which is new; and every workman who discovers, as he thinks, an opportunity to make an improvement, and sets himself to work out that improvement, whether he succeeds or not, rises from his effort a more intelligent man than when he sat down—rises from it with some addition to what he knew before. His failures are by no means utter losses.

If for no other reason than because it promotes general intelligence among the great mass of the laboring men, and gives them a mental training of the highest character, and that highest result of education, the power of original research, I hold that the patent law should be amended with caution, and that nothing should be done to impair the security with which an inventor may hold the fruits of his labor, or the certainty with which he may reap its rewards.

About the commencement of the present century, Prussia put into operation a military system, which she has been steadily perfecting ever since. Under it, not only is every man made liable to render military service, but he is actually trained to be a soldier. Under this system she has become the first military power in the world. Now, it is not the victories which she has won, great as they are. over France and Austria, which has given to that system its chief value as a national institution. Its chief value lies in the military training which every man receives, and which makes Prussia a nation of soldiers, and gives her the ability to win other and greater victories, if necessary. Just as she has trained a nation of men to be soldiers, we have trained a nation of men to be skillful workers in the arts of civil life; and the great advantage which we possess over other nations is, that, under the stimulus of our patent law, our workmen have acquired the habit of original and independent research into the secrets of nature. They have acquired the art of inventing, and the courage to assail any mechanical problem which may be presented to them for solution. They have come to believe that everything is possible. They are on the watch to discover opportunities to make improvements, for in those opportunities they see a chance to acquire property, and it is often their only chance. Inventions are a part of our national productions, as much so as our cotton, and wheat, and corn, and tobacco. They come, like the productions of the soil, from labor and capital; and it is idle to suppose that they will be produced, unless they have the protection of law, like other property.

But the stimulus of the law does not stop with the inventor. It reaches the capitalist, and holds out to him the same hope of gain. By giving to an invention the legal status of property, it makes it a legitimate subject for the investment of capital. By throwing around it the safeguards of the law, to protect it from invasion, it enables a capitalist to devote the necessary amount for its development and improvement, with a reasonable prospect that he may find again the bread which he casts upon the waters. It enables him to employ inventive labor, as he does other labor, with the certainty that the fruits of that labor will repay its costs.

It is sometimes said that inventions must be exhausted; that Nature has nothing left in store to reward further search. Is this so ? "Must Alexander weep because there are no more worlds to conquer?" Why, just around us everywhere lie secrets which have been hidden by nature to the present time. Take the telephone, one of the most wonderful achievements of man. Who could have believed that a little disk of iron, no larger than the "dollar of our fathers," could perform the functions both of the ear and the tongue, so that it could repeat to the human ear the words and the very tones of the human voice, to which its yoke-yoke-fellow was listening at the same instant a hundred miles away. And yet, that power, now trained to the service of man, has lain hidden in the bosom of Nature since the world's dawn.

I have spoken of the enormous power which the steam-engine has placed in the hands of man. But I believe it to be yet in its infancy. It will yet be placed in the hands of every farmer in this country, when the inventors have adapted it to the special work of the farm-house and the barn, brought its cost within the means of the farmer, and enabled it to be run without the constant oversight of a trained engineer.

But this is not all. The steam-engine, notwithstanding its wonderful efficiency, is a wonderfully wasteful engine. About one-tenth of the power due to the coal burned in the steam-engines in common use is all that is actually made available. There lies now before the inventors, and has lain since the steam-engine was brought into existence, this wonderful fact, that they have not been able to utilize much over one-tenth of the fuel consumed, and no greater invention lies in the future than this of saving this waste fuel; and the problem is one upon which men have been engaged more or less since the steam-engine was known.

There has been constant progress toward this desirable result, but more remains to be done than has been done.

In 1815 the Cornish engines were able to lift twenty millions of pounds of water one foot for one bushel of coal. This was called its "duty," and Watt himself thought nothing more was to be expected. But, in 1820 the "duty" had gone up to 28,000,000; in 1826 it had reached 30,000,000; in 1839, 54,000,000; and in 1850, 60,000,000. Constant advance has been made since 1850.

A MEMBER OF THE COMMITTEE. If Mr. Keeley succeeds in perfecting his motor, it will revolutionize the world, will it not?

Mr. SMITH. *If.*

These improvements have been effected, not by long steps, by what are called great improvements, but by small steps, by what are often called small inventions; by an attentive study of each part of the engine, and by improvements in the smallest details.

The locomotive has been the subject of constant improvement, and every year inventions are brought forward to increase its efficiency, or reduce its cost, or adapt it to special kinds of work. Every part of a railroad has in like manner been the subject of invention, and so also has every detail of the passenger and freight cars. The result appears in a statement contained in the last report of the Western Railroad Association, as follows: "The great reduction which has taken place in the last decade, in transportation charges, has been due largely to the improvements which have been from time to time introduced."

The facts laid before you by Mr. Coffin and Mr. Storrow are sufficient to show that they are being made quite as rapidly as ever before. Not long since, a very intelligent inventor and capitalist informed me that he was about to introduce inventions, which he had just perfected, which he believed would add one hundred millions of dollars, annually, to the value of the cotton-crop at the South.

I will spend no further time upon this subject. I wish to call attention to one or two provisions of the bill. I may here remark, that a large amount of careful labor has been bestowed upon the bill by those who have been associated with me in its preparation, by the committee at the other end of the Capitol, and by gentlemen who were not in ac-

cord with us at the commencement of our efforts. It is in many respects
a very important modification of the patent law. I do not suppose it is
of the slightest importance to this committee, or any one else, what my
opinion may be of this bill. If, however, any man would be influenced
by a knowledge of what my own experience in the patent law leads me
to expect from the bill, I frankly say that every part of the bill has my
hearty approval. I believe there is not a section of it which will not
work advantageously for the country, and for the inventor also.* All
legislation must undoubtedly look first to the interest of the country.
It must look to the inventor only as a means for promoting the interests
of the country.

I believe that it is for the interest of the inventor that a good law
should be in force. He suffers if the law is a bad one. I have had no
difficulty in reconciling the interests of inventors and the users of inventions.

Many of the provisions of this bill, it is said by way of objection, are
framed especially for the interests of defendants, or, rather, for the interests of infringers. Even if this were so, I do not think that inventors
and those interested in patent property could for that reason object to
the provisions of the bill. They in fact form the great bulk of infringers
in patent causes. I think they are more liable to be charged with infringement than any other persons. A large part of the patent litigation of the country arises between those who are interested in patents.
So that the inventors themselves have just as much interest in its provisions that look to the benefit of defendants as any other class possibly can have.

The law of mortgages might be so framed that when security was
taken upon mortgage the advantage should be altogether in favor of
the mortgagor, the man who borrowed the money. If it were so, does
not any one see that in the long run it would operate against those who
desired to borrow money? Because the owners of money would not
lend it upon a security which placed them at a disadvantage. So, on
the other hand, if the advantage was the other way, with the lender of
the money, does not any one see that it would be in the long run a great
disadvantage for all lenders, because they would not be able to get the
security? If mortgaged property were forfeited upon default in payment, according to the technical terms of mortgages, would anybody
borrow money, except under the direst distress, unless he got the full
value of the property, so that, if the property were forfeited by default
of payment, it would go for what it was worth? Each class, borrowers
as well as lenders, has an interest that the law shall be one which works
well for both parties, in order that both classes may take the benefit of
it. So of the patent law. Inventors and the owners of patents have a

---

* Since the above statement was made, Mr. Walker has handed to the committee a paper
in which he claims that I did not deny his previous statement, that I had informed him
that my real opinion was that the 2d section of the bill is unconstitutional, and that my
neglect to say that he had misstated what I said was to be taken as an admission that I
was urging upon Congress the enactment of a section which I know to be unconstitutional.
I certainly thought that what I said was a most emphatic denial of the last part of the
charge; for it never entered my mind that any one could assume or suspect that I could
give my support to a provision in the bill which I believed to be unconstitutional. I did
not care to refer to the first part of the charge, as to what I had informed Mr. Walker; for
a specific denial might seem to imply a charge of intentional misstatement on the part of
Mr. Walker—a charge which I should be slow to make. I do now say, however, that Mr.
Walker certainly misunderstood me, if he understood me to say what he asserts that I said.
I may properly add that in my argument before the Senate committee I stated distinctly
my conviction that the section is not open to the objection that it affects vested rights, and
I think Mr. Walker was then present.

common interest with the community at large that the law shall work no unnecessary hardship to any one.

Some criticism has been made upon the provisions for the reissue of patents. Not a few people have entertained the conviction that reissues of patents should be prohibited. The number of patents actually reissued is small in proportion to the whole number granted—not over four per cent.; but about three-fifths of the litigation of the country, I think, arises upon reissued patents.

About three-fifths of the suits, so far as I have been able to ascertain, which have been reported in the books, are upon reissued patents, and two-fifths upon original patents.

Before considering fully the sections which relate directly to reissues, I wish to bring to the attention of the committee one section, which, though it does not in terms speak of reissues, does in fact go far to remedy any evils which may attend them, and goes farther to remedy the many other alleged evils than any other remedy which has been proposed. I refer to the section which provides that patents shall be subject to the payment of fees of fifty dollars after an interval of five years, and of a hundred dollars at the end of ten years. In England, the effect of the law requiring the payment of a much larger fee at the expiration of three years and seven years, where the patents are granted for fourteen years, is that the average life of a patent is only three and one-third years. That, however, takes into account quite a large number of patents which lapse from the want of complete specification. A patent there takes date from the time of filing what is called the provisional specification, and at the end of six months it lapses if a complete specification is not filed. Quite a percentage, therefore, expire at the expiration of six months. I think that fifty per cent. of the patents granted will, under the operation of this law, expire at the end of four and a half years on an average, and that fifty per cent. of the remander will expire at the end of the second period. I believe that, under the operation of this law, the average duration of patents will be less than ten years.

I believe there is a bill before this committee providing that patents shall not be granted for more than ten years, but that extensions for a further term of five years shall be allowed. This provision of the law which I am now considering will give a shorter life on the average to patents, but it will give the short life to the worthless patents and the long life to those which deserve it. Now, observe the operation of this. If I am correct in my estimate, half of the patents will be placed beyond the chance of doing any mischief which may attend reissues, if mischief there is, at the end of the first period, and another half of the remainder at the end of the next five years. It has been a subject of frequent complaint that old patents which have been idle and worthless in the hands of their owners have often been revived so as to cover subsequent patents and the industries which have grown up under them. It is certain that a large part of such patents will be swept away under the provisions of this bill. The fees will become payable generally before it is discovered that they can be used to embarrass subsequent inventors or manufacturers who have unwittingly used what might be covered by the reissues; and as they are worthless for legitimate purposes at the time, they will to a large extent be allowed to expire.

A MEMBER OF THE COMMITTEE. Why do you name the period at four and a half years as the time when half the patents will expire?

Mr. STORROW. Because that is the time when the first fee becomes due.

Mr. SMITH. The fee is payable at the end of five years—or rather, on the 1st of January four years after the patent is granted; so that it does not operate upon all alike. For certain reasons we thought it better to make the fees upon all the patents granted during a year payable on the 1st of January occurring next after the expiration of four years, than to make them payable during the whole year and exactly at the expiration of four years from the date of the patent.

The CHAIRMAN. Are you perfectly satisfied, Mr. Smith, with those fees of $50 and $100? Is your mind perfectly clear upon that?

Mr. SMITH. My mind is perfectly clear on the $50 fee. I will frankly say that if I had exercised my own judgment, without regard to the judgment of others, I should have fixed the second fee at the same sum. But I do not think $100 onerous for a patent which at the expiration of the second period is found to be valuable, or that the hardship of paying that sum on a patent which has not proved valuable enough to keep it alive overbalances the evil to which the community is exposed by keeping it alive.

The CHAIRMAN. You think, if it is valuable to the public he certainly ought to be able to pay it?

Mr. SMITH. Yes, sir.

Mr. RAYMOND. It is proper to say on this question of reissue, that the Senate committee have stricken out the word "models" in the 5th section of the bill. As the bill stood originally, a reissue could be obtained only when the new thing claimed was indicated by a model, drawings, or specifications. I have just been asked by a member of the committee whether we consented that the word "model" should be stricken out in section 5.

Mr. STORROW. Nearly all of us have proposed it before the House committee.

Mr. SMITH. Allow me to say one thing more in regard to section 5. There is another provision which will, in my judgment, eliminate all the mischief from reissues, and that is the provision that no machine put into operation under the original patent, which did not infringe the original patent, shall be held to infringe the reissued patent. There is where the difficulty is now—that machines have been bought and put into operation when they might lawfully be bought, as they did not infringe any claim in the original patent, and after the reissue has been granted the owner has been able to restrain the use of such machines. This has been a hardship. The operation of sections 5 and 6, I think, is such as to remove all just causes of complaint from reissues.

There will always be one class of persons who will complain of reissues; those who have infringed, those who often appear as defendants, and who have unlawfully appropriated a substantial part of the plaintiff's invention, and who have no defense on the merits, like to find some defect in the language of the specification which will enable them to escape, and they will almost think they are defrauded of a right if their loophole of escape is closed to them by an amendment; and, so I suppose men felt when amendments first began to be freely allowed in pleadings. But no one doubts the necessity and the justice of allowing them.

I simply now desire to say, in regard to the second section, that while it is a section about which men may well differ as to the remedies which it provides, yet it is one which has been framed with care, after much reflection, and I believe it will be found beneficent in its operation. The only observation, however, that I desire to make is this, that while some gentlemen have appeared before you and the Senate committee to criticise the terms of that section, yet no one, I believe, has appeared (unless it may be Mr. Walker) to contend that the rule of law laid down in *Mowry* v. *Whitney* ought to stand as applicable to all cases. All the attorneys with whose opinions I am acquainted agree to this : That the operation of that rule is one which is calculated to work great hardship and great injustice in many cases, and whether the remedy provided in this bill is the best or not, it is the best which has been suggested. That the rule ought to be changed as to many cases, seems to be admitted.

Mr. WALKER. Can you not explain to the committee in a word what your objection to the rule in *Mowry* v. *Whitney* is?

Mr. SMITH. The rule laid down in that case is, a party who infringes by the use of an invention is to be charged with all the advantage which the use of the invention gives over the use of what was known before. Now, the false assumption which lies at the bottom of that is—1st, that the patent law in its natural operation secures to the inventor all the advantage which the invention gives over what was known before; and, 2d, that the infringer, to the extent of his use of the invention, receives all the advantage which the use of the invention gives over the use of what was open to him to use.

This assumption is not true in fact. The evidence which has been presented to this committee goes to show that the inventor, under the operation of the laws of trade, gets but a small proportion of the whole advantage due to the invention. The community, or that portion of it which uses the invention or its products, reaps the largest share of the value of the invention.

In other words, under the relations which the patent law establishes between the owner of a patent and the public, the advantages which are due to the invention are naturally divided between the owner and the public.

Now, when you charge an infringer, as trustee of the owner of the patent, with the value of the whole advantage which the use of the invention gives over the use of what was known before, you charge him not only with that share of the advantages which naturally and legitimately go to the owner and user, but with that share also which just as naturally and legitimately go to the public.

Mr. WALKER. Is the defendant or any other man entitled to any share of the invention until after the expiration of the patent?

Mr. SMITH. The public are entitled to all the benefits of the invention under the practical workings of the law, except such as the owner, in the full and undisturbed enjoyment of his patent, can put into his pocket as the fruits of it. Now, he can never, under the natural operations of the laws of trade, put all the advantages due to his invention into his pockets as its profits; but the rule of *Mowry* v. *Whitney* sweeps into the hands of the plaintiff an amount of money which never belonged to him; which he never could have had if he had had the full enjoyment of the patent himself, and which the defendant may never in fact have received.

More than that, the Supreme Court of the United States have applied this rule to a case where the defendant had lost money in the use of the invention (an invention for splitting wood). The defendant had split his wood at half a dollar a cord less by the use of the machine than he could have done by hand, and the court held that he must account for that fifty cents on every cord, although he sold his wood at a loss, on the ground that he had reaped that advantage from the use of the invention. I suppose he sold the wood at the market price, and it is quite conceivable that the market price had been fixed, not by his acts, but by the use of the invention in the hands of other men, or by causes

which would have compelled the owners of the patent to sell wood at a
loss; such as another invention which did the work still cheaper. An
illustration of the manner in which this rule may work in particular
cases, is presented in an actual case with which I was connected as
counsel. It was a machine for working eight-sided piano-legs.

Before the invention of the machine, most of the legs used were
round legs turned in a lathe. A few of the kind subsequently made by
the machine were made by hand at a cost of thirty-five dollars a set.
With the machine they could be made and sold at five dollars a set, and
the inventor was compelled to sell them at this price to compete with
turned legs. After a while another invented a different machine to make
the same kind of legs, and he also sold them for five dollars. He was sued
by the first patentee as an infringer. The court held that his machine
was not an infringement; but if he had been charged as an infringer,
and the rule in the case of *Mowry* v. *Whitney* had been applied in accounting, he would have had to pay over thirty dollars on each set, although he sold them for five dollars a set, and although the plaintiff
also did so, and was compelled by the state of the market to do so in
order to reap the advantage which his invention gave over hand-labor.

Mr. WALKER. Could not this infringer save himself from that hardship by allowing the other man to use his own patent?

Mr. SMITH. Certainly he could. But how could that circumstance
give the owner of the patent a right to recover from him as profits six
times the price he got for the legs? The patentee could not have obtained any such sum from the use of his invention. Why should the
law give it to him? An account of profits is not taken to punish an infringer by way of penalty, but to compel him to give up profits made
from the invention. There can be no possible reason for the application
of such a rule in such cases.

Mr. HUBBELL. How is it where the case is accompanied by proof of
resultant damages?

Mr. SMITH. That never comes into account in taking an account of
profits; damages are also allowed where the profits do not afford a sufficient recovery, but they are assessed and allowed *as damages*. I am
now talking about the rule in *Mowry* v. *Whitney* for taking an account
of profits. I said that I believed no gentleman, except Mr. Walker,
perhaps, had defended that rule. I am not certain that he has defended it.

Mr. WALKER. Yes, sir; I did in this hearing.

Mr. SMITH. I am quite certain that he defended before the Senate
committee his right to damages if they had accrued, whether the rule
was just or unjust; but I have seen no intelligent exposition of the
principle from anybody upon which that rule is entitled to stand as a
general rule.

A MEMBER OF THE COMMITTEE. I would like if, in your printed
argument, you would elaborate that point a little further, as you have
not time here.

Mr. SMITH. I will endeavor to do so.

A MEMBER OF THE COMMITTEE. Please explain the reasons upon
which you say that only from two to five per cent. of the actual benefit
goes to the inventor.

Mr. SMITH. I only speak of that as an average result of a great many
instances which have occurred. The evidence has been submitted by
Mr. Storrow.

A MEMBER OF THE COMMITTEE. You stated a while ago that there
were so many thousand patents issued every year, and that if this clause in

the bill (section 11) becomes a law, fixing fifty dollars as a fee to be paid at the expiration of four and a half years for the continuance of the patent, half those patents will be dead at the expiration of that time, and at the expiration of nine years probably half the balance will be dead. What source of income would that be to the government? What revenue would it bring in annually?

Mr. SMITH. From 13,000 to 15,000 patents are granted annually. I think half that number, say 7,000, would expire at the end of the first period, and 3,500 at the end of the second.

A MEMBER OF THE COMMITTEE. How is it for the future?

Mr. SMITH. I suppose the number of patents will be as large as it has been for the last seven or eight years; that is, from twelve to thirteen thousand.

A MEMBER OF THE COMMITTEE. It would be somewhere from $30,000 to $40,000?

Mr. SMITH. It would unquestionably be a large sum.

Mr. HUBBELL. If this country has prospered so long, and so well, as compared with other nations, and small patent-fees only have been required by inventors, so that we have superseded England, who, under her prerogative right, has taken excessive fees from inventors, why do you want to crush down inventors by exacting fees that will put them in the same condition as they are in England? Answer that question.

Mr. SMITH. I will answer it. I answer it in this way: that these worthless patents stand in the way of inventors themselves, and it is for their interest that they shall be gotten out of the way.

It is important that inventors should have the opportunity to protect their inventions if they think them worth protecting. If they do not deem them worth preserving, it is important that they should not stand in the way of other inventors, and the requirement of a small fee after the lapse of a few years will make it necessary for the owner of a patent to decide for himself whether he thinks it is worth preserving, and, if it is, the profits of the patent will enable him to pay it.

Mr. WALKER. Mr. Smith has said that none of the lawyers, except Mr. Walker, contended for the justice of the rule in the case of *Mowry* v. *Whitney*. How does it happen that the Supreme Court of the United States unanimously approved and sustained that ruling?

Mr. SMITH. I am not bound to answer that. I can easily see how they came to do it, because in the particular case in which they applied it, it did not work any hardship. They did not look far enough to see that in a large class of cases it would work an enormous hardship. I do not object to the rule in cases like *Mowry* v. *Whitney*, but I object to its general application. I think the Supreme Court has indicated its own distrust of the rule.

Mr. WALKER. In what case was that?

Mr. STORROW. In the case of *The Packet Company* v. *Sickles*.

Mr. SMITH. There is no question, I think, that the Supreme Court regard that rule as one which is calculated to work hardship in many cases.

Mr. WALKER. Will you mention a case, except the case of *The Packet Company* v. *Sickles*, and is it not true that that case was decided before *Mowry* v. *Whitney*?

Mr. SMITH. It was decided after that case (*Mowry* v. *Whitney* is in 14 Wall., and *Packet Company* v. *Sickles* is in 19 Wall.), and I think there have been repeated references to that rule, I think, in a way which shows that the court questioned it. But whether they questioned it or not, having once laid it down, they probably do not feel at liberty to throw it aside. This thing I feel well assured of: that it is not in ac-

cordance with the true principles of equity. The court went wrong
when they laid down the rule as a general rule, and they now feel themselves bound by it, and I think Congress should now step in and change
the rule.

I am sorry to have troubled the committee so long.

Mr. HURLBUT. The fact is that Mr. Justice Miller admits the absurdity of the rule by which they have bound themselves.

ARGUMENT OF HON. S. A. HURLBUT.

MR. CHAIRMAN AND GENTLEMEN OF THE COMMITTEE : The pending bill had its origin somewhere about three years ago. I was then a
member of the House, and at the request of patentees and heavy manufacturers, residing in my district, together with original owners of
patents upon important machinery, I presented in the House of Representatives a bill which contained two features that are embodied in
this bill ; one the limitation of actions, and the other establishing the
same rule both in law and equity—that is, a reasonable license fee.
That bill passed the House late in the session, after having been reported from the Judiciary Committee. It was then sent over to the
Senate, and there it met with some discussion and opposition. It came
in very late in the session, and could not possibly have passed any way.
From that has originated the meeting of the parties on both sides of
these questions.

A MEMBER OF THE COMMITTEE. That bill would have passed if it
had not been for the opposition of one Senator.

Mr. HURLBUT. It might have passed. This bill is a result of a compromise of the different conflicting interests.

Some comment has been made here which is hardly worth an answer,
and yet it may have some effect. I wish you gentlemen to consider
that all cases of amendments of laws come from particular grievances
suffered by some particular party, which causes that party to seek a
remedy by an amendment or change of the law. This bill comes here
as a compromise between the interests of the persons who use patents—
by whom I mean the general public—and persons who claim to represent, and, so far as I know, do represent, to a very large extent the inventors and owners of patents.

The bill occupies middle ground. With my personal notions, it is
not entirely satisfactory to me, but I do not expect any law that would
be completely satisfactory to me to pass. There are points in it which,
if I were at liberty, I might suggest an improvement upon, but I do not
think I will.

I have accepted this bill in good faith, and all I have to do is to urge
its passage upon the committee and upon the House.

There has been a great deal of very valuable and interesting information given you here in regard to the extent and value of the patent
system, its influence upon the community in the useful arts and sciences;
and the argument seems to me to proceed not so much upon the basis
of what this bill requires as if there were some covert proposition to
destroy the patent system itself. No man understands the value of the
patent system any better than I do.

I do not agree with what I consider the extravagant statistics that
have been given on the other side, because my observation does not
concur. I do not agree that in all cases labor-saving machinery is nec-

essarily an advantage. I think that in all cases it is limited, upon this one condition, that when you increase by labor-saving machinery the facilities and cheapness of production, you must necessarily enlarge the area of consumption of the product, or you must throw men out of employment. It seems to me that that is as certain as a mathematical proposition; and the history that has been given here by Mr. Coffin, Mr. Hyde, and others, shows that this condition is universal. Take the shoe interest, which was so clearly shown to this committee by Mr. Hyde (if I remember correctly). They have kept their number of employés, notwithstanding the introduction of labor-saving machinery, because they have extended the area of the consumption of their products. Just so far as you can do that, there is an unqualified benefit derived from the use of labor-saving machinery to the public. But it is not so in agricultural matters. I regret to differ from those gentlemen. I say to you that the present effect—I will not say the future effect—of the universal use of labor-saving machinery in the cultivation of the land and the production of crops, has been to throw many men out of employment. This is shown by this fact—that the consumption of agricultural products in the United States has not at all increased in proportion to the machinery. The time may come, however, when the one will overlap the other. I think it will, probably; but at present one of the great causes of what is known as the army of tramps in the United States, so far as it is drawn from the agricultural population, is the undue development of labor-saving machinery in the cultivation of land.

I had intended to argue the legal questions in this bill. I came here for that purpose, but I am very glad that that labor has been saved me, and that I have been anticipated in that respect by my friend, Mr. Payson, whose argument on that subject is, in my judgment, the most lucid and fair exposition of the existing evils of the patent law and the effect of the proposed remedies that I have ever heard.

There are just two principal causes which influence me to retain the same interest now in these matters that I did three years ago, and those are, first, rendering the reward of the inventor a thing which he is sure to recover—not involving it in expensive or extraordinary litigation; and, secondly, taking away from him the thing which more demoralizes that class of industry than anything I know of, and that is the gambling notion of the enormous, unwise, and improper profits to be derived. If I am correct in my observation, the great evil of our society now, and which has been the great evil for ten or fifteen years—and it pervades all society—is this undue and unsound desire, which amounts to a mania among the people, to grow suddenly rich without work. I think that is at the bottom of nearly all our social troubles. I think that the present patent law, as it is administered—not in the law itself, but as it is administered—tends to create that appetite, and foster that gambling spirit. I think it holds out the same temptation in the instances of these enormous profits, that have been made from time to time, that are held out by the lottery, and as there are hundreds of thousands of men even now who will put their hard earnings in a lottery, with 999 chances against them, in the hope that they will draw the capital prize, so there are in the patent business.

It has been stated to you by all the gentlemen, I believe, who have argued this question from its legal aspect, that there exists in our courts, in their application of the law, a different measure of damages, depending upon whether you bring your action upon the common-law side or equity side of the court. If you bring it upon the common-law side

you recover a reasonable license fee; if on the equity side of the court
you recover an unreasonable, unjust, and inequitable amount. The absurdity has thus come to pass that the court of equity, in administering
the principle of equity, does what it, itself, confesses to be inequitable;
and every lawyer who has practiced at the bar knows of innumerable
instances where the result is wholly wrong.

A good deal has been said here to the effect that all these parties who
stand as defendants in patent causes are *tort feasors*, willful infringers.
It is not true as a matter of fact, as five-sixths of all the patent cases
reported in the books will show. I will go further than Mr. Smith, and
say that in the five-sixths of all the patent cases reported in the books
the trouble is between two different parties, each claiming the same
right, and claiming under the same title; that is, each party has a patent from the United States, and the question is one of interference, or
of date of the patent.

Some unwise remarks were made here the other day about the railroad association. Now, the railroad association is simply a body of
men who unite themselves together for mutual protection. They do not
make patents, they use them; and in every instance where an action
has been brought, so far as I know, in which the railroad association of
the West (in whose direct interest I am standing here) has defended, it
defended under some purchased patent. It is not their interest to seek
occasion for litigation or to invite heavy penalties. But something was
said about their being monopolies. Now, sir, I have lived through two
or three granger movements in our country, and assisted to put in operation the first laws which asserted the jurisdiction of the State of Illinois over the railroads of the State, yet I never heard of any man yet
so wild as not to know that whatever inequitable burden you put upon
the railroads of the country is paid, in the end, from the pockets of the
people. It is simply shifted over upon the shoulders of the people
themselves.

This bill is not to be measured by the personal animus of one man,
who feels that he has been wronged, like my friend, Mr. White, who, as
I happen to know, from having examined into his matters two or three
years ago, has been greatly wronged; nor, on the other hand, by personal expressions against any other man who may represent the other
side. The art of statesmanship, the duty of this committee and the
House, is to bring the public good out of these conflicts of private interest, and your first consideration should be the public good, and the
second, that the burdens that are created by this bill shall bear as equitably as possible.

Take the statute of limitations as provided in this bill. Is there any
man who does not know that from the time of the old Roman law, as
long ago as the time of Cicero, the adage has come down to us that it
is good for the republic that there shall be an end to litigation? (I will
not be pedantic enough to quote the Latin) That principle has come
down in all our jurisdiction everywhere. You find these bills denomi-
nated, more particularly in the Southern States, where they adhere to
the English formula (or did formerly) more than they do in the West
and North—you find these bills headed as bills to quiet title, to produce
peace, bills to stop litigation. Is there any reason why the patentee
shall not be subject to the same limitation—shall not be required to exercise somewhat of the same diligence in asserting his rights that are
imposed upon any other citizen? Is it not a just thing to say to him,
"You shall not sleep sixteen years upon your rights, and let people
suppose that you have abandoned them?" Why, under the existing

law there is no limitation but the common-law limitation to the patent; and, if I understand it correctly, that is now twenty years.

Mr. ELDRIDGE. The Supreme Court of the United States cannot, nor any other court, go beyond the common-law limitation.

Mr. STORROW. The witnesses in these cases would all be dead, at any rate.

Mr. HURLBUT. The witnesses in these cases never die. As the law stands now, a man may have taken out a patent sixteen years ago, and still have twenty years in which to bring his action.

There is another thing which I will suggest to you: when a man comes forward and asks for a monopoly upon an invention he has made, and files his application, it has always seemed to me that the thing which that man ought to do was to state right there, when he makes his application, just exactly the date when that invention first came into his mind and was put by him into shape, and thus give notice to the public of the actual date of the invention. That has never been done. It is not asked in this bill, and I do not propose to ask it now. I simply state it as one of the evils of this system. This is an example of its working: A man sues for an infringement of his patent. Upon the trial he produces the patent which gives him a *prima-facie* title. When the defendant comes to answer he proves that two or three or four years before the plaintiff's patent was issued the principle was used by somebody else. Most people would suppose that that was a sufficient answer, but it is not; because the plaintiff can then come in, and, being advised of what the defense is, he can prove that although it was used three or four years prior to the issue of the patent, yet, as a matter of fact, he invented it two years before that prior use. It seems to me that it would be strictly right that the man who seeks protection for his rights should, when he files his application for a patent, name the exact date when that invention came into his mind, and then stand by it.

There has been a great deal said here about the extent of the patent system. It seems to me useless to argue that. All of us know it. Sidney Smith once wrote a celebrated article about the state of the English people in regard to taxation—how they were taxed from their cradles to their graves. It is so in the United States in regard to patents. There is as yet no patent on either extremity of human life. Men are born and go to their graves, and it is conducted on the old-fashioned method, without any patent. I am told that there are patented apparatuses used sometimes during the birth process, but after the birth, and until the death, there is not a step in the existence of that child, from the time that by patent pins his clothing is hooked together up to the time you carry him to his grave, an old man, in a patented coffin and in a patented hearse, that he can escape the operations of the Patent Office. They have even gone so far now that actually his gravestone is made by a patent process. The sand-blast does all that now.

Mr. SMITH. Is it any the worse for that?

Mr. HURLBUT. Not a bit. So I say, surrounded by all these evidences, there is no use talking about the importance of the measure. We all know it. It is wonderfully important and far-reaching in its effects. It affects more or less, directly or indirectly, every pursuit in life. There is not a single thing in ordinary use, that I know of, that is not more or less hedged about by these patent devices. And it is for these reasons that it is important that the committee should carefully consider the questions raised by this bill.

I take it that the rule you should adopt is this: You should say to the patentee, " We recognize the duty that is imposed upon us by the

Constitution," for when the Constitution says that the Congres shall have power to make these laws, I think it implies, not quite a command, but a very strong recommendation that that power shall be used. I think that by the exercise of that constitutional power benefits to an enormous extent have already accrued to this country, and will continue to accrue in the future; and that the wisest, best, and most beneficent legislation that can accrue, at this or any other near session of Congress, is to simplify and make clear, by some distinct and substantial enactments, the mystery that is thrown over the patent system.   There is not a patent lawyer in this country to-day who dares to give an opinion upon any new invention.

Mr. SMITH. Try me.

Mr. HURLBUT. Will you stake your reputation on its success?

Mr. SMITH. I will stake my reputation on my opinion.

Mr. WHITE. You will have to wait until the people are educated.

Mr. HURLBUT. It is not the people. The people are all right.

They have gone on now at the Patent Office so that they have educated a body of examiners there who can discriminate where there is no difference; and that is how the land comes to be flooded with these conflicting patents.   The ingenuity of man runs in a particular channel, and when a thing becomes popular men work to get a share in the profits; and the Patent Office is flooded with patents so that a plain and ordinary man cannot, for the life of him, see the difference between one thing which has been patented and another which has been patented; and therefore the task of deciding is transferred to the courts.

Why, we educate in our Patent Office, every year, from one to a dozen men, who, after receiving their education from the United States, go out and establish themselves as patent experts, and are regularly sworn, as such experts, to explain these differences, which, as a rule, ought to be so palpable that a common eye could see them.

Now, all these uncertainties, all this gambling tendency, all this extreme reward that is tendered, works practically against the interest of the inventors just as much as it does against the interest of the public, and for these reasons I think it is incumbent on this committee to give their full, free, and careful consideration to this bill.   There is no doubt about the extent of the information you have received, for I question if ever any committee in Congress has been flooded with such a mass of material, and so much of it that was valuable.   Out of this you should be able to construct a law which shall give justice to the owner of a patent and to the inventor, as well as to the user, and through him to the public.   And in the construction of such a law, if you make one, I believe this bill, as it now stands, will very largely bring about those results, and you will have done more for the development of the country than has been done by any one measure that I know of that has occurred within the last ten years.

APPENDIX.

The following extracts from the correspondence of the State Department, published in the appendix to the President's message of December 3, 1877, show how our progress in the industrial arts is universally recognized, the effect which it is having, and the causes of it.

Charles Bartlett, consul at Martinique, to the State Department:

Furniture.—There has been formerly imported to this island a small amount of American furniture, which is much cheaper than any made here, and in my opinion is better-styled than the French furniture, owing to which facts two firms have commenced importing American furniture largely during the past year, to whom I have given all the information I could on the subject.

Agricultural implements.—Formerly, articles of this description have been mostly imported from France, but lately quite an amount has been imported from the United States, and which, on being used, have been much liked, owing, perhaps, partly to the fact that they are cheaper than those of French manufacture.

Carriages.—Ten years since there was scarcely a carriage in Martinique; but since, the number of them has been constantly increasing, and for the past two years the number of carriages imported has been nearly doubled, and at present a large number of merchants (and many others) keep a carriage. Nearly all the carriages in Martinique are of American manufacture—in fact, there are very few French carriages in use.

Alfred E. Lee, consul-general at Frankfort-on-the-Main, to the State Department:

Through the reports of European visitors to the Centennial Exposition, our people have established a reputation on this side the Atlantic as skilled producers, which it is of the highest importance for them to maintain.

Agricultural implements.—In this branch of manufactures the Americans indisputably lead. Many reaping and mowing machines, horse-rakes, and a large variety of harvest hardwares are sold in this city, all of American manufacture. The testimony of dealers is that the American machines and tools easily outsell the German of the same kind.

Boot and shoe machines.—The New England inventors and manufacturers of these machines are represented by a branch established in Frankfort, from which large numbers of their contrivances are being sold in all parts of the Empire.

Wooden ware.—Americans have a great advantage in this line of manufacture, on account of the abundance and superior quality of their woods.

Rubber goods.—These and kindred articles of American make have been favorably received in Germany, and doubtless the trade might be considerably increased.

Shirtings.—American shirtings have been profitably sold in Frankfort for two years past, and are found to be cheaper than the English. American shirtings are being extensively introduced, also, in other parts of Germany.

Prints.—In this line there would seem to be a chance of successful competition with the English article. The very low cost at which the best prints are now made in the United States encourages this idea.

Dead meat.—The American dead-meat trade in England has attracted attention all over Europe, and its success there justifies the expectation that it may yet be extended to this continent.

Watches.—In a national convention of watch manufacturers, held at Wiesbaden, recently, the following declarations were made: "The International Exposition at Philadelphia has shown that the Americans have, within a few years, established watch manufactories in their country which, with their energy and use of machines, have superseded the Swiss watch industry for cheap watches. There is every reason to believe that the Swiss manufacturers cannot any longer compete with the Americans, and that they are almost forced to adopt the American system of fabrication."

Petroleum lamps and pendants.—These articles of American manufacture are now having a fair sale in this city. The same is true of some varieties of gas-fixtures and nickel-plated ware.

Carpenter's tools.—In the improved styles of American make there ought to be a larger

Paper-hangings.—These articles, brought from the United States, are extensively sold here, in spite of the formidable competition and the admirable varieties made in Germany.

Dental instruments.—The American inventions and patterns are unequaled. They ought to *monopolize* the market.

Scores of other American articles might be added to this list, which are either now sold in Germany or might be, or the sale of which might be greatly increased were their merits known.

A gentleman described by Mr. Lee as of " rare intelligence and large business experience," writes to him from Bielefield, Prussia, as follows :

The import of American articles of industry into Germany has been slowly but steadily increasing, and it seems as though the two countries might, in future, reverse the trade relations that have heretofore existed between'them. Ten years ago North America was the best market for German goods ; but now such articles mainly find their way across the Atlantic as are not yet manufactured in the United States. The Americans are already sending to Germany many articles of their skill and invention ; American machinery and tools, particularly, are much in demand here, and have been brought over in large quantities.

The superiority of the American people as a manufacturing nation, over all nations of the Old World, particularly in the mode of working, has been clearly proved by the Centennial Exposition at Philadelphia. The comprehension of this fact can be found in almost all the reports of the European commissioners to their respective governments. The consequence is that the German authorities, and all classes concerned, are discussing the measures to be taken to protect the industries of this country against a new and powerful competitor.

It has been further understood that one of the main reasons for the decline of German industry has been *the want of a useful and practical patent law*. This omission has now been supplied. The new German patent law, which has now been in existence since last July, is necessarily formed after the patent institutions of the United States, and gives full protection to the inventor and patent owner.

H. J. Wiuser, consul of Sonneberg, to the State Department :

There appears to be no question now in Germany as to the excellence of various kinds o American productions, mechanism, and manufactures, and as to the advantages which they possess over all others in the German market.

The latest important public witness to this fact is a profusely illustrated volume of nearly 400 pages, just published in Berlin, by Dr. Hermann Grothe, of that city, a political economist of repute. In the preface he says :

" The descriptions, reports; and notices which filled the publications of every European nation shortly before the opening of the Philadelphia Exhibition drew public attention more than ever before to the state of the industries of America. It was acknowledged that a development must have taken place on the other side of the ocean, of the magnitude of which Europe has been hitherto sadly ignorant, and of the value and peculiarities of which reports had suddenly appeared which sounded almost fabulous. Accustomed to connect American performances with the character of swindlers, or, at least, to regard them as eccentricities, and to undervalue the *intrinsic high worth of the American inventive faculty*, the industrial states of Europe have now to confess that their previous suppositions in this regard were false, that their opinions were unfounded, and that their real knowledge of American industries was grossly inexact. The World's Exhibition at Philadelphia was an event of the highest advantage to Europe, inasmuch as it was calculated to draw energetic and expert men over the ocean to obtain by personal observation correct views of the condition of the industries of the United States and of their subsidiary aids. That most of the reports of these men sound as though they had discovered a new world is well known, and there is, indeed, spread out in America, before the eyes of the observing European, a new world of industry, with new forms, new methods of work and traffic, new auxiliaries, and under new aspects and conditions.

" To me, also, this world on the other side of the ocean appeared new, although I was perfectly informed, before my visit to the United States, upon many branches of their industry and its development. I was particularly induced to make the visit in order to study the principles which had operated so powerfully in bringing about this rapid and high development, and from a conviction that without a prompt and honest exposition of the condition and results of American industrial relations, our German industries in future would suffer still *l* more. * * *

" I assert with emphasis that I have come to the same conclusions with regard to the development of American industry which have been reached by other German, Austrian, French, and Belgian commissioners who have formed a judgment in part from another politico-economical stand-point."

Mr. Winser continues :

Long chapters are devoted to the auxiliaries which aid the industries of the United

States, and among these great importance is attached to the stimulating effect of the patent laws.

In the second part of the book, each prominent branch of industry is treated separately and thoroughly, and the principal labor-saving machines and inventions which have contributed so greatly to the progress of the United States in all the avenues of business are carefully described and illustrated.

The superiority of our textile fabrics, our hardware, our agricultural implements, our craftsmen's tools, our machinery, and of many classes of our useful and ornamental fancy goods, is generally acknowledged. Their perfection in finish, their durability, their ingenuity, their practical character, are some of the qualities which commend them and which place them in favorable contrast to the productions of other lands. Moreover, owing to the use of labor-saving machinery and finer and better-adapted tools, the cost of manufacture, in spite of higher wages at home, is lessened to the point where competition with other nations in supplying foreign markets may fairly be tried; and there can be no doubt that a great many lines of American wares will eventually find ready sale in the German market, in some cases to the exclusion of the same classes of goods of English, French, and even of home manufacture. All this is granted.

James M. Wilson, consul at Nuremberg, to the State Department:

Mr. Frederick Haag, a German-American citizen from Auburn, New York, emigrating to America as a practical mechanic and millwright, there became familiar with American tools and machinery, and conceived the idea of introducing into Germany our modern tools, taking especial fancy to a turbine water-wheel known as the "Little Giant Turbine." Mr. Haag knew that it was just the thing wanted on the small streams of his native kingdom of Bavaria, where they still used wheels of the old pattern handed down from a remote ancestry. He purchased the patent right of this wheel for the continent of Europe, and, after much difficulty, succeeded in introducing a few of his wheels, the fame of which soon spread and secured to him a lucrative business. He has introduced, mostly in Germany, over four hundred, which are working to the entire satisfaction of their users. He has sold the patent right for Austria, whence the reported success is also very cheering.

I am of opinion that a practical farmer who understood the German language and character could introduce here our improved farming implements with great profit. * * *

In connection with our Centennial Exhibition, I may mention that the German commissioners, and very many of the visitors from this country to our Exhibition, were cultured and enlightened gentlemen, who, since their return home, have written much for publication, delivered lectures, etc., and, without an exception, so far as I know, have been unstinted in their praise of our country and our Centennial Exhibition. Notably Dr. George Seelhorst, secretary of the Industrial Museum of this city. He was one of the judges sent from Germany to the Philadelphia Exhibition, and before returning to Bavaria he visited the different industrial centers of our country, and returned enthusiastic in his praise of our country and the success of her great Exhibition, during which he purchased for his museum here a great variety of our superior mechanical tools. During the last winter, 1876–'77, Dr. Seelhorst delivered a course of lectures in this and twenty-seven cities of Bavaria, upon the Philadelphia Exhibition, and was especially eloquent over the remarkable developments our country has made during the first century of its existence. He illustrated his lectures by exhibiting to his audience specimen models of our superior mechanical tools, miniature machines, etc., and pointed out their peculiar excellence. At the present time he is occupied in writing an illustrated catalogue of the tools named, to be sent by the Nuremburg Museum throughout the country without cost, in order to introduce them into common use.

I may here add that at the request of the German Government these lectures are to be continued through this fall and coming winter, and the expenses of Dr. Seelhorst are borne by the government. The tools excited the greatest admiration. The learned doctor earnestly pressed upon his hearers the importance of shaking off their lethargy, and making the greatest possible exertions in their different industries, if they would not be outdone. He told his hearers that the United States of America already outstripped most of the older nations, except in matters of art, and as art required time, America would eventually not be behind other nations even in that.

After our productions have once had a fair trial there will be no danger of our losing the foreign markets, and we can reasonably expect increased demand from year to year, provided, always, that our manufacturers do not rest on the laurels already won, but continue to improve in the future as in the past.

It is well known that Dr. Reulaux, president of the Imperial German Commission at Philadelphia, reported to his government that the German display was "cheap, but bad." I may add that Dr. Seelhorst, in substance, indorsed that report. At the time, this report of the chief commissioner created a profound sensation throughout the German Empire, and could not have been tolerated from any other source. Time has made it plain to all that Dr. Reulaux was correct; and it is to the credit of the German manufacturers, that, looking facts squarely in the face, their leading men are organizing societies and holding conferences with a view to place their productions upon a higher plane, and to secure greater prosperity for their industrial interests.

It is pleasant to hear one's country referred to in such complimentary terms as are now heard in all circles, and the praise is not the less agreeable because of its novelty.

Mr. Badeau, consul-general at London, to the State Department, December 12, 1877:

I beg to call attention to the portion of the Times' article referring to the United States, in which it is distinctly admitted that American manufactures of tools, locomotive-engines, and many other kinds of hardware are now obtained in Canada and Australia almost exclusively from the United States, while it is also stated that not only do we produce at home all the manufactured goods we at one time bought from England, but that we have been able to exclude British manufactures from foreign markets.

Mr. Dockery, consul at Leeds, to the State Department, October 17, 1877:

From conversation with leading merchants here, I am justified in saying that they have virtually abandoned the hope of ever again seeing their manufactures exported in large quantities to the United States. * * *

They are forced to admit that even with a free entry they are not certain that they could advantageously compete in America with the home manufacturers.

It is said that an American artisan will do twice as much work in a given time as an English artisan, and that the workmanship is superior. This will explain why the difference in the price of labor should not be considered in any comparison of the productive resources of the two countries.

Again, while the cost of production in the United States has been gradually diminishing, there has been a steady improvement in the manufacturing industry.

It is a fact that, through American enterprise, England has not only lost her best customer, but that customer is competing with her in India, Brazil, and other markets, and nothing is more certain than that the Americans will never come back to this market. So that England has not only lost an important market, but she has met with an active, shrewd, and powerful competitor, which produces as well as manufactures.

Mr. Shaw, consul at Ontario, Canada, to the State Department, October 3, 1877:

The enterprise shown by American manufacturers in adopting new and attractive styles, and in the use of labor-saving machinery, combined with great natural advantages for manufacturing cheaply, all contribute to the success which their productions are meeting with in Ontario and elsewhere.

Mr. Chance, consul at Nassau, to the State Department, October 23, 1877:

Even now the Bahamas purchase largely from the United States, and are entirely dependent upon the latter for nearly all of the necessaries of life.

Great Britain formerly supplied the Bahamas with manufactured goods and hardware entirely, but the American articles, such as these lately introduced, are growing in favor, and in the future will be largely imported. It is acknowledged that in pattern and finish they are superior, for the prices, to the English goods.

Extracts from the reports to the British Parliament on the Philadelphia International Exhibition, page 90, textiles:

The American display of textile manufactures was extensive and diversified, presenting a large collection of different fabrics produced in the numerous mills of the New England States, New York, New Jersey, and other great centers of the Union, and affording a striking proof of their capability for entering into competition with the manufacturers of other countries.

The goods exhibited, though not of equal quality, were, for the most part, pure, firm, and well manufactured, and noticeable for the evenness of the yarn. The excellence of the weaving, the bleaching, dyeing, and finishing of the various grades and styles of cotton-cloths manifested superiority attributable in some degree to the excellent water found throughout the Union.

The extensive and complete representation thus made of the textile manufactures of the United States shows the rapid progress which the cotton industry has made, and the vast proportions which it has attained, whilst the character and qualities of the goods produced demonstrate that whenever the swaddling bands of protection shall be burst asunder the rest of the world will encounter a more formidable competitor than has hitherto appeared. (Page 97.)

As regards extent of invention and ingenuity, the United States was far ahead of other nations. I do not remember an exhibitor who had not some features of novelty and ingenuity to claim in the machines he exhibited.

The extraordinary extent of ingenuity and invention existing in the United States, and manifested throughout the exhibition, I attributed to the natural aptitude of the people, fostered and stimulated by an admirable patent law and system, and to the appreciation of inventions by the people generally. (Page 135.)

A great part of the marked advance in the improvement of workmen's tools, which has been made during recent years, is justly due to the inventive genius of American citizens, and, in the section of planes exhibited in the Centennial, this is fully confirmed by an important change in the structure of the tool. (Page 211.)

Speaking not only of these classes which fell more immediately under the observation of the judges in committee B, but also from general observation of other classes in the group, one cannot fail to notice the great fertility of invention displayed in America, and the excellent workmanship obtained by the joint effect of their tools, machinery, and skilled workmen.

As a whole, the Machinery Hall gave me a high opinion of the mechanical skill of the Americans. There is great inventive power, and a ready and fearless adaptation of the means to the end sought. In the machines and apparatus from the larger establishments and more favorable localities, the workmanship is admirable, and every working part, down to the smallest detail, bears evidence of thought and study. (Page 233.)

The impression is left upon the minds of European visitors that American competition in machine tools will soon be upon us, and that the competition will be for high quality and productiveness, and the capability of doing more work with a given expenditure of labor. (Page 234.)

No department of the exhibition created greater astonishment in the minds of European visitors than the saw-mill annex. The sawing machinery came chiefly from the timber districts of the West, and has a character of its own, distinguished by daring boldness. There were nearly twenty of these mills, provided each with from twenty to forty horse-power concentrated on a single saw, the limit of velocity being the tenacity of iron to resist centrifugal force. The most daring saw-miller at the Centennial was E. P. Ellis, from Milwaukee. He required a stream of water to keep down the temperature of his saw. The sawing of his mill was a sight not easily to be forgotten.

It was not at the exhibition, however, that the application of machine tools by the Americans was seen to the best advantage. To realize the nature of the competition that awaits us, their factories and workshops have to be inspected, in order to see the variety of special tools that are being introduced, both to insure precision and to economize labor. This system of special tools is extending into almost every branch of industry where articles have to be repeated. The articles made are not only good in quality, but the cost of production is extremely low, notwithstanding that those employed earn high pay. (Page 271.)

Looking to practical applications of science generally in the United States department of the exhibition, no one can fail to be struck with the great and successful activity in the application of science to useful purposes in America. Thoroughly in harmony with this very valuable development of national energy, was the exhibition, in the United States Government building, of objects illustrating the efficiency of the Washington Patent Office. Judged by its results in benefiting the public, both by stimulating inventors and by giving a perseveringly practical turn to their labors, the American patent law must be admitted to be most successful, and the beneficence of its working was very amply illustrated throughout the American region of the exhibition, where, indeed, it seemed that every good thing deserving a patent was patented. I asked one inventor of a very good invention, "Why do you not patent in England?" He answered: "The conditions in England are too onerous." Meaning, no doubt, that the cost of a patent in England is too great, and the time for which it is granted too short. It is not merely on account of the extreme injustice of such an enormous tax, as is implied in the £175 of government stamp duties, charged according to our present law, that a diminution to something nearer the American charge of $35 is urgently needed. England undoubtedly loses much of the benefit which might be had from the inventiveness of Englishmen, through the want, in English patent law, of encouragement and protection to inventors unsupported by capitalists.

Sir William Thomson, president of the Mathematical and Physical Section of the British Association, September, 1876 :

If Europe does not amend its patent laws (England in the opposite direction to that proposed in the bills before the last two sessions of Parliament), America will speedily become the nursery of useful inventions for the world.

Mr. St. John V. Day, in a paper on patent legislation, read before the British Association, September 12, 1876, speaking of the same English bill, which the government has since withdrawn, spoke of the disapproval of that law by—

Those who really of all men are best able to pronounce upon the importance of inventions, great or small, by virtue of their daily exercise of both, who alone of all men possess the requisite class of facts by which to estimate the economies which have been effected in the cost of production by the mere introduction or application of what to these outside would appear insignificant, and by the lord chancellor's last bill be styled "frivolous," and "not worthy of a patent;" those who really know what it is, not merely to work at, but more particularly to work out an invention, and not unfrequently tolerate the opposition of such incalculable factors as prejudice, vested interests, and the education up to an advanced point of perception of the public mind, in order to bring an invention into commercial use, &c.

As to points upon which the examiners are to report, there is no serious objection to those set forth as *a, b,* and *c,* in clause 10 of the bill; but as to *d,* by which they are to be called upon to report whether an invention is frivolous or not, it is impossible that without experiment that can be determined. Many inventions, as they are represented in the documents filed at the Patent Office, appear frivolous and insignificant by virtue of their very simplicity. Of such a class was Neilson's invention for using hot instead of cold air in iron-smelting—so simple-looking a matter on paper that it would almost to a certainty be viewed by an examiner as frivolous; yet the practical effect of this simple-looking invention was at one state to reduce the quantity of coal required for smelting a ton of iron from 7.5 tons to 2.5 tons. Another of such patents, which from an examiner's point of view would be deemed frivolous, is Young's patent, the essence of which was the carrying on of the destructive distillation of bituminous substances at a certain temperature, the result of which has been to convert a vast industry out of what was previously known as a chemical curiosity. Numerous other analogous instances might be noted, but it will be clear from the two I have cited that to allow an examiner to decide whether what appears in the papers before him to be frivolous or not, would be calling upon him to exercise a function which he would never properly discharge, and the effect of which must be to nip in the bud a class of inventions which have often proved of far greater industrial importance than many others which on paper have a much more specious appearance.

See pp. 120, 482, *supra.*

There certainly can be no occasion for speculation when a result may be seen in the future as certain to happen, as it surely will if the provisions of the bill of 1876, or others analogous to them, without some powerful counter-check, should ever pass into the law of a nation so much of whose whole prosperity in the past and whose position in the future to a great extent rests upon one of the mainsprings of commerce, namely, industrial development.

After a discussion, the chairman proposed and Mr. Bramwell seconded the following resolution, which was put to the meeting and unanimously adopted:

That a committee of the British Association be appointed to watch legislation with reference to patents, and to take such steps as may be deemed expedient to promote an efficient patent law.

Extracts from a paper upon the industries and manufactures in the United States, addressed to Swiss manufacturers, by Edward Bally, the largest manufacturer of boots and shoes in Switzerland, and one of the Swiss commissioners to the Philadelphia Exhibition:

Another factor which favors the education of the people (of the United States) is the excellent system of patents, by means of which, at a very moderate expense, a patent is obtained; not only the inventor is protected against infringement, but the invention is made known; and the American, more than any one else, loves innovations, and adopts them the moment they are recognized as good.

Many European states have also a patent system, but as they see in it, first of all, a source of revenue to the state, those of moderate fortune can hardly obtain a patent. In Europe the inventor anxiously hides his secret from all eyes until he is in possession of a patent. The Americans do not know this uneasiness, because there the inventor alone can take a patent, which he afterwards has the right to sell, if he pleases.

Every intelligent man has thus before him the possibility of fortune, often by a very slight improvement, and this keeps in ceaseless activity the intelligent part of the population.

I am satisfied from my knowledge that no people have made, in so short a time, so many useful inventions as the Americans; and if to-day machinery apparently does all the work, it, nevertheless, by no means reduces the workman to a machine. He uses it as a machine, it is true, but he is always thinking about some improvement to introduce into it, and often his thoughts lead to fine inventions or useful improvements.

American industry has taken a lead which in a few years may cause Europe to feel its consequences in a very marked degree. The Universal Exhibition of Philadelphia has been, so to speak, the key by which American industry will unlock for itself the road to Europe and to its colonies. Visitors from the Old World, although few, have been able to appreciate the activity of America in the dominion of industry, and they will bring back from there many lessons which will make astonished Europe open its eyes.

At this moment there are at Manchester, in England, the principal center for cottons,

40,000 men out of work because the Manchester shippers can order their goods more advantageously in America.

European sea-ports have become in part great depots for American leather. Certainly it is not pleasant to be compelled to recognize the fact that a former market has become a dangerous competitor.

If to-day a manufacturer wishes to contend only against competition, he is obliged to bring his machinery from America.

When one examines the merchandise and looks over the prices-current which were distributed among the visitors, one is almost obliged to admit that in a few years Americans will furnish Germans with shoes instead of buying their shoes from Germans.

We must introduce the patent system. All our production is more or less a simple copy. The inventor has no profit to expect from his invention, no matter how useful it may be. It is evident that this absolute want of protection will never awaken in a people the spirit of invention, but, on the contrary, accustoms them to copy more and more that which belongs to their neighbors, and that is not to the honor of the country. The want of protection for new inventions is a disadvantage to us. The state ought not to hesitate to add to its resources this new resource; but at the same time we must remember that an invention is valuable in proportion to the facility with which it can be made available, and so it is essential that the grant of patents be accessible to inventors of the most moderate fortunes.

America has shown us how in a few years a people, in the midst of circumstances often embarrassing, can merit by its activity, its spirit of enterprise, and its perseverance, the respect and the admiration of the whole world, and acquire in many respects an incontestable superiority. May our sister republic serve as our model in this.

S. Mis. 50——29

INDEX OF SECTIONS TO ARGUMENTS BEFORE SENATE COMMITTEE.

INDEX TO ARGUMENTS BEFORE HOUSE COMMITTEE.

MISCELLANEOUS.

Objections to patent laws—source of.
   Mr. Christy. The complaints against patents arises largely from the fact that the things invented are so convenient that everybody finds that they do not want to do without them ; but that is the last reason for abolishing the patent or not paying the inventor.. 464
   Mr. Storrow. Knowledge of the subject-matter, in its practical effect upon the community, should precede legislation upon it.................................... 265
   Objections to the patent law largely come from those who do not know what it

o